LAW

FOR A LEVEL YEAR 2

Jacqueline Martin
Nicholas Price
Richard Wortley

HODDER
EDUCATION
AN HACHETTE UK COMPANY

This resource is endorsed by OCR for use with OCR A Level Law specification H415.

In order to gain OCR endorsement, this resource has undergone an independent quality check. Any references to assessment and/or assessment preparation are the publisher's interpretation of the specification requirements and are not endorsed by OCR. OCR recommends that a range of teaching and learning resources are used in preparing learners for assessment. OCR has not paid for the production of this resource, nor does OCR receive any royalties from its sale. For more information about the endorsement process, please visit the OCR website, www.ocr.org.uk.

The Publishers would like to thank the following for permission to reproduce copyright material.

Text acknowledgements

p.155 Zealous parking wardens under attack; Darlington & Stockton Times, 25th Nov, 2016. © Newsquest Media Group Ltd.; **p.168** Bowcott, Owen (2016). Birmingham pub bombings inquest: families to meet home secretary over funding. Copyright Guardian News & Media Ltd 2017; **p.179** Campbell, Duncan (2016). The rules on questioning criminal suspects are there for a reason. Copyright Guardian News & Media Ltd 2017; **p.212** What are the consequences for human rights if we change our relationship with the EU? 'The UK in a Changing Europe'; **p.274** Adam Ramsay (2011), Why the Fortnum & Mason protesters' case matters, *New Statesman*; **p.346** Damien Gayle (2011). 'He lives in a parallel universe': Judge slams lies of schemer's £5m Toad Hall property scam. Used with permission from *Daily Mail*.

Photo acknowledgements

p.120 © Sailesh Patel/Shutterstock; **p.130** *t* © incamerastock/Alamy Stock Photo, *b* © jennyt/Shutterstock; **p.143** © Motoring Picture Library/Alamy Stock Photo; **p.145** © Phil Wills/Alamy Stock Photo; **p.154** © Copyright Colin Smith and licensed for reuse under https://creativecommons.org/licenses/by-sa/2.0/); **p.156** © Lordprice Collection/Alamy Stock Photo; **p.162** © Science & Society Picture Library/Getty Images; **p.172** © Steven Purcell/Alamy Stock Photo; **p.184** © chombosan/Shutterstock; **p.185** © Mark Agnor/Shutterstock; **p.187** © Stephen Barnes/Alamy Stock Photo; **p.189** © Drobot Dean/stock.adobe.com; **p.190** © punghi/Shutterstock; **p.201** © GL Archive/Alamy Stock Photo; **p.206** © The United Nations; **p.207** © Hadrian./Shutterstock; **p.209** © Gary Lucken/Alamy Stock Photo; **p.220** © Janine Wiedel Photolibrary/Alamy Stock Photo; **p.242** © Crown Copyright; **p.253** © David Ball/Alamy Stock Photo; **p.256** © TopFoto.co.uk; **p.271** © Lee Martin/Alamy Stock Photo; **p.290** © Eric James/Alamy Stock Photo; **p.294** © Lordprice Collection/Alamy Stock Photo; **p.331** © Stephen Barnes/Alamy Stock Photo; **p.355** © Robert Przybysz/Shutterstock; **p.359** © ZUMA Press, Inc./Alamy Stock Photo.

Crown copyright material is reproduced under Class Licence Number C02P0000060 with the permission of the Controller of HMSO.

Every effort has been made to trace all copyright holders, but if any have been inadvertently overlooked, the Publishers will be pleased to make the necessary arrangements at the first opportunity.

Although every effort has been made to ensure that website addresses are correct at time of going to press, Hodder Education cannot be held responsible for the content of any website mentioned in this book. It is sometimes possible to find a relocated web page by typing in the address of the home page for a website in the URL window of your browser.

Hachette UK's policy is to use papers that are natural, renewable and recyclable products and made from wood grown in sustainable forests. The logging and manufacturing processes are expected to conform to the environmental regulations of the country of origin.

Orders: please contact Bookpoint Ltd, 130 Milton Park, Abingdon, Oxon OX14 4SE. Telephone: +44 (0)1235 827720. Fax: +44 (0)1235 400401. Email: education@bookpoint.co.uk. Lines are open from 9 a.m. to 5 p.m., Monday to Saturday, with a 24-hour message answering service. You can also order through our website: www.hoddereducation.co.uk

ISBN: 978 1 5104 0177 8

© Richard Wortley, Nicholas Price 2018

First published in 2018 by

Hodder Education,

An Hachette UK Company

Carmelite House

50 Victoria Embankment

London EC4Y 0DZ

www.hoddereducation.co.uk

Impression number   10 9 8 7 6 5 4 3 2 1

Year   2022 2021 2020 2019 2018

Cover photo © Shutterstock/focusimage

Illustrations by Aptara Inc., Peter Lubach and Ian Foulis

Typeset in Bliss/Light, 10.75/13.5 pts. by Aptara Inc.

Printed in Italy

A catalogue record for this title is available from the British Library.

Contents

Component 3 Section A

Component 3 Section B Option 1

Component 3 Section B Option 2

Preface

This book, and *OCR AS/A Level Law Book 1,* are written for the OCR specification for A Level Law. The order of topics covered follows that of the OCR specification. There is also a chart setting out the coverage of the specification and where to find the related material in this book.

As well as the factual material on the topics, evaluation is included for all areas where it is required by OCR's specification.

The text is broken up into manageable 'bites' and throughout the text we have used features which have proved popular in previous texts for A and AS Level Law. These include key facts charts, case charts, highlighting cases and diagrams.

Activities for students are also included. These are based on a variety of material such as newspaper and internet articles, research material and decided cases. There are also application tasks for students to practice applying the law to given scenarios.

The law is as we believe it to be on 1 March 2018.

Jacqueline Martin
Nick Price
Richard Wortley

Tables of legislation

Acts

Statutory instruments

Conventions

Table of cases

Introduction

This book has been written and designed for the new OCR Law specifications introduced for first teaching in September 2017. It supplements *OCR A Level Law for Year 1/AS* and together the books cover the content required for OCR A level Law for first examination in 2019.

Book 1 covers the content that teachers are likely to cover in the first year of the course including an introduction to the nature of law, the civil and criminal court systems, alternatives to the courts, the personnel involved in the legal system and how cases are funded. It also deals with how laws are made both within and outside parliament and how laws are made and used in court. The book also contains some specific areas of criminal and civil law.

In the criminal law section the rules and content of criminal offences are covered, together with the general rules on sentencing guilty offenders. There is particular emphasis on non-fatal offences against the person. In the civil law section the emphasis is on the rules of negligence and occupier's liability in the law of tort or civil wrongs and the remedies that can be claimed.

In this book the content of Book 1 is developed further and it is likely that teachers will cover its content in the second year of the course. Criminal law is developed further as the book considers fatal and some property offences together with the rules of some part and full defences. Tort law is further developed by considering some civil actions relating to land and of vicarious liability. Different detailed topics of Contract law and Human Rights are encompassed. Some theoretical issues are also covered including issues of law and morality, law and justice, law and society and considering how law will adapt to the introduction of certain new forms of technology.

As stated, both this book and Book 1 cover the content required for the OCR A Level Law specification. To view the full specification, and examples of assessment material for OCR A Level Law please visit OCR's website at www.ocr.org.uk.

How to use this book

Each chapter has a range of features that have been designed to present the course content in a clear and accessible way, to give you confidence and to support you in your revision and assessment preparation.

Learning objectives
Each chapter starts with a list of what is to be studied and how these relate to the specification.

Key terms
Key terms, in bold in the text, are defined.

Key case
Description of a case and a comment on the point of law it illustrates.

Tips
These are suggestions to help clarify what you should aim to learn.

Extension tasks
These include challenging activities for students striving for higher grades.

Look online
These weblinks will help you with further research and reading on the internet.

News story
Real events relating to specific areas of law are covered.

Summary
These boxes contain summaries of what you have learned in each section.

Activities
Activities appear throughout the book and have been designed to help you apply your knowledge and develop your understanding of various topics.

Practice questions
These are questions to help you get used to the type of questions you may encounter in the exam.

Book coverage of specification content

CONTENT AREA	Coverage
H415/01 Section B: CRIMINAL LAW	
The rules and theory of criminal law	
An overview of the theory of criminal law	Book 2, Chapter 1
Fatal offences against the person	
Murder: *actus reus* and *mens rea*	Book 2, Chapter 2
Voluntary manslaughter: defences of loss of control and diminished responsibility under Coroners and Justice Act 2009	Book 2, Chapter 3
Involuntary manslaughter: unlawful act manslaughter and gross negligence manslaughter	Book 2, Chapter 4
Offences against property	
Theft under s 1 Theft Act 1968	Book 2, Chapter 5
Robbery under s 8 Theft Act 1968	Book 2, Chapter 6
Burglary under s (1)(a) and s 9(1)(b) Theft Act 1968	Book 2, Chapter 6
Mental capacity defences	
Insanity, automatism, intoxication	Book 2, Chapter 7
General defences	
Self-defence, duress by threats, duress of circumstances and necessity	Book 2, Chapter 8.1, 8.2, 8.3, 8.5
Consent	Book 2, Chapter 8.6
Preliminary offences	
Attempts: the *actus reus* and *mens rea*; impossibility	Book 2, Chapter 9
Evaluation	
Critical evaluation of offences against the person, offences against property and defences including ideas for reform	Offences against the person: Book 2, Chapter 2, 2.4 (murder); Chapter 3, 3.2.8 and 3.2.9; 3.3.6 and 3.3.7 (voluntary manslaughter); Chapter 4, 4.4 (involuntary manslaughter); Chapter 5, 5.7 (theft); Chapter 6, 6.3 (robbery and burglary). Mental capacity defences: Book 2, Chapter 7, 7.1.6 and 7.1.7 (insanity), 7.2.3 and 7.2.4 (automatism), 7.3.4 and 7.3.5 (intoxication) General defences: Book 2, Chapter 8, 8.1.3 (self-defence), 8.4 (duress by threats and of circumstances), 8.5.1 (necessity) 8.6.6 (consent)
H415/02 Section B: THE LAW OF TORT	
Torts connected to the land	
Public and private nuisance	Book 2, Chapter 10
Rylands v Fletcher	Book 2, Chapter 11
Vicarious liability	Book 2, Chapter 12
Critical evaluation of liability in negligence, occupiers' liability, torts connected to land and vicarious liability, including ideas for reform	Book 2, 10.1.4 (public nuisance), 10.2.5 (private nuisance), 11.6 (*Rylands v Fletcher*), 12.6 (vicarious liability)
2C. CONTENT OF H415/03 – FURTHER LAW	
Section A: THE NATURE OF LAW	
Law and morality	
The distinction between law and morals	Book 2, Chapter 13.1
The diversity of moral views in a pluralist society	Book 2, Chapter 13.2

CONTENT AREA	Coverage
The relationship between law and morals and its importance	Book 2, Chapter 13.3
The legal enforcement of moral values	Book 2, Chapter 13.4
Law and justice	
The meaning of justice	Book 2, Chapter 14.1
Theories of justice	Book 2, Chapter 14.2
The extent to which the law achieves justice	Book 2, Chapter 14.3
Law and society	
The role law plays in society	Book 2, Chapter 15.1
The law as a social control mechanism	Book 2, Chapter 15.2
The way in which the law creates and deals with consensus and conflict	Book 2, Chapter 15.3
The realist approach to law making	Book 2, Chapter 15.4
Law and technology	
The intersection of law and technology	Book 2, Chapter 16.2
Key issues, including privacy and data protection and cyber-crime	Book 2, Chapter 16.3
Cross-border issues and future challenges	Book 2, Chapter 16.4
Section B Option 1: HUMAN RIGHTS LAW	
Rules and theory	
An outline of the rules of human rights law	Book 2, Chapter 17.1
An overview of the theory of human rights law	Book 2, Chapter 17.2
Protection of the individual's human rights and freedoms in the UK	
An overview of the development of human rights in the UK, including Magna Carta 1215 and the Bill of Rights 1688	Book 2, Chapter 18.1
The history of the European Court of Human Rights	Book 2, Chapter 18.2
The impact of the Human Rights Act 1998	Book 2, Chapter 18.3
The entrenched nature of the Human Rights Act 1998 in the devolution settlements of Scotland, Wales and Northern Ireland	Book 2, Chapter 18.5
Key provisions of the European Convention on Human Rights including restrictions on Human Rights law	
Article 5: the right to liberty and security	Book 2, Chapter 19
Article 6: the right to a fair trial	Book 2, Chapter 20
Article 8: the right to respect for family and private life	Book 2, Chapter 21
Article 10: the right to freedom of expression	Book 2, Chapter 22
Article 11: freedom of assembly	Book 2, Chapter 23
Restrictions on human rights law	
Restrictions permitted by the European Convention on Human Rights	Book 2, Chapters 19–22
Public order offences	Book 2, Chapter 19.2
Police powers	Book 2, Chapter 19.2.5
Interception of communications	Book 2, Chapter 21.4.5
Duty of confidentiality	
Obscenity	Book 2, Chapter 22.3.4
Torts of defamation and trespass	Book 2, Chapter 22.3.5 (defamation), 23.3.1 (trespass)
Harassment	Book 2, Chapter 21.4.2

CONTENT AREA	Coverage
Enforcement of human rights law	
Role of domestic courts	Book 2, Chapter 24.1
The process of judicial review	Book 2, Chapter 24.2
The role of the European Court of Human Rights	Book 2, Chapter 24.3
Evaluation	
Critical evaluation of human rights protection in the UK, the European Convention on Human Rights and the Human Rights Act 1998, including ideas for reform	Book 2, Chapter 18.4
Critical evaluation of Article 5	Book 2, Chapter 19.8
Critical evaluation of Article 6	Book 2, Chapter 20.6
Critical evaluation of Article 8	Book 2, Chapter 21.5
Critical evaluation of Article 10	Book 2, Chapter 22.4
Critical evaluation of Article 11	Book 2, Chapter 23.4
Section B Option 2: THE LAW OF CONTRACT	
Rules and theory	
An outline of the rules of the law of contract	Book 2, Chapter 25.2
An overview of the theory of the law of contract	Book 2, Chapter 25.3
Formation of contract	
Offer and acceptance, including the rules of communication and revocation	Book 2, Chapter 26
Intention to create legal relations: domestic and commercial, presumptions and rebuttals	Book 2, Chapter 27.1
Consideration: adequacy, sufficiency, past consideration, pre-existing duties	Book 2, Chapter 27.2
Privity: the rights of third parties under the Contract (Rights of Third Parties) Act 1999 and common law exceptions	Book 2, Chapter 27.3
Terms	
Express and implied terms, including the Consumer Rights Act 2015	Book 2, Chapter 28.1, 28.4, 28.4.3
Types of term: conditions, warranties, innominate terms	Book 2, Chapter 28.2
Exclusion and limitation clauses, including the Unfair Contract Terms Act 1977 and the Consumer Rights Act 2015	Book 2, Chapter 29
Vitiating factors	
Misrepresentation, including omission in consumer contexts	Book 2, Chapter 30.2–30.3
Economic duress	Book 2, Chapter 30.4
Discharge	
Performance	Book 2, Chapter 31.2
Frustration	Book 2, Chapter 31.3
Breach of contract: actual and anticipatory breach	Book 2, Chapter 31.4
Remedies	
Damages: compensatory damages; causation and remoteness of damage; mitigation of loss	Book 2, Chapter 32.2
Equitable remedies	Book 2, Chapter 32.3
Consumer remedies under the Consumer Rights Act 2015	Book 2, Chapter 28.4.3
Evaluation	
Critical evaluation of formation and contract terms, including ideas for reform	Book 2, 26.3 and 27.4 (formation of contract), 29.3 (contract terms)

Overview of the theory of criminal law

After reading this chapter you should be able to:
- Have an overview of the theory of criminal law, including:
  - harm as the basis of criminalising conduct
  - autonomy of the individual
  - the need for fault
  - principles in formulating criminal law

1.1 Rules and theory of criminal law

Chapter 12.1 in *OCR AS/A Level Law Book 1* (ISBN 9781510401761) contains an outline of the rules and theory of criminal law.

It sets out that crimes are acts or omissions that are morally wrong, that the aim of criminal law is to provide justice in one form or another and that criminal law provides a form of social control which may reflect the morality of the time, but which may also help to change public attitudes towards certain standards of behaviour.

Most criminal laws are made by Parliament, though there are a few examples of judges making law through judicial precedent.

Most crimes require an *actus reus* and a *mens rea*, unless they are offences of strict liability. The standard of proof to be satisfied in court is 'beyond reasonable doubt' and it is for the prosecution to prove the offence to that standard.

In this chapter the outline from *OCR AS/A Level Law Book 1* is developed further to consider factors such as:
- What should be the basis for criminalising conduct?
- What is the purpose of criminal law?
- How far should individuals have autonomy to do what they wish, or should the welfare of the community as a whole take priority?

1.2 What conduct ought to be criminalised?

There are two main conditions that need to be satisfied before criminalisation of conduct is justified. These are:
- the conduct must be wrongful, and
- it must be necessary to use the criminal law to forbid the conduct.

1.2.1 Wrongful conduct

There are different views on what is 'wrongful' conduct. One main view is that conduct is only wrongful if it causes harm or serious offence to others.

Under this view offences such as murder, manslaughter and rape are clearly wrongful. So, too, are offences against property such as theft, burglary and robbery. These are less disruptive than offences against the person but are still of serious concern to the victim. Another area is public security. Riot and public disorder come within this as well as terrorism. These crimes are intrinsically wrong; they can be described as *mala in se*.

Key term

Mala in se – this term means 'intrinsically wrong'.

However, there are many other crimes which are regulatory rather than intrinsically wrong. These offences are of forbidden conduct; also known as *mala prohibita*. Examples include conduct as diverse as prostitution, illegal drug use, causing pollution, road traffic offences and regulations on the sale of unfit or out-of-date food.

Should these regulatory offences be described as 'criminal'? Some countries have a mid-range category of 'violations' or 'administrative wrongs' rather than class all such conduct as criminal. This is not the situation in English law.

Key term

Mala prohibita – this term means 'forbidden conduct'.

There is a view that criminal offences should be wrongdoings which are public in the sense that they properly concern the public and merit a formal response of censure and condemnation.

The wrongdoings must do more than just interfere with private rights. Private rights can be enforced through other areas of law such as tort, contract and human rights. Criminal law should not be used to enforce these rights.

In 1931, Sir Carleton Allen wrote in an article, 'The nature of a crime', that:

> Crime is crime because it consists in wrong doing which directly and in serious degree threatens the security or well-being of society, and because it is not safe to leave it redressable only by compensation of the party injured.

1.2.2 Paternalistic law

There is also the view that some conduct should be criminalised in order to protect us from ourselves. This is the idea of 'paternalistic' law. For example, the use of certain drugs such as cannabis and heroin is illegal. The reason for this is that such drugs are addictive and, in the long term, deprive people of the control over their lives. They can also lead to drug users committing crime such as theft in order to buy more drugs.

Interestingly, it is not a crime to buy or smoke cigarettes even though nicotine is an addictive drug and can cause serious health problems to smokers.

Similarly consuming alcohol can cause health problems. It can lead to other crimes being committed by a drunken person, in particular assaults. Possession or consumption of alcohol is a crime in some, mostly Muslim, countries. There are specific alcohol-related offences in England such as being drunk in a public place and driving while over the blood alcohol limit.

There are also other actions which, it could be argued, should not be criminal when committed by consenting adults in private. An example is the case of *R v Brown* (1994).

Case study

R v Brown (1994)

Five men in a group of consenting adult sado-masochists were convicted of offences of assault causing actual bodily harm (s 47 of the Offences Against the Person Act (OAPA) 1861) and malicious wounding (s 20 OAPA 1861). They had carried out acts which included applying stinging nettles to their genitals and inserting map pins or fish hooks into each other's penises. All the victims were adults, had consented, the actions were carried out in private, and none had needed medical attention. Their convictions were upheld by the House of Lords.

The Law Lords clearly made this decision as a matter of public policy. Lord Templeman actually said:

> The question whether the defence of consent should be extended to the consequences of sado-masochistic encounters can only be decided by consideration of policy and public interest ... Society is entitled and bound to protect itself against a cult of violence.

This case contrasts with the decision in *R v Wilson* (1996).

Case study

R v Wilson (1996)

D had branded his initials on his wife's buttocks with a hot knife at her request. The Court of Appeal held that this was not an unlawful act, even though she had to seek medical attention for the burns caused. It held that it was not in the public interest that such consensual behaviour should be criminalised. The court thought it was a situation of 'personal adornment' like having a tattoo.

1.2.3 Legal moralism

This is the principle that conduct is wrongful if it is morally wrong as in the sense of legal moralism. The case of *R v Brown* set out above can also be viewed as conduct being criminalised because of this principle. In this case Lord Mustill dissented, pointing out that:

> " I do not invite your Lordships to endorse [the conduct] as morally acceptable. Nor do I pronounce in favour of a libertine doctrine specifically related to sexual matters ... What I do say is that these are questions of private morality; the standards by which they fall to be judged are not those of the criminal law. "

It could be argued that the majority of Law Lords were taking a moral stand against sado-masochistic homosexuals, whereas the Court of Appeal judges were of the view that the law should not interfere in the private affairs of a married heterosexual couple. There are also other areas of law where the courts have ruled that conduct is criminal through legal moralism. The majority decision in the case of *R v Hinks* (2000) can be viewed in this way.

Case study

R v Hinks (2000)

D was a 38-year-old woman who had befriended a very naïve man with a low IQ. He was, however, mentally capable of understanding the concept of ownership and of making a valid gift. Over a period of months D accompanied the man on numerous occasions to his building society where he withdrew about £60,000, which D paid into his own account. The man also gave D a television set. D was charged with theft of the money and the television. The judge directed the jury to consider whether the man was so mentally incapable that D herself realised that ordinary and decent people would regard it as dishonest to accept a gift from him. D was convicted.

On appeal, it was argued that if the gift was valid, the acceptance of it could not be theft. The House of Lords dismissed the appeal by a majority of three judges to two.

Lord Hobhouse said in his dissenting judgment:

> " An essential function of the criminal law is to define the boundary between what conduct is criminal and what merely immoral. Both are the subject of the disapprobation of ordinary right-thinking citizens and the distinction is likely to be arbitrary or at least strongly influenced by considerations subjective to the individual members of the tribunal. To treat otherwise lawful conduct as criminal merely because it is open to such disapprobation would be contrary to principle. "

This case is discussed further in Chapter 5.

1.3 Autonomy of the individual

Autonomy means that individuals should have freedom to do what they want. Any attempt to limit autonomy should only be where it is necessary to limit harm. So where a defendant has chosen to attack another person, then the defendant's autonomy in that choice can be limited.

Under this principle of autonomy, it can be argued that the parties in *Wilson* should have been free to do what they wanted to each other and the acts in *R v Brown* should not have been criminalised as they were carried out by consenting adults in private.

Another area of law where autonomy of the individual is an important issue is that of assisting suicide, where the person who wishes to commit suicide is so physically disabled that they cannot do it without the help of another person.

Committing suicide is not a crime, but if another person assists with the suicide then that person can be charged with assisting suicide. This is so even if the victim has requested his assistance. It is argued that this takes away the autonomy of a disabled person to choose to take their own life. As a result of challenges to this law, the DPP has issued a Policy Guidance Statement about the factors to be considered when deciding whether a prosecution should take place.

Autonomy also means that individuals should be treated as responsible for their own behaviour. This links into the idea of fault – see section 1.4 below.

1.3.1 Limited autonomy

There are some groups of people whose ability to make choices is weaker, such as those under age and those suffering from a mental disorder. The criminal law is used to protect such people as they are not in a position to make reasoned decisions from activities with significant consequences. This is seen in the criminalisation of under-age drinking, smoking, gambling and sexual activities. So, those who sell alcohol or cigarettes to under-age children are committing a strict liability offence. An example of this type of offence is seen in the case of *Harrow London Borough Council v Shah & Shah* (1999) where the defendants were convicted of selling a lottery ticket to an under-age child.

See *OCR AS/A Level Law Book 1* at section 14.6.3 for further details.

1.4 Fault

In deciding whether a defendant is to be blamed for his conduct, the criminal law generally presumes that a defendant is responsible for his actions and the consequences of his actions.

1.4.1 Lack of fault

However, there are four main ways when the courts will recognise that the defendant is not to blame, or not fully to blame for the consequences of his actions.

- First, the law recognises that some people are properly exempt from criminal prosecution. In this category are children under the age of criminal responsibility. In England and Wales this is the age of ten. This is the lowest age of criminal responsibility in Europe. Also in this category are those who are insane. However, if it is decided that they committed an unlawful act, they can be dealt with by detention in a hospital under the Mental Health Act 1983.
- Second, the law accepts that a defendant may not be liable for some involuntary acts. An example of this is the case of *R v Mitchell* (1983), discussed in *OCR AS/A Level Law Book 1* at section 13.1.4, where D punched a man in a post office queue, causing him to stagger backwards into an 89-year-old woman. The woman was knocked over and injured, and a few days later died of her injuries. D was convicted of unlawful act manslaughter. The man who was punched by D was not charged with any criminal offence. When he staggered into the woman he was not in control of what he was doing.
- A third way in which a person may not be to blame for their actions is where they lack the required mental state (*mens rea*) for the particular offence. They are in control of their actions but do not have the required mental state for the offence. For example, if a man takes a coat from the coat rack at a restaurant, genuinely, but mistakenly, believing that it is his own coat, he is not liable for theft as he does not have the intention necessary for theft.
- Finally, there are some defences where, even though the defendant had the necessary mental state for the offence, they are not to be blamed. These defences include self-defence or defence of another, and duress where the defendant had been threatened with death or serious injury if they did not commit the crime.

1.4.2 Punishing fault

Where the defendant has been at fault and committed an offence the court will impose a punishment that reflects the level of fault. The most severe punishment – a mandatory life sentence – will be imposed on those who commit the most serious of offences – an unlawful killing – intentionally.

A maximum life sentence will be imposed on those who commit an unlawful killing but with lesser *mens rea*. So unlawful act manslaughter and gross negligence manslaughter have this as a maximum sentence but the judge can impose any sentence up to this maximum depending on the level of the defendant's fault.

The link between fault and punishment is also shown when death is caused by committing a driving offence. Examples include:

- causing death by dangerous driving, which has a maximum punishment of 14 years;
- causing death by careless driving, which has a maximum punishment of 5 years;
- causing death by careless driving when under the influence of drink or drugs, which has a maximum punishment of 14 years.

There are regular criticisms of these punishments, especially by families of victims, as the result of the offence is the same as other forms of unlawful homicides but the punishments are lower.

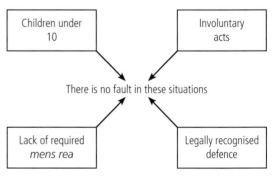

Figure 1.1 Situations where there is no fault

1.4.3 Strict liability

Although English law generally recognises that people are safeguarded from being found liable for an offence when their conduct has been without fault, there is one category of offences which appears to clash with this principle. These are offences of strict liability which are discussed in detail in *OCR AS/A Level Law Book 1* at section 14.6.

1.5 Principles in formulating criminal law

There are also principles which should be followed when the law for criminal offences is drawn up. There must be fair labelling. The law should be drafted so that the elements of the offence are clear and the law should not create retrospective liability.

1.5.1 Fair labelling

It is important that the law should be fair to the offender in that the level of offence should be in proportion to the type of offence. In the English legal system there are three categories of offence recognised: summary, triable-either-way and indictable. Indictable offences are the most serious and can only be tried at the Crown Court. This labels these offences as serious. So lesser offences carry a lower 'label'.

Another way that the law should be fair to the offender is that the punishment should be in proportion to the offence.

The labelling should also indicate to the public how the offence is viewed. This is fair to the public as well as the offender.

1.5.2 Maximum certainty

The law should be as certain as possible. If it is not known what elements constitute a crime, then it is not fair that a person could be convicted. Legal scholar Tony Honoré in his book, *About Law*, points out that:

> It is generally agreed that, as part of the rule of law, a person should not be punished by the state except for a crime defined by law in advance. But crimes can be very vaguely defined. In some countries there are crimes like 'bringing the state into disrepute', or 'corrupting public morals'. Can anyone be certain that what he does will not be held by the courts of his country to come under one of these headings?

In *R v Misra and Srivastava* (2004) discussed at 4.3.3 the defendants challenged their convictions for gross negligence manslaughter on the basis that the elements of this offence were too uncertain. The Court of Appeal rejected the challenge on the basis that the earlier case of *R v Adomako* (1995), decided by the House of Lords, had made the elements clear.

1.5.3 No retrospective liability

Where the unlawful conduct is not an offence at the time, it is clearly unfair to convict the defendant of the offence. This idea of not being liable retrospectively for crimes is set out in the European Convention on Human Rights at Article 7(1):

> No one shall be held guilty of any criminal offence on account of any act or omission which did not constitute a criminal offence under national or international law at the time when it was committed.

This prevents a government from creating a law to make someone guilty even though the act was not an offence when it was done.

In the case of *CR v United Kingdom* (1995) the defendant had been convicted of raping his wife and challenged the conviction under Article 7. The challenge was made on the basis that the offence did not exist until he was convicted of it. The challenge was unsuccessful on two grounds:
1 There had been earlier cases where the offence was beginning to be recognised.
2 The offence was one which supported fundamental objectives of the Convention.

Summary

- Criminal law generally prohibits conduct which is 'wrongful'. This can be conduct that:
  - causes harm or serious offence to others, including regulatory offences, or
  - is criminalised in order to protect us from ourselves – 'paternalistic', or
  - is legally morally wrong.

- Autonomy – the freedom of individuals to make their own choices and decisions – is important. It should only be limited where.
  - it is necessary to prevent harm
  - it interferes with the autonomy of other people
  - the people involved have weaker ability to make their own choice and need to be protected from potentially harmful activity.

- Fault should be the basis of criminal liability.
- In the English legal system it is recognised that there is no fault in the following situations:
  - children under ten
  - involuntary acts
  - where the defendant lacks the required *mens rea*
  - where the defendant can argue a recognised legal defence.

- Strict liability offences are an exception to the requirement for fault.
- The principles to be followed in formulating new criminal laws include:
  - fair labelling
  - maximum certainty in the elements
  - no retrospective effect.

Chapter 2

Murder

After reading this chapter you should be able to:
- Understand the *actus reus* of murder
- Understand the *mens rea* of murder
- Evaluate the law on murder
- Apply the law on murder to scenario-based situations

2.1 Definition of 'murder'

Homicide is the unlawful killing of a human being. There are different offences of homicide depending on the *mens rea* of the defendant and whether there is a special defence available. The most serious homicide offence is murder.

Murder is a common law offence. This means that it is not defined by any Act of Parliament. It has been defined by the decisions of judges in different cases, and the accepted definition is based on one given by a seventeenth-century judge, Lord Coke: 'Murder is the unlawful killing of a reasonable person in being and under the King's (or Queen's) Peace with malice aforethought, express or implied.'

The different elements of this definition are considered in detail under the *actus reus* and *mens rea* of murder below at sections 2.2 and 2.3.

Key term

Murder – 'the unlawful killing of a reasonable person in being and under the King's (or Queen's) Peace with malice aforethought, express or implied'.

2.1.1 Jurisdiction

Obviously, a person can be charged with a murder committed anywhere in England and Wales. But murder is unusual in that jurisdiction over it also includes any murder in any country by a British citizen. This means that if the defendant is a British citizen, s/he may be tried in an English court for a murder s/he is alleged to have committed in another country.

2.2 *Actus reus* of murder

The *actus reus* of murder is the unlawful killing of a reasonable creature in being and under the Queen's Peace. Breaking this down, it has to be proved that:
- the defendant killed
- a reasonable creature in being
- under the Queen's Peace and
- the killing was unlawful.

2.2.1 'Killed'

Act or omission

The *actus reus* of killing can be by an act or omission, but it must cause the death of the victim. Usually in murder cases, the *actus reus* is an act. But remember that an omission (a failure to act) can make a person liable for an offence.

This rule applies to murder, as seen by the case of *R v Gibbins and Proctor* (1918).

See *OCR AS/A Level Law Book 1* Chapter 13 for more information on *actus reus* of crimes generally.

Case study

R v Gibbins and Proctor (1918)

The father of a seven-year-old girl and his mistress kept the girl separate from the father's other children and deliberately starved her to death. The father had a duty to feed her because he was her parent and the mistress was held to have undertaken to look after the children, including the girl, so she was also under a duty to feed the child. The omission or failure to feed her was deliberate with the intention of killing or causing serious harm to her. In these circumstances they were guilty of murder. The failure to feed the girl was enough for the *actus reus* of murder.

Causation

Murder is a result crime. The defendant cannot be guilty unless his act or omission caused the death. In most cases there is no problem with this. For example, the defendant (D) shoots the victim (V) in the head and V is killed instantly. However, in some cases there may be other causes contributing to the death, such as poor medical treatment. This type of situation raises questions of causation.

The law on causation was considered fully in *OCR AS/A Level Law Book 1* at section 13.3.

2.2.2 'Reasonable creature in being'

This phrase means 'a human being'. So, for murder, a living person must be killed. Normally, this part of the definition does not cause any difficulties. The only two problem areas are:

- Is a foetus in the womb a 'reasonable creature in being'?
- Is a victim still considered to be alive (and so a 'reasonable creature in being') if they are 'brain-dead' but being kept alive by a life-support machine?

Foetus

A homicide offence cannot be charged in respect of the killing of a foetus. The child has to have an 'existence independent of the mother' for it to be considered a 'creature in being'. This means that it must have been expelled from her body and have an independent existence.

Brain-dead

It is not certain whether a person who is 'brain-dead' would be considered as a 'reasonable creature in being' or not. Doctors are allowed to switch off life-support machines without being liable for homicide. This suggests that 'brain-death' is the recognised test for death, but

there has been no case on this point. It is possible that the courts might decide that a defendant who switches off a life-support machine, not as a medical decision but intending to kill the victim, could be guilty of murder.

Time limit

By the Law Reform (Year and a Day Rule) Act 1996 there is no time limit on when a death may occur after an unlawful act but, where it is more than three years after the act, the consent of the Attorney-General is needed for a prosecution.

2.2.3 'Queen's Peace'

'Under the Queen's Peace' means that the killing of an enemy in the course of war is not murder.

2.2.4 'Unlawful'

The killing must be unlawful. If the killing is in self-defence or defence of another or in the prevention of crime and the defendant used reasonable force in the circumstances, then the killing is not unlawful. (See 8.1 for a detailed discussion of the rules of the defence of self-defence.)

Activity

Read the following situations and explain whether the *actus reus* for murder is present.

1. Anya is offered a lift home by Barnaby. After a few minutes, she realises he is driving away from her home. He then puts his hand on her thigh as he is driving and says that they can enjoy themselves. Anya is so afraid that she jumps out of the car while it is going at about 40 mph. She is hit by another car and killed.

2. Boris has been threatened by Clint in the past. He knows that Clint often carries a knife. One day Clint runs towards Boris shouting, 'You're for it now!' Boris picks up a heavy piece of concrete and throws it at Clint's head. Clint suffers head injuries and dies as a result.

3. Lily decides to kill Kevin. She takes his shotgun and loads it. She waits until he has gone to sleep, then she goes into his bedroom and shoots him in the head. Unbeknown to her, Kevin died from a drug overdose 20 minutes before she shot him.

4. Martha has an argument with her husband, Desmond. Desmond then goes into the kitchen and a few minutes later comes out shouting abuse at her. Martha sees what she thinks is a knife in his hand, although it is actually a child's toy. Believing that he is about to stab her, Martha throws an ash-tray at Desmond's head. This hits him on the temple and kills him.

2.3 *Mens rea* of murder

The *mens rea* for murder is stated as being 'malice aforethought, express or implied'. This means that there are two different intentions, either of which can be used to prove the defendant guilty of murder:
- express malice aforethought, which is the intention to kill, or
- implied malice aforethought, which is the intention to cause grievous bodily harm.

A defendant has the *mens rea* for murder if he has either of these intentions. This means that a person can be guilty of murder even though he did not intend to kill. This was decided in *R v Vickers* (1957).

The other issue is what is meant by 'grievous bodily harm'. In *DPP v Smith* (1961) the House of Lords decided that 'grievous bodily harm' has the natural meaning of 'really serious harm'. However, even if the judge directed the jury leaving out the word 'really' and just says 'serious harm', this is not a misdirection.

2.3.1 Intention to injure a foetus

In *Attorney-General's Reference (No. 3 of 1994)* (1997) it was held that it was not possible for a defendant to have the *mens rea* to kill or seriously injure a foetus. This was because a foetus does not have a separate existence from its mother.

2.3.2 Intention

The general rules on intention apply to murder.

These were discussed in *OCR AS/A Level Law Book 1* at section 14.3.

The main problem with proving intention is in cases where the defendant's main aim was something quite different from causing the death or serious injury of the victim, but in achieving the aim a death is caused. This is referred to as oblique intent. The defendant does not have the *mens rea* for murder unless he or she foresaw that he would also cause death or serious injury. This is known as foresight of consequences.

Foresight of consequences was considered in detail in *OCR AS/A Level Law Book 1* at section 14.3.2.

As the law in this area is complex and important, the three main cases are set out here again.

Foresight of consequences

The main rule is that foresight of consequences is not intention.

2.3.3 Transferred malice

The general rule on transferred malice applies to murder. So, if D fires a shot at V1 but misses and hits and kills V2, D is guilty of murder. It does not matter that D did not intend to kill V2. The intention to kill (or seriously injure) V1 is transferred.

See *OCR AS/A Level Law Book 1* Chapter 14.8 for more detail on transferred malice.

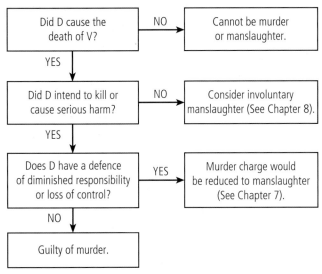

Figure 2.1 Flowchart on homicide

Activity

In each of the following situations, explain whether the defendant has the required intention for murder.

1   Jamie is annoyed because Harry has being trying to date his girlfriend. Jamie sees Harry in a local pub and goes over and punches him hard in the face, saying, 'Perhaps that will make you leave my girlfriend alone.' Harry dies as a result of the punch.
2   Diana intends to kill Edward. She fixes an explosive booby trap to the front door of his house, so that when he opens it the explosive will go off. Unknown to Diana, Edward has given Felix the keys to his house and told him to collect some papers from there. Felix opens the door and is killed by the explosion.
3   Ravinder's business has been losing a lot of money. He decides to set fire to one of the smaller buildings in the unit so that he can claim insurance on it. Ravinder knows that there is no one in his building, so he sets it alight. Unfortunately, the fire spreads to another building on the site. Nancy, who is working in that building, is trapped by the fire and dies.

	Law	Source/Case
Definition	'The unlawful killing of a reasonable person in being and under the King's (or Queen's) Peace, with malice aforethought, express or implied.'	Lord Coke (17th century)
Actus reus	Must unlawfully kill a person under the Queen's Peace. Can be an act or an omission.	*R v Gibbins and Proctor* (1918)
	A foetus is not considered a person for the purposes of murder.	*Attorney-General's Reference (No. 3 of 1994)* (1997)
Mens rea	Intention to kill *or* intention to cause grievous bodily harm.	*Vickers* (1957)
	Foresight of consequences is evidence of intention.	*Cunningham* (1981)
	Jury can find intention if death or serious injury was a virtual certainty as a result of D's actions and D appreciated this.	*Moloney* (1985) *Woollin* (1998)

Figure 2.2 Key facts chart for murder

2.4 Evaluation of the law on murder

In 2006 the Law Commission published a report, 'Murder, Manslaughter and Infanticide' (Law Com No. 304). In this report the Law Commission pointed out that there were many problems with the law on murder.

In its general comments on the law of murder, the report said (at paragraph 1.8):

> The law governing homicide in England and Wales is a rickety structure set upon shaky foundations. Some of its rules have remained unaltered since the seventeenth century, even though it has long been acknowledged that they are in dire need of reform. Other rules are of uncertain content, often because they have been constantly changed to the point that they can no longer be stated with any certainty or clarity.

The following problems were identified:

- The law on murder has developed bit-by-bit in individual cases and is not a coherent whole.
- A defendant can be convicted of murder even though he or she only intended to cause serious harm (the serious harm rule).
- There is no defence available if excessive force is used in self-defence.
- The defence of duress is not available as a defence to murder.
- The mandatory life sentence and the government's sentencing guidelines do not allow sufficient differentiation in sentencing to cover the wide variety of levels of blameworthiness in the current law of murder.

Each of these problems is discussed below.

The Law Commission also pointed out that there are problems with the special defences to murder of diminished responsibility and loss of control.

These problems are considered in Chapter 3, sections 3.2 and 3.3.

2.4.1 Meaning of intention

One of the main areas where the law has had piecemeal, or bit-by-bit, development by the courts, and which has caused problems, is the meaning of the word 'intention'. It is a concept which affects all specific intent offences but most of the cases which have been heard by the House of Lords have involved murder.

This issue has been discussed in detail at 14.3.2 of *OCR AS/A Level Law Book 1*.

The majority of murders involve the jury deciding if the defendant had direct intent – an intent to kill or commit grievous bodily harm.

If the prosecution cannot prove the defendant had direct intent they must prove he had indirect, or oblique, intent. Following the decision in *R v Woollin 1998* the judge should direct the jury that if a consequence (the death of the victim) is a virtually certain result of the defendant's act and the defendant foresaw that consequence as a virtually certain result, then the jury is entitled to find that the consequence was intended even though it was not the defendant's purpose to cause it. For example, if a person owns a small plane and plants a bomb aboard the plane which is timed to blow up in mid-flight. The bomb does explode, destroying the plane and killing the pilot. The person stated that the purpose of planting the bomb was because he was in financial trouble and wanted to claim money from the plane's insurance cover but he did not want to kill the pilot. However, he foresaw that it was virtually certain that the pilot would be seriously injured or killed by an explosion. In such case the jury, following the *Woollin* direction, is entitled to find that the person had an intention to kill or commit grievous bodily harm, and to convict them of murder.

However, in some cases there may be some 'moral elbow-room' where the law will recognise the existence of a moral dilemma or a good motive. For example, in the Herald of Free Enterprise disaster, a man (X) was blocking an escape ladder and refused to move, thereby preventing the escape of others. He was pushed off the ladder (by Y) and drowned. The defence of duress of circumstances (see Chapter 8.3) is not available for the offence of murder. However, if Y had been charged with murder it is likely that he would be acquitted as a jury, following the decision in *Woollin*, would have been able to exercise its entitlement not to find an indirect intention to kill. They could have recognised the moral dilemma between Y's main purpose of clearing the ladder, and thereby saving others, and his foresight of X's virtually certain death by drowning.

2.4.2 The serious harm rule

In its report, the Law Commission pointed out that Parliament, when it passed the Homicide Act 1957, never intended a killing to amount to murder unless the defendant realised that their conduct might cause death. It stated that, in its view, the present offence of murder is too wide.

Under the present law on murder, a defendant is guilty of murder if they had the intention to cause grievous bodily harm and actually cause the victim's death. In some of these cases the defendant may not even realise that death could occur. Yet they are just as guilty of murder as someone who deliberately sets out to kill their victim.

The following example was given in paragraph 1.17:

> D intentionally punches V in the face. The punch breaks V's nose and causes V to fall to the ground. In falling, V hits his or her head on the kerb causing a massive and fatal brain haemorrhage.

It was pointed out that if the jury decides that the harm the defendant intended the punch to cause can be described as 'serious', then this would be murder. Yet, most people would agree that this should not be the most serious offence of homicide and the defendant should not receive a mandatory life sentence for it.

Not only is the Law Commission very critical of this rule, but the problem had already been pointed out by judges as far back as 1981 in the case of *R v Cunningham* (1981). When the law was considered by the House of Lords, Lord Edmund Davies stated that he thought the *mens rea* for murder should be limited to an intention to kill. He said:

> [It is] strange that a person can be convicted of murder if death results from, say, his intentional breaking of another's arm, an action which, while undoubtedly involving the infliction of 'really serious harm' and as such, calling for severe punishment, would in most cases be unlikely to kill.

Although he was very critical of the law, Lord Edmund Davies felt that any change to the law had to be made by Parliament. This was because the law has been the same for over 200 years and it would therefore be wrong for judges to change such a well-established law.

As yet no reform to the law has been made, but the Law Commission made very specific proposals for how the law could be reformed.

2.4.3 Mandatory life sentence

For offenders aged 10–17 who are found guilty of murder, the judge has to order that they be detained at Her Majesty's Pleasure. For offenders aged 18 or over, the judge has to pass a sentence of life imprisonment.

Because the judge has no discretion, these sentences are known as the mandatory life sentence. The judge will then decide the minimum time the offender has to serve. The conditions of this time

are set out below. The judge cannot give a different sentence even if he or she feels that the defendant is not as blameworthy as a deliberate killer.

For other offences, including attempted murder, the judge can decide what the most appropriate sentence is for the offence and the offender. This makes it possible for a judge to give even a community sentence where the circumstances justify it. This happened in the case of *R v Gotts* (1992).

It is because of the mandatory life sentence for murder that the special defences of diminished responsibility and loss of control exist.

These defences reduce the charge to voluntary manslaughter. This allows the judge flexibility in passing sentence which he or she does not have when the defendant is convicted of murder.

See Chapter 3 for an explanation of voluntary manslaughter.

Minimum sentences

When sentencing, the judge will impose the mandatory life sentence and will fix the minimum number of years the offender must serve before being released on licence.

The sentencing problems have been aggravated by the government's guidelines on these minimum sentences as laid down in the Criminal Justice Act 2003. This gives three starting points for adult offenders:

- A whole life term for exceptionally serious cases, such as premeditated killings of two or more people, sexual or sadistic child murders or politically motivated murders.
- Thirty years' minimum for serious cases such as murders of police or prison officers, murders involving firearms, sexual or sadistic killings or killings aggravated by racial or sexual orientation.
- Fifteen years' minimum for murders not falling within the two higher categories.

Under these rules the defendant in *R v Martin (Anthony)* (2002) (see Chapter 8, section 8.3) who shot and killed a burglar would have had to have been given a minimum sentence of 30 years. This is the same length of sentence as a contract killer, who is paid to kill a victim deliberately, would receive. The guidelines do not allow sufficient differentiation between levels of blameworthiness.

The Law Commission was not asked to consider sentencing. However, in its proposals for making murder into a two-tier offence, it states that the mandatory life sentence and the guidelines on minimum sentences should only apply to first degree murder. This would create a fairer sentence structure.

2.4.4 Law Commission's proposals for reform

The Law Commission proposed that murder should be reformed by dividing it into two separate offences:
- first degree murder, and
- second degree murder.

First degree murder would cover cases in which the defendant intended to kill. It would also cover situations where the defendant intended to cause serious harm and was aware that his conduct posed a serious risk of death.

Cases in which the defendant intended to do serious injury, but was not aware that there was a serious risk of death, would be second degree murder. By dividing murder into two separate categories, the mandatory life sentence would apply only to first degree murder. Second degree murder would carry a maximum of a life sentence but would allow the judge discretion in sentencing.

Extension question

Find the Law Commission report, 'Murder, Manslaughter and Infanticide' (2006) (Law Com No. 304), online at www.lawcom.gov.uk. Look at paragraphs 163 to 170 where the proposals are summarised. Then choose one issue and read the main report on that.

2.4.5 Government's response to the Law Commission's proposals

In July 2008 the government issued a consultation paper, 'Murder, Manslaughter and Infanticide: Proposals for Reform of the Law' (CP 19/08). This paper rejected the Law Commission's proposal of completely reforming murder by making it a two-tier offence.

The only area where the government accepted that reform was needed was the lack of a defence for those who use excessive force in self-defence. This reform was implemented as part of the Coroners and Justice

Act 2009. Under this Act there is a defence of 'loss of control' where the defendant kills through loss of control due to fear of serious violence. If this defence is established the charge of murder is reduced to voluntary manslaughter

See Chapter 3 for more detail on this defence.

This might allow defendants in cases such as *Clegg* (1995) and *Martin (Anthony)* (2002) (see Chapter 8, section 8.3) to have a partial defence to a charge of murder which could reduce the offence to manslaughter. However, they would have to prove 'loss of control' as well as the fear of serious violence.

The Coroners and Justice Act 2009 does not address the problems of no intent to kill, the difficulty of the meaning of intention, the lack of a defence of duress and the mandatory life sentence. These will continue to be problems in the law of murder.

Tip

Questions on murder often require knowledge of the issues of *mens rea* and/or causation. Make sure you know these. They are dealt with in detail in *OCR AS/A Level Law Book 1*.

Activity

1   Carlo goes into a small shop, points a gun at the sales person and demands that he gives him all the money in the till. At that moment, Dean, a customer, enters the shop. Carlo panics and hits Dean on the head with the gun. Carlo then runs away.

Dean has serious head injuries and is taken to hospital by ambulance. On the way to the hospital, the ambulance is involved in a collision. This causes further injury to Dean. It also delays getting him to hospital and Dean dies.

Advise whether Carlo is liable for the offence of murder.

2   Discuss whether the law on murder is in need of reform.

Summary ✎

- Murder is the 'unlawful killing of a reasonable person in being and under the King's (or Queen's) Peace with malice aforethought, express or implied'.
- For the *actus reus* of murder it has to be proved that:
  - D killed
  - a reasonable creature in being
  - under the Queen's Peace and
  - the killing was unlawful.

- For the *mens rea* of murder there must be:
  - express malice aforethought, which is the intention to kill, or
  - implied malice aforethought, which is the intention to cause grievous bodily harm.

- Foresight of consequences is only evidence of intention so that:
  - a jury should be directed that they cannot find the necessary intention unless they feel sure that death or serious injury was a virtual certainty as a result of the defendant's actions, and that the defendant appreciated that such was the case.

- There are a number of problems in the law on murder:
  - The law has developed bit-by-bit.
  - Is it right that someone who did not intend to kill should be guilty of murder?
  - There is no defence where excessive force is used in self-defence.
  - The defence of duress is not available for murder.
  - There is a mandatory sentence of life imprisonment.

Chapter 3

Voluntary manslaughter

After reading this chapter you should be able to:
- Understand the partial defence of diminished responsibility
- Understand the partial defence of loss of control
- Evaluate the law on the defences of diminished responsibility and loss of control
- Apply the law of these two defences to scenario-based situations

3.1 Partial defences to murder

There are special defences to a charge of murder. These are where the killing occurs when the defendant is under:
- diminished responsibility, or
- loss of control.

Diminished responsibility is set out in the Homicide Act 1957 as amended by s 52 of the Coroners and Justice Act 2009. Loss of control is set out in the Coroners and Justice Act 2009. These defences are available only to a charge of murder. They are also only partial defences. This means that the defendant is not completely acquitted. Instead, when one of these defences is successful, the offence of murder is reduced to voluntary manslaughter. It is known as voluntary manslaughter because the defendant had the necessary *mens rea* for murder.

This verdict of manslaughter instead of murder is important because it means that the judge has discretion in the sentence which he imposes. When a person is found guilty of murder the judge has to pass a sentence of life imprisonment – the mandatory life sentence. However, for manslaughter the judge can give an appropriate sentence. For a defendant suffering mental problems this could be a hospital order. For a defendant acting under loss of control this could be a short term of imprisonment. The imposition of an appropriate punishment links to the theory of fair labelling referred to at Chapter 1, section 1.5.1.

3.2 Diminished responsibility

This defence was introduced for the first time by the Homicide Act 1957. Before 1957 if a person with mental problems killed, then their only defence was insanity. The test for insanity is a very narrow one and many defendants who clearly suffer from a mental illness do not always come within it. This is why the defence of diminished responsibility was created.

See Chapter 7 for further information on the defence of insanity.

3.2.1 Definition of diminished responsibility

The defence is set out in s 2(1) of the Homicide Act as amended by s 52 of the Coroners and Justice Act 2009. The effect of this section is that a person who kills or is a party to the killing of another is not to be convicted of murder if he was suffering from an abnormality of mental functioning which:

(a) arose from a recognised medical condition,

(b) substantially impaired D's ability to—

    (i) understand the nature of his conduct, or

    (ii) form a rational judgment, or

    (iii) exercise self-control, and

(c) provides an explanation for D's acts and omissions in doing or being a party to the killing.

The burden of proving the defence is on the defendant, but the defendant need only prove it on the balance of probabilities.

3.2.2 Abnormality of mental functioning

What is meant by 'abnormality of mental functioning'? Before s 52 of the Coroners and Justice Act 2009 amended the definition of diminished responsibility, the law required the defendant to be suffering from an 'abnormality of mind'. In *R v Byrne* (1960) the Court of Appeal described this as 'a state of mind so different from that of ordinary human beings that the reasonable man would term it abnormal'.

Case study

R v Byrne (1960)

The defendant was a sexual psychopath who strangled a young woman and then mutilated her body. The medical evidence was that because of his condition, he was unable to control his perverted desires. He was convicted of murder but the Court of Appeal quashed the conviction and substituted a conviction for manslaughter.

Although this case was decided on the old definition, it is likely that the courts will still use the same standard of abnormality. So the test will probably be that D's mental functioning was so different from that of ordinary human beings that the reasonable man would term it abnormal.

3.2.3 Cause of the abnormality of mental functioning

Under s 2(1) of the Homicide Act 1957, as amended, the cause of the abnormality of mental functioning must arise from a 'recognised medical condition'.

This is wide enough to cover both psychological and physical conditions. It obviously covers any recognised mental disorder. These can be wide-ranging such as depressive illness, paranoia or Battered Woman's Syndrome. It also covers any physical condition which affects mental functioning such as epilepsy, sleep disorders or diabetes.

There must be medical evidence given at the trial of an abnormality of mental functioning arising from a recognised medical condition.

3.2.4 Substantially impaired

The abnormality of mental functioning must substantially impair the defendant's mental responsibility for his acts or omissions in doing or being a party to the killing.

In *R v Byrne* (1960) the appeal court said that the question of whether the impairment was substantial was one of degree and that it was for the jury to decide.

In *R v Lloyd* (1967) it was held that 'substantial' does not mean total, nor does it mean trivial or minimal. It is something in between and it is for the jury to decide if the defendant's mental responsibility is impaired and, if so, whether it is substantially impaired. However, as it is a question of fact, the judge can withdraw the point from the jury if there is no evidence on which a reasonable jury could conclude that the defendant's mental responsibility was substantially impaired.

These two cases were decided on the law before it was amended in 2009. However in *R v Golds* (2016) the Supreme Court pointed out that there is no indication in the 2009 Act that Parliament wished the words to carry a different meaning. So the pre-2009 law is still relevant.

Case study

R v Golds (2016)

D killed his partner. He admitted the killing. The medical evidence was that he had an abnormality of mental functioning arising from a medical condition. The only issue was whether he was in a psychotic state at the time of the killing.

On the issue of substantial impairment, the judge told the jury that he would not give them specific guidance on the meaning of the everyday word 'substantially' unless they requested assistance. He was convicted of murder.

On appeal the Supreme Court upheld the conviction and said that the judge is not ordinarily required to attempt to define the meaning of 'substantially'. This should only be done where there is a risk that the jury will not understand the meaning of the word.

If a definition is given, the judge must direct that, while an impairment must be more than merely trivial to be substantial, it is not the case that any impairment that is more than trivial will suffice.

3.2.5 What must be substantially impaired?

The defendant's ability to do one of three things must be substantially impaired. These things are set out in s 2(1A) of the Homicide Act 1957. They are:

- to understand the nature of his conduct
- to form a rational judgement
- to exercise self-control.

These three points were used in the case of *R v Byrne* (1960) (see section 3.2.2 above). In the judgment in that case the court said that 'abnormality of mind' (the then test for diminished responsibility) was wide enough:

> to cover the mind's activities in all its aspects, not only the perception of physical acts and matters, and the ability to form a rational judgement as to whether an act is right or wrong, but also the ability to exercise will power to control physical acts in accordance with that rational judgement.

The amendments to the definition made by the Coroners and Justice Act 2009 have effectively put the decision in *Byrne* into statutory form. So what does each of these three things mean?

Ability to understand the nature of his conduct

This covers situations such as where D is in an automatic state and does not know what s/he is doing. It also covers cases where D suffers from delusions and believes, for example, that s/he is killing the devil when in fact s/he is killing a person. In this type of situation D does not understand the nature of what s/he is doing.

It could also cover defendants with severe learning difficulties whose mental age is so low that they do not understand the nature of what they are doing.

Ability to form a rational judgement

Even if D does know the nature of his/her conduct, s/he may not be able to form a rational judgement about his/her acts or omissions. Those suffering from paranoia or schizophrenia may well not be able to form a rational judgement. Another recognised medical condition where D may not be able to form a rational judgement is Battered Women's Syndrome.

Ability to exercise self-control

This was the situation in *R v Byrne* (1960). Byrne was a sexual psychopath. The medical evidence was that this condition meant he was unable to control his perverted desires. The defence of diminished responsibility was therefore available to him.

3.2.6 Provides an explanation for D's conduct

In order to come within the defence of diminished responsibility, D has to prove that the abnormality of mental functioning provides an explanation for his/her acts and omissions in doing or being a party to the killing (s 2(1B) of the Homicide Act 1957).

This is a new principle of diminished responsibility introduced by the Coroners and Justice Act 2009. There must now be some causal connection between D's abnormality of mental functioning and the killing.

Section 2(1B) of the Homicide Act explains this principle further as it states: 'an abnormality of mental functioning provides an explanation for D's conduct if it causes, or is a significant contributory factor in causing, D to carry out that conduct.'

So the abnormality of mental functioning need not be the only factor which caused D to do or be involved in the killing. However, it must be a significant factor. This is particularly important where D is intoxicated at the time of the killing.

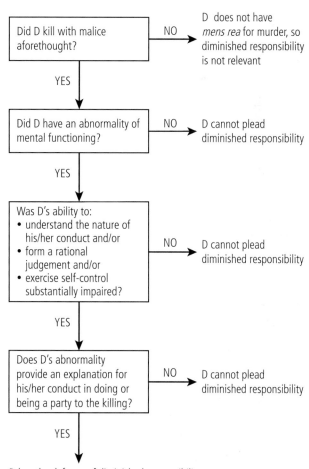

Figure 3.1 Flowchart on diminished responsibility

3.2.7 Diminished responsibility and intoxication

The defence of diminished responsibility becomes more complicated when the defendant was also intoxicated at the time of the killing.

There are three possibilities to consider:

- that the defendant was intoxicated at the time of the killing and tries to use the defence of diminished responsibility;
- that the defendant was intoxicated and has a pre-existing abnormality of mental functioning;
- that the intoxication is due to an addiction.

The defendant was intoxicated at the time of the killing and tries to use the defence of diminished responsibility

Intoxication on its own cannot be used as the basis of a defence of diminished responsibility. The defence requires that the abnormality of mental functioning must be due to a recognised medical condition and intoxication does not fall within this. This was the position under the Homicide Act 1957 and is still the position after the Coroners and Justice Act 2009. This was confirmed in *R v Dowds* 2012 when the Court of Appeal stated that if Parliament had meant to change the law, then they would have introduced changes in the 2009 Act.

The defendant was intoxicated and has a pre-existing abnormality of mental functioning

This was the situation in *R v Dietschmann* (2003).

Case study

R v Dietschmann (2003)

D was upset because, in his view, V was behaving in a way which was disrespectful to the memory of D's aunt who had just died. He killed V by repeatedly kicking him and stamping on him. The psychiatrists called by both the prosecution and the defence agreed D was suffering from an adjustment disorder in the form of depressed grief reaction to the death of his aunt. However, they disagreed on whether this had substantially impaired his mental responsibility for the killing. D had also drunk large amounts of alcohol before the killing. He was convicted and appealed.

Lord Hutton said, on the appeal to the House of Lords, that the question was not simply whether D would have killed had he not been intoxicated and he gave the following model direction to be given to juries:

'Has D satisfied you that, despite the drink, his mental abnormality substantially impaired his mental responsibility for his fatal acts, or has he failed to satisfy you of that?'

Lord Hutton also observed that if the jury decided that D would not have killed without taking the drink or drugs, it was unlikely it would find that the abnormality on its own was sufficient to impair his responsibility.

The intoxication is due to an addiction

There is a recognised medical condition called Alcohol Dependency Syndrome (ADS) which means that a person cannot control their drinking and this can be used for the defence of diminished responsibility. The leading case on this point is *R v Wood* (2008).

Case study

R v Wood (2008)

D was an alcoholic and after drinking heavily, had gone to V's flat. D claimed he had fallen asleep there and been woken by V trying to perform oral sex on him. D repeatedly hit V with a meat cleaver, killing him. At the trial medical experts agreed that D was suffering from ADS, but disagreed as to whether this had damaged his brain.

The judge directed the jury that if they found that D had suffered brain damage from his long-term abuse of alcohol then the defence of diminished responsibility was available to him. But if they found that he had not suffered brain damage, they then had to decide whether the drinking had been voluntary or not. If it was voluntary then D could not use the defence of diminished responsibility.

D was convicted of murder and appealed to the Court of Appeal who reduced the conviction to voluntary manslaughter on the grounds of diminished responsibility.

In cases where the defendant has an addiction the jury have to consider the effect of the alcohol consumed because of the addiction as this is classed as involuntary drinking.

If the consumption is not due to the addiction it is classed as voluntary drinking and its effects cannot be considered.

If there is both voluntary and involuntary drinking, so not all the consumption is due to the addiction, the defence can still be pleaded but the jury can only consider the effects of the involuntary drinking, and they have to decide whether this substantially impaired his mental functioning.

The issue was considered again in *R v Stewart* (2009) when the Court of Appeal set out a three-stage test for juries in such cases to consider:

1 Was D suffering from an 'abnormality of mind' (now mental functioning)? They pointed out that the mere fact that D has ADS would not automatically amount to an abnormality. The nature and the extent of the ADS had to be considered.
2 If so, was D's abnormality caused by the ADS?
3 If so, was D's mental responsibility substantially impaired? To decide this, all the evidence, including the medical evidence, should be considered. Relevant issues to be considered may include:
   (a) the extent and seriousness of D's dependency,
   (b) the extent to which D's ability to control his drinking, or to choose whether to drink or not, was reduced,
   (c) whether D was capable of abstinence from alcohol, and if so, for how long,
   (d) whether D was choosing for a particular reason, such as a birthday celebration, to decide to get drunk, or to drink even more than usual,
   (e) D's pattern of drinking preceding the killing, and
   (f) D's ability, if any, to make decisions about ordinary day-to-day matters.

3.2.8 Reform of the law

The original law of diminished responsibility was reformed by the Coroners and Justice Act 2009.

The Law Commission, in their report, 'Murder, Manslaughter and Infanticide' (2006), had recommended that the definition of diminished responsibility should be modernised so as to take into account changing medical knowledge.

The changes made by the 2009 Act have done that. By using the phrase 'recognised medical condition' the definition should now be flexible enough to allow for future developments in medical knowledge.

The definition also now sets out clearly what aspects of the defendant's mental functioning must be substantially impaired in order for the partial defence of diminished responsibility to succeed. This

	Law	Act/Case
Definition	Suffering from an abnormality of mental functioning which: • arose from a recognised medical condition • substantially impaired D's ability to do one or more of the following: – understand the nature of the conduct – form a rational judgement – exercise self-control, and • provide an explanation for D's conduct.	s 2(1) of the Homicide Act 1957 (as amended by the Coroners and Justice Act 2009)
Abnormality of mental functioning	A state of mind so different from that of ordinary human beings that the reasonable man would term it abnormal.	*Byrne* (1960)
Substantially impaired	A question of degree for the jury to decide. 'Substantial' does not mean 'total' nor 'trivial' or 'minimal' but something in between.	*Byrne* (1960) *Golds* (2016)
Provides an explanation for D's conduct	The abnormality of mental functioning provides an explanation for D's conduct if it causes, or is a significant contributory factor in causing, D to carry out that conduct.	s 2(1B) of the Homicide Act 1957
Effect of intoxication	• Transient effect of drink or drugs on brain cannot found the defence of diminished responsibility. • Where the defendant has a pre-existing mental disorder, intoxication does not prevent him using the defence; the abnormality of mental functioning does not have to be the sole cause of the defendant doing the killing. • Alcohol Dependency Syndrome can be an abnormality of mental functioning.	*Dowds* (2012) *Dietschmann* (2003) *Wood* (2008)
Burden of proof	It is for the defence to prove on the balance of probabilities.	s 2(2) of the Homicide Act 1957
Effect of defence	The charge of murder is reduced to manslaughter.	s 2(3) of the Homicide Act 1957

Figure 3.2 Key facts chart on diminished responsibility

incorporates the decision in *Byrne* (1960) into the statutory definition of diminished responsibility.

3.2.9 Evaluation of the law on diminished responsibility

Although the Coroners and Justice Act has resolved many of the previous problems in the law, there are still some areas where difficulties remain.

Burden of proof

A main point is that the burden of proof should not be on the defendant. For most other defences the defendant only has to raise the issue and the prosecution has to disprove it. This should also apply to diminished responsibility. At the moment, defendants pleading diminished responsibility are at a disadvantage which is not faced by those raising loss of control as a defence.

It has also been argued that putting the burden of proof on the defendant could be a breach of Article 6(2) of the European Convention on Human Rights, which states that 'everyone charged with a criminal offence shall be presumed to be innocent until proven guilty according to law'. Making the defendant prove diminished responsibility could be considered a breach of this right to be presumed innocent. However, the courts have consistently held that there is not a breach of Article 6.

Developmental immaturity

The Law Commission in its 2006 report had also recommended that developmental immaturity in those under 18 should also be included within the definition of diminished responsibility. The reason for this was because there is evidence to show that frontal lobes of the brain, which play an important role in the development of self-control and in controlling impulsive behaviour, do not mature until the age of 14.

The government took the view that there was no need to include 'developmental immaturity' as a specific cause of diminished responsibility. It thought that conditions such as learning disabilities and autism spectrum disorders were recognised medical conditions and that these were particularly relevant in the context of juvenile offenders. This is true but 'developmental immaturity' is not the same as learning disability.

If there is no such defence, children as young as ten may be convicted of murder when they are developmentally immature. They cannot use the defence of diminished responsibility under the existing law as they are not suffering from an abnormality of mental functioning.

3.3 Loss of control

Loss of control is a partial defence to a charge of murder. If it is successful, D will be found guilty of manslaughter instead of murder. This allows the judge discretion in sentencing.

Loss of control replaced the former defence of provocation. Provocation as a defence had many problems and the Law Commission recommended reform. The law on loss of control is set out in s 54 of the Coroners and Justice Act 2009. Section 54(1) states:

> Where a person (D) kills or is a party to the killing of another (V), D is not to be convicted of murder if:
>
> (a) D's acts and omissions in doing or being a party to the killing resulted from D's loss of self-control,
>
> (b) the loss of self-control had a qualifying trigger, and
>
> (c) a person of D's sex and age, with a normal degree of tolerance and self-restraint and in the circumstances of D, might have reacted in the same or in a similar way to D.

So, the following points are essential for the defence to be successful:

- D must have lost self-control
- there must be a qualifying trigger (see section 3.3.2 below)
- a person of the same sex and age would have reacted in the same way as D in the same circumstances.

Note that all cases decided under the former defence of provocation are no longer good law. However, some are included as they are useful for discussion and comparison purposes.

Key term

Loss of control – a partial defence to a charge of murder which reduces the offence to one of voluntary manslaughter under s 54(1) of the Coroners and Justice Act 2009.

3.3.1 Loss of self-control

The first matter to be proved is that the defendant lost his or her self-control when doing the act or acts which caused death.

Under the old defence of provocation the loss of control had to be sudden and temporary. However, s 54(2) of the 2009 Act sets out that the defendant's loss of self-control does not have to be sudden.

Whether the defendant lost self-control will be a matter for the jury to decide and will have to be a total loss of self-control – a partial loss will not be sufficient. The jury is entitled to draw upon their life experiences when considering the evidence to decide if this requirement is satisfied. Apart from not having to be sudden there has not yet been any statutory or judicial interpretation as to the meaning of loss of self-control.

However, it could mean:

- that the defendant D lost their ability to maintain their action in accordance with considered judgment, or
- that the defendant lost their normal powers of reasoning, or
- that the defendant's behaviour was atypical, or out of character, and normally they would not have acted in this way.

Temper or anger or a reaction out of character, or even acting spectacularly out of character, are not sufficient. D must have really 'lost it', or 'snapped'. In *R v Jewell* (2014) the fact that the defendant was unwell, sleeping badly, tired, depressed and 'unable to think straight was insufficient to amount to a loss of control.'

Case study

R v Jewell (2014)

D shot V at point blank range using a shotgun and fled the scene. He was subsequently arrested in his car which contained weapons, ammunition and what was described as a 'survival kit' including spare clothes, a tent, a passport, a driving licence and a cheque book. At his trial D told the jury that when he got out of his car outside V's house, 'I did it because I lost control. I could not control my actions. I could not think straight. My head was fucked up. It was like an injection in the head, an explosion in my head.' The judge considered that there was insufficient evidence of D having lost his self-control and this decision was supported by the Court of Appeal.

3.3.2 Qualifying trigger

There has to be a qualifying trigger for the loss of control to come within the defence. Section 55 sets out the qualifying triggers which are permitted. These are where the loss of control was attributable to:

- D's fear of serious violence from V against D or another identified person (s 55(3)), or
- a thing or things done or said (or both) which –
  (a) constituted circumstances of an extremely grave character, and
  (b) caused D to have a justifiable sense of being seriously wronged (s 55(4)).

Alternatively, the qualifying trigger can be a combination of these two matters (s 55(5)).

Fear of violence

Section 55(3) states that 'This subsection applies if D's loss of self-control was attributable to D's fear of serious violence from V against D or another identified person'.

D does not have to fear violence by V: fear of violence on another person can amount to a qualifying trigger. This was illustrated in *R v Ward 2012*

Case study

R v Ward 2012

D, his brother and V became friends. They spent much of a day and night drinking and taking drugs. The following morning V waited outside the house for a taxi, but because it was cold tried to come back into the house. There was some pushing and shoving and V head-butted D's brother. D came to his brother's aid and hit V with a pickaxe handle causing severe injuries from which he later died. D pleaded guilty to manslaughter on the grounds of loss of control, which was accepted by the prosecution.

D had not feared serious violence towards himself but s 55(3) applied as he feared that V would use serious violence to his brother

In *R v Lodge* 2014 D also pleaded Loss of Control successfully on the basis that he had lost his self-control and killed V, who was described as a 'small scale drugs dealer' after V had attacked him with a baseball bat.

Note that the other person who D fears is going to use violence has to be identified. It cannot be a general fear of violence.

However, under s 55(6)(a) where D has incited the violence, D cannot rely on the qualifying trigger of fear of violence. This was emphasised in *R v Dawes* (2013).

R v Dawes (2013)

D had returned home to find his wife and V asleep on the sofa with their legs entwined. There was an altercation and D stabbed V, killing him.

D was convicted of murder. On appeal, he put forward the argument that the judge should have left the defence of loss of control to the jury. The Court of Appeal upheld his conviction and pointed out that a defendant could not rely on sexual infidelity as a qualifying trigger. Nor could he rely on fear of violence where he had induced that violence. The Coroners and Justice Act was quite clear on both those points.

The Court of Appeal also pointed out that where D has the normal capacity of self-restraint and tolerance then, unless the circumstances were extremely grave, any normal irritation or even serious anger will not come within 'loss of control' for the Act's purposes.

Things said or done

Under s 55(4), there are two points which have to be shown if D is relying on things said or done. These are that:

- they were of an 'extremely grave character', and
- they caused D to have a justifiable sense of being seriously wronged.

The question of whether the circumstances are extremely grave and whether D had a justifiable sense of being seriously wronged should be judged objectively. The break-up of a relationship will not normally constitute circumstances of an extremely grave character nor entitle the aggrieved party to have a justifiable sense of being seriously wronged. It was observed in *R v Hatter 2013* that the circumstances must be *extremely* grave and D's sense of being seriously wronged by them must be *justifiable*. This requires an objective assessment by the judge and/or the jury. If it were otherwise it would mean that a qualifying trigger would be present if D were to give an account to the effect that, 'the circumstances were extremely grave to me and caused me to have what I believed was a justifiable sense that I had been seriously wronged' which was not the purpose of the legislation.

The interpretation of s 55(4) has been considered in the following cases of *R v Zebedee 2012, R v Hatter 2013* and *R v Bowyer 2014*.

R v Zebedee (2012)

D lost control when his 94-year-old father, who suffered from Alzheimer's and was doubly incontinent, repeatedly soiled himself. D killed his father. D put forward the defence of loss of control, but was convicted of murder and his conviction upheld.

The appeal court ruled that in order for 'things done or things said' to be a qualifying trigger they must constitute circumstances of an extremely grave character and D must have a justifiable sense of being seriously wronged. Neither of these two conditions was present in this case.

R v Hatter (2013)

D began a relationship with B but eventually the relationship phased out and she started seeing another man although she never told D it was over. He went to her house at midnight with a knife and climbed through an upstairs window. He claimed he had taken the knife to lift the carpets and had accidentally stabbed her in the chest and wrist when he spun around whilst holding the knife. He then stabbed himself in the chest but he survived. The judge held that there was no loss of control defence available to D as there was no evidence that he had lost his control, the circumstances were not of an extremely grave nature, nor did he have a justifiable sense of being seriously wronged. D was convicted of murder and appealed against the judge's ruling but his appeal was dismissed.

R v Bowyer (2013)

D and V were both having a relationship with W who was a prostitute and V was her pimp. D was not aware she was a prostitute. D and V were both aware of the other's relationship with W. D went to V's house to burgle him. In the course of the burglary D was disturbed by V and a fight developed. V revealed that W was a prostitute and taunted D that she was his best earner. D lost his control, beat V and tied him up. He was left alive by D but was found dead the following afternoon. D was convicted of murder.

On appeal it was decided that D had no justifiable sense of being wronged as he was committing a burglary. The court decided that he deliberately entered V's home, which he had targeted, to steal property to feed his drug habit. The court concluded that V was entitled to say and do anything reasonable, including using force, to eject a burglar from his home and that this did not give V any justifiable sense of being wronged, let alone seriously wronged. As a result, one essential ingredient of this defence was entirely absent.

Excluded matters

The 2009 Act specifically states that sexual infidelity can never be a qualifying trigger. Under the old law on provocation, sexual infidelity was allowed as a reason for provocation. However, the government felt that provocation allowed a defence to a jealous man who killed his wife or girlfriend because she was having an affair. They also felt that such male violence against women is not acceptable in the twenty-first century.

In *R v Clinton* (2012), the Court of Appeal held that the Coroners and Justice Act 2009 makes it quite clear that sexual infidelity alone cannot amount to a qualifying trigger for the defence of loss of control. However, sexual infidelity did not have to be completely disregarded. It could be considered if it was integral to and formed an essential part of the context where there were other factors which could be qualifying triggers.

In *R v Dawes* (2013) (see above) the Court of Appeal confirmed that sexual infidelity alone cannot amount to a qualifying trigger.

Case study

R v Clinton (2012)

D was suffering from depression and took medication. His wife told him she was having an affair and taunted him about looking up suicide websites, saying he had not got the courage to commit suicide. They argued and the following day D killed her. He was convicted of murder but appealed on the basis that the defence of loss of control should have been left to the jury. The Court of Appeal agreed and quashed the conviction.

Considered desire for revenge

The defence cannot be allowed if D acted in a 'considered desire for revenge' and here the defence is similar to provocation when there had to be a sudden and temporary loss of self-control.

3.3.3 Standard of self-control

The 2009 Act requires that, whichever 'qualifying trigger' is relied on, it is necessary for D to show that:

> a person of D's sex and age, with a normal degree of tolerance and self-restraint and in the circumstances of D, might have reacted in the same or similar way.

D is expected to show a normal degree of tolerance and self-control. The fact that D is particularly hot-tempered cannot be taken into account when looking at the level of self-control expected.

Although the Act refers to the accused's circumstances, s 54(3) emphasises that circumstances whose only relevance to D's conduct is that they bear on D's general capacity for tolerance or self-restraint are not to be considered. There is an objective test for this part of the defence and, apart from sex and age, the jury cannot consider any circumstance of D which might have made him or her have less self-control.

3.3.4 Circumstances of the defendant

Although only age and sex can be considered in deciding the level of self-control expected from D, other circumstances of D may be taken into consideration in deciding whether such a 'normal' person might have reacted in the same or in a similar way to D in those circumstances. These circumstances could include:

- depression,
- epilepsy, or
- any history of sexual abuse.

Voluntary intoxication

Voluntary intoxication is not a matter to be considered as part of D's circumstances. The Court of Appeal in *R v Asmelash* (2013) refused to allow D's voluntary intoxication to be considered. The court said that if Parliament had meant that to be the position, then it would have been clearly stated in the 2009 Act. The court also pointed out that voluntary intoxication could not found the other partial defence of diminished responsibility, as we saw in section 3.2.7 above. It was inconceivable that different criteria should govern the two defences.

However, if a sober person in the defendant's circumstances, with normal levels of tolerance and self-restraint, might have behaved in the same way as the defendant when confronted by the relevant qualifying trigger, then the defendant might still be able to use the defence of loss of control, even though they were intoxicated.

Also if a defendant with a severe problem with alcohol or drugs was mercilessly taunted about the condition, so that it was a qualifying trigger, the alcohol or drug problem would then form part of the circumstances for consideration.

Might have reacted in the same or similar way to D

The jury then has to consider whether the normal person in the circumstances of D would have reacted as D did. The defence will fail if the jury considers that the 'normal person' might have lost control but would not have reacted in the same way.

3.3.5 Sufficient evidence

In provocation, the judge was bound to leave the defence to the jury if there was any evidence that the defendant was provoked to lose his self-control, however improbable the defence may have appeared. The Law Commission, when considering reform of the law, had felt that this did not 'serve the interests of justice' because the need to put the defence to the jury in these circumstances increases the likelihood that an unmeritorious claim may succeed. It had recommended that the trial judge should have the task of 'filtering out purely speculative and wholly unmeritorious claims'.

Although the reforms made by the Coroners and Justice Act 2009 did not follow all the recommendations made by the Law Commission, the Act has given the trial judge the task of deciding if there was sufficient evidence to leave the defence of loss of control to the jury.

Section 54(5) of the Coroners and Justice Act 2009 states that:

> On a charge of murder, if sufficient evidence is adduced to raise an issue with respect to the defence ... [of loss of control], the jury must assume that the defence is satisfied unless the prosecution proves beyond reasonable doubt that it is not.

This is further qualified by s 54(6) which states:

> sufficient evidence is adduced to raise an issue with respect to the defence if evidence is adduced on which, in the opinion of the trial judge, a jury, properly directed, could reasonably conclude that the defence might apply.

These provisions were considered in *Dawes* (2013) where the cases of three separate defendants were considered. In all three cases, the trial judge had refused to leave the defence of loss of control to the jury. The Court of Appeal dismissed all the appeals. The court held that the matters put forward by the defence 'required objective assessment by the judge at the end of the evidence'. In all cases the judge was quite right to rule that there was not sufficient evidence to leave the defence to the jury.

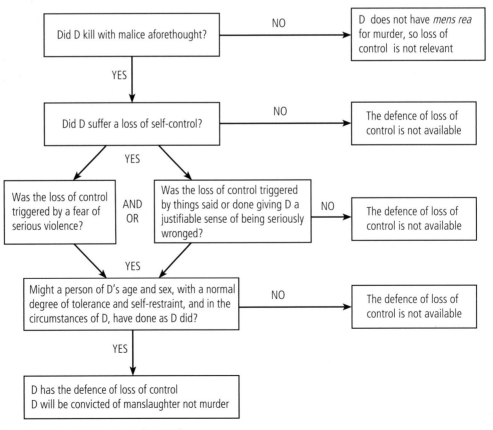

Figure 3.3 Flowchart on loss of control

3.3.6 Reform of the law

The Coroners and Justice Act 2009 abolished the old defence of provocation and replaced it with the defence of loss of control. This reform was made because there had been many problems with the law on provocation.

Problems with provocation

Provocation was originally a common law defence. The Homicide Act set out some of the tests for the defence, but did not give a complete definition. This created problems as the law in previous cases had to be considered as well as the test in the Homicide Act.

One problem was the wording of the test, which stated that the jury had to decide whether D was provoked to lose his self-control and, if so, whether provocation was enough to make a 'reasonable man' do as D did.

The use of the term 'reasonable man' initially created problems as it was held that this meant a reasonable adult. However, in *DPP v Camplin* (1978), where D was a 15-year-old boy, it was held that the age and sex of D could be considered. Age and sex are now considered in the loss of control defence.

It was also held in *Camplin* that other characteristics of D could be considered in regard to the gravity of the provocation to him. In the defence of loss of control, this has been changed to 'circumstances'. This is wider than characteristics, though the courts had been generous in their interpretation of characteristics. This was shown by the fact that D's history of sexual abuse was allowed to be considered in the case of *R v Hill* (2008).

In fact, in another old case under the law of provocation, the House of Lords had even allowed the fact that D was addicted to glue-sniffing to be considered when deciding the gravity of the provocation to him. This will probably be 'circumstances' that would also be considered in the defence of loss of control.

Comparison of provocation and loss of control

In some ways, the defence of loss of control is wider than provocation. In particular, the loss of control does not have to be sudden. Also fear of serious violence is a matter which can be considered.

In other ways the defence of loss of control is narrower than the defence of provocation. In particular, sexual infidelity is no longer allowed as a qualifying trigger.

Also where the defendant is relying on things said and/or done, then they must be of an extremely grave character. This was not the situation in provocation and some of the cases where that defence was allowed would not come within the new defence of loss of control.

The things said and/or done must also cause D to have a justifiable sense of being seriously wronged.

	Law
Main points of defence	D must have lost self-control. There must be a qualifying trigger. A person of the same sex and age would have reacted in the same way as D in the same circumstances.
Loss of control	This need not be sudden.
Qualifying triggers	Either or both of the following: • fear of serious violence • a thing or things done or said which constituted circumstances of an extremely grave character and caused D to have a justifiable sense of being seriously wronged.
Standard of self-control	That of a person of D's sex and age, with a normal degree of tolerance and self-restraint.
Circumstances of D	Circumstances of D (which do not have a bearing on capacity for self-control) can be taken into consideration in deciding whether a normal person might have reacted in the same way.
Effect of defence	Reduces charge of murder to manslaughter.

Figure 3.4 Key facts chart on loss of control

3.3.7 Evaluation of the law on self-control

The reform of the law did not follow all of the Law Commission's proposals. This means that problems still remain in the law.

Loss of self-control

Under s 54(2) of the 2009 Act the loss of self-control does not have to be sudden. This is different from the previous defence of provocation, which required the defendant to suffer a sudden and temporary loss of self-control. This requirement led to some defendants being unable to use the defence of provocation as their loss of control was not sudden.

This was seen especially in battered women cases where the reaction to threats or abuse came some hours later. In these cases the defence was not allowed as it was sufficiently 'sudden'.

The Law Commission, in their 2006 report *Murder, Manslaughter and Infanticide*, had proposed removing the loss of self-control criteria completely because it recognised that women in abusive relationships may kill from 'a combination of anger, fear, frustration and a sense of desperation'. The Government decided not to follow this proposal. The only concession given in the new law was that the loss of control need not be sudden. If a similar case came to court now it is possible that someone in the same situation as Mrs Ahluwalia would be able to use the defence.

Sexual infidelity

This is no longer allowed as a qualifying trigger for the defence. Yet the defence of provocation was largely created for just such situations. If someone unexpectedly finds their partner having sex with another person, they are very likely to lose their self-control. But if this leads to them killing their partner, they will not be able to use the defence of loss of self-control.

Fear of serious violence

Section 55(4) sets a very high threshold for the circumstances in which the defence is available where a person loses self-control in response to words or actions. The effect is to substantially narrow the potential availability of this defence in cases where a loss of control is attributable to things done or said compared to provocation (where no threshold existed in relation to the provoking circumstances). As a result many cases where the defendant was able to use the former defence of provocation would not now come within loss of control.

Excluded matters

In the defence of provocation, sexual infidelity was allowed as grounds for the defence as the law had been developed over centuries to give a defence in cases involving murder based on sexual infidelity. When drafting the new rules the Government considered that provocation allowed a defence to a jealous man who killed his wife or girlfriend because she was having an affair and that such male violence against women was not acceptable in the 21st century.

As a result the Coroners and Justice Act states, in s 55(6)(c) that, in deciding whether a loss of self-control has a qualifying trigger, the fact that a thing done or said amounted to sexual infidelity is to be disregarded.

So, if a thing done or said (as referred to in s 55(4)), amounts to sexual infidelity, that fact is disregarded in deciding whether the qualifying trigger in s 55(4) applies. The effect is that, if the defendant kills his wife or partner because they have been unfaithful, he will not be able to claim loss of control. It is the fact of sexual infidelity that is to be disregarded under the provision, so the thing done or said can still potentially amount to a qualifying trigger if (ignoring the sexual infidelity) it still amounts to 'circumstances of an extremely grave character causing the defendant to have a justifiable sense of being seriously wronged'. This may arise only rarely, but an example of where it might be relevant is where the defendant discovers his wife or partner (V) sexually abusing their young child (an act that amounts to sexual infidelity) and loses self-control and kills. The fact that V's act amounted to sexual infidelity must be discounted but the abuse may still be claimed to amount to the qualifying trigger.

Standard of self-control

Although the Act refers to the defendant's circumstances, s 54(3) emphasises that circumstances whose only relevance to the defendant's conduct is that they bear on the defendant's general capacity for tolerance or self-restraint are not to be considered. In other words, apart from sex and age, the jury cannot consider any circumstance of the defendant which might have made them have less self-control.

A jury could consider any of the following:
- any history of abuse towards the defendant by a partner,
- any addiction that the defendant may have, or
- any illness or condition such as epilepsy, or
- any external feature such as unemployment that may have caused the defendant to be depressed.

The jury cannot consider matters such as if the defendant was bad tempered, or hot tempered as these conditions would affect a person's capacity for tolerance and self-restraint.

Tip

When answering questions based on a scenario, look carefully at the facts given. There may be clear pointers as to what you need to consider. For example, the scenario may say 'suffering from depression' (or another medically recognised condition) – this is a pointer to diminished responsibility as a possible defence.

Summary

- Diminished responsibility and loss of control are partial defences to a charge of murder – if successful, they reduce the charge to one of manslaughter.
- For diminished responsibility the defendant must show that:
  - they were suffering from an abnormality of mental functioning and that this arose from a recognised medical condition, and that this substantially impaired D's ability to:
    - understand the nature of his conduct, or
    - form a rational judgement, or
    - exercise self-control, and
  - the substantial impairment provides an explanation for D's conduct.

- There are problems with the law of diminished responsibility:
  - The burden of proof is on the defendant.
  - The law does not allow for developmental immaturity.

- For loss of control there must be:
  - actual loss of control
  - which must be due to a qualifying trigger, and
  - a person of D's sex and age with a normal degree of tolerance and self-restraint and in the circumstances of D, might have reacted in the same or a similar way.

- There are problems with the law on loss of control:
  - It does not cover situations where a woman in an abusive situation kills through a 'combination of anger, fear, frustration and a sense of desperation'.
  - It no longer covers sexual infidelity.
  - Fear of serious violence is not enough; D must also show loss of control.

Chapter 4

Involuntary manslaughter

After reading this chapter you should be able to:
- Understand the elements of unlawful act manslaughter
- Understand the elements of gross negligence manslaughter
- Evaluate the law on both types of involuntary manslaughter
- Apply the law on both types of involuntary manslaughter to scenario-based situations

4.1 Involuntary manslaughter

Involuntary manslaughter is an unlawful killing where the defendant does not have the intention, either direct or oblique, to kill or to cause grievous bodily harm. The lack of this intention is what distinguishes involuntary manslaughter from murder.

It is also important not to confuse involuntary manslaughter with voluntary manslaughter. For voluntary manslaughter, the defendant has the intention to kill or cause grievous bodily harm but the charge is reduced from murder because the defendant can use one of the special defences to murder.

4.1.1 Range of involuntary manslaughter

Involuntary manslaughter covers a wide range of circumstances. At the top end of the range, the behaviour of the defendant which caused the death can be highly blameworthy, as there was a high risk of causing death or serious injury. At the bottom end of the range, the defendant's behaviour may verge on carelessness and only just enough to be considered blameworthy. There have been criticisms that the same offence covers such a wide range of behaviour, and proposals for reform are considered at section 4.4.4.

The maximum sentence for involuntary manslaughter is life imprisonment. This gives the judge a discretion to impose a sentence which is suitable for the particular circumstances of the offence. In some cases the judge may even pass a non-custodial sentence. This links to the level of the defendant's fault discussed in Chapter 1, section 1.4.2.

4.1.2 Ways of committing involuntary manslaughter

There are two main ways of committing involuntary manslaughter. These are:
- unlawful act manslaughter
- gross negligence manslaughter.

4.2 Unlawful act manslaughter

This is also known as 'constructive manslaughter' because the liability for the death is built up or constructed from the fact that the defendant has done a dangerous unlawful act which caused the death. This makes the defendant liable even though they did not realise that death or injury might occur.

The elements of unlawful act manslaughter are:
- The defendant must do an unlawful act (which is a crime).
- That act must be dangerous on an objective test.
- The act must cause the death.
- The defendant must have the required *mens rea* for the unlawful act.

Key term

Unlawful act manslaughter – where the defendant causes a death through doing an unlawful act that is objectively dangerous with the necessary *mens rea* for the unlawful act.

4.2.1 Unlawful act

The death must be caused by an unlawful act. The unlawful act must be a criminal offence. A civil wrong (tort) is not enough. In *R v Franklin* (1883) the defendant threw a large box into the sea from the West Pier at Brighton. The box hit and killed a swimmer. It was held that a civil wrong was not enough to create liability for unlawful act manslaughter. Another case illustrating that there must be a criminal unlawful act is *R v Lamb* (1967).

Case study

R v Lamb (1967)

Lamb and his friend were fooling around with a revolver. They both knew that it was loaded with two bullets in a five-chamber cylinder but thought that it would not fire unless one of the bullets was opposite the barrel. They knew that there was no bullet in this position, but did not realise that the cylinder turned so that a bullet from the next chamber along would be fired. Lamb pointed the gun at his friend and pulled the trigger, killing him. It was held that the defendant had not carried out an unlawful act. The pointing of the gun at the friend was not an assault as the friend did not fear any violence from Lamb.

There must be an act. An omission cannot create liability for unlawful act manslaughter. This was shown by the case of *R v Lowe* (1973).

Case study

R v Lowe (1973)

The defendant was convicted of wilfully neglecting his baby son and of his manslaughter. The trial judge had directed the jury that if they found the defendant guilty of wilful neglect he was also guilty of manslaughter. The Court of Appeal quashed the conviction for manslaughter because a finding of wilful neglect involved a failure to act, and this could not support a conviction for unlawful act manslaughter.

In many cases the unlawful act will be some kind of non-fatal offence, but any criminal offence can form the unlawful act, provided that it involves an act which is dangerous in the sense that it is likely to cause some injury. Examples of the offences which have led to a finding of unlawful act manslaughter include:

- arson – *R v Goodfellow* (1986) (see section 4.2.2)
- criminal damage – *DPP v Newbury and Jones* (1976) (see section 4.2.4)
- burglary – *R v Watson* (1989) (see section 4.2.2).

4.2.2 Dangerous act

The unlawful act must be dangerous on an objective test. In *R v Church* (1965) it was held that it must be 'such as all sober and reasonable people would inevitably recognise must subject the other person to, at least, the risk of some harm resulting therefrom, albeit not serious harm'.

From this, it can be seen that the risk need only be of 'some harm'. The harm need not be serious. If a sober and reasonable person realises that the unlawful act might cause some injury, then this part of the test for unlawful act manslaughter is satisfied. It does not matter that the defendant did not realise there was any risk of harm to another person. The case of *R v Larkin* (1943) illustrates both the need for an unlawful act and for there to be, on an objective viewpoint, the risk of some harm.

Case study

R v Larkin (1943)

D threatened another man with an open cut-throat razor, in order to frighten him. The mistress of the other man tried to intervene and, because she was drunk, accidentally fell onto the open blade which cut her throat and killed her. On appeal, D's conviction for manslaughter was upheld. The act of threatening the other man with the razor was a technical assault. It was also an act which was dangerous because it was likely to injure someone.

Humphries J explained this in the judgment when he said:

> Where the act which a person is engaged in performing is unlawful, then, if at the same time it is a dangerous act, that is, an act which is likely to injure another person, and quite inadvertently he causes the death of that other person by that act, then he is guilty of manslaughter.

It is clear that the act need not be aimed at the victim. This was the situation in *Larkin* where the assault was against the man but the woman died. It is also shown by the case of *R v Mitchell* (1983) discussed in *OCR AS/A Level Law Book 1* at section 13.1.4 and in this book at section 1.4.1.

I'm only playing dominoes.

Some harm

It is not necessary for the sober and reasonable person to foresee the particular type of harm that the victim suffers. It is enough that the sober and reasonable person would foresee some harm. This was stated in *R v J M and S M* (2012).

Case study

R v J M and S M (2012)

J M lit a cigarette inside a nightclub and was asked to leave. J M and his brother S M left but later returned. A fight broke out between the brothers and doormen. During the fight V, one of the doormen, collapsed and died. V's renal artery had ruptured due to a weakness in the artery wall, causing his death. The rupture was extremely unlikely to have occurred spontaneously and it was accepted that the fight was a substantial cause of V's death. The judge stopped the trial as, in his opinion, the rupture of the artery was a completely different form of harm from that foreseeable by a reasonable and sober person.

The prosecution appealed against this ruling. The Court of Appeal held that a sober and reasonable person only had to foresee some harm; they did not have to foresee any specific type of harm. A sober and reasonable person would 'have recognised that all the doormen ... were at risk of some harm'.

Act against property

The unlawful act need not be aimed at a person; it can be aimed at property, provided it is 'such that all sober and reasonable people would inevitably recognise must subject another person to, at least, the risk of some harm'. This was illustrated by *R v Goodfellow* (1986).

Case study

R v Goodfellow (1986)

D decided to set fire to his council flat so that the council would have to rehouse him. The fire got out of control and his wife, son and another woman died in the fire. He was convicted of manslaughter and appealed. The Court of Appeal upheld the conviction because all the elements of unlawful act manslaughter were present.

If you look at the facts of *Goodfellow* you can see the elements of unlawful act manslaughter. These were:
- The act was committed intentionally: Goodfellow intended to set the flat on fire.
- It was unlawful: it was arson, an offence under the Criminal Damage Act 1971.
- Reasonable people would recognise that it might cause some harm to another person: there was an obvious risk that someone in the flat might be hurt.
- The unlawful act caused the death.

Physical harm

The 'risk of harm' refers to physical harm. Something which causes fear and apprehension is not sufficient. This is so even if it causes the victim to have a heart attack. This meant that in the case of *R v Dawson* (1985) convictions for manslaughter were quashed.

Case study

R v Dawson (1985)

Three defendants attempted to rob a petrol station. They were masked and armed with pick-axe handles. The petrol station attendant managed to sound the alarm but then dropped dead from a heart attack. Causing him fear through the attempted robbery was not a 'dangerous' act and did not make this manslaughter.

However, where a reasonable person would be aware of the victim's frailty and the risk of physical harm to him, then the defendant will be liable. This was stated in *R v Watson* (1989).

Case study

R v Watson (1989)

Two defendants threw a brick through the window of a house and entered it, intending to steal property. The occupier was a frail 87-year-old man who heard the noise and came to investigate what had happened. The two defendants physically abused him and then left. The man died of a heart attack 90 minutes later. The Court of Appeal quashed the convictions for manslaughter as it could not be established that the break in was the cause of the heart attack. However, the court stated that the act of burglary could be 'dangerous' as soon as the old man's condition became apparent to the reasonable man.

Case	Facts	Law
Lamb (1967)	D fired gun at a friend. Both thought it was safe because there was no bullet in the firing chamber.	There must be an unlawful act. In this case there was no assault as the friend did not fear violence.
Lowe (1973)	Failed to care properly for baby.	There has to be an act – unlawful act manslaughter cannot be committed by an omission.
Larkin (1943)	Threatened a man with a razor – a woman fell on blade and died.	The unlawful act need not be aimed at V but it must be objectively dangerous in the sense that it is likely to cause harm.
Goodfellow (1986)	Set fire to flat, causing three deaths.	The unlawful act can be aimed at property. The test is whether it is objectively dangerous in the sense that it is likely to cause harm.
Dawson (1985)	Petrol station attendant died of a heart attack when his petrol station was robbed.	Causing fear is not enough. The unlawful act must put V at risk of physical harm.
Newbury and Jones (1976)	Pushed a paving stone onto a passing train, killing the guard.	D need only have the intention to do the unlawful act. There is no need for D to foresee that it might cause some harm.

Figure 4.1 Key cases chart on unlawful act manslaughter

Burglary is an unlawful act which is not normally dangerous under the Church definition with a risk of some harm resulting therefrom. However, if a burglary is carried out in such a way that the circumstances of the commission of the offence make it dangerous, then this may amount to an unlawful act. This was the situation in *R v Bristow, Dunn and Delay* (2013).

Case study

R v Bristow, Dunn and Delay (2013)

Ds were part of a gang of at least six men who had agreed to burgle V's workshop. The workshop was down a long drive so there was a risk of someone discovering the burglary and trying to prevent the burglars from escaping. Ds used at least two vehicles to get to the workshop. V was found dead near the workshop a few hours after the burglary. There was evidence that he had been hit by one or both of the vehicles used by Ds to commit the burglary. Ds were convicted of V's manslaughter. The Court of Appeal upheld their convictions on the basis that the circumstances of the burglary meant that a reasonable and sober person would recognise the risk of some harm resulting from the burglary.

4.2.3 Causing the death

The unlawful act must cause the death. The rules on causation are the same as for murder and are set out in Chapter 13 of *OCR AS/A Level Law Book 1* at section 13.3. An important point is that if there is an intervening act which breaks the chain of causation, then the defendant cannot be liable for manslaughter.

This point has caused problems in cases where the defendant has supplied V with an illegal drug. If the defendant also injects the drug into V, then there is no break in the chain of causation. This was shown in the case of *R v Cato* (1976).

Case study

R v Cato (1976)

D and V each prepared an injection of a mix of heroin and water. They then injected each other. V died. By injecting V with heroin D had committed the unlawful act of administering a noxious substance to V, contrary to s 23 of the Offences Against the Person Act (OAPA) 1861. As V died from the effects of the injection, D was convicted of unlawful act manslaughter.

After this case two points at issue were raised:

- whether the defendant has committed an unlawful act, and
- whether the defendant caused the victim's death, or whether the self-injection is an intervening act.

A subsequent case was *R v Dalby* (1982).

Case study

R v Dalby (1982)

D supplied a drug called Diconal which V self-injected and subsequently died. D's conviction for manslaughter was quashed by the Court of Appeal which held that although supplying the drug was an unlawful act, it was not the supplying that had caused the death. The injection was the cause of the death and, as this was a voluntary act by the victim, the chain of causation had been broken.

This approach was confirmed by the decision in *R v Kennedy* (2007) referred to in Book 1 at section 13.3.5.

Case study

R v Kennedy (2007)

D had prepared an injection of heroin and water for V to inject himself. V self-injected and subsequently died. Initially, D was convicted of manslaughter and the Court of Appeal upheld his original and subsequent appeals on the basis that filling the syringe and handing it to V was administering a noxious substance and an unlawful act.

However, the case was then appealed to the House of Lords who quashed the conviction. They ruled that V's act in injecting the heroin himself was an intervening act which broke any chain of causation.

The House of Lords pointed out that the criminal law generally assumes the existence of free will. In this case V had freely and voluntarily administered the injection to himself. D could only be guilty if he was involved in administering the injection. D had not committed an unlawful act which caused the death as he had not administered a noxious substance for an offence under s 23 OAPA 1861.

The House of Lords did accept that there could be situations in which it could be regarded that both defendant and victim were involved in administering the injection. However, they did not give any examples of when this could be considered to have happened.

It is possible that in situations where the defendant has supplied the victim with drugs, the defendant could be liable for gross negligence manslaughter as in *R v Evans 2009* referred to below in 4.3.1.

4.2.4 *Mens rea*

It must be proved that the defendant had the *mens rea* for the unlawful act. It is not necessary for the

defendant to realise that the act is unlawful or dangerous. This was made clear in the case of *DPP v Newbury and Jones* (1976).

Case study

DPP v Newbury and Jones (1976)

The defendants were two teenage boys who pushed a paving stone from a bridge onto a railway line as a train was approaching. The stone hit the train and killed the guard. They were convicted of manslaughter and the House of Lords was asked to decide the question of whether a defendant could be convicted of unlawful act manslaughter if he did not foresee that his act might cause harm to another. The House of Lords confirmed it was not necessary to prove that the defendant foresaw any harm from his act.

So, a defendant can be convicted provided that the unlawful act was dangerous and the defendant had the necessary *mens rea* for that act.

4.3 Gross negligence manslaughter

Gross negligence manslaughter is committed where the defendant owes the victim a duty of care but breaches that duty in a very negligent way, causing the death of the victim. The negligence has to be more than just civil negligence. It has to be so bad as to amount to criminal negligence. It can be committed by an act or an omission, neither of which has to be unlawful. The leading case on gross negligence manslaughter is *R v Adomako* (1994).

Case study

R v Adomako (1994)

D was the anaesthetist for a patient who was having an operation on a detached retina. During the operation, one of the tubes supplying oxygen to the patient became disconnected. D failed to notice this until some minutes later when the patient suffered a heart attack caused by the lack of oxygen. The patient suffered brain damage and died six months later as a result. Doctors giving evidence in the trial said that a competent anaesthetist would have noticed the disconnection of the tube within 15 seconds and that D's failure to react was 'abysmal'. The conviction for gross negligence manslaughter was upheld by the House of Lords.

Elements	Comment	Cases
Unlawful act	Must be unlawful. A civil wrong is not enough. It must be an act; an omission is not sufficient.	*Lamb* (1967) *Franklin* (1883) *Lowe* (1973)
Dangerous act	The test for this is objective – would a sober and reasonable person realise the risk of some harm? The risk need only be of some harm – not serious harm. There is no need to foresee the specific type of harm. The act need not be aimed at the final victim. An act aimed at property can still be such that a sober and reasonable person would realise the risk of some harm. There must be a risk of physical harm; mere fear is not enough. Burglary is not normally a dangerous act, but can be carried out in such a way as to make it dangerous.	*Church* (1966) *Larkin* (1943) *J M and S M* (2012) *Mitchell* (1983) *Goodfellow* (1986) *Dawson* (1985) *Bristow, Dunn and Delay* (2013)
Causes death	Normal rules of causation apply; the act must be the physical and legal cause of death. An intervening act such as the victim self-injecting a drug breaks the chain of causation. But merely preparing the injection is not a cause of death. V's self-injection breaks the chain of causation.	*Dalby* (1982) *Kennedy* (2007)
Mens rea	D must have *mens rea* for the unlawful act but it is not necessary to prove that D foresaw any harm from his act.	*Newbury and Jones* (1976)

Figure 4.2 Key facts chart on unlawful act manslaughter

Key term

Gross negligence manslaughter – a form of involuntary manslaughter committed where D is grossly negligent in breach of a duty of care towards V and this results in V's death.

From *Adomako* (1994) it appears that the elements of gross negligence manslaughter are:

- the existence of a duty of care by the defendant towards the victim
- a breach of that duty of care which causes death
- gross negligence which the jury considers to be so bad as to be criminal.

4.3.1 Duty of care

A duty of care has been held to exist for the purposes of the criminal law in various situations. These include the duty of a doctor to his patient, as in *Adomako*. In that case Lord Mackay said that the ordinary principles of negligence in tort applied to ascertain whether there was a duty of care and whether that duty had been breached.

The civil principles come from the three stage test of *Caparo v Dickman* 1990 which require:

- proximity of relationship,
- reasonable foreseeability of harm, and
- it being fair, just and reasonable to impose a duty of care.

Note that an act *or* an omission can form the basis of negligence.

The tort of negligence is discussed in *OCR AS/A Level Law Book 1* in Chapter 23.

Case examples of duty of care in gross negligence manslaughter

Since the case of *R v Adomako* (1994), the criminal courts have decided that a duty of care exists in very different situations. Some of these are set out below.

Case studies

R v Singh (1999)

D was the landlord of property in which a faulty gas fire caused the deaths of tenants. It was recognised that there was a duty on D to manage and maintain property properly.

R v Litchfield (1997)

D was the owner and master of a sailing ship. He sailed knowing that the engines might fail because of contamination to the fuel. The ship was blown onto rocks and three crew members died. It was held that D owed a duty to the crew.

In both of these cases there was a contractual duty of care. An actual extension of the type of duty recognised by the courts occurred in *R v Wacker* (2002).

Case study

R v Wacker (2002)

D agreed to bring 60 illegal immigrants into England. They were put in the back of his lorry for a cross-channel ferry crossing. The only air into the lorry was through a small vent and it was agreed that this vent should be closed at certain times to prevent the immigrants from being discovered. D closed the vent before boarding the ferry. The crossing took an hour longer than usual and at Dover the Customs officers found that 58 of the immigrants were dead. D argued that it was impossible to determine the extent of his duty, but the Court of Appeal held it was a simple matter on the facts. D knew that the safety of the immigrants depended on his own actions in relation to the vent and he clearly assumed the duty of care. D's conviction for manslaughter was upheld by the Court of Appeal.

An interesting point in *Wacker* was that the victims were parties to an illegal act. In the civil law of negligence this would have meant that the victims (or their dependants) could not have made a claim against the defendant. However, the Court of Appeal held that for the criminal law, it was irrelevant that the victims were parties to an illegal act. It pointed out that the purposes of civil and criminal law were different and public policy demanded that defendants in this type of situation were liable under the criminal law.

D has created a state of affairs

The Court of Appeal has also held that a duty of care can exist where the defendant has created a state of affairs, which s/he knows, or ought reasonably to know, has become life-threatening and has broken that duty. This was seen in the case of *R v Evans* (2009) which was discussed in *OCR AS/A Level Law Book 1* at section 13.2.1. In this case both the mother and D, the half-sister of V, were convicted of gross negligence manslaughter when they failed to call for help after V had overdosed. The mother clearly owed a duty of care to V. D claimed that she did not owe a duty of care to her half-sister. The Court of Appeal upheld the conviction on the basis that D had created a state of affairs, supplying her with a drug, which she knew or ought reasonably to have known was threatening the life of V. D had failed in that duty by not calling for help.

D owes a duty because of a relationship with the victim

The unfair decision in *R v Stone and Dobinson* (1977) is discussed in *OCR AS/A Level Law Book 1* at section 13.2.1.

Case study

R v Stone & Dobinson (1977)

Stone's sister came to live with the defendants who were mentally slow and barely able to look after themselves. She was anorexic and eventually became bedridden and incapable of looking after herself. Neither defendant was able to summon medical help. The sister eventually died from malnutrition. The defendants were charged with gross negligence manslaughter. Stone owed a duty of care towards his sister. Dobinson had undertaken some care of the sister so she, too, owed a duty towards her. The duty was to help her and/or to call for help. The failure to do either of these meant, unfairly, that both Stone and Dobinson were guilty of manslaughter.

In the news

Honey Rose, an optometrist working for Boots, failed to spot a brain condition in an eight-year-old boy she examined in a routine eye test. She did not inspect the back of the boy's eyes and failed to notice signs of optic disc swelling caused by fluid in the skull. The boy died five months later from swelling in his brain. She was charged with gross negligence manslaughter. The jury at her trial was told that the death could have been prevented if she had done her job properly. She was convicted and sentenced to a 2-year suspended sentence. She appealed against her conviction to the Court of Appeal who quashed the conviction. In its judgment the appeal court ruled that it was inappropriate for the court to take into account what Ms Rose would have known if she had examined the boy properly. It ruled that there needed to be a 'serious and obvious risk of death at the time of breach (the examination)'. In this case that was not present.

The court observed that 'The implications for medical and other professions would be serious because people would be guilty of gross negligence manslaughter by reason of negligent omissions to carry out routine eye, blood and other tests which, in fact, would have revealed fatal conditions, notwithstanding that the circumstances were such that it was not reasonably foreseeable that failure to carry out such tests would carry an obvious and serious risk of death'.

4.3.2 Breach of duty causing death

Once a duty of care has been shown to exist, it must be proved that the defendant was in breach of that duty of care and that this breach caused the death of the victim.

Whether there is a breach of duty is a factual matter for the jury to decide. Did the defendant negligently do or fail to do something? Causation is important, as it must be proved that the breach of duty caused the death. The general rules on causation apply.

Rules on causation are covered in detail in *OCR AS/A Level Law Book 1* at section 13.3.

4.3.3 Gross negligence

The fact that a defendant has been negligent is not enough to convict him of gross negligence manslaughter. The negligence has to be 'gross'. This was first explained in *R v Bateman* (1925) which involved negligent treatment of a patient by a doctor.

Case study

R v Bateman (1925)

D was a doctor who attended a woman for the birth of her child at her home. During childbirth, part of the woman's uterus came away. D did not send V to hospital for five days, and she later died. D's conviction was quashed on the basis that he had carried out the normal procedures that any competent doctor would have done. He had not been grossly negligent.

In his judgment Lord Hewart said:

> The facts must be such that, in the opinion of the jury, the negligence of the accused went beyond a mere matter of compensation between subjects and showed such disregard for the life and safety of others as to amount to a crime against the State and conduct deserving of punishment.

In *R v Adomako* (1994) the House of Lords approved this test and stressed that it was a matter for the jury. The jury has to decide whether, having regard to the risk of death involved, the conduct of the defendant was so bad in all the circumstances as to amount, in their judgment, to a criminal act or omission.

There have been criticisms of this test because it is left to individual juries to decide the appropriate standard for 'gross' negligence. This may lead to inconsistent decisions as there is little guidance on what should be considered as 'gross' negligence.

Risk of death

In *R v Adomako* (1994) it was not totally clear whether there has to be a risk of death through the defendant's conduct or whether the risk needs only be to 'health and welfare' of the victim. Previously in *R v Stone and Dobinson* (1977), where the defendants had undertaken the care of Stone's sister, the test was expressed as the risk being to the 'health and welfare' of the sister who died.

When Lord Mackay gave judgment in *Adomako*, he approved this way of explaining the matter. However, Lord Mackay also approved the test in *Bateman* (1925) where the test is 'disregard for the life and safety of others'. In addition, Lord Mackay specifically mentioned 'a risk of death' on two occasions in his judgment.

The matter has now been resolved in *R v Misra and Srivastava* (2004).

Case study

R v Misra and Srivastava (2004)

V had an operation on his knee. The two defendants were senior house doctors who were responsible for the post-operative care of V. They failed to identify and treat V for an infection which occurred after the operation. V died from the infection. The defendants were convicted and appealed on the basis that the elements of gross negligence manslaughter were uncertain and so breached Article 7 of the European Convention on Human Rights. This says that no one shall be guilty of any criminal offence on account of an act or omission which did not amount to a criminal offence at the time when it was committed.

The Court of Appeal held that *Adomako* had clearly laid down the elements of the offence of gross negligence manslaughter, so there was no breach of Article 7. The defendants' conviction was upheld.

4.3.4 *Mens rea*

The *mens rea* of the offence is gross negligence.

Elements	Comment	Cases
Duty of care	D must owe V a duty of care.	*Adomako* (1994)
	The civil concept of negligence applies.	*Adomako* (1994)
	Covers wide range of situations, e.g. maintaining a gas fire.	*Singh* (1999)
	The fact that V was party to an illegal act is not relevant.	*Wacker* (2003)
Breach of duty	This can be by an act or an omission.	
Gross negligence	Beyond a matter of mere compensation and showed such disregard for the life and safety of others as to amount to a crime.	*Bateman* (1925)
	Conduct so bad in all the circumstances as to amount to a criminal act or omission.	*Adomako* (1994)
Risk of death	There must be a risk of death from D's conduct.	*Adomako* (1994)
		Misra (2004)

Figure 4.3 Key facts chart on gross negligence manslaughter

Activity ❓

Consider whether the following situations could be unlawful act manslaughter and/or gross negligence manslaughter.

1   Asif is throwing stones at passing cars. One of the stones goes through the open side window in Dawn's car and hits her on the side of the head. She loses control of the car and hits a pedestrian, Keith, who is killed.

2   Justine and Oliver have spent the evening at Justine's flat, drinking heavily. Oliver has not taken any drugs but he knows that Justine has taken an Ecstasy tablet. Justine passes out and Oliver, who is afraid he may get into trouble, decides to leave. The next morning, Justine is discovered dead.

3   Liam is very angry with Sam and kicks out at him. This causes Sam to trip and fall down some steps, breaking his neck and killing him.

4   Patsy has been caring for her elderly aunt who is very frail and unable to walk without assistance. Patsy goes away on a fortnight's holiday, leaving her aunt on her own. The aunt dies through lack of food and cold.

4.4 Evaluation of the law of manslaughter

4.4.1 Unlawful act manslaughter

The main criticisms of this offence are:
- it covers a very wide range of conduct,
- death may be an unexpected result, and
- a defendant who did not realise there was risk of any injury to the victim is still guilty of manslaughter because of the objective test.

Wide range of conduct

Unlawful act manslaughter covers a very wide range of conduct. The unlawful act can be as minor as pushing V or it may be only just short of murder as an unlawful killing has taken place but the prosecution are unable to prove the *mens rea* of murder. As a result, the defendant's level of blameworthiness can vary enormously. If there were different levels of offence, then the defendant could be charged with a more appropriate offence.

It would also help a judge when sentencing as s/he has to decide on the level of blameworthiness of the defendant. If there were separate categories of offence, each would have a narrower band of sentences available.

Death an unexpected result

In many cases of unlawful act manslaughter, death is an unexpected result of D's conduct. An example was the situation in *R v Mitchell* (1983) above. The victim's death was an unexpected result of Mitchell's conduct in punching another man. If the victim had not died then Mitchell would have been charged with a less serious, non-fatal offence.

The objective test

In 1994 the Law Commission in their consultation paper, 'Involuntary Manslaughter' (Law Com consultation paper No. 135), recommended the abolition of unlawful act manslaughter. It criticised the concept of unlawful act manslaughter, pointing out:

> It ... is inappropriate to convict a defendant for an offence of homicide where the most that can be said is that he or she ought to have realised that there was the risk of some, albeit not serious, harm to another resulting from his or her commission of an unlawful act.

Having an objective test poses the question – why should a defendant be guilty of manslaughter when he or she did not realise the risk of some harm occurring to the victim?

This objective test conflicts with other offences where recklessness is required for the *mens rea*. In these offences it must be shown that the defendant is aware of the risk but goes ahead with the action – in other words a subjective test. It seems inconsistent that this serious offence should require a different form of *mens rea* from all offences requiring recklessness.

4.4.2 Reform of unlawful act manslaughter

Although in 1996 the Law Commission recommended abolishing unlawful act manslaughter, it did not recommend abolition in its later 2006 report, 'Murder, Manslaughter and Infanticide'. Instead, it recommended a three-tier structure of homicide offences. These were:

- first degree murder
- second degree murder, and
- manslaughter.

Under these proposals manslaughter would cover:

1 killing another person through gross negligence (this proposal is discussed at section 4.4.4), or

2 killing another person–
   (a) through the commission of a criminal act intended by the defendant to cause injury, or
   (b) through the commission of a criminal act that the defendant was aware involved a serious risk of causing some injury.

This second category would be known as 'criminal act manslaughter'. It would be different to unlawful act manslaughter as a defendant could only be convicted using a subjective test; that is, he must either intend to cause injury or be aware that the act involved a serious risk of causing some injury. This would prevent defendants being convicted where they did not intend any injury and were unaware of the risk of injury.

In addition, more serious situations which at the moment are classed as manslaughter could become second degree murder. These are killings where the defendant intended to cause injury or fear or risk of injury and was aware that their conduct involved a serious risk of causing death.

This suggestion allows for greater differentiation between the blameworthiness of defendants.

4.4.3 Evaluation of the law on gross negligence manslaughter

The main criticisms of gross negligence manslaughter are:

- The test is circular, as the jury is directed to convict if they think that the conduct was criminal.
- The test may lead to inconsistent verdicts, as it depends on what different juries think.
- The civil test for negligence should not be used in criminal cases: the purpose of the two branches of law is quite different.

Circular test

The fact that the jury has to decide whether to convict the defendant of manslaughter (a criminal offence) by deciding whether his/her conduct was criminal is regarded as a circular test.

In other words, the starting point of 'is the defendant's conduct criminal?' is almost the same as saying 'has s/he committed a crime?' There is no sequence of reasoning, and instead the argument goes round in a circle. It's a crime because it's criminal!

Inconsistency of verdicts

The other problem with this test is that it leaves the jury to decide a question of law. Normally, the judge decides if the defendant's conduct is capable of being a crime and the jury then decides on the facts whether the defendant has committed the alleged crime. In gross negligence manslaughter the jury decides whether the conduct is capable of being criminal.

This may lead to different decisions in very similar circumstances. It would make the law fairer if the judge made the decision as to whether the defendant's conduct was capable of amounting to gross negligence manslaughter.

Civil or criminal negligence

In *R v Adomako* (1994), Lord Mackay said that the ordinary principles of negligence applied in deciding whether D had broken a duty of care owed to V.

This appears to say that the tests for negligence in civil law apply to criminal law. Yet negligence in criminal law has not developed in the same way as in civil law. This is clear from the case of *R v Stone and Dobinson* (1977) when the defendants were guilty of gross negligence manslaughter where they had given very limited care to Stone's adult sister and failed to obtain medical help.

It is probable that such a situation would not give rise to liability in civil negligence. So, if the civil tests for negligence apply in criminal cases, could this mean that a defendant in the same situation would not now be found guilty of gross negligence manslaughter?

The Law Commission in its report on manslaughter in 1996 pointed out that this area of law is uncertain.

Risk of death

There also used to be a criticism that it was unclear whether the risk had to be of death or whether risk of serious injury was sufficient to prove gross negligence manslaughter. This point was clarified in *R v Misra and Srivastava* (2004) where the Court of Appeal held that the test for gross negligence manslaughter involves consideration of the risk of death. It is not sufficient to show a risk of bodily injury or injury to health.

4.4.4 Reform of gross negligence manslaughter

In 1996, the Law Commission proposed that instead of gross negligence manslaughter there should be two categories of killing involving negligence.

The proposed offences were 'reckless killing' and 'killing by gross carelessness'.

Although the government issued a paper on reform in 2000, no other action was taken on the Law Commission's proposals. However, the government did later ask the Law Commission to review the whole of law of homicide.

Law Commission Report of 2006

In its report, 'Murder, Manslaughter and Infanticide' (Law Com No. 304) 2006 (also referred to at 2.4 above), the Law Commission did not continue its previous recommendation of having two categories of killing where there had been negligence.

Instead, it recommended that there should only be gross negligence manslaughter which would be committed where:

- a person by their conduct causes the death of another
- a risk that their conduct will cause death would be obvious to a reasonable person in their position

- they are capable of appreciating that risk at the material time, and
- their conduct falls far below what can reasonably be expected of them in the circumstances.

This recommendation largely restates the existing law. It makes it absolutely clear that the risk must be to cause death. A risk of serious injury is not sufficient.

However, the Law Commission recommended keeping the rule that gross negligence manslaughter can be committed even when D was unaware that his or her conduct might cause death. It justified this by pointing out:

> This is because negligence, however gross, does not necessarily involve any actual realisation that one is posing a risk of harm. It is a question of how glaringly obvious the risk would have been to a reasonable person.

The prosecution would have to prove that the defendant was capable of appreciating the risk at the material time. This would prevent those with mental disabilities or younger defendants being convicted if they were not capable of appreciating the risk.

Although Parliament implemented the Law Commission's recommendations on voluntary manslaughter (see Chapter 3) they did not implement the recommendations for involuntary manslaughter and there appears to be no sign of change of law in the near future.

4.4.5 Subjective reckless manslaughter

After the decision in *R v Adamako* it was thought that reckless manslaughter no longer existed. However there is one case, *R v Lidar* (2000), where the Court of Appeal confirmed the defendant's conviction for manslaughter where the judge, in his directions to the jury, referred to recklessness rather than gross negligence and where the defendant could have been convicted of gross negligence manslaughter. It could be said that until or unless *Lidar* is specifically overruled, it is uncertain whether there is an offence of subjective reckless manslaughter. Technically, such an offence may exist due to the *Lidar* decision but, if so, it is not relied upon by the CPS when bringing involuntary manslaughter prosecutions.

Summary

- There are two types of involuntary manslaughter:
  - unlawful act manslaughter
  - gross negligence manslaughter.

- For unlawful act manslaughter the following conditions must exist:
  - There must be an unlawful act – a crime.
  - That act must be objectively dangerous.
  - The act must cause the death.
  - The defendant must have the *mens rea* of the unlawful act.

- For gross negligence manslaughter there must be:
  - the existence of a duty of care by the defendant to the victim
  - a breach of that duty of care which causes death
  - gross negligence which the jury considers to be criminal.

- The *mens rea* is gross negligence.
- The maximum sentence for both forms of manslaughter is life imprisonment.
- The main problems with the law of unlawful act manslaughter are:
  - it covers a very wide range of conduct
  - de-ath may be an unexpected result
  - a defendant who did not realise there was risk of any injury is still guilty because of the objective nature of the test.

- The main problems with the law on gross negligence manslaughter are:
  - the test is circular, as the jury is directed to convict of a crime if they think that the conduct was criminal
  - the test may lead to inconsistent verdicts
  - the civil test for negligence should not be used in criminal cases.

Chapter 5

Theft

After reading this chapter you should be able to
- Understand the *actus reus* of theft
- Understand the *mens rea* of theft
- Evaluate the law on theft
- Apply the law on theft to scenario-based situations

5.1 Definition of theft

Theft is defined in s 1 of the Theft Act 1968: 'A person is guilty of theft if he dishonestly appropriates property belonging to another with the intention of permanently depriving the other of it.'

The Act in ss 2–6 helps with the meaning of the words or phrases in the definition. They do not themselves create any offence. This is done in the order that the words or phrases appear in the definition, making it easy to remember the section numbers. They are:
- s 2 – dishonestly (part of the *mens rea*)
- s 3 – appropriates (part of the *actus reus*)
- s 4 – property (part of the *actus reus*)
- s 5 – belonging to another (part of the *actus reus*)
- s 6 – with the intention of permanently depriving the other of it (part of the *mens rea*).

The *actus reus* of theft is made up of the three elements in the phrase 'appropriates property belonging to another'. So, to prove the *actus reus* it has to be shown that there was appropriation by the defendant of something which is property within the definition of the Act and which, at the time of the appropriation, belonged to another.

There are two elements which must be proved for the *mens rea* of theft. These are that the appropriation of the property must be done 'dishonestly' and there must be the intention of permanently depriving the other person of it. This chapter covers the *actus reus* elements first and then the *mens rea*.

Key term

Theft – A person is guilty of theft if they dishonestly appropriate property belonging to another with the intention of permanently depriving the other of it.

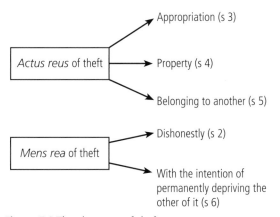

Figure 5.1 The elements of theft

5.2 'Appropriation'

The more obvious situations of theft involve a physical taking, for example a pickpocket taking a wallet from someone's pocket. But appropriation is much wider than this.

Section 3(1) of the Theft Act 1968 states that:

> Any assumption by a person of the rights of an owner amounts to an appropriation, and this includes, where he has come by the property (innocently or not) without stealing it, any later assumption of a right to it by keeping or dealing with it as owner.

The important words are 'any assumption by a person of the rights of an owner amounts to appropriation'. The rights of the owner include selling the property or destroying it as well as possessing it, consuming it, using it, lending it or hiring it out. So for there to be appropriation, the thief must do something which assumes (takes over) one of the owner's rights.

An appropriation by assuming the right to sell is demonstrated by the case of *Pitham v Hehl* (1977).

Case study

R v Pitham and Hehl (1977)

D offered to sell furniture in a house belonging to a friend who was in prison. The offer to sell was an assumption of the rights of the owner and the appropriation took place at that point. It did not matter whether the furniture was removed from the house or not. Even if the owner was never deprived of the property, D had still appropriated it by assuming the rights of the owner to offer the furniture for sale.

Taking goods from a shelf in a supermarket and placing them in one's pocket or own shopping bag is an appropriation as there is an assumption of the rights of an owner. The issue of the shop's consent to this normal action of shopping is discussed at section 5.2.1 below.

The right to destroy property is also an owner's right. This means that if D destroys property belonging to another person, D can be charged with theft, although D has also, of course, committed the offence of criminal damage. Similarly, if the property is not destroyed but merely thrown away.

Theft can also be charged where D does not destroy the other's property but throws it away. For example, if D threw a waterproof watch belonging to another into the sea, this could be theft. Again, only the owner has the right to do this to the property.

The wording in s 3(1) is 'any assumption by a person of the rights of an owner'. Does the assumption have to be of all of the rights or just any of the rights? This was considered in *R v Morris* (1983) where Lord Roskill stated that 'It is enough for the prosecution if they have proved ... the assumption of any of the rights of the owner of the goods in question.'

Case study

R v Morris (1983)

D had switched the price labels of two items on the shelf in a supermarket. He had then put one of the items, which now had a lower price on it, into a basket provided by the store for shoppers and taken the item to the checkout, but had not gone through the checkout when he was arrested. His conviction for theft was upheld as the owner's right to put a price label on the goods was a right that had been assumed.

This is a sensible decision since in many cases the defendant will not have assumed all of the rights.

Quite often, only one right will have been assumed, usually the right of possession.

5.2.1 Consent to the appropriation

Can a defendant appropriate an item when it has been given to him by the owner? The Theft Act 1968 does not state that the appropriation has to be without the consent of the owner. So, what is the position where the owner has allowed the defendant to take something because the owner thought that the defendant was taking what was owed to him? This point was considered in *Lawrence v Commissioner for Metropolitan Police* (1972).

Case study

Lawrence v Commissioner for Metropolitan Police (1972)

An Italian student, who spoke very little English, arrived at Victoria Station and showed an address to Lawrence who was a taxi driver. The journey should have cost 50p, but Lawrence told him it was expensive. The student got out a £1 note and offered it to the driver. Lawrence said it was not enough and so the student opened his wallet and allowed Lawrence to help himself to another £6. Lawrence put forward the argument that he had not appropriated the money as the student had consented to him taking it. The court stated that there was appropriation in this situation.

You can't have it – the House of Lords says I've appropriated it.

The issue of consent to the taking was also present in *R v Morris* (1983). The whole system of self-service retailing relies on the customer taking goods from shelves or petrol from a pump, which is consented to by the retailer.

The point was considered again in the case of *R v Gomez* (1993). The effect of the decision in *R v Gomez* is that any removal of goods from a shelf in a shop is an appropriation. However, theft requires all five elements of the *actus reus* and *mens rea* to be proved so appropriation alone is not a criminal offence.

5.2.2 Consent without deception

In *Gomez* (1993) there was a deception used to appropriate the goods but in the case of *R v Hinks* (2000) there was no deception.

A major argument against the ruling in *Hinks* is that in civil law the gift was valid, and the £60,000 and the television set belonged to the defendant. Lord Steyn, in the leading judgment, accepted that this was the situation but he considered it to be irrelevant to the decision.

5.2.3 Appropriation at one point in time

Another effect of the decision in *Gomez* is that the appropriation is viewed as occurring at one point in time. This is illustrated by the case of *R v Atakpu and Abrahams* (1994).

5.2.4 A later assumption of a right

Section 3(1) makes it clear that there can also be an appropriation where the defendant acquires property without stealing it, but then later decides to keep or deal with the property as owner. The appropriation in this type of situation takes place at the point of 'keeping' or 'dealing'.

An example is where the defendant hires a digger from a tool-hire shop, but instead of returning it decides to keep it or sell it. They are acting as though they are the owner with the right to keep the digger.

Activity

Discuss whether there has been an appropriation in each of the following situations:

1 Jake has had an argument with his neighbour. When his neighbour is out, Jake holds an auction of the neighbour's garden tools. The neighbour returns before any of the tools are taken away.
2 Saskia goes shopping at the local supermarket and takes her five-year-old son, Tom with her. While at the checkout Tom takes some bars of chocolate from a shelf and puts them in his pocket. Saskia does not realise Tom has done this until she finds the chocolate when they get home. Saskia decides she will not take the chocolate back to the supermarket.
3 The owner of a shop asks Parvati, who is a lorry driver, to pick up a load of computer equipment and take it to a warehouse. Parvati agrees to do this but, after collecting the equipment, she decides not to take it to the warehouse but to sell it for cash.
4 Otto, aged 18, is infatuated with Harriet, a married woman aged 32. Otto uses his student loan to buy expensive presents for Harriet. She knows he is a student and has very little money but she accepts the gifts from him.

5.3 'Property'

For there to be theft the defendant must have appropriated 'property'. Section 4 gives a very comprehensive definition of property which means that almost anything can be stolen. The definition is in s 4(1) of the Theft Act 1968: ' "Property" includes money and all other property real or personal, including things in action and other intangible property.'

Section 4 lists five types of items which are included in the definition of 'property'. These are:

- money
- real property
- personal property
- things in action
- other intangible property.

In this list money is self-explanatory. It means coins and banknotes of any currency.

Personal property includes all moveable items such as books, jewellery, clothes and cars, as well as trivial items such as a sheet of paper. In *R v Kelly and Lindsay* (1998) it was held that dead bodies and body parts can be personal property for the purposes of theft. And the law has also recognised that regenerative body materials, such as hair (*R v Herbert* (1961)), blood (*R v Rothery* (1976)) and urine (*R v Welsh* (1974)), can be the subject of property rights and are capable of being stolen.

Case study

R v Kelly and Lindsay (1998)

Kelly was a sculptor who asked Lindsay to take body parts from the Royal College of Surgeons where he worked as a laboratory assistant. Kelly made casts of the parts. They were convicted of theft and appealed on the point of law that body parts were not property. The Court of Appeal held that, though a dead body was not normally property within the definition of the Theft Act 1968, the body parts were property as they had acquired 'different attributes by virtue of the application of skill, such as dissection or preservation techniques, for exhibition or teaching purposes'.

5.3.1 Real property

Real property is the legal term for land and buildings. Under s 4(1) land can be stolen, but s 4(2) states that this can only be done in three circumstances. These are where:

- a trustee or personal representative takes land in breach of his duties as a trustee or personal representative

- someone not in possession of the land severs anything forming part of the land from the land
- a tenant takes a fixture or structure from the land let to him.

Under the second point, it is theft to dig up turf from someone's lawn or to dismantle a wall and take the bricks. In 1972 a man was prosecuted for stealing Cleckheaton railway station by dismantling it and removing it. He was in fact acquitted by the jury as he said he was acting under a claim of right, but there was no doubt that the station could be property under the Theft Act 1968 definition.

5.3.2 Choses in action (Things in action)

A thing in action is a right which can be enforced against another person by an action in law. The right itself is property under the definition in s 4. An example of property that is a thing in action is a bank account. So, if D causes the bank to debit another person's account he has appropriated property, a thing in action.

A cheque itself is a thing in action, but it is also a piece of paper – this is property which can be stolen, and it is a 'valuable security' which can also be stolen under the definition of property.

5.3.3 Other intangible property

This refers to other rights which have no physical presence but can be stolen under the Theft Act 1968. In *Attorney-General for Hong Kong v Chan Nai-Keung* (1987) an export quota for textiles was intangible property which could be stolen. A patent is also intangible property which can be stolen.

However, there are some types of intangible property which have been held not to be property within the Theft Act 1968 definition. In *Oxford v Moss* (1979), knowledge of the questions on an examination paper was held not to be property.

Case study

Oxford v Moss (1979)

D was a university student who acquired a proof of an examination paper he was due to sit. It was accepted that D did not intend to permanently deprive the university of the piece of paper on which the questions were printed, so he was charged with theft of confidential information (i.e. the knowledge of the questions). He was found not guilty as the confidential information contained in the paper did not amount to intangible property for the purposes of the Theft Act 1968.

5.3.4 Things which cannot be stolen

There are some things which cannot be stolen. These are set out in ss 4(3) and 4(4) of the Theft Act 1968. These include plants and fungi growing wild, unless done for resale or payment, and wild animals.

Activity ❓

Explain whether the items in each of the following situations would be property for the purposes of theft.

1   Arnie runs a market stall selling flowers. Just before Christmas, he picks a lot of holly from a wood, intending to sell it on his stall. He then digs up a small fir tree for his own use. On his way home, he sees some late flowering roses in a garden and picks them to give to his girlfriend.
2   Della discovers the examination papers she is to sit next week in the next-door office. She writes out the questions from the first paper on her own notepad. The second paper is very long, so she uses the office photocopier to take a copy, using paper already in the machine.

5.4 'Belonging to another'

In order for there to be a theft of the property, that property must 'belong to another'. However, s 5(1) of the Theft Act 1968 gives a very wide definition of what is meant by 'belonging to another' so that possession or control of the property or any proprietary interest in it is sufficient. One reason for making it wide-ranging is so that the prosecution does not have to prove who is the legal owner.

5.4.1 Possession or control

Obviously, the owner of property normally has possession and control of it, but there are many other situations in which a person can have either possession or control of property. Someone who hires a car has both possession and control during the period of hire. If the car is stolen during this time, then the thief can be charged with stealing it from the hirer. Equally, as the car hire firm still owns the car (a proprietary right), the thief could be charged with stealing it from them.

The possession or control of the item does not have to be lawful. Where B has stolen jewellery from A and subsequently C steals it from B, B is in possession or control of that jewellery and C can be charged with stealing it from B. This is useful where it is not known who the original owner is, as C can still be guilty of theft.

This wide definition of 'belonging to' has led to the situation in which an owner was convicted of stealing his own car, in *R v Turner (No. 2)* (1971).

Case study

R v Turner (No. 2) (1971)

D left his car at a garage for repairs. It was agreed that he would pay for the repairs when he collected the car after the repairs had been completed. When the repairs were almost finished the garage left the car parked on the roadway outside their premises. D used a spare key to take the car during the night without paying for the repairs. The Court of Appeal held that the garage was in possession or control of the car because, as repairers, they have a right to retain possession of the item being repaired until payment is made (a repairer's lien). Therefore D was guilty of stealing his own car.

It is possible for someone to be in possession or control of property even though s/he does not know it is there. This happened in *R v Woodman* (1974).

Case study

R v Woodman (1974)

A company had sold all the scrap metal on its site to another company, which arranged for it to be removed. However, a small amount of the scrap had been left on the site. The company was in control of the site itself as it had put a fence round it and had notices warning trespassers to keep out. D took the remaining scrap metal. He was convicted of theft even though the company was unaware there was any scrap left.

An interesting case on possession of property is *R (on the application of Ricketts) v Basildon Magistrates' Court* (2010). It follows that items left for someone on a doorstep are in the possession of the person for whom the goods are left and that the contents of a dustbin are in the possession of the person whose bin it is until collected by the waste collection service, who then are in possession of the contents.

Case study

R (on the application of Ricketts) v Basildon Magistrates' Court (2010)

In the first offence, Ricketts had taken bags containing items of property from outside a charity shop. He argued that the original owner had abandoned the property and, therefore, it did not belong to another. The court ruled that the goods had not been abandoned – the giver had attempted to deliver them to the charity and delivery would only be complete when the charity took possession. Until then they were the property of the giver.

In the second offence, Ricketts had taken bags of goods from a bin at the rear of another charity shop. These goods were still in the possession of the charity at the time they were appropriated by Ricketts.

5.4.2 Proprietary interest

Where the defendant owns property and is in possession and control of property, they can still be guilty of stealing it if another person has a proprietary interest in it. This point was the key matter in the case of *R v Webster* (2006).

Case study

R v Webster (2006)

D was an army sergeant who had served in Iraq. He had been awarded a medal for his service there. By mistake the Ministry of Defence sent him a second copy of the medal. D sold this second medal on eBay. He was convicted of theft of the medal. On appeal his conviction was upheld on the basis that the Ministry of Defence had retained an equitable interest in the medal. In other words, the Ministry still had a proprietary interest in the medal.

Section 5 makes it clear that in certain situations a defendant can be guilty of theft even though the property may not 'belong to another'. These are situations in which the defendant is acting dishonestly and has caused a loss to another or has made a gain. These are:

- trust property, where a trustee can steal it
- property received under an obligation
- property received by another's mistake.

5.4.3 Property received under an obligation

There are many situations in which property (usually money) is handed over to D on the basis that D will keep it for the owner or will deal with it in a particular way. Subsection 5(3) of the Theft Act 1968 tries to make sure that such property is still considered to 'belong to the other' for the purposes of the law of theft.

Under this subsection there must be an obligation to retain and deal with the property in a particular way. So, where money is paid as a deposit to a business, the prosecution must prove that there was an obligation to retain and deal with those deposits in a particular way. If the person paying the deposit only expects it to be paid into a bank account of the business, then if that is what happens, there cannot be theft, even if all the money from the account is used for other business expenses and the client does not receive the goods or service for which they paid the deposit. This is what happened in *R v Hall* (1972).

Case study

R v Hall (1972)

D was a travel agent who received deposits from clients for air trips to America. D paid these deposits into the firm's general account but never organised any tickets and was unable to return the money. He was convicted of theft but on appeal his conviction was quashed because when D received the deposits he was not under an obligation to deal with them in a particular way. The Court of Appeal stressed that each case depended on its facts.

In *R v Klineberg and Marsden* (1999) there was a clear obligation to deal with deposits in a particular way.

Case study

R v Klineberg and Marsden (1999)

The two defendants operated a company which sold timeshare apartments in Lanzarote to customers in England. Each purchaser paid the purchase price on the understanding that the money would be held by an independent trust company until the apartment was ready for the purchaser to occupy. Over £500,000 was paid to the defendants' company but only £233 was actually paid into the trust company's account. The defendants were guilty of theft as it was clear that they were under an obligation to the purchasers 'to retain and deal with that property or its proceeds in a particular way', and that they had not done this.

There can be an obligation in less formal situations. This was shown by *Davidge v Bunnett* (1984).

Davidge v Bunnett (1984)

D was given money by her flatmates to pay the gas bill but instead she used it to buy Christmas presents. There was a legal obligation to deal with the money in a particular way and, as she had not, she was guilty of theft.

In *Davidge v Bunnett* there was an intention to create legal relations under contract law, so the obligation was clear. However, it is not certain whether there would be a legal obligation (and so theft) if the situation happened between members of the same family. This might be considered as a domestic arrangement without the intention to create legal relations, so that there would not be theft.

5.4.4 Property received by a mistake

Section 5(4) also provides for situations where property has been handed over to D by another's mistake and so has become D's property.

This section was considered in *Attorney-General's Reference (No. 1 of 1983)* (1985).

Attorney-General's Reference (No. 1 of 1983) (1985)

The defendant, a police woman, had received an overpayment of wages when her pay went into her bank account. She recognised it was an overpayment. She did not withdraw any part of the money, but did not return it. She was convicted of theft of the property (a thing in action) as she was under an obligation to return it.

There must be a legal obligation to restore the property. In some situations there is no legal obligation to restore money. This is shown by *R v Gilks* (1972).

Case	Facts	Law
Turner (No. 2) (1971)	D left his car for repair at a garage. He agreed he would pay for the repairs when he collected the car. He used a spare key to take the car from the garage without their knowledge.	An owner can steal their own property if another has possession and control of it.
Woodman (1974)	Site-owners had arranged for all scrap metal on the site to be removed. Unknown to them a small amount was left on the site.	A person (or company) can be in possession or control of property even though they do not know the property is on their land.
Webster (2006)	An army sergeant sold a duplicate medal on eBay.	The Ministry of Defence retained an equitable interest in the medal and so D was guilty of theft.
Hall (1972)	A travel agent received deposits from customers. He put these deposits into the firm's general account. He did not arrange the tickets for the customers and was unable to repay the money.	D was not under an obligation to deal with the deposits in a particular way under s 5(3), so he was not guilty of theft.
Klineberg and Marsden (1999)	Money was paid for timeshare apartments on the understanding that the money would be held in an independent trust. The money was instead paid into the company's general account.	Where there was a clear obligation to deal with property in a certain way, D was guilty of theft if the property was dealt with in another way.
Davidge v Bunnett (1984)	D was given money by her flat mates to pay the gas bill. She did not pay the bill but used the money to buy Christmas presents.	Even though it was an informal arrangement, there was a clear obligation to deal with property in a certain way. D was guilty of theft when the property was dealt with in another way.
Attorney-General's Reference (No. 1 of 1983) (1985)	An overpayment was made by D's employers into her bank account.	By s 5(4) D was under an 'obligation to make restoration'. If she did not then there was an appropriation of the property. Whether D was guilty of theft would depend on whether or not she acted dishonestly.
Gilks (1972)	D was overpaid for winnings on a bet. He realised the error and decided not to make repayment.	There was no legal obligation to restore the money as betting transactions are not enforceable at law. This meant that s 5(4) did not apply and D was not guilty of theft.

Figure 5.2 Key cases chart on belonging to another

R v Gilks (1972)

D had placed a bet on a horse race. The bookmaker made a mistake about which horse D had backed (two horses had similar names) and overpaid D. D realised the error and decided not to return the money. The ownership of the money had passed to D, so the only way he could be guilty of theft was if s 5(4) applied. It was held that as betting transactions are not enforceable at law, s 5(4) did not apply and D was not guilty.

5.5 'Dishonestly'

The first point which needs to be proved for the *mens rea* of theft is that when the defendant appropriated the property he did it dishonestly. There is no definition of what is meant by this in the Act but s 1(2) states that 'it is immaterial whether the appropriation is made with a view to gain, or is made for the thief's own benefit'.

In other words, if all the elements of theft are present, the motive of the defendant is not relevant. This means that a modern-day Robin Hood stealing to give to the poor could be guilty of theft. The defendant does not have to gain anything from the theft.

5.5.1 Behaviour which is not dishonest

The Theft Act 1968 does not define dishonesty, though it does give three situations in which D's behaviour is not considered dishonest. Section 2(1) of the 1968 Act provides that a person's appropriation of property belonging to another is not to be regarded as dishonest if s/he appropriates the property in the belief that:

- s 2(1)(a) – s/he has in law the right to deprive the other of it, on behalf of him/herself or of a third person, or
- s 2(1)(b) – s/he would have the other's consent if the other knew of the appropriation and the circumstances of it, or
- s 2(1)(c) – the person to whom the property belongs cannot be discovered by taking reasonable steps.

All these three situations depend on D's belief. It does not matter whether it is a correct belief or even whether it is a reasonable belief. If D has a genuine belief in one of these three, then s/he is not guilty of theft.

Unreasonable belief

It has been held in *R v Small* (1987) that the fact that the belief was an unreasonable one does not prevent the defendant from relying on these sections. If the jury decides that the defendant did have a genuine belief, even though an unreasonable one, in one of the three situations, then the defendant must be found not guilty.

R v Holden (1991)

D was charged with the theft of scrap tyres from Kwik Fit where he worked. He claimed that other people had taken tyres with the permission of the supervisor. However, taking tyres was a sackable offence. The Court of Appeal quashed his conviction. As the test is subjective a person was not dishonest if he believed, reasonably, or not, that he had a legal right to the property, providing that belief is genuinely held.

R v Robinson (1977)

D was owed £7 by the victim's wife. When he went to collect the money, a fight developed between D and the victim's husband during which a £5 note dropped out of the husband's pocket. D kept this. His conviction for robbery was quashed by the Court of Appeal as there was no theft (an underlying part of robbery), as he had an honest belief that he was entitled to the money.

R v Small (1987)

D took a car. He said he believed it to be abandoned as it had been left for two weeks in the same place. It was unlocked with the keys in the ignition. There was no petrol in the tank, the battery and tyres were flat. D put petrol in the tank, and drove it off. As he was driving away he saw police flashing their lights at him. He panicked and ran away. He said it was not until he saw the police that he thought the car might have been stolen. He was convicted of theft.

The conviction was quashed because the question to consider was whether D had an honest belief that the owner could not be found.

5.5.2 Willing to pay

Section 2(2) states that 'a person's appropriation of property belonging to another may be dishonest notwithstanding that he is willing to pay for the property'.

This prevents D taking what he or she likes, regardless of the owner's wishes.

5.5.3 The *Ghosh* test

The case of *R v Ghosh* (1982) is the leading case on what is meant by 'dishonestly'. In this case the Court of Appeal set out the tests to be used.

> **Tip** 💬
>
> You need to know the *Ghosh* test precisely as it is used for the offences of theft, burglary and robbery (among others).

Case study

R v Ghosh (1982)

D was a doctor acting as a locum consultant in a hospital. He claimed fees for an operation he had not carried out. He said that he was not dishonest as he was owed the same amount for consultation fees. He was convicted and appealed against the conviction.

The Court of Appeal decided that the test for dishonesty has both an objective and a subjective element to it:

- Was what was done dishonest according to the ordinary standards of reasonable and honest people?
- Did the defendant realise that what he was doing was dishonest by those standards?

The *Ghosh* test means that the jury has to start with an objective test. Was what was done dishonest by the ordinary standards of reasonable and honest people? If it was not dishonest by those standards, the defendant is not guilty.

The first stage of the test requires the jury to consider whether what was done was dishonest according to the ordinary standards of reasonable and honest people. This has the odd effect that if the jury thinks it is not dishonest, then the defendant will be found not guilty even though they may have thought they were being (and intended to be) dishonest.

The second part of the test is not totally subjective as the defendant is judged by what they realised ordinary standards were. This prevents a defendant from saying that, although they knew that ordinary people would regard their actions as dishonest, they did not think that those standards applied to them.

In a trial the judge will use the *Ghosh* test to direct the jury only where there is an issue about dishonesty.

However, the second part of the Ghosh test is now in doubt following the unanimous decision of the Supreme Court decision in the civil case of *Ivey v Genting Casinos Ltd t/a Crockfords* (2017). As this is a civil case, the decision is only *obiter* with respect to the criminal law, although it is likely that it will eventually become a criminal law precedent. The Supreme Court did away with the second limb of the Ghosh test, thus making what the defendant thought about how others would regard his actions irrelevant.

Lord Hughes (with whom Lord Neuberger, Lady Hale, Lord Kerr and Lord Thomas agree) stated in paragraph 74:

> [There are] convincing grounds for holding that the second leg of the test propounded in *Ghosh* does not correctly represent the law and that directions based upon it ought no longer to be given. The test of dishonesty is as set out by Lord Nicholls in *Royal Brunei Airlines Sdn Bhd v Tan* and by Lord Hoffmann in *Barlow Clowes* (referred to at) para 62. When dishonesty is in question the fact-finding tribunal must first ascertain (subjectively) the actual state of the individual's knowledge or belief as to the facts. The reasonableness or otherwise of his belief is a matter of evidence (often in practice determinative) going to whether he held the belief, but it is not an additional requirement that his belief must be reasonable; the question is whether it is genuinely held. When once his actual state of mind as to knowledge or belief as to facts is established, the question whether his conduct was honest or dishonest is to be determined by the fact-finder by applying the (objective) standards of ordinary decent people. There is no requirement that the defendant must appreciate that what he has done is, by those standards, dishonest.

As this was a civil judgement this statement is, at present, *obiter* as far as criminal law is concerned.

5.6 'Intention of permanently depriving'

The final element which has to be proved for theft is that the defendant had the intention permanently to deprive the other of the property. In many situations there is no doubt that the defendant had such an intention; for example, where an item is taken and sold to another person or where cash is taken and spent by the defendant. This last example is true even if the defendant intends to replace the money later, as was shown in *R v Velumyl* (1989).

R v Velumyl (1989)

D, a company manager, took £1,050 from the office safe. He said that he was owed money by a friend and he was going to replace the money when that friend repaid him. The Court of Appeal upheld his conviction for theft as he had the intention of permanently depriving the company of the banknotes which he had taken from the safe, even if he intended replacing them with other banknotes to the same value later.

Another situation where there is a clear intention to permanently deprive is where the defendant destroys property belonging to another. This can be charged as theft, although it is also criminal damage.

There are, however, situations where it is not so clear and, to help in these, s 6 of the Theft Act 1968 explains and expands the meaning of the phrase. It provides that, even though a person appropriating property belonging to another does not mean the other permanently to lose the thing itself, they can be regarded as having the intention to permanently deprive the other of it if their intention is to treat the thing as their own to dispose of, regardless of the other's rights.

In *DPP v Lavender* (1994) the court ruled that the dictionary definition of 'dispose of' was too narrow, as a disposal could include 'dealing with' property.

DPP v Lavender (1994)

D took doors from a council property which was being repaired and used them to replace damaged doors in his girlfriend's council flat.

The doors were still in the possession of the council but had been transferred without permission from one council property to another. Here he is dealing with the doors as his own by moving them from one property to another without permission.

Section of Theft Act 1968	Definition	Comment/Cases
s 1	A person is guilty of theft if he dishonestly appropriates property belonging to another with the intention of permanently depriving the other of it.	Full definition of theft. D is charged under this section.
s 2	**Dishonesty** 1 Not dishonest if D believes: – he has a right in law (s 2(1)(a)) – he would have the other's consent (s 2(1)(b)) – the owner cannot be discovered (s 2(1)(c)). 2 Can be dishonest even if D intends to pay for property.	No definition of 'dishonesty' in the Act. *Ghosh* (1982): two-part test: • Is it dishonest by ordinary standards? • If so, did D know it was dishonest by those standards?
s 3	**Appropriation** 'any assumption of the rights of an owner' Includes a later assumption of rights.	Held to be assumption of any of the rights of an owner: *Gomez* (1993). Given 'neutral' meaning, so consent irrelevant: *Lawrence* (1972), *Hinks* (2000).
s 4	**Property** Includes money and all other property real or personal, including things in action and other intangible property. Land cannot be stolen except by trustee or tenant or by severing property from land. Wild mushrooms, fruit, flowers and foliage cannot be stolen unless done for commercial purpose. Wild animals cannot be stolen unless tamed or in captivity.	
s 5	**Belonging to another** Property is regarded as belonging to any person having possession or control or any proprietary right. Property belongs to the other where it is received under an obligation to retain and deal with it in a particular way. Property received by a mistake where there is a legal obligation to make restoration belongs to the other.	Not limited to owner: *Turner (No. 2)* (1972) stole own car. *Hall* (1972), *Klineberg and Marsden* (1999) *A-G's Reference (No. 1 of 1983)* (1985) Must be a legal obligation: *Gilks* (1972).
s 6	**Intention to permanently deprive** Treat the thing as his own to dispose of regardless of the other's rights. Dispose of includes 'dealing with' property.	The 'goodness' or practical value must have gone from the property: *Lloyd* (1985). *DPP v Lavender* (1994)

Figure 5.3 Key facts chart on theft

In each of the following situations, explain whether all the elements of theft are present.

1   Roland works in a small factory where there are only 20 employees. One day he finds a small purse in the washroom. He opens it. It contains a £10 note and some coins. There is no name or other identification in it. Roland decides to keep the money as he does not think he can find the owner.

2   Venus comes from a country where property placed outside a shop is meant for people to take free of charge. She sees a rack of clothes on the pavement outside a shop and takes a pair of jeans from it.

3   Natalie is given a Christmas cash bonus in a sealed envelope. She has been told by her boss that the bonus would be £50. When she gets home and opens the envelope she finds there is £60 in it. She thinks her employer decided to be more generous and so keeps the money. Would your answer be different if:
   ● Natalie realised there had been a mistake but did not return the money, or
   ● the amount in the envelope was £200?

4   Errol is given permission by his employer to borrow some decorative lights for use at a party. Errol also takes some candles without asking permission. When putting up the lights Errol smashes one of them. He lights two of the candles so that by the end of the evening they are partly burnt down. One of the guests admires the remaining lights and asks if he can have them to use at a disco at the weekend. Errol agrees to let him take the lights.

5   Jabez is late for work one day so he takes his neighbour's bicycle to get to work on time. His neighbour is away, but Jabez has used the bicycle on previous occasions. He intends returning it that evening when he comes home from work. Jabez parks the bicycle at the back of the shop where he works. When he leaves work in the evening he finds that the lamp and the pump have been taken from the bicycle and it has been damaged. He is frightened to return the bicycle in this state so he throws it into the local canal.

5.6.1 Borrowing or lending

Another difficulty with s 6 is the point at which 'borrowing or lending' comes within the definition. Normally borrowing would not be an intention to permanently deprive such as where a student takes a textbook from a fellow student's bag in order to read one small section and then replaces the book. However, if that student also took a photocopying card, which had a limit placed on its use, used it, then returned it, the photocopy card has been returned but it is no longer as valuable as it was. So is there an intention to permanently deprive so far as the card is concerned?

Section 6 states that borrowing is not theft unless it is for a period and in circumstances making it equivalent to an outright taking or disposal. In *R v Lloyd* (1985) it was held that this meant borrowing the property and keeping it until 'the goodness, the virtue, the practical value ... has gone out of the article'. However, there are usually offences that can be used in these sorts of circumstances.

R v Lloyd (1985)

The projectionist at a local cinema gave D a film that was showing at the cinema so that D could make an illegal copy. D returned the film in time for the next screening at the cinema. His conviction for theft was quashed because, by returning the film in its original state, it was not possible to prove an intention to permanently deprive. The goodness, the virtue, the practical value of the films to the owners has not gone out of them.

Conditional intent

Another difficulty is where the defendant examines property to see if there is anything worth stealing. What is the position if s/he decides it is not worth stealing and returns it? This is what happened in *R v Easom* (1971).

Case study

R v Easom (1971)

D picked up a handbag in a cinema, rummaged through the contents and then replaced the handbag without having taken anything. His conviction for theft of the handbag and its contents was quashed. There was no evidence that the defendant had intended to permanently deprive the owner of the bag or items in it so he could not be guilty of theft.

See Chapter 9 on the point of whether a defendant in the situation of *Easom* can be guilty of attempted theft.

5.7 Evaluation of the law on theft

When the Theft Act 1968 was passed, the definition of 'theft' was meant to be in simple everyday language that ordinary people could understand. However, there have been some case decisions on the elements of theft which make it more difficult to understand the law. The main problems with each element are discussed below.

5.7.1 Appropriation

There are a number of problems with the concept of appropriation in the law of theft. These include:

- the width of the acts which can be considered as appropriation
- the problem of appropriation being regarded as occurring at one point in time
- the implication of the one-point concept for robbery and the conflict with decisions in robbery cases
- the difficulty of being able to appropriate even though the owner has consented to the act
- the conflict between civil and criminal law on gifts
- the reliance on dishonesty, a difficult concept of itself, to distinguish between innocent appropriations and appropriations which are theft
- the need for clarity and certainty in the law.

Width of appropriation

As already seen in section 5.2 above, a wide variety of acts can be considered as appropriation. They include the physical picking up of an item, destroying property, throwing items away, selling property, switching price labels on items, giving worthless cheques in payment for goods, receiving a gift, and deciding to keep an item.

All these are considered to be the assumption of the rights of an owner. This width of acts is as a result of the decision in *Morris* that what needed to be proved was the assumption of any of the rights of an owner.

This leads to the question of whether this is the correct test. The Theft Act 1968 uses the phrase 'any assumption of the rights of an owner'. It can be argued that by interpreting the phrase as 'the assumption of any of the rights', the courts have gone beyond what was intended by Parliament.

Assumption at one point in time

The decision in *Gomez* means that appropriation is considered to have occurred at one point in the whole process of theft. As seen in section 5.2.3 above, this led to the acquittal of the defendants in *Atakpu and Abrahams*. Yet the defendants in that case were bringing the cars into this country to sell them. Surely this was an ongoing part of the theft? Why should the appropriation be regarded as only occurring when they hired the cars in Germany?

The defendants were still assuming the right of an owner by continuing to drive the cars and by bringing them into this county. It seems more sensible to say that the appropriation was continuing. This is a view taken by judges in cases of robbery.

There has to be a theft immediately before or at the time of the stealing for the offence of robbery to have been committed. One would assume that the definition of appropriation would be the same for robbery as for theft. Yet in two cases, *R v Hale* (1979) and *R v Lockley* (1995), it has been held that theft is an ongoing process.

See Chapter 6, section 6.1.3 for these cases.

Consent to appropriation

A major criticism of the law is that there can be an appropriation, even though the owner of the goods has consented to the act the defendant has done in relation to the goods.

This appears to be particularly odd in relation to items in shops. Lord Roskill's view of the matter that the honest shopper is only doing what the shop expects and so has not assumed any of the rights of an owner is a very strong argument.

There is also the argument that where an owner consents to the taking of property due to a false statement, then it is more appropriate to charge the defendant with an offence of fraud under the Fraud Act 2006. For cases prior to 2006 defendants could have been charged with the old offence of obtaining property by deception under s 15 of the Theft Act 1968.

If this had been done, then the law on theft would not have needed to be made so complicated.

Theft of gifts

The problems caused by the decisions in *Lawrence* and *Gomez* that there could be an appropriation even though the owner consented to the taking have become even greater since the decision of the House of Lords in *Hinks* (2000) (see section 5.2.2 above).

In *Hinks* the owner had given the property to the defendant. It is difficult to understand how a defendant can have assumed the rights of an owner when the property has actually been given to him.

Conflict of civil and criminal law

The decision in *Hinks* also means that the civil law and criminal law are in conflict.

Lord Hobhouse, one of the judges in the case, stated that in his opinion there was no appropriation. This was because the civil law on gifts involves conduct by the owner who transfers the ownership of the gift to the donee (the person receiving the gift). Once this is done the gift is the property of the donee. The donee does not have to do anything for the gift to become his property. It is not even necessary that the donee should know of the gift. For example, money could be transferred to the donee's bank account without the donee's knowledge. In view of this Lord Hobhouse thought that it was impossible to say that there was any appropriation by the defendant.

Reliance on dishonesty to prove theft

Because of the problems arising from making appropriation so wide, proof of dishonesty is now the only distinguishing point between theft and an honest appropriation. This causes further difficulties as the law on dishonesty also causes problems. These are discussed in section 5.7.3 below.

Need for clarity and certainty in the law

It is important that all law should be as clear and certain as possible. This is especially important for the criminal law. A conviction for theft carries a social stigma. It may even lose a person his job. Yet, as we can see from the above point, the law on theft is not clear.

Remember that appropriation on its own is not enough for theft. All the other elements of theft must be present; in particular there must be dishonesty. There are many situations where there is appropriation but there is no dishonesty so that there cannot be theft. For example, all honest shoppers who place items in a basket or trolley provided by the store are appropriating the items, but because they intend to pay for them, they are not dishonest and so there is no offence of theft.

5.7.2 Property belonging to another

The word 'property' has not caused any real problems. The definition in the Act is so very wide, it includes almost everything. The Act itself sets out detailed rules on when land, animals and plants can or cannot be stolen. The decision that knowledge cannot be stolen in *Oxford v Moss* (1979), where information on examination questions was obtained, does not normally cause any problems as most instances are covered by other offences such as copyright laws.

'Belonging to another'

The Act states that 'belonging to another' includes situations where property is in the possession or control of another, or where another person had any proprietary right or interest in the property. This wide definition of 'belonging to another' is needed since in many cases it might be difficult for the prosecution to prove that the victim was the legal owner. However, this phrase has caused some surprising decisions, in particular the decision in *Turner (No. 2)* (1971) (see section 5.4.1 above for full case details).

In this case the owner of a car took it from a garage without paying for repairs. The garage clearly had a lien (a legal right to retain the car until payment was made) and it could have been held that this gave the garage control of the car. However, the judge at the trial had directed the jury to ignore any question of a lien. On appeal to the Court of Appeal the judges simply based their decision to uphold the conviction on the fact that the garage had possession and control. In fact, if the question of lien is ignored, then Turner had the right to take the car back.

5.7.3 Dishonesty

There are criticisms of the *Ghosh* test (1982) for dishonesty. The main criticism is that it leaves too much to the jury, so that there is a risk of inconsistent decisions with different juries coming to different decisions in similar situations. It has been argued that it would be better for the judge to rule on whether there was dishonesty as a point of law rather than leave it as a matter of fact for the jury. However, this overlooks the fact that members of the jury still need to decide whether they believe what the defendant says.

Another criticism of the test is that it places too much emphasis on objective views of what is dishonest rather than the defendant's intentions. The first stage of the test requires the jury to consider whether what was done was dishonest according to the ordinary standards of reasonable and honest people. This has the odd effect that if the jury thinks it is not dishonest, then the defendant will be found not guilty even though s/he may have thought s/he was being (and intended to be) dishonest.

The points above were emphasised by Professor Griew in an article he wrote in 1985. He put forward several problems with the definition of theft following the decision in *Ghosh*. As well as the points above he also pointed out that:

● the *Ghosh* test leads to longer and more difficult trials
● the idea of standards of ordinary reasonable and honest people is a fiction
● the *Ghosh* test is unsuitable in specialised cases.

Longer trials

The complicated nature of the *Ghosh* test means that trials take longer. The jury has first to decide if the defendant's behaviour is dishonest according to the ordinary standards of reasonable and honest people. This is not always a straightforward matter.

Then the jury has to decide if the defendant realised that what they were doing was dishonest by those standards. This is another difficult point as evidence of a state of mind is not easy to prove.

Griew also thought that the nature of the test meant that more defendants might decide to plead not guilty in the hope that a jury would decide their behaviour was not dishonest.

Fiction of community standards

Griew points out that using a test of ordinary standards of reasonable and honest people assumes that there is a common standard. In fact society is very diverse and different sections of the community may well have slightly varying standards.

Griew's view is supported by the Law Commission in its report on the law of fraud in 2002 when it said, 'There is some evidence that people's moral standards are surprisingly varied'.

This creates problems when the jury has to decide on the ordinary standards. The jurors are likely to come from different backgrounds with different experiences

of life. They can also vary in age from 18 to 70. All these factors may mean that the jury disagree on what the ordinary standards are.

The problems of applying the *Ghosh* test of dishonesty were shown in the case of *DPP v Gohill and another* (2007).

Case study

DPP v Gohill and another (2007)

The defendants were manager and assistant manager of an outlet hiring plant and equipment to customers. Ds had allowed some customers to borrow equipment for periods of less than two hours without charge. These hirings were recorded by Ds on the computer. However, when the customer returned the item within two hours, Ds had either recorded that it had been returned as faulty or incorrectly chosen (for which no charge was made under the company's rules) or, in some cases, Ds altered the computer records to show that the item had only been reserved and not actually borrowed.

Ds stated that they regarded this as good customer service which kept customers who frequently hired happy. It was not done for personal gain and they did not ask for any money for doing this. Sometimes the customer would tip them £5 or £10 but at other times they were not given any money by the customer.

The magistrates acquitted Ds of theft and false accounting on the basis stating that they

> were not satisfied beyond reasonable doubt that by the ordinary standards of reasonable and honest people the [Ds] had acted dishonestly.

The Divisional Court allowed the prosecution's appeal against the acquittal. The court held that the behaviour of the Ds was dishonest by the ordinary standards of reasonable and honest people and they sent the case back for retrial by a new bench of magistrates.

This case shows that even magistrates and judges cannot agree on what is dishonest. So it is even more likely that juries will have very different views on what is dishonest.

Research

Online research by Finch and Fafinsky of Brunel University in 2009 gave several examples and asked people to say whether they thought that the examples were dishonest or not. The views of those responding varied enormously. However, it might be argued that as it was an online questionnaire, some of the people answering may not have taken it seriously and have given unreal answers.

Specialised cases

It is even more difficult to apply ordinary standards where the offence involves a specialised area such as futures trading or other complex financial dealing. The first part of the *Ghosh* test is even more unsuitable in such cases.

Ordinary people have no experience of such financial dealing, so how can they say what is 'honest' or 'not honest' in such cases?

Whether the defendant is being dishonest has become much more important in view of the ruling in *Hinks* (2000) that appropriation is a neutral word. This means that whether a theft has occurred or not is dependent on whether the appropriation was dishonest. The whole of the illegality of the act is based on the *mens rea* of the defendant.

The effect of *Ivey v Genting*

However, many of these problems may now by resolved given Sir Brian Leveson's comments in *DPP v Patterson* (2017). With respect to the decision in *Ivey v Genting* and the comments therein about the Ghosh test he said:

> 16. These observations were clearly *obiter*, and as a matter of strict precedent the court is bound by Ghosh, although the Court of Appeal could depart from that decision without the matter returning to the Supreme Court. This much is clear from *R v Gould* [1968] 2 QB 65, in which Diplock LJ observed at 68G that:
>
> 'In its criminal jurisdiction, ... the Court of Appeal does not apply the doctrine of *stare decisis* with the same rigidity as in its civil jurisdiction. If upon due consideration, we were to be of opinion that the law has been either misapplied or misunderstood in an earlier decision of this court or its predecessor, the Court of Criminal Appeal, we should be entitled to depart from the view expressed in that decision ...'
>
> Given the terms of the unanimous observations of the Supreme Court expressed by Lord Hughes, who does not shy from asserting that Ghosh does not correctly represent the law, it is difficult to imagine the Court of Appeal preferring Ghosh to Ivey in the future.

5.7.4 Intention to permanently deprive

The first point that can be made on this part of the definition of theft is whether it is necessary to include it as part of the law of theft. If someone dishonestly takes property belonging to another, does it matter whether they intend permanently to deprive that person of the property? This would make it possible to convict of theft in situations such as *Lloyd* (1985) where a film was copied and then returned. On the present law Lloyd was not guilty, yet he had appropriated property belonging to another, was being dishonest as the only reason for the appropriation was to take an illegal copy, and temporarily deprived the other of his property. Abolishing the need for an intention permanently to deprive would include this behaviour within the law of theft.

It is because of this need to prove an intention permanently to deprive another of property that the Theft Act 1968 includes a separate offence of taking vehicles without consent. It is recognised that in many cases where a car or other vehicle is taken there is no intention permanently to deprive. This can be seen in the robbery case of *R v Zerei* (2012).

Case study

R v Zerei (2012)

D and another man approached V, whom they knew, and told him that they were going to take his car. D then pulled a knife, punched V and took his car keys. D drove the car off. The car was found abandoned (but undamaged) about one kilometre away. D was convicted of robbery (which requires a theft) but the conviction was quashed on appeal. The Court of Appeal held that the trial judge had misdirected the jury on the issue of intention to permanently deprive. The judge had given the jury the impression that a forcible taking was enough to show an intention to permanently deprive and this is not the law. Also the judge had failed to deal with the fact that D had abandoned the car not far away.

The taker merely wants to drive the vehicle, but will then abandon it, often not far from where it was originally parked. It could be argued that there is theft of the petrol used.

The other problem is what can be called 'conditional' intention to deprive. This is where the defendant examines property to see if it is worth stealing. If he or she then decides it is not worth stealing and returns it, there is no theft. This happened in *Easom* (1971) where the defendant picked up a handbag, looked in it, could not find anything worth stealing and put the bag back. Easom was not guilty of theft because a conditional intention to deprive is not enough to convict the defendant of theft. Again, if in the definition of theft, the word 'permanent' were replaced with the word 'temporary', defendants behaving in this way could be convicted.

This would also bring the law into line with the law on burglary where the courts have ruled that a conditional intention to steal anything worth stealing in the building which the defendant is entering, is sufficient for the defendant to be guilty of burglary under s 9(1)(a) Theft Act 1968.

See Chapter 6 for more information on burglary and robbery.

Tip

You will need to know the relevant sections of the Theft Act 1968 and also to be able to illustrate answers with reference to suitable cases.

Summary

- Theft is defined by s 1 of the Theft Act 1968.
- In order to prove theft there must be:
  ○ appropriation
  ○ of property
  ○ belonging to another
  ○ with the intention of permanently depriving that other of it, and
  ○ dishonesty.

- Appropriation occurs where there is an assumption of the rights of an owner.
- Property includes money and all other property real or personal.
- Things which cannot be stolen include:
  ○ knowledge
  ○ mushrooms, flowers, fruit and foliage growing wild (unless taken for commercial purposes)
  ○ wild creatures who are not in captivity
  ○ electricity.

- Property belongs to another if they have possession or control of it or any proprietary interest in it or it has been received under an obligation or by mistake.
- Dishonesty is not defined in the Theft Act 1968. The *Ghosh* test states that D is dishonest if:
  ○ what was done was dishonest according to the ordinary standards of reasonable and honest people, and
  ○ D realised that what they were doing was dishonest by those standards.

- D is regarded as having the intention to permanently deprive if it is their intention to treat the thing as their own to dispose of.

Chapter 6

Robbery and burglary

After reading this chapter you should be able to:
- Understand the *actus reus* and *mens rea* of robbery under s 8 of the Theft Act 1968
- Understand the *actus reus* and *mens rea* of burglary under s 9 of the Theft Act 1968
- Evaluate the law on robbery and burglary
- Apply the law on robbery and burglary to scenario-based situations

6.1 Robbery

Robbery is an offence under s 8 of the Theft Act 1968. In effect it is a theft which is aggravated by the use or threat of force. Section 8 states:

> A person is guilty of robbery if he steals, and immediately before or at the time of doing so, and in order to do so, he uses force on any person or puts or seeks to put any person in fear of being then and there subjected to force.

So the elements which must be proved for robbery are for the *actus reus*:
- theft
- force or putting or seeking to put any person in fear of force.

In addition, there are two conditions on the force: it must be immediately before or at the time of the theft, and it must be in order to steal.

For the *mens rea* of robbery it must be proved that the defendant:
- had the *mens rea* for theft, and
- intended to use force to steal.

Key term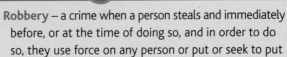

Robbery – a crime when a person steals and immediately before, or at the time of doing so, and in order to do so, they use force on any person or put or seek to put any person in fear of using force.

6.1.1 Completed theft

There must be a completed theft for a robbery to have been committed. This means that all the elements of theft have to be present. If any one of them is missing then, just as there would be no theft, there is no robbery. For example, there is no theft in the situation where D takes a car, drives it a mile and abandons it because D has no intention permanently to deprive. Equally there is no robbery where D uses force to take that car. There is no offence of theft, so using force cannot make it into robbery, as in *R v Zerei* (2012).

See Chapter 5, section 5.7.4 for details of this case.

Another case on this point is *R v Waters* (2015).

Case study

R v Waters (2015)

D snatched V's phone from her and told her that she could have it back if one of her friends would speak to D. The police were immediately called to the scene and D was charged and convicted of robbery. The Court of Appeal quashed the conviction because the evidence did not establish an intention to permanently deprive V of her phone. D's condition for returning the phone could have been 'fulfilled in the near future'. This meant that there was no theft and, therefore, no robbery.

The case of *R v Robinson* (1977), seen above in Chapter 5, section 5.5.1, also demonstrates that if the elements of theft are not complete, then there cannot be robbery.

Where force is used to steal, then the moment the theft is complete there is a robbery. This is demonstrated by the case of *Corcoran v Anderton* (1980).

Case study

Corcoran v Anderton (1980)

One of the defendants hit a woman in the back and tugged at her bag. She let go of the bag and it fell to the ground. The defendants ran off without the bag (because the woman was screaming and attracting attention). It was held that the theft was complete so the defendants were guilty of robbery.

However, if the theft is not completed, for instance if the woman in the case of *Corcoran v Anderton* had not let go of the bag, then there is an attempted theft and the defendant could be charged with attempted robbery.

6.1.2 Force or threat of force

As well as theft, the prosecution must prove force or the threat of force. The amount of force can be small. This is clearly shown by the case of *R v Dawson and James* (1976).

Case study

R v Dawson and James (1976)

One of the defendants pushed the victim, causing him to lose his balance which enabled the other defendant to take his wallet. They were convicted of robbery. The Court of Appeal held that 'force' was an ordinary word and it was for the jury to decide if there had been force.

This decision was confirmed in *R v Clouden* (1987).

Case study

R v Clouden (1987)

The Court of Appeal held that D was guilty of robbery when he had wrenched a shopping basket from the victim's hand. The Court of Appeal held that the trial judge was right to leave the question of whether D had used force on a person to the jury.

It can be argued that using force on the bag was effectively using force on the victim as the bag was wrenched from her hand. However, if a thief pulls a shoulder bag so that it slides off the victim's shoulder, would this be considered force? Probably not. It would certainly not be force if a thief snatched a bag which was resting (not being held) on the lap of someone sitting on a park bench.

This view is supported by *P v DPP* (2012).

Case study

P v DPP (2012)

D snatched a cigarette from V's hand without touching V in any way. It was held that as there had been no direct contact between D and V, it could not be said that force had been used 'on a person'; therefore D was not guilty of robbery.

The situation in *P v DPP* is similar to pickpocketing where D is unaware of any contact. However, where the pickpocket (or accomplice) jostles V to distract him while the theft is taking place, there is force which could support a charge of robbery rather than theft.

The definition of robbery makes clear that robbery is committed if D puts or seeks to put a person in fear of force. It is not necessary that the force be applied. Putting V 'in fear of being there and then subjected to force' is sufficient for robbery. This covers threatening words, such as 'I have a knife and I'll use it unless you give me your wallet', and threatening gestures, such as holding a knife in front of V.

Robbery is also committed even if the victim is not actually frightened by D's actions or words. If D seeks to put V in fear of being then and there subjected to force, this element of robbery is present. So if V is a plain-clothes policeman put there to trap D and is not frightened, the fact that D sought to put V in fear is enough.

A case illustrating the fact that the victim does not have to be frightened and also that the amount of force does not have to be great is *B and R v DPP* (2007).

Case study

B and R v DPP (2007)

The victim, a schoolboy aged 16, was stopped by five other school boys. They asked for his mobile phone and money. As this was happening, another five or six boys joined the first five and surrounded the victim. No serious violence was used against the victim, but he was pushed and his arms were held while he was searched.

The defendants appealed against their convictions for robbery on the basis that no force had been used and the victim had not felt threatened. The Divisional Court upheld the convictions for robbery on the grounds that:

- there was no need to show that the victim felt threatened; the defendant only has to 'seek to put any person in fear of being then and there subjected to force'
- there could be an implied threat of force; in this case, surrounding the victim by so many created an implied threat
- in any event, there was some limited force used by holding the victim's arms and pushing him.

'On any person'

This means that the person threatened does not have to be the person from whom the theft occurs. An obvious example is an armed robber who enters a bank, seizes a customer and threatens to shoot that customer unless a bank official gets money out of the safe. This is putting a person in fear of being then and there subjected to force. The fact that it is not the customer's property which is being stolen does not matter.

6.1.3 Force immediately before or at the time of the theft

The force must be immediately before or at the time of stealing. This raises two problems. First, how immediate does 'immediately before' have to be? Consider the situation where a bank official is attacked at his home by a gang in order to steal keys and security codes from him. The gang then drives to the bank and steals money. The theft has taken place an hour after the use of force. Is this 'immediately before'? It would seem sensible that the gang should be convicted of robbery. But what if the time delay were longer, as could happen if the attack on the manager was on Saturday evening and the theft of

the money not until 24 hours later. Does this still come within 'immediately before'? There have been no decided cases on this point.

The second problem has come in deciding the point at which a theft is completed, so that the force is not 'at the time of stealing'. This was considered in *R v Hale* (1979).

Case study

R v Hale (1979)

The two Ds forced their way into V's house. One put his hand over V's mouth to stop her screaming while the other went upstairs and took a jewellery box. Before they left the house they tied up V.

Here there was force immediately before the theft when D put his hand over V's mouth. Tying up V could also be force in order to steal, as the theft was still ongoing.

The decision in *Hale* was followed in *R v Lockley* (1995).

Case study

R v Lockley (1995)

D was caught shoplifting cans of beer. He used force on the shopkeeper who tried to stop him from escaping. D appealed on the basis that the theft was complete when he used the force, but the Court of Appeal followed the decision in *Hale* (1979) and upheld his conviction for robbery.

But there must be a point when the theft is complete and so any force used after this point does not make it robbery. What if in *Lockley* the defendant had left the shop and was running down the road when a passer-by (alerted by the shouts of the shopkeeper) tried to stop him, and the defendant then used force on the passer-by to escape? Surely the theft is completed before this use of force. The force used is a separate act to the theft and does not make the theft a robbery. The force will, of course, be a separate offence of assault and/or battery.

6.1.4 Force in order to steal

The force must be used in order to steal. So if the force was not used for this purpose, then any later theft will not make it into robbery. Take the situation where D has an argument with V and punches him, knocking him out. D then sees that some money has

Activity

Explain whether or not a robbery has occurred in each of the following situations.

1 Albert holds a knife to the throat of a three-year-old girl and orders the child's mother to hand over her purse or he will 'slit the child's throat'. The mother hands over her purse.
2 Brendan threatens staff in a post office with an imitation gun. He demands that they hand over the money in the till. One of the staff presses a security button and a grille comes down in front of the counter so that the staff are safe and Brendan cannot reach the till. He leaves without taking anything.
3 Carla snatches a handbag from Delia. Delia is so surprised that she lets go of the bag and Carla runs off with it.
4 Ellie breaks into a car in a car park and takes a briefcase out of it. As she is walking away from the car, the owner arrives, realises what has happened and starts to chase after Ellie. The owner catches hold of Ellie, but she pushes him over and makes her escape.
5 Freya tells Harmid to hand over his Rolex watch and that, if he does not, Freya will send her boyfriend, Grant, round to beat Harmid up. Harmid knows that Grant is a very violent man. Harmid takes his watch off and gives it to Freya.

Element	Law	Case
Theft	There must be a completed theft; if any element is missing there is no theft and therefore no robbery.	*Robinson* (1977)
	The moment the theft is completed (with the relevant force) there is robbery.	*Corcoran v Anderton* (1980)
Force or threat of force	The jury decides whether the acts were force, using the ordinary meaning of the word.	*Dawson and James* (1976)
	It includes wrenching a bag from V's hand.	*Clouden* (1987)
On any person	The force can be against any person. It does not have to be against the victim of the theft.	
Immediately before or at the time of the theft	For robbery, theft has been held to be a continuing act.	*Hale* (1979)
	Using force to escape can still be at the time of the theft.	*Lockley* (1995)
In order to steal	The force must be in order to steal. Force used for another purpose does not become robbery if D later decides to steal.	
Mens rea	Mens rea for theft plus an intention to use force to steal.	

Figure 6.1 Key facts chart for robbery

fallen out of V's pocket and decides to take it. The force was not used for the purpose of that theft and D is not guilty of robbery, but guilty of two separate offences: an assault and theft.

6.1.5 *Mens rea* for robbery

D must have the *mens rea* for theft: this means s/he must be dishonest and s/he must intend to permanently deprive the other of the property. He or she must also intend to use force to steal.

6.2 Burglary

This is an offence under s 9 of the Theft Act 1968. Section 9 provides two different ways in which burglary can be committed. Under s 9(1)(a) a person is guilty of burglary if they enter any building or part of a building as a trespasser with intent to steal, inflict grievous bodily harm, or do unlawful damage to the building or anything in it.

Under s 9(1)(b) a person is guilty of burglary if, having entered a building or part of a building as a trespasser, they steal or attempt to steal anything in the building or inflict or attempt to inflict grievous bodily harm on any person in the building.

The chart in Figure 6.2 shows these different ways of committing burglary.

Burglary	
s 9(1)(a)	s 9(1)(b)
Enters a building or part of a building as a trespasser.	Having entered a building or part of a building as a trespasser:
With intent to: • steal • inflict grievous bodily harm • do unlawful damage.	• steals or attempts to steal, or • inflicts or attempts to inflict grievous bodily harm.

Figure 6.2 Different ways of committing burglary

Although ss 9(1)(a) and 9(1)(b) create different ways of committing burglary, they do have common elements. There must be:

• entry
• of a building or part of a building
• as a trespasser.

The difference between the subsections is the intention at the time of entry. For s 9(1)(a), the defendant must intend to do one of the three listed offences (known as ulterior offences) at the time of entering. However, there is no need for the ulterior offence to take place or even be attempted. For s 9(1)(b) what the defendant intends on entry is irrelevant, but the prosecution must prove that D actually committed or attempted to commit theft or grievous bodily harm.

Key terms

Burglary (1) – a crime when a person enters any building or part of a building as a trespasser with intent to steal, inflict GBH, or damage the building or anything in it.

Burglary (2) – a crime when a person, having entered a building or part of a building as a trespasser, steals or attempts to steal anything in the building or inflicts or attempts to inflict GBH on any person in the building.

6.2.1 Entry

Entry is not defined in the Theft Act 1968, but there have been several cases on the meaning of the word. The first main case on this point was *R v Collins* (1972); see section 6.2.3 below for the facts of this case. In this case the Court of Appeal said that the jury had to be satisfied that D had made 'an effective and substantial entry'.

However, in *R v Brown* (1985) this concept of 'an effective and substantial entry' was modified to 'effective entry'.

Case study

R v Brown (1985)

D was standing on the ground outside but leaning in through a broken shop window rummaging through goods. His feet and lower part of his body were outside the shop, but the top part of his body and his arms were inside the shop. The Court of Appeal said that the word 'substantial' did not materially assist the definition of entry and his conviction for burglary was upheld as clearly in this situation his entry was effective.

However, in another case, *R v Ryan* (1996), the need for an 'effective' entry does not appear to have been followed.

Case study

R v Ryan (1996)

D was trapped when trying to get through a window into a house at 2.30 a.m. His head and right arm were inside the house but the rest of his body was outside. The fire brigade had to be called to release him. The Court of Appeal upheld his conviction for burglary saying that there was evidence on which the jury could find that the defendant had entered the house.

6.2.2 Building or part of a building

The Theft Act 1968 gives an extended meaning to the word 'building' so that it includes inhabited places such as houseboats or caravans, which would otherwise not be included in the offence.

A case in which the defendant was convicted of burgling two houseboats moored on the Grand Union canal was *R v Coleman* (2013).

However, the Act does not give any basic definition for 'building'. Usually there is no problem. Clearly houses, blocks of flats, offices, factories and so on are buildings. The word also includes outbuildings and sheds. In *R v Rodmell* (1994) there was the burglary of a garden shed, and the theft of power tools. The shed stood in three and a quarter acres of grounds of a house, and some 60 yards from the house. The Court of Appeal approved these remarks in the context of sentencing:

> A garden shed is part of a person's home. Burglars should be under no illusion that burglary of outbuildings is just as much burglary of domestic premises as breaking into the front door, although it can be said to be not quite as serious as breaking into the place where people live.

This may help reconcile the difficulties arising from the cases of *B and S v Leathley* (1979) and *Norfolk Constabulary v Seekings and Gould* (1986).

Case studies

B and S v Leathley (1979)

A 25-foot-long freezer container had been kept in a farmyard for over two years. It was used as a storage facility. It rested on sleepers, had doors with locks and was connected to the electricity supply. This was held to be a building.

Norfolk Constabulary v Seekings and Gould (1986)

A lorry trailer with wheels, which had been used for over a year for storage, had steps providing access and was connected to the electricity supply, was held not to be a building. The fact that it had wheels meant that it remained a vehicle.

'Part of a building'

The phrase 'part of building' is used to cover situations in which the defendant may have permission to be in one part of the building (and therefore is not a trespasser in that part) but does not have permission to be in another part.

A case example to demonstrate this is *R v Walkington* (1979).

Case study

R v Walkington (1979)

D went into a counter area in a shop and opened a till. This area was clearly marked by a three-sided counter. D's conviction for burglary under s 9(1)(a) was upheld as he had entered part of a building (the counter area) as a trespasser with the intention of stealing.

The critical point in this case is that the counter area was not an area where customers were permitted to go. It was an area for the use of staff, so D was a trespasser.

Other examples include storerooms in shops where shoppers would not have permission to enter, or a hall of residence where one student would be a trespasser if they entered another student's room without permission.

6.2.3 'As a trespasser'

In order for D to commit burglary, they must enter as a trespasser. If a person has permission to enter they are not a trespasser. This was illustrated by the unusual case of *R v Collins* (1972).

Case study

R v Collins (1972)

The defendant, having had quite a lot to drink, decided he wanted to have sexual intercourse. He saw an open window and climbed a ladder to look in. He saw there was a naked girl asleep in bed. He then went down the ladder, took off all his clothes except for his socks and climbed back up the ladder to the girl's bedroom. As he was on the window sill outside the room, she woke up, thought he was her boyfriend and helped him into the room where they had sex.

Collins was convicted of burglary under s 9(1)(a), that is that he had entered as a trespasser with intent to rape. (Note that before 2004 entering as a trespasser with intent to rape was also included under s 9(1)(a), but is now an offence under the Sexual Offences Act 2003.) He appealed on the basis that he was not a trespasser as he had been invited in. The Court of Appeal quashed his conviction because there was no evidence that he was a trespasser; the girl had invited him into the room.

The court said that there could not be a conviction for entering premises 'as a trespasser' unless the person entering did so either knowing he was a trespasser or was reckless as to whether or not he was entering the premises of another without the other person's consent.

So, to succeed on a charge of burglary, the prosecution must prove that the defendant knew s/he was trespassing or that the defendant was subjectively reckless as to whether s/he was trespassing.

'Going beyond permission'

Where the defendant is given permission to enter but then goes beyond that permission, they may be considered a trespasser. This was decided in *R v Smith and Jones* (1976).

There are many situations where a person has permission to enter for a limited purpose. For example, someone buys a ticket to attend a concert in a concert hall, or to look round a historic building or an art collection. The ticket is a licence (or permission) to be in the building for a very specific reason and/or time. If D buys a ticket intending to steal one of the paintings from the art collection, these cases mean that they are probably guilty of burglary.

Shoppers have permission to enter a shop. It is obvious that if a person has been banned from entering a shop they will be entering as a trespasser if they go into that shop. Such a person would be guilty of burglary if they intended to steal goods (s 9(1)(a)) or if, having entered, they then stole goods (s 9(1)(b)).

The case of *Smith and Jones* (1976) takes matters further than this as it means that any person who enters a shop intending to steal is going beyond the permission to enter the shop in order to buy goods. They will be guilty of burglary under s 9(1)(a). However, it is rare for anyone to be charged with this as, unless D admits s/he intended to steal when s/he entered, it is difficult for the prosecution to prove the intent.

The law is also clear where D gains entry through fraud, such as where they claim to be a gas meter reader. There is no genuine permission to enter and D is a trespasser.

6.2.4 *Mens rea* for burglary

There are two parts to the *mens rea* in burglary. These are in respect of:
- entering as a trespasser, and
- the ulterior offence.

First, for both ss 9(1)(a) and 9(1)(b) the defendant must know, or be subjectively reckless, as to whether they are trespassing. In addition, for s 9(1)(a) the defendant must have the intention to commit one of the three offences at the time of entering the building.

Where D is entering intending to steal anything s/he can find which is worth taking, then this is called a conditional intent. This is sufficient for D to be guilty under s 9(1)(a) even if there is nothing worth taking and he does not actually steal anything.

For s 9(1)(b) the defendant must also have the *mens rea* for theft or grievous bodily harm when committing (or attempting to commit) the *actus reus* of one of these offences.

Figure 6.3 helps to make sure you understand the separate ways of committing burglary.

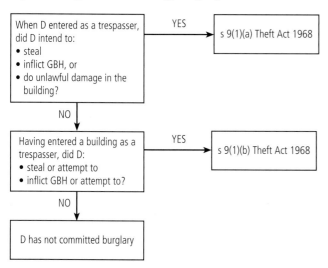

Figure 6.3 Flowchart on different ways of committing burglary

6.3 Evaluation of the law on robbery and burglary

6.3.1 The element of theft in robbery

Robbery requires a theft to be completed. However, there is a difference in the way that the law on theft is applied in robbery to the way the courts have applied it in theft cases. In theft cases it has been held that appropriation occurs at one point in time

> See Chapter 5, section 5.2.3 for more information on appropriation at one point in time.

However, in robbery in the cases of *Hale* (1979) and *Lockley* (1995), the courts have been prepared to view appropriation as a continuing act. In *Lockley* the defendant used force to escape after he had stolen. Despite the fact that the appropriation for the theft occurred before the force, the Court of Appeal still held that the defendant was guilty of robbery. This conflicts with the courts' approach in theft cases.

The theft has to be completed; otherwise there is no robbery. It can be argued that a completed theft should not be necessary. This would bring the law into line with burglary. In burglary a defendant is guilty under s 9(1)(a) where s/he intends to steal (or do

Elements	Comment	Case/Section
Entry	This has changed from: • 'effective and substantial' entry to • 'effective' entry to • evidence for the jury to find D had entered.	*Collins* (1972) *Brown* (1985) *Ryan* (1996)
Building or part of a building	Must have some permanence. Includes inhabited vehicle or vessel. Can be entry of part of a building.	*B and S v Leathley* (1979) *Norfolk Constabulary v Seekings and Gould* (1986) s 9(4) of the Theft Act 1968 *Walkington* (1979)
As a trespasser	If D has permission s/he is not a trespasser. If D goes beyond permission then s/he can be a trespasser.	*Collins* (1972) *Smith and Jones* (1976)
Mens rea	D must know or be subjectively reckless as to whether s/he is a trespasser PLUS EITHER Intention at point of entry to commit: • theft, or • grievous bodily harm, or • criminal damage OR	s 9(1)(a) of the Theft Act 1968
	Mens rea for theft or grievous bodily harm at point of committing or attempting to commit these offences in a building.	s 9(1)(b) of the Theft Act 1968

Figure 6.4 Key facts chart for burglary

various other offences) at the moment s/he enters as a trespasser. Also, in s 9(1)(b) a defendant is guilty if having entered as a trespasser s/he attempts to steal. If it is thought to be just that a defendant can be guilty of burglary where s/he intends or attempts, then there seems no reason why the same rules should not have been applied to robbery. To bring the law into line with burglary, the law would need to be altered to include that a person would be guilty of robbery if s/he used force intending to steal or if s/he attempted to steal using force for that purpose.

6.3.2 Level of force in robbery

The level of force required for robbery is very low. There is also the problem that in *Dawson and James* (1976) the Court of Appeal held that 'force' was an ordinary word and it was for the jury to decide if there had been force. There are not likely to be any problems in deciding whether there had been force where higher levels of force have been used, such as pointing a gun at the victim or punching him. The problems arise where the force is minimal, and different juries may come to different decisions as to whether or not there has been force.

In fact some of the decisions on the amount of force seem to contradict what was intended by the Criminal Law Revision Committee when it proposed the law. It said in its report that it would not regard 'mere snatching of property, such as a handbag, from an unresisting owner as using force for the purpose of the definition [of robbery], though it might be so if the owner resisted'. Despite this, the Court of Appeal in *Clouden* (1987) upheld the defendant's conviction for snatching a handbag from the victim.

6.3.3 Intention in burglary

There are anomalies between the different ways of committing burglary under ss 9(1)(a) and 9(1)(b). Under s 9(1)(a) the defendant at the time of entering must have the intention to inflict grievous bodily harm, steal something from inside the building, or damage the building or anything in it. For s 9(1)(b) there is no need to prove the defendant's intention at the time of entry, but it must be shown that once in the building they stole (or attempted to) or inflicted grievous bodily harm (or attempted to).

Protecting people or property

The first point is that the defendant need only intend some damage (even slight) to be guilty under s 9(1)(a). Yet so far as injuring a person is concerned, the prosecution must prove an intention to inflict grievous bodily harm. This difference appears to be placing the protection of property above the protection of people.

Sections 9(1)(a) and 9(1)(b)

However, under s 9(1)(b) only theft or inflicting grievous bodily harm (GBH) will trigger the required elements for burglary. This has the effect that under s 9(1)(a) a defendant who enters a building as a trespasser with the intention of causing damage is guilty of burglary, while under s 9(1)(b) a defendant who enters a building as a trespasser with no particular intention and then when in the building damages it or other property, has not committed burglary.

There seems no reason why damage should not be included as one of the 'trigger' offences for s 9(1)(b). The point of s 9(1)(b) is to catch the opportunist burglar: that is, the person who only decides to steal or cause damage after s/he has entered. So it would be logical to include criminal damage as one of the 'trigger' offences under s 9(1)(b).

Another comparison between the two subsections is that it is easier to prove a s 9(1)(b) burglary than s 9(1)(a). This is because for s 9(1)(a) the defendant's intention has to be proved, while for s 9(1)(b) the commission of one of the 'trigger' offences has to be proved. Proving a fact is easier than proving intention.

Conditional intention

As already pointed out, a defendant can be guilty of burglary based on their intention when they enter the building as a trespasser. The courts have interpreted this as including where the defendant only intends to steal if there is something worth taking, as in *Walkington* (1979) where the defendant would have stolen from the till in the shop if there had been anything in it to steal. This is known as conditional intention. It can be argued that convicting of the completed offence of burglary on conditional intention is unjust. Conditional intention does not permit a conviction for the full offence in other situations. In particular, in robbery there must be a completed theft as intention to steal is not sufficient for the offence.

Lack of definitions

The Theft Act 1968 does not define key elements of the offence of burglary. There is no definition of 'entry', 'trespasser' or 'part of a building'. 'Building' is only defined to extend its meaning to include inhabited places such as houseboats and caravans. There is no other definition of 'building'.

This lack of definitions means that the courts have had to decide what the Act was meant to cover. This has created difficulty in some cases and inconsistent decisions, especially on what is meant by 'entry'.

Entry

The law on entry has changed through the cases of *Collins*, *Brown* and *Ryan*. In *Collins* the Court of Appeal clearly stated that there had to be 'an effective and substantial entry'. However, in *Brown* the Court of Appeal discarded the 'substantial' element of entry and ruled that Brown was guilty of burglary as his entry was 'effective'.

In the case of *Ryan*, even the need for the entry to be 'effective' was abandoned. Ryan's conviction was upheld on the basis that there was evidence on which the jury could find that the defendant had entered the house.

The decisions in these cases are inconsistent and leave the law uncertain. The problems might have been avoided if the Theft Act had given a definition of 'entry'.

Building

Generally the meaning of building has not caused problems in cases. There are only a few instances where it has been difficult to decide if the place the defendant has entered is a building or not.

The main problems have come where the place was not originally intended as a building but its use has become that of a building. This was seen in the cases of *B and S v Leathley* (1979) and *Norfolk Constabulary v Seekings and Gould* (1986). It appears from these two cases that it will depend on the exact facts of the case as to whether the court will take the view that the place is a building or not. Again, this leaves the law uncertain.

Part of a building

The Act included this phrase as it is clear that there are many situations when a defendant can be lawfully in one part of a building, but not in another part. There is no problem with most of the situations that can arise: for example, a resident in a block of flats entering a neighbouring flat and stealing property from there, or someone entering a room clearly marked 'private' or 'staff only'.

The only case in which the decision can be criticised is *Walkington*. This extended 'part of a building' to include an area which had a counter around three sides but was open on one side. There were no walls or

partitions clearly separating the place out from the rest of the store floor area. The argument was that it was sufficiently clearly defined by the counter and that the counter area was intended only for staff use.

The problem arose because, as the till was empty, the defendant did not actually steal anything. This meant he could not be charged with theft. Also, at the time, the law was that it was impossible to be guilty of attempted theft if there was nothing to steal.

So Walkington at that time could not have been guilty of attempted theft either. This meant that unless he could be charged with burglary he would not have been guilty of any offence. However, the law on attempts has been changed by the Criminal Attempts Act 1981 and Walkington's actions would now constitute attempted theft. So this decision is irrelevant today as there is another and, arguably, more accurate offence with which someone could now be charged.

See Chapter 9 for more information on attempts.

Trespasser

The original use of the word 'trespasser' in law comes from the civil law. When the Theft Act was first passed, it was assumed that the meaning of 'trespasser' would be the same as in the civil law. This is that trespass is entry without the consent of the lawful occupier of the building.

However, in *Collins* the Court of Appeal made it clear that more than this is required. The defendant must enter 'knowing he was a trespasser or was reckless as to whether or not he was entering the premises of another without the other party's consent'.

This element of knowledge of trespassing or being reckless as to whether he is a trespasser is important in the criminal law. It is part of the *mens rea* of the offence of burglary.

The main problems on the issue of 'trespasser' come where the defendant has gone beyond the permission he was given to enter the building.

Going beyond permission

Another area of the law on burglary which can be criticised is where judges have decided that a person who is not a trespasser can become one when he goes beyond the permission given to him. In *Smith and Jones* (1976) the Court of Appeal ruled that the son of the householder was a trespasser where he had entered and stolen two television sets even though the father stated that his son would not be a trespasser in the house; he had a general permission to enter. This decision could mean that a guest at a dinner party in someone's house may become a trespasser if he goes into another room, such as a bedroom, uninvited. If he then steals in that room, he could be guilty of burglary.

The concept of burglary originally was to protect people's homes and other buildings from trespassers who intended to (or did) steal and so on. There is no need to extend the law on burglary to include people who have permission to be in the house, even though they have gone beyond their permission. A thief, as in *Smith and Jones* (1976), can still be charged with theft.

This concept of going beyond the permission has also been applied to shoplifters on the basis that the permission to enter a shop is only given for legitimate shopping purposes. Where someone enters and then steals, he can be considered to have gone beyond the permission given to him when he entered.

As with the *Smith and Jones* case, there is no need to charge such a person with burglary. The obvious and correct charge for this behaviour is theft.

Tip

Make sure you understand the difference between the two types of burglary – s 9(1)(a) and s 9(1)(b).

Summary

Robbery
- It is defined by s 8 of the Theft Act 1968 as stealing and using or threatening force immediately before or at the time.
- There must a completed theft.
- D must use force or put or seek to put any person in fear of force.
- The force must be immediately before or at the time of the theft.
- The amount of force can be small.
- D must intend to steal and intend to use force to steal.

Burglary
- It is defined by s 9 of the Theft Act 1968.
- There are two ways of committing burglary:
  - Section 9(1)(a) – entering a building or part of a building as a trespasser intending to steal, inflict GBH or do unlawful damage
  - Section 9(1)(b) – having entered a building or part of a building as a trespasser, steals or attempts to steal or inflicts or attempts to inflict GBH.
- Being a trespasser includes where D goes beyond the permission to enter.
- Building includes inhabited vehicles and boats.

Chapter 7

Mental capacity defences

After reading this chapter you should be able to:
- Understand the defence of insanity
- Understand the defence of automatism
- Understand the defence of intoxication
- Evaluate the defences of insanity, automatism and intoxication
- Apply the law on these defences to scenario-based situations

7.1 Insanity

For this defence the defendant has to prove that he or she comes within the legal rules of insanity. If successful, there is a special verdict of 'Not guilty by reason of insanity'. It used to be thought that insanity was a defence to all offences. However, in *DPP v H* (1997), where the defendant was charged with driving with excess alcohol, it was held that insanity is not a defence to offences of strict liability where no mental element is required.

7.1.1 The *M'Naghten* Rules

The rules on insanity are based on the *M'Naghten* Rules (1843).

The answers that the House of Lords gave in the case of *M'Naghten* (1843) created the rules on insanity. The main rule is that 'in all cases every man is presumed to be sane and to possess a sufficient degree of reason to be responsible for his crimes'.

The legal definition is that the defendant must be:

> labouring under such a defect of reason, from disease of the mind, as not to know the nature and quality of the act he was doing, or if he did know it, that he did not know he was doing what was wrong.

From this it can be seen that three elements need to be proved. These are:
- a defect of reason
- which must be the result of a disease of the mind
- causing the defendant not to know the nature and quality of their act or not to know they were doing wrong.

Key term

Insanity – a full defence to a criminal offence requiring *mens rea*. The defendant must be labouring under such a defect of reason, from disease of the mind, as not to know the nature and quality of the act they were doing, or if they did know it, that they did not know they were doing what was wrong.

The burden of proving insanity is on the defence, who must prove it on the balance of probabilities.

7.1.2 Defect of reason

This means that the defendant's powers of reasoning must be impaired. If the defendant is capable of reasoning but has failed to use those powers, then this is not a defect of reason. This was decided in *R v Clarke* (1972) where it was held that the defect of reason must be more than absent-mindedness or confusion.

Case study

R v Clarke (1972)

D went into a supermarket, picked up three items including a jar of mincemeat, put them into her bag and then left the store without paying. She was charged with theft but claimed in her defence that she lacked the *mens rea* for theft as she had no recollection of putting the items into her bag. Indeed, she did not even want the mincemeat as neither she nor her husband ate it. She said she was suffering from absent-mindedness caused by diabetes and depression. The trial judge ruled that this amounted to a plea of insanity. D pleaded guilty to the theft but appealed against it.

The Court of Appeal quashed the conviction. They held that the phrase 'defect of reason' in the *M'Naghten* Rules applied only to 'persons who by reason of a "disease of the mind" are deprived of the power of reasoning'. The Court of Appeal also said that the rules of insanity do not apply to people who simply have moments of confusion or absent-mindedness.

7.1.3 Disease of the mind

The defect of reason must be due to a disease of the mind. This is a legal term, not a medical one. The disease can be a mental disease or a physical disease which affects the mind. An example of this is seen in *R v Kemp* (1956).

Case study

R v Kemp (1956)

D was suffering from hardening of the arteries which caused a problem with supply of the blood to the brain. This caused D to have moments of temporary loss of consciousness. During one of these he attacked his wife with a hammer causing her serious injury. He was charged with inflicting grievous bodily harm under s 20 of the Offences Against the Person Act (OAPA) 1861.

At his trial the question arose as to whether this condition came within the rules on insanity. D admitted that he was suffering from a 'defect of reason' but said that this was not due to a 'disease of the mind' as it was a physical illness causing the problem and not a mental illness. He was found 'not guilty by reason of insanity' and appealed against this finding. The Court of Appeal upheld this finding, stating that the law was not concerned with the brain but with the mind. Kemp's ordinary mental faculties of reason, memory and understanding had been affected and so his condition came within the rules on insanity.

In *R v Sullivan* (1984) the House of Lords was asked to decide whether epilepsy came within the rules of insanity.

Case study

R v Sullivan (1984)

D, aged 51, had suffered from epilepsy since childhood. He was known to have fits and had shown aggression to those trying to help him during a fit. He injured an 80-year-old man during a friendly visit to a neighbour's flat. The trial judge ruled that on the facts he would be directing the jury to return a verdict of 'not guilty by reason of insanity'. As a result of this, D pleaded guilty to ABH (s 47 OAPA 1861). D then appealed. Both the Court of Appeal and the House of Lords confirmed the conviction.

The House of Lords ruled that the source of the disease was irrelevant. It could be 'organic, as in epilepsy, or functional', and it did not matter whether the impairment was 'permanent or transient and intermittent', provided that it existed at the time at which the defendant did the act.

This ruling means that for the purpose of the *M'Naghten* Rules, the disease can be of any part of the body provided it has an effect on the mind. In *R v Hennessy* (1989) high blood sugar levels because of diabetes were classed as insanity because the levels affect the mind.

Case study

R v Hennessy (1989)

D was a diabetic who had not taken his insulin for three days. He was seen getting into a car which had been reported stolen and driving off. He was charged with taking a motor vehicle without consent and driving while disqualified. He had no recollection of taking or driving the car. The judge ruled that on these facts D was putting forward a defence of insanity (and not non-insane automatism which the defendant wanted to use as a defence (see section 7.2 below)). D then pleaded guilty, rather than have a verdict of not guilty by reason of insanity. He appealed on the basis that he should have been allowed to put forward the defence of non-insane automatism. The Court of Appeal held that the correct defence was insanity as the disease of diabetes was affecting his mind.

As a result of this decision diabetes was brought within the definition of insanity.

Another case in which it was held that the correct defence was insanity was *R v Burgess* (1991). In this case it was decided that, in some instances, sleep-walking was within the legal definition of insanity.

Case study

R v Burgess (1991)

D and his girlfriend had been watching videos. They fell asleep and in his sleep D attacked her. There was no evidence of any external cause for the sleep-walking and a doctor at the trial gave evidence that in this instance it was due to an internal cause: a sleep disorder. The judge ruled that this was evidence of insanity and the defendant was found 'not guilty by reason of insanity'. The Court of Appeal upheld the finding.

However, if the sleep-walking is due to an external cause, such as a blow to the head, then it is not insanity but will allow the defendant the defence of automatism (see section 7.2).

External factors

Where the cause of the defendant being in a state where s/he does not know what s/he is doing is not a disease but an external cause, then this is not insanity. This was shown in *R v Quick* (1973).

Case study

R v Quick (1973)

D was a nurse working in a psychiatric hospital and assaulted a patient who suffered a fractured nose, a black eye and bruising. D was charged with ABH (s 47 OAPA 1861). His defence was that he was a diabetic who had taken his normal insulin dose but then had eaten insufficient food and claimed his low blood sugar level was the cause of his aggression. The trial judge ruled that his defence should be insanity. However the Court of Appeal ruled that his condition did not come within the definition of insanity. It was caused by an external matter, in this case the taking of insulin. This meant that D could rely on the defence of automatism (see section 7.2) and he was acquitted.

Voluntary intoxication

Where the defendant voluntarily takes an intoxicating substance and this causes a temporary psychotic episode, the defendant cannot use the defence of insanity. This is because the intoxicating substance is an external factor. The case of *R v Coley* (2013) illustrates this.

Case study

R v Coley (2013)

D, aged 17, was a regular user of cannabis and one evening watched a violent video game. Later that night he entered a neighbour's house and attacked her and her partner with a knife. When arrested he was calling for his mother and threatening suicide. He said he had blacked out and had no recollection of what had happened. The psychiatric evidence was that he could have suffered a brief psychotic episode induced by the taking of cannabis and that he might have been acting out the role of a character in the video game he had been playing.

The judge refused to leave the defence of insanity to the jury and D was convicted of attempted murder. The Court of Appeal upheld the conviction as the situation was one of voluntary intoxication and the abnormality of mind had been caused by an external act. Nor could D rely on automatism as he had induced any automatic state by his own fault. (See section 7.2.2 for further discussion on automatism and section 7.3.1 on intoxication.)

7.1.4 Not knowing the nature and quality of the act

Nature and quality refer to the physical character of the act. There are two ways in which the defendant may not know the nature and quality of the act. These are:

- because s/he is in a state of unconsciousness or impaired consciousness, or
- when s/he is conscious but due to his/her mental condition s/he does not understand or know what s/he is doing.

If the defendant can show that either of these states applied to him at the time he did the act, then he satisfies this part of the *M'Naghten* Rules.

An example of not knowing the nature and quality of the act is where a nurse threw a baby onto a fire believing it to be piece of wood.

A case of a defendant not knowing the nature and quality of his act was *R v Oye* (2013).

Case study

R v Oye (2013)

The police were called to a café where D was behaving oddly. He threw crockery at the police and was arrested and taken to a police station. At the police station D continued to behave oddly including drinking water out of a lavatory cistern. When the police moved D to the custody suite he became aggressive and punched a woman officer, breaking her jaw. D was charged with ABH (s 47 OAPA 1861) and two charges of affray.

D's defence was that he believed the police had demonic faces and were agents of evil spirits. Medical evidence at the trial was that D had had a psychotic episode and that he had not known what he was doing and/or that he was doing wrong. Despite this evidence and the judge pointing out the defence of insanity, the jury convicted D. On appeal the Court of Appeal substituted a verdict of not guilty by reason of insanity.

This case also raised issues regarding the defence of self-defence that are dealt with in Chapter 8.

Where the defendant knows the nature and quality of the act s/he still can use the defence of insanity if s/he does not know that what s/he did was wrong. Wrong, in this sense, means legally wrong not morally wrong. If the defendant knows the nature and quality of the act and that it is legally wrong, s/he cannot use the defence of insanity. This is so even if the defendant

is suffering from a mental illness as shown by *R v Windle* (1952).

Case study

R v Windle (1952)

D's wife constantly spoke of committing suicide. One day the defendant killed her by giving her 100 aspirins. He gave himself up to the police and said, 'I suppose they will hang me for this.' He was suffering from mental illness, but these words showed that he knew what he had done was legally wrong. As a result he could not use the defence of insanity and was found guilty of murder.

Note that this case was in 1952 and the special defence of diminished responsibility to a charge of murder did not exist. That defence was only created in 1957, so Windle could not use it.

The case of *Windle* was followed in *R v Johnson* (2007).

Case study

R v Johnson (2007)

D forced his way into a neighbour's flat and stabbed him. D was charged with wounding with intent (s 18 OAPA 1861). At his trial two psychiatrists gave evidence that he was suffering from paranoid schizophrenia and suffering from hallucinations. However, they both agreed that, despite this, D knew the nature and quality of his acts and that they were legally wrong. One psychiatrist was of the view that D did not consider that what he had done was wrong in the moral sense. The judge ruled that the defence of insanity was not available to D and D was convicted of wounding with intent. The Court of Appeal upheld the judge's ruling that insanity was not available as D knew the nature and quality of his acts and that they were legally wrong. They followed the decision in *Windle* (1952) where the court had held that the word 'wrong' meant knowing that the act was contrary to law.

In their judgment, the Court of Appeal pointed out that there had been a case in which an Australian court had refused to follow *Windle* (1952). The view of the Australian court was that if a defendant believed their act to be right according to the ordinary standard of reasonable people, then they were entitled to be acquitted even if they knew that it was legally wrong.

The Court of Appeal felt obliged to follow *Windle* (1952), but they did express the opinion that the Australian case contained 'illuminating passages indicating the difficulties and internal inconsistencies which can arise from the application of the *M'Naghten* Rules if the decision in *Windle* is correct'.

7.1.5 The special verdict

When a defendant successfully proves insanity, then the jury must return a verdict of 'not guilty by reason of insanity'. Up to 1991 the judge then had to send the defendant to a mental hospital regardless of the cause of the insanity or the offence committed. This was clearly not suitable for cases where the defendant suffered from diabetes, epilepsy or hardening of the arteries. So, in 1991 the Criminal Procedure (Insanity and Unfitness to Plead) Act was passed to extend the options for the judge.

The judge can now impose:

- a hospital order (with or without restrictions as to when the defendant may be released)
- a supervision order
- an absolute discharge.

If the defendant is charged with murder then the judge must impose an indefinite hospital order. This means that the hospital can only release the defendant from the hospital if the Home Secretary gives consent.

7.1.6 Evaluation of the law on insanity

The *M'Naghten* Rules

The first major problem is that the definition of insanity was set by the *M'Naghten* Rules in 1843. At that time medical knowledge of mental disorders was very limited. Much more is known today about mental disorders and a more modern definition should be used.

The only area which Parliament has reformed is the options available to judges when dealing with those found not guilty by reason of insanity.

At least this wider range of options has stopped the injustice of epileptics and diabetics having to be sent to a mental hospital.

Legal definition of insanity

Another major problem is that the definition is a legal one rather than a medical one. This causes two problems.

People suffering from certain mental disorders do not come within the definition, for example those suffering from irresistible impulses and who are psychopaths such as *Byrne* (1960). They do not come within the *M'Naghten* Rules as they know what they

	Law	Case
Definition	D must be labouring under a defect of reason, from disease of the mind; AND must either not know the nature and quality of the act s/he was doing, or not know s/he was doing wrong.	*M'Naghten* (1843)
Defect of reason	D's powers of reasoning must be impaired. Absent-mindedness is not enough.	*Clarke* (1972)
Disease of the mind	This is a legal term NOT a medical one. There must be an internal cause. It need not be permanent; it can be 'transient and intermittent'. An external cause is not sufficient.	*Kemp* (1956) *Sullivan* (1984) *Quick* (1973) *Coley* (2013)
Not know nature and quality of act OR Not know he is doing wrong	This means that D must not know it is legally wrong: if s/he does s/he cannot rely on the defence of insanity.	*Oye* (2013) *Windle* (1952) *Johnson* (2007)
Special verdict	Not guilty by reason of insanity. Judge can impose: • a hospital order • a guardianship order • a supervision and treatment order • an absolute discharge.	Criminal Procedure (Insanity and Unfitness to Plead) Act 1991

Figure 7.1 Key facts chart on insanity

are doing and that it is wrong. However, they cannot prevent themselves from acting and have a recognised mental disorder.

On the other hand those suffering from physical illnesses such as diabetes (*Hennessy* (1989)), brain tumours or hardening of the arteries (*Kemp* (1957)) are considered to be legally insane. Even a sleep-walker has come within the definition (*Burgess* (1991)). The justification for this is that there is an internal cause of their actions: the behaviour may recur and it may be possible to treat it.

The overlap with automatism

Insanity overlaps with automatism. It is necessary to decide whether the defendant's automatic state is due to a mental illness or due to external factors. The courts have decided that those suffering from any illness, mental or physical, which affects their mind or puts them into an automatic state amounts to insanity. This means that the defence of non-insane automatism has been removed from such people as epileptics and diabetics.

This has serious consequences, as those successfully using the defence of automatism are entitled to a complete acquittal. Whereas, on a finding of not guilty by reason of insanity, the judge has to impose some form of order on the defendant.

It may be argued that the reason the courts are reluctant to allow defendants to use the full defence of automatism is because it will lead to an acquittal and the defendant will be free from any order or supervision. There is the argument that, even though the cause of the erratic behaviour may be a physical illness, there is still the risk that such a person may commit further offences. Extending insanity to cover those who commit an offence because of a physical illness means that these people can be supervised.

The decisions in *Hennessy* (1989) and *Quick* (1973) referred to in section 7.1.3 highlight the problems with the law. People with diabetes can go into an automatic state in which they do not know what they are doing. This state can be caused by:

- the disease itself, which causes high levels of blood sugar (hyperglycaemia), or
- the drug, insulin, which is used to control the levels of blood sugar. If, after taking insulin, D fails to eat, the blood sugar level will become too low (hypoglycaemia).

If it is the disease which causes the automatic state then, as shown in *Hennessy* (1989), the defendant is considered to come within the rules of insanity as it is an internal cause. If it is the drug which causes the automatic state then, as shown in *Quick* (1973), the defendant is not within the rules on insanity but can rely on the defence of automatism.

It seems ridiculous that a physical disease such as diabetes is classed as insanity, but it is even more ridiculous that diabetics have to rely on different defences available according to whether it was the drug or the disease itself which caused the automatic state.

Decision in *Windle* (1952)

Following the decision in *Windle* (1952), a defendant who is suffering from a serious recognised mental illness and who does not know that his or her act is morally wrong cannot have a defence of insanity when s/he knows that the act is legally wrong. An Australian case refused to follow this decision. In *Johnson* (2007) the Court of Appeal clearly thought that the Australian case had some merit, but they were obliged to follow *Windle*.

Social stigma

Even the use of the word 'insanity' is unfortunate. It carries a social stigma. It is bad enough to apply it to people who are suffering from mental disorders, but it is entirely inappropriate to apply it to those suffering from such diseases as epilepsy or diabetes.

In 2013 the Law Commission issued a Discussion Paper, 'Criminal Liability: Insanity and Automatism'. In this it suggests that a new defence of 'Not criminally responsible by reason of a medical condition' should replace the defence of insanity. This would avoid the stigma of the word 'insanity'. It would also be more appropriate for those suffering from a physical condition that affects the mind. No action has been taken on this suggestion at the time of writing.

Proof of insanity

The defendant has to prove that he or she is insane. This places the burden of proof on them. It is possible that this is in breach of Article 6 of the European Convention on Human Rights, which states that the defendant is innocent until proven guilty.

There is also the point that the jury is required to decide if the defendant is insane or not. This is not an appropriate function for a jury. It is a matter which should be decided by medical experts. Where there is dispute, the jury has to listen to medical evidence and try to understand technical and complex psychiatric issues.

The role of the jury

As jurors have to decide if the verdict should be not guilty by reason of insanity, this means that ordinary people with no medical knowledge have to make what is, in effect, a medical decision. This means there is potential for jurors to be confused over the medical evidence due to the technical terminology of psychiatric medicine.

There is also the possibility that jurors may be so revolted by the crimes committed that they will refuse to return the verdict of not guilty by reason of insanity. Especially in murder cases, jurors may disregard the medical evidence and, instead of returning the special verdict, find the defendant guilty of murder.

This actually happened in the case of Peter Sutcliffe, the 'Yorkshire Ripper', in 1981 where the defendant was charged with the murder of several women but wanted to plead diminished responsibility. All the doctors giving evidence agreed that the defendant was suffering from paranoid schizophrenia, a recognised serious mental illness. Despite this, the jury found Sutcliffe guilty of murder.

Another case where the jury found the defendant guilty despite clear medical evidence on his mental state was *Oye* (2013). When the case was appealed to the Court of Appeal they substituted a verdict of 'not guilty by reason of insanity'.

Overlap with diminished responsibility

Since 1957, for defendants with mental illness charged with murder, there has been an alternative defence of diminished responsibility. If successfully pleaded the charge of murder is reduced to voluntary manslaughter which allows the judge a wider range of sentencing options.

Diminished responsibility covers a wider range of mental illnesses than insanity. It is much more likely to be used as a defence to a murder charge than insanity. In recent years there have been about 20 cases each year where the defendant relies on diminished responsibility. However, there are only one or two cases a year where the defendant relies on the defence of insanity.

This shows that for murder, insanity is not particularly important as a defence as there is a better alternative which does not carry the stigma of insanity.

Case	Facts	Law
M'Naghten (1843)	Suffering from paranoia, shot Sir Robert Peel's secretary. Acquitted but House of Lords asked to clarify the law on insanity.	D must be labouring under a defect of reason, from disease of the mind; AND must either not know the nature and quality of the act he was doing, or not know he was doing wrong.
Clarke (1972)	Absent-mindedly took items from a supermarket.	Mere absent-mindedness or confusion is not insanity.
Kemp (1956)	Suffering from hardening of the arteries which causes blackouts.	Was within the rules of insanity as his condition affected his mental reasoning, memory and understanding.
Sullivan (1984)	Injured friend during epileptic fit.	Insanity included any organic or functional disease. It also applied even where it was temporary.
Hennessy (1989)	Diabetic who took a car after failing to take his insulin.	If the disease affects the mind then it is within the definition of insanity.
Burgess (1991)	Injured his girlfriend while he was asleep.	If the cause of sleep-walking is internal, it is a disease within the definition of insanity.
Quick (1973)	Diabetic who failed to eat after taking his insulin.	This was an external cause (the effect of the drug) and so not insanity.
Windle (1952)	Was suffering from a mental disorder and killed his wife, who had constantly spoken of committing suicide.	Because he knew what he had done was legally wrong, he was not insane by the *M'Naghten* Rules.
Johnson (2007)	D, who was suffering from paranoid schizophrenia and hallucinations, stabbed his neighbour.	Because he knew what he had done was legally wrong, he was not insane by the *M'Naghten* Rules.

Figure 7.2 Key cases on insanity

7.1.7 Proposals for reform

There have been several proposals for reform of the law on insanity. In 1953, the Royal Commission on Capital Punishment suggested that the *M'Naghten* Rules should be extended so that a defendant would be considered insane if he or she 'was incapable of preventing himself' from committing the offence. If this had been acted upon, then those suffering from 'irresistible impulses' would have come within the definition of insanity.

However, instead of making this reform, the defence of diminished responsibility was introduced. This gives a special defence to those charged with murder but does not give a defence to any other offence.

In 1975, the Butler Committee suggested that the verdict of not guilty by reason of insanity should be replaced by a verdict of not guilty on evidence of mental disorder.

In 1989, the Law Commission's Draft Criminal Code proposed that a defendant should be not guilty on evidence of severe mental disorder or severe mental handicap.

None of these proposals has been made law. However, changes to the ways in which judges can deal with a defendant after they are found not guilty by reason of insanity has improved matters. As explained in section 7.1.5, a judge can now make a supervision and treatment order or even give an absolute discharge where that is suitable.

Recent proposals

In 2013, the Law Commission published a Discussion Paper, 'Criminal Liability: Insanity and Automatism'. This sets out the law as it currently is and discusses the problems with the law. As stated above, the paper proposes a new defence of 'Not criminally responsible by reason of a medical condition' to replace the defence of insanity.

> ### Extension question
>
> Research the Law Commission's Discussion Paper 'Criminal Liability: Insanity and Automatism' at www.lawcom.gov.uk. Chapter 1, paragraphs 1.30–1.77 set out problems with the law on insanity. Make your own notes on the problems identified.

7.2 Automatism

In *Bratty v Attorney-General for Northern Ireland* (1963) automatism was clearly defined as:

> An act done by the muscles without any control by the mind, such as a spasm, a reflex action or a convulsion; or an act done by a person who is not conscious of what he is doing such as an act done whilst suffering from concussion or whilst sleep-walking.

In fact this definition covers two types of automatism:

1 Insane automatism
   This is where the cause of the automatism is a disease of the mind within the *M'Naghten* Rules. In such a case the defence is insanity and the verdict not guilty by reason of insanity. An example is where the defendant commits a crime while sleepwalking.
2 Non-insane automatism
   This is where the cause is an external one. Where such a defence succeeds, it is a complete defence and the defendant is not guilty.

> ### Key term
>
> **Automatism** – a complete defence where the defendant proves that the body acted without any control by the mind due to an external factor

7.2.1 Non-insane automatism

This is a defence because the *actus reus* of a crime committed by the defendant is not voluntary. In addition the defendant does not have the required *mens rea* for the offence.

The cause of the automatism must be external. Examples of external causes include:

- a blow to the head
- an attack by a swarm of bees
- sneezing
- hypnotism
- the effect of a drug.

This concept of no fault when the defendant was in an automatic state through an external cause was approved in *Hill v Baxter* (1958).

Case study

Hill v Baxter (1958)

D drove through a halt sign without stopping, and collided with another car. He was charged with dangerous driving but acquitted by the magistrates who accepted that he remembered nothing from some distance before reaching the halt sign. The Divisional Court allowed the prosecution's appeal and sent the case back to the magistrates with a direction to convict as there was no evidence to support a defence of automatism.

The court approved the judgment in the earlier case of *Kay v Butterworth* (1945) where the judge said:

> A person should not be made liable at the criminal law who, through no fault of his own, becomes unconscious when driving, as, for example, a person who has been struck by a stone or overcome by a sudden illness, or when the car has been put temporarily out of his control owing to his being attacked by a swarm of bees.

In *R v T* (1990) it was accepted that exceptional stress or post traumatic stress disorder (PTSD) can be an external factor which may cause automatism.

Case study

R v T (1990)

D was raped. Three days later she took part in a robbery and an assault. She claimed that at the time of the robbery she was suffering from PTSD as a result of the rape and that she had acted in a dream-like state. The trial judge allowed the defence of automatism to go to the jury, but D was convicted.

Reduced or partial control of one's actions is not sufficient to constitute non-insane automatism. In *Attorney-General's Reference (No. 2 of 1992)* (1993) the Court of Appeal held that there must be 'total destruction of voluntary control'.

Case study

Attorney-General's Reference (No. 2 of 1992) (1993)

D was a lorry driver who, after driving for several hours, drove along the hard shoulder of a motorway for about half a mile. He hit a broken-down car which was stationary on the hard shoulder, killing two people. He said that he was suffering from a condition of 'driving without awareness' which puts a driver into a trance-like state. This condition may be brought on by driving for long distances on motorways. The jury acquitted him. The Attorney-General referred a point of law to the Court of Appeal who ruled that because this condition only causes partial loss of control (he was still driving) it did not amount to automatism.

7.2.2 Self-induced automatism

This is where the defendant knows that their conduct is likely to bring on an automatic state. Examples include a diabetic, who knows the risk of failing to eat after taking insulin, or a man who drinks after taking medication when he has been told by his doctor that he must not take alcohol while on that medication. This law comes from the case of *R v Bailey* (1983).

Case study

R v Bailey (1983)

D was a diabetic who had failed to eat enough after taking his insulin to control his diabetes. He became aggressive and hit someone over the head with an iron bar. The trial judge ruled that the defence of automatism was not available. The Court of Appeal held that this ruling was wrong but upheld D's conviction as there was insufficient evidence in the case to raise the defence of automatism.

Although the appeal was dismissed in *Bailey*, the Court of Appeal set out the rules on self-induced automatism. The first point was that there is a difference in the way the defence applies to specific intent offences and basic intent offences.

Specific intent offences

If the offence charged is one of specific intent, then self-induced automatism can be a defence. This is because the defendant lacks the required *mens rea* for the offence.

> **Specific intent offences** – offences for which the *mens rea* required is specific intent. Specific intent offences are those with the *mens rea* of intent only, such as murder or s 18 OAPA 1861.

Basic intent offences

If the offence charged is one of basic intent then the law is more complicated. The main rule is that the defendant cannot use the defence of automatism if s/he has brought about the automatic state by being reckless. The law set out in *Bailey* (1983) states:

1 If the defendant has been reckless in getting into a state of automatism, self-induced automatism cannot be a defence. Subjective recklessness is sufficient for the *mens rea* of crimes of basic intent.

2 Where the self-induced automatic state is caused through drink or illegal drugs or other intoxicating substances, the defendant cannot use the defence of automatism. This is because *DPP v Majewski* (1977) decided that becoming voluntarily intoxicated is a reckless course of conduct (see section 7.3).

3 Where the defendant does not know that their actions are likely to lead to a self-induced automatic state in which they may commit an offence, they have not been reckless and can use the defence of automatism.

> **Basic intent offences** – offences where recklessness is sufficient for the *mens rea*. These include offences such as assault, battery, ss 47 and 20 OAPA 1861 and manslaughter.

The second point is illustrated by *Coley* (2013) where the defendant had been taking cannabis which led him to attack his neighbours. The Court of Appeal pointed out that automatism was not available as a defence to a defendant who had induced an acute state of voluntary behaviour by his own fault (see section 7.1.3 for fuller discussion of this case).

The third situation was seen in *R v Hardie* (1984).

Case study

R v Hardie (1984)

D was depressed because his girlfriend had told him to move out of their flat. He took some Valium tablets which had been prescribed for his former girlfriend. She encouraged him to take the tablets, stating that it would calm him down. He then set fire to a wardrobe in the flat. He said he did not know what he was doing because of the Valium. The trial judge directed the jury to ignore the effect of the tablets and he was convicted of arson.

The Court of Appeal quashed his conviction as the defendant had taken the drug because he thought it would calm him down. This is the normal effect of Valium. So the defendant had not been reckless and the defence of automatism should have been left to the jury.

7.2.3 Evaluation of the law on automatism

There is some dispute whether the defence of automatism is a denial of *actus reus* or of *mens rea*. The present use of the defence is for the defendant to show that he could not form the *mens rea* of an offence due to an external factor. However the Law Commission considers that the correct classification of the defence is as a denial of *actus reus* as they consider the true basis of the defence as a denial of voluntary 'action' due to an external factor. This approach means that the defence could be available for people charged with offences of strict liability, which is not the case at present.

Where there is a finding of insanity the defendant can be made subject to forms of supervision or to treatment orders. But, as automatism is a complete defence, the defendant cannot be made subject to any such orders. For example, if a motorist crashes into another vehicle and there is expert evidence that he was suffering from undiagnosed sleep apnoea he may successfully plead automatism, but the court will not be able to order medical treatment for the condition to prevent possible future recurrences.

The distinction between insane and non-insane automatism is incoherent and arbitrary. It was set for reasons of social protection as it could be considered unsafe for someone who is considered to be insane to be allowed on the streets without treatment as there is a greater possibility that they could lose control and harm other members of the public. Some defendants who are currently classed as insane pose little or no continuing danger to the public while others who are acquitted on the basis of sane automatism may in fact be liable to react in the same way again. Further there is no medical support for the distinction and it can produce conflicting and arbitrary results, especially in the case of persons suffering from diabetes. For example, A is a diabetic who lapses into a hyperglycaemic coma having not taken insulin, has to plead insane automatism and receives the special verdict regardless of whether he has been at fault in failing to take the insulin.

On the other hand B is a diabetic who takes his insulin but fails to eat and lapses into a hypoglycaemic coma is treated as a sane automaton and can plead not guilty.

When the defendant commits a crime while sleepwalking, according to the decision in *R v Burgess 1991*, the case is treated as one of insane automatism requiring confinement and treatment. The court considered that, while sleep itself was a normal condition, sleepwalking, in particular violent sleepwalking, was not normal, and constituted a 'disease of the mind' within the M'Naghten test. According to Lord Chief Justice Lane in that case:

> It seems to us that if there is a danger of recurrence that may be an added reason for categorising the condition as a disease of the mind.

However, this precedent may not be applied in every case and some courts have taken a generous approach, treating sleepwalking as a plea of sane automatism. An example was in Rv *Bilton* 2005 where the defendant, who had a history of sleepwalking, was acquitted of rape after the jury accepted his claim that he had been sleepwalking at the time.

There has also been inconsistency of approach where the defendant has been sleepwalking but was also voluntarily intoxicated. In *R v Lowe* 2005 the defendant fatally attacked his aged father one night while voluntarily intoxicated. The defence argued that the attack occurred while sleepwalking or, alternatively, when he was in a confused state of arousal. The defendant's plea of insane automatism was accepted and he was hospitalised for eight months. By contrast in *R v Pooley 2007* the defendant was acquitted of rape after he successfully proved that he was suffering an episode of parasomnia, a sleep disorder which can include sleepwalking, despite his own voluntary intoxication.

7.2.4 Proposals for reform in the law on automatism

In the Draft Criminal Code (1989) the following definition was suggested:

> A person is not guilty of an offence if—
>
> **(a)** he acts in a state of automatism, that is, his act—
>
> **(i)** is a reflex, spasm or convulsion; or
>
> **(ii)** occurs while he is in a condition (whether of sleep, unconsciousness, impaired consciousness or otherwise) depriving him of effective control of his act; and
>
> **(b)** the act or condition is the result neither of anything done or omitted with the fault required for the offence nor of voluntary intoxication.

This definition would include those who act during an epileptic convulsion, so that cases such as *Sullivan* (1984) would be able to use the defence of non-insane automatism instead of insanity. Also cases of sleepwalking would come under this defence. This would have given *Burgess* (1991) the defence of non-insane automatism. In both these cases the defendants would have had a full defence.

Insanity	Automatism
For defence to prove, on the balance of probabilities.	For defendant to raise; the prosecution must then disprove.
Must have a defect of reason due to disease of the mind: *M'Naghten* Rules. Example: Diabetic affected by disease: *Hennessey* (1989).	Must be caused by an external factor. Example: Diabetic affected by (drug) insulin: *Quick* (1973).
Verdict: not guilty by reason of insanity. Judge must make one of the following four orders: • a hospital order (with or without restrictions as to when the defendant may be released) • a guardianship order • a supervision and treatment order • an absolute discharge.	Verdict: not guilty. Defendant is free.

Figure 7.3 Comparison of insanity and automatism as defences

On the other hand, the present system allows a judge to order medical treatment for those who are found not guilty by reason of insanity. Should there be some way of making sure that those who commit dangerous offences while in an automatic state, and who would benefit from treatment, do in fact receive treatment? It can be argued that a complete acquittal leaves a possibly dangerous person (although not intentionally) to do the same thing again.

Recent proposals

As pointed out at section 7.1.7 the Law Commission in 2013 published a Discussion Paper, 'Criminal Liability: Insanity and Automatism'. It had already pointed out in an earlier Scoping Paper that the two defences are so closely related that if there is to be reform of insanity, then automatism must be reformed at the same time.

The Discussion Paper sets out the present law and the problems with it.

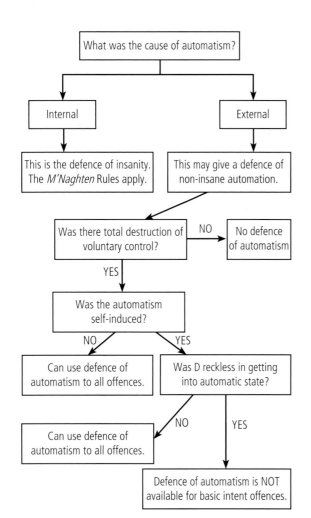

Figure 7.4 Flow chart on automatism

However, it recommends that where the accused's loss of capacity to control his or her actions is due to something the accused culpably did or failed to do, then liability will still turn on the principles of prior fault. In this respect the Law Commission is not proposing any change to the law.

7.3 Intoxication

Intoxication may come about by alcohol, drugs or other substances, such as glue-sniffing. Intoxication does not provide a defence as such, but is relevant as to whether the defendant has the required *mens rea* for the offence. If he or she does not have the required *mens rea* because of his/her intoxicated state, s/he may be not guilty.

Whether the defendant is guilty or not depends on:
- whether the intoxication was voluntary or involuntary, and
- whether the offence charged is one of specific or basic intent.

As with Automatism at section 7.2.2, specific intent offences are those which require specific intention, or intent only, for their *mens rea*. Relevant specific intent offences are murder, s 18 OAPA 1861, theft, robbery and burglary.

Basic intent offences are those for which recklessness is sufficient for the *mens rea*. Relevant basic intent offences are manslaughter, ss 20 and 47 OAPA 1861, assault and battery.

7.3.1 Voluntary intoxication

Voluntary intoxication is where the defendant has chosen to take an intoxicating substance. This can be by taking alcohol, illegal drugs or other intoxicants such as through sniffing glue. It can also occur where the defendant knows that the effect of a prescribed drug will be to make him intoxicated.

Voluntary intoxication and specific intent offences

Voluntary intoxication can negate the *mens rea* for a specific intent offence. If the defendant is so intoxicated that they have not formed the *mens rea* for the offence, they are not guilty. This rule comes from *DPP v Beard* (1920).

Case study

DPP v Beard (1920)

Beard had been charged with murder and had put forward as his defence the fact that he was too intoxicated to have formed the *mens rea* for murder. He was convicted but on appeal, Lord Birkenhead considered previous decisions and stated:

> Where a specific intent is an essential element in the offence, evidence of a state of drunkenness rendering the accused incapable of forming such an intent should be taken into consideration in order to determine whether he had in fact formed the intent necessary to constitute the particular crime.

Lord Birkenhead then stated the rule which still stands today:

> If he was so drunk that he was incapable of forming the intent required, he could not be convicted of a crime which was committed only if the intent was proved.

An example of where it was found that the defendants were so drunk that they did not have the *mens rea* for murder is *R v Sheehan and Moore* (1975). The defendants were very drunk when they threw petrol over a tramp and set fire to him. They were too drunk to have formed any intent to kill or cause grievous bodily harm. It was held that because they did not have the *mens rea* for murder, their intoxication was a defence to that offence. However, they were found guilty of manslaughter as that is a basic intent offence.

Where the defendant has the necessary *mens rea* despite their intoxicated state, then they are guilty of the offence. The intoxication does not provide a defence. It has been held that a drunken intent is still an intent. This was shown by *A-G for Northern Ireland v Gallagher* (1963).

Case study

A-G for Northern Ireland v Gallagher (1963)

D decided to kill his wife. He bought a knife to do the killing and also a bottle of whisky. He drank a large amount of the whisky to give himself 'Dutch courage' before killing his wife. His conviction for murder was upheld as he had formed the intent before becoming intoxicated and committing the murder.

A more recent case on this is *R v Coley* (2013) (see section 7.1.3 above for full case details). Coley had taken cannabis and attacked his neighbours. The trial judge ruled that the case was one of involuntary intoxication and the jury found him guilty of attempted murder. The Court of Appeal upheld the conviction as the verdict of guilty involved a clear finding that, despite Coley's state of mind, he intended to kill.

Voluntary intoxication and basic intent offences

Where the offence charged is one of basic intent then intoxication is not a defence. This is because voluntarily becoming intoxicated is considered a reckless course of conduct, and recklessness is enough to constitute the necessary *mens rea*. The leading case on this is *DPP v Majewski* (1977).

Case study

DPP v Majewski (1977)

D had consumed large quantities of alcohol and drugs and then attacked the landlord of the public house where he was drinking and damaged the premises. The landlord called the police and D also attacked the police officers who tried to arrest him. He was charged with assault, ABH under s 47 OAPA 1861 and criminal damage, all basic intent offences. The Law Lords held that becoming intoxicated by drink and drugs was a reckless course of conduct, and recklessness is enough to constitute the necessary *mens rea* in assault cases.

Past intoxication

Where the defendant is suffering from a mental disorder brought on by past voluntary intoxication, he can use this as a defence.

Case study

R v Harris (2013)

D was convicted of arson being reckless as to whether the life of another was endangered. D started a fire in his own house which potentially endangered his neighbours in the adjoining semi-detached house. He had previously been a heavy drinker but a few days before the incident he had stopped drinking. This had caused alcohol psychosis or alcohol-induced hallucinations as he said he had heard voices telling him to burn the house down. The Court of Appeal allowed his appeal against conviction as his condition was caused by past voluntary intoxication which had caused mental disorder. He was not intoxicated at the time of the offence.

The Court of Appeal rejected the prosecution's argument that an illness caused by D's own fault ought as a matter of policy to be treated in the same way as drunkenness. The court held that this would be too great an extension of the principles in *Majewski*. The defendant was entitled to have the question of whether, in the condition he was in, he was actually aware that his action might endanger life.

7.3.2 Involuntary intoxication

Involuntary intoxication covers situations where the defendant did not know he or she was taking an intoxicating substance. This may be where, for example, a soft drink has been 'laced' with alcohol or drugs. It also covers situations where prescribed drugs have the unexpected effect of making the defendant intoxicated.

The test is, did the defendant have the necessary *mens rea* when he or she committed the offence? If so, as decided in *R v Kingston* (1994), he or she will be guilty. The involuntary intoxication will not provide a defence. This is so even though the defendant would not have committed the offence without the intoxication lowering his or her resistance to committing the offence.

Case study

R v Kingston (1994)

The defendant's coffee was drugged by someone who wanted to blackmail him. He was then shown a 15-year-old boy who was asleep and invited to abuse him. The defendant did so and was photographed by the blackmailer.

The House of Lords upheld his conviction for indecent assault. They held that if a defendant had formed the *mens rea* for an offence then the involuntary intoxication was not a defence.

Where, however, the defendant did not have the necessary intent s/he will be not guilty. He or she has no *mens rea* and so cannot be guilty of a specific intent offence. Neither can s/he be guilty of a basic intent offence. This is because the defendant has not been reckless in getting intoxicated. An example of this is *R v Hardie* (1984) (see section 7.2.2) where the

defendant took Valium tablets, not knowing they could make his behaviour unpredictable.

7.3.3 Intoxicated mistake

If the defendant is mistaken about a key fact because s/he is intoxicated, then it depends on what the mistake was about as to whether s/he has a defence or not.

Where the mistake is about something which means that the defendant did not have the necessary *mens rea* for the offence, then for specific intent offence s/he has a defence. However, where the offence is one of basic intent then the defendant has no defence. An example of this was the case of *R v Lipman* (1970).

Case study

R v Lipman (1970)

D and his girlfriend had taken the drug LSD before falling asleep at her flat. LSD causes people to have hallucinations. D thought that he was at the centre of the earth and being attacked by snakes. When he awoke he found his girlfriend was dead. He had strangled her and stuffed a sheet into her mouth believing she was a snake attacking him. He was charged with murder and manslaughter.

Lipman did not have the specific intention for murder as he thought he was killing a snake. He did not intend to kill or cause grievous bodily harm to any human being. However, he had voluntarily taken the drug LSD which was 'a reckless course of conduct' and so was guilty of manslaughter.

If the mistake is about another aspect, for example the amount of force needed in self-defence, the defendant will not have a defence. This was stated in *R v O'Grady* (1987) and confirmed in *R v Hatton* (2005).

Case study

R v O'Grady (1987)

After D and V, who was a friend, had been drinking heavily, they fell asleep in D's flat. D claimed that he awoke to find V hitting him. D picked up a glass ashtray and hit V with it, and then went back to sleep. When he woke the next morning, he found that V was dead. D was charged with murder but was convicted of manslaughter. The Court of Appeal upheld this conviction.

O'Grady was convicted of manslaughter which is a basic intent offence. This is clearly in line with the decision in *DPP v Majewski* (1977) as getting drunk is a 'reckless course of conduct' and recklessness is sufficient for a basic intent offence such as manslaughter.

The interesting point in the case was that the Lord Chief Justice, Lord Lane, also stated that an intoxicated mistake as to the amount of force needed in self-defence was not a defence to a specific intent offence. This has been confirmed by *R v Hatton* (2005).

Shorry, I thought you were a martian.

Case study

R v Hatton (2005)

D had drunk over 20 pints of beer. He and another man (V) went back to D's flat. In the morning D claimed he found V dead from injuries caused by a sledgehammer. D said he could not really remember what had happened but thought V had hit him with a five-foot-long stick and he had defended the attack. D was convicted of murder. The Court of Appeal held that the decision in *O'Grady* (1987) was not limited to basic intent crimes, but also applied to specific intent crimes. A drunken mistake about the amount of force required in self-defence was not a defence.

Exception

An exception to the rule on intoxicated mistake is *Jaggard v Dickinson* (1980).

Case study

Jaggard v Dickinson (1980)

D, who was drunk, went to what she thought was a friend's house. There was no one in so she broke a window to get in as she believed (accurately) her friend would consent to this. Unfortunately in her drunken state she had mistaken the house and had actually broken into the house of another person.

The Divisional Court quashed her conviction holding that she could rely on her intoxicated belief as Parliament had 'specifically required the court to consider the defendant's actual state of belief, not the state of belief which ought to have existed'.

Criminal Justice and Immigration Act 2008

This Act now makes it clear that a mistaken belief caused through the defendant's voluntary intoxication cannot be used for of self-defence, defence of another or prevention of crime.

Further, s 76 of the Criminal Justice and Immigration Act 2008 states that reasonable force may be used for purposes of self-defence, defence of another or prevention of crime. However, s 76(5) says that this 'does not enable D to rely on any mistaken belief attributable to intoxication that was voluntarily induced'.

This exception is because s 5 of the Criminal Damage Act 1971 allows an honest belief that the person to whom the property belonged would have consented to the damage or destruction as a lawful excuse to a charge of criminal damage, whether or not the belief is justified. This has been interpreted as giving a defendant a defence even where the mistake was made through intoxication.

	Specific intent crimes	Basic intent crimes
Voluntary intoxication	If defendant has *mens rea* s/he is guilty: *Gallagher* (1963). If defendant has no *mens rea* s/he is not guilty.	Becoming intoxicated is a reckless course of conduct: *Majewski* (1977). The defendant is guilty of the offence.
Involuntary intoxication	If defendant has *mens rea* s/he is guilty: *Kingston* (1994). If defendant has no *mens rea* s/he is not guilty: *Hardie* (1984).	The defendant has not been reckless in becoming intoxicated, so is not guilty: *Hardie* (1984).
Drunken mistake	If the mistake negates *mens rea* the defendant is not guilty. If the mistake is about the need to defend oneself, it is not a defence. The defendant will be guilty. This is so for both specific and basic intent offences: *O'Grady* (1987), *Hatton* (2005). For self-defence, defence of another or prevention of crime, s 76(5) of the Criminal Justice and Immigration Act 2008 does not allow D to rely on 'any mistaken belief attributable to intoxication that was voluntarily induced'.	This is a reckless course of conduct, so the defendant is guilty.

Figure 7.5 Key facts chart on intoxication as a defence

7.3.4 Evaluation of the law on intoxication

The interests competing in the operation of this defence are those of personal autonomy and social paternalism.

On the one hand an adult can make a choice to spend as much of their own money on buying intoxicating substances as they wish. Subject to some timing restrictions, an adult can spend as much time as they choose consuming alcohol in public – in pubs, bars and restaurants.

On the other hand there is the view that excessive consumption of alcohol, and particularly consumption of drugs, causes problems with health and welfare of the individual and potentially requires reliance on the health service, on social services and, at times, the intervention of the criminal justice system. Intoxication is a major factor in the commission of many crimes and in social disorder. Statistics suggest that half of all violent crimes are committed by people who are intoxicated by drink and/or drugs. It can result in considerable money and resources being used by the police and the health service. As a result it is considered that the state has a duty to control consumption and to limit the opportunities to use a defence of intoxication to criminal offences. There is a need to balance the rights of the defendant and the victims of crime. If intoxication was always allowed to be a defence, then victims' rights would not be protected.

Statutory intervention has also followed the paternalistic approach. An example is s 76(5) of the Criminal Justice and Immigration Act 2008 which provides, in relation to the defence of self-defence, that a person cannot rely on 'any mistaken belief attributable to intoxication that was voluntarily induced' when claiming this defence.

Mens rea

Some areas of the law on intoxication appear to be contrary to the normal rules on *mens rea* and *actus reus*. In particular this is seen in the decision in *DPP v Majewski* (1977). The decision in this case, that the defendant is guilty of a basic intent offence because getting drunk is a 'reckless course of conduct', ignores the principle that *mens rea* and *actus reus* must coincide. The decision to drink may be several hours before the defendant commits the *actus reus* of any offence. For example, in *O'Grady* (1987), the defendant had fallen asleep and only committed the act of hitting his friend some hours afterwards.

In addition, the recklessness in becoming intoxicated means that the defendant takes a general risk of doing something 'stupid' when drunk. At the time of becoming intoxicated the defendant has no idea that he or she will actually commit an offence. Normally, for offences where recklessness is sufficient for the *mens rea* of an offence, it has to be proved that D knew there was a risk of the specific offence being committed.

This point was considered by the Law Commission in a Consultation Paper in 1993. It said in that paper that the *Majewski* rule was arbitrary and unfair. However, the Law Commission's proposals for changing the law were severely criticised and by the time it published firm proposals for reform of the law in 1995 it had changed its opinion. By this time it thought that the present law operated 'fairly, on the whole, and without undue difficulty'.

Specific intent/basic intent

Where a defendant is charged with murder or a s 18 offence they can use intoxication as a defence. However, because intoxication is not a defence to a basic intent offence, a defendant can be found guilty of a lower level offence. These include manslaughter or s 20 OAPA 1861.

However, for other crimes, there is often no 'fall-back' offence. If a defendant is charged with theft and successfully claims that they did not form the *mens rea* for theft because they were too intoxicated, they will be not guilty of any offence.

Involuntary intoxication

A final point where the law could be thought to be in need of reform is where the defendant's inhibitions are broken down by being made intoxicated involuntarily. The decision in *Kingston* (1994) makes such a defendant guilty if they formed the necessary *mens rea*. This ignores the fact that the defendant was not to blame for the intoxication. Such a defendant would be not guilty of a basic intent offence where the prosecution relied on recklessness (as in *Hardie* (1984)). This appears to be unfair to defendants in Kingston's situation.

7.3.5 Proposals for reform

After previous proposals to reform the law on intoxication were rejected or abandoned the Law Commission looked again at the defence in its 2009 report, 'Intoxication and Criminal Liability', (Law Com No. 314).

This report recommended that:
- the distinction between voluntary and involuntary intoxication should be kept

- the use of the terms 'specific intent' and 'basic intent' should be abolished;
- instead offences should be categorised as those where *mens rea* is an integral fault element (e.g. where there has to be intention as to a consequence) and those where *mens rea* is NOT an integral fault element (e.g. because the offence merely requires proof of recklessness).

Voluntary intoxication

Where D was voluntarily intoxicated, the Law Commission proposed the following:
- There should be a general rule that where D is charged with an offence for which *mens rea* is not an integral fault element, then D should be treated as being aware of anything he would have been aware of if he had been sober.
- This rule would not apply to offences where the required *mens rea* involved intention as to a consequence, knowledge, fraud or dishonesty.

Involuntary intoxication

The Law Commission proposed that there should be a list of situations which would count as involuntary intoxication. It suggested that these should include spiked drinks, D being forced to take an intoxicating substance, D reasonably believing that the substance was not an intoxicant, and situations where the substance was taken for a 'proper medical purpose'.

Where D was involuntarily intoxicated, then this should be taken into account in deciding whether D acted with the required *mens rea*. This effectively confirms the law as set out in *Kingston* (1995).

At the time of writing no action has been taking on any of these proposals.

  Tip

When answering scenario-based questions which involve one or more defences, look for key words such as 'has drunk seven pints of beer' (intoxication) or 'taken a drug' (intoxication or perhaps automatism). This should help you to decide which defences are relevant.

Explain whether there would a defence available in the following situations.

1   Alice took some illegal drugs. She is told that while she was under the influence of the drugs, witnesses saw her hit Peter in the face with a saucepan, breaking his jaw. Alice cannot remember doing this. What defence(s) might be available to her if she is charged with offences under ss 18 and 20 OAPA 1861?

2   Courtney is a diabetic. One morning he gets up late and in his rush to get to work he forgets to take his insulin. As a result he becomes violent later in the day and punches Jemima in the face. What defence(s) might be available to him if he is charged with an offence under s 47 OAPA 1861?

3   Zahir is hit on the head by a slate which accidentally falls off a building. He loses consciousness briefly but is then able to walk home. Later that day he attacks his partner, Lynne, causing serious injuries to her. He has no recollection of doing this. What defence(s) might be available to him if he is charged with offences under ss 18 and 20 OAPA 1861?

Summary

Insanity
●   The definition of insanity is based on the *M'Naghten* Rules.
●   D must prove that s/he was 'labouring under such a defect of reason, from disease of the mind, as not to know the nature and quality of the act he was doing, or if he did know it, that he did not know he was doing what was wrong'.
●   Disease of the mind includes physical diseases which affect the mind: it does not include the effect of an external factor.
●   If D knows the act is legally wrong then they cannot use the defence of insanity.
●   If the defence is successful the verdict is not guilty by reason of insanity.

Automatism
●   This is an act done by the muscles without any control by the mind.
●   Automatism can be categorised as insane (covered by the defence of insanity) or non-insane.
●   Where D is not at fault in getting into a non-insane automatic state then there is defence and D is not guilty.
●   If the automatism is self-induced, D will be able to use the defence for a specific intent offence.
●   If the automatism is self-induced because of D's recklessness, D will have no defence for a basic intent offence.

Intoxication
●   Voluntary intoxication can only be a defence to a specific intent offence where D is so intoxicated that he does not have the necessary *mens rea* for the offence.
●   Voluntary intoxication is not a defence to a basic intent offence as becoming intoxicated is a reckless course of conduct.
●   Involuntary intoxication is a defence to a specific intent offence where D did not have the necessary *mens rea* for the offence.
●   Involuntary intoxication can be a defence to a basic intent offence as D has not been reckless in becoming intoxicated.
●   Where D makes a mistake because s/he is intoxicated, then if the mistake means that D did not have necessary *mens rea* for the offence D can use intoxication as a defence.

Chapter 8

General defences

After reading this chapter you should be able to:
- Understand the defence of self-defence
- Understand the defence of duress by threats
- Understand the defence of duress of circumstances
- Understand the defence of necessity
- Understand the defence of consent
- Evaluate all these defences
- Apply the law of these defences to scenario-based situations

8.1 Self-defence

This defence covers not only actions which are needed to defend oneself from an attack, but also actions taken to defend another person. The defences of self-defence and defence of another are common law defences which justify the defendant's actions. In addition there is a statutory defence of prevention of crime under s 3(1) of the Criminal Law Act 1967 which states that 'a person may use such force as is reasonable in the circumstances in the prevention of crime.'

The Criminal Justice and Immigration Act (CJIA) 2008, which now sets out what is 'reasonable force', acknowledges that the defences are common law as it states it applies to the common law defence of self-defence and the common law defence of defence of property (s 76(2)).

8.1.1 Degree of force

The amount of force which can be used in self-defence, defence of another or in prevention of crime is now set out in s 76 CJIA 2008. This states that, in deciding whether the force used is reasonable in the circumstances:

" (a) that a person acting for a legitimate purpose may not be able to weigh to a nicety the exact measure of any necessary action; and

(b) that evidence of a person's having only done what the person honestly and instinctively thought was necessary for a legitimate purpose constitutes strong evidence that only reasonable action was taken by that person for that purpose. "

This allows for the fact that a person who is facing an attack by another is under stress and cannot be expected to calculate the exact amount of force which needs to be used in the circumstances. If there is evidence that the person 'honestly and instinctively' thought the level of force s/he used to protect him/herself or another or to prevent crime was reasonable, then this provides strong evidence that the defensive action taken was reasonable in the circumstances.

However, if the force is used after all danger from the assailant is over (i.e. as retaliation or revenge), the defence is not available. Also, where the attack is over and the attacker is running away, then it is highly unlikely that force will be considered necessary. This was shown in the case of *R v Hussain* (2010).

Case study

R v Hussain (2010)

D's house was broken into by a group of armed men and D and his family were threatened. One of D's sons managed to escape from the house and told his uncle (T) of the attack. D and another son also escaped and the intruders ran from the house, chased by D and T. They caught one of the men and beat him up, inflicting serious injuries. D and T were charged with s 18 OAPA 1861. It was held they could not use the defence of self-defence as all danger to D from the original attack was over.

Look online

What sentences were imposed on D and T? Do you agree with those sentences?

Householder cases

The Crime and Courts Act 2013 under s 43 has amended s 76 CJIA 2008 to give a wider defence to householders where an intruder enters their property. The normal rule for other cases is that the degree of force will not be regarded as reasonable if it was 'disproportionate'.

Section 76(5A) states that in a householder case the degree of force will not be regarded as reasonable only where it was 'grossly disproportionate'.

To be a householder case:
- the force must be used by D while in or partly in a building that is a dwelling
- D must not be a trespasser
- D must have believed V to be a trespasser.

This is intended to cover situations where a burglar or other intruder enters D's house. It also applies where a building has a dual purpose as a place of residence and of work, and there is an internal means of access between the two parts. For example, where a shopkeeper is confronted by an intruder in the shop area, there could be a risk to his family in the adjoining residential part. But this extended defence does not apply to customers who happen to be in the shop. The normal rules apply to them.

In *Collins v Secretary of State for Justice* (2016) there was a challenge to the householder defence in s 76(5A) on the basis that it was in breach of the right to life in Article 2 of the European Convention on Human Rights.

Case study

Collins v Secretary of State for Justice (2016)

At about 3 a.m., C broke into B's house where B, his wife, three children and three friends were sleeping. One of the children confronted C on the stairs and chased him downstairs where B, who had fallen asleep on the sofa, caught C and forced him into a headlock. B's wife called the police and told them to hurry. B could be heard in the background shouting to tell the police to get there now 'or else I'll break his fucking neck'.

When the police arrived C was purple in the face and not breathing. He had been held in a headlock for about six minutes and he suffered irreversible brain damage. Following the police investigation, the Crown Prosecution Service (CPS) decided not to prosecute B. C's father sought a judicial review of the CPS decision claiming that the householder defence was a breach of the right to life.

The High Court rejected the claim, holding that the effect of s 76(5A) was to allow 'a discretionary area of judgment in householder cases with a different emphasis to that which applied in other cases'.

So s 76(5A) does not give householders the right to use any degree of force they choose. Where a householder puts forward this defence it will be for the jury to decide whether the householder's actions were reasonable in the circumstances as they believed them to be. In *Collins* the court pointed out that:

> there may instances when a jury may consider the actions of a householder in self-defence to be more than what might objectively be described as the minimum proportionate response but nevertheless reasonable given the particular and extenuating circumstances of the case.

The court went on to say:

> This does not weaken the capacity of the criminal law of England and Wales to deter offences against the person in householder cases. The headline message is and remains clear: a householder will only be able to avail himself of the defence if the degree of force he used was reasonable in the circumstances as he believed them to be.

8.1.2 Mistaken use of force in self-defence

In looking at the circumstances, the defendant must be judged on the facts as s/he genuinely believed them to be. In *R v Gladstone Williams* (1987) it was ruled that the defendant should be judged according to his or her genuine mistaken view of the facts, regardless of whether this mistake was reasonable or unreasonable. This allowed Williams to use the defence of protection of others.

Case study

R v Gladstone Williams (1984)

D was on a bus when he saw what he thought was a man assaulting a youth in the street. In fact it was a man trying to arrest the youth for mugging an old lady. D got off the bus and asked what was happening. The man said that he was a police officer arresting the youth, but when D asked him to show his police ID card he could not do so. There was then a struggle between D and the man in which the man was injured. D was convicted of ABH under s 47 OAPA 1861 after the judge directed the jury that D only had a defence if his mistake was a reasonable one.

The Court of Appeal quashed his conviction because the jury should have been told that if they thought the mistake was genuine they should judge the defendant according to his genuine mistaken view of the facts, regardless of whether this mistake was reasonable or unreasonable.

Section 76 CJIA 2008 puts the decision in *Gladstone Williams* onto a statutory footing. The section states:

> **(3)** The question whether the degree of force used by D was reasonable in the circumstances is to be decided by reference to the circumstances as D believed them to be ...
>
> **(4)** If D claims to have held a particular belief as regards the existence of any circumstances–
>
> **(a)** the reasonableness or otherwise of that belief is relevant to the question whether D genuinely held it; but
>
> **(b)** if it is determined that D did genuinely hold it, D is entitled to rely on it for the purposes of subsection (3), whether or not–
>
> **(i)** it was mistaken, or
>
> **(ii)** (if it was mistaken) the mistake was a reasonable one to have made.

So in each situation, the important point is to establish the facts as the defendant genuinely believed them to be. If the defendant genuinely made a mistake, then s/he is to be judged on the facts as s/he believed them to be. This is so, even if the mistake was unreasonable.

Drunken mistake

Section 76(5) CJIA 2008 makes it clear that a defendant cannot rely on any mistaken belief, if that mistake is made due to the defendant being voluntarily intoxicated.

If the defendant made the mistake because s/he had voluntarily got drunk or taken drugs, and makes a mistake because of his/her intoxicated state, then s/he cannot rely on his mistaken belief. An example would be where a defendant had taken drugs which caused hallucinations causing him/her to believe that s/he was being attacked by snakes. If the defendant then assaults someone believing that that person is a snake, then the defendant cannot use the defence of self-defence. He or she genuinely believes s/he is being attacked by a snake, but this mistake has been caused by the defendant's voluntary intoxication.

So the rules on when use of force can justify the defendant's actions are as follows:

- The defences of self-defence/defence of another/ prevention of crime are full defences which justify D's actions so that he or she is held not to have acted unlawfully.
- The force used must be reasonable in the circumstances.
- The circumstances include what D genuinely believed to be the situation. This is so even if that belief was mistaken or unreasonable, provided the jury accepts that D genuinely believed it.
- However, a personality disorder which affects D's perceptions of the situation cannot be taken into account.
- The amount of force must not be excessive in the circumstances as D believed them to be.

8.1.3 Evaluation of the law on self-defence

Is force necessary?

This is a question for the jury. In many cases it is straightforward. For example, if the facts are that the victim had a knife in their hand and came towards the defendant saying 'I'm going to slash you to pieces', it is quite clear that force is necessary in self-defence in this situation.

However, there can be problems deciding when force is necessary. In particular, does a victim have to retreat before using force as in *R v Bird* (1985) below?

Section 76(6A) CJIA 2008 (an amendment added by s 148 of the Legal Aid, Sentencing and Punishment of Offenders Act 2012) now makes it clear that a person is not under a duty to retreat when acting for a legitimate purpose. But the possibility that the defendant could have retreated is to be considered as a relevant factor in deciding whether the degree of force was necessary.

Section 76 CJIA 2008 makes it clear that, provided the mistake was not made due to intoxication, then D can rely on their mistake.

And what of householder cases? It can be said that a householder is morally justified in using force to defend him or herself, others in the house and their property against an intruder. But is a householder morally justified in using any amount of force? Is a householder acting wrongfully in defending him or herself or his/her property, whatever the force used? As set out in 8.1.1 above, Section 76(5A) now states that in a householder case the degree of force will not be regarded as reasonable only where it was 'grossly disproportionate'. The law now appears to support the view that a householder has a moral right to defend him or herself or his/her property using force, but only to a certain level, which level is higher than before the 2008 Act was introduced.

The defence is too generous to the defendant

The defence is available even where the mistake the defendant made is unreasonable. Is it too generous to judge defendants on the basis of facts they unreasonably believe to be true? If the defence is not allowed where the defendant honestly believed (however unreasonably) s/he was about to be attacked, then the defendant is at risk of being imprisoned when s/he really was not at fault. Against this, there is the need to protect the innocent victim whom the defendant has assaulted due to a mistaken belief.

Pre-emptive strike

Do defendants have to wait until they are attacked before they can use force? The law appears to be clear that they can act to prevent force. It is not necessary for an attack to have started. This appears to be a sensible rule, since it would be ridiculous if people had to wait until they were stabbed or shot before being allowed to defend themselves.

In *Attorney-General's Reference (No. 2 of 1983)* (1984) it was held that someone who fears an attack can make preparations to defend him/herself. This is so even if the preparations involve breaches of the law.

Case study

Attorney-General's Reference (No. 2 of 1983) (1984)

D's shop had been attacked and damaged by rioters. Fearing further attacks, he made petrol bombs. D was charged with possessing an explosive substance in such circumstances as to give rise to a reasonable suspicion that he did not have it for a lawful object (contrary to s 4(10) of the Explosive Substances Act 1883). D pleaded self-defence and the jury acquitted him. The Attorney-General referred the point of law to the Court of Appeal which decided that it was correct that D could make preparations in self-defence.

Case study

R v Bird (1985)

D was at a party celebrating her birthday. Her ex-boyfriend, V, arrived with his new girlfriend. A heated argument developed between D and V and D asked him to leave. He did so but later returned. A further argument occurred and D poured a glass of spirit over him. V slapped her and pinned her against a wall. D punched him in the face and claimed that she had forgotten that she had a glass in her hand. The glass broke causing V to lose his eye. She was charged with wounding under s 20 OAPA 1861. She argued she acted in self-defence. The trial judge directed the jury that in order to rely on self-defence, D must show that she did not want to fight. The jury convicted her and she appealed arguing that she did not have to show an unwillingness to fight. The Court of Appeal decided that withdrawing from an attack or showing an unwillingness to fight is good evidence that D is acting reasonably and in good faith, but there was no absolute requirement to show an unwillingness to retreat. D's conviction was quashed.

Excessive force

As set out above, an issue is where a defendant uses excessive force in self-defence. It can be said to be morally right that a person should be able to use force to defend him/herself and/or his or her property. This should apply whether the person who uses force is a householder or acting outside of a house. However limits have to be set on what force can be used to prevent people from taking the law into their own hands. If the limits are exceeded then self-defence cannot be used and the person who uses force will be at fault. However, the level of fault can be taken into account by the judge when passing sentence.

This can be particularly unfair for a person who kills another while claiming to act in self-defence. If convicted, they must be given a life sentence. However, the level of their fault can be reflected in the tariff period.

This was seen in the cases of *R v Clegg* (1995) and *R v Martin (Anthony)* (2002).

Case study

R v Clegg (1995)

D was a soldier on duty at a checkpoint in Northern Ireland. A car came towards the checkpoint at speed and with its headlights full on. One of the soldiers shouted for it to stop but it did not. D fired three shots at the windscreen of the car and one as it passed him. This final shot hit a passenger in the back and killed her. The evidence showed that by the time this last shot was fired the car had gone past D. It was ruled that he could not use self-defence as a defence because there was no danger when he fired that shot. The force was excessive in the circumstances and his conviction for murder was upheld.

Note that in 1999 Clegg's case was referred back to the Court of Appeal by the Criminal Case Review Commission. His conviction was quashed because new forensic evidence cast doubt on whether the fatal shot had actually been fired by Clegg.

Case study

R v Martin (Anthony) (2002)

D shot two burglars who had broken into his farmhouse, one of whom died. The evidence was that the burglars were leaving when D shot them, and the burglar who died had been shot in the back. D was found guilty of murder. He appealed on the basis that the defence of self-defence should have been allowed as he was suffering from a paranoid personality disorder which meant that he may have genuinely (but mistakenly) thought he was in an extremely dangerous situation.

The Court of Appeal rejected the appeal on this basis as they held that personality disorders could not be taken into account when considering the defence of self-defence. However, the conviction was reduced to manslaughter on the grounds that D was suffering from diminished responsibility.

This leads critics to say that the defence is an 'all or nothing' defence. That is, the defendant either succeeds completely with the defence and is found not guilty, or s/he fails and is found guilty. It can be argued that there should be a partial defence where the use of force in self-defence was justified, but the defendant used excessive force in the circumstances.

Relevance of D's characteristics

Another point is whether D's characteristics can be taken into account in deciding if D thought that he or she needed to defend him/herself.

In *R v Martin (Anthony)* (2002) the Court of Appeal held that psychiatric evidence that D had a condition entailing that he perceived much greater danger than the average person was not relevant to the question of whether D had used reasonable force. One of the reasons for this decision was that self-defence is usually raised in cases of minor assault and it would be 'wholly disproportionate to encourage medical disputes in cases of that sort'.

Also in *R v Cairns* (2005) the Court of Appeal followed the decision in *Martin* (2002) and held that when deciding whether D had used reasonable force in self-defence, it was not appropriate to take into account whether D was suffering from a psychiatric condition (such as paranoid schizophrenia) which may have caused him to have delusions that he was about to be attacked.

In *R v Oye* (2013) the Court of Appeal held that the law in *Martin* and *Cairns* still applied.

See Chapter 7, section 7.1.4 for full details of *R v Oye* (2013).

The Criminal Justice and Immigration Act 2008 was passed to clarify the common law on self-defence and it has not altered this point. There is an objective element to the defence of self-defence. In particular, s 76(6) of the Act requires that the amount of force used in the circumstances as the defendant believed them to be should be reasonable.

Also the Crime and Courts Act 2013 now gives a wider defence to householders where an intruder enters their property. They can use the defence of self-defence provided that the degree of force was not 'grossly disproportionate'. For other cases, the degree of force used in self-defence must not be 'disproportionate'. However, again it is probable that Martin would not have been able to use the defence, as shooting someone in the back is likely to be regarded as 'grossly disproportionate'.

	Comment	Source
Self-defence	Degree of force used must be reasonable and not disproportionate.	s 76 CJIA 2008
	Doing what the person honestly and instinctively thought was necessary for a legitimate purpose.	
Self-defence in householder cases	Degree of force must not be 'grossly disproportionate'.	s 76(5A) CJIA 2008
Mistaken use of force	D is judged on the facts as s/he genuinely believed them to be.	ss 76(3) and 76(4) CJIA 2008
Drunken mistake	If mistake is made because D is intoxicated, then s/he cannot rely on this mistake.	s 76(5) CJIA 2008
Should D retreat?	D is not under a duty to retreat when acting for a legitimate purpose.	s 76(6A) CJIA 2008
	But the possibility that D could have retreated is considered when deciding whether the degree of force used was reasonable.	

Figure 8.1 Key facts chart on self-defence

8.2 Duress by threats

Duress is a defence based on the fact that the defendant has been effectively forced to commit the crime. The defendant has committed the offence because s/he has been threatened with death or serious injury. The law therefore allows a defence. The defendant has to choose between being killed or seriously injured, or committing a crime. In such a situation there is no real choice. The defendant can be considered as so terrified that s/he ceases 'to be an independent actor'. However, despite this the defendant knowingly does the *actus reus* for the offence and has the required *mens rea*. So, if the law did not allow the defence, s/he would be liable for the offence.

> **Key term**
>
> **Duress (1)** – a full defence to certain crimes where the defendant alleges they have been forced to commit the crime

8.2.1 For which crimes is duress available?

Duress can be used as a defence to all crimes, except murder, attempted murder and, possibly, treason.

Murder

It was originally held in *DPP for Northern Ireland v Lynch* (1975) that the defence of duress was available to a secondary party on a charge of murder. This meant it was available for defendants who had participated in a murder, such as a getaway driver, but had not actually performed

the act of killing. However in *R v Howe* (1987) the House of Lords ruled that the defence was not available to anyone charged with murder, even if he or she was only a secondary party and had not done the killing him/herself.

> **Case study**
>
> ### *R v Howe* (1987)
>
> D, with others, took part in torturing and abusing a man who was then strangled by one of the others. On a second occasion another man was tortured, abused and then strangled by D. D claimed that he took part in the killings because of threats to him. The trial judge ruled that duress was available to D for the first killing where D was only a secondary party to the killing, but that it was not available for the second killing where D was a principal offender, that is had carried out the actual killing. The Court of Appeal ruled that this was correct but the House of Lords held that duress was not available as a defence for any defendant on a murder charge.
>
> The reason why duress was held not to be a defence was explained by Lord Hailsham when he said in the judgment:
>
> > I do not at all accept in relation to the defence of murder it is either good morals, good policy or good law to suggest ... that the ordinary man of reasonable fortitude is not to be supposed to be capable of heroism if he is asked to take an innocent life rather than sacrifice his own.

The rule that duress cannot be a defence to murder applies even where the defendant is young and less able to resist pressure. This was confirmed in *R v Wilson* (2007).

R v Wilson (2007)

D, who was aged 13, and his father were charged with the murder of D's mother. D stated that he had helped with the murder because he was too frightened to disobey his father. The Court of Appeal held that D did not have a defence as the rule that duress provided no defence to murder applied, however susceptible D might be to duress.

Attempted murder

In the case of *R v Howe* (1987) the House of Lords said they thought the defence should not be available on a charge of attempted murder. This was an *obiter dicta* statement and so not binding. However, in *R v Gotts* (1992) the Court of Appeal decided to follow this *obiter* statement.

Case study

R v Gotts (1992)

D was a 16-year-old boy whose parents were separated. D was threatened with violence by his father unless he agreed to stab his mother. D attacked his mother but did not kill her. He was convicted of attempted murder. The Court of Appeal upheld his conviction on the basis that the defence of duress was not available to him.

8.2.2 Threats

The threat has to be of death or serious injury. It must cause D's will to be so overborne by the threats that they commit an act which they would not otherwise do. So, where another person threatens the defendant with serious violence unless the defendant commits an offence, and the defendant then commits the offence, they are acting under duress. For example, if an armed man pointed a gun at the defendant, gave them a fake credit card, and ordered them to use it in a cashpoint machine to get money, the defendant is stealing the money but they are only doing it because of the threat.

The threat of violence is directed at the defendant by another person who demands that the defendant commit a specific crime or else they will be shot.

Seriousness of the threat

The threat must be of death or serious injury; lesser threats do not provide a defence. For example, a threat to disclose a previous conviction is not sufficient for duress. However, provided there are serious threats, then the cumulative effect of the threats can be considered. This was decided in *R v Valderrama-Vega* (1985).

Case study

R v Valderrama-Vega (1985)

The defendant illegally imported cocaine. He claimed he had done this because of death threats made by a mafia-type organisation involved in drug-smuggling and also because of threats to disclose his homosexuality and because of financial pressures. The trial judge said that the defence was only available to him if the death threats were the sole reason for his committing the offence. The Court of Appeal quashed his conviction as they considered that the jury was entitled to look at the cumulative effects of all the threats.

If there had not been a threat of death, then the other threats in this case would not be enough on which to base a defence of duress. But as there had been a threat of death, the jury was entitled to consider the whole of the threats.

Threat to whom?

The threat had to be to the defendant, his partner or his immediate family. There has been no decision on whether a threat to a complete stranger would be enough to give a defence of duress, but it is possible that this would now be allowed as the draft Criminal Code proposed that this should be the rule.

8.2.3 Subjective and objective tests

In deciding if the defence should succeed, the jury must consider a two-stage test. This involves both subjective and objective tests. These are:

- Was the defendant compelled to act as they did because they reasonably believed they had good cause to fear serious injury or death (a mainly subjective test)?
- If so, would a sober person of reasonable firmness, sharing the characteristics of the accused, have responded in the same way (an objective test)?

These tests were laid down by the Court of Appeal in *R v Graham* (1982) and approved by the House of Lords in *Howe* (1987).

R v Graham (1982)

D was a homosexual who lived with his wife and another homosexual man, K. K was violent and bullied D. After both D and K had been drinking heavily, K put a flex around the wife's neck and told D to pull the other end of the flex. D did this for about a minute. The wife died. D claimed he had only held the flex because of his fear of K. D's conviction for murder was upheld.

Subjective test

The first part of the test is based on whether the defendant did the offence because of the threats they believed had been made. This is subjective, but it was thought that this had to be a reasonable belief in the sense that an ordinary person would have believed it. This made it a partially objective test.

However, in *R v Martin (D P)* (2000), the Court of Appeal interpreted this part of the two-stage test as being whether the defendant may have reasonably feared for his safety. So, in considering this test, the jury could take into account any special characteristic of the defendant which may have made him more likely to believe the threats.

Case study

R v Martin (D P) (2000)

The defendant suffered from a condition known as schizoid-affective state, which would lead him to regard things said to him as threatening and to believe that such threats would be carried out. He claimed he had been forced to carry out two robberies by two men who lived on the same estate. The judge ruled that the schizoid-affective disorder was irrelevant to the first part of the test, although it was a characteristic which could be included in the second part of the test.

The defendant appealed, saying that the correct test should have been whether, in view of his condition, he may have reasonably feared for his own or his mother's safety.

The Court of Appeal allowed the appeal and quashed his conviction. The court held that duress and self-defence should be treated in the same way in regard to belief of the circumstances. In self-defence, a mistaken belief by the defendant can be a defence provided it is a genuine mistake. The same applies to duress and so the defendant's mental condition is relevant in deciding whether he reasonably believed that his (or his family's) safety was at risk.

This decision is now in doubt following the House of Lords' decision in *R v Hasan (formerly Z)* (2005) (see section 8.2.8 below), which confirmed the decision in *Graham* (1982) that the defendant's belief in the threats must be reasonable and genuine.

Objective test

The second part of the test is based on whether the reasonable man would have responded in the same way. However, the jury is allowed to take certain of the defendant's characteristics into account, as the reasonable man is regarded as sharing the relevant characteristics of the defendant.

What characteristics can be taken into account was decided in *R v Bowen* (1996). In this case the defendant had a low IQ of 68 and he obtained goods by deception for two men who had told him they would petrol-bomb him and his family unless he carried out this offence. It was held that this was irrelevant in deciding whether the defendant found it more difficult to resist any threats. The relevant characteristics must relate to the ability to resist pressure and threats. In *Bowen* it was accepted that the following could be relevant:

- Age: very young people and the very old could be more susceptible to threats.
- Pregnancy: there is the additional fear for the safety of the unborn child.
- Serious physical disability: this could make it more difficult for the defendant to protect himself.
- Recognised mental illness or psychiatric disorder: this could include post-traumatic stress disorder or any other disorder which meant that a person might be more susceptible to threats. This did not include a low IQ.
- Gender: although the Court of Appeal thought that many women might have as much moral courage as men.

8.2.4 No safe avenue of escape

Duress can only be used as a defence if the defendant is placed in a situation where they have no safe avenue of escape. In *R v Gill* (1963) the defendant claimed that he and his wife had been threatened unless he stole a lorry. However, there was a period of time during which he was left alone and so could have raised the alarm. As he had a 'safe avenue of escape' he could not rely on the defence of duress.

It has also been held that if police protection is possible then the defendant cannot rely on duress.

However, in the case of *R v Hudson and Taylor* (1971) it was accepted that police protection might not always be effective.

R v Hudson and Taylor (1971)

The defendants were two girls, aged 17 and 19, who were prosecution witnesses in a case against a man called Wright who was charged with wounding another man. When giving evidence in court they lied and said they could not identify Wright as the attacker. They were then charged with perjury (lying in court under oath). In their defence at their trial for perjury they said they lied because a man called Farrell, who had a reputation for violence, had told Hudson that if she gave evidence against the attacker, he would cut her up. They were convicted and appealed. The Court of Appeal quashed their conviction.

At the appeal the prosecution argued that the girls could have sought police protection. On this point the Court of Appeal pointed out that there were cases in which the police could not provide effective protection. They said that in deciding whether going to the police for protection was a realistic course, the jury should consider the age of the defendant, the circumstances of the threats and any risks which might be involved in trying to rely on police protection.

However, the decision in *Hudson and Taylor* was criticised by the House of Lords in *R v Hasan (formerly Z)* (2005) (see section 8.2.8 below). It is now doubtful that a defendant could use the defence of duress where there was opportunity to go to the police.

8.2.5 Imminence of threat

The threat must be effective at the moment the crime is committed, but this does not mean that the threats need to be able to be carried out immediately. In *Hudson and Taylor* (1971) the trial judge ruled that the defence of duress was not available to the two girls. This was because the threat could not be immediately put into effect while the girls were giving evidence, so there was no reason for them not to have given truthful evidence.

On this point the Court of Appeal said that the threat had to be a 'present' threat but that this was in the sense that it was effective to neutralise the will of the defendant at the time of committing the offence. If the threat is hanging over the defendant at the time he or she commits the offence, then the defence of duress is available.

This was further considered in *R v Abdul-Hussain* (1999), a case on duress of circumstances.

R v Abdul-Hussain (1999)

The defendants, who were Shi'ite Muslims, had fled to Sudan from Iraq because of the risk of punishment and execution because of their religion. They feared that they would be sent back to Iraq and so they hijacked a plane. The plane eventually landed in the UK. The defendants were charged with hijacking and pleaded duress. The trial judge decided that the danger they were in was not sufficiently 'close and immediate' as to give rise to a 'virtually spontaneous reaction' and he ruled that the defence of duress could not be considered by the jury. The defendants were convicted and appealed.

The Court of Appeal quashed their convictions, holding that the threat need not be immediate but it had to be imminent in the sense that it was hanging over them.

The Court of Appeal in *Abdul-Hussain* (1999) ruled that:

- There must be imminent peril of death or serious injury to the defendant, or to those for whom he or she has responsibility.
- The peril must operate on the defendant's mind at the time of committing the otherwise criminal act, so as to overbear his or her will; this is a matter for the jury.
- Execution of the threat need not be immediately in prospect.

8.2.6 Threat to make defendant commit a specific offence

The defendant can only use the defence if the threats are in order to make him or her commit a specific offence.

R v Cole (1994)

D claimed that he and his girlfriend and child had been threatened (and he had been actually hit with a baseball bat) in order to make him repay money he owed. As he did not have the money, D carried out two robberies at building societies to get sufficient money to repay the debt. D said he only did this because of the threats of violence to him and his family.

His conviction was upheld because he had not been told to commit the robberies. The threats to him were directed at getting repayment and not directed at making him commit a robbery. This meant there was not a sufficient connection between the threats and the crimes he committed, so the defence of duress was not available to him.

This applies only to duress by threats. In duress of circumstances the defence may be used for any offence which is an appropriate response to the danger posed by the circumstances. As seen in *R v Abdul-Hussain* (1999) above, the danger was of torture and execution, and the offence committed was hijacking which enabled the defendants to get to a safe venue.

8.2.7 Intoxication and duress

If the defendant becomes voluntarily intoxicated and mistakenly believes s/he is being threatened, s/he cannot use duress as a defence. A mistake in these circumstances is unreasonable. However, if there is no mistake and the intoxication is irrelevant to the duress, the defendant can use the defence of duress. This could be, for example, where s/he is threatened by a man with a gun. In this situation there is duress and it is irrelevant whether the defendant is intoxicated or not.

8.2.8 Self-induced duress

This is where the defendant has brought the duress on himself through his own actions. For example, a defendant voluntarily joins a criminal gang and commits some offences, but then is forced under duress to commit other crimes which he or she did not want to do.

The normal rule is that where the defendant is aware that s/he may be put under duress to commit offences, s/he cannot use the defence. This has been held to apply to the following situations:

- The defendant joins a criminal gang which he or she knows is likely to use violence.

- The defendant puts him/herself in a position where s/he knows that s/he is likely to be subjected to threats of violence or actual violence. This could be by being involved in criminal activity although not part of a gang, or by becoming indebted to a drug dealer.

These situations can be illustrated by specific cases.

R v Sharp (1987)

D joined a gang which carried out robberies. D claimed that he had wanted to withdraw from the robberies before the last one where a sub-postmaster was shot dead. The Court of Appeal ruled that he could not use duress as a defence. D knew when he joined the gang that it was likely to use violence, so he could not claim duress when the gang threatened him with violence.

A contrasting case to *R v Sharp* is the case of *R v Shepherd* (1987).

R v Shepherd (1987)

D had joined an organised gang of shoplifters. A group of them would enter a shop and while one of them distracted the shopkeeper, the others would steal as much as they could, usually boxes of cigarettes. This activity was non-violent. D said he wanted to stop taking part but was then threatened with violence unless he continued. The Court of Appeal allowed his appeal and quashed his conviction. If he had no knowledge that the gang was likely to use violence then the defence of duress was available to him.

The rule that duress is not available where it is self-induced has been extended to situations where the defendant associates with violent criminals. For example, in *Heath* (2000) the defendant owed money to a drug dealer. He was then threatened and made to help in the supply of cannabis. He could not use the defence of duress as he knew that by becoming indebted to a drugs dealer he was putting himself at risk of being threatened or having violence used on him.

However, in other cases, the courts had allowed a defendant who associated with violent people to use the defence of duress. This conflict of whether self-induced duress could be a defence was resolved in *R v Hasan (formerly Z)* (2005).

Case study

R v Hasan (formerly Z) (2005)

D associated with a violent drug dealer. This drug dealer told D to burgle a house in order to steal a large amount of money that was in a safe there. The dealer threatened that if D did not do this, then D and his family would be harmed. D, carrying a knife, broke into the house but was unable to open the safe. He was convicted of aggravated burglary. The Court of Appeal quashed the conviction but certified the following question for the consideration of the House of Lords:

> Whether the defence of duress is excluded when as a result of the accused's voluntary association with others:
>
> (i) he foresaw (or possibly should have foreseen) the risk of being then and there subjected to any compulsion by threats of violence; or
>
> (ii) only when he foresaw (or should have foreseen) the risk of being subjected to compulsion to commit criminal offences; and, if the latter
>
> (iii) only if the offences foreseen (or which should have been foreseen) were of the same type (or possibly the same type and gravity) as that ultimately committed.

The House of Lords reinstated his conviction. They took the view that option (i) in the certified question correctly states the law. The defence of duress is excluded where D voluntarily associates with others who are engaged in criminal activity and he foresaw or ought reasonably to have foreseen the risk of being subjected to any compulsion by threats of violence.

So self-induced duress is no longer available where a defendant realises or ought to have realised that he or she may be threatened with violence and compelled to commit an offence.

	Law	Case
Availability	All offences EXCEPT: ● murder ● attempted murder ● treason (possibly).	*Howe* (1987) *Gotts* (1992)
Seriousness of threat	Must be of death or serious injury BUT can consider cumulative effect of other threats with threat of injury.	*Valderrama-Vega* (1985)
Subjective and objective tests	There are two tests: ● Was D compelled to act because s/he feared serious injury or death? (subjective) ● Would a sober person of reasonable firmness have responded in the same way? (objective). Some of D's characteristics can be taken into account, especially: ● age ● pregnancy ● serious physical disability ● recognised mental illness.	*Graham* (1982) *Bowen* (1996)
Avenue of escape	Duress is NOT available as a defence if there is a safe avenue of escape.	*Gill* (1963)
Imminence of threat	The threat need not be immediate but it must be imminent.	*Hudson and Taylor* (1971), *Abdul-Hussain* (1999)
Self-induced duress	Duress is NOT available where: ● D joins a criminal gang which s/he knows is violent ● D puts himself in a position where s/he foresaw (or should have foreseen) the risk of being subjected to compulsion.	*Sharp* (1987) *Hasan* (2005)

Figure 8.2 Key facts chart on duress by threats

Duress can be by threats or circumstances. **Duress is not available for murder (*Howe* (1987)) or attempted murder (*Gotts* (1992)).**		
Case	**Facts**	**Law**
Valderrama-Vega (1985)	Smuggled cocaine because of death threats and threats to disclose homosexuality.	Must be a threat of death or serious injury but can consider cumulative effect of threats.
Graham (1982)	Helped kill his wife because he was threatened by his homosexual lover.	Two-stage test: • Was D compelled to act as he did because he reasonably believed he had good cause to fear serious injury or death? • If so, would a sober person of reasonable firmness, sharing the characteristics of the accused have responded in the same way?
Martin (DP) (2000)	Suffered from a schizoid-affective state which would make him see things as threatening and believe the threats would be carried out.	Correct test should have been whether, in view of his condition, he may have reasonably feared for his own or his mother's safety.
Bowen (1996)	Had a low IQ (68). Obtained goods by deception for two men because of petrol bomb threat.	Cannot take low IQ into account. Can consider: • age • pregnancy • recognised mental illness • gender.
Gill (1963)	Threatened so he stole a lorry, but had time to escape and raise the alarm.	Cannot use duress if has a 'safe avenue of escape'.
Hudson and Taylor (1971)	Two girls lied on oath because of threats to cut them up.	The threat need not be capable of being carried out immediately. Also recognised that police protection cannot always be effective. Take into account age and gender.
Hasan (2005)	D tried to burgle a safe after he was threatened by a drug dealer associate.	Criticised *Hudson and Taylor* (1971) saying that D should seek police protection.
Abdul-Hussain (1999)	Hijacked plane to escape from persecution in Iraq.	Threat must be 'imminent' and operating on D's mind when he commits the offence.

Figure 8.3 Key cases on general principles of duress

8.3 Duress of circumstances

Although duress by threats has been recognised as a defence for a long time, it is only since the 1980s that the courts have recognised that a defendant may be forced to act because of surrounding circumstances. This is known as duress of circumstances.

The first case in which this was recognised was *R v Willer* (1986).

Case study

R v Willer (1986)

D and a passenger were driving down a narrow alley when the car was surrounded by a gang of youths who threatened them. D realised that the only way to get away from the gang was by driving on the pavement. He did this quite slowly (about 10 mph) and having made his escape he drove to the police station to report the gang.

The police charged him with reckless driving for having driven on the pavement and he was convicted.

He appealed and the Court of Appeal said that the jury should have been allowed to consider whether the defendant drove 'under that form of compulsion, that is, under duress'.

This case was followed by *R v Conway* (1988) where the threats were to a passenger in the defendant's car.

Case study

R v Conway (1988)

A passenger in D's car had been shot at by two men a few weeks earlier. The car was stationary when the passenger saw two men running towards the car. He thought they were the two men who were after him (in fact they were plain-clothes policemen) and he yelled at D to drive off. D did so very fast and was charged with reckless driving. The trial judge refused to leave duress for the jury to consider and D was convicted. On appeal the Court of Appeal quashed his conviction and ruled that a defence of duress of circumstances was available if, on an objective standpoint, the defendant was acting in order to avoid a threat of death or serious injury.

There was then a third case involving a driving offence. This was *R v Martin* (1989) where the wife of the defendant threatened to commit suicide unless he drove while disqualified.

Case study

R v Martin (1989)

D's wife became hysterical and threatened suicide unless he drove her son (who was late and at risk of losing his job) to work. D was disqualified from driving but he eventually agreed to do this. He was convicted of driving while disqualified. On appeal it was ruled that duress of circumstances could be available as a defence and the same two-stage test put forward in *Graham* (1982) for duress by threats applied. So the tests were:

- Was the defendant compelled to act as he did because he reasonably believed he had good cause to fear serious injury or death?
- If so, would a sober person of reasonable firmness, sharing the characteristics of the accused have responded in the same way?

Although these cases established that there was a defence of duress of circumstances, all the cases involved driving offences. It was not until the decision in *R v Pommell* (1995) that it became clear that duress of circumstances could be a defence to all crimes except murder and attempted murder and some forms of treason.

Case study

R v Pommell (1995)

D was found by police at 8 a.m. lying in bed with a loaded sub-machine gun against his leg. He told police that at about 1 a.m. he had taken it from another man who was going to use it 'to do some people some damage'. D said he had intended getting his brother to hand the gun in to the police that morning. At his trial for possessing a prohibited weapon the judge ruled that his failure to go to the police straight away prevented him having any defence. D was convicted. He appealed to the Court of Appeal who held that the defence of duress of circumstances was available for all offences except murder and attempted murder and some forms of treason. They quashed D's conviction and sent the case for retrial.

In *R v Cairns* (1999) the court had to consider whether there had to be a real threat to the defendant or whether the defence was available where the defendant reasonably perceived a threat of serious physical injury or death, even though there was no actual threat.

Case study

R v Cairns (1999)

V threw himself across the bonnet and windscreen of D's car. Several of V's friends were nearby shouting and D felt threatened. D drove off with V on his bonnet and some of V's friends following. These friends were in fact trying to help rather than threaten D. When D braked for a speed hump, V fell under the car and was seriously injured. At the trial the judge directed the jury that they had to consider whether D's actions were 'actually necessary'. D's conviction was quashed as he reasonably perceived a threat of serious physical injury or death.

It is sufficient for the defendant to show that they acted as they did because they reasonably perceived a threat of serious physical injury or death. They are not required to prove that the threat was an actual or real threat.

8.4 Evaluation on the law of duress by threats and duress of circumstances

Most of the following points relate to the defence of duress by threats. However similar issues arise for duress of circumstances.

8.4.1 Unavailability for murder

The ruling in *R v Howe* (1987) that duress is not available on a charge of murder ignores situations such as a motorist being hijacked and forced to act as getaway driver and a person is killed during the hijack. In that case Lord Griffiths simply dismissed such examples on the basis that it was inconceivable that such a person would be prosecuted. However, it is possible that a prosecution could take place and duress would not be a defence.

What if a young mother's car is hijacked and she is told her two young children will be killed unless she helps terrorists to plant a bomb? Lord Hailsham thought that the ordinary person should be capable of heroism if she is asked to take an innocent life rather than sacrifice her own. But in this situation the mother is being asked to sacrifice her two children, yet again she would have no defence.

The age and/or susceptibility of a defendant to duress are also ignored as shown by the case of *R v Wilson* (2007). The Court of Appeal in that case accepted that there might be grounds for criticising the rule that did not allow a 13-year-old boy any defence to a charge of murder, even though he was only doing what his father told him when he was too frightened to refuse to obey.

There is also an anomaly in that duress is not available for murder but is available for a charge of s 18 OAPA 1861 – crimes which have similar *mens rea*. Remember that the *mens rea* of murder could be the intention to cause grievous bodily harm.

There is an additional problem where a defendant is convicted of murder, as this offence carries a mandatory life sentence. The judge has to send the defendant to prison for life, and cannot take the duress into account when passing sentence except when setting the tariff period. Where the defendant is convicted of attempted murder, which has a maximum sentence of life imprisonment, the judge has discretion in setting the sentence. For example, in the case of the 16-year old defendant in *R v Gotts* (1992), the judge placed him on probation.

8.4.2 No allowances for low IQ

In *R v Bowen* (1996) the Court of Appeal refused to allow the fact that the defendant had a very low IQ to be taken into account in deciding whether he found it more difficult to resist any threats. This decision may be seen as harsh. A very low IQ can mean that the defendant fails to understand the true nature of matters. It is suggested that it is a factor that should be taken into account.

8.4.3 Police protection

In *R v Hudson and Taylor* (1971) the Court of Appeal accepted that police protection could not be completely fool-proof. Even where a defendant had the opportunity to go to the police and tell them of the threats, many people might be so afraid of the consequences that they would not contact the police.

Unfortunately the decision in *Hudson and Taylor* (1971) has been called into question by the House of Lords' judgment in *R v Hasan* (2005). This means it is uncertain whether a person who is threatened and who does not contact the police, can rely on the defence of duress.

8.4.4 Proposals for reform

The Law Commission in its report, 'Legislating the Criminal Code: Offences Against the Person and General Principles' (1993) (Law Com No. 218), proposed that the defence of duress should be available for all crimes. In 2006, the Law Commission's report, 'Murder, Manslaughter and Infanticide' (Law Com No. 304) proposed that duress should be allowed as a defence to murder. However, as with many Law Commission proposals, neither of these have been acted upon.

Explain whether a defence of duress would be available in the following situations.

1   Clancy is threatened by Neil, a fellow employee, who tells Clancy that he will tell their boss about Clancy's previous convictions for theft. Neil orders Clancy to help him shoplift from a small corner shop by distracting the counter-staff while Neil does the stealing. Clancy feels obliged to do this as he does not want to lose his job.

2   Joseph, who is of a timid nature and low intelligence, is told by Katya that she will beat him up unless he obtains goods for her from a shop using a stolen credit card. He does this and obtains a DVD player for her.

3   Natasha's boyfriend, Ross, is a drug dealer. She also knows that he has convictions for violence. He threatens to beat her 'senseless' unless she agrees

to take some drugs to one of his 'customers'. She is caught by the police and charged with possessing drugs with intent to supply.

4   Sanjeet's wife has tried to commit suicide previously. She is very depressed because they are heavily in debt. She tells Sanjeet that she will throw herself under a train unless he can get the money to pay off their debts. Sanjeet obtains the money by robbing a local off-licence.

5   Tamara is due to give evidence against Alexia's boyfriend who is facing a trial for attempted murder. A week before the trial is due to take place, Alexia sends Tamara a text message saying that Tamara will be killed if she gives evidence. Tamara attends the court but lies in evidence saying, untruthfully, that the man she saw was much shorter than Alexia's boyfriend.

8.5 Necessity

This is where circumstances force a person to act in order to prevent a worse evil from occurring. The defence has similarities with the defence of duress of circumstances, yet the courts have been reluctant to recognise necessity as a defence in its own right. The leading case is *R v Dudley and Stephens* (1884).

Case study

R v Dudley and Stephens (1884)

The two defendants were shipwrecked with another man and V, a 17-year-old cabin boy, in a small boat about 1600 miles from land. After drifting for 20 days, and having been nine days without food and seven days without water, the two defendants killed and ate the cabin boy. Four days later they were picked up by a passing ship and on their return to England were convicted of murder. Their claim of necessity to save themselves from dying was rejected.

It is interesting to note that although Dudley and Stephens were convicted of murder and sentenced to be hanged, their sentence was commuted to a mere six months' imprisonment.

In this case the charge was of murder, so it can be argued that the law on necessity is in line with the law on duress, as duress is not available on a charge of murder.

It is interesting to note that the defence has been recognised by courts when making an order in certain civil cases. One example is *Re F (mental patient: sterilisation)* (1990).

Case study

Re F (mental patient: sterilisation) (1990)

A health authority applied for a declaration that it was lawful to sterilise a girl who had a very severe mental disability. The girl had formed a sexual relationship with another patient, putting her at risk of becoming pregnant. Doctors said that she would not be able to understand pregnancy and it could be disastrous for her precarious mental health. The girl's mother supported the application, but the Official Solicitor, who was acting on behalf of the girl as she was unable to give consent to an operation herself, thought that performing such an operation would be illegal.

The House of Lords granted the application and Lord Brandon stated:

> In many cases ... it will not only be lawful for doctors, on the ground of necessity, to operate on or give other medical treatment to adult patients disabled from giving their consent, it will also be the common duty to do so.

Another case in which doctors sought a declaration that it would be lawful for them to operate was *Re A (Conjoined Twins)* (2000). In this case the defence of necessity was considered and held to be available as a defence even to a potential charge of murder.

Case study

Re A (conjoined twins) (2000)

Conjoined twins were born with one of them having no proper heart or lungs. She was being kept alive by the other twin, whose heart circulated blood for both of them. Their parents refused to consent to an operation to separate them. Doctors applied for a declaration that it was lawful to operate to separate the twins, even though the weaker twin would certainly die. The Court of Appeal gave the declaration. The three judges gave very different reasons for why the operation would be lawful, but one of them, Brooke L, J said that the defence of necessity would be available to the doctors were they to be charged with murder of the weaker twin. He approved the following four principles of the defence of necessity as set out in *Stephen's Digest of Criminal Law* (1883):

1 The act was done only in order to avoid consequences which could not otherwise be avoided.
2 Those consequences, if they had happened, would have inflicted inevitable and irreparable evil.
2 No more was done than was reasonably necessary for that purpose.
4 The evil inflicted by it was not disproportionate to the evil avoided.

Necessity was also considered in the case of *R v Shayler* (2001).

Case study

R v Shayler (2001)

D was a former member of the British Security Service (MI5). He was charged with disclosing confidential documents in breach of the Official Secrets Act 1989. He claimed the defence of necessity. His conviction was upheld by both the Court of Appeal and the House of Lords. The Court of Appeal discussed the defences of necessity and duress of circumstances, and concluded that they were in effect the same defence. Lord Woolf stated:

> the distinction between duress of circumstances and necessity has, correctly, been by and large ignored or blurred by the courts. Apart from some of the medical cases like *Re F* (1990), the law has tended to treat duress of circumstances and necessity as one and the same.

The Court of Appeal held that the tests for duress of circumstances and/or necessity were as follows:

- The act must be done only to prevent an act of greater evil.
- The evil must be directed towards the defendant or a person or persons for whom s/he was responsible.
- The act must be reasonable and proportionate to the evil avoided.

8.5.1 Evaluation of necessity

In the case of *Buckoke v Greater London Council* (1971) Lord Denning stated *obiter* that he thought the defence of necessity would not be available to emergency service drivers (fire-fighters or ambulance drivers) if they broke traffic laws in an attempt to arrive at an emergency quickly. He said that such a driver should be congratulated for his action and he hoped that anyone in that situation would not be prosecuted.

Nevertheless, the law seems to be that such a person could be prosecuted and would not have a defence of necessity. As there is no general defence of necessity in emergency situations, traffic laws have been changed to give emergency service drivers a special defence in certain circumstances.

It can be seen that the tests set out in *Shayler* are very similar to both defences of necessity and duress of circumstances. There are, however, some differences.

The important one is that the evil must be directed towards the defendant or a person or persons for whom s/he was responsible. This demonstrates that it is wrong to treat necessity as being the same as duress of circumstances. In 'pure' necessity situations there is no requirement for this. In the case of *Re A (conjoined twins)* (2000), the evil was not directed at the doctors, nor were they responsible for the twins; the parents maintained responsibility for them.

The other major difference between duress of circumstances and necessity is that duress of circumstances cannot be used as a defence to murder, yet in *Re A (Conjoined Twins)* (2000) it was accepted that necessity could be a defence to the murder of the weaker twin. In that case, performing an operation which the doctors knew would kill the weaker twin was an act which would prevent the greater evil of both twins dying.

	Law	Case
Definition	Circumstances force a person to act in order to prevent a worse evil from occurring.	
Existence	Only recognised as duress of circumstances in criminal cases. Civil cases have recognised the defence of necessity.	*Dudley and Stephens* (1884) *Re F (mental patient: sterilisation)* (1990), *Re A (conjoined twins)* (2000)
Tests	These were set out in *Stephen's Digest of Criminal Law* and approved in *Re A (conjoined twins)* (2000): • Act was done only to avoid consequences which could not otherwise be avoided. • Those consequences would have inflicted inevitable and irreparable harm. • No more was done than was necessary. • The evil inflicted was proportionate to the evil avoided.	*Re A (conjoined twins)* (2000)

Figure 8.4 Key facts chart on necessity

8.6 Consent as a defence to non-fatal offences

Consent may be a defence to some non-fatal offences against the person. However, it is never a defence to murder or to offences where serious injury is caused.

Key term

Consent – where the victim agrees to suffer an injury. It is a defence to some, less serious, non-fatal offences.

Consent is strictly speaking not a defence, as where the other person consents, there is no offence. For example, where the other person consents to being touched, there is no battery as there is no unlawful force. This is illustrated by *R v Donovan* (1934).

Case study

R v Donovan (1934)

D caned a 17 year-old-girl for the purpose of sexual gratification. This caused bruising and he was convicted of indecent assault and a common assault. D appealed on the basis that V had consented to the act. His conviction was quashed.

A more extreme case illustrating the same point is *R v Slingsby* (1995) where the defendant was charged with manslaughter.

Case study

R v Slingsby (1995)

D was charged with involuntary manslaughter by an unlawful act. D and the victim had taken part in sexual activity which was described as 'vigorous' but which had taken place with the victim's consent. During this, a signet ring which D was wearing caused small cuts to the victim and this led to blood poisoning from which she died. The victim's consent meant that there was no battery or other form of assault and so D was held to be not guilty of manslaughter as there was no unlawful act.

8.6.1 Real consent

There must, however, be real consent. In *R v Tabassum* (2000) the defendant had persuaded women to allow him to measure their breasts for the purpose of preparing a database for sale to doctors. The women were fully aware of the nature of the acts he proposed to do, but said they consented only because they thought that D had either medical qualifications or medical training. He had neither. The Court of Appeal approved the trial judge's direction when he said:

> I should prefer myself to say that consent in such cases does not exist at all, because the act consented to is not the act done. Consent to a surgical operation or examination is not consent to sexual connection or indecent behaviour.

The fact that the victim submits to the defendant's conduct through fear also means that the consent is not real. This was shown by *R v Olugboja* (1982).

R v Olugboja (1982)

The victim had already been raped by D's companion and seen her friend raped by the same man. When D tried to have sexual intercourse with her, she submitted. D claimed that this meant she had consented. The Court of Appeal held that there was a difference between real consent and mere submission. It was for the jury to decide if the consent was real.

In *R v Dica* (2004), the Court of Appeal had to consider the position where V had consented to sexual intercourse but did not know that the defendant was HIV positive.

Case study

R v Dica (2004)

D, who knew he was HIV positive, had relationships with two women. They had unprotected sex with him and both became infected. They claimed that they did not know he was HIV positive and that if they had known they would not have agreed to unprotected sex. D was charged with s 20 OAPA 1861. At his trial, the judge did not allow the issue of consent to go to the jury.

The Court of Appeal held there was no consent to the risk of infection. They quashed the conviction and ordered a retrial.

The decision in this case makes it clear that even though V has consented to sexual intercourse, D can be guilty of an offence under s 20 OAPA 1861. This overruled the decision in *R v Clarence* (1888), where unknown to the wife, the husband was suffering from a venereal disease and the wife became infected when they had sexual intercourse. It was held that a wife's consent to sexual intercourse with her husband meant that there was no assault.

Another recent case is *R v Golding 2014* which confirms that the herpes virus may be added to the list of communicable diseases that are considered sufficiently serious to constitute really serious harm.

Case study

R v Golding 2014

D started a sexual relationship with V and infected her with the herpes virus. When she confronted him, he denied responsibility for infecting her and the relationship continued. He subsequently admitted

to her that he had caught the virus from a previous partner and had attended clinics for treatment. The prosecution case was that D recklessly caused V to become infected in circumstances where he was aware that he was infected with herpes and where she had not consented to the risk of becoming infected through intercourse. D pleaded guilty on the basis that he had previously suffered from herpes and was aware that this was a sexually transmitted virus which once caught never left the carrier, and could be transmitted from the carrier to others by a number of means including sexual intercourse. He did not intend V to catch the virus from him, but accepted that he behaved recklessly.

8.6.2 Implied consent

There are situations in which the courts imply consent to minor touchings, which would otherwise be a battery. These are the everyday situations where there is a crowd of people and it is impossible not to have some contact. In *Wilson v Pringle* (1987) it was held that the ordinary 'jostlings' of everyday life were not battery. Nobody can complain of the jostling which is inevitable from his presence in, for example, a supermarket, an underground station or a busy street; nor can a person who attends a party complain if his hand is seized in friendship, or even if his back is (within reason) slapped.

This also applies to contact sports. When people take part in organised sport such as football, rugby or judo, they are agreeing to the contact which is part of that sport. However, if the contact goes beyond what is allowed within the rules, then it is possible for an offence to be committed. For example, a rugby player consents to a tackle within the rules of the game, but s/he does not consent to an opposition player stamping on his/her head.

The breach of the rules of the sport must be a serious one. The Court of Appeal said in *R v Barnes* (2004) that where an injury is caused during a match, then a criminal prosecution should be reserved for those situations where the conduct was sufficiently grave to be properly categorised as criminal.

Case study

R v Barnes (2004)

D made a late tackle on V during an amateur football match. V suffered a serious leg injury. D's conviction of an offence under s 20 OAPA 1861 was quashed.

8.6.3 Consent to minor injuries

There have been arguments as to whether consent could be a defence to an offence under s 47 OAPA 1861. It used to be thought that consent could be a defence where the injuries were not serious. However, in *Attorney-General's Reference (No. 6 of 1980)* (1981) where two young men agreed to fight in the street to settle their differences following a quarrel, the Court of Appeal held that consent could not be a defence to such an action as it was not in the public interest. They said:

> It is not in the public interest that people should try to cause, or should cause, each other bodily harm for no good reason. Minor struggles are another matter. So, in our judgment, it is immaterial whether the act occurs in private or public; it is an assault if actual bodily harm is intended and/or caused. This means that most fights will be unlawful regardless of consent.

So it is now accepted that consent is not a defence to a s 47 offence, unless the situation is one of the exceptions which have been recognised by the courts. In *Attorney-General's Reference (No. 6 of 1980)* the Court of Appeal gave the following list of exceptions: 'properly conducted games and sports, lawful chastisement or correction, reasonable surgical interference, dangerous exhibitions, etc.'

The court added 'etc.' to the end of the list to show that there may be other situations where consent would be permitted to be a defence. It is a question of whether it is in the public interest or not.

In deciding what was in the public interest, the courts have come to decisions which are difficult to reconcile. In *R v Brown* (1993) the House of Lords held that consent was not a defence to sado-masochistic acts done in private by homosexuals, even though all the participants were adult and the injuries inflicted did not require medical attention.

Case study

R v Brown (1993)

Five men in a group of consenting adult sado-masochists were convicted of offences of assault causing actual bodily harm (s 47 OAPA 1861) and malicious wounding (s 20 OAPA 1861). They had carried out acts which included applying stinging nettles to the genital area and inserting map pins or fish hooks into the penises of each other. All the victims had consented and none had needed medical attention. Their convictions were upheld by the House of Lords.

The Law Lords clearly made this decision as a matter of public policy. Lord Templeman actually said:

> The question whether the defence of consent should be extended to the consequences of sado-masochistic encounters can only be decided by consideration of policy and public interest ... Society is entitled and bound to protect itself against a cult of violence.

However, in *R v Wilson* (1996), the Court of Appeal held that where a defendant branded his initials on his wife's buttocks with a hot knife at her request, this was not an unlawful act, even though she had to seek medical attention for the burns caused. It held it was not in the public interest that such consensual behaviour should be criminalised. This was a situation of 'personal adornment' like having a tattoo.

8.6.4 Mistaken belief in consent

Where the defendant genuinely, but mistakenly, believes that the victim is consenting, then there is a defence to an assault.

In this area the decisions of the courts are even more difficult to reconcile with the general principle that 'it is not in the public interest that people should try to cause, or should cause, each other bodily harm for no good reason'. In the following two cases the courts held that mistaken belief in consent was a defence to the offences charged.

Case study

R v Jones (1986)

Two schoolboys aged 14 and 15 were tossed into the air by older youths. One victim suffered a broken arm and the other a ruptured spleen. The defendants claimed they believed that the two victims consented to the activity. The Court of Appeal quashed their convictions for s 20 OAPA 1861 because the judge had not allowed the issue of mistaken belief in consent to go to the jury. The court held that a genuine mistaken belief in consent to 'rough and undisciplined horseplay' could be a defence, even if that belief was unreasonable.

A similar decision was reached in *R v Aitken* (1992).

Case study

R v Aitken (1992)

RAF officers poured white spirit over a colleague who was wearing a fire-resistant flying suit, but who was asleep and drunk at the time that this was done. He suffered 35 per cent burns. Their convictions under s 20 OAPA 1861 were quashed as the mistaken belief in the victim's consent should have been left to the jury.

If consent is obtained by fraud, as in *Tabassum*, duress or influence – because of the victim's age or lack of mental capacity, that will not amount to true consent.

8.6.5 The need for a defence of consent

It is important to allow a defence of consent in some situations. For example, if there was no defence of consent, then contact sports would all be illegal. This is why the Court of Appeal in *Attorney-General's Reference (No. 6 of 1980)* (1981) stated that, although consent was not a defence to street fights, there were exceptions where consent was a defence.

The list of exceptions that the Court of Appeal gave in that case was 'properly conducted games and sports, lawful chastisement or correction, reasonable surgical interference, dangerous exhibitions, etc'. These exceptions are based on public policy.

Sport

If there was no defence of consent in 'properly conducted games and sports' then team games such as football, rugby and hockey could never be played. There would also be a large number of individual sports which would be prevented, such as judo, karate and boxing.

The important phrase in the judgment is 'properly conducted games and sports'. There has to be a distinction between playing within the rules and behaviour which is outside the rules. A deliberate 'off-the-ball' tackle aiming at another player's legs with the intention of causing serious injury must surely be considered as criminal behaviour. A player who is injured in this way has not consented to such behaviour.

The case of *R v Barnes* (2004) set out matters which were to be considered in deciding whether an assault in the course of a match was criminal. The court said that in deciding whether conduct in the course of a sport is criminal or not, the following factors should be considered:
- Intentional infliction of injury will always be criminal.
- For reckless infliction of injury, did the injury occur during actual play, or in a moment of temper or over-excitement when play had ceased?
- 'Off-the-ball' injuries are more likely to be criminal.
- The fact that the play is within the rules and practice of the game and does not go beyond them will be a firm indication that what has happened is not criminal.

By applying these factors a good balance should be achieved between allowing contact sports to be played without unnecessary restrictions on their rules and upholding the criminal law on assault. Only those who deliberately inflict injury or who go beyond the rules of the game should be liable under the criminal law.

Offence	Can consent be a defence?	Comment/Case
Murder **s 18 OAPA 1861**	Never a defence to these crimes.	Not in the public interest.
s 20 OAPA 1861 **s 47 OAPA 1861**	Generally not a defence.	Not in public interest, e.g. fighting (*Attorney-General's Reference (No. 6 of 1980)* (1981)) OR sado-masochistic acts (*Brown* (1993)).
	BUT there are exceptions where consent is a defence.	Properly conducted sports, surgery, dangerous exhibitions (*Jones* (1986)) OR personal adornment such as tattoos (*Wilson* (1996)).
Battery	Always allowed as a defence.	Consent can also be implied to the 'jostlings' of everyday life (*Wilson v Pringle* (1986)).

Figure 8.5 Key facts chart on consent as a defence

Medical procedures

Another exception where consent is allowed as a defence is 'reasonable surgical interference'. Clearly where the surgery is needed to save the patient's life or to improve a patient's health in some way, then consent to the operation is a defence to any charge of assault.

Mentally capable adults can consent to reasonable medical treatment or they can refuse it. If they refuse consent, then if surgery or other treatment was performed it would be a criminal act. For example, if a person refuses a blood transfusion because of his religious beliefs, then such treatment cannot be given.

If a patient is unconscious so that his consent cannot be asked, medical staff will try to obtain consent from relatives. If this is not possible then, where treatment is necessary and must be performed quickly, such an operation can be performed without actual consent.

8.6.6 Evaluation of the law on consent

It is difficult to reconcile some decisions by the courts when considering the defence of consent, for example, when comparing the cases of *Brown* (1994) and *Wilson* (1996).

In *Brown* the House of Lords ruled, by a majority, that consent could not be a defence to sado-masochistic behaviour between consenting adult homosexuals because of the cruelty and degradation involved. In *Wilson* the Court of Appeal ruled that consent could be a defence where a husband had branded his wife's buttocks with his initials. These decisions were made despite the fact that none of the 'victims' in *Brown* had needed medical attention whereas the wife in *Wilson* had had to receive medical attention. The autonomy of the participants to suffer injury appeared to receive limited support in *Brown*, though Lord Slynn suggested that 'it is not for the courts in the interests of paternalism or to protect people from themselves to introduce into statutory crimes concepts that do not properly fit there.'

Policy considerations

One view of these conflicting decisions is that the courts are prepared to condone acts where the parties are consenting adult heterosexuals (and the injuries are not too serious), but not where the parties are consenting adult homosexuals (as in *Brown*).

There are also contradictory decisions within cases involving heterosexual couples. This was shown by *R v Emmett* (1999).

Case study

R v Emmett (1999)

'High-risk' sexual activity between D and his partner (later his wife) had resulted in the woman suffering haemorrhages to her eyes on one occasion and burns to her breast on another occasion. She had to consult her doctor on both occasions. D was charged with ABH s 47 OAPA 1861. The Court of Appeal held that her consent to the injuries could not be a defence where the harm caused is more than 'transient or trivial' injury.

This case contrasts with *R v Wilson* (1996), where consent was allowed as a defence even though the wife had needed medical attention.

It could be said, in the cases when consent could not be used, that the courts are trying to impose their own moral values. Public policy issues were important considerations in the decision of the House of Lords in *Brown*. In the judgment in *Brown* it was said that 'In principle there is a difference between violence which is incidental and violence which is inflicted for the indulgence of cruelty. In a civilised society, cruelty should not be tolerated.' This was a main reason for the House of Lords' decision that victims could not consent to injuries caused by the deliberate infliction of cruelty.

The Law Lords also felt that the violence involved the degradation of the victims. They were treated in a humiliating and uncaring way. In addition, there was also no way of knowing what injuries might result to the victim from the conduct.

All these points meant that, in the view of the courts, it was in the public interest, and morally right, for the law to interfere with the autonomy and freedom of individuals to do what they chose, especially in private.

Horseplay

Another area of law where the courts are prepared to accept consent as a defence is in what is called 'horseplay'. That is where those involved in a 'game' use 'friendly' violence to each other.

Even where such behaviour results in serious injury, the courts have ruled that consent can be a defence. This is the legal basis that the aggressor does not have the *mens rea* for assault. Even more surprisingly, the courts have held that honest belief in consent provides a defence although the victim in fact has not consented.

This is shown in *Jones* (1986) and *Aitken* (1992). Serious injuries were caused to the victims in both cases. Yet the courts accepted that the defence of consent was available, even though there was a mistaken belief in the existence of consent.

When these cases are contrasted with *Brown* (1994) and *Emmett* (1999), there appear to be further inconsistencies in the law. Why should real consent be refused as a defence for disapproved types of sexual behaviour and yet allowed for horseplay which results in serious injury, even where the victim was not actually consenting?

> **Tip**
>
> Consent, as an issue, can arise in scenario-based questions which involve non-fatal offences. Check to see if the scenario is about an incident in a 'game' or if there is mention of the people involved 'agreeing'. Check also the injuries suffered as this could to lead to a discussion of whether the defence would be available.

8.6.7 Consent and euthanasia

No one can consent to another person assisting in bringing about their own death. This means that if a terminally ill patient wishes to die, they must take their own life. If anyone helps bring about the death they will face a charge of murder or assisting suicide. This was decided in *R (on the application of Pretty) v DPP* (2001). This decision leads to the situation where the law recognises the personal autonomy of a person being entitled to take their own life and not committing any crime by trying to do so.

> **Case study**
>
> ### *R (on the application of Pretty) v DPP* (2001)
>
> Mrs Pretty was suffering from motor neurone disease. As a result she was becoming more and more incapable of movement. She knew that eventually she would suffocate to death. She wanted her husband to be able to assist her to take her own life when she felt that her life had become intolerable.
>
> She applied to the courts for a judicial declaration that, if her husband assisted her to commit suicide, he would not be prosecuted. The House of Lords refused the declaration on the basis that any assistance of the husband would be a criminal act.

But in cases where people who wish to commit suicide are physically incapable of doing so, then they are denied their wishes as anyone who helps them will be guilty of an offence. There have been several attempts to challenge this rule including Tony Nicklinson in 2014. In this and other cases that have come to court it has been said that this is an issue for Parliament to consider. However, at the time of writing, Parliament has been unwilling to legislate, despite there being broad public support for their doing so.

> **Case study**
>
> ### *R (on the application of Nicklinson and another) v Ministry of Justice* 2014
>
> In 2005 Tony Nicklinson suffered a severe stroke and became paralysed from the neck down. He described his life following the stroke as a 'living nightmare'. He wanted to end his life but was unable to commit suicide without assistance, which was an offence under s 2 of the Suicide Act 1961. He applied for a declaration that either:
>
> - It would be legal for a doctor to assist in his suicide; or
> - The present legal regime concerning assisted suicide is incompatible with Article 8 of the European Convention on Human Rights (Right to respect for private and family life).
>
> The case was appealed to the Supreme Court (though Mr Nicklinson refused food and died during the course of the proceedings). The courts refused his request for a declaration saying that this issue is a matter for Parliament (not the courts) to legislate on. The request for a declaration of incompatibility was also refused as the court considered that the issue was within the UK's margin of appreciation, and was therefore a question for the UK to decide.

Article 8 ECHR is discussed in detail in Chapter 21; social control through law in Chapter 15.2.1

> **Look online**
>
> Read the following article and make notes on the reasons given by the judges in the Supreme Court for their decisions.
>
> https://ukhumanrightsblog.com/2014/06/25/supreme-court-rejects-right-to-die-appeals/

Summary

Self-defence

- This includes the need to defend oneself and action taken to defend another.
- Section 76 of the Criminal Justice and Immigration Act 2008 sets out rules:
  - Degree of force must be reasonable and not disproportionate.
  - In householder cases the degree of force must not be 'grossly disproportionate'.
  - Where D is acting under a mistake s/he is judged on the facts as s/he genuinely believed them to be.
  - Where D is acting under a drunken mistake s/he cannot use the defence.

Duress

- This is where D is effectively forced by threats to commit an offence.
  - Not available for murder, attempted murder and, possibly, treason.
  - Threat must be of death or serious injury – but cumulative effect of threats can be considered.
  - Threat must be to D or his family.
  - There are two tests:
    - Subjective – was D compelled to act as s/he did because s/he reasonably believed that s/he had good cause to fear death or serious injury?
    - Objective – if (a) is satisfied, would a sober person of reasonable fitness, sharing the same characteristics as D, have responded in the same way?
  - Relevant characteristics include age, pregnancy, gender, serious physical disability, recognised mental illness or psychiatric disorder (low IQ is not included).

Duress of circumstances

- This is where D is forced to act because of circumstances.
  - The defence is not available for murder or attempted murder or, possibly, treason.
  - The circumstances must mean that there is a threat of death or serious injury.

Necessity

- This is where circumstances force a person to act to prevent worse evil.
  - Criminal courts have been reluctant to recognise the defence.
  - Civil courts have recognised the defence.
  - In the criminal case of *R v Shayler* (2001) it was concluded that necessity and duress were the same defence.

Consent

- Consent can be a defence to some offences against the person.
  - It cannot be a defence to murder nor where serious injury is caused.
  - The consent must be real.
  - V must have knowledge of relevant facts, such as D being HIV positive.
  - There is implied consent to ordinary 'jostlings' of everyday life.
  - In sport there is consent to contact which is within the rules of that sport.
  - For minor injuries it has been held that it is not in the public interest that people should try to cause each other bodily harm for no good reason.
  - The exceptions to this rule include properly conducted games and sports, lawful chastisement, reasonable surgical interference, dangerous exhibitions.
  - A genuine mistaken belief that V is consenting can be a defence.

After reading this chapter you should
- Understand the *actus reus* of attempts
- Understand the *mens rea* of attempts
- Understand the problems that arise with impossibility of the completed offence being committed
- Evaluate the law on attempts
- Apply the law on attempts to scenario-based situations

9.1 What is meant by 'an attempt'?

An attempt is where a person tries to commit an offence but, for some reason, fails to complete it. For example, D fires a gun at V, intending to kill V. Just as D pulls the trigger, V stoops to tie his shoelace. The bullet misses V and goes over his head. D intended to kill V but has not succeeded, so D cannot be charged with murder as V is still alive. However, it is obvious that D ought to be criminally liable for some offence. It would be ridiculous if D were just allowed to go free. D is clearly a dangerous person and should be liable under the criminal law. In this type of situation D can be charged with attempted murder.

A case example of an attempt to murder is *R v White* (1910).

Case study

R v White (1910)

D put cyanide in his mother's drink, intending to kill her. She died of a heart attack before she could drink it. He tried to commit murder but did not actually kill his mother. He was convicted of attempted murder.

9.1.1 Definition of 'attempt'

'Attempt' is now defined by s 1(1) of the Criminal Attempts Act 1981 which states:

> If, with intent to commit an offence to which this section applies, a person does an act which is more than merely preparatory to the commission of the offence, he is guilty of attempting to commit the offence.

As with all offences, the prosecution must prove the *actus reus* and the *mens rea*. The definition above sets these out. They are:
- *Actus reus* – a person does an act which is more than merely preparatory to the commission of the offence.
- *Mens rea* – with intent to commit that offence.

Key term

Attempt – in criminal law an attempt occurs where a person with the relevant *mens rea* does an act which is more than merely preparatory to the commission of an offence.

9.2 *Actus reus* of attempt

Before 'attempt' was defined in the 1981 Act, the courts used several different tests to decide whether the defendant had actually done enough towards the commission of the main offence for him to have committed the *actus reus*.

The courts have held that the previous common law tests are irrelevant, the important point being whether the defendant has done an act which is 'more than merely preparatory' to the commission of the main offence.

9.2.1 'More than merely preparatory'

The act that the defendant commits has to be more than merely preparation for the main crime. Some acts are obviously mere preparation, but other acts are more difficult to categorise.

Let's take the example where a man decides to rob a bank. First, he buys himself a shotgun and converts it into a sawn-off shotgun. Both the buying and the converting are 'merely preparatory'. Next, he drives around the area, checking escape routes. Again, this is 'merely preparatory'.

On the day of the robbery, D steals a car ('merely preparatory') and drives to the bank (still 'merely preparatory'). He stands on the pavement outside the bank, carrying the sawn-off shotgun in a bag. This is getting nearer, but, according to the case of *Campbell* (1990) (see below), is still only 'merely preparatory'. Then he walks into the bank. Now he has gone beyond mere preparation and can be charged with attempted robbery.

There have been many cases on the meaning of 'merely preparatory'. It is difficult to draw any general principle from them. In *Attorney-General's Reference (No. 1 of 1992)* (1993) it was decided that D need not have performed the last act before the crime proper, nor need he or she have reached the 'point of no return'.

Case study

Attorney-General's Reference (No. 1 of 1992) (1993)

D dragged a girl up some steps to a shed. He lowered his trousers and interfered with her private parts. His penis remained flaccid. He argued that he could not therefore attempt to commit rape. His conviction for attempted rape was upheld. Attempted rape can be complete before the attempt at physical penetration.

Looking at the whole of D's acts, this seems a sensible decision. However, if he had been stopped immediately after he had dragged the girl to the shed, and before he lowered his trousers or interfered with her, then it is unlikely that he could have been convicted. His act of dragging her was probably 'merely preparatory'.

In *R v Gullefer* (1987) the Court of Appeal held that 'more than merely preparatory' means that the defendant must have gone beyond purely preparatory acts and be 'embarked on the crime proper'.

Case study

R v Gullefer (1987)

D jumped onto a race track in order to have the race declared void and so enable him to reclaim money he had bet on the race. His conviction for attempting to steal was quashed because his action was merely preparatory to committing the offence.

9.2.2 Cases showing mere preparation

The case of *R v Gullefer* (above) illustrates a situation in which D's acts were mere preparation. Although D had tried to interfere with the race, he had several other acts to do before the theft (the point at which he would get his betting money back). He had to go to one of the betting points and ask for his money back. Even just going towards the point would not be sufficient. However, asking for the money would change his actions into 'more than merely preparatory'. He would be guilty of attempted theft. It is worth noting that when the money was handed to him, he would then be guilty of the main offence of theft.

The Court of Appeal stated that an attempt begins when 'the merely preparatory acts have come to an end and the defendant embarks upon the crime proper'. It also pointed out that when this moment occurs will depend on the facts in any particular case.

The case of *R v Geddes* (1996) also illustrates acts which were only preparatory.

Case study

R v Geddes (1996)

D was found in the boys' toilet block of a school, in possession of a large kitchen knife, some rope and masking tape. He had no right to be in the school. He had not contacted any of the pupils. His conviction for attempted false imprisonment was quashed.

This case is difficult to justify. D had no right to be on the premises. He had entered the school with all the equipment for falsely imprisoning a student. The next step would be for him to approach one of the students. If the law of attempt is to be effective in protecting people from the main offence, then surely he should have been guilty of an attempt at that point. Is it sensible to wait until he approaches one of the students?

However, the Court of Appeal thought that attempts should be considered by asking two questions:

- Had the accused moved from planning or preparation to execution or implementation?
- Had the accused done an act showing that he was actually trying to commit the full offence, or had he got only as far as getting ready, or putting himself in a position, or equipping himself, to do so?

Using these two questions, it can be seen that *Geddes* had not quite moved from planning or preparation to execution. Also, it can be argued that he had got only as far as getting ready, or putting himself in a position, to commit the full offence.

Another case which is perhaps even more difficult to justify is *R v Campbell* (1990).

Case study

R v Campbell (1990)

D, who had an imitation gun, sunglasses and a threatening note in his pocket, was in the street outside a post office. His conviction for attempted robbery was quashed.

The next step in this case would have been for D to enter the post office. Again, if the law of attempt is to be effective in protecting people from the main offence, surely he should have been guilty of an attempt at that point? Is it sensible to wait until he enters the post office? If the gun had been real then customers and staff in the post office would have been put at risk.

No, I'm not attempting to rob the bank.

9.2.3 Cases in which there was an attempt

The following three cases show situations where the defendant had gone beyond mere preparation. In each case the defendants were held to be guilty of an attempt to commit the full offence.

Case studies

R v Boyle and Boyle (1987)

The defendants were found standing by a door of which the lock and one hinge were broken. Their conviction for attempted burglary was upheld.

The Court of Appeal held that the test to use was whether the defendant was embarking on the crime proper. In this case, once the defendants had entered they would be committing burglary, so trying to gain entry was an attempt.

R v Tosti (1997)

D intended to burgle premises. He took metal cutting equipment with him and hid it behind a hedge near to the premises. He then examined the padlock on the door. He did not damage the padlock. He was found guilty of attempted burglary.

The difference from *Campbell* for both these cases is that burglary is committed at the moment D enters as a trespasser with intent to steal (or do certain other offences). Robbery is not committed until D uses force in order to steal. Walking into a building still leaves another step before the crime proper is committed.

In the next case, *R v Jones* (1990), the defendant had done almost everything he could before committing the full offence.

Case study

R v Jones (1990)

D's partner told him that she wanted their relationship to end and that she was seeing another man, V. D bought a shotgun and shortened the barrel. D then found V, who was in his car. D, who was wearing a crash helmet with the visor down, got into V's car and pointed the gun at V. V grabbed the gun and managed to throw it out of the car window. D's conviction for attempted murder was upheld.

D tried to argue that, as the safety catch was still on, he had not done the last act before the crime proper. The Court of Appeal said that buying the gun, shortening it, loading it and disguising himself with the visor were all preparatory acts. But once D got into V's car and pointed the gun at V, then there was sufficient evidence to leave to the jury the question of whether there was an attempt.

Case	Facts	Offence attempted	Law
Cases where there was sufficient evidence for an attempt			
A-G's reference (No. 1 of 1992) (1993)	D tried to rape a girl but could not get an erection.	Rape	Need not have performed the last act.
Boyle and Boyle (1987)	Standing by door with broken lock.	Burglary	Had done part of a series of acts.
Jones (1990)	Gun safety catch was left on.	Murder	Sufficient evidence to leave the question of whether there was an attempt to the jury.
Cases which were merely preparatory			
Gullefer (1987)	Disrupted race intending to reclaim bet.	Theft	Has D 'embarked upon the crime proper'?
Geddes (1996)	In school with knife, rope and tape.	False imprisonment	Has D 'actually tried to commit the offence in question'?
Campbell (1990)	Outside post office with imitation gun and threatening note.	Robbery	Merely preparatory.

Figure 9.1 Key cases chart on 'merely preparatory' in attempts

9.3 *Mens rea* of attempt

For an attempt, the defendant must normally have the same intention as would be required for the full offence. If the prosecution cannot prove that D had that intention then D is not guilty of the attempt. This was shown by the case of *R v Easom* (1971).

Case study

R v Easom (1971)

D picked up a woman's handbag in a cinema, rummaged through it, then put it back on the floor without removing anything from it. His conviction for theft of the bag and its contents was quashed. The Court of Appeal also refused to substitute a conviction for attempted theft of the bag and specific contents (including a purse and a pen), as there was no evidence that D intended to steal the items.

In this case there was no evidence that the defendant had intended to permanently deprive the owner of the bag or items in it (part of the required *mens rea* for theft). As a result, he could not be guilty of attempted theft.

A similar decision was made in the case of *R v Husseyn* (1977).

Case study

R v Husseyn (1977)

D and another man were seen loitering near the back of a van. When the police approached, they ran off. D was convicted of attempting to steal some sub-aqua equipment that was in the van. The Court of Appeal quashed his conviction.

The decisions by the Court of Appeal in both these cases can be criticised. Surely the defendant did intend to steal something. The fact that Easom did not do so (presumably because there was nothing really worth stealing) should not make him not guilty of attempting to steal. Equally, in the case of Husseyn, the fact that he ran off because the police arrived does not mean that he was not trying to steal.

These problems were resolved in *Attorney-General's Reference (Nos 1 and 2 of 1979) (1979)* where the Court of Appeal decided that if D had a conditional intent (i.e. D intended stealing if there was anything worth stealing), D could be charged with an attempt to steal some or all of the contents. This is a technical procedural way around the problem.

So, Eason would now be charged with attempting to steal some or all of the contents of the bag, rather than the bag itself and specific items in it. Husseyn would be charged with attempting to steal some or all of the contents of the van. In this way they could be found guilty of attempted theft.

9.3.1 *Mens rea* of attempted murder

The *mens rea* for attempted murder involves proving a higher level of intention than for the full offence of murder. The full offence requires that the prosecution proves the defendant had the intention either to kill or to cause grievous bodily harm. However, for attempted murder, the prosecution must prove an intention to kill. An intention to cause serious harm is not enough. This means that the prosecution always has to prove the higher level of intention for attempted murder. This was shown by the case of *R v Whybrow* (1951).

Case study

R v Whybrow (1951)

The defendant wired up his wife's bath and caused her an electric shock. He was convicted of attempted murder. When he appealed, the court, although upholding his conviction, criticised the trial judge's summing up and stressed that only an intention to kill was sufficient for the *mens rea* of attempted murder.

9.3.2 Is recklessness enough for the *mens rea*?

What if it can be proved that the defendant was reckless? Is this sufficient for him to be guilty of an attempt? In *R v Millard and Vernon* (1987) it was decided that it was not sufficient.

Case study

R v Millard and Vernon (1987)

Ds repeatedly pushed against a wooden fence on a stand at a football ground. The prosecution alleged that they were trying to break it and they were convicted of attempted criminal damage. The Court of Appeal quashed their convictions.

Recklessness is not normally sufficient *mens rea* for an attempt. This is so even where recklessness would suffice for the completed offence. However, there is an exception in that recklessness as to one part of the offence can be sufficient. This is illustrated by *Attorney-General's Reference (No. 3 of 1992)* (1994).

Case study

Attorney-General's Reference (No. 3 of 1992) (1994)

D threw a petrol bomb towards a car containing four men. The bomb missed the car and smashed harmlessly against a wall. D was charged with attempting to commit arson with intent to endanger life. The trial judge ruled that it had to be proved that D intended to damage property and to endanger life. D was acquitted.

The Court of Appeal held that the trial judge was wrong. It was necessary to prove that D intended to damage property, but it was only necessary to prove that he was reckless as to whether life would be endangered.

9.4 Impossibility

In some situations people may intend to commit an offence and may do everything they possibly can to commit it, but in fact the offence is impossible to commit.

An example of this would be where D goes to V's room and stabs V as he lies in bed. In fact, V died of a heart attack two hours before D stabbed him. D has merely stabbed a dead body. Murdering V is physically impossible so D cannot be guilty of his murder, but can D be guilty of attempting to murder V?

Another example is where D thinks that the goods s/he is buying very cheaply are stolen goods. He or she is willing to go ahead, thinking s/he is 'handling stolen property'. In fact, the goods are not stolen, so the offence of handling stolen property is legally impossible in this situation. Should D be guilty of attempting to handle stolen property?

Under the common law before 1981, the House of Lords had held that where a crime was legally or physically impossible to commit, then the defendant could not be guilty of attempting to commit it. When the Criminal Attempts Act 1981 was passed, it contained a subsection (s 1(2)) which was intended to close this loophole and make defendants guilty of an attempt even though the full offence was impossible.

Section 1(2) of the Criminal Attempts Act 1981 states: 'A person may be guilty of attempting to commit an offence ... even though the facts are such that the commission of the offence is impossible.'

After the Act was passed, the House of Lords had to consider this section and the problem of attempting the impossible in the case of *Anderton v Ryan* (1985).

Case study

Anderton v Ryan (1985)

Mrs Ryan bought a video recorder very cheaply. She thought it was stolen. Later she admitted this to police who were investigating a burglary at her home. Her conviction was quashed because the video recorder was not in fact stolen.

The House of Lords held that even though Mrs Ryan had gone beyond merely preparatory acts, in fact all her acts were innocent. The video recorder was not stolen. On this basis, they thought that s 1(2) did not make her guilty.

However, less than a year later, the House of Lords overruled this decision in *R v Shivpuri* (1986).

Case study

R v Shivpuri (1986)

D agreed to receive a suitcase which he thought contained prohibited drugs. The suitcase was delivered to him, but it contained only snuff and harmless vegetable matter. D was convicted of attempting to be knowingly concerned in dealing with prohibited drugs.

This time the House of Lords said that both ss 1(2) and 1(3) were relevant. Section 1(3) states:

> In any case where—
>
> (a) apart from this subsection a person's intention would not be regarded as having amounted to an intent to commit an offence; but
>
> (b) if the facts of the case had been as he believed them to be, his intention would be so regarded, then, for the purpose of subsection (1) he shall be regarded as having an intent to commit that offence.

The combined effect of ss 1(2) and 1(3) of the Criminal Attempts Act 1981 meant that a person could be guilty of an attempt even if the commission of the full offence was impossible. In *R v Shivpuri* the facts as he believed them to be were that the suitcase contained prohibited drugs. He intended dealing in drugs so his intention, under s 1(3), was regarded as being an intention to commit that offence.

The House of Lords accepted that its decision in *Anderton v Ryan* (1985) had been wrong and they used the Practice Statement to overrule that decision.

Activity

Explain whether in each of the following scenarios there is an attempt to commit an offence.

1. Amir knows his girlfriend has been going out with Blake. Amir plans to disfigure Blake. He buys some acid which he intends to throw in Blake's face and then drives to Blake's house. As he is about to get out of the car, he sees a police car nearby. Amir immediately drives off.

2. Connor puts some poison in Donna's drink, intending to kill her. The amount he puts in the drink is insufficient to kill and Donna survives.

3. Faye sees a handbag in the ladies' cloakroom. She hopes there will be some money in it, so she opens it. In fact, the bag contains only make-up and tissues. Faye closes the bag and replaces it.

4. Greg and Hans are found in the garden of a house with masks, a torch and screwdrivers in their pockets. They admit they intended to burgle the house.

5. Ian fires a shot at Jani but misses her. He admits he intended to kill her.

	Attempt	Case or statute
Definition of 'attempt'	With intent to commit an offence, a person does an act which is more than merely preparatory to the commission of the offence.	s 1(1) of the Criminal Attempts Act 1981
'More than merely preparatory'	D must have embarked on the crime proper OR D must be trying to commit the full offence.	*Gullefer* (1987) *Geddes* (1996)
Mens rea of attempt	D must have intention for the full offence. A conditional intention is sufficient. Recklessness is not normally sufficient BUT recklessness as to part of the offence may be sufficient.	*Easom* (1971) *Attorney-General's Reference (Nos 1 and 2 of 1979) (1979)* *Millard and Vernon* (1987) *Attorney-General's Reference (No 3 of 1992) (1994)*
Attempting the impossible	ss 1(2) and 1(3) of the Criminal Attempts Act 1981 mean that D is guilty even if the full offence is legally or physically impossible.	*Shivpuri* (1986)

Figure 9.2 Key facts chart on attempts

Summary

Attempt
- Defined by s 1(1) of the Criminal Attempts Act 1981.
- The *actus reus* of attempt is doing an act which is more than merely preparatory to the commission of the offence.
- Prior to the 1981 Act the courts had used several different tests of the *actus reus*. These tests are no longer law: the only test is the 'more than merely preparatory'.
- The *mens rea* of attempt is that D must have the *mens rea* required for the full offence.
- For murder there must be an intention to kill.
- There can be a conditional intent, i.e. where D intends to steal if there is something worth stealing.
- Recklessness is not normally sufficient for the *mens rea* of attempt.

Impossibility
- Originally the courts held that if the full offence was impossible to commit, then D could not be guilty of an attempt.
- In *R v Shivpuri* the courts overruled their previous decision and held that a person could be guilty of an attempt even though the commission of the full offence was impossible.

Evaluation
- The courts have not been very clear in deciding the dividing line between what is 'merely preparatory' and what is an attempt.
- Some of the decisions in this area are not effective for protecting the public.
- An attempt cannot be committed by an omission.
- Is only direct intention sufficient for the *mens rea* of attempt?
- The early decisions on *mens rea* left a loophole where D intended to steal if he or she could find anything worth stealing.
- Should D be guilty because of his intention, although it is impossible for him to commit the full offence?

Chapter 10

Torts connected with land: private and public nuisance

After reading this chapter you should be able to:
- Understand the tort of public nuisance
- Understand the tort of private nuisance
- Evaluate the law relating to these torts
- Apply the law to factual situations

In general people have the right to do whatever they want in their own homes provided it is reasonable and does not cause a nuisance or annoyance to their neighbours. Tort law provides the possibility of actions if the nuisance or annoyance continues beyond what is reasonable. Public nuisance applies where a number of people are affected – but only the claimant suffers damage over and above that of others. Private nuisance applies where only one neighbour is affected. In addition, various statutes have made actions a nuisance in areas such as protection of the environment. In these cases the person who has caused the nuisance is likely to be prosecuted in criminal courts.

10.1 Public nuisance

Public nuisance is different from private nuisance as it potentially affects more people than just immediate neighbours. It has been defined by Romer LJ in *Attorney-General v PYA Quarries Ltd* (1957) as 'something which materially affects the reasonable comfort and convenience of a class of Her Majesty's subjects'.

Key term

Public nuisance – where a group of people is affected by the use of land in the locality.

115

It does not have to be an interference with the use and enjoyment of land, so it is not based on property rights or ownership.

It has also developed as a crime, and will be prosecuted by the Attorney-General. In this chapter we are only concerned with its use as a civil action.

10.1.1 The requirements for proving public nuisance

A class of people

It is essential for an action to be successful for there to be a class of people affected by the nuisance. How many should be within that class is a question of fact in each case. It is likely to be more than two or three but there is no set minimum number. It is not necessary to show that every member of the class is affected – it is sufficient to show that a representative cross section has been affected.

> ## Case study
>
> ### Attorney-General v PYA Quarries Ltd (1957)
>
> Thirty local residents complained of noise, dust and vibrations coming from the defendant's quarry which affected them and the enjoyment of their properties. It was suggested that too few people were affected. According to Lord Denning,
>
> " a public nuisance is a nuisance which is so widespread in its range or so indiscriminate in its effect that it would not be reasonable to expect one person to take proceedings on his own responsibility to put a stop to it but that it should be taken on the responsibility of the community at large. "
>
> The court decided that the defendant's activities amounted to a (public) nuisance and an injunction was granted.

Special damage

To succeed, the claimant must be able to show that they suffered special damage over and above that which other members of the class have suffered. This special damage might include personal injury suffered by a member of the class.

> ## Case study
>
> ### Castle v St Augustine Links (1922)
>
> A golf club had sited a golf tee next to a public road that went through the club grounds. Golfers often sliced balls onto the highway, sometimes hitting cars. On one occasion a taxi was hit, breaking the windscreen, and injuring the driver in the eye. The golf club was found liable for public nuisance. The class of people affected were car drivers who drove along the road. The claimant suffered special damage over and above that of the class.

The principle that a claimant can claim damages for personal injury due to a public nuisance has been confirmed in *Corby Group Litigation v Corby Borough Council* (2008).

> ## Case study
>
> ### Corby Group Litigation v Corby Borough Council (2008)
>
> The local authority intended to redevelop a former steel works, the soil of which was eventually shown to be toxic. As a result of the work on the site several local children were born with deformed limbs.
>
> The Court of Appeal decided that a public nuisance is not confined to loss of enjoyment of land. It is an unlawful act or omission which endangers the life, safety, health, property or comfort of the public.

It can also include damage to goods, as with the damage to car paintwork in *Halsey v Esso Petroleum Co. Ltd* (1961).

> ## Case study
>
> ### Halsey v Esso Petroleum Co. Ltd (1961)
>
> An oil refinery discharged oily smuts which damaged the paintwork of the claimant's car parked in the street outside his house. Other cars in the vicinity may have been affected but the claimant suffered damage over and above that of others and was able to claim for repairs to his car's paintwork.

Note that this case is an example of an action amounting to both public and private nuisance.

A public nuisance claim could also be for financial loss. In *Rose v Miles* (1815) the defendant's barge blocked a navigable river. As a result, the claimant was forced to empty his barge and pay for alternative transport and the defendant was liable for the additional cost incurred. A further example of special damage might be a loss of trade connection, as when shops lose trade during a long-term blockage of the highway such as road repairs.

Most commonly, the tort involves use and abuse of the highway. Interference can arise in a number of ways.

Examples of public nuisance claims

- Obstruction to a highway – perhaps due to queues at a football match, concert or theatre performance.
- A picket line.
- Projections over a highway, which cause damage, e.g. clocks, hoardings, signs and other artificial structures.
- Noise and traffic disruption at a badly organised pop festival.

10.1.2 Defences

The general defences of consent and contributory negligence apply.

Statutory authority to carry out the activity may be relevant – see *Allen v Gulf Oil Refining* (1981) referred to in section 10.2.3 below. The defence of prescription, which is available for private nuisance actions, is not available for public nuisance.

10.1.3 Remedies

Both an injunction and the award of damages are available for a public nuisance action.

- An injunction will benefit all those affected by an action, though only one of the group affected has to take action.
- Damages can be claimed for any special damage suffered by the claimant, which include any personal injury.

10.1.4 Evaluation

While the *Corby* case was perhaps unique in that it involved a large contaminated former steelwork site very close to a town centre, there are many other contaminated 'brown-field' sites in the UK. The judgment opens up the possibility that similar public nuisance actions may be brought against other councils and landowners, and the legal principles in the case may be of great use to those who might seek to take action in the future. This might apply when premises are demolished or where brownfield sites are cleared and where there is potential for exposure of noxious substances into the atmosphere.

In these cases regard should be had, not just to the onsite workforce, but also to those living and working in the surrounding area. In the *Corby* case, the area of risk was four kilometres from the site, though the area for potential exposure will clearly vary depending on each case. To avoid any action for public nuisance landowners must carry out a proper risk assessment and employ competent workers to do the job and not cut corners as happened in the *Corby* case.

Although it has been accepted for some time that it is possible to claim damages for personal injury in a public nuisance claim, there has been limited authority to support this. In the *Corby* case the Court of Appeal confirmed the accepted view that it is only open to the Supreme Court to depart from accepted practice. This means that different rules apply for public and private nuisance. In a claim for public nuisance it is possible to claim for personal injury, while in private nuisance it is not.

In the *Corby* case the Court of Appeal pointed out that the scope of public nuisance is broader than private nuisance; in particular public nuisance is not confined to the protection of the use or enjoyment of land. On this basis the functions of the two torts are different so it is not inconsistent for personal injury damages to be claimable in public nuisance but not in private nuisance.

Private nuisance	Public nuisance
Only one person, a neighbour, is affected.	A class of people has to be affected, one of whom has to suffer special damage.
Claimant requires an interest in the land affected.	Claimant does not have to have an interest in land, *Castle v St Augustine Links* (1922).
Nuisance arises from defendant's unreasonable use of land.	It can arise from an activity not related to land.
Injunction and damages for property damage can be claimed.	Injunction and property damage can be claimed and personal injury, if suffered.

Figure 10.1 The differences between private and public nuisance

Case	Facts	Legal principle
Attorney-General v PYA Quarries Ltd (1957)	Work at a quarry caused noise, dust and vibration nuisance to at least 30 local homes.	A public nuisance is widespread in its range or indiscriminate in its effect so that it is unreasonable to expect one person to take action to stop it.
Castle v St Augustine Links (1922)	Car windscreen hit by golf ball and driver injured.	Only those who have suffered injury or damage over and above the general public can sue.
Corby Group Litigation v Corby Borough Council (2008)	Children born deformed by work on toxic site.	Personal injury damages can be claimed.
Halsey v Esso Petroleum Co. Ltd (1961)	Car paintwork damaged by oily smuts.	Claim can be made in both public and private nuisance. Claim can be made for damage to property.

Figure 10.2 Key cases on public nuisance

10.2 Private nuisance

The usual definition of private nuisance is that it is 'an unlawful interference with a person's use or enjoyment of land coming from neighbouring land'.

In most cases the word 'indirect' must be added, because any interference is likely to be caused by noise, smell or smoke. However an action for nuisance by direct interference would be possible if, for example, the roots of trees encroached from one property into the neighbouring property, perhaps causing damage to foundations.

Key term

Private nuisance – where an action will be taken because someone's use or enjoyment of their property is affected by the unreasonable behaviour of a neighbour.

Private nuisance concerns neighbours. It will almost always involve the competing claims of neighbours to do as they wish on their own land. It is not unreasonable to expect to be able to do what you like on your own land. Problems only arise when this affects a neighbour's ability to enjoy his land and when the use is termed unreasonable. What is reasonable depends not so much on the conduct of the defendant, but whether the interference caused by that conduct is sufficient to give

rise to a legal action. Not every intentional interference with the enjoyment of land will be classed as a nuisance, only that which is classed as unreasonable.

Extension question

A court action to stop a nuisance should be considered a last resort. How else might a problem with a neighbour be resolved?

10.2.1 The parties to an action

The claimant

Since nuisance involves the competing rights of neighbours to use their land how they wish, the basic rule is that anyone who has the use or enjoyment of the land and is affected by the interference may claim. It is important to note that the claimant must have an interest in the land. This will include being an owner or a tenant but not a member of the owner's family, such as a child who has no legal interest in the property. This was confirmed in *Hunter v Canary Wharf* (1997) covered in section 10.2.2 below.

The defendant

The person who is causing, or allowing, the nuisance can be sued. For example, in *Tetley v Chitty* (1986) a local authority who allowed go-kart racing on its land was held liable for a nuisance.

Where the occupier is not responsible him/herself for creating the nuisance, s/he might still be liable as a result of 'adopting' the nuisance, in other words failing to deal with the problem, even if it was caused by a previous owner or a trespasser. This can be seen in the case of *Sedleigh Denfield v O'Callaghan* (1940).

Case study

Sedleigh Denfield v O'Callaghan (1940)

The defendants were an order of monks who occupied land where there was a ditch. The local authority, without the knowledge of the defendants, laid a pipe to take water away from the ditch. The pipe had a grate to stop leaves blocking it but the grate was situated in the wrong place and became blocked. As a result the neighbouring land became flooded. By this time the defendants knew of the pipe. The defendants were liable in nuisance as the House of Lords decided that an occupier who knows of a danger and allows it to continue is liable, even if he has not created the danger himself.

A defendant can also be liable where the nuisance is the result of natural causes which he or she is aware of but fails to deal with.

Case study

Leakey v National Trust (1980)

The defendants owned land on which there was a large natural mound on a hillside. They were aware that it could slip and following a hot summer it did slip, damaging the claimant's cottage. The defendants were held liable as they knew that a slippage might happen and they failed to prevent it.

Anthony v Coal Authority (2005)

The defendant took over responsibility for a former colliery. It was later landscaped and sold as common land. A fire started through spontaneous combustion which lasted for three years, causing fume and smoke interference to people living in the area. The defendant was liable because it was aware of the problem while the tip was still in its control and failed to prevent the nuisance.

Note that the defendant who is causing the nuisance does not have to have an interest in the land from which the nuisance is coming so that a short-term tenant or a member of the neighbour's family can be liable.

10.2.2 The elements of private nuisance

The definition of the tort again is 'an unlawful interference with a person's use or enjoyment of land coming from neighbouring land'.

Unlawful

Mere interference on its own is insufficient for an action. The claimant must prove that the defendant's activity amounts to an unlawful use of land. 'Unlawful' here does not mean illegal, but rather means that the court accepts that the defendant's use of land is unreasonable in the way that it affects the claimant.

The proper question for the court is: 'in all of the circumstances, is it reasonable for the claimant to have to suffer the particular interference?' There is a certain amount of fault involved by the defendant not having regard for his neighbour. However, fault, in the sense of how, and why, the interference occurred does not have to be proved.

Indirect interference

Over the years a variety of actions have been decided as amounting to a nuisance:
- fumes drifting over neighbouring land
- smell from farm animals
- noise – from a children's playground, due to gunfire, and from a speedway and motor racing circuit
- vibrations from industrial machinery
- hot air rising into other premises
- oily smuts from chimneys
- fire
- cricket balls being hit into a garden.

However, some forms of interference will not be protected. A claimant cannot take action to protect a right to a view of the surrounding countryside or the right to light, nor can interference with television reception be protected, as shown in the case of *Hunter v Canary Wharf Ltd* (1997).

Case study

Hunter v Canary Wharf Ltd (1997)

The claimants were a number of people who were living in the Docklands area of East London when the Canary Wharf office tower was being built. They claimed that the building affected their television reception. The House of Lords decided that the loss of this kind of recreational facility was not sufficient interference to give rise to an action in nuisance. This was partly because other forms of reception such as cable and satellite were available.

The court also confirmed the rule that only those with an interest in the land, and not members of families, had the right to bring an action.

However, the courts are prepared to protect feelings of emotional distress. For example, in *Thompson-Schwab v Costaki* (1956) the Court of Appeal decided that the running of a brothel in a respectable residential area of London amounted to a nuisance. In *Laws v Florinplace Ltd* (1981) an injunction was awarded where a shop in an area of shops, restaurants and some housing was converted into a sex shop.

Factors of reasonableness

Because the tort is all about balancing competing interests of the claimant and the defendant, the court will take into account any relevant factors to decide whether the use of land by the defendant is unreasonable.

Buildings in Canary Wharf, London

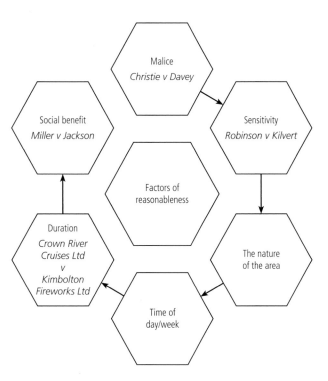

Figure 10.3 Factors of reasonableness considered by the court

Locality

Nuisance is all about the use of land in the area where it is situated, so the character of the neighbourhood has to be considered. The court will consider questions such as whether the area is purely residential, if it is partly residential and partly commercial or industrial,

if it is situated in the town or country and whether the character of the area has changed over time. As Thesiger LJ stated in *Sturges v Bridgman* (1879), 'what would be a nuisance in Belgrave Square would not necessarily be so in Bermondsey.'

The duration of the interference

To be actionable, the interference is likely to be continuous and at unreasonable hours of the day. In this way, a noisy one-off party to celebrate a special occasion may not be a nuisance, but if regular, noisy, late-night parties are held, this may amount to a nuisance. However, in *Crown River Cruises Ltd v Kimbolton Fireworks Ltd* (1996), an event lasting for a maximum of 20 minutes was held to be a nuisance.

Case study

Crown River Cruises Ltd v Kimbolton Fireworks Ltd (1996)

A river barge was set alight by flammable debris, resulting from a firework display lasting only 20 minutes. It was said that the display amounted to an actionable nuisance.

If the interference is only temporary, this is not a sufficient reason to avoid a claim if it is of a kind and, at times, when it is an unreasonable interference.

The sensitivity of the claimant

If it can be shown the claimant is particularly sensitive, then the action may not be a nuisance.

Case study

Robinson v Kilvert (1889)

The claimant stored brown paper on the ground floor of a building. The defendant stored paper boxes in the basement. He needed the conditions to be hot and dry. The heat in the basement caused the brown paper to dry out and the claimant sued for its loss in value. The court decided that the brown paper was particularly delicate and the heat from the basement would not have dried out normal paper. The court did not grant an injunction or damages.

The law on nuisance is moving away now from the idea of 'abnormal sensitivity' to a general test of foreseeability.

Case study

Network Rail Infrastructure v Morris (2004)

The claimant ran a recording studio near the main London to Brighton railway line. The railway company installed new track circuits which interfered with the amplification of electric guitars causing him to lose business. The Court of Appeal considered that the use of amplified electric guitars was abnormally sensitive equipment and as the interference was not foreseeable, the defendants were not liable.

Malice

A deliberately harmful act will normally be unreasonable behaviour and considered a nuisance.

Case study

Hollywood Silver Fox Farm v Emmett (1936)

The claimant bred mink on his farm. The defendant had a disagreement with the claimant and told his son to shoot his guns near to the property to frighten the animals so they would not breed. This was a deliberate and unreasonable act, and amounted to a nuisance.

Christie v Davey (1893)

The claimant was a music teacher who held musical parties and lessons in his house. The defendant became annoyed by the noise and responded by banging on the walls with his hands and with trays, blowing whistles and shouting. An injunction was granted against him due to his deliberate and malicious behaviour.

Social benefit

If it is considered that the defendant is providing a benefit to the community, the court may consider the actions reasonable.

Case study

Miller v Jackson (1977)

The claimants' use of their garden was disrupted by cricket balls being hit into it from the adjoining recreation ground. The cricket club tried to compromise with the claimants by erecting high fencing and instructing batsmen to hit the ball on the ground. However the claimants continued with their action to stop cricket being played. The court weighed up the use of the ground and the benefit of sport to the community as against the claimants' use of their garden. They decided that the community use of the ground outweighed the private use and refused an injunction.

However, the opposite view was taken in *Adams v Ursell* (1913), when a well-used fish and chip shop was found to be causing a nuisance to local residents due to smells coming from it, and it was forced to close. It is unlikely that a similar decision would be reached today as the court could make a positive order to fit extractors to remove excessive smells.

Tip

You will not need to discuss every factor of reasonableness. From the facts of the scenario you should be able to identify the relevant factors to explain. Use the relevant cases to help explain the factor.

Activity

Consider whether there is a possible claim for nuisance in the following situations:

1 Raj and Jas recently received successful A Level results and held a very noisy party that lasted till 3 a.m. Ada and Florence who live next door were kept awake and were quite annoyed.

2 Tara lives next door to Albert, an amateur shortwave radio enthusiast. When he is using his equipment, it causes interference to both sound and vision on Tara's television.

3 Ricky, a music promoter, proposes to hold an open-air pop concert lasting one week in parkland at the head of a residential cul-de-sac.

4 Norris is annoyed because Rita's cat regularly comes into his garden and messes on his flowers, some of which have died.

5 Residents in a private home for the elderly object to the noise from junior football matches played on local authority playing fields near to the home.

10.2.3 Defences

Unlike other torts, the defendant can argue any one of a number of defences.

Prescription

This is a defence that is unique to nuisance. Prescription may be a defence to a nuisance action – if the action has been carried on for at least 20 years, and there has been no complaint between the parties in that time, then the defendant may be said to have a prescriptive right to continue. It has to be between the same parties.

Case study

Sturges v Bridgman (1879)

The claimant, a doctor, had lived and worked next to the defendant's confectionery factory. The claimant then built a consulting room in his garden on the boundary to the factory. He then complained of a nuisance in his rooms due to vibrations from the defendant's machinery. The defendant argued that he had a prescriptive right to continue as he had been using the factory without complaint for over 20 years. The court decided that the defence of prescription failed as the nuisance only began when the consulting room was built.

The operation of the defence has been considered in the case of *Coventry v Lawrence* (2014). The Supreme Court confirmed that the defence only applied to an activity that was an actionable nuisance for at least the last 20 years – not just that an activity had been carried on for that time without complaint.

Linked to this defence, the defence of *volenti non fit injuria* – consent by the claimant to the nuisance – can apply.

See *OCR AS/A Level Law Book 1* Chapters 23 and 24 for more information on the defence of *volenti non fit injuria*.

Moving to the nuisance

The defendant may argue that the claimant is only suffering the nuisance as they have moved closer to the alleged problem (as in *Sturges v Bridgman*), or moved into the area (*Miller v Jackson*) and that there was no issue previously. This argument will not give a defence to the defendant.

Statutory authority

Since many of the activities that can amount to a nuisance are now regulated or licensed by environmental or other laws, then statutory authority is likely to be one of the most effective defences.

Case study

Allen v Gulf Oil Refining (1981)

Residents in the area where the defendants were operating an oil refinery brought an action in private and public nuisance. The defendants had been given statutory authority to acquire the site and build a refinery, but not express permission to operate it. The House of Lords said that it must have been Parliament's intention when it gave permission for the defendants to operate a refinery. As the nuisance was an inevitable consequence of operating the refinery the defence of statutory authority succeeded. Note that this defence applies to public nuisance as well as private nuisance.

If a statute provides the only possible remedy, an action in nuisance may not be possible as an alternative.

Case study

Marcic v Thames Water plc (2003)

Through the failures of the defendants, the claimant's home became flooded with sewage on many occasions. The Water Industry Act 1991, which governed the conduct of the defendants, provided appropriate remedies and procedures and excluded a private action in nuisance. The House of Lords decided that as there were clear statutory procedures, there could be no nuisance action. If such action was allowed it would conflict with the intentions of Parliament.

It was also argued that there was a breach of Article 8 of the European Convention on Human Rights (ECHR) – particularly the right to respect for the home, which includes a right not to have one's home life interfered with. The Lords considered that Article 8 requires a fair balance to be struck between the interests of persons whose homes and property are affected and the interests of other people, such as customers and the general public. His case was that he had a Convention right to have the decision as to whether new sewers should be constructed for his property made by a court in a private action for nuisance rather than under the statutory scheme. However the Lords considered he had no such right.

See Chapter 21 for Article 8 ECHR.

Local authority planning permission can in some circumstances act in the same way, as lawful justification for a nuisance.

Case study

Gillingham Borough Council v Medway (Chatham) Dock Co (1993)

Planning permission was granted to use part of a dockyard as a commercial port. Access was only available by residential roads which caused noise disturbance from heavy lorries to residents. The court decided that as the character of the neighbourhood had been changed by the planning permission, what could have previously been a nuisance could now be considered reasonable. It was held not to be an actionable nuisance because of the grant of planning permission changing the character of the neighbourhood.

However, if the planning permission does not change the character of the neighbourhood, it will not operate as a defence.

Case study

Wheeler v Saunders (1996)

A pig farmer was granted planning permission to expand by building two more pig houses, each containing 400 pigs. One pig house was only 11 metres from the cottage of a neighbour who then took action in nuisance due to the strong smells he experienced. The Court of Appeal confirmed that the grant of planning permission could only be a defence if its effect was to change the character of the neighbourhood so that the nuisance was not unreasonable. This had not been the case here and the planning permission was not a defence.

This principle has been confirmed again in a case about a sporting venue.

Case study

Watson v Croft Promo-Sport (2009)

Planning permission was granted in 1963 to use a former aerodrome as a motor racing track, and it was then used as a track for 16 years. Racing then ceased but in 1995 new owners reopened the track and it became a very popular circuit. The new owners reapplied for planning permission for 210 days per year and following a public inquiry this was granted. The claimant, who lived about 300 metres from the circuit, brought an action in private nuisance claiming noise disturbance, an injunction and damages. The defendant argued that the planning permission had changed the character of the area and so the use of the circuit was reasonable. However, the Court of Appeal granted an injunction restraining the defendant from using the race track for more than 40 days per year. They considered that the area remained essentially rural and that there was an actionable nuisance.

The Supreme Court has considered the law of nuisance more recently, in the case of *Coventry v Lawrence* (2014).

Case study

Coventry v Lawrence (2014)

The claimant bought a house in 2006, 864 metres from the defendant's motor sport stadium. Planning permission had originally been granted in 1975 for speedway use and subsequently for other motor sport use including stock cars, bangers and motorcross. The claimant brought an action based on noise nuisance requiring an injunction limiting the use of the track. The Supreme Court confirmed the existence of a noise nuisance and granted an injunction limiting the use of the track. They decided that:

- the rule in *Sturges v Bridgman* – about considering the character of neighbourhood – still applies; further, provided the claimant uses his property for the same purposes as his predecessor, the defendant cannot use the defence of coming to the nuisance, but
- where a claimant builds on his property or changes the use of his property after the defendant has started his use of the activity complained of, then the defence of coming to the nuisance may fail, and
- damages may be considered as a remedy more often in nuisance cases, especially where planning permission has been awarded to the defendant for the use of his land, or where the public interest is involved, such as employees losing their jobs if an injunction is awarded.

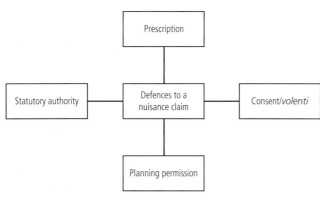

Figure 10.4 Defences to a nuisance claim

Look online

Research to find a report of a neighbour dispute. What was the cause of the dispute? If it is an ongoing dispute how do you think it can be resolved? If the dispute is over, do you think it has been resolved to the satisfaction of both parties?

10.2.4 Remedies

Injunction

Until the case of *Coventry v Lawrence* (2014) the most common remedy for a nuisance claim, and the point of bringing an action, was an injunction. This would generally be prohibitory, ordering the defendant to stop causing the nuisance. An injunction could also be positive in nature – for example, to order the defendant to install a filter to prevent the escape of smell or smuts. The injunction could be linked to the award of damages where a loss has occurred.

This approach followed the '*Shelfer* test' (from *Shelfer v City of London Electric Lighting Co.* (1895)) which set out that damages should only be awarded over an injunction when:

- the injury to the claimant's rights was small
- the claimant can be compensated by money
- a small payment is adequate, and
- it would be unfair on the defendant to grant an injunction.

Now, in *Coventry v Lawrence* (2014) the Supreme Court has laid down guidance as to the future use of injunctions and the award of damages in nuisance. They considered that:

- an injunction could be the default order in a nuisance claim
- it is open to the defendant to argue that an award of damages would be a suitable alternative,
- the *Shelfer* test should not be applied rigidly, and
- an injunction will not automatically be granted, even if the *Shelfer* test is satisfied.

One of the judges, Lord Sumption, suggested that damages would ordinarily be an appropriate remedy in nuisance.

For the future, following this guidance, the courts may award fewer injunctions in nuisance claims and be prepared to award damages instead.

See *OCR AS/A Level Law Book 1* Chapter 25 for information on remedies in tort.

Abatement

A further remedy available to a claimant in nuisance is 'abatement'. This could involve entering the defendant's premises in order to prevent further nuisance. For example, a claimant could enter a defendant's land in order to chop down overhanging branches, although these would need to be returned to the defendant.

10.2.5 Evaluation of the tort of private nuisance

Disputes between neighbours can lead to very strained relations, and indeed a number of television programmes have been made about neighbour disputes that have got out of hand. The courts in recent times have encouraged the use of Alternative Dispute Resolution (ADR) in general in civil disputes. Negotiation and mediation are especially useful in dealing with neighbour disputes. They allow both parties to put their case and the parties themselves come to a resolution. This is a better way of neighbours approaching and dealing with the problem than resorting to court actions. A court case will often lead to confrontation between the parties who still have to live alongside each other when the court case is finished.

The definition of nuisance is an unreasonable interference with the claimant's use or enjoyment of land. This could come about from interference with a view, light or a recreational facility such as television signal. The interference could be caused by the placing of a high boundary or a new building on an adjoining site. Many people will have bought their house because of the quality of its recreational facility. The courts, perhaps with a view to discouraging too many claims, have decided, most recently in *Hunter v Canary Wharf* (1997) that this loss of a recreational facility cannot be claimed for. However this approach does seem inconsistent with cases such as *Thompson-Schwab v Costaki* (1956) and *Laws v Florinplace Ltd* (1981), where the courts were prepared to protect residents from potentially immoral changes to an area.

In *Hunter v Canary Wharf* (1997) the House of Lords confirmed that members of a household who do not have an interest in the land cannot claim. More people now work or study from home and hours of work are more flexible. It seems unfair to restrict claims only to those who have an interest in the land affected and not to extend the ability to claim to any member of the household who may be affected.

However this restriction may be overtaken by the establishment of a right under Article 8 of the European Convention on Human Rights, which states that everyone has the right to respect for his private and family life, his home and correspondence. In *McKenna v British Aluminium* (2002) over 30 claimants, including some children, who had no interest in the land affected, were able to claim in nuisance for the noise and fumes that came from the defendant's factory.

In many areas, the rights of landowners are protected by statute. For example, high boundaries are covered by the Anti-social Behaviour Act 2003, and the Water Industry Act 1991 covers blocked sewerage services. On the one hand, these statutes prevent claims in common law nuisance but may give house owners specific rights in the event of a problem. These specific rights may not involve civil court action.

Many people would think that if the defendant is providing a public, or social, benefit this would be a defence to a nuisance claim. This was not the case in *Adams v Ursell* (1913) when a fish and chip shop was forced to close despite providing a service to the local community. Supporting the benefit to the public was certainly behind the decision of the Court of Appeal not to grant an injunction to Mr and Mrs Miller to stop the playing of cricket on the adjoining recreation ground, in *Miller v Jackson* (1977). The decision of the majority was to provide justice and equity, rather than to decide the case on strict legal grounds. The decision perhaps also reflected the behaviour of the parties. Mrs Miller, in particular, had been confrontational and unwilling to compromise. The cricket club had tried many approaches to deal with the problem, and it was perhaps rewarded by its conciliatory approach.

The court in *Dennis v MOD* (2003) considered that the benefit to the public should be a reason to award compensation to the claimants rather than an injunction. The claimants brought an action because of fighter jets constantly flying low over their property. The MOD defended on the basis that the training of pilots was for the benefit of the public and the country. The court awarded substantial compensation without limiting the flying.

This decision perhaps was a forerunner to the decision in *Coventry v Lawrence* (2014) when comments were made that an injunction should not automatically be ordered in a nuisance case. Many claimants will take court action, as a last resort, to stop a nuisance continuing and will not be looking for compensation. However, in the light of this decision, this cannot now be guaranteed for a successful applicant.

Nuisance and negligence

There is a considerable amount of overlap and relationship between the torts of nuisance and negligence. There can be times when negligence and nuisance both arise together in a situation. In such cases, the claimant has to choose whether to file a case under nuisance or negligence. However, over the years, some distinctions have been highlighted between the two torts.

The law of nuisance mainly deals with interference with enjoyment of land and is not designed to cover claims for personal injuries, which negligence does.

While nuisance protects interests for the enjoyment of land, negligence deals with a breach of duty of care which a person owes to another and which results in loss, injury or damage. In nuisance a claimant will generally be seeking a remedy in the form of an injunction in order to stop unreasonable behaviour rather than damages. This is because the main aim in nuisance is that the neighbour, against whom a complaint is made, should be stopped from continuing an activity which is causing unreasonable interference. In nuisance there cannot be an objective standard as the amount of interference with enjoyment and the unreasonableness of behaviour depend on each situation. Nuisance is not concerned with whether the defendant passes the 'reasonable man' test or not. It deals with the unreasonableness of the outcome and the effect on the claimant, rather than the unreasonableness of the defendant's act. However in negligence, the standard of care is set from a reasonable person's point of view.

In *Cambridge Water Co. v Eastern Counties Leather* (1994) Lord Goff considered the relationship between the two torts and particularly whether foreseeability of harm to another was a requirement in nuisance.

In his view, where a claim for an injunction was made, the defendant who is causing the nuisance must be, or become aware of, the harm (loss of enjoyment) s/he is causing another. However, where the claimant is claiming damages in nuisance the situation is different. In Lord Goff's view it does not follow that the defendant should be held liable for damage of a type which s/he could not reasonably foresee. He considered that the developments in the law of negligence point towards a requirement that foreseeability should be a requirement for liability in damages for nuisance and negligence. It would be unfair to require a claimant in a personal injury claim to prove foreseeability of harm but not to require foreseeability when the claim involves interference with the enjoyment of land.

Nuisance and strict liability

It can be said that liability in nuisance is strict. It is strict in the sense that, although a defendant may take all reasonable care to prevent any interference to the neighbour, s/he would still be liable. This is kept 'under control' by the principle that a defendant is not liable for actions a reasonable user takes on his land. This means that if the use is reasonable, the defendant will not be liable for loss of his enjoyment of his land; but if the user is not reasonable, the defendant will be liable, even though he or she may have taken reasonable care and skill to avoid it.

The claimant in a nuisance action will not have to prove that the neighbour was at fault. However where the claimant alleges malice on the part of the neighbour, as in *Hollywood Silver Fox Farm v Emmett* (1936) or *Christie v Davey* (1893), the defendant's deliberate actions will be evidence of his fault.

Tip

Identify how many people are affected by the activity in the scenario to decide whether the action is a public or private nuisance.

Activity

Consider whether any defence to a claim for nuisance is possible in the following situations:

1   The noise from a busy railway line distresses homeowners living in houses next to the railway line.
2   Burglars break into Ravinder's home while he is spending six months in India and leave his radio, TV and hi-fi all playing on maximum volume.
3   Anna lives in a block of flats in the flat beneath Roger. Anna is very distressed because she has to get up at 6 a.m. to go to work, and when Roger returns from his work at around 1 a.m. she can hear his footsteps walking around for hours after.
4   Residents of a small estate want to have a nearby local authority playground shut down because of the noise from children playing.
5   For more than 15 years, Archie has kept pigs in his back yard. His neighbour Reggie eventually objects to the smell.

Case	Facts	Legal principle
Sedleigh Denfield v O'Callaghan (1940)	A pipe, laid by the local authority, but on the defendant's land, was blocked flooding the neighbouring land.	An occupier who knows of a danger and allows it to continue is liable in nuisance, even if s/he has not created the danger him/herself.
Leakey v National Trust (1980)	There was a large natural mound on a hillside on the defendants' land. They were aware that it could slip and following a hot summer it did slip, damaging the claimant's cottage.	A landowner could be liable in nuisance if he or she knows a slippage might happen and fails to prevent it.
Hunter v Canary Wharf Ltd (1997)	Residents in Docklands complained of interference with TV reception when Canary Wharf was being built.	The loss of a recreational facility is not sufficient interference to give rise to an action in nuisance. Only those with an interest in the land, not members of families, have a right to bring an action in nuisance
Crown River Cruises Ltd v Kimbolton Fireworks Ltd (1996)	A river barge was set alight by flammable debris, from a 20-minute firework display.	Even a short-term activity can amount to a nuisance.
Robinson v Kilvert (1889)	Paper boxes were stored in hot and dry conditions which caused paper stored above them to dry out.	If the claimant is unduly sensitive, a nuisance will not be found.
Christie v Davey (1893)	The defendant was annoyed by his neighbour's music and deliberately banged trays on the walls, blew whistles and shouted to disturb the neighbours.	The defendant's deliberate and malicious behaviour amounted to a nuisance
Miller v Jackson (1977)	The claimants' use of their garden was disrupted by cricket balls being hit into it from the adjoining recreation ground.	The use of a sports ground and its benefit to the community was balanced against the claimants' use of their garden. The community use outweighed the private use.
Sturges v Bridgman (1879)	A doctor built consulting rooms in his garden on the boundary to a sweet factory. He complained of vibrations from machinery.	The defence of prescription failed as the nuisance began when the consulting room was built. The period before the building was erected did not count.
Allen v Gulf Oil Refining (1981)	Residents near an oil refinery brought a nuisance as the defendants did not have express permission to operate it.	The refinery had statutory authority to operate as this must have been Parliament's intention.
Gillingham Borough Council v Medway (Chatham) Dock Co. (1993)	Planning permission was granted to use a dockyard as a commercial port but nuisance was caused when lorries accessed the port.	As the character of the neighbourhood had been changed by planning permission, what could have previously been a nuisance could now be considered reasonable.
Coventry v Lawrence (2014)	Planning permission had been given for speedway and later for other motor sports. A claim of noise nuisance was made limiting the use of the track.	The Supreme Court decided the rule in *Sturges v Bridgman* about the character of neighbourhood still applies.

Figure 10.5 Key cases on private nuisance

Public nuisance

- Public nuisance is something which affects the reasonable comfort and convenience of a class of Her Majesty's subjects.
- There is no minimum number of a class.
- Only those who have suffered over and above that of the general public can sue. They do not need to have an interest in the land affected.
- The defendant will be the person who caused the nuisance or who allowed it to continue.
- Claims can be made for an injunction to stop the nuisance continuing or damages for damage to property or personal injury.

Private nuisance

- Private nuisance is 'an unlawful (unreasonable) interference with a person's use or enjoyment of land coming from neighbouring land'.
- Any person with an interest in the land affected can claim.
- The defendant will be the person who caused the nuisance or who allowed it to continue.
- The court will take various factors into account when considering if the defendant's activities are reasonable.
- Factors include the character of the neighbourhood, duration, sensitivity of the claimant, malice and social benefit.
- Defendants can argue defences such as prescription and statutory permission but moving to the nuisance is not an arguable defence.
- Courts have a wider discretion then in the past when ordering remedy. Damages may be considered more widely than in the past as an appropriate remedy.

Chapter 11

Torts connected to land: *Rylands v Fletcher*

> After reading this chapter you should be able to:
> - Understand the tort of *Rylands v Fletcher*
> - Evaluate the law relating to this tort
> - Apply the law to factual situations

11.1 The development of strict liability

This strict liability tort was developed in the case of *Rylands v Fletcher* (1868) (see later for the facts). Blackburn said in the Court of Exchequer Chamber:

> **"** We think that the true rule of law is, that the person who, for purposes of his own, brings on his land and keeps there anything likely to do mischief if it escapes, must keep it in at his peril, and, if he does not do so, he is prima facie answerable for all the damage which is the natural consequence of its escape. **"**

This definition contains the major requirements of the tort. Lord Cairns then added, in the appeal to the House of Lords, the further requirement that, for the claimant to succeed, *D must have brought/accumulated something in the course of some 'unnatural' use of the land.* In other words there must be a 'non-natural' use of land.

> ### Key term 🔑
>
> *Rylands v Fletcher* – where a person's property is damaged or destroyed by the escape of non-naturally stored material onto adjoining property.

Traditionally, it could be said that the liability was strict because there was no particular requirement to show fault, and the defendant could be made liable even if they had taken care to avoid the escape. The tort was also originally distinguished from nuisance because of the requirement in nuisance that harm of the type caused by the nuisance should be foreseeable, but no such requirement is apparent in *Rylands v Fletcher* (1868).

This is not now the case since the House of Lords in *Cambridge Water Co. v Eastern Counties Leather plc* (1994) identified the tort as a type of nuisance, and subject to the same test of foreseeability.

11.2 Essential elements of the tort

There are essentially four elements that must be proved in order for there to be a successful claim under the tort of *Rylands v Fletcher* (1868):
- the bringing onto the land and an accumulation (or storage)
- of a thing likely to cause mischief if it escapes
- which amounts to a non-natural use of the land, and
- which does escape and causes reasonably foreseeable damage to adjoining property.

In the case of *Rylands v Fletcher*, all the elements were present and the defendants were liable.

> ### Case study
>
> #### *Rylands v Fletcher* (1868)
>
> The defendant, a mill owner, hired contractors to create a reservoir on his land to act as a water supply to the mill. The contractors negligently failed to block off disused mineshafts that they came across during their excavations. Unknown to the contractors, these shafts were connected to other mine works on adjoining land. When the reservoir was filled, water then flooded the neighbouring mines.

A disused water mill wheel, England

There was a bringing onto land and storage of water; a large volume of water which could do damage if it escaped. This storage amounted to a non-natural use of land. The water did escape through the mineshafts, causing considerable damage to the claimant.

11.3 The parties to an action

11.3.1 Potential claimants

It has traditionally been thought that a person who can take an action has to have an interest in the land affected. This means that s/he must own the land or rent it or have some sort of property interest in it.

11.3.2 Potential defendants

According to Viscount Simon's test in *Read v Lyons* (1947), a defendant to an action in *Rylands v Fletcher* (1868) will be either the owner or occupier of land who satisfies the four ingredients of the tort, all of which must be present for liability. It is assumed that the defendant must have some control over the land on which the material is stored.

11.3.3 The bringing onto the land

There must be a bringing onto land of a substance. If the thing in question is already naturally present on the land, then there can be no liability. So in *Giles v Walker* (1890) there was no liability when weeds spread onto neighbouring land as they were naturally growing.

There cannot be liability for a thing that naturally accumulates on the land. So in *Ellison v Ministry of Defence* (1997), rainwater that accumulated naturally

on an airfield at Greenham Common did not lead to liability when it escaped and caused flooding on neighbouring land.

11.3.4 The thing is likely to do mischief if it escapes

The thing which the defendant brings onto his land must be likely to do damage if it escapes. This is a test of foreseeability. It is not the escape that must be foreseeable – only that damage is foreseeable, if the thing brought onto land does escape.

Examples of things which courts have decided can do mischief are:
- gas and electricity
- poisonous fumes
- a flag pole
- tree branches, and
- an occupied chair from a chair-o-plane ride.

Case study

Hale v Jennings Bros (1938)

A 'chair-o-plane' car on a fairground ride became detached from the main assembly while in motion and injured a stallholder as it crashed to the ground. The owner of the ride was liable as the risk of injury was foreseeable if the car came loose. This is one of the few cases where a claim for personal injury using *Rylands v Fletcher* was successful. Note that in *Transco plc v Stockport Metropolitan Borough Council* (2003), the House of Lords commented, obiter, that it is not now possible to claim for personal injury under the tort.

A chair-o-plane ride

There are two recent examples of *Rylands v Fletcher* actions based on damage caused by fire. The first is *LMS International Ltd v Styrene Packaging and Insulation Ltd* (2005) where the claimant was successful. The second is *Stannard (t/a Wyvern Tyres) v Gore* (2012) where the claimant was successful at trial but the decision was reversed on appeal.

Case studies

LMS International Ltd v Styrene Packaging and Insulation Ltd (2005)

A fire started in the defendant's factory which contained a large quantity of flammable material. The fire service arrived within five minutes of being called. Despite this, the fire spread to the claimant's adjoining property causing it to be damaged. The claimant brought an action based on *Rylands v Fletcher*, nuisance and negligence.

The defendant was held liable in *Rylands v Fletcher* as it had accumulated things which were a known fire risk. They were stored in a position close to hot wire cutting machines which made ignition more likely and where any fire was likely to spread. The storage represented a recognisable risk to the claimant and a non-natural user of the land. The defendant was also liable in negligence and nuisance.

Stannard (t/a Wyvern Tyres) v Gore (2012)

The defendant stored tyres in relation to his tyre fitting business. A fire ignited and spread rapidly causing damage to the claimant's adjoining premises. The trial judge found that the defendant was not negligent, but was strictly liable in *Rylands v Fletcher*.

The judge found that tyres are not in themselves normally flammable, but they did have a special fire risk so that if a fire did develop the tyres might ignite; and if they did they may burn rapidly and intensely. Further, the tyres were stored in a haphazard manner and in a large quantity (approximately 3000) for the size of the premises. In this case the storage of tyres, in this particular situation, presented an exceptionally high risk of danger, and was a non-natural use of land.

However the Court of Appeal disagreed. The majority reasoning was that in light of *Transco v Stockport Metropolitan Borough Council* (2003), it was not possible for a *Rylands v Fletcher* claim here. In their view it is an essential requirement of the tort that the defendant has brought some exceptionally dangerous 'thing' onto his land, and that thing must escape causing damage. In this case, where the fire had escaped but not the tyres, a claim based on *Rylands v Fletcher* must fail. In any event the tyres were not exceptionally dangerous or mischievous.

Further, the commercial activity carried on by the defendant as a motor tyre supplier was a perfectly ordinary and reasonable activity to be carried on in a light industrial estate, and was not therefore a non-natural use of the land for the purposes of the rule in *Rylands v Fletcher*.

In *Wyvern*, Ward LJ concluded that in an appropriate case, damage caused by fire moving from an adjoining property can fall within a *Rylands v Fletcher* claim, but the appropriate case is likely to be very rare, because:

1. It is the 'thing' which had been brought onto the land which must escape, not the fire which was started or increased by the 'thing'.

2. While fire may be a dangerous thing, the occasions when fire as such is brought onto the land may be limited to cases where the fire has been deliberately or negligently started by the occupier or one for whom he is responsible.

3. In any event starting a fire on one's land may well be an ordinary use of the land.

Wyvern will have significant implications for damage by fire claims. In particular, it is clear from Ward LJ's comments that it will now be very difficult for a claimant to succeed in such cases without proof of negligence.

A non-natural use of land

Lord Cairns in the House of Lords in *Rylands v Fletcher* (1868) indicated the requirement of a non-natural use of land. He said:

> if the defendants, not stopping at the natural use of their close, had desired to use it for any purpose which I may term a non-natural use ... and in consequence of doing so ... the water came to escape ... then it appears to me that that which the defendants were doing they were doing at their own peril.

This concept of non-natural use was developed and explained by Lord Moulton in *Rickards v Lothian* (1913):

> it is not every use of land which brings into play this principle. It must be some special use bringing with it increased danger to others, and not merely by the ordinary use of land or such a use as is proper for the general benefit of the community.

Non-natural use of land is clearly a complex concept, and one which inevitably changes to take into account technological change and changes in lifestyle. It is inconceivable for instance that leaving a car garaged with petrol in the tank could be seen as a non-natural use of land today, though it was seen as such in 1919 at the time of *Musgrove v Pandelis* (1919).

Case law suggests that 'non-natural' refers to some extraordinary or some unusual use of land. In general, storage of things associated with the domestic use of land will not normally be classified as non-natural even though they may be potentially hazardous. The following have been decided by courts as being a natural use of land:

- a fire in a grate which spread to the claimant's premises
- defective electric wiring that caused a fire which spread to the claimant's premises
- a domestic water supply.

However, courts have been prepared to accept that certain activities may always lead to a potential level of danger, so that amounts to a non-natural use of land whatever the benefit to the public derived from the activity that has led to the danger. However, in *Cambridge Water Co. v Eastern Counties Leather plc* (1994) the storage of chemicals in a factory was a classic example of a non-natural use of land. Just because the activity was an important source of local employment did not make the storage a natural use of land.

11.3.5 The thing stored must escape and cause foreseeable damage

The stored item must escape from one property onto an adjoining property. Note the comments in *Wyvern*, above, where the Court of Appeal observed that it was not the fire that should escape but the stored tyres to come within the tort.

Note that this rule is not always strictly applied, as in *Hale v Jennings Bros* (1938) both stalls operated on the same piece of land and neither stallholder owned the land. Yet liability was imposed.

The House of Lords in *Transco plc v Stockport Metropolitan Borough Council* (2003) reviewed the past case law on the issue of escape and approved the line taken in *Read v Lyons*. This was on the basis that the court felt that the tort, being a specific form of nuisance, required a proprietary interest in land by the claimant.

Storage of non-naturally occurring material on land controlled by the defendant

Material is likely to cause damage if it escapes

Material escapes onto adjoining property

Material causes reasonably foreseeable damage to the adjoining land

Figure 11.1 Diagram showing ingredients of *Rylands v Fletcher* action

Extension question

Phil runs a microbrewery from a unit on an industrial estate. One evening his apprentice leaves the boiler running, causing the brew to overheat and overflow. A considerable quantity of beer escapes into the adjoining bakery unit owned by Mac. As a result several sacks of hops and malt were damaged.

Advise Mac whether he can take a *Rylands v Fletcher* action against Phil for the damage to the hops and malt.

Discuss advantages and disadvantages of making a claim in *Rylands v Fletcher* as opposed to making a claim in negligence.

11.4 Defences

Despite the tort being described as strict liability, many defences are possible in the event of a claim.

- *Volenti non fit injuria* (consent) – there will be no liability where the claimant has consented to the thing that is accumulated by the defendant.
- Act of a stranger – if a stranger over whom the defendant has no control has been the cause of the escape causing the damage, then the defendant may not be liable.

Case study

Perry v Kendricks Transport Ltd (1956)

The defendants parked their bus on their parking space, having drained the tank of petrol. A stranger removed the petrol cap and a child was injured when another child threw a match into the tank which ignited fumes. A claim was made in *Rylands v Fletcher*. There was a valid defence of an act of a stranger and no liability.

- Act of God – this defence may succeed where there are extreme weather conditions that 'no human foresight can provide against'. It is only likely to succeed if there are unforeseeable weather conditions.

Case study

Nichols v Marsland (1876)

The defendant made three artificial ornamental lakes by damming a natural stream. Freak thunderstorms accompanied by torrential rain broke the banks of the artificial lakes, which caused the destruction of bridges on the claimant's land. There was no liability because the weather conditions were so extreme and amounted to an Act of God.

- Statutory authority – if the terms of an Act of Parliament authorise the defendant's action, this may amount to a defence.
- Contributory negligence – where the claimant is partly responsible for the escape of the thing, then the Law Reform (Contributory Negligence) Act 1945 applies and damages may be reduced according to the amount of the claimant's fault.

11.5 Remedies

A claimant must show damage to, or destruction of, his property in order to succeed in a claim for damages. The level of damages will be the cost of repair or replacement of the property damaged or destroyed.

11.6 Evaluation

When *Rylands v Fletcher* was first decided, there was a view that it was a broad, strict liability action covering both damage to property and personal injury. However as time went by, the courts, as seen in cases such as *Rickards v Lothian*, took a restrictive approach and claimants were encouraged to use the tort of negligence, even though it required the proof of fault. As a strict liability tort, where fault does not have to be proved, it should have been easier for a claimant to prove *Rylands v Fletcher* action than using the alternative of negligence. However, unlike some other strict liability actions, it allows a number of defences which limit its usefulness.

There are other factors which make the tort difficult to prove. Lord Cairns added the requirement that there be a non-natural use of land. So the simplest way to defeat a claim is to show that the use of land in question is a natural use.

Moreover, judges have shown hostility to the general principle of strict liability in the tort and have restricted the application of the rule still further:

- First, according to *Read v Lyons* (1947), there can only be liability if the thing brought onto the defendant's land escapes from that land.
- Second, according to *Rickards v Lothian* (1913), there must be a 'special use of land bringing with it increased danger to others'.
- Third, the recent return to foreseeability of type of damage, as in *Cambridge Water Co. v Eastern Counties Leather plc* (1994).

Over the years there have been calls for *Rylands v Fletcher* to be abolished as an action altogether. For example, the Pearson Commission report in 1978 recommended it should be replaced with a statutory scheme for injuries suffered in hazardous activities which required those who engaged in them to pay compensation for injuries caused in true strict liability fashion. This approach has been developed by Parliament, which has developed a number of specific, true strict liability actions, which may reflect the increasing technology present in today's society. These actions include the Reservoirs Act 1975, when water has been accumulated, the Nuclear Installations Acts 1965 and 1969, which cover the escape of radioactive substances, and even the Health and Safety at Work Act 1974. A claimant would be encouraged to use a specific action under one of these statutes rather than a *Rylands v Fletcher* action.

The House of Lords took the opportunity to review the use of the tort in the case of *Transco v Stockport Metropolitan Borough Council* (2003). In the nuisance case of *Hunter v Canary Wharf Ltd* (1997) it was doubted whether personal injury was recoverable in private nuisance and so it is unlikely now to be possible in *Rylands v Fletcher*.

Case study

Transco v Stockport Metropolitan Borough Council (2003)

The council was responsible for a high pressure water pipe supplying multi-storey flats. The pipe had leaked over time and caused an embankment to collapse, exposing the claimant's gas pipeline and leaving it in a dangerous condition. The claimant sought the cost of repairs from the council. The House of Lords held that there was no accumulation of a thing likely to cause mischief if it escaped, and that also the use of land by the council was a normal use.

In the case the Lords were invited to consider whether there was still a need for a *Rylands v Fletcher* tort or whether claims for damage caused by the movement of material from one property to another should be made using negligence.

Lord Bingham considered that:

- there are still cases deserving compensation in the absence of fault – this included the *Cambridge Water* case,
- Parliament has legislated to allow strict liability claims in certain areas because of the existence of the rule in *Rylands v Fletcher*,
- the House of Lords was invited in the *Cambridge Water* case to dispense with *Rylands v Fletcher* but did not do so; there should be a consistency of approach, and
- introducing a fault-based approach would bring English law in line with Scotland but it would be different from other systems such as in France and Germany. He was inclined to follow a wider approach of consistency.

In conclusion he considered that the test of use of the land from where the thing escaped should be that of 'ordinary user' as opposed to 'natural user'; this makes it clear that the rule in *Rylands v Fletcher* is engaged only where the defendant's use is shown to be extraordinary and unusual. What amounts to an ordinary user will have to be considered in each case.

Lord Hoffman considered that even though there are restrictions on the operation of the rule and there are very few cases where it has proved to be successfully used, it was not the role of the House of Lords to remove a rule that had been in operation for over 150 years.

Lord Hobhouse considered that the rule (as a branch of nuisance) should not be repealed. He considered that the rationale for it was and remains valid. The content of the rule was, in his view, clearly spelled out in the original case. In his view the academic and judicial criticisms of the rule are largely the result of later confusions. The rule allows for sufficient control mechanisms to be allowed to continue in existence.

So, as a result of the judgments in this case, the tort only applies when the defendant's use of land is extraordinary or unusual in the particular circumstances and at the particular point in time. An interest in the land affected by the escaping material is needed and personal injury is not within the scope of a claim. Overall the House rejected the idea of abandoning the tort or that it should be treated as having been absorbed within the general law of negligence.

Case	Facts	Legal principle
Rylands v Fletcher (1868)	The defendant made a reservoir as a water supply for his mill. Mineshafts were not blocked off causing flooding to a mine.	A claim could be made if material was brought onto land and stored, it was likely to cause mischief if it escapes, which amounted to a non-natural use of the land, and which escaped.
Rickards v Lothian (1913)	An unknown person turned on water taps and blocked plugholes causing damage to the flat below.	There has to be a non-natural use of the land – not present in this case as domestic pipes were a natural use of land.
Read v Lyons (1947)	An explosion took place in a munitions factory, causing injury.	The material has to escape from one property onto adjoining property – no liability here as there was no escape.
Cambridge Water Co. v Eastern Counties Leather (1994)	Stored chemicals seeped through the concrete floor of a factory into the soil below, polluting an area where water was extracted.	Damage has to be reasonably foreseeable and not too remote from the escape.

Figure 11.2 Key cases for the tort of *Rylands v Fletcher*

Summary

- The tort of *Rylands v Fletcher* was developed in the case of the same name.
- It was a strict liability tort, providing a claim could be made if material was brought onto land and stored, it was likely to cause mischief if it escapes, which amounted to a non-natural use of the land, and which escaped causing damage to adjoining land.
- A person who can take an action has to have an interest in the land affected.
- A defendant will be the owner or occupier who satisfies the four ingredients of the tort, and he or she must have some control over the land on which the material is stored.
- The storage of material which escapes must be a non-natural use of the land.
- The material must escape from one property onto adjoining property.
- The damage caused to the adjoining property has to be reasonably foreseeable.
- Various defences are available including act of a stranger, act of God, statutory authority to storage, consent and contributory negligence.
- The claimant can claim damages for the cost of repairing his property.

Chapter 12

Vicarious liability

After reading this chapter, you should be able to:
- Understand the nature and purpose of vicarious liability
- Understand liability for employees, including testing employment status and torts in or not in the course of employment
- Understand liability for the crimes of employees and liability for independent contractors
- Evaluate the law relating to this liability
- Apply the law to factual situations

12.1 The nature and purpose of vicarious liability

Vicarious liability is not an individual tort claim such as a claim for negligence or nuisance. It is a way of imposing liability for a tort onto someone who did not commit the tort.

It was originally based on the idea that an employer has control over his employees at work, and should therefore be responsible for any torts committed by the employee at work.

In a less sophisticated society, with less diverse types of work, control by an employer was more possible. Modern methods of employment and the different possible locations where work can be carried out make an employer's control of employees less clear. For example, the work done by a surgeon at a hospital cannot be said to be under the control of a manager with no medical expertise. Should an employer be responsible for the actions of an employee who is working from home?

However, it is important to understand the reasons for the development of this liability, as most examples of it will exist in an employment relationship.

The rule can be criticised for applying liability unfairly as an apparently innocent party is liable for something which he or she has not personally done or failed to do. It also imposes liability when the employer has not been directly at fault and is an example of strict (or no fault) liability.

However, the liability is justified for the following reasons, which mainly ensure that the victim of a tort is able to receive compensation for the injury or damage suffered:
- Traditionally, an employer may have had a greater degree of control over the activities of employees in the workplace. Indeed, it may well be that an employee has carried out the instructions of the employer which led to the tort. In this case it is only fair that the employer should bear the cost of the employee's actions.
- Employers are responsible for hiring, firing and disciplining their staff. An employer may have been careless in selecting staff, and, if employees are either careless or likely to cause harm, and the employer is aware of this, the employer has the ability to do something about it. Internal disciplinary systems allow the employer to ensure that lapses of behaviour are not repeated. There is the ultimate sanction of dismissing a member of staff who refuses to, or is unable to follow set procedures.
- An employer is responsible for making sure that all employees are trained so that work is done safely and that safe procedures are followed.
- The major concern of a victim is whether they will receive compensation and whether the defendant is worth suing. An employer will usually be in a better financial position to pay than one of his employees. In addition, an employer is required to take out public liability insurance to cover, among other things, injuries in the workplace.

Key term 🔑

Vicarious liability – where a third person has legal responsibility for the unlawful actions of another. It is commonly seen in the workplace where the employer is responsible for the actions of an employee who acted in the course of their employment.

There are two main tests required to prove vicarious liability:

- Was the person alleged to have committed the tort an employee? Generally there will be no vicarious liability for the tort committed by an independent contractor who will be legally responsible for his own actions.
- Did the employee commit the alleged tort 'during the course of his employment'?

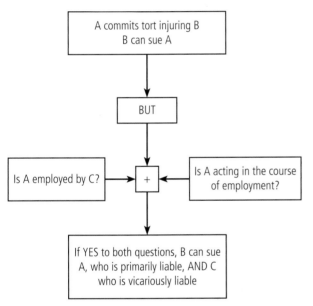

Figure 12.1 The operation of vicarious liability

12.2 Liability for employees

12.2.1 Testing employment status

The old test of employment was whether a person was providing a contract of service – in which case he or she would be an employee – or a contract for services – in which case he or she would be an independent contractor (see section 12.5 below). An employer can be vicariously liable for the actions of his employees, but not an independent contractor.

It is not always possible to easily decide whether a person is employed or an independent contractor and different tests may be used according to who is doing the testing. For example, the only concern of HM Revenue and Customs is to decide liability for payment of tax and not for any other purpose. So the fact that a person is paying Schedule D tax, or is subject to self-assessment, is not necessarily a legal test of self-employed status. Health and Safety inspectors may have less concern with the status of an injured victim and more with any regulations that have been broken.

Various different forms of working relationships have developed in recent times which may not fit into traditional definitions. Full-time and part-time work will often indicate employment, but what of casual, temporary or seasonal work or 'zero hours' contracts? And what of workers carrying out internships or volunteering? Should an employer be legally responsible then?

Over the years the courts have developed several methods of testing employee status.

The control test

The oldest of these is the 'control test'. In *Yewens v Noakes* (1880) the test was whether the master (the employer) had the right to control what the employee did and the way in which it was done. According to McArdie J in *Performing Rights Society v Mitchell and Booker* (1924), the test concerns 'the nature and degree of detailed control'.

Lord Thankerton in *Short v J W Henderson Ltd* (1946) identified many key features which would show that the master had control over the servant. These included the power to select the servant, the right to control the method of working, the right to suspend and dismiss, and the payment of wages.

Such a test is virtually impossible to apply accurately today. Nevertheless, there are circumstances in which a test of control is still useful, in the case of borrowed workers.

A more recent development of the control test concerns the activities of bouncers.

The integration or organisation test

Lord Denning in *Stevenson Jordan and Harrison Ltd v McDonald and Evans* (1969) established this test. It provides that a worker will be an employee if his work is fully integrated into the business. If a person's work is only accessory to the business, that person is not an employee.

According to this test, the master of a ship, a chauffeur and a reporter on the staff of a newspaper are all employees. On the other hand the pilot bringing a ship into port, a taxi driver and a freelance writer are not employees.

The test can work well in some cases but there are still problems. Teachers who are examiners for exam boards may be classed as employed persons as tax and pension contributions may be deducted, but the terms of contracts specify that examiners are not to be considered as employees and there are no rights to dismissal or redundancy pay when their services are no longer required.

The economic reality or multiple test

In view of problems with these two tests, courts recognise that a single test of employment status is not satisfactory and may produce confusing results. This test considers various factors which may indicate employment or self-employment. It was established in *Ready Mixed Concrete (South East) Ltd v Minister of Pensions and National Insurance* (1968).

The test has been updated so that all factors in the relationship should be considered and weighed according to their significance. They might include:

- the ownership of any tools, plant or equipment – an employee is less likely to own the plant and equipment used at work
- the method of payment – a self-employed person is likely to take a payment for a whole job where an employee will usually receive regular payments (salary) for the period of employment
- if tax, National Insurance and pension contributions are deducted from an employee's wages. A self-employed person will have to submit self-assessments and pay tax annually under Schedule D
- any description of role – a person may describe himself as an employee or as self-employed. This will usually, but not always, be an accurate description
- any independence in doing a job – probably one of the most important tests of self-employed status is the amount of independence and flexibility in being able to take work from different sources, and when to do it.

All of these factors are useful in identifying the status of the worker, but none are an absolute test or are definitive on their own and cases can still bring conflicting decisions. For example, in *Carmichael v National Power* (2001) tour guides employed on a casual basis were not employees as there was no formal contractual arrangement between the parties. In *Ferguson v Dawson* (1976) there was a contract which stated that a building labourer was self-employed, but the court decided he was employed and the employers were required to protect him under safety laws.

12.2.2 Recent developments

A number of cases have reached the appeal courts in recent years testing whether the tortfeasor was an employee or not. There was often no traditional employment relationship and it had to be decided whether 'the employer' should be vicariously liable. Several of the cases involved claims of historic abuse.

Case studies

McE v De La Salle Brothers (2007)

In *McE v De La Salle Brothers* (2007) (a Scottish case), the claimant claimed damages for physical abuse to which he had been subjected by a De La Salle brother, while he attended their school. This was a test case as there were some 150 other potential claims depending on this decision. The court held that there was no basis upon which the allegation of vicarious liability could succeed, and the claim was dismissed.

E v English Province of Our Lady of Charity (2012)

The claimant alleged that she had been sexually abused by a nun in charge of a children's home and by a visiting priest. The question for the court was whether they were employees and if the bishop of the diocese could be vicariously liable for their actions.

The Court of Appeal stated that the court was required to look for:

1. a relationship akin (or similar) to employment
2. which was established by a connection between a putative defendant and an 'actor' which was sufficiently close, so that
3. it was fair and just to impose liability on the defendant.

Several questions could be considered which might point to vicarious liability:

1. control by the 'employer' of the 'employee'
2. control by the contractor of himself
3. the organisation test (how central was the activity to the organisation?)
4. the integration test (whether the activity was integrated into the organisational structure of the enterprise), and
5. the entrepreneur test (whether the person was in business on his own account).

Applying such tests to the facts of the case, the majority decided that the priest was more like an employee than an independent contractor, and he had been in a relationship with his bishop which was close enough and so akin (similar) to that of employer/employee as to make it just and fair to impose vicarious liability.

JGE v Trustees of the Portsmouth Roman Catholic Diocesan Trust (2012)

The claimant alleged that, when she was very young, she was sexually abused and raped by a Roman Catholic priest while living in a children's home. She brought an action against the church for the acts of the priest. The church argued that it was not liable for the acts of the priest as he was not an employee, only an office holder following his vocation and not subject to the level of control required to demonstrate an employment relationship.

➜

The Court of Appeal held that, even though the priest was not an employee of the church, his relationship with the church was sufficiently akin (close) to one of employment that it was fair and just to hold the church vicariously liable for damages as a result of his conduct. The court held that this test was met in the case of the priest performing his duties within the context of the Roman Catholic Church. The court based its holding on an analysis of several factors, including the level of control and supervision exercised by the church and the role of the priest within the organisational structure of the church.

Catholic Child Welfare Society v Various Claimants (FC) and the Institute of the Brothers of the Christian Schools (2012)

A group of 170 men alleged that they were physically and sexually abused by their teachers while living at a school for boys in need of care. The teachers were members of the Brothers of the Christian Schools (the 'Institute'), a religious organisation that sent its members to the school as part of its mission to 'teach children, especially poor children, those things which pertain to a good and Christian life'. The members had contracts of employment with the school. The court had to decide whether the Institute could be held liable for the abuse perpetrated by its members. The school argued that the Institute should share responsibility for the acts of its members. The Institute responded that only a body managing a school and employing a brother in that school as a teacher should be vicariously liable for his wrongdoing.

The court held that the Institute could be held liable for the alleged sexual abuse committed by its members because the relationship between the Institute and its members was sufficiently akin to one of employer and employee, and there was a close connection between that relationship and the sexual abuse allegedly committed by the brothers while teaching in the school.

The court examined the school's claim against the Institute under a two part test: (1) whether the relationship between the Institute and its members was capable of giving rise to vicarious liability, and (2) whether the alleged acts of sexual abuse were connected to that relationship in such a way as to give rise to vicarious liability.

The court held that the first element of vicarious liability can be based on a relationship that, while not arising under a formal contract of employment, is sufficiently 'akin to that between an employer and an employee'. The court explained that the Institute's relationship with its members was sufficiently akin to one of employment based on the hierarchical structure of the Institute, the ability of the Institute to direct where its members taught, the importance of teaching activity in the organisation's mission, and the manner in which its members were bound by its rules. The second element was also satisfied based on the close connection between the Institute's relationship with its members, and the alleged sexual abuse its members committed while pursuing their mission to provide an education to vulnerable students living on the premises of the school.

As a result, the court decided that the Institute should be responsible for the acts of its members even though they were employees of the school.

In *Mohamud v Morrison's Supermarkets plc* (2016) (see below) Lord Toulson in the Supreme Court restated the test of whether the tortfeasor is employed or not as follows:

> 44. In the simplest terms, the court has to consider two matters. The first question is what functions or 'field of activities' have been entrusted by the employer to the employee, or, in everyday language, what was the nature of his job. As has been emphasised in several cases, this question must be addressed broadly ...
>
> 45. Secondly, the court must decide whether there was sufficient connection between the position in which he was employed and his wrongful conduct to make it right for the employer to be held liable under the principle of social justice ...

The case of *Cox v Ministry of Justice* (2016) was heard alongside *Mohamud*.

Case study

Cox v Ministry of Justice (2016)

The claimant was employed in a prison as a catering manager. She was negligently injured by a prisoner who dropped a sack of rice on her back. She claimed compensation from the Ministry of Justice. At first instance, the court held that the Ministry of Justice was not vicariously liable for the negligence of the prisoner. However, the Court of Appeal disagreed, stating that the relationship between the prisoner and the prison service was similar to that of employer and employee. The Supreme Court agreed noting that:

> a relationship other than one of employment is in principle capable of giving rise to vicarious liability where harm is wrongfully done by an individual who carries on activities as an integral part of the business activities carried on by a defendant and for its benefit (rather than his activities being entirely attributable to the conduct of a recognisably independent business of his own or of a third party)...

In other words, the Supreme Court recognised that today many workers may, in reality, be part of the workforce of an organisation without having a contract of employment with that organisation. Further, the word 'business' did not necessarily require the carrying out of commercial activities, nor the pursuit of profit. It was enough here that the prison carried on activities in the furtherance of its own interests; in this case, rehabilitating prisoners.

The most recent case following *Mohamud* is *Fletcher v Chancery Supplies Ltd* (2017).

Case study

Fletcher v Chancery Supplies Ltd (2017)

The claimant, who was a police officer, was riding his police issue mountain bike along a cycle lane alongside a busy main road. A man, T, suddenly emerged from behind a stationary van on the road and collided with the claimant in the cycle lane. The claimant fell to the floor and suffered severe leg injuries.

T had been working that morning, was wearing a work polo shirt and work boots, and told attending police officers, 'I have attempted to cross the road to where my shop is' and he had given the shop as his home address. At trial the judge found T's employer vicariously liable.

Applying the questions in *Mohamud*, the Court of Appeal decided that, as there was no explanation why T had previously left the shop, there was no sufficient connection between his work and him causing the accident to make T's employer vicariously liable.

The principles from these cases will apply when it is not obvious that the tortfeasor is an employee or not.

Case	Principles
E v English Province of Our Lady of Charity (2012)	The court has to look for: (i) a relationship akin (or similar) to employment, (ii) which was established by a sufficiently close connection so that (iii) it was fair and just to impose liability on the defendant.
JGE v Trustees of the Portsmouth Roman Catholic Diocesan Trust (2012)	Being an office holder, as opposed to an employee, could make the church vicariously liable for the actions of a priest as the priest's relationship with the church was sufficiently akin (close) to one of employment and it was fair and just to hold the church vicariously liable.
Catholic Child Welfare Society v Various Claimants (FC) and the Institute of the Brothers of the Christian Schools (2012)	Was the relationship between the Institute and its members akin to an employer and employee relationship, and was the sexual abuse connected to that relationship in such a way as to give rise to vicarious liability?
Mohamud v Morrison's Supermarkets plc (2016)	● What functions or 'field of activities' have been entrusted by the employer to the employee – what was the nature of his job? This question should be addressed broadly. ● Was there a sufficient connection between the position in which he was employed and his wrongful conduct to make it right for the employer to be held liable under the principle of social justice?
Cox v Ministry of Justice (2016)	Many workers today may be part of the workforce of an organisation without having a contract of employment with the organisation. It does not have to be carrying out a commercial activity or making a profit. It is enough for the organisation to carry on activities furthering its own interests.

Figure 12.2 Key cases on whether the tortfeasor is an employee or not

12.3 Can more than one employer be vicariously liable?

This was a question for the Court of Appeal in *Viasystems (Tyneside) Ltd v Thermal Transfer (Northern) Ltd* (2005).

Case study

Viasystems (Tyneside) Ltd v Thermal Transfer (Northern) Ltd (2005)

The claimants contracted with D1 to install air conditioning in their factory. D1 subcontracted some work to D2. D2 agreed with D3 to provide fitters and fitters' mates on a labour only basis. S was a fitter's mate who damaged some ducting that came into contact with a sprinkler which fractured causing a flood.

It had to be decided whether D2 or D3 were both vicariously liable for S's negligence.

The leading authority was *Mersey Docks and Harbour Board v Coggins & Griffith (Liverpool) Ltd* (1946). That case was authority for the principle that decisions as to employment depended on the particular facts but certain considerations might be relevant.

There was a long standing assumption, not a legal principle, that a finding of dual vicarious liability was not possible. The basis for the assumption appeared to be the idea that to find a temporary employer vicariously liable there would have to be a transfer of employment. The core question for the court was 'who was entitled and in theory obliged to control the employee's negligent act in order to prevent it'. There could be some cases in which the sensible answer would be each of two 'employers' so D2 and D3 were both liable.

Where there was dual vicarious liability arising out of the negligence of a single employee it followed that the responsibility of each employer for the purposes of contribution must be equal and D2 and D3 should each contribute 50 per cent to the claimant.

Activity

Complete a table of two columns showing whether the following aspects of work are characteristics of being employed or being an independent contractor (self-employed)?

- set hours of work
- use own tools or equipment in work
- paid a regular salary
- holiday is taken at time of choice
- manager directs how work is done
- keep own financial records
- health and safety training is provided
- tax and pension contributions are deducted
- send out invoices for work completed
- maternity/paternity leave is available
- can employ workers when required
- uniform is provided
- have own liability insurance policy
- have dismissal/redundancy rights
- provide a contract for services
- enter a contract of service.

In the news

Although not involving vicarious liability, the employment status of certain delivery drivers has recently been considered and whether they are entitled to the benefits of being employed.

Activity

K is a private hire driver working for a business providing a 24-hour service at an airport. The business has an exclusive contract with the airport to provide a taxi service. K owns and is responsible for his own vehicle, has to obtain an operating licence and pays his own tax and National Insurance. He collects fares from passengers, but pays a percentage of each fare to the business. K can work as and when he wishes.

Is K an employee of the business or an independent contractor?

Tip

If you are presented with a scenario in which vicarious liability is a possible issue, start by finding out whether the person who caused the injury is an employee. You can then consider the second part of liability – whether the employee is acting in the course of employment.

12.4 Acting in the course of employment

In order for the employer to be liable the employee has to commit the tort 'in the course of the employment'.

What is in the course of employment or not is a question of fact for the court to determine in each case. It is often difficult to see consistency in the judgments and recent judgments appear to be weighted in favour of claimants who have been injured by the employee.

Regardless of the reasoning applied in them, there are two lines of cases:
1. those where there is vicarious liability because the employee is acting in the course of the employment
2. those where there is no vicarious liability because the employee is said not to be in the course of employment.

12.4.1 Acting against orders

If the employee is doing his or her job but acts against orders in the way he or she does it, the employer can be liable for any tort committed by the employee.

Case study

Limpus v London General (1862)

The employer instructed its bus drivers not to race other drivers when collecting passengers. One driver caused an accident when racing. The employer was liable to the injured claimant as the driver was doing what he was employed to do – even against orders.

A more recent example is *Rose v Plenty* (1976).

Case study

Rose v Plenty (1976)

A dairy instructed its milkmen not to use child helpers on their milk rounds. One milkman did use a boy to help him but the boy was injured on the round due to the milkman's negligent driving of the electric milk float. The dairy was vicariously liable for the milkman's negligence as one judge suggested that the dairy was benefiting from the work done by the boy.

An electric milk float from the 1960s

However if the employee gives an unauthorised lift, the employer will not be liable.

Case study

Twine v Beans Express (1946)

The claimant's husband was killed through the negligence of a driver who had been forbidden to give lifts. This instruction was supported by notices on the side of the van stating who could be carried in it. The employers were not liable as the driver was doing an unauthorised act and the employers were gaining no benefit from it.

12.4.2 Acting outside employment

If the employee causes injury by doing something outside his employment, the employer will not be liable. This is shown in *Beard v London General Omnibus Co.* (1900).

Case study

Beard v London General Omnibus Co. (1900)

A bus conductor, employed to collect fares, drove a bus without the authority of his employer, injuring the claimant. The employer was not liable as the conductor was doing something outside the course of his employment.

12.4.3 Employee committing a criminal act

If the employee commits a crime during his work, the employer may be liable to the victim of the crime if there is a 'close connection' between the crime and what the employee was employed to do.

> ### Case study
>
> #### Lister v Hesley Hall (2001)
>
> The warden of a school for children with emotional difficulties sexually assaulted some of the children. He was convicted of criminal offences. The House of Lords decided there was a close connection between his job and what he did as the assaults were carried out on the school premises when he was looking after the children.

On the other hand, the fact that a police officer uses his uniform to gain the trust of a victim will not necessarily give rise to vicarious liability if the officer commits a crime. This was shown in *N v Chief Constable of Merseyside Police* (2006).

> ### Case studies
>
> #### N v Chief Constable of Merseyside Police (2006)
>
> Two hours after he had gone off duty, D was parked outside a club still in uniform. D offered to take to the police station a young woman, about whom a first aider from the club was worried, because the woman was very drunk and had taken the drug ecstasy. D, in fact, took the woman to his house where he committed various sexual assaults on her including rape. The court held that there was no close connection between his employment and the assaults. D had merely made use of his uniform to gain trust and abuse it. The Chief Constable was not liable for his officer's actions.
>
> #### Mattis v Pollock (2003)
>
> A bouncer was employed to keep order outside a nightclub. The bouncer inflicted serious injuries on a customer and was jailed for committing serious criminal offences. The nightclub was held vicariously liable for the bouncer's actions as he was encouraged to use force and to be violent and intimidating, and his criminal actions were closely connected to his work. The club was liable to pay damages to the injured claimant.

This principle of employees committing a criminal act has been looked at again in *Mohamud v Morrison's Supermarkets* (2016) by the Supreme Court.

> ### Case study
>
> #### Mohamud v Morrison's Supermarkets (2016)
>
> A man employed at the defendant's petrol station assaulted a customer, causing him serious injuries. The Supreme Court considered the job that had been given to the employee and whether there was a sufficient connection between the employee's job and what he did to the customer. The court decided that as the employee was acting within the field of his employment – it was at work, within working hours and there was a close connection between what he did and what he was required to do in his job – the employer was vicariously liable.

12.4.4 Employee committing a negligent act

If the employee does a job badly, the employer can be liable for his actions which cause injury to another. This was shown in *Century Insurance v Northern Ireland Road Transport Board* (1942).

> ### Case study
>
> #### Century Insurance v Northern Ireland Road Transport Board (1942)
>
> A petrol tanker driver was delivering petrol to a petrol station when he lit a cigarette and threw a lit match on the ground. This caused an explosion which destroyed several cars and damaged some houses. The employer was liable to pay compensation as the driver was doing his job, even though negligently.

12.4.5 Employee acting on a 'frolic' of their own

If the employee causes injury or damage to another while doing something, or at a time, outside the area or time of their work, the employer will not be liable.

Case studies

Hilton v Thomas Burton (Rhodes) Ltd (1961)

Some employees were working away from their workplace. They took an unauthorised break by driving the firm's van to a café for tea but had an accident on the way back. One of the workmen was killed and his widow sued the employer. The employers were not liable to pay compensation to the victim of the accident as the workmen were on an unauthorised 'frolic' of their own and not acting in the course of employment.

Smith v Stages (1989)

The employee was driving back to his place of work after working elsewhere and caused an accident. The employer was liable here because the court decided that he was acting in the course of employment as he was being paid during his travelling time.

If the tort is committed by an employee acting in the course of employment, the employer will be liable to pay compensation to the injured person. By the Civil Liability (Contribution) Act 1978 the employer can recover any compensation paid out from the employee by, for example, deduction from wages.

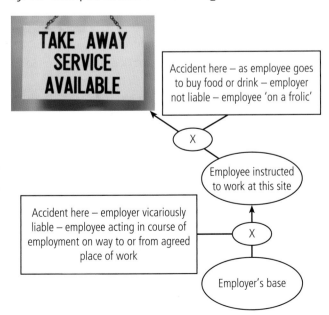

Figure 12.3 Acting 'on a frolic'

12.5 Liability for independent contractors

In section 12.2 above, we looked at the difference between a worker being an employee and an independent contractor. You will remember that an employee is employed under a contract of service and an independent contractor offers a contract for services.

The distinction is important because an employer can be vicariously liable for the actions of his employees, but an independent contractor, also known as a self-employed person, is legally responsible for his own actions and can be sued by the victim of a tort committed by him. An independent contractor should therefore have his own liability insurance cover and has limited employment rights. Whether or not a worker is an independent contractor is usually a question of fact.

Activity

Decide whether each of the following workers are employed or self-employed, giving reasons for your answers:

1 C is a caddie at a golf club. The club provides him with a number, a uniform and a clothes locker. Caddying work is allocated according to a strict rotation and at set rates. Caddies can choose when they work and there is no guarantee of work. The club charges members and passes payment to the caddies.

2 Q is a lap dancer performing for guests at a private member's club. She pays the club a fee for each night that she performs. In return, she decides for whom she dances, for how long and the fee.

3 M is a driver who owns his own car. He pays a mini-cab operator a weekly fee and in return has a radio installed and access to the computer system which allocates customers to drivers. He is required to wear a uniform and is prohibited from working for any other operator. He can choose when to work and for how long, and he keeps all the fares he collects.

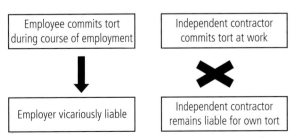

Figure 12.4 Employee and independent contractor liability

12.6 Evaluation of the tort of vicarious liability

1   A justification of vicarious liability is that it gives a victim a just and practical remedy – that, in the event of a successful claim, the claimant is more likely to receive compensation than if they pursued just the employee. This is because an employer is more likely than an employee to have the financial means to pay any award. In addition, and more likely, the employer will have liability insurance cover which will pay any damages awarded. These reasons justified the imposition of liability in *Limpus v London General* (1862) and *Rose v Plenty* (1976).

2   On the one hand, the principle of vicarious liability is justified as the employer is receiving a benefit from an employee's work and has to accept the liability of an employee's tortious action. However the principle appears to contradict the concept of fault-based liability. The employer may have taken all steps to choose, train and supervise its employees but will still be liable for their acts and omissions. The operation of the principle appears to be justified for the reason set out in point 1 above.

3   There have been some inconsistent and unfair decisions relating to road accidents and whether they were carried out in the course of employment. If an employee is acting 'on a frolic' as in *Hilton v Thomas Burton (Rhodes)* (1961) the victim, or the victim's relatives, will be unsuccessful in claiming compensation. This is obviously unfair as someone such as Mrs Hilton clearly suffered a loss, and her husband was killed in his work time and in the employer's van, but she was unsuccessful in proving vicarious liability.

   The decision in this case clearly contrasts with *Smith v Stages* (1989) where, on similar facts, the victim was able to claim vicarious liability. The difference in the decisions was merely related to the purpose of the employee's journey. In *Beard v London General* (1900) the injured victim would not have been aware that the employee was not authorised to drive the bus, and as a result was not able to prove vicarious liability.

4   In contrast, where the employee commits a crime in the course of employment, the courts are more prepared to make the employer vicariously liable. The concept of 'close connection' with the employment has been developed to allow claims in cases such as *Lister v Hesley Hall* (2001), *Mattis v Pollock* (2003), *Hawley v Luminar Leisure Ltd* (2006) and *Mohamud v Morrisons* (2016). It is obviously fair for the victims of the crimes that they should receive compensation for the injuries suffered, and they would be unlikely to obtain compensation from the person who inflicted those injuries as they were serving prison sentences.

5   The principle of vicarious liability should encourage employers to take greater care when selecting their employees and on providing suitable training and supervision in the workplace. The decision in *Century Insurance v Northern Ireland Road Transport Board* (1942) is an example of this as the employer should have made it totally clear to its employee that smoking while delivering petrol was dangerous. It shows that employers have a social responsibility for their position and a business should see this responsibility as one of the underlying costs of being an employer. However, modern methods of working from home or flexibly mean that it is not always possible for employers to closely supervise their workforce, and it could be said to be unfair on them to accept liability for an employee's actions when he or she is working away from the employer's eyes.

6   An employer, or their insurer, can use the Civil Liability (Contribution) Act 1978 to recover from an employee any compensation paid out. If this message was given to employees, it could act as a deterrent to committing wrongs in the workplace. However, this right of recovery is unlikely to be effective in practice. The employee is unlikely to be earning sufficient to make it worth the employer pursuing him for large amounts of money. Also, the employee could leave the employment, or be dismissed and the employer's rights of recovery will be difficult or impossible to enforce. This would certainly be the case if the employee has committed a crime during the employment and is serving a sentence of imprisonment. Rogue employees will know that there is little chance of them being sued or financially penalised by their employer, so there is little incentive to take care at work.

Case	Facts	Legal principle
Mersey Docks & Harbour Board v Coggins and Griffiths (Liverpool) Ltd (1947)	Hired crane driver negligently injured a person.	If worker and equipment are hired out, there is the presumption that the original employer is liable. If worker only is hired, the presumption is that the hirer is liable.
Hawley v Luminar Leisure Ltd (2006)	A bouncer assaulted a customer outside a club. He was employed by specialist suppliers.	The club employed him and was vicariously liable for his actions.
Ready Mixed Concrete (South East) Ltd v Minister of Pensions and National Insurance (1968)	Should the company be liable for the payment of National Insurance contributions or a driver?	Three conditions to be met to show an employment relationship: 1 a relationship similar to employment 2 which was established by a close connection 3 it was fair and just to impose liability on the employer.
E v English Province of Our Lady of Charity (2012)	Claimant alleged that she had been sexually abused when she was being looked after in a home and the bishop of the diocese was vicariously liable.	The court had to look for: (i) a relationship akin (or similar) to employment, (ii) which was established by a sufficiently close connection so that (iii) it was fair and just to impose liability on the defendant. These tests were satisfied in this case.
JGE v Trustees of the Portsmouth Roman Catholic Diocesan Trust (2012)	Claimant alleged she had been raped by a priest when she was being looked after in a home.	As an office holder, not an employee, the priest's relationship with the church was sufficiently akin (close) to one of employment that it was fair and just to hold the church vicariously liable for damages as a result of his conduct.
Catholic Child Welfare Society v Various Claimants (FC) and the Institute of the Brothers of the Christian Schools (2012)	Members of the Institute sexually abused pupils at the school where they were employed.	Was the relationship between the Institute and its members akin to employer and employee, and was the sexual abuse connected to that relationship in such a way as to give rise to vicarious liability? Both tests were satisfied to make the Institute vicariously liable.
Cox v Ministry of Justice (2016)	A prison employee was negligently injured by a prisoner. Was the employer liable for the actions of the prisoner?	An organisation can be vicariously liable for the actions of its workers even though they do not have a contract of employment with the organisation; it is not necessary for the organisation to be carrying out a commercial activity or making a profit. It is enough for the organisation to carry on activities in the furtherance of its own interests.
Fletcher v Chancery Supplies Ltd (2017)	T emerged from behind a stationary van colliding with the claimant riding his police mountain bike causing severe leg injuries. Was T's employer vicariously liable?	In the absence of explanation why T had left his workplace, there was no sufficient connection between his work and him causing the accident to make T's employer vicariously liable.
Viasystems (Tyneside) Ltd v Thermal Transfer (Northern) Ltd (2005)	The claimants contracted with D1 to install air conditioning in their factory. D1 subcontracted some work to D2. D2 agreed with D3 to provide fitters and fitters' mates. S was a fitter's mate who damaged some ducting that came into contact with a sprinkler which fractured causing a flood.	More than one 'employer' could be vicariously liable and the court had to consider 'who was entitled and in theory obliged to control the employee's negligent act in order to prevent it'. Here D2 and D3 were each 50% liable.
Limpus v London General (1862)	A bus driver caused an accident when racing, despite being instructed by the employer not to race.	The employer was liable to the injured claimant as the driver was doing what he was employed to do – even against orders.
Rose v Plenty (1976)	A dairy instructed its milkmen not to use child helpers on their milk rounds. A boy was injured when he helped a milkman.	The dairy was vicariously liable for the milkman's negligence as the dairy was benefiting from the work done by the boy.
Twine v Beans Express (1946)	The claimant's husband was killed through the negligence of a driver who had been forbidden to give lifts.	The employers were not liable as the driver was doing an unauthorised act and the employers were gaining no benefit from it.

Case	Facts	Legal principle
Beard v London General Omnibus Co. (1900)	A bus conductor drove a bus without the authority of his employer, injuring the claimant.	The employer was not liable as the conductor was doing something outside the course of his employment.
Lister v Hesley Hall (2001)	The warden of a school for children with emotional difficulties was convicted of sexually assaulting some of the children.	The House of Lords decided there was a close connection between his job and what he did.
N v Chief Constable of Merseyside Police (2006)	An off-duty policeman offered to take a drunk woman to the police station but instead committed sexual assaults on her, including rape.	There was no close connection between the employment and the assaults.
Mattis v Pollock (2003)	A bouncer inflicted serious injuries on a customer and was jailed for committing serious criminal offences.	The nightclub was vicariously liable for the bouncer's actions as he was encouraged to use force and his criminal actions were closely connected to his work.
Mohamud v Morrison's Supermarkets (2016)	A man employed at the defendant's petrol station assaulted a customer causing him serious injuries.	The Supreme Court decided that as the employee was acting within the field of his employment, the employer was vicariously liable.
Century Insurance v Northern Ireland Road Transport Board (1942)	A petrol tanker driver was delivering petrol to a petrol station when he lit a cigarette and threw a lighted match on the ground.	The employer was liable to pay compensation as the driver was doing his job, even though negligently.
Hilton v Thomas Burton (Rhodes) Ltd (1961)	Some employees took an unauthorised break by driving the firm's van but had an accident. One of the workmen was killed and his widow sued the employer.	The employers were not liable to pay compensation to the victim of the accident as the workmen were on an unauthorised 'frolic' of their own and not acting in the course of employment.

Figure 12.5 Key cases on vicarious liability

Summary

- Vicarious liability means that someone other than the person who committed the tort is responsible for his actions, and has to pay compensation.
- It usually applies where an employer has to pay for a tort committed by an employee.
- Two conditions have to be satisfied:
  - the person who committed the tort is an employee as opposed to an independent contractor, and
  - he or she was acting in the course of his or her employment.
- Whether a person is employed or is self-employed is a legal test which may involve:
  - the control test – how much control the employer had over the employee in the way, and how the employee worked
  - the integration test – if a person's work is fully integrated into the business, he or she will be considered an employee
  - the economic reality or multiple test – looks at the whole situation between the worker and the employer including ownership of tools, equipment or uniform, payment of wages, deductions from wages, job description, taking of orders and hours to be worked.
- An employer will be liable:
  - for a criminal act of an employee if there is a close connection between the crime and the work he or she is required to do
  - for an employee who is doing his job but acts against orders
  - if the employee does his job negligently.
- An employer will not be liable:
  - for an employee who is 'on a frolic of his own'
  - for the tort of an independent contractor.
- If the employer has to pay compensation it can be recovered from the employee under the authority of the Civil Liability (Contribution) Act 1978.

Chapter 13

Law and morality

After reading this chapter you should be able to:
- Understand the distinction between law and morals
- Understand the diversity of moral views in a pluralist society
- Understand the relationship between law and morals and its importance
- Understand the legal enforcement of moral values

Introduction to Chapters 13–16

The following four chapters deal with topics that follow from the material in Chapter 1 of *OCR AS/A Level Law Book 1* – the nature of law. The concept of law can be examined in great detail, but this brief introduction should set the scene for:
- law and morality
- law and justice
- law and society
- law and technology.

Some laws are laws relating to the operation of the universe such as the three laws of thermodynamics. These laws are immutable – they are unchanging and cannot be broken. The set of rules we are concerned with is English law. It is a starting point to define law as:

Law is a body of rules supported by sanctions administered by the state.

There are two main theories relating to the nature of law:
- legal positivism
- natural law.

Legal positivism

Legal positivists believe that laws are valid where they are made by the recognised legislative power in the state; they do not have to satisfy any higher authority.

 Key term

Legal positivism – the theory of law that is based on the idea that laws are valid where they are made by the recognised legislative power in the state and do not have to satisfy any higher authority.

Each legal positivist has his own individual explanation of the theory. The nineteenth-century philosophers are often referred to as classical legal positivism. Jeremy Bentham and John Austin are the best known of them. Criticisms of Austin and his rather simplistic view have been made by the modern legal positivists, in particular Professor H.L.A. Hart. Other modern legal positivists include Hans Kelsen and Joseph Raz. Kelsen argues that morality is no part of law.

Law is autonomous – we can identify its content without recourse to morality.

As a legal positivist, Hart insists on the separation of law and morality. His model of law is more sophisticated than that of Austin. He argues that there are two categories of rules, primary and secondary which combine to form the basis of a workable legal system.

Legal philosopher	Basic premise
Jeremy Bentham	A utilitarian who wrote about what the law is, and a commentary on its merits or otherwise. He believed that the philosophy of law should be concerned purely with what law is.
John Austin	He developed the command theory of law with its three main principles.
Prof. H.L.A. Hart	A legal positivist who believes in the separation of law and morality. He argues that there are two categories of rules, primary and secondary. These combine to form the basis of a workable legal system.
Joseph Raz	A legal positivist who argues that the identity and existence of a legal system may be tested by reference to three elements. Law is autonomous – we can identify its content without recourse to morality.
Hans Kelsen	A legal positivist who argues that morality is no part of law.

Figure 13.1 Key facts chart about legal philosophers who are utilitarian and legal positivists

Natural law

Natural lawyers reject legal positivism. They believe that the validity of man-made laws depends upon the laws being compatible with a higher, moral authority. Where laws do not satisfy the requirements of this higher moral authority, the laws lack validity. There are different views on natural law, reflected in the work of Thomas Aquinas and Lon Fuller.

> **Key term**
>
> **Natural law** – a moral theory of jurisprudence, which maintains that law should be based on morality and ethics.

Thomas Aquinas combined the philosophy of Aristotle with Christian theology, including the Bible and the Ten Commandments, and Catholic Church tradition. He saw in Aristotle's philosophy a rational foundation for Christian doctrine. These principles help people work out our moral principles that should be reflected in man-made laws.

Fuller wrote *The Morality of Law* in 1964. He rejected legal positivism and also traditional religious forms of natural law theory. He argued that law serves a purpose. That purpose is 'to achieve social order through subjecting people's conduct to the guidance of general rules by which they may themselves orient their behaviour'.

Legal philosopher	Basic premise
Thomas Aquinas	Combined the philosophy of Aristotle with Christian theology, including the Bible and the Ten Commandments, and Catholic Church tradition. He sets out four kinds of law.
Lon Fuller	Argued that law serves the purpose: 'to achieve social order through subjecting people's conduct to the guidance of general rules by which they may themselves orient their behaviour.' If law is to achieve this purpose, it must satisfy eight principles which make up an inner morality of law.

Figure 13.2 Key facts chart about legal philosophers who are natural lawyers

13.1 The distinction between law and morals

13.1.1 What is law?

Rules exist in many contexts. A rule is something that determines the way in which we behave, whether

because we submit ourselves to it voluntarily, as would be the case with moral rules, or because it is enforceable in some general way, as would be the case with laws.

> **Key term**
>
> **Rule** – this has been defined by Twining and Miers in *How to Do Things with Rules* (2014) as 'a general norm mandating or guiding conduct'.

Some rules are not based on law or morality, but are often referred to as laws. These might be the laws of football or the laws of chess. They are generally observed in the context in which they operate. If these laws are broken, there are sanctions in the context of the sport. Many would view any form of cheating in a sport or game as wrong and possibly as immoral.

Some laws are laws relating to the operation of the universe such as the three laws of thermodynamics. These laws are immutable – they are unchanging and cannot be broken. The rules we are concerned with is English law. It is a starting point to define law as:

Law is a body of rules supported by sanctions administered by the state.

There are two main theories relating to the nature of law:

- legal positivism
- natural law.

13.1.2 What is morality?

Hart's criticism of Fuller raises the question of what is morality. Morality is defined in the Oxford English Dictionary as 'a particular system of values and principles of conduct, especially one held by a specified person or society'.

Morality can be a personal morality or a collective morality of society as a whole.

Morality is 'normative' or prescriptive; that is, it specifies what ought to be done and delineates acceptable and unacceptable behaviour. In our society and in many others, morality has been influenced to a large extent by religious beliefs. The Bible provides a moral code for Christian communities, both in the very basic and strict rules of the Ten Commandments, and in the more advanced socially aware teachings of Christ. In Islam, the Koran provides a very extensive moral code for Muslims.

Morality is the moral code that touches virtually every area of our lives – behaviour towards fellow human beings, money and property, and sexuality. There are 'core' moral beliefs such as issues surrounding birth, death and families.

Although morality is concerned with issues of 'right' and 'wrong', it is not at all black and white. Mary Warnock, an academic who has been predominantly concerned with moral issues, said:

> I do not believe that there is a neat way of marking off moral issues from all others; some people, at some time, may regard things as matters of moral right and moral wrong, which at another time or in another place are thought to be matters of taste, or of no importance at all.

Moral attitudes change over time. This can be seen in attitudes to issues such as abortion, homosexuality, drugs and drink-driving. Morality was easy to see as a common morality when societies were insular, structured and not exposed to different beliefs and values. The customs of that society formed the basis of a code of conduct that reflected that society, and members of the society accepted these customs in large measure. It was therefore part of the morality of that age. However, we now live in a multicultural society where there are a wide range of views.

Sociologist Emile Durkheim identified a range of factors as potentially contributing to the breakdown of a common morality. These included:

- the increasing specialisation of labour
- the growing ethnic diversity within society
- the fading influence of religious belief.

All of these factors are increasingly apparent in pluralist societies today. Under Durkheim's analysis, we should not be prised to discover a parallel growth in the diversity of moral outlook and in norms of behaviour in modern Britain. There is, therefore, a more obvious difference between an individual's moral code and that of society as a whole.

13.1.3 Characteristics of legal and moral rules

In order to discover the characteristics of legal and moral rules, it is useful to compare them under a number of headings:

- their origins
- their date of commencement
- their enforcement
- their ease of change
- their certainty of content
- the way the rules are applied.

These characteristics help to identify the rules and distinguish legal and moral rules.

Their origins

It is generally possible to trace legal rules back to a source. Originally this was the common law. The law of tort and contract have been developed incrementally by judges. Today, statutes have become an increasingly large source of law, together with delegated legislation. European Union law has become a major source of law making in the UK through treaties, directives, regulations and decisions.

Conventions that the UK subscribes to such as the European Convention on Human Rights (ECHR) also play their part in the origin of law in the UK today.

Moral rules are more difficult to trace back to a precise origin. The Bible and the Koran form the basis for many individuals of their moral outlook. Codes such as these inform attitudes towards issues such as premarital sex, theft and how one treats fellow humans. For those who do not follow religious teaching, morality is based upon upbringing, education, peer views, or the leanings of their own consciences. For most people, their morality is based on a combination of all these influences.

Their date of commencement

Legal rules generally have a start date. Acts of Parliament come into force at a specific time. Precedents operate from the date of the decision, although it can be argued they have retrospective effect as with the decision in *R v R* (1991).

Moral rules are less straightforward. For example, Western attitudes towards pre-marital sex have undergone significant change in the last 100 years. It is not possible to attach a date to this change, as it is part of a wider change in social attitudes towards matters of sexual morality. Similarly, it is not possible to fix a date when a person's particular morality came into being – it evolves over time.

Their enforcement

Legal rules can be enforced by the courts following a designated procedure and with appropriate sanctions such as criminal penalties or civil damages.

Sanctions may also be available for those who breach moral codes. Someone who uses offensive language may be excluded from a sports or social club. Moral rules are usually enforced through public disapproval through the media or privately – social ostracism rather than a formal sanction. Moral rules are less enforceable than legal rules, but it is often easier to show views about them.

Their ease of change

In theory, legal rules are relatively easy to change. Parliament has authority to pass a law whenever it wants. In practice, however, Parliament is often slow to respond to change.

As we have seen, courts also have the power to change legal rules.

Moral rules tend to change gradually, perhaps over decades or centuries. It is often only in hindsight that we become aware of such change.

Sometimes the law leads morality, and sometimes the law follows the lead of morality.

Their certainty of content

It is normally possible to discover the precise content of legal rules through published statutes, delegated legislation and law reports.

The content of moral rules may also be clear. However, knowledge of the content of moral rules can often only be acquired informally through exposure to them in the setting where they are applied, such as the home.

Application of the rules

Legal rules generally apply to everyone in a situation covered by the law. The only difference is the ability of every individual to access the law.

Moral rules, on the other hand, range in application from enjoying almost universal adoption to having only marginal acceptance. Differing views are taken by different individuals and different sectors of society. This is particularly apparent in a pluralist society.

13.2 The diversity of moral views in a pluralist society

We have explored the distinction between law and morals and the views of legal positivists and natural lawyers. We have also considered the characteristics of legal and moral rules. This section now considers the fact that there is likely to be a variety of moral views in a pluralist society.

Key term

Pluralist society – a diverse society, where minority groups maintain their independent cultural traditions and all members tolerate each other's beliefs even when they don't match their own.

13.2.1 Pluralism in the UK

The UK has a multicultural society, with individuals having different or no religious beliefs. This leads to a great variety in the moral values of the individuals in society. Often these individuals group together as a result of their moral views whether as a collective view that binds them or because of common purpose in promoting their views. An individual's views are protected under the ECHR as is his right to express his views and assemble with others to express the collective views.

The country in which we live plays a significant role in shaping our lives. Both other members of society and the laws of the country shape our views. The kinds of lives we can lead are constrained by the state which has the right to punish individuals if we go beyond what the state deems to be appropriate limits.

One example is that of the conscientious objector who, when the country is at war, refuses to fight. The large majority of society accept that they must be prepared to fight and may not fully accept the views of those who will not. Conscientious objectors believe it to be completely wrong in any circumstance and accept that the state may punish them and much of society will shun them. Such a view is not necessarily a judgement about a government's policy but a moral judgement, drawn from personal beliefs. The difficulty arises when an individual changes their views.

Example

Conscientious objection in the UK armed forces

Conscientious objection to military service is a subtle concept. Broadly speaking, it arises when a serving or prospective member of the armed forces finds that his work cannot/could not be done in good conscience. When the claim of conscience is sufficiently powerful for the person to seek to remove himself from his work, then a conscientious objection can be said to exist. This could arise in relation either to specific orders or military operations, or to military service in all its aspects.

Source: 'Informed Choice? Armed Forces Recruitment Practice in the UK', David Gee (2007)

So how does this work in practice?

The case of *R v Lyons* (2011) shows that refusal of a lawful order even on the grounds of conscientious objection is a punishable offence in the UK armed forces under the Armed Forces Act 2006.

R v Lyons (2011)

Lyons, aged 18, had joined the Royal Navy and became a Leading Medical Assistant in submarines. Five years later, he was told that he would be deployed to Afghanistan. He applied for discharge from the Royal Navy on the basis that he objected to the UK's role in Afghanistan. His application on grounds of conscientious objection was refused. Before his appeal against this refusal was decided he was ordered to undertake a pre-deployment weapons training course, because of the risk all personnel faced in that theatre, combatant or not. On refusing to submit to this he was convicted of insubordination.

He argued that Article 9 ECHR (freedom of thought, conscience and religion) protected him from active service from the moment when he told his commanding officer of his objections, until his appeal on grounds of conscientious objection was finally determined.

The court decided that moral objections to the UK's involvement in Afghanistan do not constitute a defence to an insubordination charge. The appellant was not entitled to disobey a lawful command on the ground of conscientious objection.

Similarly, there is the criminal who is prepared to steal but is not prepared to kill in order to steal. The majority of society and the state would agree with him that killing is wrong, but a small proportion would consider that stealing is not wrong.

13.2.2 Pluralism in Europe and the ECHR

The attempt to keep morality and religions out of politics and the law arises from the worry that, for example, religious fundamentalists will impose intolerant and coercive laws and practices on all of society. We have seen this in various countries with respect to attitudes towards abortion, stem-cell research on embryos and in-vitro fertilisation (IVF).

In Ireland, when abortion was illegal, the case of *Open Door Counselling and Dublin Woman Well Centre v Ireland* (1992) was heard by the ECtHR. The court found that the Ireland Supreme Court's injunction restraining counselling agencies from providing pregnant women with information concerning abortion facilities abroad violated Article 10 ECHR (right to freedom of expression).

See Chapter 22 for more details about the case and the relationship between Article 10 and health and morals.

In *Evans v United Kingdom* (2007) the ECtHR stated that for the right to respect for the decision to become a parent in the genetic sense, the margin of appreciation to be afforded to the respondent state under Article 8 (right to respect for private and family life) has to be a wide one. This case involved the refusal of one partner to the destruction of frozen embryos following the ending of the parents' relationship.

Extension question

There are many cases relating to this area that are further examples of different countries' laws reflecting one particular moral view. Consider, for example: *A, B and C v Ireland* (2010), *Vo v France* (2004), *Boso v Italy* (2002), *Tysiac v Poland* (2007), *RR v Poland* (2011), *P and S v Poland* (2012) and *H v Norway* (1992).

In a group, take one each of these cases and prepare a summary for presentation or display that shows:

- the issue in question
- the applicable Article of ECHR
- the moral view taken by the state, the applicant in the case and the ECtHR.

This will aid your understanding of the issues relating to pluralism in society and different sectors of society's moral views.

13.2.3 Pluralism in other areas of law

The collective moral views of society are reflected in many areas of law. The change in the moral view of society as a whole changes. Issues such as child protection, euthanasia and assisted dying, the death penalty, same sex marriage, LGBT issues, equality of pay and legalisation of drugs are all the subject of the effect of changes in the views of how the law should be reflected in morality.

Extension question

Select an area which you have studied or are interested in and write notes to argue whether the law is satisfactory in this area given the view of morality in the UK today. The list set out above gives some suggestions.

With respect to LGBT rights, the Hart–Devlin debate, considered below at section 13.4.2, was sparked as a result of the Wolfenden Report in 1957 on Homosexual Offences and Prostitution. This eventually led to the Sexual Offences Act 1967 which decriminalised homosexual activity in certain circumstances. The reduction in the age of consent for sexual activity between those of the same sex was not brought into line with that for heterosexual relations until 2001. It was not until 2003 that sex specific sexual offences were removed from the statute book under the Sexual Offences Act 2003.

The Policing and Crime Act 2017 gave posthumous pardons to the thousands of homosexual men from England and Wales who had been convicted under the old law. This Act is sometimes called Alan Turing's law after the effect his conviction under the then homosexual laws had on his life and work.

Statue of Alan Turing at the university of Surrey

Other legislation in this area includes the Civil Partnership Act 2004, the Gender Recognition Act 2004, the Human Fertilisation and Embryology Act 2008 and the Marriage (Same Sex Couples) Act 2013. Not all of this legislation remains satisfactory and much of it continues to be strongly opposed by some sectors of society.

Look online

The Parliamentary Women and Equalities Committee reported on many of the remaining issues in the area of equality and transgender people in 2015.

The report can be found at **www.publications. parliament.uk/pa/cm201516/cmselect/ cmwomeq/390/39001.htm**.

You can use this to research how law and morality are reflected today.

13.2.4 Summary

John Stuart Mill said, 'All silencing of discussion is an assumption of infallibility'.

When people are silenced or coerced while wanting to express an opinion, they are often trying to voice positions that should be heard. In a democracy, minorities can become majorities. The tyranny of the majority can undermine the very nature of democracy and its search for the best way of living together. This is reflected in ECHR and should be reflected in UK law.

Freedom of thought and expression is frequently restricted as being contrary to the moral views of the majority. The difficulty is deciding when the greater good of society as a whole should prevent the individual's view which is not being considered acceptable, be it on the grounds of protection (anti-terrorism, online bullying), obscenity (likely to deprave or corrupt) or sexual matters (same-sex relationships, abortion, contraception).

13.3 The relationship between law and morality, and its importance

Law and morality often overlap, although there is often a period where one leads and the other follows. This relationship coincides for much of the time, and at other times the one influences the other.

This can be seen in the coincidence of legal and moral rules and the influences of law and morality on each other

13.3.1 The coincidence of legal and moral rules

Legal and moral rules, though distinctive, share certain characteristics. They are both concerned with setting standards, which are essential for governing the behaviour of individuals within society. They both dictate the way in which people are expected to behave.

Legal and moral rules employ similar language: they distinguish between right and wrong, and they speak of duties, obligations and responsibilities.

Legal rules are strengthened when they are the same as moral rules, and their enforcement can more readily be justified and is accepted by society.

Sometimes legal rules possess no obvious moral content. Parking a car on a double yellow line in an empty town centre at 4 a.m. does not seem to infringe any moral code (other than the act itself of breaking the law). Most would think it was immoral to impose a parking fine in that situation, merely a money-raising exercise on behalf of a local council.

Activity

Think about areas where law and morality coincide and be able to state the relevant law. One example is murder. Then think about areas where law and your morality do not coincide and the reasons for that.

In the news

Zealous parking wardens under attack

A publican was handed a fixed penalty notice for parking at 9.15 p.m. in the loading bay outside his pub that he had used without any problems for 13 years, and a motorist was fined after breaking down on double yellow lines at 8.30 p.m.

Other instances of overly-zealous enforcement in the town, a Thirsk Town Council meeting heard, included a delivery driver being told he could not unload 11 boxes from his van, and another driver being fined for parking on yellow lines while getting change for a parking meter.

Members of North Yorkshire and Hambleton District councils, which employ wardens hired by Scarborough Borough Council, said that, while motorists who block key access points need to be dealt with, the style of enforcement is not in keeping with market towns and is causing significant embarrassment.

Scarborough Council has carried out an investigation into the actions of one parking warden after receiving complaints, but found no wrongdoing.

Source: Adapted from an article in the *Darlington and Stockton Times* online, 25 November 2016

It is not surprising that the principle of strict liability is controversial as legal rules are given greater validity by their moral content.

There are many moral rules that are not part of the law. Most people would agree that adultery is immoral and indeed may be the basis of a divorce, but it is not illegal in the UK, even though it is in some other countries of the world.

Some acts that may be considered immoral are not criminal but may be sufficient to support a claim in civil law. The line between them is blurred, as might be seen in some cases of gross negligence manslaughter.

Tip

As you revise material for the exams, list areas of law and cases you have studied that show acts which are not criminal but are immoral, and where civil law provides a remedy.

13.3.2 The influences of law and morality on each other

Changing moral values can lead to developments in the law. This can be seen in the historical development of the law relating to rape within marriage. It was ruled in 1736 that 'a man cannot rape his wife', yet in *R v R* (1991) Owen J stated: 'I find it hard to believe that it ever was common law that a husband was in effect entitled to beat his wife into submission to sexual intercourse.'

In this way, the law eventually caught up with perceived public morality.

Extension question

Research and make a list of key developments in other areas of law that have changed to reflect changing morality. You could use abortion or homosexuality for this.

Then perform the same research for areas of law where public morality has followed the lead of the law such as discrimination on the grounds of gender or race.

Ideally the law and morality change in harmony with little lead or lag. For example, the Sexual Offences Act 1967 was passed following the Wolfenden Report. However, there were many more influences in the public's view at the time. There had been the famous case of *R v Penguin Books Ltd* (1961) which considered the novel *Lady Chatterley's Lover* by D.H. Lawrence not to be obscene under the Obscene Publications Act 1959. So-called underground magazines became available, such as *OZ* and *IT*; satirical magazines such as *Private Eye* developed a large circulation, reporting and commenting on current issues and scandals which many considered immoral and required action by the state and a change of the law.

Cover of *OZ* magazine from April 1969

13.4 The legal enforcement of moral values

As the UK is a multicultural society, it contains a diversity of moral views. This section explores the questions of whether, and to what extent, the law should seek to enforce any particular moral views. This is not just a subject of academic debate as judges are often forced to consider these questions before determining the law. There are two starting points for this debate:

- The law, as the guardian of public morals, should intervene to ensure the continuation of the dominant morality within the state.
- Individuals should be left free to decide their own morality.

These starting points appear to be diametrically opposite, but, in practice, both these positions are modified so that they tend towards convergence.

13.4.1 The influence of John Stuart Mill

In his book *On Liberty*, John Stuart Mill, a nineteenth-century philosopher, explored the nature and limits

of the power which can be legitimately exercised by society over the individual.

He stated that there is a limit to the legitimate interference of collective opinion with individual independence. Nevertheless, Mill accepted that rules governing an individual's conduct must be imposed upon him. The problem, though, is identifying where society should or should not be permitted to interfere with individual liberty. Therefore, Mill developed the harm principle as the appropriate test to be used when considering this issue. He wrote:

> The only purpose for which power can be rightfully exercised over any member of a civilised community, against his will, is to prevent harm to others. His own good, either physical or moral, is not a sufficient warrant ... Over himself, his own body and mind, the individual is sovereign.

Under this principle, an individual should be allowed to harm himself and society can only intervene where his conduct harms others.

Mill does, however, limit the application of the harm principle in one significant way. He states it does not apply to those who are not in the maturity of their faculties. In other words, it does not apply to children, over whom society enjoys absolute power and presumably also those suffering a severe mental disability. They must be protected against their own actions as well as against the actions of others.

Mill recognised that others might refuse to admit this distinction between that part of a person's life which concerns only himself and that which concerns others. One such objector was the nineteenth-century judge, Sir James Stephen, who opposed the liberalism of Mill. Stephen argued that there is no distinction between acts that harm others and acts that harm oneself. He wrote: 'There are acts of wickedness so gross and outrageous that they must be punished at any cost to the offender'.

He went on to argue that the prevention of wickedness and immorality is a proper end in itself and justifies state action. The law, Stephen argued, has a duty to proscribe behaviour condemned by society at large.

Mill answered such objections by making a distinction between the harmful act itself and its particular consequences.

In summary, Mill argued that society should not impose morality on individuals. Individuals should be free to choose how they behave provided that no harm is caused to other members of society. If harm is done, he argued, this should not outweigh the harm that denying individual liberty would do.

Problems with Mill's approach

Mill's approach raised questions. It is not clear what constitutes 'harm', physical or otherwise; does it include, for example, pornography, drug-taking or sexual practices when carried out consensually or alone? Equally, it is not clear whether an embryo or a foetus falls within the definition of other members of society.

A logical extension of Mill's approach is that crimes without victims should not really be crimes at all. Edwin Schur and Hugo Bedau in their book, *Victimless Crimes: Two Sides of a Controversy*, argue that a victimless crime is a term used to refer to actions that have been made illegal but which do not directly violate or threaten the rights of any other individual. It often involves consensual acts, or solitary acts in which no other person is involved. Such acts would not lead to any person calling for help from the police. This would include recreational drug use. The argument is that some of these laws produce secondary crime, and all create new criminals, many of whom are otherwise law-abiding citizens and people in authority. These victimless crimes that only do harm to the criminal should be decriminalised. They cite as examples drug use, homosexuality and abortion (these being illegal at the time of the book's publication). If such activities are criminalised, demand will still be there and the activities will be pushed underground.

13.4.2 The Hart–Devlin debate

This debate between an eminent law lord, Patrick Devlin, and the academic Professor H.L.A. Hart was sparked by the publication of the Wolfenden Report. The report concluded that the law has a role in preserving public order and decency, but

> it is not, in our view, the function of the law to intervene in the private life of citizens, or to seek to enforce any particular pattern of behaviour ... [There] must remain a realm of private morality and immorality which is, in brief and crude terms, not the law's business.

In his book, *The Enforcement of Morals*, published in 1965, Lord Devlin wrote: 'Without shared ideas on politics, morals, and ethics, no society can exist.'

Society, therefore, is constituted in part by its morality. Lord Devlin argued that the fabric of society is dependent upon a shared or common morality. Where the bonds of that morality are loosened by private immoral conduct, the integrity of society will be lost and society will be liable to disintegrate. Society therefore has the right to defend itself against immorality. Even private wickedness and immorality may be punished because they are harmful to society. Lord Devlin stated: 'The suppression of vice is as much the law's business as the suppression of subversive activities.'

Lord Devlin also recognised that there are limits to the right of society to interfere with private immoral conduct. He believed that 'There must be toleration of the maximum individual freedom that is consistent with the integrity of society'. He accepted that personal preferences, or likes and dislikes, should not form the basis for decisions about what immoral conduct should be outlawed. He therefore developed an apparently objective test, that of the reasonable or ordinary man, to help decide where the boundaries are to be drawn. Only where immoral conduct is regarded by this ordinary man with 'intolerance, indignation or disgust', should it be prohibited by law.

Professor Hart proposed a more limited role for the law in the enforcement of morality. Whereas Lord Devlin started from the general principle that society has a duty to enforce its dominant morality, and then limited the application of this general principle to acts that the ordinary man regards with intolerance, Professor Hart started from the opposite end of the spectrum – that society should not interfere with private moral or immoral conduct. However, Hart then limited the application of this general principle by sanctioning the enforcement of morality in certain situations.

He accepted that enforcement is permitted when one of society's dominant moralities is being eroded by a true threat to the cohesion of society. Such a threat, though, has to be more than merely a challenge to society's code of conduct. There must be evidence that it creates a genuine public nuisance.

Issues reflecting the Hart–Devlin debate and the relationship between law and morality

Judges and Parliament are often forced to confront complex moral issues. Parliament can choose whether to legislate. Judges have no choice. If a case comes to court they have to make a decision, and of course if a case reaches the higher appeal courts, it becomes a precedent.

Judges often have to confront 'new' issues affecting public morality. In *Shaw v DPP* (1962), the case concerned a magazine advertising the services of prostitutes, and Shaw was convicted of 'conspiracy to corrupt public morals' – a previously unknown offence. The House of Lords confirmed the existence of this 'new' common law offence. Viscount Simonds declared:

> There remains in the courts a residual power to enforce the supreme and fundamental purpose of the law, to conserve not only the safety and order, but also the moral welfare of the State.

Lord Devlin would have approved of this paternalistic approach.

Extension question

There are many other examples of judges making decisions which have a moral background. Consider how Hart and Devlin would view the following cases and other similar cases that you come across:

- *DPP v Knuller (Publishing, Printing and Promotions) Ltd* (1971)
- *R v Gibson* (1990)
- *R v Brown* (1993)
- *R v Wilson* (1996)

The overlap with criminal law, morality and human rights can be seen in *R v G* (2008).

Case study

R v G (2008)

G was a boy aged 15 who had had sexual intercourse with a girl aged 12. He was charged under s 5 of the Sexual Offences Act (SOA) 2003 with rape of a child under 13. The girl was actually 12, but G believed on reasonable grounds that she was 15. She had told him so on an earlier occasion. G was held to be guilty as the offence is one of strict liability and may be committed irrespective of:

- consent
- reasonable belief in consent
- a reasonable belief as to age.

G appealed on the basis that making s 5 a strict liability offence was a breach of his human rights, in particular Article 8, the right to respect for his private life. In the House of Lords, Baroness Hale pointed out that the physical and moral integrity of the complainant, vulnerable by reason of her age, was worthy of respect. She thought the state would have been open to criticism if it did not provide the complainant with adequate protection. This shows the court upholding the moral values set by the Act.

In civil law, the principle that promises should be kept lies beneath the law of contract. Much of the law of equity was historically founded upon principles of conscience with maxims such as 'equity will not allow a statute to be used as a cloak for fraud' and 'he who comes to equity must come with clean hands'.

In the law of negligence, Lord Atkin's famously Biblical description of the duty of care as one owed to one's fellow man as a 'neighbour' in *Donoghue v Stevenson* (1932) reworked the parable of the Good Samaritan.

Historically, certain contracts can be declared void because of their association with immorality. For example:

- *Pearce v Brooks* (1866): a cab owner failed to enforce a contract with a prostitute who used his cabs for trade because the courts were not prepared to allow contracts for immoral purposes.
- *Parkinson v The College of Ambulance* (1925): the contract was void because its whole purpose was corruption in public life.

In more recent times, the courts have produced conflicting views on the relationship between law and morality. In *Otkritie International Investment Management Ltd v Urumov* (2013) the court specifically made the connection between morality and the law when it said:

> public policy requires that the courts will not lend their aid to a man who founds his action upon an immoral or illegal act. The action will not be founded upon an immoral or illegal act, if it can be pleaded and proved without reliance upon such an act.

However, in *MacFarlane v Tayside Health Board* (1999) (a case where, despite a vasectomy, Mr MacFarlane fathered a child, and he and his wife sought damages for the cost of care among other claims), the claim for damages in respect of the rearing of the child was dismissed. Lord Steyn stated:

> It may be objected that the House must act like a court of law and not like a court of morals. That would only be partly right. The court must apply positive law. But a judge's sense of the moral answer to a question, or the justice of the case, has been one of the great shaping forces of the common law. What may count in a situation of difficulty and uncertainty is not the subjective view of the judge but what he reasonably believes that the ordinary citizen would regard as right.

So the situation is still conflicted. Whether one talks of 'morals' or 'values', judges have to apply themselves to real cases with real facts and real people and reflect the situation as they perceive it as to any moral or values issues.

Summary

- There are two main theories relating to the nature of law: legal positivism and natural law.
- Legal positivists believe that laws are valid where they are made by the recognised legislative power in the state; they do not have to satisfy any higher authority.
- Natural law is a moral theory of jurisprudence, which maintains that law should be based on morality and ethics.
- Morality is 'normative' or prescriptive; that is, it specifies what ought to be done and delineates acceptable and unacceptable behaviour.
- There are six characteristics which help to identify the rules and distinguish legal and moral rules.
- Legal and moral rules, though distinctive, share a number of characteristics.
- Changing moral values can lead to developments in the law and vice versa.
- Judges and Parliament are often forced to confront complex moral issues. Parliament can choose whether to legislate. Judges have no choice.

Chapter 14

Law and justice

After reading this chapter you should be able to:
- Understand the meaning of justice
- Understand theories of justice
- Understand the extent to which the law achieves justice

14.1 The meaning of justice

Justice is a concept that can be described simply by a synonym such as fairness, equality or even-handedness. We have a sense of justice from a very young age. The idea includes treating like cases in a like manner, showing impartiality and acting in good faith. However, the term 'justice' has occupied the minds of some of the greatest thinkers across the ages. As a result, there is a wide range of theories available to explain its meaning and application.

For the purpose of this chapter, the word 'law' refers not only to the substantive law – for example, criminal law, tort law or the law of contract, as developed in court decisions, by Parliament or through other sources, but also to procedural rules and principles by which the laws themselves are made and the legal system administered, known as procedural justice or formal justice.

Substantive justice can be seen in the way in which the rules work in different areas of law. You can see this in the evaluation of areas of law you have studied such as contract, tort, crime or human rights.

Procedural justice is concerned with legal institutions such as the courts and the appeal system, the judiciary and juries and the police. The failings of the system seen in miscarriages of justice is pertinent here as are bodies such as the Criminal Case Review Commission. Much of this has been dealt with in *OCR AS/A Level Law Book 1*.

Distributive justice is concerned with the fair allocation of resources among different areas of society and can be seen through the law on equal pay and minimum wages, taxation and the benefits system, and the way in which the law deals with those who fail to comply with the law – the corrective justice related

to individual failings and the balancing of interests between consumers and traders in contract law and the award of damages.

14.1.1 Legal philosophers and justice

One of the earliest attempts to define justice was set out by the fourth century BC Greek philosopher Plato. He saw justice as being harmony between the different sectors or classes in society. He regarded justice as an overarching virtue of both individuals and societies, so that almost every issue he would classify as ethical comes in under the notion of justice. For example, it is unjust for a person to steal from someone else, or not to give them what s/he owes them; these concepts are reflected in both criminal and civil law today.

Plato's work was continued by his pupil, Aristotle, who stressed the need for proportionality and for achieving the middle way – a balance between extremes. This can be seen today in the law's efforts to balance competing interests; for example, freedom of contract and protection of consumers or the individual's right to freedom of expression and protection of society from extreme views.

In the thirteenth century, Thomas Aquinas continued attempts to define justice. He described justice in language similar to that of Aristotle. Aquinas considered justice as governing our relationships with other people. It is the constant willingness to deal with other people as they deserve. The end result of justice is the common good, for the individual and for the community (society).

From the eighteenth century onwards, legal philosophy developed quickly. We will consider these areas in the next section:
- distributive justice, which is concerned with the fair allocation of the benefits (e.g. money, property,

family life) and responsibilities (e.g. taxes, civic duties) of life
- utilitarianism, where maximising happiness is the object of justice
- social justice, which is concerned with equal justice, not just in the courts, but in all aspects of society.

Tip

Make sure you can explain the meaning of each type of justice and can link relevant philosophers to each.

14.2 Theories of justice

There are many theories relating to justice. Above, we have noted the Greek philosophers and the idea of justice as harmony. We will now consider the philosophies behind the following theories:
- distributive justice
- utilitarianism
- social justice.

14.2.1 Distributive justice

Distributive justice is concerned with the fair allocation of the benefits (e.g. money, property, family life) and responsibilities (e.g. taxes, civic duties) of life. There are several philosophers who have expounded this view including:
- Aristotle
- Thomas Aquinas
- Karl Marx
- Chaim Perelman.

Aristotle

Aristotle identified particular examples of justice that apply to different situations. Among these is distributive justice. Aristotle argued that a just state will distribute its wealth on the basis of merit, giving to each according to his 'virtue' and to his contribution to society.

To allocate resources on the basis of people's needs would be unjust, as it would reward the lazy at least as much as the hard-working. We might consider how this would apply today to paying for care for the elderly or by providing social security benefits to all without question.

Thomas Aquinas

Aquinas identified particular forms of justice that govern our dealings with others, which help put into practice the general principle that people are given what is due to them. First of all, distributive justice concerns the fair allocation of goods and responsibilities throughout the community. This is governed by the principle of due proportion. This means that people receive what they are due in accordance with their merit, rank and need.

Concerning merit, it would be wrong to pay workers an equal amount for unequal work, or an unequal amount for equal work.

Aquinas based his doctrine on natural law.

See Chapter 13, section 13.1.1 for more information on natural law.

Karl Marx

Karl Marx, regarded as the nineteenth-century founder of communism, developed a radically different model of distributive justice. This model was embodied in his slogan, 'from each according to his ability, to each according to his need'. This enshrines two principles of the ideal of communism:
- Each will maximise his/her contribution to the common wealth by making full use of his/her abilities.
- Each will receive according to his/her need, irrespective of the personal contribution he or she has made to the production process.

Aristotle would have regarded this model of distribution as unjust in that it has the potential for giving the greatest rewards to the least productive, and therefore least deserving, members of society.

The main criticism of Marx's views is that no country has so far been able to put them into practice with sufficient success to bring about the just society envisaged by Marx. However, capitalist societies that follow principles of distributive justice, closer to those held by Aristotle and Aquinas, are also criticised for social injustice.

Chaim Perelman

The models of distributive justice described above are among those identified by Chaim Perelman. In 1944, Perelman produced a study of justice, entitled *De la Justice*. He concluded that justice cannot be studied logically, as each attempt to define it is based upon a person's subjective values.

In *De la Justice* he discusses different understandings of justice:
1 'To each according to his merits'
2 'To each according to his needs'
3 'To each according to his works'

4 'To each equally'

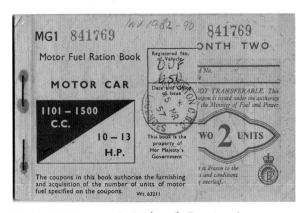

Petrol rationing ensured a fair (equal) allocation of scarce resources

5 'To each according to his rank'
6 'To each according to his legal entitlement'

	Basic premise
Aristotle	An ancient Greek philosopher. He described justice as referring to individuals in their dealings with each other, and to the state in making and enforcing laws.
Thomas Aquinas	A 13th-century theologian. He stated that justice governs our relationships with other people. It is the constant willingness to deal with other people as they deserve. The end result of justice is the common good, for the individual and for the community.
Karl Marx	Widely regarded as the founder of communism, he developed a radically different model of distributive justice. This model was embodied in his slogan, 'from each according to his ability, to each according to his need'.
Chaim Perelman	He produced a study of justice, entitled *De la Justice*. He concluded that justice cannot be studied logically, as each attempt to define it is based upon a person's subjective values. He saw six possible models of distributive justice.

Figure 14.1 Key facts about legal philosophers concerned with distributive justice

Extension question

Research each of the philosophers that have been discussed. How much do you think that their views were influenced by the times in which they lived? You can continue this process with other philosophers that will be studied later.

14.2.2 Utilitarianism

Utilitarianism is a philosophy that developed in the nineteenth century from the writings of Jeremy Bentham and John Stuart Mill.

Jeremy Bentham

Jeremy Bentham was a social reformer who developed the theory known today as utilitarianism. This philosophy is centred around this concept: the more an action increases overall happiness, the more valuable it is; and the more it decreases happiness, the more reprehensible. Utilitarians are only interested in the outcome of an act, regardless of the act itself. For a utilitarian, maximising happiness is the object of justice.

One of the criticisms of utilitarianism is that the interest of an individual may be sacrificed for greater community happiness. For example, if a drunk man announces that he is about to drive home to see his child who has suddenly fallen ill, would you be justified in stealing his car keys so he could not set off? Not having the car keys may well cause distress and inconvenience. Would it be different if the person was about to set off to take part in a demonstration or a terrorist attack? The greater happiness brought to the larger community by your action might outweigh the pain of the individual.

Consider this in the light of the Investigatory Powers Act 2016 which, according to the government, aims to be:

> an Act to make provision about the interception of communications, equipment interference and the acquisition and retention of communications data, bulk personal datasets and other information; to make provision about the treatment of material held as a result of such interception, equipment interference or acquisition or retention; to establish the Investigatory Powers Commissioner and other Judicial Commissioners and make provision about them and other oversight arrangements; to make further provision about investigatory powers and national security; to amend sections 3 and 5 of the Intelligence Services Act 1994; and for connected purposes.

Another view of the Investigatory Powers Act 2016 can be seen from whistle-blower Edward Snowden's tweet: 'The UK has just legalised the most extreme surveillance in the history of western democracy. It goes further than many autocracies.'

John Stuart Mill

John Stuart Mill was a nineteenth-century liberal, whose pamphlet, *Utilitarianism*, published in 1861, supported the basic principles of utilitarianism put forward by Bentham.

Mill wrote that actions are right 'in proportion as they tend to promote happiness, wrong as they tend to produce the reverse of happiness'. However, he focused upon the quality of happiness rather than merely upon its quantity. He wrote: 'Better to be a human being dissatisfied than a pig satisfied.'

Mill also linked utilitarianism to justice. Justice, he explained, includes respect for people, for property and for rights, as well as the need for good faith and impartiality. All of these are consistent with the principle of utility, since their application brings the greatest happiness to the greatest number.

It could also be argued that punishing wrongdoers also brings happiness to the greatest number. However, Mill argued that punishment is in itself an evil as it involves inflicting harm or pain, and can only be justified where it brings a greater benefit, such as public order.

Act and rule utilitarianism

The theory of utilitarianism has developed since Bentham and Mill. Under act utilitarianism, the rightness of an act is judged in isolation to see whether it adds to, or subtracts from, the sum of human happiness. For example, when I drive my car at 130 mph on an empty motorway, I am increasing my own happiness and causing pain to nobody else: the sum of human happiness is increased.

According to rule utilitarianism, the rightness of an action is judged according to whether the sum of human happiness would be increased if everyone acted in the same way. Developing the example, if all car owners tried to drive along the same stretch of motorway at the same speed and at the same time, an accident might well occur, resulting in pain and misery: the sum of human happiness would decrease.

	Basic premise
Jeremy Bentham	He developed the legal and moral principle of utility: what makes an action right or wrong is the usefulness, or value, of the consequence it brings. The more an action increases overall happiness, the more valuable it is; and the more it decreases happiness, the more reprehensible.
John Stuart Mill	Justice, he explained, includes respect for people, for property and for rights, as well as the need for good faith and impartiality. All of these are consistent with the principle of utility, since their application brings the greatest happiness to the greatest number.

Figure 14.2 Key facts about legal philosophers concerned with utilitarianism

14.2.3 Social justice

Social justice can be said to be the ability which people have to realise their potential in the society where they live. It is concerned with equal justice, not just in the courts, but in all aspects of society. This concept demands that people have equal rights and opportunities; everyone, from the poorest person on the margins of society to the wealthiest, deserves an even playing field.

The Department for Work and Pensions published a paper on this topic in 2012. In the document the key expression was 'Social Justice is about making society function better – providing the support and tools to help turn lives around'.

Look online

Read the introduction to 'Social Justice: Transforming Lives' on pages 4 and 5 to gain an insight about social justice: www.gov.uk/government/publications/social-justice-transforming-lives.

This is not a new idea, as it has been expounded by philosophers including John Rawls and Robert Nozick.

John Rawls

John Rawls published *A Theory of Justice* in 1971, which set out the concept of social justice. Rawls described justice as fairness, and then presented a hypothetical society where each member would distribute its resources in a disinterested manner. To make this possible, nobody would know in advance what their position in that society would be, nor what stage of that society's development they would be born into. They would operate behind a 'veil of ignorance'. Rawls stated:

> No one knows his place in society, his class position or social status, nor does anyone know his fortune in the distribution of natural assets and abilities, his intelligence, strength, and the like.

Rawls believed that, on this basis, benefits and burdens would be distributed justly and therefore fairly.

He argued that two basic principles of justice would be evident within this society:

● Each person would have 'an equal right to the most extensive scheme of basic liberties compatible with a similar scheme of liberties for others'. This would include certain basic freedoms, such as the right to own property, freedom of speech, freedom of association, and freedom from arbitrary arrest, which we can see as many of the freedoms under the ECHR.

- Social and economic inequalities may exist, but only:
  - where they benefit the least advantaged members of society, and
  - provided all offices and positions are open to everyone.

This would mean that it is acceptable for a surgeon to earn several times the average wage, live in a large detached house and drive a luxury car, etc., because his work benefits disadvantaged members of society. In addition, his work would encourage others to imitate his example, further benefiting the disadvantaged. It is only acceptable provided that everyone with skills and abilities comparable to those of the neurosurgeon has a reasonable opportunity to pursue a similar path.

In employing the fiction of the 'veil of ignorance' to develop a society based upon consent, Rawls was promoting a rights-based system. So basic human rights such as freedom of speech and association are 'inalienable': they can never be sacrificed for the common good.

The state must always respect the autonomy of the individual. Rawls wrote:

> Each person possesses an inviolability founded on justice that even the welfare of society as a whole cannot override. Therefore, in a just society the rights secured by justice are not subject to political bargaining or to the calculus of social interests.

This distinguishes Rawls from Bentham and the utilitarians, against whom the final comment is directed, for utilitarians might allow individual freedoms to be sacrificed where this is considered necessary to promote wider benefits for the greater number.

Robert Nozick

Robert Nozick published *Anarchy, State and Utopia* in 1974, in which he developed an entitlement theory of justice, which consisted of three principles:

- A principle of justice in acquisition, dealing with how property is initially acquired.
- A principle of justice in transfer, dealing with how property can change hands.
- A principle of rectification of injustice, dealing with injustices arising from the acquisition or transfer of property under the two principles above. This third

principle would not be required if the world was entirely just.

Where a person obtains property in accordance with the principles of acquisition or transfer, s/he is entitled to keep that property. Where a person obtains property by fraud or theft or other unjust means, the third principle provides a remedy.

This is different from Rawls, who argued that inequalities may exist only where they benefit the most disadvantaged members of society. Nozick places no limits upon private ownership. Property justly acquired may not be appropriated simply as a form of redistribution of wealth, to reduce inequalities. He wrote: 'No one has a right to something whose realisation requires certain uses of things and activities that other people have rights and entitlements over.'

This is a free-market, libertarian form of justice.

Nozick revives John Locke's theory of justice. He argues that state interference should be kept to a minimum to achieve a just society and that it should be restricted to the basic needs – protecting the individual against force, theft/fraud and enforcing contractual obligations. The emphasis is on protecting the individual's rights, particularly one's property rights. Nozick does not believe that property can be owned by the state, but by individuals.

Nozick's theory may be criticised, but many of the recent political moves in our society show this theory in practice:

- privatisation of state-owned facilities
- making the individual more responsible for his own welfare – this can be seen in the tightening of the welfare net in terms of social security and pension provision
- reducing the dependence of the individual on the state.

	Basic premise
John Rawls	He described justice as fairness. He argued that two basic principles of justice would be evident within society.
Robert Nozick	In his book, *Anarchy, State and Utopia*, he developed an entitlement theory of justice, which consisted of three principles. This contrasts with Rawls who provided a philosophical basis for the welfare state and the redistribution of wealth to help the disadvantaged in his book, *A Theory of Justice*.

Figure 14.3 Key facts about legal philosophers concerned with social justice

The criminal process

Trial by jury enables the jury members to use their view of justice rather than adhere strictly to the rules of law and the evidence presented to them. In *Ponting* (1985) a civil servant was charged under the Official Secrets Act for releasing secret information about the sinking of the Argentinian warship, *General Belgrano*. The judge told the jury that any public interest in the information did not provide a defence but the jury acquitted him. The rules of evidence adopted in criminal trials seek to balance the interests of the parties to the action.

For this reason, evidence of previous convictions is not generally admissible unless the facts are strikingly similar to those in the instant case.

On the other hand, even illegally obtained evidence may be admissible. In *Jeffery v Black* (1978) the police arrested a student for the theft of a sandwich, and then conducted an illegal search of his flat, where they discovered some drugs. The magistrates threw out the case after ruling the evidence inadmissible. However, the Divisional Court ruled that the illegality of the search did not justify excluding the evidence it had exposed. This may at first seem to be unjust.

However, consider a situation where the police had discovered plans and materials to commit a terrorist attack. They would surely be justified in relying upon the material found in the 'illegal' search in court.

In general justice is served by the criminal process, but individual cases may expose a lack of justice that is not always remedied at a later date.

Appeals in criminal cases

In criminal cases heard in the Magistrates' Court, the defendant may appeal against conviction or sentence or on a point of law.

Under the Criminal Justice Act 1998, the prosecution may appeal against 'unduly lenient' sentences. Convicted criminals appeal less frequently now that an appeal may result in a more severe sentence.

Under the Criminal Justice Act 1972, the Attorney-General may appeal on a point of law to the Court of Appeal where s/he wishes to question the judge's direction that has led to an acquittal.

For example, in *Attorney-General's Reference (No. 2 of 1992)* (1993) the Court of Appeal considered the defence of automatism.

See the case study in Chapter 7, section 7.2.1.

Appeals with respect to substantive law are always seen as achieving justice, but not necessarily for those who have been convicted under the 'old' law. In the interests of justice, today's sentencing guidelines are not applicable to offences committed before new guidelines came into force.

Miscarriages of justice in criminal cases

In spite of this system of appeals, injustices arise where people serve prison sentences for crimes they are not guilty of. Famous cases include the Birmingham Six and the Guildford Four. The publicity of these and other similar cases led to the establishment in 1997 of the Criminal Cases Review Commission (CCRC), whose role is to review the cases of those it feels have been wrongly convicted of criminal offences, or unfairly sentenced.

Look online

Look at cases that the CCRC has been involved with and its successes, at: **www.ccrc.gov.uk/case-library/**.

The CCRC does not consider innocence or guilt, but whether there is new evidence or argument that may cast doubt on the safety of the original decision. Derek Bentley and Sally Clark are among those who have had their convictions quashed by the Court of Appeal following reference from the CCRC.

The only comfort in terms of justice is the fact that systems exist to bring miscarriages of justice to the attention of the appeal courts, even if in some cases a considerable period of time can lapse before the miscarriage is put right, and in Bentley's case, many years after he had been hanged. Even then, compensation is unlikely to be paid unless it can be shown that their innocence was beyond all reasonable doubt as a result of fresh evidence.

Public funding for many aspects of this is limited. Procedural justice relies very heavily upon the integrity of those responsible for the investigation and prosecution of crime.

Birmingham pub bombings inquest: families to meet home secretary over funding

Relatives of victims of the IRA's 1974 Birmingham pub bombings are to meet the home secretary, Amber Rudd to request funding for legal representation at the resumed inquest.

The private discussions on Monday come amid mounting concern over the way police, prison officers and local authority staff are invariably provided with lawyers at coroners' courts whereas the families of those who died are repeatedly denied legal aid.

...

For the Hillsborough inquest, the Home Office did eventually provide discretionary payments for legal representation for families at the second inquest into the deaths of 96 men, women and children in the 1989 stadium disaster ...

The Birmingham families hope to persuade Rudd that a similar funding approach should be taken by the Home Office for their resumed inquest.

Source: Taken from an article by Owen Bowcott in the *Guardian* online, 5 September 2016

Follow this link to read the complete article: **www.theguardian.com/uk-news/2016/sep/05/birmingham-pub-bombings-inquest-families-to-ask-home-secretary-for-funding**.

14.3.4 Rules of natural justice

Natural justice is often described as containing two basic principles. The first is that the court must not only be impartial, but also seen to be so. Judges should have no personal interest in a case. In the *Pinochet* case (1998), the House of Lords ruled that General Pinochet, the former dictator of Chile, could be extradited to Spain to stand trial for his alleged involvement in the torture and death of Spanish citizens in Chile.

The House of Lords initially included Lord Hoffman. He was a director of one part of Amnesty International who had been given permission to take part in the appeal. Clearly this infringed the principle of impartiality.

The second principle is that each party to the dispute must have a fair opportunity to present his own case and to answer the case of his opponent. In *Ridge v Baldwin* (1964) the House of Lords ruled that the decision by a police authority to dismiss its chief constable without a personal hearing contravened natural justice.

The rules of natural justice are designed to protect the interests of individuals against arbitrary decisions. In both the *Pinochet* case and *Ridge v Baldwin*, the original decision may have been correct. However, each was unreliable because of the breach of the rules of natural justice.

The application of justice must be fair, and must be seen to be fair.

14.3.5 Contract law

Formation of contract

In *Reveille Independent LLC v Anotech International (UK) Ltd* (2016) the court had to consider if a contract has come into existence between commercial parties when they were apparently still in negotiation. In examining the rules on offer and acceptance by conduct, the court was keen to preserve certainty and give due attention to what it considered to be the reasonable expectations of honest, sensible business people. This was stressed in order to achieve justice in these business situations.

Exclusion clauses

Parties to a contract may try to limit their liability by relying upon exclusion clauses. The traditional rule of *caveat emptor* (let the buyer beware) can work against the interests of the weaker bargaining party or where there is a pre-printed standard form of contract. The courts try to achieve a more just result.

Case study

Olley v Marlborough Court Hotel (1949)

The exclusion clause was invalid as it had not been brought to Mrs Olley's attention when she booked in at reception.

Spurling v Bradshaw (1956)

Lord Denning observed that some exclusion clauses were written in 'regrettably small print', and stated that the more harsh or unusual the term was, the more it needed to be brought to the attention of the person signing it – for example by being 'printed in red ink, with a red hand pointing to it'.

The Unfair Contract Terms Act 1977 restricts the use of exclusion clauses. A person cannot exclude liability for death or personal injury resulting from his negligence, and other exclusion clauses are subjected to the test of reasonableness. This Act aims to prevent those with strong bargaining power from taking unfair advantage of weaker parties and to provide a fairer balance between the bargaining parties.

Further protection is given to consumers by legislation such as the Consumer Rights Act 2015 which sets out both rights and remedies in consumer transactions.

Penalty clauses

The justice of penalty clauses depends on the view of how far a person can force someone else to comply with what they have promised. European and international law allow a court to modify an excessive penalty in a contract term. Under UK law, the penalty clause is either invalid or not.

Case study

Cavendish Square Holding BV v Talal El Makdessi and ParkingEye Ltd v Beavis (2015)

The Supreme Court decision widened the previously applied tests in relation to the enforceability of penalty clauses. Lord Hodge stated that:

> the correct test for a penalty is whether the sum or remedy stipulated as a consequence of a breach of contract is exorbitant or unconscionable when regard is had to the innocent party's interest in the performance of the contract.

This suggests an idea of justice being applied.

In *El Makdessi*, the court held that the provisions contained in the agreements were there to protect the legitimate interests of the buyer.

In *ParkingEye* it was held that although £85 may have been perceived to be an unreasonably high sum, there were clear legitimate commercial interests that were to be protected by the fine.

Third party rights

Traditionally, a person could not sue unless they were a party to the contract. However, in *Jackson v Horizon Holidays* (1975) the claimant succeeded in seeking damages for himself and for members of his family after a package holiday failed to match the advertised description, even though only he, and not his family members, had made the contract. This is not too surprising given the law of agency and the doctrine of the undisclosed principal.

In 1999, Parliament passed the Contract (Rights of Third Parties) Act, allowing third parties to make a claim where the contract expressly provided for this, or where the contract purported to confer a benefit on them. These provisions were designed to avoid the obvious injustices caused in cases such as *Tweddle v Atkinson* (1861), and the subterfuges that were necessary to obtain a just result which occurred in *Beswick v Beswick* (1967).

It does appear that the Contracts (Rights of Third Parties) Act 1999 would now allow the *Beswick* claim even if she had not been an executor of the will. However, if it appears the parties did not intend the term to benefit a third party then the Act will not apply. The parties to the contract have therefore the right to exclude the Act from benefiting a third party. Most commercial contracts now include such a term so the Act is not as useful as might be hoped.

Frustrated contracts

Parliament again was responsible for legislating to ensure that, where a contract is frustrated through no fault of either party, a just outcome can be reached. The Law Reform (Frustrated Contracts) Act 1943 enabled the courts to apportion the losses more fairly between the parties: the court may order 'a just sum' to be paid where either expenses have been incurred or a valuable benefit obtained.

However, the courts seem reluctant to find frustration of contract. This can be seen in the case of *Armchair Answercall v People in Mind* (2016) where the court made the inference that 'one or other party [had] assumed the risk of the occurrence of the event' and so there was no frustration of contract.

14.3.6 Tort

Duty and breach in negligence

Within the tort of negligence, a duty of care will not be imposed unless it is fair, just and reasonable to do so. In *Hill v Chief Constable for West Yorkshire* (1988) the mother of the Yorkshire Ripper's final victim sued the police for damages for not preventing her daughter's death. The House of Lords decided that it would not be fair or just for the police to owe a duty of care to every potential victim of crime, as it could lead to defensive policing practices. This decision appears to be harsh on this claimant but could be considered just, as making the police liable could lead to defensive policing practices and lead the police away from their role of public protection and the detection of crime. However, where the victim is known to the police, such as in *Swinney v Chief Constable of Northumbria* (1996), it will be fair, just and reasonable for the police to owe a duty of care and to be liable for any loss suffered as a result of their negligence. This seems just, as the police in this case had accepted responsibility to the claimant.

The decision in *Nettleship v Weston* (1971) might also be regarded as unfair: a learner driver was judged according to the objective standard of a competent driver, and so was liable for injuries caused to her instructor. However, leaving an innocent victim without a remedy is probably the cause of an even greater injustice. In such situations, justice can only be achieved where the potential for injustice to each party is weighed in the balance. This could also be seen as just because the motorist's insurance policy could compensate the injured claimant.

It could be argued that an unjust verdict was arrived at in *Bolton v Stone* (1951). The innocent claimant was injured by a cricket ball hit out of a ground. This decision might be fair for the club but was unjust on the injured claimant, who received no compensation.

Occupier's liability

The decision in *British Railways Board v Herrington* (1972) illustrates how justice is achieved when the claims of the two parties to the dispute are weighed in the balance. This result appeared to be just, as it compensated the injured boy. Also, social conditions had changed. *Robert Addie & Sons Ltd v Dumbreck* in 1929 ruled that the occupiers owed no duty to child trespassers. It was just for the court to decide that owners of land owed a responsibility to visitors, including trespassers.

Strict liability in tort

In *Rylands v Fletcher* (1868) liability was imposed even though the defendant was unaware of the danger.

In *Abouzaid v Mothercare (UK) Ltd* (2000) the claimant used the strict liability provisions of the Consumer Protection Act 1987 to claim damages for personal injury. Under the Act, the claimant only has to prove that they were injured as a result of using a faulty product which is easier to prove than negligence. The Court of Appeal found that although the product supplier was not negligent, the claimant had proved his strict liability claim and was entitled to damages. This result appeared to be just, as it compensated the injured boy.

Summary

- Justice is a concept that can be described simply by a synonym such as fairness, equality or even-handedness.
- There are many theories and aspects of justice including: justice as harmony; distributive justice; utilitarianism; social justice; procedural justice; corrective justice; natural justice; substantive justice.
- Justice is essential in the law. The extent to which it is achieved varies with respect to different aspects of procedural and substantive law.
- Examples can be seen in both civil and criminal law.
- Judges are increasingly aware of the concept of justice and use the law to achieve justice even if this means overruling a previous case or distinguishing previous decisions on surprising grounds.

Chapter 15

Law and society

After reading this chapter you should be able to:
- Understand the role law plays in society
- Understand the law as a social control mechanism
- Understand the way in which the law creates and deals with consensus and conflict
- Understand the realist approach to law making

15.1 The role law plays in society

15.1.1 What is society?

We have considered the nature of law in Chapter 13, and examined the concepts of legal positivism and natural law. Law is just one aspect of social structure. According to sociologists, a society is a group of people with common territory, interaction and culture.

Countries normally have formal boundaries and territory that the world recognises as theirs. However, a society's boundaries don't have to follow these boundaries, such as the one between Ulster and the Republic of Ireland.

Members of a society must come in contact with one another. If a group of people within a country has no regular contact with another group, those groups cannot be considered part of the same society. Geographic distance and language barriers can separate societies within a country. This occurred when Pakistan, which was a country both to the west and the east of India, separated into Pakistan and Bangladesh in 1971. There had been little interaction between the two parts that were separated geographically.

People of the same society share aspects of their culture, such as language or beliefs. Culture refers to the language, values, beliefs, behaviour and material objects that constitute a people's way of life. It is a defining element of society. Members of a society will not necessarily have every aspect of culture in common. This may appear to give separate societies within a geographical country such as where there is apartheid. This is known as pluralism.

15.1.2 Pluralism

Pluralism has many definitions. In the context of this chapter, pluralism may be defined as a form of society in which the members of minority groups maintain their independent cultural traditions. A pluralist is, therefore, a person who believes that the existence of different types of people, beliefs, and opinions within a society is a good thing. This requires tolerance from everyone concerned.

The United Kingdom is a society composed of many groups of people, some of whom originally belonged to other societies. There is a long history of invasion such as the Romans, the Vikings and the Norman Conquest. Since the Norman Conquest there have been many examples of relatively large immigrations to the United Kingdom such as the Huguenots who, in the seventeenth and eighteenth centuries, left their homes in France to escape persecution. The influence of the British Empire and Commonwealth enabled immigration from many parts of the world. Successive governments from the time of the Norman Conquest have either encouraged or discouraged immigration from different countries and of different groups. For example, the Jewish community has since grown, swelled by the Nazi policies in Germany during the 1930s and the subsequent war. This is just one example of religious tolerance in the UK helping to establish a pluralist society of Christians, Jews, Muslims and Hindus among others in today's pluralistic society.

Members of a particular culture, religion or immigrant society tend to congregate together for comfort and also to preserve the cultural identity of their society.

Some practices that are common in other societies will inevitably offend or contradict the values and

Chinese New Year parade in Manchester

beliefs of the new society. Groups seeking to become part of a pluralistic society often have to give up many of their original traditions in order to fit in. This is known as assimilation, and can be seen in the gradual loss of immigrants' language as they assimilate society's use of English as the language of society in the UK.

However, in pluralistic societies, groups do not have to give up all of their former beliefs and practices. Many groups within a pluralistic society retain their traditions such as Chinese communities celebrating the Lunar New Year.

UK society has people from different societies who blend together into a single mass. This is often referred to as multicultural, as even if a group has been in this country for many generations, it probably still retains some of its original heritage. The term 'multiculturalism' recognises that those who are originally from other societies do not necessarily have to lose their individual markers by becoming part of the mainstream. In a pluralistic society, no one group is officially considered more influential than another. However, powerful informal mechanisms, such as prejudice and discrimination, work to keep many

groups out of the political process or out of certain neighbourhoods, or to prevent free expression of their values and beliefs.

15.1.3 The role of law in society

The rule of law cannot exist without a transparent legal system. This requires a clear set of laws that are freely and easily accessible to all, strong enforcement structures, and an independent judiciary to protect citizens against the arbitrary use of power by the state, individuals or any other organization.

Lord Bingham set out the rule of law through eight principles which society, the state and the judiciary must embrace. His principles are:

- The state must abide by both domestic and international law. This means no government has the ability to act by whim.
- People should only be punished for crimes set out by law.
- Questions on the infringement of rights should be subject to the application of law, not discretion.
- The law should be accessible, clear, precise and open to public scrutiny.

- All people should be treated equally.
- There must be respect for human rights.
- Courts must be accessible and affordable, and cases should be heard without excessive delay.
- The means must be provided for resolving, without prohibitive cost or inordinate delay, bona fide disputes which the parties themselves are unable to resolve.

Law plays four primary roles in society:

1 To protect people from harm – typically by the mechanisms of the criminal law with respect to harm by other people or by dangerous things such as unsafe machinery or pollution.
2 To ensure a common good – by providing facilities for all such as education and health care.
3 To settle arguments and disputes regarding finite resources – this is the idea of a civil justice system.
4 To persuade people to do the right thing – by giving nudges through the law such as encouraging giving to charity through gift aid.

This can be seen in the effect of law on the balance between competing interests within society and the importance of fault as a basis for law in society. The law has a role in shaping social norms and behaviour. Society can shape the law through protests, strikes and civil disobedience. These link to examples from the influences on Parliament and law reform topics set out in *OCR AS/A Level Law Book 1*. There is therefore a two-way movement between law and society.

The difficulty is that the threats from small sectors of society are often exaggerated by the media either because of their own views or because the media outlet hopes to increase its influence and sales through sensationalism. Examples of the media influence can be seen from the mods and rockers of the 1950s. Stanley Cohen in his book *Folk Devils and Moral Panics* (1972) points out that if someone is acting in a way that is not typical to what society is used to, then the media tends to overreact extremely about it. The more the media cover this new behaviour (in this case, the mods and rockers fighting), the more it becomes established. So rather than stopping it, which they were trying to do, they actually helped it to grow. Then government becomes enjoined to act.

This is further exemplified by the consequences of the Castlemorton Common festival, which ran for seven days in May 1992. This was the tipping point for the government's full-blown assault on the free party scene, and it was certainly the excuse. The giant party set in motion the moral panic that led to the Criminal Justice and Public Order Act 1994. The excessive powers proposed by this Act were soon the subject of protest, notably by the publication of SchNEWS which pointed out examples of abuse of power. This organisation continued for 20 years highlighting injustice and ecological issues among others.

Look online

The following link shows how the influence of a small number of people can try to affect the law: www.theecologist.org/campaigning/campaigning_the_basics/988474/schnews_how_road_protesters_ravers_and_gm_activists_fought_back_with_direct_action_tabloid.html.

Knee-jerk reactions can be seen in the media campaigns to identify paedophiles in society leading to the so-called 'Sarah's law' permitting disclosure of the whereabouts of some sex offenders in certain circumstances, albeit after some disastrous attempts by vigilantes to take the law into their own hands. This includes one case where a paediatrician was attacked as the attacker was unable to distinguish paediatrician from paedophile.

The Dangerous Dogs Act 1991 came about as a result of media attention arising from the attack on six-year-old Rucksana Khan in a park in Bradford and another ten dog attacks at around the same time. The Home Secretary promised action and the Act was rushed through, banning four named breeds of dog. The legislation has not been considered a success as many healthy and safe dogs have been destroyed and an average of one person per year has been killed by dogs from breeds other than those prohibited.

Look online

For an example of media reporting of a recent dog attack see: www.liverpoolecho.co.uk/news/liverpool-news/dogs-mauled-toddler-were-not-13004563

Tip

When considering law and society, consider the balance of interests between the state, the majority of society and minorities within society. Does the state protect minorities or does it persecute them?

15.2 The law as a social control mechanism

Social control may be either informal or formal. Informal social control occurs through the family, the peer group, the local community and societal group. Formal social control occurs through specific social agencies which have the role of maintaining order in society. This is the criminal justice system including the police force, the judiciary, the probation and prison services as well as law makers – Parliament through Acts of Parliament and through delegating its powers to local law makers such as local councils and the judiciary in its interpretation and application of the law. The civil justice system also does this so that disputes can be settled through formal mechanisms in which society trusts.

> ## Key term
>
> **Social control** – the ways in which our behaviour, thoughts and appearance are regulated by the norms, rules, laws and social structures of society.

15.2.1 Social control through law

Rosco Pound's book, *Social Control Through Law*, was published in 1942. He suggested that the subject matter of law involves examining manifestations of human nature which require social control to assert or realise individual expectations. Pound formulated a list of social-ethical principles, with a three-fold purpose:

1 They identify and explain human claims, demands, or interests of a given social order.
2 They express what the majority of individuals in a given society want the law to do.
3 They guide the courts in applying the law.

He states that individual interests, public interests and social interests overlap and that claims, demands and desires can be placed in all three categories. Rights, unlike interests, have many different meanings.

The increasing rate of litigation in society can be seen as a result of the decline of the family and religious institutions over an individual's behaviour. The result is that the law courts exert greater control over the public and private lives of most members of society. Law is now the paramount agency of social control.

Social control entails rules of behaviour that should be followed by the members of a society. Some of the rules of conduct fall into the realm of good manners as the culture defines them. As such they describe behaviour that is socially desirable but not necessarily compulsory. Other rules of conduct are not optional and are enforced by laws.

Some areas of law are confusing because they are inconsistent or open to interpretation in different situations. Killing another individual is considered to be a serious crime except when it is done in battle during a war. There is a distinction between murder, manslaughter and other crimes where a death has occurred such as causing death by dangerous driving. The offence of murder has a mandatory life sentence. Other offences involving death do not. There is a wide disparity in sentencing for the same offence.

Social control is necessary to maintain social order. Society will then function without chaos or continual disruption. It ensures that only the values and norms of society are acceptable. It provides predictability. When there is no predictability as to how others will act, peaceful and productive interaction between people becomes virtually impossible. Social control, therefore, makes society possible by policing the boundaries and dealing with deviant behaviours.

The consequences of a breakdown of social order are lawlessness and a descent into anarchy. Social control can be informal or formal. The law provides the formal aspects. Some members of society need protection such as children and vulnerable adults, particularly those with mental health issues. We therefore have laws ensuring social services can take action where there is the potential for harm, abuse or neglect. Assisted suicide is forbidden because of the potential for abuse.

Public safety is important regardless of the age and vulnerability of individual members of society. For this reason we have, for example, health and safety at work legislation and controls on driving and the legality of drugs.

> ## Look online
>
> Read this article online and discuss whether the sentence was appropriate for this crime: www.thestar.co.uk/whats-on/out-and-about/death-crash-driver-freed-1-316624.

Social control fails where the law is weak or enforced without any degree of consistency. Eventually the law may be changed when society's view has changed and the inconsistent approach to enforcement has meant the law has fallen into disrepute. It is arguable that this eventually happened with respect to the law on homosexuality.

Where an area of law is of interest only to a small number of people in society, it becomes of less public importance and the possibility of change is diminished. If there is illogicality and inconsistency, it is seen as just 'one of those things' and those not directly involved ae not interested. This can be seen with the law on suicide which is aimed at reflecting traditional views of the sanctity of life and protecting the most vulnerable.

Suicide is no longer a crime, but aiding suicide is. The law on assisted suicide indicates the confusion there is in the law. Those convicted of aiding suicide could face up to 14 years in prison. Whether there is a prosecution is a matter of prosecution policy.

The policy includes a list of public interest factors that will influence whether or not someone is prosecuted for assisting suicide. In cases of encouraging or assisting suicide, prosecutors must apply the public interest factors in making their decision. A prosecution will usually take place unless the prosecutor is sure that there are sufficient public interest factors against it.

A prosecution is less likely if the person made a voluntary, informed decision to end his life, and if the assister was wholly motivated by compassion. Also, if the assister tried to discourage the person from suicide and if his actions could be seen as reluctant encouragement or assistance, prosecution is less likely.

The policy says that police and prosecutors should take a common sense approach to financial gain. If compassion was clearly the only reason behind the assister's actions, the fact that s/he may have gained some benefit will not usually be a factor in favour of prosecution. This is hardly clear for a situation like that of Debbie Purdy who had Multiple Sclerosis (MS). Shortly after her diagnosis in 1995, she began to think about how to have choice and control over her death. She argued that it was against her human rights not to know if her husband would be prosecuted if he went abroad with her so that she could die in a country where assisted suicide is legal. In 2009, Debbie won her case in the House of Lords. The judges said that the law was not clear enough about when people would be prosecuted for encouraging or assisting suicide and guidelines have been drawn up.

Criminal and civil disputes are rarely simple matters in any society. Laws may be open to interpretation, and there often is a difference of opinion about the evidence. In criminal law, when guilt is established, there can be a difference of opinion about the appropriate punishment. In civil law, there may be disagreement about the quantum of damages or

the wording of an injunction. Because these issues are open to differing conclusions, most societies settle legal cases in a manner agreed by the entire community or at least a representative sample of it.

The jury system is based on this idea, but jurors do not choose the sentence, only whether or not the defendant is guilty. The assumption is made that jurors will come to an understanding that would be acceptable to a 'reasonable man'. In most societies in the past, the reasonable man was thought to be a man and judges were also almost exclusively male. Women and children were not thought to be reasonable, nor were uneducated poor men. Subsequently, they were excluded from being jurors and judges. Society today has changed and the law recognises this. However, although the law recognises equality, it does not always enforce it.

15.2.2 Social control through the civil and criminal process

This can be seen in examples taken from both substantive law and procedure.

Look online

Read the following articles online and consider the defendants' sentences and whether they protect society and help maintain social control:
- www.theguardian.com/uk/2009/dec/14/jail-brothers-burglar-cricket-bat
- www.yorkshirepost.co.uk/news/crime/yorkshire-farmer-83-cleared-of-shooting-suspected-thief-on-his-property-1-8432452.

Many argue that the balance between the interests of the householder and of the burglar needs to be realigned, allowing the householder to decide the appropriate degree of force to be used when confronting burglars. All members of society want to feel safe when at home and when outside the home. In an unsafe situation, different people will react in different ways to protect themselves, others and their own and others' property. Juries and magistrates will take a view in each individual case so the law reflects their views. Advice comes from the state which helps form the views of those trying the cases where the defence has been raised.

This balance between the law and society has been recognised by the revised statement issued in 2013 entitled 'Householders and the Use of Force Against Intruders' which was a Joint Public Statement from the Crown Prosecution Service and the Association of Chief Police Officers. In that statement it is clear that no prosecution will be started in most circumstances for self-defence against a personal attack in your own home:

> The force you use must always be reasonable in the circumstances as you believe them to be. Where you are defending yourself or others from intruders in your home, it might still be reasonable in the circumstances for you to use a degree of force that is subsequently considered to be disproportionate, perhaps if you are acting in extreme circumstances in the heat of the moment and don't have a chance to think about exactly how much force would be necessary to repel the intruder: it might seem reasonable to you at the time but, with hindsight, your actions may seem disproportionate. The law will give you the benefit of the doubt in these circumstances.
>
> This only applies if you were acting in self-defence or to protect others in your home and the force you used was disproportionate – disproportionate force to protect property is still unlawful.

Consent

Where the victim consents to an assault, the defendant may escape liability. Two cases illustrate how the courts balance the interests of the defendant against those of their victims: *Wilson* (1996) and *Brown* (1993).

See Chapter 1 for full case details of *Wilson* (1996) and *Brown* (1993).

The main distinction between these two cases is circumstantial. On the one hand a married couple were engaging in an extreme form of tattooing, where the pain was incidental to the desired outcome. On the other hand, a group of sado-masochists were engaged in forms of torture, where inflicting pain was their purpose. In *Brown*, Lord Templeman spoke of the need for issues of policy and public interest to be weighed in the balance. Lord Mustill, however, spoke of the rights of an individual to live his life as he chooses in *Wilson*.

Clearly, these judges had different views about which considerations should form part of the balancing exercise they were performing and how society views activities that may revolt or disgust many people but are apparently consensual activities.

Contract law

In contract law, the courts are often confronted with the interests of two innocent parties, both of whom believe they have a plausible legal argument. There are many issues which illustrate the problems that the courts have faced when balancing the interests of businesses in society, and those that run them, and the ordinary citizen who uses those businesses. This is often with respect to consumer protection and the validity of terms in a contract imposed by the business sector on individual members of society. Law controls the way in which sectors of society can impose their will and profit from others through legislation such as the Consumer Rights Act 2015. This Act is sometimes criticised for protecting consumers in society at the expense of business.

We have seen a shift in the law as stated by judges with respect to third party rights in contract over the years from the approach in *Tweddle v Atkinson* (1861), where the claim failed as the claimant was not a party to the contract and so had no legal interest in the case. However, in *Jackson v Horizon Holidays* (1975) the House of Lords awarded the claimant damages on his own behalf and on behalf of his family for their disappointment over a package holiday that failed to match the advertised description. This award was made even though Mr Jackson was the only member of his family who was a party to the contract for the holiday. This confusion was apparently addressed in Contract (Rights of Third Parties) Act 1999. However, business merely excludes the operation of the Act by a contract term and so defeats the object of the exercise.

The law of tort

Tort law is concerned with obligations or duties owed by one party to another. It seeks to provide a remedy, usually damages, for the harm that is caused by the wrongdoing of one person to another. Often it is difficult to decide which party's interest should take precedence. The following issues illustrate the courts' concern to find the appropriate balance between the interests of the claimant and defendant who are often ordinary members of society.

We can see this by comparing *Bolton v Stone* (1951) and *Miller v Jackson* (1977). Both cases involved cricket and the interests of a small sector of society, the cricket club, and the individual in society as a whole.

See *OCR AS/A Level Law Book 1* Chapter 23 for full case details of *Bolton v Stone* (1951) and Chapter 10 of this book for details of *Miller v Jackson* (1977).

In *Bolton v Stone* (1951) the balance was in favour of the cricket club at the expense of the innocent victim. The Lords believed there were policy implications in terms of the message of what liability would have meant in creating restrictions in what we can do in our everyday lives in an urbanised modern society.

However, in *Miller v Jackson* (1977) the court had to weigh up the claimants' private interest to peacefully enjoy their own home against the defendant's enjoyment of a valuable recreational activity. There was, in addition, the interest of the local community in enjoying the open space. Roscoe Pound had warned against this balancing of a private with a social interest.

When the state is the other interested party, the situation appears to change. In *Dennis v Ministry of Defence* (2003), the private interest of the Dennises had to be balanced with the public interest of the MOD and society as a whole. Here it was decided that although there was a public benefit to the continued training of Harrier pilots, the Dennises should not be required to bear the cost of the public benefit. In contrast to *Miller v Jackson*, the private interest outweighed the public interest.

The balance between the individual in society and society as a whole as represented by the state can be seen in the increased desire of the individual member of society to gain compensation from the state whatever the overall effect on the state and society as a whole. Many local authorities bemoan the compensation culture as defending claims, particularly spurious claims, is costly. The insurance industry takes the same view as all of society is affected by these claims in the form of higher Council Tax and insurance premiums.

In February 2016 the NHS Litigation Authority released figures on medical negligence claims made in 2014/15. Just over 10,000 claims were lodged with another 900 pending; and the amount paid out during the year (but not necessarily related to the claims lodged in the same period) amounted to £1.3 billion. If financial squeeze on the NHS and social services continues, the number of claims and subsequent compensation payments will continue to rise relentlessly. There are those that argue that barring all such claims would go a long way to restoring NHS funding at the expense of some unfortunate members of society.

Area of law	Brief legal rule	Case examples
Criminal law – consent	Where the victim consents to an assault, the defendant may escape liability.	*Wilson* (1996) *Brown* (1993)
Contract law – third party rights	The shift in the law as stated by judges with respect to third party rights in contract over the years.	*Tweddle v Atkinson* (1861) *Jackson v Horizon Holidays* (1975)
The law of tort – negligence	The balance between the individual in society and society as a whole.	*Bolton v Stone* (1951) *Miller v Jackson* (1977)

Figure 15.1 Key facts about social control through the civil and criminal law

15.3 The way in which the law creates and deals with consensus and conflict

The way in which the law deals with consensus and conflict has already been seen to some extent in the cases discussed in the previous section. Judges clearly come to different opinions, deciding the cases on the facts presented to them and in accordance with their interpretations of the law with those facts. Procedural law also creates and deals with conflict, but perhaps in a more negative way.

Both the criminal and civil processes have to balance the interests of those involved in a case and particularly the trial. Achieving that balance flags up imbalances in the system or, more often, how one sector of society finds its interests subjugated to another's interests so as to provide social control.

There are three theories that need to be considered here:

- consensus theory
- conflict theory
- labelling theory.

Key terms

Consensus theory – consensus theory is a social theory that holds that a particular political or economic system is a fair system, and that social change should take place within the social institutions provided by it.

Conflict theory – society is in a state of perpetual conflict due to competition for limited resources.

Labelling theory – most people commit deviant and criminal acts but only some are caught and berated, ostracised or punished for them.

According to consensus theories, for the most part society works because most people are successfully socialised into shared values through the family and education. Socialisation produces agreement or consensus between people about appropriate behaviour and beliefs without which no human could survive. According to consensus theorists this process starts from a young age in the family and education. These institutions enforce what are known as positive and negative sanctions, or rewarding good behaviour and punishing bad behaviour. Both of these institutions perform the function of social control, and this is a good thing for both the individual and society.

Consensus theory is a social theory that holds that a particular political or economic system is a fair system, and that social change should take place within the social institutions provided by it. Consensus theory contrasts sharply with conflict theory, which holds that social change is only achieved through conflict. Consensus theory is concerned with the maintenance or continuation of social order in society.

Durkheim's work is based upon the assumption that there exists a consensus within society. The importance of the presence of a consensus is that it provides people with an understanding as to the forms of behaviour and conduct that are acceptable and those that are not.

The conflict theory of Karl Marx claims society is in a state of perpetual conflict due to competition for limited resources. It holds that social order is maintained by domination and power, rather than consensus and conformity. According to conflict theory, those with wealth and power try to hold on to it by any means possible, chiefly by suppressing the poor and powerless.

The labelling theory suggests that most people commit deviant and criminal acts but only some are caught and berated, ostracised or punished for them. These individuals are stigmatised for their behaviour. Most of us commit deviant and criminal acts at one time or another. However we regard those who are categorised as 'criminal' as somehow different from the rest of us and the only difference between the bulk of the population and criminals is that criminals are the ones who got caught. When sufficient people committing this behaviour have similarities such as age, race or appearance, they become stereotypes

and society then expects those that conform to that stereotype to be deviant or criminal.

An example of this is the use of stop and search laws. Between April 2015 and March 2016 the Home Office National Statistics show that in that year searches had fallen across all ethnicity groups to a total of 387,448. This is encouraging. However searches on white individuals fell by the largest amount (38 per cent), while searches on Black and Minority Ethnic (BME) individuals fell by only 13 per cent. Those from BME groups were three times as likely to be stopped and searched as those who are white. In particular, those who are black were over six times more likely to be stopped. In both cases these figures were higher than the previous year, and reflect the fact that although stops of all ethnicities have fallen, stops of white individuals have fallen by more than stops of BME individuals. This may be an example of stereotyping.

The law treats different members of society differently and this may be as a result of a number of factors drawn from those who make and enforce the law.

15.3.1 Magistrates and stereotyping

The idea of trial by one's peers suggests that there will be a balance found because those deciding on guilt or innocence will be members of society just like the accused. A House of Commons Select Committee reported in October 2016 on the role of the magistracy. Among the recommendations are the following:

- Steps to increase the diversity of magistrates, including wider and more proactive advertising, a streamlined recruitment process, additional funding for magistrates in the community and consideration of the introduction of 'equal merit' provisions for magistrates' recruitment.
- Rebalancing the age profile of the magistracy is unlikely to happen unless more is done to overcome the barriers facing employed magistrates. The following examples illustrate this balancing exercise.
  - ○ The number of magistrates has fallen significantly over the past ten years. The current total of 17,552 compares to around 30,000 in 2006. Judicial diversity statistics for 2016 show that 53 per cent of magistrates are female

and 89 per cent are white. While the latter figure is similar to the proportion of the overall population that is white (86 per cent), many benches have no, or very few, Black, Asian and Minority Ethnic (BAME) magistrates. So in some areas there are sectors of society that are not part of the peer group trying cases in the Magistrates' Court.

○ The statistics also indicate that, among serving magistrates, 86 per cent are aged 50 and over, with only 4 per cent under 40 and less than 1 per cent under 30; well over half of magistrates (57 per cent) are within ten years of the retiring age of 70. The age profile of offenders is possibly the mirror image of this age profile.

○ Only 4 per cent of magistrates declared themselves to be disabled, in comparison to 16 per cent of working age adults and 45 per cent of adults over state pension age. The Ministry of Justice statistics on disabled magistrates provide no further breakdown as to the nature of their impairment or the extent to which reasonable adjustments would help them to carry out their duties.

Of course magistrates do not only deal with criminal cases as they have a major part in the operation of the Family Court. Here age may be less of an issue but the racial background may well cause disquiet in those using the Family Court even if the training of those magistrates was excellent with respect to different communities in their locality.

The balance between state and society appears to be maintained by the use of people making decisions in legal cases who are supposed to reflect the society whose disputes and activities are in question. However, it is clear that there is disquiet at the imbalance of those who make the decisions and those about whom decisions are made. This disquiet arises as it appears that the decisions are made by sectors of society that are often very different from those about whom the decisions are made.

The suggestion that you should be tried by your peers who are of the same sector of society is unworkable. However, magistrates, like judges, need to be aware of the facts of life in different communities within society and be seen to act accordingly, although it is not always viewed in that way by those involved in the case.

In the news

The rules on questioning criminal suspects are there for a reason

After the conviction this week of taxi driver Chris Halliwell for the murder of Becky Godden, there has been much anger over what happened to the detective, Steve Fulcher. He obtained a confession from Halliwell that was deemed inadmissible as he had not yet been given access to a lawyer. This meant that Halliwell initially escaped justice for Godden's murder but it also had serious repercussions for Fulcher's career; he was found guilty of misconduct and given a final written warning. As a consequence he resigned from the police and now works as a security consultant in Somalia.

Halliwell was one of the most odious and devious of killers, and it would be hard not to feel both sympathy and admiration for Fulcher. He was clearly driven by the best of motives, and perhaps the police disciplinary process could have been handled with greater understanding.

However, Fulcher's actions were described by the IPCC as 'catastrophic'. They said that 'it is not possible to determine what may or may not have happened if Mr Halliwell had been immediately conveyed to custody. The Police and Criminal Evidence Act and its codes of practice are not optional. They are a fundamental part of the criminal justice process.'

Source: Adapted from an article by Duncan Campell in the *Guardian* online, 20 September 2016

Case study

R v Samuel (1988)

A man was arrested and interviewed four times over two days. He was denied access to a solicitor on the grounds that it would lead to the alerting of other suspects. At his fourth interview, he confessed to two offences of burglary, and was charged with these. He continued to be denied access to his solicitor. He was then interviewed a fifth time, and confessed to a robbery. The Court of Appeal quashed his subsequent conviction for robbery. It described the right to legal advice as 'one of the most important and fundamental rights of a citizen'. This fired a warning shot across the bows of the police, who had acted in breach of their duty in denying the suspect his legal right.

The right to legal advice should balance the individual with the power of the state and the needs of society as a whole. The fact that we are appalled by the occasional failure of the system as in *Samuel* suggests that the system works adequately. However, many are surprised that the right may be delayed and in many cases requires private funding to ensure a solicitor is present rather than just giving telephone advice.

15.3.2 Access to justice and society

In a democratic society all citizens have a right to access justice, to receive a fair hearing and to understand their legal rights and obligations. However exercising the right is difficult for those who are not confident and articulate and who cannot afford to pay for a lawyer or get other funding for their claim.

The Law Society has mounted a campaign about this stating the need to improve access to justice for all, regardless of social background or wealth. Ordinary people are finding it more difficult to access justice because of issues including legal aid cuts, court closures and increased court fees, as well as changes to the rules regarding the legal costs a client can recover. During 2017 it intends to launch a series of initiatives focused on improving access to justice.

The fact that this has been seen to be necessary indicates how society's relationship with the law is in danger of becoming even more lopsided and not reflecting the needs of society. This would appear to be trying to recover consensus and avoid conflict.

Look online

Read about the Law Society's campaign in more detail at this link: **www.lawsociety.org.uk/news/press-releases/time-to-restore-access-to-british-justice/**.

The first of these initiatives focused on ending legal aid deserts – these are areas where those entitled to legal aid can no longer access it due to a shortage of specialist advice providers.

15.4 The realist approach to law making

Legal realism is the view that we should understand the law as it is practised in the courts, law offices and police stations, rather than as it is set out in statutes or books.

For legal realists such as Oliver Wendell Holmes, who wrote *The Common Law* in 1923, if the law were merely a system of rules, we would not need lawyers conducting adversarial proceedings, because judges could just apply the rules. However, judges have discretion with which they can decide a case in a number of ways, so the outcome is not certain.

Key term

Legal realism – an understanding of the law as it is practised in reality, not presented in statutes or academic theories.

Legal realism is positivist in that it first considers the law as it is. On the other hand, the law as it stands is the product of many factors. The realists are interested in the law rather than society.

Realists do not give any importance to laws enacted by Parliament as they uphold only judge-made law as genuine law.

A judge's understanding about law, society and psychology affects any judgment given by them. At the same time, in the same case, applying the same law, two different judges can give different judgments. This is seen in dissenting judgments in the Court of Appeal, Supreme Court and the ECtHR. Realism denounces traditional legal rules and concepts and concentrates more on what the courts actually do in reaching the final decision in the case. They define law as a generalised prediction of what the courts will do.

Realists believe that certainty of law is a myth. Law is intimately connected with society and since society changes faster than law, there can never be certainty about law. This can be seen in the change (or lack of change) with respect to the law on homosexuality and assisted suicide. The difficulty is that this view results in absurdity because a judge pondering what rights an accused has is, in fact, deciding what rights the judge is going to let the parties have. This can be seen in the way in which different interests in a case are balanced.

Many philosophers have written theories about balancing interests in society. As each member of society has a number of interests, some of them cannot be exercised without affecting others. The way in which the law deals with this is by allowing some interests at the expense of other members of society. Some of these theorists are Rudolf von Jhering, Roscoe Pound and Wesley Hohfeld, whose ideas are summarised in Figure 15.2 below.

	Basic premise
Rudolf von Jhering	Law is a means of ordering a society in which there are many competing interests that require regulation.
Roscoe Pound	Claims or demands or desires seeking legal recognition can be classified in one of three ways – individual interests, public interests and social interests.
Wesley Hohfeld	Distinguished between rights and liberties. He categorised relationships as jural correlatives and jural opposites.

Figure 15.2 Key facts about legal philosophers

Extension question

Research and write brief notes about an area where you think that a sector of society is poorly protected by the law. You might review your initial belief following your research. You might consider areas such as wearing particular clothing such as a hijab, niqab or burka, orthodox Jewish dress codes including a kippah or yarmulke, or Rastafarians with dreadlocks and a tam.

Summary

- Law plays four primary roles in society:
  - protect people from harm
  - ensure a common good
  - settle arguments and disputes regarding finite resources
  - persuade people to do the right thing.
- This can be seen in the effect of law on the balance between competing interests within society and importance of fault as a basis for law in society.
- Different areas of law reflect this balance which is often unequal, particularly from the point of view of some communities and some sectors of society.
- Legal realism is the view that we should understand the law as it is practised in the courts rather than as it is written.

Chapter 16

Law and technology

After reading this chapter you should be able to:
- Understand the intersection of law and technology
- Understand key issues, including privacy, data protection and cyber-crime
- Understand cross-border issues and future challenges

16.1 Law and technology – the challenges

Traditionally, rules of law have dealt with physical matters such as:
- the ownership of goods, services or property by a person
- property crimes such as theft or robbery or causing injury to another
- causing injury, loss or damage by an accident.

The question to ask in this topic is, how should the law deal with future technologies and their use? We live in a world where machines are carrying out functions traditionally done by humans, there are no physical borders, no single set of laws apply, physical products are replaced by information, and this information has to be stored and used. How should English laws deal with these evolving issues?

The focus of this chapter is on privacy, data protection and cyber-crime. For each of these forms of technology we will consider how, currently, law and the technology intersect with each other, the key issues with the use of that form of technology, and, finally, what cross-border issues and future challenges can be foreseen.

However there are other issues that you may wish to investigate where laws will have to be developed to cover the use of new forms of technology. These include driverless cars and vehicles, the use of robots and e-commerce.

The main issue that confronts lawyers is that, currently, traditional rules of law have to be used to deal with new forms of technology that are being developed. In the last 30 years the speed of innovation has been phenomenal and has given us a much greater range of products to use and rely on at home and at work. For example, the World Wide Web (www) was invented by Sir Tim Berners-Lee, a British scientist at CERN, in 1989. It was originally conceived and developed to meet the demand for automatic information-sharing between scientists in universities and academic institutions around the world. Mobile phones and individual computers became more common from the mid-1990s and the first smartphone, the Apple iPhone, was released in 2007, giving access to the internet while the user was on the move. In just a few years, an estimated 80 per cent of the UK adult population now owns a smartphone.

On the other hand, making law is a much slower process. First, there has to be an idea that a law is needed. Consultation and debate will take place on the form of that law, and it needs to pass through the legislative process during which there will be further debate and possible amendment. Arrangements might have to be made to operate the new law, and training might have to take place. In many cases a number of years will pass between the original thought and full implementation of a law. The alternative is making law through judicial precedent – this requires a case to come to court and for it then to reach the higher appeal courts.

Often a law will be reactive in nature, dealing with issues that are known about at the time of its passing or the issues in the case. Legislators are unlikely to have sufficient knowledge to frame laws that can deal with future technologies, even if they can anticipate what future technologies can be developed. Equally, judges have to rely on the expertise of the lawyers, parties and witnesses in the case, and the judicial decision will focus narrowly on the issues raised in that case. Most developments in technology will, for some time following their introduction, have to fit into current laws and be interpreted by them.

16.2 The intersection of law and technology

16.2.1 Robots and advanced computer systems

In the United States the Boston Dynamics company is one of the leaders in developing robots. In February 2016 they published a video on YouTube entitled 'Atlas, The Next Generation' showing a robot in humanoid form performing a number of tasks that would have been difficult or impossible for previous generation robots. These tasks included walking over uneven and treacherous snow-covered terrain, lifting boxes onto shelves and getting up quickly when knocked over.

An earlier version of Atlas was also able to negotiate rough terrain, to climb using hands and feet and to pick its way through congested spaces.

Method-2 is in its early stages of development in South Korea. It is over 13 feet tall and weighs 1.5 tonnes. It walks like a human. The pilot sits in the torso and moves his limbs which are then mimicked by the robot. It is suggested that the robot can be used by the armed forces, or in hazardous industrial environments or by search and rescue forces.

Activity

On YouTube, watch the Boston Dynamics video of Atlas in operation and the video of Method-2.

An advanced computer system is IBM Watson, which is a question answering computer system capable of answering questions posed in natural language. The system was originally developed to answer questions on the quiz show Jeopardy!

In 2013, IBM announced that Watson software system's first commercial application would be for helping to make management decisions in lung cancer treatment. It is being investigated to see how Watson may contribute to clinical decision support systems for use by medical professionals. Once a doctor has posed a query to the system describing symptoms and other related factors:

- Watson identifies the most important pieces of information
- it considers patient data to find facts relevant to the patient's history

- it examines available data sources to form and test hypotheses
- it finally provides a list of recommendations.

It has been suggested that Watson could be used for legal research and in other information-intensive fields, such as telecommunications, financial services, and government.

16.2.2 Driverless vehicles

A driverless vehicle is a self-driving or robotic vehicle that is capable of sensing its environment and navigating without any human input. Surroundings can be detected using techniques such as radar, lasers, GPS, motion sensors, and computer vision. Control systems can interpret sensory information to identify appropriate navigation paths, as well as obstacles and relevant signage.

There are five levels of autonomous driving. At the lowest level is cruise control which is available in many cars today. The next level is 'hands off' where the driver is in the car and vigilant; the next level is where the driver has eyes off; the fourth level is where the 'driver' is not involved in the driving – they may be working on a laptop for example. The highest level is where the vehicle does not have anyone in it and is driving itself which could be, for example, in a parking area.

Among the potential benefits of automated cars is a significant reduction of traffic accidents, with a decrease in deaths and injuries, and related costs. This could result in lower insurance costs. There could be less traffic congestion; enhanced mobility for the elderly or disabled. It is suggested that they will relieve travellers from driving and navigation chores with the result of freeing commuting time. From a business point of view, different models of service could be developed such as car sharing or ride hailing services, and other services, contributing to reduced personal car ownership.

Among the main obstacles and disadvantages, in addition to the initial technological challenges, are disputes concerning liability; the time needed to convert the existing stock of vehicles; concerns about their safety and the implementation of an alternative legal framework to cover their use. There may also be concerns about loss of privacy and security, for example by hacking systems or terrorist activity. There may be further long-term concerns about loss of driving-related jobs in the transport and delivery industry.

In a driverless car, the 'driver' is free to do other things

From a legal view, the main issue is tort liability in the event of an accident. As has been established in *OCR AS/A Level Law Book 1* Chapter 23, claims of personal injury and damage to property in the event of an accident depend on proof of fault. Fault may be due to driver error, other road users, the vehicle or a component such as a defective tyre. Payment of compensation will fall on the person or company who was at fault for the accident.

One manufacturer, Tesla, has announced that all of its new vehicles will come with built-in self-driving hardware and the company would not be liable if there was an accident with a car in self-driving mode. If the accident was due to design issues, then the company would accept liability, but otherwise, liability would be for the individual 'in charge or control' of the vehicle. On the other hand Volvo has announced it would take full liability for any of its cars while they are in autonomous mode.

It is not just these two manufacturers who are considering the issue of liability. Motor insurers and car companies are not certain who will be liable in the event of an accident – and they may not be until these cars have been on the market for a while. Lawyers and the insurance industry have decades of claims experience with driven cars and very little, if

any, experience of dealing with claims generated by self-driving cars. Initially some cases may be very complicated, where car companies, lawyers, insurers and drivers try to work out who, or what, was at fault for the crash and precedents are set.

The first fatal accident involving a semi-autonomous Tesla car, in May 2016 in the USA, caused concerns over driverless car safety. In that case, the car did not use its automatic braking system because it did not detect a lorry that came from two lanes away turning in front of it. In that case, Tesla claimed it was not the fault of its Autopilot system. One option to deal with liability is to install a black box in every driverless vehicle (just like in planes) to see who is at fault for an accident.

Some jurisdictions are already passing laws to deal with the development of driverless cars and liability. In Michigan in the USA laws were passed in 2016 allowing the use of driverless cars on public roads. There, regulations have been established for the testing, use, and eventual sale of autonomous vehicle technology and are meant to more clearly define how self-driving vehicles can be legally used on public roads. Liability in the event of an accident is placed on the driver or operator of the car. But the definition of 'operator' does not appear to be clear. The term could possibly include a company running a driverless taxi service, an engineer who started the vehicle, a passenger who is being driven in it, or the manufacturer of the automated driving system.

Finally, there may be a question of ownership. Many of the companies developing the technology claim that they should be considered the owners of both the software and the cars themselves, and consumers would simply license the product. Their argument is that private ownership would allow an individual to change the software, thereby decreasing the safety of the vehicle. This issue would have to be widely debated as it could affect all aspects of the automobile industry from dealerships to insurance companies, transportation services to repair shops.

16.2.3 The use of drones

Drones, also known as unmanned aerial vehicles (UAVs), are small aircraft either controlled by 'pilots' from the ground or increasingly, autonomously following a pre-programmed route. As well as their increasing use in a military context, there are a number of uses for drones in civilian life. These uses include:

- being flown for pleasure or competition
- documenting the aftermath of crashes or disasters
- using cameras for taking photos and filming aerial videos, or for domestic surveillance, surveying or farming
- the delivery of medical supplies to remote or otherwise inaccessible regions. DHL Parcel fly drones regularly to a sparsely inhabited German island in the North Sea for scheduled deliveries of medications and 'other urgently needed goods' for the local community.

Several companies have future plans for the use of drones, including:

- Amazon plans to use drones for small package delivery called 'Prime Air', a delivery system, which will allow packages to get into customers' hands within 30 minutes or less of placing the order.
- Amazon is also applying for permission to build and fly delivery drones and flying warehouses, from which drones are dispatched to individual houses.
- Google is also planning a drone delivery service called Wing.

Section 16.3.1 below examines the legal challenges posed by the use of drones.

Drones can be used to deliver parcels

Activity ❓

Driverless vehicles

- How is it suggested that driverless vehicles be used in the future? You may wish to investigate how driverless vehicles are being developed for use in the USA, particularly in California.
- What laws do you think currently exist in England covering their use on public roads?
- What legal issues might affect the use of driverless cars on public roads in England?
- How are other legal jurisdictions dealing with driverless vehicles? How do these laws differ from current English law?

16.2.4 Privacy – the use of CCTV and surveillance systems

Closed-circuit television (CCTV) is a TV system in which signals are not publicly distributed but are monitored, primarily for surveillance and security purposes. It relies on the placement of cameras, followed by observation of the camera's images. Because the cameras communicate with monitors and/or video recorders across private cable runs or wireless communication links, they are designated 'closed-circuit' to show that access to their content is limited only to those able to see it. In addition to fixed cameras on buildings, the use of body-worn video cameras is being increasingly introduced, especially by police forces, as a new form of surveillance.

CCTV is used widely, including:

- Traffic-monitoring in cities and on motorways to detect congestion and notice accidents.

Cameras are used to enforce the London congestion charge. Some cameras may be owned by private companies and can transmit data to drivers' GPS systems.

- Recording passing vehicles using automatic number plate recognition (ANPR) cameras in mobile police cars and vans or in fixed positions. This information is added to a national database and is available to be searched by police officers. The record is stored for a maximum of two years. In addition some local councils operate ANPR cameras, as do private companies for supermarkets and petrol stations to reduce the number of customers who leave without paying.
- By transport operators, for example on buses and trains, to allow the operator to confirm that passengers are clear of doors before closing them and starting off.
- By stadiums and event venues to track movement of fans into and away from the venue and the behaviour of users. With all-seater stadiums, fans can be identified and their names and addresses found to contact them with regard to possible criminal offences.
- For home and building safety and security as part of an alarm monitoring package that can include fire and flood detection.
- In commercial premises, CCTV may be used to maintain security, to observe the behaviour of incarcerated inmates and potentially dangerous patients in medical or prison facilities, and to oversee locations that would be hazardous to a human, for example, in highly radioactive or toxic industrial environments.
- To obtain a visual record of activities in situations where it is necessary to maintain proper security or access controls such as in banks, casinos, or airports.

Look online

To read more about the use of ANPR cameras, visit www.anpr.org.uk.

Section 16.3.2 below explores the legal issues raised by the use of CCTV.

16.2.5 Data protection

During the second half of the twentieth century, businesses, organisations and the government began storing information about their customers, clients and staff in databases. This information could include:

- names
- addresses
- contact information
- employment history
- medical conditions
- any criminal convictions
- credit history.

Databases can be easily accessed, searched and edited. Information can be cross-referenced if stored in two or more computer-based databases, especially if the computers are networked. This sharing can allow organisation-wide access to the information, which could also be shared with other organisations.

With more and more organisations storing and processing personal information, there is a danger the information could be misused or get into the wrong hands. Concerns include:

- Who could access this information?
- How accurate is it?
- Could it be easily copied and shared?
- Is it possible to store information about a person without their knowledge or permission?
- Are records kept of any changes to information stored?

The Data Protection Act 1998

This Act was passed to control the way in which information is handled and to give legal rights to people who have personal information stored about them. It covers information held on computers and paper-based records.

Personal information is not limited to a person's name and address. It can include any data that could reasonably be put together with other information to divulge personal information about a person.

The processing of information covered by the Act includes any operation on data involving a computer. This could range from selecting a name for a mail shot, to reading it from a screen during a sales call.

A company or organisation that wants to process data needs to notify the Office of the Information Commissioner (a government body) that it is doing so. That way, it is possible to know who is legitimately processing data and who is not. The Information Commissioner has powers to enforce the Act. The Act

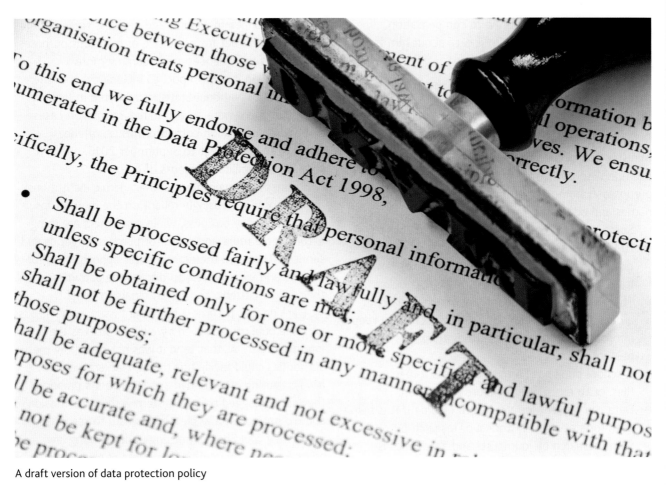

A draft version of data protection policy

does not stop companies storing information about people – it just makes them follow rules.

The rules for storage and processing of data are contained in the following eight principles:

1 It must be collected and used fairly and inside the law.
2 It must only be held and used for the reasons given to the Information Commissioner.
3 It can only be used for those registered purposes and can only be disclosed to those people mentioned in the register entry. A company cannot give away or sell information unless it has disclosed this.
4 The information held must be adequate, relevant and not excessive when compared with the purpose stated in the register.
5 It must be accurate and kept up to date. An example is changing an address when notified. A company can inform its data subjects by a Fair Processing Notice what it will do with their data and of any changes in the arrangements.
6 It must not be kept longer than is necessary for the registered purpose.
7 It must be kept safe and secure. This includes keeping information backed up and away from any unauthorised access.

8 The files may not be transferred outside of the European Economic Area (the EU and some other European countries) unless the country that the data is being sent to has a suitable data protection law.

A person whose data has been collected (a 'data subject') has a number of rights which include:
- a right to be supplied with the personal data held about them (a charge can be made for giving this information)
- any mistakes found in the data can be corrected
- the use of information can be prevented if it would be likely to cause distress
- a data subject may stop their data being used if there are attempts to sell them products, for example by junk mail or cold calling
- a data subject can specify that they do not want a data user to make 'automated' decisions about them, for example where, by point-scoring, a computer decides on an application for a loan
- a data subject can ask for the use of their personal data to be reviewed by the Information Commissioner

- the data subject is entitled to compensation for damage caused to him if data about him is inaccurate, lost, or disclosed.

There are some exemptions from the Act. Complete exemptions include any personal data held for national security reasons. The security services do not have to follow the rules but they do need to get a government minister to sign a certificate saying that they are exempt. Also any personal data held for domestic purposes at home is exempt, such as a list of friends' names and addresses.

Some personal data is partially exempt, such as:

- HM Revenue & Customs and the police do not have to disclose information held to prevent crime or taxation fraud. Convicted offenders cannot see their police files.
- There is no right to see information stored about a data subject's health. This allows doctors to keep information from patients if they think it is in their best interests.
- A school pupil has no right of access to personal files, or to exam results before publication.
- Data can be kept for any length of time if it is being used for statistical, historical or research purposes. Some research by journalists and academics is exempt if it is in the public interest or does not identify individuals.

Activity

Investigate the increasing use of robots in the home and in the workplace. Consider the following issues:

- What laws do you think currently exist in England covering the use of robots in the home?
- What laws do you think currently exist covering the use of robots in the workplace?
- What legal issues can you see will affect the use of robots at home?
- What legal issues can you see will affect the use of robots in the workplace?
- How are other legal jurisdictions dealing with the use of robots?

16.2.6 Cyber-crime

Cyber-crime can be defined as a crime in which a computer is the object of the crime. Examples of such crimes include hacking, phishing and spamming. It includes crimes where a computer is used as a tool to commit an offence such as viewing child pornography, or spreading material which amounts to a hate crime. Cyber-criminals may use computer technology to access personal information and business trade secrets, or use the internet for exploitive or malicious purposes.

Cyber-crime offences are becoming more widespread. In its first report to include cyber-crime, the Office for National Statistics reported in January 2017 that there were an estimated 3.6 million cases of fraud and 2 million computer misuse offences committed in the year to September 2016, out of a total of 11.8 million incidents of crime.

Businesses, government and academic institutions have become increasingly reliant on the internet for their day-to-day business, while consumers are using e-commerce more and more for purchasing goods and services. There are therefore greater opportunities for hackers and virus-writers to disrupt the activities of their fellow citizens, and for criminals to benefit.

Hacking first became a prominent issue in the 1980s, with the publicity achieved by exploits such as the Internet Worm. At that time it was not clear how the authorities could tackle this threat. Hackers were not always causing physical damage to anyone's property; if they simply logged on to a system without permission and did not access any files, it was hard to see what crime they could be committing under existing law apart from the theft of tiny amounts of electricity.

As the problem grew, it was clear that legislation was needed to enable hackers to be prosecuted. So, in 1990, the Computer Misuse Act was passed. It created the following new offences:

- Unauthorised access to computer material – this is the lowest level of offence. It can be committed by finding, guessing or using another person's password to log on to their user area. Merely looking at files and not changing, deleting or damaging anything is an offence. There is a maximum sentence of six months' prison and/or a fine.
- Unauthorised access with intent to commit or facilitate a crime – this offence is committed when the person gaining access to another person's system is doing so with the sole purpose of doing something illegal. Examples of ways of committing this offence are using spyware or keylogging software or by 'phishing'. There is a maximum sentence of five years' prison and/or a fine.

Key term

Phishing – a form of online fraud when an attacker represents him or herself as being reputable and tries to learn information in order to defraud an innocent victim.

Phishing

- Unauthorised modification of computer material – this offence relates to the deletion or changes made to files with the intent to cause damage to an individual or company. The difference is 'the intent to cause damage'. It includes deliberately introducing or transmitting viruses to other systems. There is a maximum sentence of five years' prison and/or a fine.
- Making, supplying or obtaining anything which can be used in computer misuse offences – writing or supplying can include programs such as computer viruses, worms, trojans, malware and malicious scripts. Supplying includes the distribution of any of this material, whether it is self-created or obtained from elsewhere. Obtaining is committed if you deliberately obtain malicious files such as computer viruses or scripts that you know could damage a computer system. There is a maximum sentence of five years' prison and/or a fine for any of these versions of the offence.

Fraudsters use people's personal information to obtain money

Over time, other types of cyber-crime have developed including:

Mail bombing

A mail bomb is the sending of a massive amount of email to a specific person or system. It may fill up the recipient's disk space on his server or, in some cases, may be too much for a server to handle and may cause the server to stop functioning. Variations of this type of cyber-attack include list listing and zip bombing.

Website defacement

This is an attack on a website that changes the visual appearance of the site or a webpage. A website will represent the image of a company or organisation, and if there is a defacement it can suffer financial losses while repairs are carried out. Defacement is a form of electronic graffiti. It can be used to spread messages by politically motivated 'cyber protesters' or activists. The sites most often targeted are religious and government sites. Disturbing images or offensive words might be posted.

Identity fraud

This is a crime where one person uses another person's personal data, without authorisation, to deceive or defraud someone else. For example, it is identity fraud to use someone's personal information to open a credit card account without permission, and then charge goods to that account.

Fraudsters can use false identity details to:
- open a bank account or take over existing accounts
- obtain credit cards, loans and state benefits
- order goods
- obtain genuine documents such as passports and driving licences.

Stealing another person's identity details is not, by itself, identity fraud. But using that identity for any of these activities is a crime.

16.3 Key issues

16.3.1 Privacy – the use of drones

One issue raised by the use of drones is the expansion of surveillance and the recording of images without consent. In the future it may be possible for drones to carry equipment to allow facial recognition of individuals on the ground, and the monitoring of individual behaviour and conversation. This has implications for individual privacy as the recording of these images could amount to a breach of the Data Protection Act 1998, or of the CCTV code of practice. This code has been extended to include public use of drones where they are collecting information about individuals and states:

> it will be good practice for domestic users to be aware of the potential privacy intrusion which the use of drones can cause to make sure they're used in a responsible manner.

In addition, there has to be considered the possibility of sharing images or recordings on social media, as these can quickly transfer from being private to public property. Consideration may have to be given as to whether the use or sharing of material could amount to a form of harassment.

with the case of *Wood v Commissioner of Police for the Metropolis* (2009).

See Chapter 21, section 21.4.3 for full case details of *Wood v Commissioner of Police for the Metropolis* (2009).

Case study

Ryneš v Urad (2014)

A Czech journalist, František Ryneš, installed a CCTV camera outside his front door to protect his property. The camera recorded the entrance to his home, the public footpath and the entrance to the house opposite.

Footage from the camera was used to identify two possible suspects after the windows of his home were broken. One of the suspects complained that Czech data protection law had been infringed by the collection and use of the images. Mr Ryneš argued that the recording fell within the household exemption, but the European Court of Justice (ECJ) upheld the complaint.

Although this case was specifically related to CCTV camera images, it is possible that the impact of the decision is wider and could equally apply to images captured through drone technology.

Activity ❓

As well as the issue of privacy, there are a number of other issues that could result from the use of drones, including flying them close to commercial aircraft, delivering prohibited items to prisons and flying over secure establishments, and the responsibility for damage caused to property on the ground when a drone crashes.

- What other issues can you identify from the use of drones?
- What laws apply in England to the issues identified above, and to those other issues you have identified?

16.3.2 Privacy – the use of CCTV and surveillance systems

There are real concerns about invasion of privacy. The British Security Industry Authority has estimated there are up to 5.9 million CCTV cameras in the country, including 750,000 in 'sensitive locations' such as schools, hospitals and care homes. This could work out at one camera for every 11 people living in the country. The indiscriminate use of CCTV in public could be a breach of Article 8 ECHR (right to private life), and parallels can be seen

CCTV is in widespread use in the UK

However, there have been no reported challenges to the use of CCTV under Article 8. As it is accepted that CCTV cameras are an invaluable source of crime detection, it is likely that judges will back the public interest view. This view is supported by an estimate that in 2009, 95 per cent of Scotland Yard murder cases used CCTV footage as evidence. On the other hand there are concerns about the extent of the surveillance and monitoring in a democratic society, with cameras in virtually every high street, in shopping centres and local shops.

There could be a further concern about the admissibility of CCTV recordings in court. In criminal cases, any use of a digital image as evidence must be accompanied by a certificate under s 69 of the Police and Criminal Evidence Act 1984. This certificate, given by a person responsible for the computer system in question, must state that either the computer system was at all times operating properly, or that any defect in its operation did not affect the accuracy of the record. In addition there is a British Standard Code of Practice for the Legal Admissibility of Information on Electronic Document Management Systems (DISC PD 0008, February 1996). This sets out procedures and documentation required for the audit of systems producing documents or other images that may be used as evidence in court. There have been no reported cases where defence teams have requested an audit trail be produced in any case where video images were being used by the prosecution. This may change as defendants and their lawyers become more familiar with the technology.

16.3.3 Data protection and retention

In the past different police forces had problems interpreting the requirements of the Data Protection Act 1998. Sometimes this caused confusion when some forces tried to build psychological profiles of suspects. For example, after Ian Huntley was convicted of the murders of Holly Wells and Jessica Chapman in 2003, it was revealed that Humberside police had deleted records of previous sexual allegations about him because they thought that was what was required by the Act. This could have been because the Act states that information should be kept 'no longer than necessary' without giving any precise time limits. The data user has to interpret the law and might take a cautious approach, which means that records might be deleted too quickly.

The Act applies to almost every organisation, whether commercial or voluntary, and even those holding what may be thought of as harmless information. Organisations may be cautious in deciding what information they hold to ensure that they do not break the rules. The Act does not define what 'appropriate' security measures have to be taken by an organisation to protect data held by it. But it does say that an assessment of the appropriate security measures in a particular case should consider technological developments and the costs involved. The Act does not require an organisation to have state-of-the-art security to protect the personal data but there should be regular reviews of the security measures.

There are categories of data such as photographs, video and audio which can be interpreted by machines to identify facts about a person and therefore can fall into the realm of data protection. These were not envisaged when the Act was passed. For example:

- Google's Streetview program can potentially reveal location and other data about individuals.
- Web browsing histories could be used to infer information that is currently regarded as sensitive, such as political and religious beliefs, health and sexuality.
- Biometric data is being collected with increasing frequency.

Fair Processing Notices are usually long and difficult to read, and they often leave users no other choice but to agree to them. A company can change the terms of use without notifying data subjects; see for example Facebook or Google's multiple change of policies without prior notification.

The Act could be improved by restricting the types of information which the Act applies to and removing some of the bureaucracy. Also industry bodies, including the police, could be encouraged to develop specific guidance and codes of practice for their members on what data can be held and for how long.

The Data Retention and Investigatory Powers Act 2014 regulated the interception of communications on public or private networks. Monitoring was allowed only if the controller had obtained a warrant from a designated official, if both parties to the call/email consented. This Act has now been replaced by the Investigatory Powers Act (IPA) 2016.

It was found by the Investigatory Powers Tribunal in a case in October 2016 that the security services, both in the UK and in the USA, had been collecting and retaining bulk communications data from 1998 until 2015. This included the who, where, when and what of personal phone and web communications. This was in breach of Article 8 ECHR. Also, bulk personal datasets – which might include medical and tax records, individual biographical details, commercial and financial activities, communications and travel data – had been retained by the security services for ten years prior to 2015. Again this was found to be in breach of Article 8. This had not been made clear to either the public or Parliament before this case.

16.3.4 Cyber-crime

It is a good thing to have the legislation in place, but in practice the police have other priorities and very few cases of cyber-crime are actually prosecuted. And even when a case is pursued, sentences tend to be lenient.

One problem is the proving of intent. Many people challenged will say that they were not aware what they were doing was illegal, or that they didn't realise they were in possession of, or passing, a virus.

Another problem issue is tracing who was actually responsible. When challenged, many people pass the blame on to others, saying that they were not logged on and that someone else must have carried out the action using their details. Although the USA will pursue alleged hackers living in the UK, such as Gary McKinnon and Lauri Love, under reciprocal arrangements, there have been no reported cases of any US residents being extradited to the UK on hacking charges.

By the time an offender is caught, damage to a system has already been done. Data may have been lost or irretrievably damaged, or it may have already been sold on. Companies can lose revenue if customers desert them following a hacking. Even multi-national companies such as Yahoo have suffered. In September 2016 it was revealed that half a billion international users, including about eight million in the UK, had had their names, email addresses, passwords, telephone numbers and more stolen. Even if the company does not lose money directly there can be considerable damage to its reputation – such as suffered by Talk Talk and Ashley Madison – which could in time cause a loss of revenue and a fall in the share price.

The number of computer misuse offences seems large, but this could be minute compared to the real extent of UK cyber-crime. The figures are likely to increase over time as more people recognise they have been targeted and the police get better at detecting cyber-crime.

The Computer Misuse Act was passed over 20 years ago, which in technological terms is an age. It is perhaps time for the law to be updated to cover practices that have developed since that time.

16.4 Cross-border issues and future challenges

16.4.1 Privacy – the use of drones

A number of areas of law are potentially in issue with the use of drones. They include:

- aviation law
- data protection
- privacy
- confidentiality
- harassment.

The rules governing the civilian use of drones are still developing, and public understanding of how to use drones safely might not keep pace with the desire to fly them. As more and more people acquire drones, there are likely to be many more cases of people using them in circumstances that present risks, or which involve a variety of legal issues. That

is why the House of Lords EU Committee made a strong recommendation that all drone flights must be traceable through an online database, which the general public could access via an app. Modern technology could be used creatively, not just to manage the skies, but to help police them as well. Consideration will have to be given to the question of whether existing laws cover the responsibility of the drone operator for damage caused to property on the ground and the need for compulsory liability insurance cover.

16.4.2 Privacy – the use of CCTV and surveillance systems

One of the latest developments in catching offenders is being developed and trialled. The system can identify a whole face from a tiny fragment, such as a piece of forehead which may be the only part of a face visible if an offender is wearing a hood. As well as using images of offenders arrested in the past, the police will take photographs of offenders presently held in custody. Each part of the image including skin colour and texture, eye, nose, mouth, shape and other features will be allocated a number. When a suspect is captured on CCTV the system will compare the image with those images held on the database and will be able to identify the suspect. This system could help the police identify the small number of people responsible for committing a large proportion of all crime. It has been estimated that about 500,000 crimes each year are committed nationally by repeat offenders – people who have committed more than 25 offences.

However, the use of the system has alarmed civil rights campaigners. Big Brother Watch has commented that the police have a poor record of deploying intrusive forms of surveillance technology, and that the system should be subject to stringent oversights on the retention and deletion of images.

Forms of surveillance can also be used by criminals. For example, a hidden camera at a cashpoint can capture customers' PINs as they are entered, without their knowledge. The devices are small enough not to be noticed, and are placed where they can monitor the keypad of the machine as a user enters his PIN. Images showing the PIN may then be transmitted wirelessly, allowing unlawful access to bank accounts.

The police view is that the use of ANPR cameras has proved to be important in the detection of offences such as locating stolen and uninsured vehicles and speeding up investigations leading to the solving of cases of terrorism, major and organised crime. Further, it allows officers' attention to be drawn to offending vehicles while allowing law-abiding drivers to go about their business unhindered.

There is strong anecdotal evidence that the use of CCTV helps in the detection and conviction of offenders, and most police forces routinely seek CCTV recordings after crimes have been reported. CCTV has also played a crucial role in tracing the movements of suspects or victims and is widely regarded by anti-terrorism officers as a key tool in tracking terrorist suspects. It is suggested that the presence of CCTV helps prevent crime, especially on public transport and in public car parks.

Developments in the use of CCTV have included the hiring of deaf police officers to lip read conversations to help uncover criminal conspiracies, and an 'Internet Eyes' website which would pay members of the public to view CCTV camera images from their homes and report any crimes they witness. The site aimed to add 'more eyes' to cameras which might be insufficiently monitored. This use of the general public in this way has been severely criticised by civil liberties campaigners.

On the other hand, there are few checks on the images once they are stored, and there are concerns about the loss or unauthorised use of database records and the accuracy of information. There are also concerns about the invasion of privacy by recording and storing information about innocent members of the public for the duration of their journey, and whether this is in breach of Article 8 EHCR.

Also, there is the question of whether public CCTV is cost-effective. The installation and maintenance of high-definition CCTV is expensive, and if it is a deterrent, many crimes prevented result in little monetary loss. There is also a question of the cameras being a target of attacks themselves.

16.4.3 Data protection and retention

The Investigatory Powers Act 2016 provides a new framework to govern the use and oversight of investigatory powers by law enforcement, security and intelligence agencies.

1 It brings together all of the powers already available to the agencies to obtain communications and data about communications. It will make these powers and the safeguards that apply to them clear and understandable.

2 It overhauls the way these powers are authorised and overseen. It introduces a 'double-lock' for interception warrants, so that, following Secretary of State

authorisation, these (and other warrants) cannot come into force until they have been approved by a judge. And it creates a powerful new Investigatory Powers Commissioner to oversee how these powers are used.

3 It ensures that powers are fit for the digital age. It provides for the retention of internet connection records for law enforcement to identify the communications service to which a device has connected. This will restore capabilities that have been lost as a result of changes in the way people communicate.

The legislation sets out for the first time the surveillance powers available to the intelligence services and the police. It legalises hacking by the security agencies into computers and mobile phones of individuals, and allows them access to masses of stored personal data, even if the person under scrutiny is not suspected of any wrongdoing. The government's view is that these powers of collection and retention are necessary to continue the fights against terrorist attacks. Other countries such as Germany and the USA have given their security services similar powers.

Benefits of IPA 2016

On the one hand, the Act has benefits:

- It introduces a new standard of openness, accepting, for example, equipment interference or legalised government hacking which few countries even acknowledge.
- It gives approval to a range of powers, such as bulk collection of information, which have already proved valuable in counter-terrorism and the fight against sexual exploitation and serious and organised crime.
- It provides greater safeguards, including the need for judicial approval for the issue of a warrant.
- It is written in technology-neutral language which should last for the next 10–15 years.
- It does everything possible to ensure that in the future, intelligence and law enforcement agencies use only such powers as Parliament has approved.
- The Investigatory Powers Commission will flag any unsatisfactory features of the Act, for the attention of the government and, if necessary, Parliament, in its annual reports.
- The operation of the Act must be reviewed within six years.

Drawbacks of IPA 2016

On the other hand, there are concerns. Jim Killock, the executive director of Open Rights Group, has said:

> The UK now has a surveillance law that is more suited to a dictatorship than a democracy. The state has unprecedented powers to monitor and analyse UK citizens' communications regardless of whether we are suspected of any criminal activity.

At least 48 bodies, including GCHQ, the National Crime Agency, the Foods Standards Agency and the NHS, will have power under IPA 2016 to check a person's internet-searching records. However, due to the ECJ's ruling that indiscriminate collection of data is illegal, the Act may need to be amended.

A bill is currently under consideration in Parliament that will supplement IPA 2016 and allow government agencies to share more widely consumer data, but there are no safeguards contained about the safety and security of shared information. The bill also provides for compulsory age verification to access adult websites, and users might be required to provide passport or credit card details.

A potential conflict for many data-storing companies may come in 2018 when the EU's General Data Protection Regulation comes into force. It will give individuals greater power to control how their data can be used – and could include the right to have certain data completely erased. This will cause problems for many companies. On the one hand, data subjects will have the right to consent to the storage of their data and its use and the right to be forgotten. On the other hand, there is pressure from UK laws for the sharing of information. The result may be sanctions on companies which fail to enforce the laws, though there is doubt which laws will apply.

Renate Samson, the chief executive of Big Brother Watch, said:

> The passing of the Investigatory Powers Act has fundamentally changed the face of surveillance in this country. None of us online are now guaranteed the right to communicate privately and, most importantly, securely.

The most serious challenge to IPA 2016 has come from the decision in December 2016 of the ECJ in the joined cases of *Tele2* and *Watson*. The case involved a challenge to the collection of bulk data under the predecessor to IPA 2016, the Data Retention and Investigatory Powers Act 2014. The court ruled that general and indiscriminate retention of emails and electronic communications by governments is illegal. This could bring challenges against IPA 2016 which continues to allow the practice. The court ruled that only targeted interception of traffic and location data in order to combat serious crime – including terrorism – is justified.

In a summary the court said electronic communications allow

> very precise conclusions to be drawn concerning the private lives of persons whose data has been retained. The interference by national legislation that provides for the retention of traffic data and location data with that right must therefore be considered to be particularly serious. The fact that the data is retained without the users of electronic communications services being informed of the fact is likely to cause the persons concerned to feel that their private lives are the subject of constant surveillance. Consequently, only the objective of fighting serious crime is capable of justifying such interference. Legislation prescribing a general and indiscriminate retention of data … exceeds the limits of what is strictly necessary and cannot be considered to be justified within a democratic society. Prior authorisation by a court or independent body to access retained data is required for each official request.

The *Watson* case will be sent back to the Court of Appeal to be resolved specifically in terms of UK legislation.

16.4.4 Cyber-crime

One major issue that applies to cyber-crime is for the authorities to decide in which jurisdiction a crime has taken place and which laws apply. In some countries it may be considered that no crime has taken place or is not actionable and different standards may apply in different countries. As can be seen from the examples of McKinnon and Love, the USA has been particularly keen on prosecuting those they allege are guilty of cyber-crimes, even though the alleged offenders have never visited the USA or had any other contact with that country.

Look online

Research the cases of Gary McKinnon and Lauri Love, and answer these questions about each case:
- What were they alleged to have done?
- What charges could they have faced in the USA?
- What sentence could they have received?
- What did the Home Secretary decide about their deportation?

Some countries may be unwilling to pursue their citizens who are alleged to be committing cyber-crimes or to shut down offending websites. This applies particularly to Russia and Eastern European countries. This inaction could encourage other offenders to set up their operations in those countries. There may also be questions asked:

- Who can be pursued?
- Is there a person behind the operation or merely a computer, perhaps programmed from another country?
- Are the authorities prepared to pursue a single hacker when there may be more and more vulnerable victims, such as children subject to abuse or pornography that they should prioritise?

- Even if a prosecution is launched, what sanctions is a convicted offender likely to face, and where will any imprisonment be served? In the Gary McKinnon case it was suggested that he could serve up to 70 years in prison in the USA, if found guilty.
- If a machine is carrying out the crime, what punishment can be imposed on it?

Tip

Do not spend too long describing the working of the technology. Your focus should be on how the law applies to the technology and the issues that can arise from its use, not the technology itself.

	Privacy	Data protection	Cyber-crime
Form of technology	Drones are increasingly being used by private and commercial operators. CCTV has been in use for some time operating in private and commercial premises and for public order purposes.	Personal information stored and used by commercial operators.	Computers are the object of crime by hacking, phishing or spamming.
The issue	Liability in event of accidental use of drones. Surveillance, recording and use of images without consent.	Stored information could be misused or stolen causing loss to the data user.	Tracing and prosecuting those responsible. Failure to keep up with new forms of fraudulent attacks.
Challenges for the future	Registering ownership of drones. Invasion of privacy due to increasing number of cameras and images.	Use of personal information; wider powers given to the enforcement and security services.	Deciding where the crime takes place and a common international approach to dealing with offenders.

Figure 16.1 Key facts on law and technology

Case	Facts	Legal principle
Ryneš v Urad (2014)	A Czech journalist installed a CCTV camera. A break-in suspect complained that Czech data protection law had been infringed.	The ECJ upheld the complaint and rejected the householder's argument that recording fell within the household exemption.
Wood v Commissioner of Police for the Metropolis (2009)	The police required a demonstrator to be photographed as a condition of leaving 'a kettle'.	The unexplained police action was a sufficient intrusion by the state into the individual's own space and integrity to breach Article 8 ECHR.

Figure 16.2 Key cases on law and technology

Summary

- This chapter raised many questions on how existing law should be used, or adapted for use, with various forms of new technology:
  - Drones – can their use amount to surveillance and breach of privacy?
  - CCTV – can its use amount to a breach of privacy?
  - Data protection – how effective are the current rules for storage of personal information?
  - Cyber-crime – how should alleged offenders across national borders be tracked and prosecuted, and how should sanctions be imposed?

Chapter 17

Rules and theory of human rights law

After reading this chapter you should:
- have an outline understanding of the rules of human rights law
- have an overview of the theory of human rights law

17.1 An outline of the rules of human rights law

Any discussion of human rights in the UK has to be considered within the constitutional position. Unlike many countries, the UK constitution is not written or contained in a single document or series of documents. Rights have been protected by:
- legislation made by Parliament such as the Human Rights Act 1998
- judicial decisions
- documents such as the Magna Carta and the Bill of Rights (see Chapter 18 for more information on these)
- conventions such as the House of Lords passing legislation that appeared in the government's pre-election manifesto
- authoritative writings.

The UK constitution is based on the doctrine of the separation of powers between Parliament, the executive and the judiciary, and on the rule of law.

A common misconception which has applied for a number of years is that the ECHR (see Chapter 18 for more information) and its institutions were forced upon an unwilling UK as part of a wider European project. But the reality is that the UK was one of the architects of the human rights agenda that followed the Second World War.

The ECHR has its roots in the philosophical tradition of universal rights which stretches back to the Enlightenment of the eighteenth century and the French Revolution. But the actual spur for creating a model set of rights in the twentieth century was the Allies' determination to bring peace to Europe in 1945.

The first international step towards codifying these rights came when the General Assembly of the United Nations adopted the Universal Declaration of Human Rights in 1948. In Europe, work was taking place (largely driven by the UK) to create a form of rights customised to the continent, and in 1950 the members of the Council of Europe signed the ECHR which came into force in 1953. The UK was one of the first members of the Council of Europe to ratify the Convention when it passed through Parliament in 1951. The ECHR allowed an individual with a grievance against a state to challenge his treatment in the European Court of Human Rights (ECtHR) at an international level.

However, it was not until 1966 that the UK granted the right to its citizens to take a case to Strasbourg. This meant that UK citizens were able to challenge the laws of the state at a European level, though it was a costly and lengthy process, and limited compensation was available if a breach of human rights was proved. Breach of ECHR rights could not be argued directly before a UK court.

The Human Rights Act 1998 was passed by Parliament to deal with this situation and allowed UK citizens to claim remedies for breach of human rights in UK courts. The ECHR was incorporated into UK law and Convention rights are directly enforceable against a public body by any individual who can show that his rights have been breached. In addition, the Human Rights Act allowed a UK court to declare that a piece of UK legislation was incompatible with a Convention right (though there is no power for a court to overrule the legislation). UK courts can also interpret legislation to be compatible with Convention rights.

The ECHR contains 14 Articles, which set out different individual rights and are mainly civil and political in nature. Some are absolute rights where a state cannot justify interfering with them. They include the prohibition of torture, inhuman or degrading treatment (Article 3) and the prohibition of slavery and forced labour (Article 4). Other rights are limited or qualified.

For the OCR specification you will need to know about the following specific rights:

- Article 5 – the right not to be arbitrarily detained. This is a limited right so that there is an absolute prohibition on detentions which are outside the scope of Article 5(1).
- Article 6 – the right to a fair trial. This again is a limited right so there is a right to a fair hearing if a case falls within Article 6(1).
- Article 8 – freedom of family life, private life, home and correspondence.
- Article 10 – freedom of expression.
- Article 11 – freedom of assembly and association.

Articles 8, 10 and 11 are all qualified rights, so that if the state can justify a limitation of these rights which is in accordance with law and meet a legitimate aim, there will be no breach of the EHCR.

17.2 An overview of the theory of human rights law

17.2.1 What are human rights?

Human rights belong to every individual regardless of sex, race, nationality, socio-economic group, political opinion, sexual orientation or any other status.

Human rights are universal. They apply to everyone simply on the basis of being human.

Human rights are inalienable. They cannot be taken away simply because the state does not like the person seeking to exercise his rights. They can only be limited in certain tightly defined circumstances and some rights, such as the prohibition on torture and slavery, can never be limited.

Key term

Human rights – rights and freedoms that everyone in a country and the world are entitled to because they are human.

Human rights are indivisible. The state cannot pick and choose which rights it accepts. Many rights depend on each other to be meaningful – so, for example, the right to free speech must go hand in hand with the right to assemble peacefully.

Human rights are owed by the state to the people. This means that public bodies must respect an individual's human rights, and the government must ensure that there are laws in place so that people

respect each other's rights. For example, the right to life requires not only that the actions of those working on behalf of the state do not lead to a person's death, but that laws are also in place to protect an individual from the actions of others that might want to cause a person harm.

In addition to these basic rights owed to every individual, the UK government has, in recent years, tried to address what it refers to as social rights granted to specific groups to improve the quality of their lives. Some of these social rights are:

- equal pay at work
- the right not to be unfairly dismissed at work
- the right not to be discriminated against on the grounds of sex, race, or disability
- the rights given to consumers when buying goods or services.

Within the concept of human rights are ideas of natural justice, universality, the rule of law and due process

Natural justice

Natural justice is shown where the criminal trial or dispute resolving process is fair and results in a decision that has been made by an objective decision-maker.

The three main principles of natural justice are that:

- the court or tribunal hearing a case is impartial and is seen to be
- judges or the decision-makers have no interest in the case. In criminal cases this will generally be by lay magistrates or a jury. In civil cases this will be by a judge who has no interest in the subject matter of the dispute and is not inclined to either party in the case
- both parties in a case are given the opportunity to be heard.

If procedures are fair in this way the rights of the individuals in the case are protected and public confidence in the process is maintained. Article 6 of the European Convention on Human Rights provides protection for these principles of natural justice.

See Chapter 14, section 14.3.4 for more detail on natural justice.

See Chapter 20 on Article 6 ECHR.

Universality

Human rights are moral principles or standards of human behaviour, which are protected by law. They are understood to be fundamental rights 'to which a person is entitled simply because he or she is a human being'.

They apply to all regardless of their race, their nationality, religion, ethnic origin or any other status. They apply everywhere and at all times and they apply in the same way to everyone. They should not be taken away except as a result of due process of law and of procedure.

Cultural Relativists object to the idea of universality, and argue that human rights are culturally dependent, and that no moral principles can be made to apply to all cultures. It means that in some cultures the concept of human rights makes no sense. It is argued that the principles contained in the Universal Declaration of Human Rights (1948) are the product of Western political history. They say that the origins of the Declaration are found in Magna Carta and the United States' Bill of Rights (1791). They argue that Universalism, in its attempt to extend a Western ideal to the rest of the world, is a form of cultural imperialism and that a body such as the International Criminal Court illustrates that. Cultural Relativists are generally supportive of 'traditional' or local approaches to justice, as they believe these will contribute more to post-conflict reconciliation.

The rule of law

The rule of law exists where:
- law and order are common
- there is efficient and predictable dispute resolution
- there is equal treatment before the law
- public bodies are bound by, and are accountable to, existing, clear and known laws, and
- human rights are protected.

It ensures that the state functions for its citizens and there is peace and security, accountability and democracy and equality and social justice. There will also be a commitment by the state to human rights and institutions that protect those rights.

Due process

The right to due process is a fundamental human right. It refers to a fair judicial process, including the right to a fair trial, qualified legal representation, and the ability to appeal against decisions of lower courts and tribunals.

Figure 17.1 What are human rights?

17.2.2 What are civil liberties?

It is important to note the difference between 'civil rights' and 'civil liberties'. The term 'civil rights' revolves around a basic right to be free from unequal treatment. 'Civil liberties' concern basic rights and freedoms that are guaranteed – either explicitly by a constitution, or interpreted as such by the legislature and courts. Civil liberties include:

- the freedom of speech
- the right to privacy
- the right to be free from unreasonable searches of your home
- the right to a fair trial in a court or tribunal
- the right to marry
- the right to vote.

Key term

Civil liberties – freedoms that are guaranteed to people to protect them from an over-powerful government. They are found in democratic states such as the UK but are not found in undemocratic states such as North Korea.

Civil liberties are distinct from human rights:
- Human rights are universal rights and freedoms to which all people throughout the world are entitled.
- Civil liberties are those rights and freedoms recognised by a particular country.

People do not earn civil rights – citizenship automatically confers them. Civil liberties prevent governments from abusing their powers and restrict the level of interference in peoples' lives.

Different countries may define civil liberties differently. They may, depending on prevailing circumstances, be more or less likely to uphold those civil liberties. For example, since the 2001 terrorist attacks in New York (9/11) several laws have been passed in the UK restricting certain liberties in order to deal with the threat of terrorism. In the UK the right to marry has been extended to all people regardless of their sexuality. In more restrictive countries, people can risk their lives in support of basic civil liberties such as free speech, the right to peaceful protest and freedom of assembly. What constitutes a civil liberty may depend very much on the country that a person calls home.

As mentioned earlier, the UK does not have a written constitution, setting out the civil liberties and rights of its citizens. It does however have a long history of recognising certain freedoms, and many written constitutions around the world are based on the rights long upheld by British courts. An example is 'Habeas corpus' – which appears to have been in effect in the UK since at least the fourteenth century and may predate the Magna Carta. Under this rule anyone who has been arrested, or deprived of their liberty, may request that they are presented before a judge so that the legality of their detention can be judicially decided. Since 9/11 it has been argued that the spirit of this ancient law has been severely undermined by the introduction of anti-terrorism legislation such as the Counter-Terrorism and Security Act 2015 which among other measures requires internet service providers to keep records showing which IP address was searched by a computer or other device. In addition the Civil Contingencies Act 2004 removes certain rights such as *habeus corpus* in the event of an emergency, though the regulations that grant these rights will only exist for a maximum of 30 days. The government argues that this approach is necessary to ensure the safety of the country and its citizens. Opponents argue that the government has overstepped the mark and has gone past the acceptable line of what a government can and cannot do within a representative democracy.

One way to consider the difference between 'civil rights' and 'civil liberties' is to look at:
- what right is affected, and
- whose right is affected.

For example, as an employee, a worker does not have the legal right to be promoted as obtaining promotion is not a guaranteed 'civil liberty'. But, a female or disabled employee has the legal right to be free from discrimination in being considered for that promotion – an employee cannot legally be denied the promotion based on gender or disability. By choosing not to promote a female or disabled worker solely because of the employee's gender or disability, the employer has committed a civil rights violation and has engaged in unlawful employment discrimination based on gender or disability.

Tip

Make sure that you can describe the difference between human rights and civil liberties.

Rights	Liberties
They are basic rights given to all citizens to be free from unequal treatment.	They are granted by a state.
They belong to everyone.	They may be granted to certain sections or groups within a country.
They are inalienable and indivisible but can be limited.	Their extent is likely to be limited by the law granting them.

Figure 17.2 The differences between rights and liberties

Summary

- As the UK does not have a written constitution, individual rights have been protected in various ways including by legislation, judicial decisions, documents, conventions and authoritative writings.
- The UK was a major force behind the development of the European Convention on Human Rights, which set out a number of basic rights given to individuals within member countries.
- UK citizens had to wait until 1966 to have the right to take the UK to the ECtHR.
- The Human Rights Act 1998 allowed UK courts to hear claims from UK citizens that their rights had been interfered with.
- Absolute rights are where a state cannot justify interfering with them.
- Limited rights are where rights are protected to a certain level.
- Qualified rights are where the state can justify their limitation if they are in accordance with law and they meet a legitimate aim.
- Human rights belong to everyone.
- Human rights cannot be removed by the state but can be limited.
- They are owed by the state to their people; they cannot be earned by individuals.
- Civil liberties are granted by the legislature or the courts.
- Civil liberties prevent governments from abusing their powers and restrict state interference in people's lives.

Chapter 18

Protection of the individual's human rights and freedoms in the UK

After reading this chapter you should be able to:
- Have an overview of the development of human rights in the UK, including the Magna Carta 1215 and the Bill of Rights 1688
- Understand the history of the European Court of Human Rights
- Understand the impact of the Human Rights Act 1998
- Understand the entrenched nature of the Human Rights Act 1998 in the devolution settlements of Scotland, Wales and Northern Ireland

18.1 An overview of the development of human rights in the UK

18.1.1 Magna Carta

The Magna Carta, one of the most important documents of Medieval England, was signed in June 1215 between the barons of Medieval England and King John. 'Magna Carta' means 'Great Charter' in Latin.

The document was a series of written promises between the king and his subjects that he, the king, would govern England, and deal with its people according to the customs of feudal law. Magna Carta was an attempt by the barons to stop King John and future kings from abusing their power over the people.

Magna Carta promised laws that were good and fair. It states that everyone shall have access to courts and that costs and money should not be a barrier if someone wanted to take a problem to the law courts.

It also states that no freeman (i.e. a person who was not a serf) will be imprisoned or punished without first going through the proper legal system. In later years the word 'freeman' was replaced by 'no one' which was taken to mean everybody.

It also dealt with how its terms would be enforced in England. Twenty-five barons were given the responsibility of making sure the king carried out what was stated in the Magna Carta – using force

if necessary. To give Magna Carta an impact, it was stamped with the royal seal of King John to show people that it had his royal support.

Magna Carta still forms an important symbol of liberty today, often cited by politicians and campaigners, and is held in great respect by British and American legal communities. Lord Denning described it as 'the greatest constitutional document of all times – the foundation of the freedom of the individual against the arbitrary authority of the despot'.

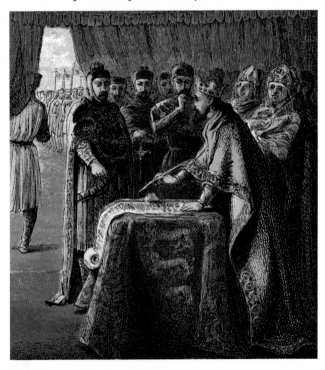

King John signs the Magna Carta

Jury trial

Trial by jury is an ancient right. Although it dates from 1215, it did not come about as a result of Magna Carta, but rather as the consequence of an order by Pope Innocent III (1161–1216). However, Magna Carta's reference to 'the lawful judgment of his peers' as a precondition for loss of liberty has helped in later centuries to entrench the right to jury trial in the English legal system.

Clause 39 of Magna Carta reflected a privilege negotiated by the barons to ensure that their disputes with the King – mainly over land – would be settled after advice from men of their own rank and status. Criminal trials at the time took the form of 'ordeals' by fire or by water, supervised by the local priest. God was the judge, and he would ensure that the innocent survived. Suspects, who were dunked in ponds, were declared guilty if they drowned.

In November 1215, Pope Innocent III, perhaps concerned that wrongful convictions were destroying faith in divine faith, forbade clerical participation. This 'trial by ordeal' was replaced by a type of fact-finding already used since the twelfth century in land disputes and by coroners. This was the summoning of local men likely to know the circumstances of the crime. In due course, 'twelve good men and true' emerged to deliver acceptable verdicts.

Article 39 of the Magna Carta read:

> No free man shall be captured, and or imprisoned, or disseised of his freehold, or of his liberties, or of his free customs, or be outlawed, or exiled, or in any way destroyed, nor will we proceed against him by force or proceed against him by arms, but by the lawful judgment of his peers, or by the law of the land.

Magna Carta further secured trial by jury by stating that:

> For a trivial offence, a free man shall be fined only in proportion to the degree of his offence, and for a serious offence correspondingly, but not so heavily as to deprive him of his livelihood. In the same way, a merchant shall be spared his merchandise, and a husbandman the implements of his husbandry, if they fall upon the mercy of a royal court. None of these fines shall be imposed except by the assessment on oath of reputable men of the neighbourhood. Earls and barons shall be fined only by their equals, and in proportion to the gravity of their offence.

Juries were then used to decide civil disputes and criminal trials. The use of juries in smaller civil cases was discontinued when county courts were introduced in 1846. Juries were still used in the High Court until 1933 when their use was curtailed, and now they can only be requested in civil claims of fraud, libel and slander. Even now their use in defamation cases is extremely limited due to the complexity of the issues. In criminal cases, juries are only used in the Crown Court to hear not guilty pleas to indictable and either-way cases, though there are now provisions for judge-only trials in certain cases where jury nobbling has taken place or where it is a strong possibility.

Habeus corpus

Habeas corpus or 'bring me the body' is a writ, issued by a judge, which requires a detained person to be brought before a court of law so that the legality of the detention may be examined.

It does not decide guilt or innocence, merely whether the person is legally imprisoned. It may also be writ against a private individual detaining another.

> ### Key term
>
> *Habeas corpus* – a writ issued by the court which required the immediate production of the detained person so the court could hear arguments for and against continued detention.

It was thought at one time to have been developed by Magna Carta but it, or its predecessor, appears to have been used before then. The Habeas Corpus Act passed by Parliament in 1679 guaranteed this right in law.

Its original use was more straightforward – a writ to bring a prisoner into court to testify in a pending trial. But what began as a weapon for the king and the courts became – as the political climate changed – protection for the individual against arbitrary detention by the state.

It is thought to have been common law by the time of Magna Carta. These days it is rarely used but it still represents the fundamental principle that unlawful detention can be challenged by immediate access to a judge – even by telephone in the middle of the night.

In relation to police detention it no longer plays a role as it has been superseded by the Police and Criminal Evidence Act 1984, which lays down precise rules about the length of pre-charge detention and the responsibility for checking them.

In the past, there have been occasions when the British Parliament has suspended its operation, usually in times of social unrest.

One example was when William Pitt, startled by the success of the French Revolution, suspended its operation after France declared war on Britain in 1793, to arrest parliamentary reformers. This was repeated by Lord Liverpool's government against the same movement in 1817.

War is a particularly fraught time for individual liberty. The Defence of the Realm Act 1914 allowed the Home Secretary to intern residents, and it was used against people of German descent, and Irish citizens suspected of involvement in the Easter Uprising. These powers were reinstated in the Second World War to detain those of German background, including Jewish refugees, as well as those with known fascist sympathies, such as Oswald Mosley. But the most recent example of its suspension took place in 1971, when the British Government introduced the internment of hundreds of Irish Republican suspects in an attempt to shut down the IRA. The tactic was abandoned four years later as it was thought to have increased support for the IRA.

More recently, following the terrorist attacks in the US on 9/11, its suspension was suggested in the debate for the making of control orders for terrorist suspects who could not be prosecuted. However, in response, the Home Office denied that its plans amount to *habeas corpus* suspension. A spokesman said at the time of the debate about their introduction: 'We are not removing *habeas corpus* rights. Everyone has a right to *habeas corpus* and that will remain the case.'

The wording of the writ of *habeas corpus* suggests that the detained person is brought to the court for the legality of the imprisonment to be examined. However, rather than issuing the writ immediately and waiting for the detained person to appear, modern practice is for the original application to be followed by a hearing with both parties present to decide the legality of the detention, without any writ being issued. If the detention is considered unlawful, the detainee can be released or bailed by order of the court without having to be produced before it. The writ, however, maintains its validity, and in *Rahmatullah v Secretary of State* (2012) was held by the Supreme Court to be available in respect of a prisoner captured by British forces in Afghanistan.

18.1.2 The Bill of Rights

In the Glorious Revolution, William III of Orange landed with his army in England on 5 November 1688.

Before William and Mary were confirmed as co-rulers of England and Ireland, they accepted a Declaration of Right drawn up by Parliament. Having accepted the Declaration of Right, William and Mary were offered the throne, and were crowned as joint monarchs in April 1689. The Declaration of Right was later embodied in an Act of Parliament, now known as the Bill of Rights, on 16 December 1689.

The Bill of Rights deals with constitutional matters and sets out certain basic civil rights. It lays down limits on the powers of the monarch and sets out the rights of Parliament, including the requirement for regular Parliaments, free elections and freedom of speech in Parliament known today as parliamentary privilege. It sets out certain rights of individuals including the prohibition of cruel and unusual punishment. The main principles of the Bill of Rights are still in force today and it is largely a statement of certain positive rights that its authors considered that citizens and/or residents of a free and democratic society ought to have. It also sets out (or in the view of its writers, restates) certain constitutional requirements where the actions of the Crown require the consent of the governed as represented in Parliament.

The Bill incorporated into law the growing conviction that, although some people may inherit privileges, all women and men enjoy the same basic rights which cannot be violated even by a head of state, who is also subject to, not above, the law. The Bill also took the view that the heads of state, and others in authority, have responsibilities towards the governed, and that they are answerable to the people, not to themselves. It was a significant legal advance in recognising individual rights and in giving them protection in law. The whole idea of inalienable human rights, championed by the Universal Declaration and other documents, may have its origin in this legislation.

The Bill of Rights 1689 is a predecessor of:
- the United States Constitution
- the United Nations Universal Declaration of Human Rights
- the European Convention on Human Rights.

For example, like the Bill of Rights, the US Constitution requires jury trials and prohibits excessive bail and 'cruel and unusual punishments'. Similarly, 'cruel, inhuman or degrading punishments' are banned under Article 5 of the Universal Declaration of Human Rights and Article 3 ECHR.

In the UK, the Bill of Rights is considered, together with Magna Carta, the Petition of Right, the Habeas

Corpus Act 1679 and the Parliament Acts 1911 and 1949, as one of the basic documents of the constitution.

Provisions of the Bill of Rights

In particular, the Bill asserted 'certain ancient rights and liberties' by declaring that, in relation to human rights:

- the power of the monarch to suspend law and dispense with laws by royal authority, without the consent of Parliament, is illegal
- it is the right of the subjects to petition the king, and prosecutions for such petitioning are illegal
- election of Members of Parliament ought to be free
- the freedom of speech and debates or proceedings in Parliament ought not to be impeached or questioned in any court or place outside Parliament
- excessive bail ought not to be required, nor excessive fines imposed, nor cruel and unusual punishments inflicted
- jurors in trials for high treason ought to be freeholders
- promises of fines and forfeitures before conviction are illegal and void
- for the redress of all grievances, and for the amending, strengthening and preserving of the laws, Parliaments ought to be held frequently.

The Bill of Rights is still law in the UK and its provisions are occasionally referred to in court. On 21 July 1995, a libel case brought by Neil Hamilton, then a Member of Parliament (MP), against the *Guardian* newspaper was stopped after Mr Justice May ruled that the prohibition on the courts questioning parliamentary proceedings contained in the Bill of Rights would prevent the *Guardian* from obtaining a fair trial. Section 13 of the Defamation Act 1996 was later enacted to permit an MP to waive his parliamentary privilege.

18.1.3 The United States Constitution and the Bill of Rights

America's first constitution, the Articles of Confederation, was ratified in 1781, when the nation was a loose confederation of states, each operating like an independent country. The national government comprised a single legislature, the Congress of the Confederation; there was no president or judiciary. The Articles of Confederation gave Congress power in foreign affairs, to conduct war and regulate currency; however, these powers were limited because Congress had no authority to enforce its requests to the states for money or for troops. It became clear that a stronger central government was needed for the nation to remain secure.

In 1787 delegates from each of the states (except one) met in Philadelphia and were tasked by Congress with amending the Articles of Confederation. However, they soon began deliberating proposals for an entirely new form of government. The US Constitution and Bill of Rights are vital points in the story of the development of the human rights we enjoy today. The founding fathers, a number of whom were lawyers, interpreted Magna Carta as a higher law, beyond the Crown. They had believed, as British colonists, that they enjoyed the rights of free Englishmen. As Americans, they established the United States as a federal republic by law, enshrining the rights of the federal government and its branches, the states and individual citizens. After intensive debate, they developed a plan that established three branches of a state – the executive (or government), a legislature and a judiciary. A system of checks and balances was put into place so that no single branch would have too much authority. The effect of the Constitution was to establish a form of higher law which could not be altered without strong popular support. Constitutional law was supreme binding all three branches of the state. Article VI provides:

> This Constitution, and the laws of the United States ... shall be the supreme Law of the Land; and the Judges in every State shall be bound thereby, any Thing in the Constitution or Laws of any State to the contrary notwithstanding.

In 1789, James Madison, introduced 19 amendments to the Constitution. Congress adopted 12 of the amendments and sent them to the states for ratification. Ten of these amendments, known collectively as the Bill of Rights, were ratified and became part of the Constitution in 1791. The Bill of Rights guarantees individuals certain basic protections as citizens, including freedom of speech, religion and the press; the right to bear and keep arms; the right to peaceably assemble; protection from unreasonable search and seizure; and the right to a speedy and public trial by an impartial jury.

The first amendment alone guarantees freedom of speech, freedom of the press, freedom of assembly and the right to petition government.

In over 200 years since its drafting, and in all the changes to the size and population of the USA, the Constitution has endured and adapted, and provides broad human rights protections. Many of the rights contained in the Constitution are equivalent to rights found in the Universal Declaration of Human Rights, especially those related to political and civil liberties. In addition, the US Supreme Court has identified fundamental rights not explicitly stated in the Constitution, such as the presumption of innocence in a criminal trial and freedom of movement. US courts provide a remedy for people whose constitutional rights have been violated. Congress has also passed laws that protect constitutional rights and provide remedies for victims of human rights violations such as laws that prohibit discrimination based on race, gender, religion, or disability.

Although the US Constitution provides protections for civil and political rights, it fails to recognise the economic, social, and cultural rights guaranteed in the Universal Declaration of Human Rights. Some rights, such as the right to education, can be found in some state constitutions; others, such as the right to an adequate standard of living including food, shelter, and medical care, have not been recognised as rights

18.1.4 The Universal Declaration of Human Rights

In April 1945 towards the end of the Second World War, delegates from 50 countries met in San Francisco. The goal of the United Nations Conference on International Organisation was to fashion an international body to promote peace and prevent future wars. The ideals of the organisation were stated in the preamble to its proposed charter: 'We the peoples of the United Nations are determined to save succeeding generations from the scourge of war, which twice in our lifetime has brought untold sorrow to mankind.'

The Charter of the new United Nations organisation went into effect on 24 October 1945. The UN came into being as an intergovernmental organisation with the purpose of saving future generations from the devastation of international conflict.

The Charter of the UN established six principal bodies, including the General Assembly, the Security Council, the International Court of Justice, and in relation to human rights, an Economic and Social Council (ECOSOC). It empowered ECOSOC to establish 'commissions in economic and social fields and for the promotion of human rights'. One of these was the United Nations Human Rights Commission, which, under the chairmanship of Eleanor Roosevelt, drafted the Universal Declaration of Human Rights.

The Declaration was referred to by Eleanor Roosevelt as the international Magna Carta for all mankind and was adopted by the UN on 10 December 1948.

In its preamble and in Article 1, the Declaration sets out the rights of all human beings:

> Disregard and contempt for human rights have resulted in barbarous acts which have outraged the conscience of mankind, and the advent of a world in which human beings shall enjoy freedom of speech and belief and freedom from fear and want has been proclaimed as the highest aspiration of the common people ... All human beings are born free and equal in dignity and rights.

The member states of the United Nations pledged to work together to promote the 30 Articles of human rights that, for the first time in history, had been codified into a single document.

It was drafted by representatives of all regions of the world covering all legal traditions. It is the most universal human rights document in existence, setting out the 30 fundamental rights that form the basis for a democratic society.

The General Assembly called upon all member countries to publicise the text of the Declaration and 'to cause it to be disseminated, displayed, read and expounded principally in schools and other educational institutions, without distinction based on the political status of countries or territories'.

It is a living document that has been accepted as a contract internationally between governments and their citizens. According to the Guinness Book of World Records, it is the most translated document in the world.

It provided a long list of rights, most of which are familiar 'political' rights, but also 'social' rights, such as the right to work.

It was not a treaty in the formal sense as it did not create legally binding obligations. It was not ratified by individual nations but approved by the General Assembly, and the UN Charter did not give the General Assembly the power to make international law. The rights were described in vague, aspirational terms, which could be interpreted in multiple ways, and national governments – even the liberal democracies – were wary of setting binding legal obligations. The US did not commit itself to eliminating racial segregation, and Britain and France did not commit themselves to liberating the populations in their colonies. Several authoritarian states – including the Soviet Union, Yugoslavia and Saudi Arabia – refused to vote in favour of the Universal Declaration and instead abstained.

In addition there was disagreement between the USA and the Soviet Union. The USA argued that human rights consisted of political rights such as the rights to vote, to speak freely, not to be arbitrarily detained and

THE UNIVERSAL DECLARATION OF Human Rights

WHEREAS recognition of the inherent dignity and of the equal and inalienable rights of all members of the human family is the foundation of freedom, justice and peace in the world,

WHEREAS disregard and contempt for human rights have resulted in barbarous acts which have outraged the conscience of mankind, and the advent of a world in which human beings shall enjoy freedom of speech and belief and freedom from fear and want has been proclaimed as the highest aspiration of the common people,

WHEREAS it is essential, if man is not to be compelled to have recourse, as a last resort, to rebellion against tyranny and oppression, that human rights should be protected by the rule of law,

WHEREAS it is essential to promote the development of friendly relations between nations,

WHEREAS the peoples of the United Nations have in the Charter reaffirmed their faith in fundamental human rights, in the dignity and worth of the human person and in the equal rights of men and women and have determined to promote social progress and better standards of life in larger freedom,

WHEREAS Member States have pledged themselves to achieve, in cooperation with the United Nations, the promotion of universal respect for and observance of human rights and fundamental freedoms,

WHEREAS a common understanding of these rights and freedoms is of the greatest importance for the full realization of this pledge,

NOW THEREFORE The General Assembly

Proclaims this Universal Declaration of Human Rights as a common standard of achievement for all peoples and all nations, to the end that every individual and every organ of society, keeping this Declaration constantly in mind, shall strive by teaching and education to promote respect for these rights and freedoms and by progressive measures, national and international, to secure their universal and effective recognition and observance, both among the peoples of Member States themselves and among the peoples of territories under their jurisdiction.

ARTICLE 1 All human beings are born free and equal in dignity and rights. They are endowed with reason and conscience and should act towards one another in a spirit of brotherhood.

ARTICLE 2 Everyone is entitled to all the rights and freedoms set forth in this Declaration, without distinction of any kind, such as race, colour, sex, language, religion, political or other opinion, national or social origin, property, birth or other status. Furthermore, no distinction shall be made on the basis of the political, jurisdictional or international status of the country or territory to which a person belongs, whether it be independent, trust, non-self-governing or under any other limitation of sovereignty.

ARTICLE 3 Everyone has the right to life, liberty and security of person.

ARTICLE 4 No one shall be held in slavery or servitude; slavery and the slave trade shall be prohibited in all their forms.

ARTICLE 5 No one shall be subjected to torture or to cruel, inhuman or degrading treatment or punishment.

ARTICLE 6 Everyone has the right to recognition everywhere as a person before the law.

ARTICLE 7 All are equal before the law and are entitled without any discrimination to equal protection of the law. All are entitled to equal protection against any discrimination in violation of this Declaration and against any incitement to such discrimination.

ARTICLE 8 Everyone has the right to an effective remedy by the competent national tribunals for acts violating the fundamental rights granted him by the constitution or by law.

ARTICLE 9 No one shall be subjected to arbitrary arrest, detention or exile.

ARTICLE 10 Everyone is entitled in full equality to a fair and public hearing by an independent and impartial tribunal, in the determination of his rights and obligations and of any criminal charge against him.

ARTICLE 11 (1) Everyone charged with a penal offence has the right to be presumed innocent until proved guilty according to law in a public trial at which he has had all the guarantees necessary for his defence. (2) No one shall be held guilty of any penal offence on account of any act or omission which did not constitute a penal offence, under national or international law, at the time when it was committed. Nor shall a heavier penalty be imposed than the one that was applicable at the time the penal offence was committed.

ARTICLE 12 No one shall be subjected to arbitrary interference with his privacy, family, home or correspondence, nor to attacks upon his honour and reputation. Everyone has the right to the protection of the law against such interference or attacks.

ARTICLE 13 (1) Everyone has the right to freedom of movement and residence within the borders of each State. (2) Everyone has the right to leave any country, including his own, and to return to his country.

ARTICLE 14 (1) Everyone has the right to seek and to enjoy in other countries asylum from persecution. (2) This right may not be invoked in the case of prosecutions genuinely arising from non-political crimes or from acts contrary to the purposes and principles of the United Nations.

ARTICLE 15 (1) Everyone has the right to a nationality. (2) No one shall be arbitrarily deprived of his nationality nor denied the right to change his nationality.

ARTICLE 16 (1) Men and women of full age, without any limitation due to race, nationality or religion, have the right to marry and to found a family. They are entitled to equal rights as to marriage, during marriage and at its dissolution. (2) Marriage shall be entered into only with the free and full consent of the intending spouses. (3) The family is the natural and fundamental group unit of society and is entitled to protection by society and the State.

ARTICLE 17 (1) Everyone has the right to own property alone as well as in association with others. (2) No one shall be arbitrarily deprived of his property.

ARTICLE 18 Everyone has the right to freedom of thought, conscience and religion; this right includes freedom to change his religion or belief, and freedom, either alone or in community with others and in public or private, to manifest his religion or belief in teaching, practice, worship and observance.

ARTICLE 19 Everyone has the right to freedom of opinion and expression; this right includes freedom to hold opinions without interference and to seek, receive and impart information and ideas through any media and regardless of frontiers.

ARTICLE 20 (1) Everyone has the right to freedom of peaceful assembly and association. (2) No one may be compelled to belong to an association.

ARTICLE 21 (1) Everyone has the right to take part in the government of his country, directly or through freely chosen representatives. (2) Everyone has the right to equal access to public service in his country. (3) The will of the people shall be the basis of the authority of government; this will shall be expressed in periodic and genuine elections which shall be by universal and equal suffrage and shall be held by secret vote or by equivalent free voting procedures.

ARTICLE 22 Everyone, as a member of society, has the right to social security and is entitled to realization, through national effort and international cooperation and in accordance with the organization and resources of each State, of the economic, social and cultural rights indispensable for his dignity and the free development of his personality.

ARTICLE 23 (1) Everyone has the right to work, to free choice of employment, to just and favourable conditions of work and to protection against unemployment. (2) Everyone, without any discrimination, has the right to equal pay for equal work. (3) Everyone who works has the right to just and favourable remuneration ensuring for himself and his family

an existence worthy of human dignity, and supplemented, if necessary, by other means of social protection. (4) Everyone has the right to form and to join trade unions for the protection of his interests.

ARTICLE 24 Everyone has the right to rest and leisure, including reasonable limitation of working hours and periodic holidays with pay.

ARTICLE 25 (1) Everyone has the right to a standard of living adequate for the health and wellbeing of himself and of his family, including food, clothing, housing and medical care and necessary social services, and the right to security in the event of unemployment, sickness, disability, widowhood, old age or other lack of livelihood in circumstances beyond his control. (2) Motherhood and childhood are entitled to special care and assistance. All children, whether born in or out of wedlock, shall enjoy the same social protection.

ARTICLE 26 (1) Everyone has the right to education. Education shall be free, at least in the elementary and fundamental stages. Elementary education shall be compulsory. Technical and professional education shall be made generally available and higher education shall be equally accessible to all on the basis of merit. (2) Education shall be directed to the full development of the human personality and to the strengthening of respect for human rights and fundamental freedoms. It shall promote understanding, tolerance and friendship among all nations, racial or religious groups, and shall further the activities of the United Nations for the maintenance of peace. (3) Parents have a prior right to choose the kind of education that shall be given to their children.

ARTICLE 27 (1) Everyone has the right freely to participate in the cultural life of the community, to enjoy the arts and to share in scientific advancement and its benefits. (2) Everyone has the right to the protection of the moral and material interests resulting from any scientific, literary or artistic production of which he is the author.

ARTICLE 28 Everyone is entitled to a social and international order in which the rights and freedoms set forth in this Declaration can be fully realized.

ARTICLE 29 (1) Everyone has duties to the community in which alone the free and full development of his personality is possible. (2) In the exercise of his rights and freedoms, everyone shall be subject only to such limitations as are determined by law solely for the purpose of securing due recognition and respect for the rights and freedoms of others and of meeting the just requirements of morality, public order and the general welfare in a democratic society. (3) These rights and freedoms may in no case be exercised contrary to the purposes and principles of the United Nations.

ARTICLE 30 Nothing in this Declaration may be interpreted as implying for any State, group or person any right to engage in any activity or to perform any act aimed at the destruction of any of the rights and freedoms set forth herein, religion or belief in teaching, practice, worship and observance.

Adopted by the United Nations General Assembly at its 183rd meeting held in Paris on 10 December 1948.

Issued by U.N. Department of Information.

UNITED NATIONS

to practise a religion of one's choice, which were set out in the US Constitution. The Soviet Union argued that human rights consisted of social or economic rights – the rights to work, to health care, and to education. Members of the UN tended to support political rights (especially liberal democracies) or economic rights (socialist countries) and negotiations to convert the Universal Declaration into a binding treaty were split. It would take another 18 years for the UN to adopt a political rights treaty and an economic rights treaty. The International Covenant on Civil and Political Rights and the International Covenant on Economic, Social and Cultural Rights finally took effect in 1976.

Look online

Research the 30 Articles of the Universal Declaration of Human Rights: **www.humanrights.com/what-are-human-rights/universal-declaration-of-human-rights/preamble.html**.

18.2 History of the European Court of Human Rights

The European Court of Human Rights (ECtHR) is an international court established by the ECHR. It hears applications alleging that a state which has subscribed to the Convention has broken a provision of the Convention.

An application to the Court can be lodged by an individual after all domestic remedies have been tried and exhausted. The Court can issue both judgments and advisory opinions. It is based in Strasbourg, France.

The Court was established on 21 January 1959 on the basis of Article 19 ECHR. The jurisdiction of the Court is recognised by all 47 member states of the Council of Europe.

The accession of new states to the ECHR following the fall of the Berlin Wall in 1989 led to a sharp increase in applications filed in the Court. The efficiency of the Court was seriously threatened by the large number of applications it received:

- In 1999 8400 applications were allocated to be heard.
- In 2003, 27,200 cases were filed and the number of pending applications was 65,000.
- In 2005, the Court opened 45,500 new case files.
- In 2009 57,200 applications were allocated, with the number of pending applications rising to 119,300.

More than 90 per cent of applications were declared to be inadmissible and about 60 per cent of the remaining cases decided by the Court were

The European Court of Human Rights, Strasbourg

repetitive cases, where there was well established case law on a similar issue. Protocol 11 tried to deal with the backlog of cases by establishing the Court and its judges as a full-time institution, by simplifying the procedure and reducing the length of proceedings.

In May 2004 the Council of Europe Committee of Ministers adopted Protocol 14 to the ECHR. This was drafted with the aim of reducing the workload of the Court and that of the Committee of Ministers of the Council of Europe, which supervises the execution of judgments, so that the Court could focus on cases that raise important human rights issues.

Before Protocol 14, judges were elected for a six-year term, with the option of renewal of this term. Now judges are elected for a non-renewable nine-year term. The number of full-time judges is 47, equal to the number of contracting states. The Convention requires that judges are of high moral character and have qualifications suitable for high judicial office. Judges are elected whenever a sitting judge's term has expired or when a new state accedes to the Covenant. The retiring age of judges is 70, but they may continue to serve as judges until a new judge is elected or until the cases in which they sit have come to an end.

The judges perform their duties in an individual capacity and are prohibited from having any institutional or other type of ties with their state. To ensure the independence of the Court, judges are not allowed to participate in activity that may compromise the Court's independence. Judges cannot hear or decide a case if they have a family or professional relationship with the parties. Judges can only be dismissed from office if the other judges decide, by two-thirds majority, that the judge has ceased to fulfil the required conditions.

18.2.1 Relationship with other courts

The European Court of Justice

The Court of Justice of the European Union (ECJ) is not related to the ECtHR. However, since all EU member states are members of the Council of Europe and have signed the Convention on Human Rights, there are concerns about consistency in case law between the two courts. The ECJ refers to the case law of the ECtHR and treats the Convention on Human Rights as though it was part of the EU's legal system, since it forms part of the legal principles of the EU member states. Even though its member states are party to the Convention, the European Union itself is not a party, as it did not have competence to do so under previous

treaties. However, EU institutions are bound under Article 6 of the EU Treaty of Nice to respect human rights under the Convention.

National courts

Most of the signatory states to the ECHR, including the UK, have incorporated the Convention into their own national legal systems, either through constitutional provision, statute or judicial decisions. In the UK, all courts are bound to give effect to decisions of the ECtHR.

An individual who argues that his human rights have been violated has to first take a case in his national courts. Only if all avenues and remedies have been exhausted in the national courts can a claim be issued in ECtHR.

Tip

Make sure that you understand the differences between the EU and the ECHR, the respective institutions and the different laws.

18.3 The impact of the Human Rights Act 1988

The UK ratified the European Convention on Human Rights in 1966. The UK is a dualist system in respect of incorporating international law into the UK legal system. This means that Parliament must pass legislation to make provisions in a treaty between the UK and another country or organisation part of UK law and so directly enforceable in a UK court. The opposite system is a monist system when a treaty with another country or organisation automatically becomes part of the domestic law.

For the UK, this meant that before 2000, a person who alleged breach of his human rights could bring a case in the ECtHR but could not argue any of his rights given by the Convention before a UK court. UK courts could use the Convention to help interpret ambiguous wording or clauses in legislation but could not decide a case based purely on a Convention right.

When Labour came to power in 1997 it kept its manifesto promise and put forward a Human Rights Bill to incorporate the ECHR into UK law. The Bill received Royal Assent in 1998 and came into effect in October 2000 allowing time for judges, lawyers and public bodies to receive training on its effects and application.

A person claiming under the Human Rights Act (HRA) 1998 can, since 2000, bring a claim by s 7

before a court or tribunal if he or she is a victim of an unlawful act. This means that he or she is directly affected by an act or measure of a public body.

An action can only be taken against a public body carrying out a public function. This has been described as a vertical relationship between the state and an individual. Relations between private individuals are described as horizontal and are not covered by HRA 1998. According to s 6 HRA 1998 a public body is a body carrying out a public function and the act must not be of a private nature, and under the section it is unlawful for a public body to act against a person's ECHR rights. Public bodies can be divided into:

- core authorities which only perform public functions – these include government departments, local authorities, courts and tribunals but not Parliament, and
- hybrid public authorities – these are bodies that may be private in nature but perform public functions. They may include bodies that carry out a public service that has been contracted out such as providing residential care or social housing.

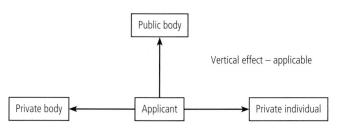

Figure 18.1 Diagram showing vertical and horizontal effect

18.3.1 Judicial powers

Case law

Under s 2, a court or tribunal deciding a case under HRA 1998 must take into account all past judgments, decisions, declarations or opinions of the ECtHR. If the court is faced with a conflicting domestic (UK) precedent and a decision of the ECtHR, it should follow the domestic precedent and refer the case to appeal.

Interpretation

According to s 3, so far as is possible, domestic laws, primary and secondary, should be read and given effect in a manner which is compatible with Convention rights. This is a major change from pre-2000 when the courts could only use the Convention to interpret ambiguous legislation.

Case study

Bellringer v Bellringer (2003)

The claimant was a transsexual woman who went through a marriage ceremony with a man in 1981. The Matrimonial Causes Act 1973 made a marriage void when the parties were not of opposite sex. The woman wanted a legal recognition of her marriage. The House of Lords decided that the marriage was not valid as, at the time of the ceremony, English law did not recognise a change of gender. Also the court could not use its powers under s 3 to interpret 'man and woman' in the 1973 Act to include a person who had undergone gender reassignment. A declaration of incompatibility was issued for the 1973 Act as it was inconsistent with Articles 8 and 12 ECHR. Parliament later passed the Gender Recognition Act 2004 to remove the incompatibility.

Declarations of incompatibility

If, as in the *Bellringer* case above, the court finds a piece of legislation is incompatible with a Convention right, it may make a declaration of incompatibility. This does not affect the original legislation so the parties in the case will still be bound by it. Parliamentary sovereignty remains as the court cannot declare a piece of legislation invalid. When a declaration of incompatibility is issued, it is for Parliament to decide whether to repeal or amend the legislation, or to ignore the court judgment.

Case studies

R (Anderson) v Secretary of State for the Home Department (2002)

Under the Crime (Sentences) Act 1997 the Home Secretary was given the power to fix a tariff period for a murderer subject to a life sentence. The House of Lords decided this power was incompatible with Article 6 ECHR. Parliament amended the law in the Criminal Justice Act 2003 and power to fix the tariff period passed to judges.

A v Secretary of State for the Home Department (2005)

The claimants were indefinitely detained under anti-terror legislation. When passing the legislation, Parliament had issued an order of derogation, as they were entitled to do under Article 15 ECHR in times of war or other public emergency. The claimants argued that there was no public emergency and powers allowing indefinite detention were disproportionate and unnecessary.

The House of Lords decided:

- that it was for the government to decide if there was an emergency situation, and
- the powers were disproportionate, discriminatory and incompatible with Articles 5 and 14 ECHR.

The government's response was to introduce legislation creating control orders – the Prevention of Terrorism Act 2005.

Key term

Derogation – in human rights where there is an exemption from, or relaxation of, rules which would otherwise apply.

A government minister can, when promoting a bill through Parliament, certify that it is necessary to depart from the ECHR – perhaps because of terrorism issues. This power has mainly been used to derogate from Articles 5 and 6.

Section 10 HRA 1998 gives relevant government ministers power to amend legislation that is subject to a declaration of incompatibility without having to go through the full parliamentary process, though it still has to be approved by a parliamentary resolution.

18.3.2 Remedies

Under s 8, if the court finds that an act by a public authority is unlawful, it may grant such relief as is just and appropriate. This may take the form of damages or an injunction

Case study

Commissioner of Police for the Metropolis v DSD, NBV (2015)

The claimants had been victims of rape by a serial offender. The court found that there had been a breach by the police of Article 3 ECHR as they owe a duty to investigate acts of alleged ill-treatment by private individuals including serious, violent crime committed by non-state agents. The failure in this case caused sufficient detriment to the claimants for them to be awarded damages.

Issue	Before HRA 1998	After HRA 1998
An Act incompatible to ECHR	Courts could not set it aside or question its validity.	Court can issue declaration of incompatibility or interpret Act in such a way to make it compatible.
Duty of court in interpretation of Act	No duty to interpret in ECHR-friendly manner.	A duty on court to interpret Act to comply with ECHR as far as possible.
Use of ECtHR cases in domestic courts	Only used in a few limited situations.	A duty is on courts to take ECtHR decisions into account.
Claimants able to argue ECHR rights in domestic courts	No right to do so.	Have directly enforceable right to do so.
Remedy for breach of ECHR	Take case to ECHR after exhausting all domestic rights.	Directly available in domestic courts.
Effect of ECHR violation by public authority	Lawful – unless unlawful on other grounds.	Unlawful.

Figure 18.2 Comparison of the law before and after HRA 1998 came into effect

Although before HRA 1998 there was no right for an individual to bring an action for breach of ECHR rights in a domestic court, this did not mean that there was no protection of individual rights. Common law, through Magna Carta, protected the right to a fair trial and other fundamental rights and freedoms. Judicial review gave individuals the right to challenge decisions of government departments and other public bodies. Statutes created express rights such as under the Police and Criminal Evidence Act 1984 for those arrested and detained by the police.

However, prior to HRA 1998 the UK's record in protecting ECHR rights was, in certain cases, found lacking. For example, in *Sunday Times v United Kingdom* (1979) the newspaper had an injunction placed on an article it had planned to publish. The article concerned the cause of birth defects in children whose mothers had used the drug thalidomide during pregnancy. The ECtHR held that such an injunction violated Article 10 ECHR because the interference did not correspond to public interests.

Case study

Malone v United Kingdom (1984)

The claimant was charged with offences relating to the dishonest handling of stolen goods; he was ultimately acquitted. During his trial, it emerged that a telephone conversation to which he had been a party had been intercepted on behalf of the police on the authority of a warrant issued by the Home Secretary. He also believed that his correspondence had been intercepted and his telephone 'tapped' and 'metered' by a device recording all the numbers dialled. The UK government accepted that as a suspected receiver of stolen goods, he was one of a class of persons who's postal and telephone communications were liable to be intercepted. The ECtHR decided that there had been a violation of the claimant's right to respect for his private life and correspondence, as guaranteed by Article 8.

Even after HRA 1998 was passed, there have been cases heard by UK courts where a breach of human rights has not been accepted and the applicant has been forced to pursue a claim to the ECtHR.

Case study

Wainwright v United Kingdom (2007)

The claimant and his mother went to visit his stepbrother in prison. Because he was suspected of taking drugs in jail, the two visitors were asked to consent to a strip search. They reluctantly consented and were searched by prison officers, which they found upsetting. In particular, the claimant was handled in a way that was later conceded amounted to a battery.

A psychiatrist concluded that the claimant (who had physical and learning difficulties) had been so severely affected by his experience as to suffer PTSD.

At first instance the judge held that the searches were wrongful because of the battery and invasion of the claimant's right to privacy and damages were awarded. The appeal court did not agree that the search amounted to trespass to the person and did not consider that (apart from the battery) the prison officers had committed any wrongful act. They set aside the judgments with the exception of the damages for battery, which was valued at £3,750.

An appeal was made to the House of Lords. Lord Hoffmann held that there was no tort for invasion of privacy, because it was too uncertain. A claim under Article 8 – the right to privacy and family life – did not help because, in his view, the ECHR was a standard which applied to whatever was currently present in the common law. Common law protection was sufficient privacy protection for the ECHR's purpose. The claim of a breach of Article 3 (inhuman and degrading treatment) was completely unfounded.

In Lord Scott's opinion the way the strip searches were carried out had humiliated and caused distress to the claimant and his mother, and was 'calculated (in an objective sense)' to do so, even if this was not the intention of the prison officers. However, that was not tortious at common law, even if the humiliation and distress were intended and the appeal was dismissed unanimously.

The claimant appealed to ECtHR who decided:

1 The treatment to which the claimant had been subjected was negligent and fell short of the level of severity required to constitute a breach of Article 3.
2 However, Article 8 also protects physical and moral integrity. As the searches had not been proportionate to the aim of preventing crime and disorder in the manner in which they had been carried out, there was a violation of Article 8.
3 The absence of an effective domestic remedy, in particular the absence of a general tort of invasion of privacy, resulted in a breach of Article 13.
4 The applicants were awarded €3,000 each in damages for the distress caused to them.

This judgment could be read as requiring the introduction into English law of a general tort of invasion of privacy. At the time of the visit (pre-2000) HRA 1998 was not in force. If it had occurred after HRA 1998, a remedy might have been available directly to the applicants.

What are the consequences for human rights if we change our relationship with the EU?

Europe consists of two separate legal systems, each of which has a separate human rights framework: the Council of Europe and the European Union.

Each has its court (the Council of Europe's in Strasbourg, and the European Union's in Luxembourg), and they adjudicate separately on human rights issues. As a member of the Council of Europe and the European Union the UK has a duty to comply with the decisions of these courts in different ways and the types of remedy available under each system differ.

It is within the power of the UK parliament to withdraw from each of the European systems – although the complexity of how the systems overlap makes exit from either or both very complicated.

If we repeal the Human Rights Act 1998 but remain a member of the ECHR system there may actually be an increase in cases going to Strasbourg, because the ECHR protects the right to a remedy (Article 13). If we remove the remedies available under the Human Rights Act then more cases may end up being admitted to the court in Strasbourg.

It is open to the UK to leave the Council of Europe system completely and to repeal the Human Rights Act. However, the ECHR is considered a fundamental part of EU law and so would continue to apply in relation to EU matters. The European Union itself is also under an obligation to sign up to the ECHR and will join as a member, just like Russia and the UK. In this sense the two European systems overlap and are intertwined.

Each of the devolved regions (of the UK) is on a very different human rights trajectory, all with moves towards stronger enforcement. Proposed reform may risk further fragmenting an already fragmented UK and could potentially leave those living in England with even less access to rights or remedies compared to other parts of the UK. On the other hand, a holistic UK approach to human rights reform might help forge stronger links between its constituent parts and could lead to a formal written constitution setting out the rights of all UK citizens.

Source: Adapted from an article by Dr Katie Boyle, University of Roehampton on *The UK in a Changing Europe* website

Follow this weblink for the complete article: http://ukandeu.ac.uk/explainers/what-are-the-consequences-for-human-rights-if-we-change-our-relationship-with-the-eu/

18.4 Evaluation of human rights protection and ideas for reform

The first practical point is that there may be a considerable delay for the resolution of any case involving human rights, especially if the case has to be referred to the ECtHR. For example, in the case of *Wainwright*, the prison visit took place in January 1997 but the decision of the ECtHR was given in 2006. The reason for this is that the case had to go through the English courts, including the House of Lords hearing in 2003, and then be referred to the ECtHR. As is stated in section 18.2 there is a considerable delay in dealings with the ECtHR because of the volume of cases referred.

The main point is the different treatment and effect of laws and rulings from the ECJ and rulings of the ECtHR.

While the UK remains a member of the EU it has to follow and implement decisions of the ECJ. As has been set out in *OCR AS/A Level Law Book 1*, Chapter 21, Parliament and the courts have no choice. The supremacy of EU law is a consequence of UK membership. However, the situation is different with decisions of the ECtHR. These are not automatically applicable in a domestic legal system and, in the UK, require Parliament to correct any incompatible primary legislation. So for example, in the case of *Hirst v United Kingdom (No. 2)* (2005), the Strasbourg court found that a blanket ban on prisoner voting was incompatible with the right to vote as it was a breach of Article 3 of Protocol 1, and the Committee of Ministers – the body responsible for overseeing the execution of Strasbourg judgments – continues to urge the UK to comply. Subsequent cases brought by serving prisoners before the ECtHR have all come to the same conclusion. However successive governments have failed to take any action to implement the judgments though it was reported in October 2017 that the Justice Secretary is considering removing the voting ban for a limited number of offenders. Any future developments on prisoner voting are likely to be closely tied to the government's proposals for reforming the Human Rights Act 1998.

Case study

Hirst v United Kingdom (No. 2) (2005)

The applicant was serving a sentence of life imprisonment for manslaughter. As a convicted prisoner, he was barred by s 3 of the Representation of the People Act 1983 from voting in parliamentary or local elections. According to UK government figures, some 48,000 other prisoners were similarly affected.

Proceedings were issued under s 4 of HRA 1998, seeking a declaration that s 3 was incompatible with the ECHR. Hirst alleged that, as a convicted prisoner in detention, he was subject to a blanket ban on voting in elections. He relied on Article 3 of Protocol 1, Article 14 and Article 10.

His application was rejected by the High Court and he appealed to the ECtHR, where his complaint was upheld.

This issue shows that the UK Government, and ultimately Parliament, retain the right to decide whether to apply decisions of the ECtHR, and no amount of pressure can force them to change the law. This is different from decisions of the ECJ which have to be implemented immediately by Parliament and the courts. Breach of EU law can have immediate consequences on the UK as was seen in the *Factortame* case.

See *OCR AS/A Level Law Book 1* section 21.5 for full details of the *Factortame* case.

However, if there is a breach of the ECHR or HRA 1998, the English courts can only issue a declaration of incompatibility, which may or may not be acted on by government and Parliament.

Following on from this, the Westminster Parliament can still pass law that is incompatible with the ECHR providing the government minister sponsoring the legislation signs a declaration of incompatibility. This has been done with anti-terrorism legislation introduced since 2001. While the UK remains a member of the EU, Parliament cannot pass legislation that goes against any EU legislation or decisions of the ECJ.

There is uncertainty on whether the UK should have a Bill of Rights, or indeed whether each constituent country should have its own Bill.

A Commission on a Bill of Rights 2012 was set up by the Conservative Government in 2012 following an election manifesto promise. It reported in 2014 but failed to reach consensus, leading to a split report. Two Conservative members argued withdrawing from the ECHR. Lord Faulks QC and Jonathan Fisher QC, the Tory members, said in their minority view:

> There are strong arguments that the cause of human rights, both in the UK and internationally, would be better served by withdrawal from the convention ... or at the very least a renegotiation of the UK's terms of membership so as to free it from the strictures of the court.

Seven members suggested there should be a new bill in principle, but could not agree precisely what form it might take. The chairman of the commission, Sir Leigh Lewis went with the majority view. He said:

> Our current human rights structures do not enjoy great public support and ownership and are seen very much as someone else's creation [from abroad]. We were struck by the fact that [within Europe] we are unique in neither having our own constitution nor our own bill of rights decided by our own parliament.

In a minority view, two of the commission members, Philippe Sands QC, a Liberal Democrat adviser, and the Labour peer Baroness Kennedy QC, opposed the introduction of a UK bill of rights for fear it would be used to lever the UK out of the ECHR. Their view was: 'We believe that such a path would be catastrophic for the UK, for Europe and for the protection of human rights around the world.'

Francesca Klug, a professor and expert in human rights laws, said:

> There is no political appetite to [change the Human Rights Act] which is only 12 years old, maintains parliamentary sovereignty and is compatible with remaining within the ECHR. That is the gist of over 80 per cent of the responses to the commission's consultation, most of which maintain that the HRA is a UK bill of rights in all but name.

Ben Emmerson QC, said:

> The Human Rights Act has been interpreted and applied by British judges in a balanced and intelligent way that reflects British legal traditions, and the judgments of our supreme court now exert a powerful influence over the court in Strasbourg precisely because they are interpreting the same set of rights, but with a distinctively British character.

His view was that 'to embark on an ill thought through process of altering the language and content of our human rights legislation at this time is irresponsible madness'.

Stephen Bowen, director of the British Institute of Human Rights, said:

> The commission asked for the public's views about whether we need a bill of rights, and the message from the majority was clear: the Human Rights Act is our bill of rights, and should remain part of our law.

The end result was a recommendation that nothing should be altered until after the outcome of the Scottish referendum on independence in 2014, when a constitutional convention should be held. However after this vote came the 2015 General Election and in 2016 the vote on the UK's continued membership of the EU. This vote in favour of withdrawing from the EU appears to have put the issue of reform of the HRA to one side and no further action is proposed at this time.

18.5 The entrenched nature of the Human Rights Act 1988 and the devolution settlements

Entrenchment is a procedure which would make an Act of Parliament difficult to repeal or amend in the future. One way of doing this would be to include a provision that would require, for example, a 75 per cent majority of votes in the House of Commons before repeal or amendment could take place.

As is well known, under the principle of parliamentary sovereignty, Parliament is the supreme law-making body in the UK, and no one Parliament can bind its successors. This means that, in theory, a future Parliament could repeal or amend HRA 1998. The Human Rights Act contains no provision to stop or limit the powers of a successor Parliament from repealing or amending it. In practice that is extremely unlikely because, in a political sense, it would suggest that the UK does not respect human rights.

In its 1997 White Paper, 'Rights Brought Home: The Human Rights Bill 1997', the government set out its view about entrenchment as follows:

> 2.16 On one view, human rights legislation is so important that it should be given added protection from subsequent amendment or repeal. The Constitution of the United States of America, for example, guarantees rights

which can be amended or repealed only by securing qualified majorities in both the House of Representatives and the Senate, and among the States themselves. But an arrangement of this kind could not be reconciled with our own constitutional traditions, which allow any Act of Parliament to be amended or repealed by a subsequent Act of Parliament. We do not believe that it is necessary or would be desirable to attempt to devise such a special arrangement for this Bill.

By three separate Acts, Parliament granted devolution, or law-making powers, to Scotland, Wales and Northern Ireland. None of these Acts contained entrenched provisions so again, in theory, these laws could be repealed by a future Westminster Parliament. However, politically, this would be extremely embarrassing and unlikely.

18.5.1 Scotland

Scotland was granted devolved powers by the Scotland Act 1998 and a Scottish Parliament was established. In constitutional terms, the Scotland Act makes provisions for the protection of human rights within Scotland. Specifically, s 57(2) states that:

> a member of the Scottish Executive, or government, has no power to make any subordinate, or delegated, legislation or to do any other act, so far as the legislation or act is incompatible with any of the ECHR rights.

Furthermore, Sch 4(1) of the Act states that 'an Act of the Scottish Parliament cannot modify the Human Rights Act 1998'. Any Act which did so would be automatically rendered invalid. A decision on whether a decision of Scottish Ministers or an Act is invalidated by being noncompliant is ultimately for the UK Supreme Court, in considering any 'devolution issues' brought before it.

18.5.2 Wales

Wales was granted devolved powers by the Government of Wales Act 2006 which established the Welsh Assembly with law-making powers. The Act provides, in s 108(6), that an Assembly Act (or Assembly Measure) which is incompatible with ECHR rights is outside the legislative competence of the National Assembly. This means that such a provision would be invalid and of no effect.

Also, by s 81 Welsh Ministers have no power to make, confirm or approve any subordinate legislation, or to do any other act, so far as that legislation or act is incompatible with any ECHR rights. The Welsh ministers must not, therefore, in exercising any of their functions breach ECHR rights.

18.5.3 Northern Ireland

Northern Ireland was granted devolved powers by the Northern Ireland Act 1998 which established an Assembly with law-making powers. The Act provides, in a similar way to the other devolved countries, in s 7, that HRA 1998 cannot be modified by an Act of the Assembly or by any subordinate legislation.

18.5.4 Recent developments

The Conservatives pledged in their manifesto for the 2015 General Election to repeal HRA 1998 and introduce a British bill of rights. This, the manifesto said, would break the formal link between the British courts and the ECtHR, making the Supreme Court the 'ultimate arbiter of human rights' in the UK.

Arguments for repeal were that the Act does little to protect the liberties or the safety of British people, and that it allows judges – who are not chosen by popular vote – to make substantive judgments about government policies. This has led, said the Conservatives, to 'perverse' rulings, such as allowing radical Islamist preacher Abu Qatada to remain in the UK, and the ban on prisoners being allowed to vote being declared unlawful.

There have been no attempts, at the time of writing, to introduce any attempt to repeal or amend the Act. It is thought that any such attempt would require the agreement of all three devolved legislatures, requiring them to pass what is known as a legislative consent motion. It is thought that this proposal would be vigorously opposed, by all the governing parties in the devolved countries.

Case	Facts	Legal principle
Bellringer v Bellringer (2003)	A transsexual woman 'married' a man. This was void as the parties were not of opposite sexes.	The House of Lords decided that the marriage was not valid: the law did not recognise a change of gender. A declaration of incompatibility was issued.
R (Anderson) v Secretary of State for the Home Department (2002)	The Home Secretary's power to fix a tariff period for a murderer subject to a life sentence was challenged.	The House of Lords decided this power was incompatible with Article 6.
A v Secretary of State for the Home Department (2005)	The claimants were indefinitely detained under anti-terror legislation. They argued there was no war or public emergency allowing derogation from the ECHR.	It was for the government to decide if there was an emergency situation; indefinite detention was disproportionate and discriminatory and incompatible with Articles 5 and 14.
Commissioner of Police for the Metropolis v DSD, NBV (2015)	The police failed to investigate offences of rape by a serial offender.	The police owe a duty to investigate acts of alleged ill-treatment by private individuals including serious, violent crime and there had been a breach of Article 3.
Malone v United Kingdom (1984)	The claimant was charged and acquitted of handling stolen goods. His telephone had been tapped and metered and letters intercepted.	The ECtHR decided there had been a violation of Article 8 – the right to respect for private life and correspondence.
Wainwright v United Kingdom (2007)	The claimant and his mother were required to undergo a strip search before visiting a relative in prison. This caused the claimant to suffer from PTSD.	The ECtHR decided there was no breach of Article 3, but as the searches had not been proportionate to prevent crime and disorder there was a violation of Article 8.

Figure 18.3 Key cases on human rights protection

Summary

- Magna Carta promised that everyone should be subject to fair laws, with access to courts and there should be no imprisonment without jury trial.
- *Habeus corpus* requires a detained person to be brought before the court for the legality of the detention to be considered.
- The Bill of Rights 1689 set out limits on the power of the monarch and the rights of Parliament.
- The European Convention of Human Rights (ECHR) set out a number of protections given to individuals.
- The ECtHR hears applications by individuals who allege that their ECHR rights have been infringed by a state.
- The ECtHR is separate from the European Court of Justice and from national courts.
- Since 2000 an individual in the UK can claim before a national court that there has been a breach of the Human Rights Act 1998 by a public body.
- Parliament can pass legislation that derogates from the ECHR if a government minister issues a certificate of incompatibility.
- UK courts can issue a certificate of incompatibility if they find a law incompatible with the ECHR.

Chapter 19

Article 5: the right to liberty and security

After reading this chapter, you should be able to:
- Understand the key provisions of Article 5 ECHR – the right to liberty and security
- Understand some of the restrictions placed on Article 5
- Apply the law to given situations
- Critically evaluate the operation and application of Article 5

19.1 Article 5 ECHR

" 1 Everyone has the right to liberty and security of person. No one shall be deprived of his liberty save in the following cases and in accordance with a procedure prescribed by law:

   a the lawful detention of a person after conviction by a competent court;

   b the lawful arrest or detention of a person for non-compliance with the lawful order of a court or in order to secure the fulfilment of any obligation prescribed by law;

   c the lawful arrest or detention of a person effected for the purpose of bringing him before the competent legal authority on reasonable suspicion of having committed an offence or when it is reasonably considered necessary to prevent his committing an offence or fleeing after having done so;

   d the detention of a minor by lawful order for the purpose of educational supervision or his lawful detention for the purpose of bringing him before the competent legal authority;

   e the lawful detention of persons for the prevention of the spreading of infectious diseases, of persons of unsound mind, alcoholics or drug addicts or vagrants;

   f the lawful arrest or detention of a person to prevent his effecting an unauthorised entry into the country or of a person against whom action is being taken with a view to deportation or extradition.

2 Everyone who is arrested shall be informed promptly, in a language which he or she understands, of the reasons for his arrest and of any charge against him.

3 Everyone arrested or detained in accordance with the provisions of paragraph 1(c) of this Article shall be brought promptly before a judge or other officer authorised by law to exercise judicial power and shall be entitled to trial within a reasonable time or to release pending trial. Release may be conditioned by guarantees to appear for trial.

4 Everyone who is deprived of his liberty by arrest or detention shall be entitled to take proceedings by which the lawfulness of his detention shall be decided speedily by a court and his release ordered if the detention is not lawful.

5 Everyone who has been the victim of arrest or detention in contravention of the provisions of this article shall have an enforceable right to compensation. "

19.2 Restrictions of Article 5 rights

There are three parts to a confinement which amounts to a deprivation of liberty:
- it is objectively thought that a person is detained for a period of time
- the detainee has not consented to the detention
- the reason for the confinement is set by the state.

Generally confinement will be due to arrest on suspicion of having committed an offence, imprisonment following conviction, or a hospital order. It does not always depend on being locked up. Lord Hope in *Austin v Commissioner of Police of the Metropolis* (2009) said:

> A person can be deprived of his liberty even if his departure is not prevented by a locked door or other physical barrier and even though he may be allowed extensive social and other contact with the outside world.

However there may be situations outside formal detention which amount to a restriction of Article 5 and a deprivation of liberty.

19.2.1 Control orders and TPIM

In 2005 the House of Lords ruled that the practice of holding foreign terror suspects in prison without charge or trial was unlawful. Rather than charge and prosecute these individuals within the criminal justice system, the government brought in the control orders scheme. Control orders enabled the Home Secretary to impose an almost unlimited range of restrictions on any person suspected of involvement in terrorism.

In January 2012 the government replaced control orders with Terrorism Prevention and Investigation Measures (TPIM). TPIMs may be thought of as 'control order-lite'. These new measures are still outside of the criminal justice system and initiated by the Home Secretary.

A TPIM:
- can include electronic tagging and an overnight residence requirement
- allows 'controlees' to use the internet, but they can be restricted on who they can meet and where they can go, including foreign travel bans
- they are limited to two years in length, but it is possible to make a new order as soon as the existing one expires (if there is new evidence to do so).

Key term

Terrorism Prevention and Investigation Measures (TPIM) – a terrorist suspect may be made subject to this order, which places conditions on their residence, movement and activities.

Case studies

Guzzardi v Italy (1981)

A man suspected of criminal activities was put under special police supervision and was sent to the isolated island of Asinara where he was, among other things, required to:
- report to the supervisory authorities twice a day and whenever called upon to do so
- not return to his residence later than 10 p.m. and not go out before 7 a.m.
- not frequent bars or night-clubs
- lead an honest and law-abiding life.

The ECtHR decided that these restrictions amounted to a deprivation of his liberty.

Secretary of State for the Home Department v J J (2007)

A deprivation of liberty took place, and subject to Article 5, when the controlees were subject to an 18-hour house curfew, visitors had to be authorised, and during the six hours the controlees were permitted to leave their house they were confined to restricted areas.

Secretary of State for the Home Department v E (2007)

A person made subject to a control order was subject to a 12-hour curfew, in his own home where he lived with his wife and family. There were no geographical restrictions when he was allowed out of his house and no restriction on who he could meet. This did not amount to a deprivation of liberty subject to Article 5.

19.2.2 Care

There will normally be no deprivation of liberty if a person of sound mind is living with and cared for by his parents, friends or relatives in a family home, foster care or in sheltered accommodation. But what if the person has learning difficulties or other needs?

Case studies

Cheshire West and Chester Council v P (2014)

P was incontinent and had developed a habit of tearing pieces off his continence pad and ingesting them. His carers had tried to intervene by getting him to open his mouth and putting in their fingers to try and sweep out the ingested material. In order to prevent him from accessing the pad he had been placed in an all-body suit like a Babygro which he could not open from the front.

P and Q by their litigation friend the Official Solicitor v Surrey County Council (2011)

P and Q were sisters and both had severe learning disabilities. P lived at a college for 38 weeks and returned to her foster mother in the holidays. She was supervised by both the college and her foster mother (to whom she was devoted). She had never attempted to leave the home by herself and showed no wish to do so, but if she did, the foster mother would restrain her. She was taken on trips and holidays by her foster mother. She was not on any medication.

Q lived in a non-secure NHS supported living placement for learning disabled adolescents with complex needs. She had occasional outbursts of challenging behaviour towards other residents and sometimes required physical restraint. She was receiving tranquillising medication. Her care needs were met only as a result of continuous supervision and control. She showed no wish to go out on her own and so did not need to be prevented from doing so, but was accompanied by staff whenever she left.

The Supreme Court decided, by a 4–3 majority that the individuals in both cases were being deprived of their liberty. The test set out by Lady Hale, in the majority, was: 'Is the patient under continuous supervision and not entitled to leave?' In her view the individuals should be reassessed to see if their condition and needs had altered.

Activity

1 In the P and Q case above the Court of Appeal had decided that for an adult with a disability, their situation was decided by comparing them with that of an adult of similar age with the same capabilities, affected by the same condition or suffering the same inherent mental and physical disabilities and limitations. In the court's view there was no deprivation of liberty for the purposes of Article 5. They were living lives which were as normal as could be for people in their situation.

Which view would you support:
- the majority of the Supreme Court who considered that there was a deprivation of liberty, or
- the view of the Court of Appeal, and the minority of the Supreme Court, who all ruled that the individuals had not been deprived of their liberty?

Decide whether any of the following would be relevant to your decision:
- the individual's happiness about his care arrangements
- the giving of medication to stop an individual from expressing himself
- the living arrangements being normal for an individual with those needs
- the ability to socialise and leave the accommodation to play sports or for recreation.

You can find the full report of this case online, at **www.supremecourt.uk/cases/docs/uksc-2012-0088-judgment.pdf**.

2 This activity is based on *Hillingdon LBC v Neary* (2011).

A young man with autism and a severe learning disability was accepted into respite care with the local authority for a few days at the request of his father.

Do you think there was a deprivation of his liberty in any of the following situations:
- he was detained for a total of a year
- the young man objected to being held in care
- the father objected to him being kept in respite care
- there was total control of his movements by carers at his every waking moment?

Now compare your thoughts with those of the judge. You can find the law report at **www.bailii.org/ew/cases/EWHC/COP/2011/1377.html**.

J E v D E, aka Re D E (2006)

D E suffered a stroke and was blind with short-term memory impairment; he had dementia and lacked capacity to decide where he should live. D E and J E moved in together in 2004. D E then lived voluntarily at a care home but was then taken home by J E. A year later he was taken back to the care home and then to another care home. He was given a fair amount of freedom within the homes. He was taken for walks, had regular telephone contact with his wife and daughter, and received visits. However, his care notes indicated his wishes to leave and live with J E.

The ECtHR decided he was deprived of his liberty as, despite his freedoms, he was not 'free to leave' and the police would be contacted if he was missing. The court also observed there is no requirement for a lock or physical barrier to be present for there to be a deprivation of liberty. For example, a Category C prisoner in an open prison is deprived of his liberty. Whether a patient is kept in locked or open conditions is not decisive.

19.2.3 Parents and children

Parental restrictions do not generally offend Article 5 but a two-year Secure Accommodation Order on a teenager imposed by a court was subject to the Article.

Activity

1   Are you still subject to parental restrictions on your movement? How are you restricted?
2   Imagine that you have a 15-year-old brother or sister. What parental restrictions do you think are reasonable to set on him or her?

19.2.4 Public order and crowd control

'Kettling' is where a group of people are held by police in an area as a means of controlling a demonstration. It is a relatively new tactic used by the police, which has no statutory authority.

Austin v Commissioner of Police of the Metropolis (2009)

The police stood in lines across the exits from Oxford Circus in London during a demonstration. People were allowed to leave the 'kettle' only with permission but many were held for over seven hours. The detention was challenged by one of the detained demonstrators. It was argued that this amounted to a deprivation of liberty and was contrary to Article 5. The House of Lords considered that if the measures were resorted to in good faith, proportionate, and enforced for no longer than necessary, the action will not offend Article 5. There was no breach found in this case.

Look online

Read more about this case at **www.humanrighteurope.org**.

After reading this article, do you think the decisions of the English and European courts are fair?

R (Moos) v Metropolitan Police Commissioner (2011)

The court ruled that the police had acted unlawfully in 'containing' (or kettling) G20 protestors. It made clear that the police must be in reasonable apprehension of an 'imminent breach of the peace' before taking 'preventative action'. Preventative action included kettling, but only 'as a last resort catering for situations about to descend into violence'. The police have no power to arbitrarily kettle protestors. The High Court confirmed its legality under these conditions.

Police kettling students in London, 2010

Mengesha v Metropolitan Police Commissioner (2013)

The police authorised a 'kettle' in a protest. About 100 people were kettled, including the claimant who was present as a legal observer. No one disputed that the containment was justified because serious damage and a breach of the peace had occurred and officers reasonably believed a further imminent breach of the peace would occur.

As people were funnelled out of the containment area, a Chief Superintendent decided to film those leaving and obtain their details. He took the view that such action would help in any subsequent post-incident investigation to identify persons involved in criminal acts. The claimant was held in a separate area, surrounded by police officers, and filmed. She was asked to give her name and address and date of birth. She attempted to ask what police power was relied upon authorising the police to film her and ask her details. Those questions were not answered until she had been filmed and given her details.

The court had to consider whether the police can lawfully require individuals 'kettled' to give their details or be videoed before they are allowed to leave the 'kettle' (or 'area of containment'). No statutory powers enabled the police to take details and video before a person was allowed to leave a containment area. However the police do have power under s 50 of the Police Reform Act 2002 for a person who has been or may have been behaving in an 'anti-social' manner to give his name and address; s 64A of the Police and Criminal Evidence Act (PACE) 1984 allows the police to photograph those who have been arrested. Neither of these applied in this case and, as the giving of the video was not voluntary, the police requirement was unlawful.

Videoing a member of the public engaged Article 8 ECHR when the video was taken as the price of being required to leave a containment area. The retention of the video was not 'in accordance with the law' and the retention was therefore a breach of Article 8.

See Chapter 21 for more information about Article 8.

19.2.5 Police powers – stop and search

A formal arrest is subject to Article 5, but what about stop and search?

Section 60 of the Criminal Justice and Public Order Act 1994 gives police the right to search people in a defined area during a specific time period when they believe, with good reason, that:

- serious violence will take place and it is necessary to use this power to prevent such violence
- a person is carrying a dangerous object or offensive weapon, or
- an incident involving serious violence has taken place and a dangerous instrument or offensive weapon used in the incident is being carried.

R (Gillan) v Commissioner of Police of the Metropolis (2006)

The claimant was stopped and searched under s 44 of the Terrorism Act 2000 when he protested about the holding of an arms fair. The House of Lords decided that the power to stop and search him did not involve a deprivation of liberty under Article 5. The procedure would usually be relatively brief, and the person stopped would not be arrested, handcuffed, confined or removed to any different place. In the absence of special circumstances, such a person should not be regarded as being detained in the sense of being confined or kept in custody; he was more properly to be regarded as being detained in the sense of being kept from proceeding or kept waiting – *Guzzardi v Italy* (1981) applied. In any event, assuming the detention was lawful, the police could rely on the exception in Article 5.

R (Roberts) v Commissioner of Police of the Metropolis (2012)

Police intelligence reports indicated a possible rise in violent crime involving offensive weapons. A police officer searched Mrs Roberts after she failed to show a valid bus ticket for her journey, or any identification, and she had given a false name to ticket inspectors. The police officer reasoned that Mrs Roberts' behaviour suggested that she might be carrying an offensive weapon and that it was not uncommon for women of her age to carry weapons for others. She was searched under the authority of s 60.

The court decided that there was no deprivation of liberty in her case as

> she was not confined, nor required to move to a police station, handcuffed or restrained and ... had she not resisted, the search would have been as short as three minutes.

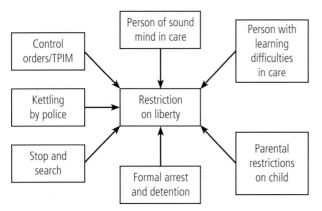

Activity

Have you, or someone you know, been subject to a stop and search? Did you, or they, feel that they had been detained during the procedure?

Alternatively, read online the experience of those who have been stopped and searched. How did they feel about their experience? Did they feel they had been detained?

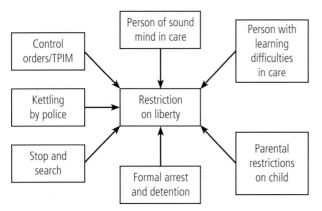

Figure 19.1 Restrictions on liberty

19.3 Article 5(1)

This Article guarantees the liberty and security of the person, with the aim of protecting an individual against arbitrary arrest and detention. The Article requires that a deprivation of liberty must follow a prescribed procedure and it must be lawful. If both of these requirements are met, there is no limit set for the length of the detention.

19.3.1 'A prescribed procedure'

This means that a measure depriving a person of his liberty should be carried out by someone or a body with the authority to do so and should not be arbitrary. A failure to allow a person to respond to the case against him may infringe Article 5(1).

19.3.2 'Lawful'

This means lawful under English law, and any detention which is unlawful under English law will automatically be contrary to Article 5(1).

A detention of a person after conviction by a lawful court is allowed but there must be a causal link between the conviction and the detention.

- Article 5(1)(b) allows for the lawful arrest or detention in cases such as arrest under a warrant for non-payment of a fine, contempt of court and breach of a bail condition.
- Article 5(1)(c) allows for the lawful arrest or detention of a person suspected of having committed an offence. There must be some facts or information which satisfy the requirement of the police having reasonable suspicion and a person can be arrested for questioning in order to obtain evidence.

Case study

Shimovolos v Russia (2011)

The applicant was Russian. The Interior Department of Transport registered his name in a surveillance database which contained information about people perceived by the authorities as 'potential extremists'. When he got on a train to travel to an EU-Russia summit and protest march, his identity documents were checked several times, and when he got off the train he was threatened with force if he did not go to the police station. He was kept at the police station for 45 minutes and questioned about the purpose of his trip and his acquaintances. The police report indicated that he had been stopped and questioned, acting on information in order to prevent him from committing administrative or criminal offences.

On his Article 5 complaint, the ECtHR ruled that as he had been taken to the police station under threat of force and had not been free to leave without permission, he had been deprived of his liberty, even for a short time.

Article 5(1)(c) did not allow detention, as a general policy of prevention, of people who were perceived by the authorities to be dangerous or likely to offend. He had been arrested arbitrarily, in violation of Article 5(1).

- Article 5(1)(d) allows for the detention of a minor for educational supervision or bringing him before a competent legal authority – a court.
- Article 5(1)(e) allows for the lawful detention of a person to prevent the spread of infectious diseases and persons of unsound mind, alcoholics, drug addicts or vagrants. A true mental disorder must be established, it must necessitate confinement and the disorder must be persistent. Expert evidence will be required to support the detention.
- Article 5(1)(f) allows for the lawful arrest or detention to stop a person unlawfully entering the country or a person subject to deportation or extradition. This covers asylum seekers while their application is being considered and in the case of deportation while their case is being investigated and a decision is being made.

19.4 Article 5(2)

The provisions of this Article are mostly covered in PACE 1984, to allow a person to know why he or she has been arrested in a language he or she understands. It does not have to be given in full at the very moment of arrest but should be given promptly. In general, an explanation by the custody officer at the police station will be sufficient.

Case study

Christie v Leachinsky (1947)

The defendant was arrested without a warrant. The police suspected he had stolen or received a bale of fabric, but he was arrested under a different charge of 'unlawful possession' under the Liverpool Corporation Act 1921. He was taken to a police station and detained in custody. The next day he was brought before the court on the charge of 'unlawful possession', remanded in custody for a week, but later released on bail. The defendant claimed false imprisonment. The House of Lords, in relation to these events, confirmed that an arrest without warrant can be justified only if it is an arrest on a charge made known to the person arrested, and the police defence of arrest due to justification failed.

The defendant was eventually brought before court on the charge of 'unlawful possession', but which was withdrawn. He was discharged, but instead of going from the dock into the body of the court, he was directed by police to the cells, detained, eventually charged with larceny and taken into custody.

The House of Lords decided, in relation to these events, that the imprisonment was justified, since the defendant then knew for what alleged felony he was being detained. They commented that it is undesirable that an arrest should be made in court, but such an arrest, will not, if otherwise justified, give rise to an action for damages.

Strict rules are laid down by PACE 1984 as to knowing the reasons for arrest, detention and charge and any breach of those rules will mean that the prosecution will fail.

Case studies

R v Samuel (1988)

The defendant was arrested on suspicion of robbery and taken to a police station. He was interviewed four times about the robbery and two burglaries but he denied the offences. During the second interview he asked for access to a solicitor. Under the Code of Practice a police officer of superintendent rank or above was allowed to delay the right of access to a solicitor if the suspect was being detained in connection with a serious arrestable offence, if he had not yet been charged with an offence and if the officer had reasonable grounds for believing that giving access to a solicitor 'will lead' to other suspects being alerted before their arrest.

He was refused access to a solicitor. At his fourth interview he confessed to two offences of burglary and he was charged with those offences. A solicitor instructed by his family was informed of the charges but was denied access to the appellant. Shortly after he confessed to the robbery in another interview and was charged with that offence. The solicitor was allowed to see him an hour later.

At his trial, he argued that the evidence of the last interview should be excluded as it had taken place in the unjustified absence of a solicitor. The trial judge ruled that there had been no breach of the Code, the evidence was admitted and he was convicted.

On appeal it was decided that:

1 The right of a person detained by the police to have access to a solicitor could not be delayed after he had been charged with any offence and certainly not after he had been charged with a serious arrestable offence in connection with which he was in police custody. Here, the defendant had already been charged with the two burglaries, one of which →

was a serious arrestable offence, before his fourth interview, and the Code was satisfied.

2   The right of a person detained by the police to have access to a solicitor was a fundamental right of the citizen, and a police officer attempting to justify his decision to delay access had to do so by reference to the specific circumstances of the case, including evidence as to the person detained or the actual solicitor sought to be consulted. In particular, not only did the officer have to believe that the access 'will', more than 'may', lead to the alerting of other suspects but he had also to believe that if a solicitor was allowed access to the detained person, the solicitor would thereafter commit the criminal offence of alerting other suspects or would be hoodwinked into doing so inadvertently or unwittingly.

3   In this case the refusal of access to the defendant's solicitor before the last interview had been unjustified and the interview should not have taken place. The conviction of robbery was quashed.

Taylor v Chief Constable of Thames Valley Police (2004)

A 10-year-old boy was arrested at the site of an anti-vivisection protest for what he had done at a previous protest. On arrest the police constable told him he was being arrested for violent disorder committed at a previous place and time. The Court of Appeal decided that sufficient information was given of the reasons for his arrest. His mother was present, and 'violent disorder' without further detail was a good enough description of what he had previously been alleged to have done.

19.5 Article 5(3)

This contains three separate parts:
- the right to be brought promptly before a judge or other officer authorised by law to exercise judicial power
- the right to release on bail, except when custody is justified
- the right to be tried within a reasonable time.

The right to bail is not absolute, but if objected to, the objection must be justified by the judge. This provision is covered by the Bail Act 1976 by which there is a presumption in favour of bail and the court must give reasons for its refusal.

The purpose of the third provision is to ensure that no one spends too long in detention before trial. There is a link here with Article 6(1). Time starts when the accused is first remanded into custody and ends when the court gives judgment. What is a reasonable time depends on the circumstances of each case including the seriousness of the charge.

See Chapter 20 for more information on Article 6.

Case study

Brogan v United Kingdom (1988)

The applicants were arrested and questioned within a few hours of their arrest about their suspected involvement in terrorist offences. They were detained for periods between four-and-a-half and six days before being released without charge. The ECtHR decided that the periods of detention were inconsistent with the idea of 'promptness'.

19.6 Article 5(4)

This provides that everyone who is deprived of his liberty by arrest or detention shall be entitled to take proceedings by which the lawfulness of his detention shall be decided speedily by a court, and his release ordered if the detention is not lawful.

19.6.1 Access to a court

This means that the detainee can challenge the lawfulness of detention. It does not necessarily extend to an application by the detainee's family, though they could help in the detainee's application. The application can be made by judicial review.

19.6.2 Lawfulness of detention

The lawfulness can be considered under Convention rights and under domestic law, and can be carried out by a court or a relevant tribunal such as a mental health review tribunal. For those of unsound mind, the detention should be reviewed regularly.

The court or tribunal must be impartial and independent. The Home Secretary used to set the minimum tariff to be served by an offender convicted of murder, which was considered in breach of this Article. This function has now been transferred to the judiciary, which is fair under the Article. The Parole Board decides on the suitability of prisoners for release once they have served the minimum term set by the court. As appointments to this body are made by the Home Secretary, there are questions as to whether the Parole Board is sufficiently independent to satisfy the requirements of the Article.

A judicial review of detention requires natural justice to be satisfied. This means that the offender is entitled to know the reasons for detention and to be able to put his case before the court, but there is no necessity for an oral hearing in every case.

Determinate and indeterminate sentences

A determinate sentence is a period fixed by the sentencing court. Once a sentence has been passed by a court, and any appeal process has finished, there is no right to have the lawfulness of the sentence reviewed by another court.

Indeterminate sentences are those where the offender is sentenced to a minimum term (the tariff) but will be released only when a body such as the Parole Board is satisfied that the offender is safe to be released and the public does not need further protection. Also covered are situations when an offender is returned to prison after early release or when licence conditions have been broken. These are considered executive actions which, under Article 5(4), will need regular review by a court to ensure that continued detention does not breach the Article.

19.6.3 Speedy decision

There is no time limit set by the Article but a hearing about the detention should be arranged as soon as reasonably practicable depending on the circumstances of the case. In *R v Secretary of State for the Home Department ex parte Noorkoiv* (2002) it was decided that a Parole Board hearing three months after the expiry of a tariff period of a life sentence breached Article 5(4) even though this was a standard practice. The requirement for a speedy decision also applied to reviews of detention.

19.7 Article 5(5)

This Article provides that everyone who has been the victim of unlawful arrest or detention shall have a right to compensation. This right arises for breach of Article 5(1) and (4), and is mandatory – if there has been a breach, compensation must be awarded. The amount of compensation will be assessed by the court finding the detention unlawful. It is unlikely that compensation will be awarded for feelings of disappointment or frustration, though actual financial loss caused by the unlawful detention can be recovered.

> **Tip**
>
> Not every scenario that you have to consider will involve a breach of Article 5. Discuss the issues both for and against a possible breach before coming to a conclusion.

19.8 Evaluation of Article 5

Article 5 contains fundamental values of liberty of the individual and the control of arbitrary state power. Any arrest or detention has to be for legal reasons, ensuring that a person loses his liberty within strict rules that have the essential qualities of law and the rule of law.

These principles have been applied by the ECtHR, although it has been prepared to offer some flexibility to the state in cases such as the prevention of terrorism. This approach has been followed by domestic courts in relation to control orders which had to be replaced with the current system of TPIM.

Both ECtHR and domestic courts have insisted that minimum standards of the right of liberty and security of the person in Article 5 should not be completely abandoned. The UK Government responded to the court's decisions in an attempt to ensure that legislation is compatible with Article 5, though this approach may alter if plans to repeal HRA 1998 are pursued.

Case	Facts	Legal principle
Guzzardi v Italy (1981)	A man suspected of criminal activities was put under supervision and sent to an isolated island subject to conditions.	This amounted to a deprivation of liberty.
Cheshire West and Chester Council v P (2011)	P was incontinent, ate pieces of his pads put in an all-body suit.	The Supreme Court using the test 'is the patient under continuous supervision and not entitled to leave' decided that the individuals were being deprived of their liberty.
P & Q by their litigation friend the Official Solicitor v Surrey CC (2011)	Two sisters with severe learning disabilities had to be continually supervised by their carers.	
J E v D E aka Re D E (2006)	D E suffered a stroke and had dementia and lived in care homes but wished to live with J E.	The ECtHR decided he was deprived of his liberty as he was not 'free to leave' and the police would be contacted if he was missing.
Austin v Commissioner of Police of the Metropolis (2009)	Police 'kettled' demonstrators for over seven hours.	The House of Lords decided there was no breach of Article 5 as the measures were taken in good faith, were proportionate and enforced for no longer than necessary.
Mengesha v Metropolitan Police Commissioner (2013)	Police required demonstrators to be filmed as a condition of leaving a 'kettle'.	The police requirement was unlawful and breached Article 8.
R (Gillan) v Commissioner of Police of the Metropolis (2006)	G was stopped and searched when he protested about the holding of an arms fair.	The House of Lords decided this did not involve a deprivation of liberty under Article 5.
R (Roberts) v Commissioner of Police of the Metropolis (2012)	Mrs R was stopped and searched as she had no valid bus ticket or ID and had given a false name.	The court decided that there was no deprivation of liberty under Article 5.
Shimovolos v Russia (2011)	S had his ID checked several times on a train journey, was forced to go to a police station and questioned about the purpose of his trip and his acquaintances.	ECtHR ruled that he had been arbitrarily arrested in breach of Article 5(1) as he had been taken to the police station under threat of force and had not been free to leave without permission.
Christie v Leachinsky (1947)	D was arrested and later charged with 'unlawful possession' and detained in custody. In court he was remanded in custody but then released on bail. He was then arrested in court on another charge. D claimed false imprisonment.	The House of Lords decided that the imprisonment was justified, since D knew for what alleged charge he was being detained.
R v Samuel (1988)	D was arrested on suspicion of robbery and interviewed four times about the robbery and two burglaries but he denied the offences. He was denied legal advice. He finally confessed to burglary and robbery and was charged. He finally received legal advice.	The Court of Appeal decided that the right of a person detained by the police to have legal advice could not be delayed after he had been charged with any offence and certainly not after he had been charged with a serious arrestable offence in connection with which he was in police custody. In this case the refusal of access to the defendant's solicitor before the last interview had been unjustified and the interview should not have taken place. The conviction of robbery was quashed.
Taylor v Chief Constable of Thames Valley Police (2004)	A 10-year-old boy was arrested at a protest for what he had done at a previous protest and he was told of the reason for the arrest.	The Court of Appeal decided that enough information was given of the reasons for the arrest. His mother was present, and 'violent disorder' without further detail was enough description of what he had previously been alleged to have done.

Figure 19.2 Key cases for Article 5 ECHR

Summary

- Article 5 ECHR protects a person's liberty and security.
- A person's liberty has been deprived when the person has not consented to being held and there is a reason for it.
- The former control orders and the current system of TPIM can amount to deprivation of liberty.
- There is no deprivation of liberty if a person of sound mind is being cared for.
- When a person in care has learning difficulties, it will be a question of fact whether there has been a deprivation of liberty.
- Parental restrictions on their children do not offend Article 5.
- The courts have decided that 'kettling' does not offend Article 5.
- Stop and search is a statutory power and does not offend Article 5.
- Formal detention by the authorities must follow prescribed procedures – in the UK laid down by PACE 1984.
- Any person detained must be brought before a court promptly, bail considered and tried promptly.

Chapter 20

Article 6: the right to a fair trial

After reading this chapter you should be able to:
- Understand key provisions of Article 6 ECHR, the right to a fair trial
- Understand the restrictions permitted by Article 6
- Understand the ways in which English law has applied Article 6
- Critically evaluate the operation and application of Article 6
- Apply the law to given situations

20.1 Article 6 ECHR

" In the determination of his civil rights and obligations or of any criminal charge against him, everyone is entitled to a fair and public hearing within a reasonable time by an independent and impartial tribunal established by law. Judgment shall be pronounced publicly but the press and public may be excluded from all or part of the trial in the interest of morals, public order or national security in a democratic society, where the interests of juveniles or the protection of the private life of the parties so require, or the extent strictly necessary in the opinion of the court in special circumstances where publicity would prejudice the interests of justice.

Everyone charged with a criminal offence shall be presumed innocent until proved guilty according to law.

Everyone charged with a criminal offence has the following minimum rights:

a   to be informed promptly, in a language which he understands and in detail, of the nature and cause of the accusation against him;

b   to have adequate time and the facilities for the preparation of his defence;

c   to defend himself in person or through legal assistance of his own choosing or, if he has not sufficient means to pay for legal assistance, to be given it free when the interests of justice so require;

d   to examine or have examined witnesses against him and to obtain the attendance and examination of witnesses on his behalf under the same conditions as witnesses against him;

e   to have the free assistance of an interpreter if he cannot understand or speak the language used in court. "

20.2 Key provisions of this Article

The core right guaranteed by this Article is the right to a fair trial and the main focus of the Article is about achieving a result, which is, and is seen to be, fair.

The point of the Article is to protect citizens against the abuse of power by state and public authorities. The importance of this principle is seen by the fact that it permits no restriction; the only qualification is on the requirement of a public hearing. However in certain situations the rights of the parties can be waived – for example, by the parties agreeing to settle a dispute by arbitration, rather than by a court hearing.

Some additional rights have been implied by the ECtHR including:
- the right not to incriminate oneself
- the right of access to a court
- equality of arms.

These implied rights are not absolute, and interference with them is possible if there is a public interest in doing so and there is proportionality between the means employed and the aim to be realised.

20.2.1 Civil rights and obligations

Paragraph 1 refers to 'civil rights and obligations ... everyone is entitled to a fair and public hearing within a reasonable time by an independent and impartial tribunal established by law'.

These include planning appeals, the right to claim compensation in tort, employment law rights and family law rights. It does not include a claim to be educated at a certain school or a claim by a prisoner to associate with other prisoners.

For this Article to apply, there must be a dispute in issue of a genuine and serious nature which directly affects civil rights and obligations. This could include a decision of a tribunal affecting the right to continue to practice – such as:

- the Solicitors Disciplinary Tribunal
- the making of a confiscation order following conviction, such as in drug supply cases
- the role of the Secretary of State in deciding planning appeals.

The Article will not apply in cases such as proceedings to decide entry, stay or deportation of foreigners, or a request for extradition of a foreigner or a decision to order the removal of a foreigner on national security grounds. It will not apply to a decision to dismiss an employee.

20.2.2 Criminal charge

Paragraph 1 also refers to:

> In the determination of ... any criminal charge against him, everyone is entitled to a fair and public hearing within a reasonable time by an independent and impartial tribunal established by law.

For criminal charges, in addition to the protection of Article 6(1), there will also be protection under 6(2) and 6(3). It also includes the sentencing of offenders.

The word 'determination' has caused issues when deciding when a criminal case should start, as in *Brown v Stott* (2001).

Case study

Brown v Stott (2001)

Mrs Brown was stopped on suspicion of drink driving. She was required by the police, in exercise of their statutory powers, to say who had been driving her car when she would have travelled in it to a supermarket car park. She replied, 'It was me'. This admission was relied on by the prosecution at her trial. She was found guilty and argued that the compulsion to answer amounted to self-incrimination and a violation of Article 6.

The Privy Council (the case was tried in Scotland) decided that this compulsion was compatible with Article 6. The right of self-incrimination was not an absolute right and could be limited for reasons of public safety on the roads. It did not undermine the right to a fair trial as other evidence (breathalyser) would be needed to be proved as well as any admission by the accused.

Whether an action is a criminal charge or not, the following will be considered:

- The domestic classification of the action – this could include whether the CPS are involved, an accusation of a crime, the taking of prints or samples. The making of an anti-social behaviour order was classed as a civil, not criminal matter in *McCann v United Kingdom* (1996).
- The nature of the offence – this is where a matter will lead to some form of punishment.
- The severity of the possible penalty – this will include where a fine can be imposed as well as other forms of punishment.

20.2.3 Access to court

This is an implied right (not an absolute right) so the state may impose some procedural restrictions. This right is a check on the use by the state of arbitrary power. It requires a state to have a fair and public judicial process, and forbids the state to deny a person access to that process for deciding their civil rights. It is a right that is available to everyone including serving prisoners. It does not give a right to appeal against an original decision where none exists. However if a right to appeal is available, Article 6 applies to the appeal as well as the original trial.

Restrictions

Limitation periods can be legitimately imposed when an action can be brought. For example, in England and Wales there is a three-year limitation period for personal injury claims in tort, and six years for property claims in tort and for claims in contract law.

It is permissible for the court to impose restrictions on who can bring a claim such as with vexatious litigants, imposing a civil restraint order or requiring leave of the court before a claim can be issued.

Key term

Vexatious litigant – a person who regularly issues civil court proceedings. Once an order is made that a person is a vexatious litigant, s/he can only bring a further action with the permission of the court.

It is permissible for there to be some types of immunity. For example, judges are said to be immune from suit in respect of their judicial decisions in court. It is permissible for the court to have a power to strike out an action if no cause of action exists.

Osman v United Kingdom (2000)

A teacher harassed a pupil and his family. The police were called on several occasions and the teacher had told the police that he was unable to control himself and would do something which was criminally insane if he was not stopped. Eventually he shot the boy and his father who died. In a criminal case the teacher was convicted of manslaughter. The boy and his mother brought civil actions against the police for their failure to apprehend the teacher earlier or to provide them with protection. The police successfully argued that the case of *Hill v Chief Constable of West Yorkshire* (1989) gave them, as a matter of public policy, a blanket immunity from being sued.

Osman appealed to the ECtHR arguing that the blanket immunity was in breach of Article 6. The Court found there had been a violation of Article 6. They decided the blanket immunity provided by *Hill* was a disproportionate restriction on the Osmans' right of access to a court. The substantive merits of the case could not be argued before a judge. It should always be open for claimants to put their case before a judge and a blanket rule which interfered with this right was not acceptable.

See *OCR AS/A Level Law Book 1* Chapter 23 for more information about *Hill v Chief Constable of West Yorkshire* (1989).

There is no right to legal representation or of financial legal aid, and a claimant may find it difficult to argue that, without financial aid, his right of access to court has been denied. See section 20.2.8 below for more information on restriction of representation.

20.2.4 A fair hearing

This is not defined in the Article but appears to include:

- equality of arms
- a presumption of innocence, and
- the privilege of self-incrimination.

If the right to a fair hearing is infringed in a criminal case, including an appeal, a conviction will be unsafe and will be set aside.

R v Bow Street Magistrate, ex parte Pinochet Ugarte (2000)

Known as the *Pinochet case*, this came before the House of Lords on the question of whether the former Chilean dictator Augusto Pinochet could claim state immunity from torture allegations made by a Spanish court and therefore evade extradition to Spain. The original decision had to be set aside because one of the judges, Lord Hoffmann, failed to declare his links to Amnesty International before or during the hearing.

20.2.5 Equality of arms

This means that there must be a fair balance between the parties.

- In civil cases the claimant must be allowed to present his case.
- In criminal cases it has to be shown that the prosecutor has enjoyed a particular advantage, for example when a prisoner, representing himself, is allowed limited computer facilities.

This equality does not extend to the defendant being allowed the same level of representation as the prosecution. In *Attorney-General's Reference (No. 82a of 2000)* (2002) the court would not allow the defendant a QC to represent him when the prosecution had employed a QC. It was decided that what was important was that an advocate of any level was allowed to ensure that the defence was properly prepared and presented. If the defendant wishes for an unqualified 'McKenzie friend' to represent him in a civil case, there is a presumption that this should be allowed. In a criminal case, the defendant will either be represented by a lawyer or unrepresented and conduct the defence himself.

Key term

'McKenzie friend' – the court may allow a legally unqualified and unpaid adviser to represent the defendant and speak for them in a civil case.

Steel and Morris v United Kingdom (2005)

McDonald's brought a libel action against Helen Steel and David Morris. The defendants had published a leaflet against the claimants making various allegations against them. Legal aid was not available for libel cases and the defendants had to represent themselves, despite each being on a low wage. McDonald's employed experienced senior barristers. The trial lasted 313 days and the defendants lost their case.

The ECtHR decided that the complexity of the case and the different levels of legal support were so great to make the case unfair under Article 6. It also decided that the level of damages awarded against the defendants was so great that it breached Article 10.

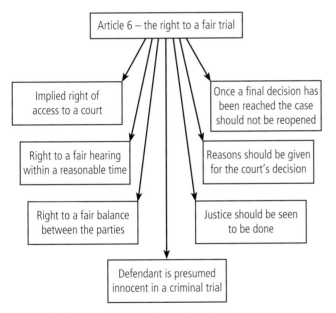

Figure 20.1 Protections given by Article 6

See Chapter 22 for more information on Article 10.

There is a breach of this equality if, in a criminal trial, the prosecution fails to disclose all material evidence but there is no absolute right for the prosecution to disclose all available evidence. This material evidence could include witness statements and information about any previous convictions of witnesses.

Restrictions

It is permissible for the state to have justified reasons, on the grounds of national security or public interest immunity, for not disclosing certain material.

In some cases of national security it is permissible for a special advocate to be appointed to represent the defendant, in so far as is possible, in parts of the case that are closed to the defendant or his representatives. This would be where the defendant is unable to know secret material or evidence relevant to the case.

A child defendant should not be subject to intimidation, humiliation or distress and all possible steps must be taken to allow a child defendant to take part in the case and to understand the proceedings. A child has a right to be heard in a case affecting him but has no right to give evidence.

T and V v United Kingdom (2000)

Two 11-year-old boys were charged and convicted of murder after a trial in a Crown Court. They appealed to the ECtHR on the grounds that in view of their young age, their trial in public in an adult court violated their Article 6 rights. The court decided that under Article 6(1) the accused must enjoy the right to understand what is happening at the trial and to play an active role in their defence, at least for children, what could reasonably be expected of a child of their age. The case was heard in a tense courtroom and under public scrutiny, and, given their immaturity and disturbed emotional state, the boys would not have been capable outside the courtroom of co-operating with their lawyers and giving them information for the purpose of their defence. The court decided the boys were denied a fair hearing in breach of Article 6. It was highly likely that a child aged 11 would find the formal setting intimidating, whether involved as a witness or a defendant.

Despite the decision of the ECtHR child defendants are still tried in adult courts by a jury when they have been charged with a serious offence.

Research the case of two boys tried for rape and attempted rape at http://news.bbc.co.uk/1/hi/uk/8692823.stm.

What measures were used to try to make the courtroom experience less difficult for:
- the defendant boys, and
- the victim?

What features can you identify from the report that makes the experience intimidating for the defendants?

After reading the report, do you think that the defendants received a fair trial?

20.2.6 A presumption of innocence

This is an express right under Article 6(2) and only an implied right under Article 6(1), but it may be important where Article 6(2) does not apply, such as in the making of a confiscation order. However in most criminal cases, such an order will only be considered after conviction and this presumption will have little influence. It is permissible for the court to assume in such a case that property held by the defendant at a relevant time was obtained or acquired through criminal activity.

20.2.7 Self-incrimination and a right of silence

This right is implied in Article 6. It is based on the presumption of innocence in Article 6(2) and the right to a fair trial in Article 6(1). It is not absolute, so interference with it may be justified if it pursues a legitimate aim. See *Brown v Stott* (2001) in section 20.2.2 above.

Obtaining a confession by oppression or compulsion is a breach of Article 6. The jury should be directed that if they think that a confession was obtained by oppression, or is in any way unreliable, they should be directed to disregard it.

20.2.8 Representation

There is no absolute right to legal representation in civil or criminal cases. Provided the court is aware of and reminds itself of the need for fairness, this part of the Article will not be infringed. However, in *Hammerton v United Kingdom* (2012) it was decided that a litigant in person who was liable to be sent to prison for contempt of court was entitled to legal representation, if necessary at public expense. And in *Benham v United Kingdom* (1996) when Stephen Benham was imprisoned by magistrates for not paying the poll tax, the ECtHR held that his rights under Article 6 had been violated because he had not been able to get representation by a solicitor under the legal aid scheme.

Restriction

Paying for a legal representation

Normally, an accused will have complete freedom to have the lawyer of his choice to represent him in court. This right will cover the right to claim financial aid to pay for the representation in a criminal case if the alleged offender cannot afford to pay the legal fees. However, in England this right is restricted by the requirement for the alleged offender to pass two tests to claim financial aid – the interests of justice test and the means test. Unless the alleged offender passes both tests, financial aid will not be available. In addition, now the accused's right of choice will also be limited as those able to offer state-funded services have to be members of a panel who have entered into contracts with the Legal Aid Agency. In civil cases, state financial aid is much more restricted and is virtually non-existent.

> See *OCR AS/A Level Law Book 1* Chapter 11 for details of the tests for claiming financial aid in civil and criminal cases.

Special advocates

A special advocate is a specially appointed lawyer (typically, a barrister) who is instructed to represent a person's interests in relation to material that is kept secret from that person (and his ordinary lawyers) but analysed by a court at an adversarial hearing held in private. Special advocates have the advantage that they can go behind the curtain of secrecy. Special advocates can be used before some specialist courts and tribunals, including certain cases of immigration and terrorism.

There are several disadvantages of involving a special advocate:

1 Once they have had sight of the secret material, they cannot take instructions from the persons they are representing or their ordinary legal representatives, who will be unable to make accurate decisions on how to conduct the case.

2 They work alone and lack the resources of an ordinary legal team for the purpose of conducting a full defence in secret (for example, for making detailed inquiries or research).

3 They have no power to call witnesses.

Giving instructions to lawyers

Normally the lawyer and client will be able to meet, even if the client is in prison, for the client to see the evidence against him and to give the lawyer instructions.

However the situation was different if the client was subject to a control order (now replaced).

Case study

Secretary of State for the Home Department v A F (2009)

The applicants were subject to control orders but some of the evidence against them was based on 'closed' material which could not be accessed by their lawyers and on which their clients could not give them instructions. The House of Lords decided that it was a breach of the right to a fair trial under Article 6 to hold someone under a non-derogating control order without sufficient information about the allegations against him, even where the case against the 'controlee' was based on closed materials, the disclosure of which would compromise the country's national security.

20.2.9 An oral hearing

This requires the decision-maker to have regard to the arguments and evidence produced by the parties before coming to a decision. If necessary, they should be carried out at an oral hearing. It is not always necessary to have an oral hearing during the preliminary stages of civil or criminal cases, but the substantive hearing should be carried out in person, together with sentencing after conviction.

It is important in every case to show that justice is being seen to be done. If a decision-maker is not showing an interest in the hearing, then justice is not being seen to be done.

Case study

Stansbury v Datapulse plc and Troy Holdings International plc (2003)

It was found that a lay member at an Employment Tribunal had consumed alcohol and had fallen asleep during the hearing. There could not have been a fair hearing.

Restrictions

The right to an oral hearing can be limited in certain circumstances, such as when it is in the best interests of children and in cases of national security.

Case study

B and P v United Kingdom (2002)

Both applicants brought cases for residence orders under the Children Act 1989. The usual practice was for those hearings to be held in private to protect the identities of those involved. The applicant claimed that this breached Article 6(1). The ECtHR decided that this provision did not breach Article 6. They ruled that:

> such proceedings are prime examples of cases where the exclusion of the press and public may be justified in order to protect the privacy of the child and parties and to avoid prejudicing the interests of justice. To enable the deciding judge to gain as full and accurate a picture as possible of the advantages and disadvantages of the various residence and contact options open to the child, it is essential that the parents and other witnesses feel able to express themselves candidly on highly personal issues without fear of public curiosity or comment.
>
> However, while the court agrees that Article 6(1) states a general rule that civil proceedings, inter alia, should take place in public, it does not find it inconsistent with this provision for a state to designate an entire class of case as an exception to the general rule where considered necessary for the interests of morals, public order or national security or where required by the interests of juveniles or the protection of the private life of the parties, although the need for such a measure must always be subject to the court's control. The English procedural law can therefore be seen as a specific reflection of the general exceptions provided for by Article 6(1).

Look online

In 2014 the prosecution applied to hold a completely secret criminal trial for the first time, excluding the press and public. The defendants were charged with terrorism offences. Some media outlets challenged the restrictions before the trial took place.

Look at reports of the Court of Appeal hearing at **www.bbc.co.uk/news/uk-27806814** or **www.theweek. co.uk/uk-news/58831/secret-trial-blocked-by-court-of-appeal**.

- What were the prosecution arguments for a trial to be held in private?
- What parts of the trial did the Court of Appeal judges order could be reported?
- Do you think that the defendants could have received a fair trial?

Activity

1 In March 2017 the Minister for Justice and Lord Chancellor announced that she was introducing plans for alleged rape victims to give evidence by way of pre-recorded video interviews rather than by oral evidence at a trial in court. What progress has been made for introducing these plans by the time you read this book?
2 There are also plans to introduce new online courts to deal with lower level criminal offences. It is estimated this will remove over 900,000 offences each year from the traditional courts.
    - What types of offences are proposed to be dealt with by these online courts?
    - Can you see any disadvantages to this proposal?

20.2.10 Evidence

Under s 76 of the Police and Criminal Evidence Act (PACE) 1984, the court has the power to exclude evidence which they consider would have an adverse effect on the fairness of the case. This may include any evidence obtained by entrapment, such as in *Attorney General's Reference (No. 3 of 2000)* (2001), illegally obtained evidence or evidence obtained by torture.

Case study

Attorney General's Reference (No. 3 of 2000) (2001)

The defendant had never dealt heroin but was induced by an undercover police officer to procure the drug as part of a deal in smuggled cigarettes. As the police had caused him to commit an offence he would not otherwise have committed, it was right to stop the case against the defendant.

Hearsay evidence cannot be admitted in criminal proceedings but may be used in some civil cases.

In general, the defendant has the right to attend his trial in person but may waive this right by deliberately and voluntarily absenting himself and/or removing instructions from his legal team. The judge has discretion whether to allow the case to continue in the absence of the defendant and, if it is decided to continue, he or she must ensure the trial is as fair as possible. In particular he or she must ensure that the jury is directed that absence is not an admission of guilt and adds nothing to the prosecution case.

In civil cases, if one of the parties cannot be present through no fault of their own then an adjournment should be ordered.

20.2.11 Reasons for a decision

The final judgment of the court must contain reasons that show that the main issues in the case have been taken into account and decided upon. There is no need to give reasons for every point on why one piece of evidence has been preferred to another. If the appeal system is to work effectively, the appeal court must be able to decide what was taken into account and how the judge reached his decision. Once a final decision has been reached by a court, and any appeals exhausted, the case should be closed.

Case study

Brumarescu v Romania (1999)

B's parents' house was nationalised by the state in 1950 without payment of compensation. In 1993 B brought an action against the state, claiming that the nationalisation was unlawful. This claim was upheld, the time limit for an appeal passed and →

ownership was transferred to B. The following year the case was reopened before the Supreme Court who set aside the previous judgment and ruled that the house had passed into state ownership under a relevant law. B complained to the ECtHR that there had been a violation of Article 6(1), and this was upheld on the grounds that there had been a final judgment in B's favour which could not be reopened.

20.2.12 Public hearing in a reasonable time

The right to a public hearing of a case is not absolute as it is recognised that a hearing in private may be needed in cases of national security or where the defendants are young. Certain hearings – such as those before a Mental Health Tribunal and a Juvenile Court – are always held in private. The main reason in favour of a public hearing is public confidence in the administration of justice by seeing that justice is being carried out impartially.

Article 6(1) also provides that the judgment be pronounced publicly.

Both civil and criminal proceedings should be heard within a reasonable time – though the actual time is not specified. In a criminal case, the reasons for an early trial include:

- the witness's memory of the incident
- the preservation of evidence
- preventing a long state of uncertainty for the accused
- the maintenance of public confidence.

Failure to hold a trial within a reasonable time would not, of itself, be a breach of Article 6. If there is delay, the court may order an early hearing or release on bail if the accused is being held in custody. It is unlikely, for public interest reasons, that an order to stop the case completely will be made.

20.2.13 An independent and impartial tribunal

In both civil and criminal cases, Article 6(1) requires that the hearing takes place before an independent and impartial tribunal, to prevent bias or prejudice. If this does not happen in a civil case then damages may be awarded. In a criminal case, any conviction must be quashed and a retrial may be ordered.

Specific reasons of partiality may be that the judge has a personal interest in the case, or knows the participants including any witnesses. In the case of jury trial it may have to be considered whether there has been any pre-trial prejudicial material published. Justice must not only be done – it has to be seen to be done.

Article 6(1) finally requires the tribunal to be established by law. This means in a serious criminal case that the case is normally heard by a judge and jury and that the judge is qualified to hear such cases.

Restriction

The Criminal Justice Act 2003 allows for judge-only criminal trials where there is a serious risk of jury tampering or where tampering has taken place. The first such case was *R v Twomey* (2011).

Look online

Read the online article about the case of *R v Twomey* (2011) at this web address: **https://theoldbailey. wordpress.com/2010/03/31/found-guilty-with-no-jury-r-vs-twomey-blake-hibberd-cameron/**.

- Why did the second trial not reach a conclusion?
- What happened during the third trial which led to the fourth trial being heard by a judge alone?
- Do you think that the four defendants eventually received a fair trial?

20.3 Article 6(2): presumption of innocence

This only applies to criminal cases and follows the principle in *DPP v Woolmington* (1935) – it is for the prosecution to prove the defendant's guilt beyond reasonable doubt.

See *OCR AS/A Level Law Book 1* Chapter 12 for more details of this case.

However, the Article is not an absolute right and a breach does not automatically mean that a conviction is unsafe.

In *Salabiaku v France* (1988) the ECtHR ruled that a strict liability drug-smuggling offence does not offend this Article as a defence was available to the charge.

20.4 Article 6(3)

This Article sets out minimum rights for everyone charged with a criminal offence:

- To be informed of the accusation promptly, in a language the accused understands, and, in detail, the nature of the accusation.

- To have adequate time and facilities to prepare a defence. This may include access to a lawyer, especially if detained before trial, to obtain expert evidence and to call witnesses.
- Legal assistance – a guarantee of defending him/herself in person or through legal assistance of his/her own choosing or, if he or she has not sufficient means to pay for legal assistance, to be given it free when the interests of justice so require. These are not alternatives so the defendant cannot be forced to defend him/herself. It is possible for the accused to waive his/her right to legal advice, and there is no rule that says that an accused must have consulted a lawyer before waiving any rights under this Article.
- The right to legal representation applies to every stage of the investigation, including interviews at the police station. If the accused is denied representation, any evidence obtained may be excluded by s 78 PACE 1984. The right to representation is not absolute and in civil cases the denial of legal aid may be reasonable. In criminal cases, especially where custody is a likely sentence, the denial of legal aid is likely to be a breach of the Article. In fact it is one of the grounds (the interests of justice) where it is likely to be granted.
- The right to examine, and have examined, witnesses. English law has always required witnesses to give their evidence in court in the presence of the accused, and no conviction should be based on the testimony of anonymous witnesses. A witness can give evidence by television link or video recording as long as the defence has the ability to question and challenge the witness at some stage.

However see the plans for the introduction of pre-recorded video interviews in rape trials referred to in section 20.2.9 above

20.4.1 Restrictions

In terrorist cases, the right of the defendant to legal assistance may be waived by the police for a longer time than in standard criminal investigations.

Case study

Ibrahim v United Kingdom (2016)

The defendants were arrested in connection with the London bombings in July 2005, when 52 people were killed and many others injured. In order for the police to conduct 'safety interviews' which were authorised by the Terrorism Act 2000, the defendants were refused legal assistance. In these interviews the defendants denied involvement in the bombings. At their trial they accepted involvement but claimed that the bombs were a hoax and it had never been intended that they should explode. The statements made in the safety interviews were admitted. The defendants claimed that their Article 6 rights had been infringed.

The ECtHR commented that the police were operating at the time under great pressure and needed to ensure public safety in case of further bombs. The police had operated under the statutory rules in place at the time and the use of the rules for 'safety interviews' were only temporary, lasting a maximum of 48 hours. In addition the use of the safety interviews was authorised by senior officers and the defendants had been informed of the reasons to restrict legal assistance. The court ruled that, in the circumstances, and because of the public interest in preventing terrorist attacks, the defendants' Article 6 rights had not been infringed.

Note: 'Safety interviews' were authorised by the Terrorism Act 2000 (now repealed) which allowed the police to conduct an urgent interview to protect life and prevent serious damage to property.

Case study

Abdurahman v United Kingdom (2016)

The defendant was convicted of assisting one of the bombers and of failing to disclose information about the plot. He told police about encountering one of the bombers and the assistance he had provided. He was questioned as a witness and gave a statement but was only subsequently arrested and told of his right to legal advice. His statement was used as evidence in his trial. He claimed that the use of his statement was a breach of his Article 6 rights. The court in this case observed that the defendant's treatment had not been authorised by any legislation and he had been misled about his rights; in this case his Article 6 rights had been breached. However, the court ruled that there was little evidence that his conviction had been prejudiced by the breach of procedure, and they refused the award of compensation.

R v Davis (2008)

Seven witnesses said they would be in fear for their lives if it was known that they gave evidence against the accused. Several methods were used to protect their identities including pseudonyms, withholding personal details, distorted voices and giving evidence from behind a screen. The House of Lords ruled that the combination of measures hampered the defence to the extent that it rendered the trial unfair, especially as it impaired the ability of defence lawyers to cross-examine the witnesses.

Finally, Article 6(3)(e) gives the accused the right to a free interpreter if he or she cannot understand or speak the language used in court.

20.5 Evaluation of Article 6

20.5.1 Access to court

It may take legislation or a later court decision to change existing law to allow a claim under Article 6. This can be illustrated in the liability of the police.

It will be recalled that the case of *Hill v Chief Constable of West Yorkshire* (1989), described in *OCR AS/A Level Law Book 1* Chapter 23, gave the police immunity from being sued where loss had been suffered due to an omission on their part. In that case it was an omission to catch the Yorkshire Ripper who then murdered the claimant's daughter. This decision was interpreted as giving the police blanket immunity from being sued. As set out at 20.2.3 the ECtHR in *Osman v UK* (2000) considered this blanket immunity breached Article 6 but until a recent case there was no change in the law to reflect the decision in *Osman*.

In *Robinson v Chief Constable of West Yorkshire Police* (2018) the Supreme Court ruled that the case of *Hill* did not confer on the police blanket immunity from being sued in negligence. Robinson concerned an injury to a bystander caused by police who were carrying out an arrest – a positive action on their part. In this case there was a reasonably foreseeable risk of injury to the claimant when the arrest was attempted. This was enough to impose a duty of care on the officers. So finally, many years after *Osman* the decision has been acted upon and the law changed.

20.5.2 Equality of arms

With the removal of state funding for civil cases, it is even more the case that there is inequality between the parties. 'No win no fee' funding requires lawyers to assess that there is a high chance of the claim succeeding before they are prepared to accept the case. In many cases the defendant will be a large company or organisation that can afford to pay expensive lawyers to defend its practice.

In criminal cases most defendants charged with a serious criminal offence will receive state funding. However their choice of lawyer is likely to be limited as only those on the Legal Aid Agency panel can be instructed. On the one hand this should ensure a certain level of quality as panel lawyers have to show expertise. On the other hand it may mean that accused persons are less likely to have representation available locally. For many lower level offences, state funding has been removed. This is likely to result in many defendants appearing in court unrepresented and pleading guilty, or being found guilty, when they may have an arguable defence.

In terrorist cases, defendants can be at a disadvantage in knowing some or most of the evidence against them, especially when special advocates are involved. Defendants and their lawyers cannot work with the special advocates, and this system appears to contravene the general principles of criminal law that an accused should know the case against him.

20.5.3 Open justice in oral hearing

The long-established principle in criminal cases of 'trial by your peers' has been removed with the introduction of judge-only trials – the judge hears the evidence, decides guilt or innocence and imposes a sentence. Judges are more likely to understand complicated evidence and therefore deal with the case quicker and at a lower cost. It should be ensured, however, that these trials remain a rarity and are only used as a last resort when there have been suggestions of jury tampering or other procedural irregularities in previous hearings.

There has been concern for some time about the nature of cross-examination of rape victims in court leading to a low conviction rate and reluctance for victims to pursue their complaint. This has led to the suggestion for introducing pre-recorded video evidence to remove the trauma of appearing in court. On the one hand it is said that this could lead to more defendants pleading guilty when they see the evidence against them. On the other hand, lawyers are concerned that they would be less able to challenge the victim's account. Also the video statement is likely to be taken soon after the alleged offence and other matters may come to light which the defence may wish to raise between the statement and the trial.

The ECtHR has generally taken a strict approach about the need for impartial and independent tribunal and such an approach helps to maintain the idea of the rule of law and justice. This approach has, at times conflicted with the approach of domestic governments who wish to deal efficiently and effectively with suspected terrorists. Decisions such as *Othman (Abu Qatada) v United Kingdom* (2012) have led to calls for repeal of HRA 1998.

On the other hand, there have been other cases where it has been found that the UK has complied with the basic principles of Article 6 and the courts have been prepared to allow some flexibility in upholding these principles.

Othman (Abu Qatada) v United Kingdom (2012)

The claimant was born in Jordan and came to the UK in 1993. He made an application for asylum and was recognised as a refugee in 1994. He was granted leave to remain until 30 June 1998. On 8 May 1998 he applied for indefinite leave to remain.

In October 2002 he was arrested and detained under the Anti-terrorism, Crime and Security Act 2001. After the Act was repealed in March 2005 he was released on bail and subjected to a control order. On 11 August 2005, while his appeal against that control order was pending, the Secretary of State served him with a notice of intention to deport. He appealed against that notice, arguing that he would not receive a fair trial in Jordan. The ECtHR ruled that, under Article 6, the UK could not lawfully deport the claimant to Jordan because of the risk of the use of evidence obtained by torture.

The claimant was eventually deported from the UK to face retrial in Jordan after an agreement between the two countries that evidence obtained by torture would be discarded.

Case	Facts	Legal principle
Brown v Stott (2001)	D admitted she was drink-driving and this admission was used in court. She argued this amounted to self-incrimination and a violation of Article 6.	The Privy Council decided Article 6 was complied with.
Osman v United Kingdom (2000)	The police were sued for failure to protect a family from harassment The police argued they had immunity from being sued for negligence.	ECtHR decided Article 6 had been violated by the blanket immunity as it was a disproportionate restriction on the claimant's right of access to a court.
R v Bow Street Magistrate, ex parte Pinochet Ugarte (2000)	One of the judges in the Pinochet case had not disclosed his links to Amnesty International.	Judges and panel members must disclose any links to anyone or any organisation with an interest in the case.
Steel and Morris v United Kingdom (2005)	S and M were sued for libel by McDonald's for publishing an alleged defamatory leaflet. S and M represented themselves in a long trial against experienced senior barristers.	The ECtHR decided that the complexity of the case and the different levels of legal support were so great to make the case unfair under Article 6.
T and V v United Kingdom (2000)	Two 11-year-old boys were tried for murder in a Crown Court room. They claimed an unfair trial in view of their age and trial in public in an adult court.	The ECtHR decided the boys were denied a fair hearing in breach of Article 6.
Secretary of State for the Home Department v A F (2009)	The applicants were subject to control orders but some of the evidence against them was based on 'closed' material.	The House of Lords decided that it was a breach of the right to a fair trial under Article 6 to hold someone under a control order without sufficient information about the allegations against him.
B and P v United Kingdom (2002)	The usual practice for hearing residence orders in family cases was to hold the hearings in private. It was claimed this breached Article 6.	The ECtHR ruled that there are certain cases, including this one, where the exclusion of the press and public may be justified. There was no breach of Article 6.
Brumarescu v Romania (1999)	B's parents' house was nationalised by the state in 1950. A later court ruled that the house had passed into state ownership under a relevant law. B complained there had been a violation of Article 6(1).	ECtHR upheld B's complaint as there had been a final judgment which could not be reopened.
Ibrahim v United Kingdom (2016)	Defendants were arrested in connection with the London bombings and were refused legal assistance to allow 'safety interviews' to be held.	The ECtHR ruled their rights had not been infringed and there was no breach of Article 6.

Case	Facts	Legal principle
R v Davis (2008)	Several methods were used to protect the identities of witnesses against D as they feared for their lives if they were identified.	The House of Lords ruled that the combination of measures used to protect identities hampered the defence to render the trial unfair.
Othman (Abu Qatada) v United Kingdom (2012)	O was arrested and detained under terrorism laws; while he was subject to a control order he was served with a deportation notice.	The ECtHR ruled that, under Article 6, the UK could not lawfully deport the claimant to Jordan because of the risk of the use of evidence obtained by torture.

Figure 20.2 Key cases on Article 6 ECHR

Summary

- Article 6 guarantees the right to a fair trial in criminal cases and a fair hearing in civil cases.
- There is an implied right of access to a court, but this may be subject to procedural restrictions such as a limitation period or immunity from being sued for the police.
- There is a right to a fair hearing by an independent panel.
- There must be a fair balance between the parties, though this can be restricted if national security is an issue.
- The defendant is presumed innocent in a criminal trial and has the right to remain silent.
- There is no absolute right to be legally represented.
- The court should hear both sides of the case before coming to a decision – justice should not only be done, it should be seen to be done.
- Any prejudicial evidence should be excluded and hearsay evidence should not be used in criminal cases.
- The court should give reasons for its decision.
- Once a final decision has been reached the case should not be reopened.
- Any hearing should take place within a reasonable time.

Chapter 21

Article 8: the right to respect for family and private life

After reading this chapter you should be able to:
- Understand the scope of Article 8(1) ECHR
- Understand the restrictions permitted by Article 8(2)
- Understand the explanations of Article 8 in the ECtHR
- Understand the ways in which English law has applied Article 8
- Critically evaluate the operation of Article 8 in English law
- Apply the law to given situations

21.1 Article 8 ECHR

1 Everyone has the right to respect for his private and family life, his home and his correspondence.

2 There shall be no interference by a public authority with the exercise of this right except such as is in accordance with the law and is necessary in a democratic society in the interests of national security, public safety or the economic well-being of the country, for the prevention of disorder or crime, for the protection of health or morals, or for the protection of the rights and freedoms of others.

21.2 General aspects of qualified rights

Article 8 is a qualified right and as such the right to a private and family life and respect for the home and correspondence may be limited. So while the right to privacy is engaged in a wide number of situations, the right may be lawfully limited. Any limitation must have regard to the fair balance that has to be struck between the competing interests of the individual and of the community as a whole.

Under Article 8(2) any limitation must be:
- in accordance with law
- necessary and proportionate

and for one or more of the following legitimate aims:
- the interests of national security

- the interests of public safety or the economic well-being of the country
- the prevention of disorder or crime
- the protection of health or morals, or
- the protection of the rights and freedoms of others.

When someone can show that there is an interference with their rights it is then up to the state to show that the interference is justified. This can only be done if it is in accordance with the law. It also has to be necessary in a democratic society and also has to be proportional.

If it is proportional, the court must ensure that:
- the objective of the legislation is sufficiently important to justify some interference with a person's basic rights
- that measure is rationally connected with the objective in question
- it is not arbitrary, unfair or based on other irrational considerations
- the limitation must impair the right as little as possible
- the interference must not be so severe in effect that it outweighs the objective for which it would otherwise be permitted.

21.3 Background to Article 8 – who is 'everyone'?

The ECtHR's view of the importance of these rights can be seen in the case of *Klass v Germany* (1993), which raised a question about mail opening and telephone tapping. The court said that the powers of secret surveillance of citizens are tolerable under the ECHR only in so far as strictly necessary for safeguarding the democratic institutions.

This also raises the question as to who is an individual – does it include a business? In certain circumstances it appears to include business life.

If businesses are entitled in certain circumstances to assert a right to privacy, then we need to establish when they should be able to do so. A lawyer's office was private in *Niemietz v Germany* (1992) (see section 21.4.2 below). Does the business itself have that right? This is important as many celebrities have corporate persona. In *Gamerco v ICM Fair Warning (Agency) Ltd and Missouri Storm Inc.* (1995) the defendant rock group, Guns 'n' Roses, had made a contract through their corporate persona, Missouri Storm Inc.

We know that limited companies are in law individuals ever since the famous case of *Salomon v Salomon and Co. Ltd* (1897), where the limited company was stated to be a completely separate legal person to Mr Salomon who owned virtually all the shares in the company and thus controlled it. It can therefore be argued that companies and other business organisations with separate legal persona have human rights under the Convention.

This seems to be the case as ECtHR has ruled in *Vinci Construction and GTM Genie Civil et Services v France* (2015) that wholly generalised document seizures during dawn raids conducted by the French Department for Competition, Consumer Affairs and Fraud Prevention violated the fundamental rights of both Vinci Construction and GTM Génie. The inspections and seizures violated Article 8 because the indiscriminate nature of the seizures was disproportionate and interfered with rights to respect for home, private life and correspondence under Article 8.

Key term

'Everyone' – so far as Article 8 is concerned, this includes businesses.

21.4 The scope of Article 8

Article 8 has four protected interests. Everyone has the right to respect for:
- private life
- family life
- home
- correspondence.

These concepts will be considered in turn together with the relevant law, although the separate interests overlap as part of the general idea behind the Article.

21.4.1 'Respect'

The word 'respect' means that primarily the state must not interfere, as stated in Article 8(1), with the qualifications in Article 8(2). It also means that the state must take positive steps to protect these rights. This was considered by the ECtHR in *Sheffield and Horsham v United Kingdom* (1999).

Key term

'Respect' – with regard to Article 8, this requires the state not to interfere and has positive aspects.

Case study

Sheffield and Horsham v United Kingdom (1999)

The two applicants had undergone gender reassignment surgery from male to female. The state would not recognise their new status as women or take steps to allow this to be officially recognised. There had been no breach of Article 8(1) as a nation could refuse to re-register birth details of people who had undergone gender reassignment surgery. Similarly, the state could refuse to permit post-operative transsexuals to marry. However the ECtHR criticised the UK's apparent failure to take any steps to keep this area of the law under review. The court recognised increased social acceptance of transsexualism and the problems which post-operative transsexual people encounter.

English law has now been changed by the Gender Recognition Act 2004, which allows transsexual individuals to apply for legal recognition for their new gender. The Marriage (Same Sex Couples) Act 2013 is also now in place, so fulfilling positive obligations.

21.4.2 'Private life'

The meaning of 'private life' is very wide, and is not the same as privacy. There is some overlap with Article 10,

Identifier _____

GRF

GENDER RECOGNITION CERTIFICATE

1.	Name	
2.	Date of Birth	
3.	Gender	
4.	Date of Issue	

The above named person is, from the date of issue, of the gender shown.

CAUTION: THERE ARE OFFENCES RELATING TO MAKING OR USING A FALSE CERTIFICATE.
©CROWN COPYRIGHT

WARNING: A CERTIFICATE IS NOT EVIDENCE OF IDENTITY.

freedom of expression. Aspects of the right to private life include:

- the physical and psychological integrity of a person
- sex life and gender
- personal data
- reputation
- names
- photos.

Key term

'**Private life**' – with regard to Article 8, this includes matters such as physical and psychological integrity; sex life and gender; personal data; reputation, names and photos.

Case study

Niemietz v Germany (1992)

The police searched a lawyer's offices to try to identify a suspect. The search was part of 'home' and the lawyer's private life.

The court attempted to define private life and said:

> It would be too restrictive to limit the notion of an 'inner circle' in which the individual may live his own personal life as he chooses and to exclude therefrom entirely the outside world not encompassed within that circle. Respect for private life must also comprise to a certain degree the right to establish and develop relationships with other human beings.

This included being at work.

Surveillance is included, as shown in *Halford v United Kingdom* (1997).

Halford v United Kingdom (1997)

Alison Halford was an Assistant Chief Constable. Her telephone calls were intercepted by senior police officers to obtain information regarding a sex discrimination claim she was pursuing in the employment tribunal. The interception of the telephone calls of an employee in a private exchange was a breach of the right of a private life under Article 8.

Personal information and data is also included. This means things such as DNA details and medical records. In *M S v Sweden* (1999) it was stated that 'respecting the confidentiality of health data is a vital principle in the legal systems of all contracting parties to the Convention'. Although these cases deal with the position of an adult, there is no good reason why they could not apply to protect the confidentiality of health information concerning a young person. This was the issue in *Axon v Secretary of State for Health* (2006). The case discussed the relationship of *Gillick* competence, Article 8 and the right to keep medical records private.

Woolf, J stated:

> Whether or not a child is capable of giving the necessary consent will depend on the child's maturity and understanding and the nature of the consent required. The child must be capable of making a reasonable assessment of the advantages and disadvantages of the treatment proposed, so the consent, if given, can be properly and fairly described as true consent.

Key term

Gillick **competence** – a term used to help assess whether a child has the maturity to make their own decisions and to understand the implications of those decisions. The term is taken from the case of *Gillick v West Norfolk and Wisbech Area Health Authority* (1984).

Case study

Axon v Secretary of State for Health (2006)

Sue Axon sought a declaration that a doctor was under no obligation to keep confidential advice and treatment proposed to a young person, under the age of 16, in respect of contraception, sexually transmitted infections and abortion. She wanted a declaration from the court that a doctor must inform the parents unless that might prejudice the child's physical or mental health. At the time, medical professionals were bound by advice contained within professional guides. The claimant sought a declaration that this guidance was unlawful.

The court rejected the claimant's argument; provided the child is *Gillick* competent, the parental right to determine medical treatment is ended.

The right to a private life also includes sexual identity. We have seen this in terms of transsexuals. Same-sex marriage need not, yet, be treated in the same way as heterosexual marriage although it is in the UK. As the ECtHR is a dynamic institution, its decisions reflect the situation at the time of a decision. The growing view of marriage being made available to all regardless of their sexual orientation is not yet sufficiently firm that the court will find that a state has an obligation to provide identical rights. However, where a state provides a civil partnership possibility, it should not do so in a discriminatory manner. This can be seen from the case of *Vallianatos v Greece* (2013).

The UK does not allow a civil partnership to be registered between persons of opposite sex. This was confirmed by the Court of Appeal in *Steinfeld v Secretary of State for Education* (2017).

Look online

Check whether *Steinfeld v Secretary of State for Education* (2017) has been appealed to the Supreme Court, and investigate the application of Article 8 in particular in this case.

Private life or privacy in the UK?

In English law there has never been a right to privacy. While there was the possibility for a claim in the tort of breach of confidence, this was restricted to confidential information and confidential relationships. However, Article 8 is not available in private disputes. It can only be raised in cases involving a public authority. The court, however, must take into account ECHR as it must not make a decision that is incompatible with ECHR.

The Data Protection Act 1998 controls how personal information is used by organisations, businesses or the government. Everyone responsible for using data has to follow the strict rules – the 'data protection principles'. We have seen this in relation to medical records in the *Axon* case, but the law has developed in other ways to give some protection from what might be considered an invasion of privacy and thus a person's right to a private life.

The intrusion into private life has always been a feature of the tabloid press. The principle of freedom of expression under Article 10 is considered in Chapter 22, but the two articles do overlap. The difficulty is in establishing what is in the public interest and what is a mere invasion of privacy. The courts have had to balance individual rights to privacy and to freedom of expression.

The cases of *Wainwright v Home Office* (2003) and *Campbell v MGN Ltd* (2004) show a contrast in the development of the law in England.

See Chapter 18, section 18.3.2 for full case details of *Wainwright v Home Office* (2003).

Case study

Campbell v MGN Ltd (2004)

Naomi Campbell was photographed coming out of a Narcotics Anonymous meeting in London. The newspaper published these photographs with the faces of others attending the meeting pixelated to protect their identities. The headline alongside the photograph read 'Naomi: I'm a drug addict'.

Because she was a model who had proclaimed publicly that she did not take drugs, this might be a legitimate matter to discuss under Article 10, freedom of expression. The question was whether this was a breach of her right to a private life and whether Article 8 takes precedence over Article 10.

The court stated that Articles 8 and 10 are now part of a claim for breach of confidence. There is no question of priority of Article 10 over Article 8 or a presumption in favour of one rather than the other. The publication of photographs of her outside a rehabilitation clinic was a disproportionate interference with her right to privacy, even though the fact that she was receiving treatment was in the public domain.

Naomi Campbell started proceedings in 2001, after the coming into force of HRA 1998. Her appeal to the House of Lords succeeded in 2004. She succeeded even though the newspaper publisher was not a public authority.

The question of priority has been raised on a number of occasions, most recently in *PJS v News Group Newspapers Ltd* (2016). Here it was stated that case law establishes that neither Article 8 nor Article 10 has preference over the other. When the court is considering an injunction with respect to the right of an individual to a private life, it focuses on the comparative rights being claimed in the individual case.

Case study

PJS v News Group Newspapers Ltd (2016)

The claimant applied to the court for an injunction to prevent publication of the fact that, in 2011, he had a three-way sexual encounter. The Supreme Court decided that neither Article 8 nor Article 10 has preference over the other. Furthermore, criticism of a person's conduct cannot be a pretext for invasion of privacy by disclosure of alleged sexual infidelity, which is of no real public interest in a legal sense. This rules out one defence to a claim for defamation.

Thus it seems that there is, as yet, no full privacy law in the UK, but Article 8 together with law on breach of confidence and defamation give adequate, if confused, protection.

Restrictions permitted by the ECHR – harassment

The Protection from Harassment Act 1997 and the Malicious Communications Act 1998 both give some additional protection.

Protection from Harassment Act 1997

The Protection from Harassment Act 1997 was originally introduced to deal with the problem of stalking. The Act in fact covers a range of conduct, including harassment motivated by race or religion, some types of anti-social behaviour, and some forms of protest.

The Act gives both criminal and civil remedies. There are two criminal offences:
- pursuing a course of conduct amounting to harassment
- a more serious offence where the conduct puts the victim in fear of violence.

Case	Facts	Law
Niemietz v Germany (1992)	Police searched a lawyer's offices to try to identify a suspect.	The search was part of home and the lawyer's private life.
Halford v United Kingdom (1997)	Telephone calls were intercepted by senior police officers to obtain information.	Interception of the telephone calls of an employee in a private exchange was a breach of the right to a private life.
Axon v Secretary of State for Health (2006)	Mrs Axon queried whether a doctor was under an obligation to keep confidential advice and treatment proposed to a young person, under the age of 16, in respect of contraception, sexually transmitted infections and abortion.	Provided the child is *Gillick* competent, the parental right to determine medical treatment is ended or else there is a potential violation of Article 8.
Wainwright v Home Office (2003)	There was a strip-search by prison officers of Mrs Wainwright and her son during a visit to Armley Prison, Leeds.	Article 8 does include touching of the body as part of the right to a private life.
Campbell v MGN Ltd (2004)	Naomi Campbell was photographed coming out of a Narcotics Anonymous meeting in London.	Articles 8 and 10 are now part of a claim for breach of confidence. There is no question of priority of Article 10 over Article 8 or a presumption in favour of one rather than the other.
PJS v News Group Newspapers Ltd (2016)	PJS applied to the court for an injunction to prevent publication of the fact that, in 2011, he had a three-way sexual encounter.	• Neither Article 8 nor Article 10 has preference over the other. • Criticism of a person's conduct cannot be a pretext for invasion of privacy by disclosure of alleged sexual infidelity, which is of no real public interest in a legal sense.

Figure 21.1 Key cases for Article 8 – the right to a private life

Harassing a person includes alarming the person or causing the person distress.

A 'course of conduct', which can include speech, must normally involve conduct on at least two occasions, although there are exceptions to this.

In addition to the criminal offences, a civil court can impose civil injunctions in harassment cases as well as awarding damages to the victim for the harassment. Breach of such an injunction is a criminal offence.

Malicious Communications Act 1998

The Malicious Communications Act 1998 states that it is an offence to send another person a letter, electronic communication or article of any description which conveys:
- a message which is indecent or grossly offensive
- a threat
- information which is false and known or believed to be false by the sender.

Guilt requires the intention to cause distress or anxiety to the recipient or any other person. This is increasingly relevant with respect to cyber bullying.

Tip

When considering problem questions, consider whether the scenario might need a discussion of both Articles 8 and 10.

21.4.3 'Family life'

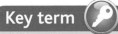

Key term

'Family life' – with regard to Article 8, the right to enjoy family relationships without interference from the state.

Under Article 8, you have the right to enjoy family relationships without interference from the state. This includes the right to live with your family and, where this is not possible, the right to regular contact with your family. 'Family life' can include the relationship between an unmarried couple, an adopted child and the adoptive parent, and a foster parent and fostered child.

There are many aspects of family life that can be affected by the state. For example:
- care proceedings and the possibility of a child being removed from the family home
- access to a child
- forced breakup of a relationship as a result of immigration rules.

The protection of Article 8 always extends to marriages which can be shown to be lawful and genuine. So, for example, a sham marriage to avoid

245

immigration rules or to acquire nationality may not be protected. A child born to parents who are married will therefore also always fall within Article 8. Unmarried couples who live together with their children fall within the Article, as the stable nature of the relationship makes it effectively the same as marriage.

Problems can arise when immigration rules cause a couple who are living together with no suggestion of a sham marriage in England, find that one of them is not permitted to remain under immigration rules, while the other is a British citizen or otherwise has indefinite right to remain in the UK.

Agyarko and Ikuga v Secretary of State for the Home Department (2015) were precariousness cases involving people who had overstayed their permits to be in the UK.

Case study

Agyarko and Ikuga v Secretary of State for the Home Department (2015)

Mrs Agyarko and Mrs Ikuga had been refused permission to remain or apply for judicial review proceedings of the Home Office's refusal to grant them leave to remain. Agyarko (a Ghanaian) and Ikuga (a Nigerian) had relied on their respective family lives to get leave to remain. However, their applications were refused because there were no insurmountable obstacles preventing them from continuing their relationships outside the UK, and no exceptional circumstances under Article 8 existed.

Extension question

Research the problems highlighted by cases such as *Singh and Khalid v Secretary of State for the Home Department* (2015) and *M M (Lebanon) v Secretary of State for the Home Department* (2017).

The scope of the margin of appreciation differs according to the context of the case. It is particularly wide in child protection cases. It takes this into account when examining such cases under the Convention by allowing states a measure of discretion. An example of this can be seen in *Gaskin v United Kingdom* (1989).

Case study

Gaskin v United Kingdom (1989)

Graham Gaskin was placed in care when he was a baby. He complained of ill-treatment while he was in the care of a local authority and living with foster parents. He wanted access to his case records held by the local authority but his request was denied. He applied to the ECtHR.

The refusal to allow him access to his records involved a breach of his rights under Article 8. This was because there was no independent mechanism to decide whether or not access should be permitted if the consent of third party contributors, such as care workers who made the decisions at the time, could not be obtained. There must be specific justification for preventing individuals from having access to information which forms part of their private and family life. The court stated that relationships between children and foster parents or carers fall within the definition of 'family' within the meaning of Article 8.

In *Johannsen v Norway* (1996) the court had to consider a permanent placement of a child with a view to adoption in opposition to the natural parents' wishes. The question was, under Article 8, how the rights of the child and the parents should be balanced.

Case study

Johannsen v Norway (1996)

The natural parents of a child were opposed the decision of the state with respect to adoption. The mother had been subject to domestic violence and suffered a chaotic lifestyle. There had been several interventions by Norwegian social services.

The court stated that particular weight should be attached to the best interests of the child, which may override those of the parent.

In *Yousef v Netherlands* (2003) the court reiterated that in judicial decisions where the rights under Article 8 of parents and those of a child are at stake, the child's rights must be the paramount consideration. This is entirely consistent with the principles in English family law.

Extension question

Look in detail at the case of *Yousef v Netherlands* (2003) for further examples of how Article 8 operates.

Case	Facts	Law
Agyarko and Ikuga v Secretary of State for the Home Department (2015)	The applicants had overstayed their permits to be in the UK, and relied on their relationships with British citizens in order to obtain leave to remain.	The claims failed as there were no insurmountable obstacles preventing them from continuing their relationships outside the UK and no exceptional circumstances under Article 8 existed.
Gaskin v United Kingdom (1989)	The applicant had been in care as a baby and then fostered. He wanted access to his case records held by the local authority to support claims of abuse, but his request was denied.	Refusal to allow him access to his records involved a breach of his rights under Article 8.
Johannsen v Norway (1996)	The natural parents of a child were opposed to the decision of the state with respect to adoption.	Particular weight should be attached to the best interests of the child, which may override those of the parent.

Figure 21.2 Key cases for Article 8 – respect for family life

These cases can be seen as the way in which different states' legal frameworks operate in a positive way to prevent harm to an individual who is part of a family.

Family and private life in the UK

The Human Rights Act 1998, along with Article 8, has influenced the development of the law in the UK. Some examples have been seen above. More recent examples often relate to immigration cases such as *Agyarko and Ikuga v Secretary of State for the Home Department* (2015).

In *Wood v Commissioner of Police for the Metropolis* (2009), the question again arose about the taking of photographs and their retention.

Case study

Wood v Commissioner of Police for the Metropolis (2009)

The taking and retention of photographs by the police of a person connected with a group opposed to the arms trade as he left the annual general meeting of a company that organised a trade fair for the arms industry was an interference with that person's right to respect for his private life under Article 8, and the police failed to justify that interference as being proportionate.

The police action was a sufficient intrusion by the state into the individual's own space and integrity as to amount to a violation of Article 8.

In terms of sexuality and gender, the courts in England have been quite clear in their engagement of Article 8. In *A B v Secretary of State for Justice* (2009) it was decided that the continued detention of a pre-operative transgender woman in a male prison breached her right to privacy under Article 8.

Case study

A B v Secretary of State for Justice (2009)

The claimant asked for judicial review of a decision to keep her in a male prison and to not transfer her to a female prison. She suffered gender dysphoria and had been granted a certificate under the Gender Recognition Act 2004. The certificate provides that for all purposes the claimant is a female. The claimant wanted to have gender reassignment surgery to complete her female transition. However, the Gender Identity Clinic would not approve her for surgery until she had lived as a woman for a period of time within a female prison. Her claim was the failure to transfer her to a female prison prevented her from attempting to meet the conditions for surgery.

The court said that the failure to transfer her violated her Article 8 rights. Justification for the infringement of her rights must be clear and weighty in order to be proportionate and there was no justification in this case.

Other UK regulations have also been questioned. Under s 82 of the Sexual Offences Act 2003 all persons sentenced to 30 months' imprisonment or more for a sexual offence become subject to a lifelong duty to keep the police notified of where they are living and of travel abroad. There is no right to a review of the necessity for the notification requirements. Is this a violation of Article 8? This was considered in *F and Thompson v Secretary of State for the Home Department* (2010).

Case	Facts	Law
Wood v Commissioner of Police for the Metropolis (2009)	The police took and retained photographs of a person connected with a group opposed to the arms trade as he left the annual general meeting of a company that organised a trade fair for the arms industry.	The photography had to be considered in context, and here it was an interference under Article 8.
A B v Secretary of State for Justice (2009)	The claimant, a pre-operative transgender woman who was in a male prison, asked for judicial review of a decision not to transfer her to a female prison.	The court said that the decision not to transfer her to a female prison was in violation of her Article 8 rights.
F and Thompson v Secretary of State for the Home Department (2010)	Two convicted sex offenders claimed that the absence of a right of review of the notification requirements was disproportionate and breached their right to privacy under Article 8.	The notification requirements may not be disproportionate, but there must be a way for the offender to seek a review of their status. The current law is incompatible with Article 8.
R (T) v Chief Constable of Greater Manchester (2013)	In *T*, the police issued warnings in 2002 to an 11-year-old boy for theft, which were disclosed in 2008 and again in 2010 when he applied for positions that might have involved contact with children.	The court agreed that the 1997 Act is incompatible with Article 8.

Figure 21.3 Key cases for Article 8 – family and private life in the UK

Case study

F and Thompson v Secretary of State for the Home Department (2010)

The two convicted sex offenders were subject to the notification requirements. They claimed that the absence of a right of review of the requirements was disproportionate to the pursuit of the legitimate aim of preventing crime and violated Article 8.

The Supreme Court stated that while the notification requirements may not be disproportionate, there must be a way for the offender to seek a review of his status. Therefore the current law was incompatible with Article 8.

Guidance was issued on this matter by the Home Office in November 2016.

The result of this and other decisions is that UK law is amended so as to comply with Article 8.

Extension question

Look at the issue of warnings and cautions that were raised in cases such as *R (T) v Chief Constable of Greater Manchester* (2013) and the Law Commission review on 'Criminal Records Disclosure' (2017) (Law Com No. 371).

Do you consider that English law breaches Article 8 now, and will recommendations made by the Law Commission be sufficient? What are the interests being balanced here?

21.4.4 'Home'

Key term

'Home' – with regard to Article 8, this is a right to enjoy your existing home peacefully, rather than a right to a house.

This is a right to enjoy your existing home peacefully, rather than a right to a house. This means that public authorities should not stop you entering or living in your home without very good reason, and they should not enter without your permission. This applies whether or not you own your home.

In *Khatun v United Kingdom* (1998) the ECtHR considered whether interference could be differentiated depending on whether the home was owned by the claimant or not. Whether or not somewhere was a home within the Article depends on the facts of each case.

Case study

Khatun v United Kingdom (1998)

The applicants suffered from pollution of the area of their home by dust caused by building works in London Docklands. A distinction had been made between those applicants with a proprietary interest in the land and those without such an interest, such as the applicants.

The court stated that:

> Article 8(1) applies to all the applicants in the present case whether they are the owners of the property or merely occupiers living on the property, for example the children of the owner of the property.

Usually the existence of sufficient and continuous links is enough to engage Article 8. In *Gillow v United Kingdom* (1986) the owners of a house in Guernsey were not given a licence to reside there by the authorities even though it was their home, so Article 8 was engaged.

Many of the cases brought against the UK with respect to 'home' relate to claims by gypsies and others, such as travelling showmen, bringing caravans on to land. *Connors v UK* (2004) and *Price v Leeds City Council* (2005) explain that Article 8 is engaged where the dispute relates to eviction from a lawful site for gypsy caravans but not where the occupation of the land is unauthorised, in the *Price* case on a playing field. Article 8 operates only with respect to an individual's claim against a public body. Bizarrely, this would appear to include publicly owned housing rented to a tenant, but not where private landlords were concerned. This is seen in the case of *McDonald v McDonald* (2016).

Case study

McDonald v McDonald (2016)

Fiona McDonald suffered with mental health issues. Her parents therefore decided to purchase a property for her to live in, with the assistance of a mortgage on the property. The parents ran into financial difficulties and therefore the mortgage company wished to evict her and then sell the property. The Supreme Court decided that HRA 1998 and Article 8 do not require a court to consider whether it is proportionate to evict a residential occupier in a possession claim brought by a private residential landlord.

21.4.5 'Correspondence'

Key term

'Correspondence' – with regard to Article 8, this means the right to uninterrupted and uncensored communications with others.

Respect for correspondence under Article 8 covers all forms of communication including phone calls, letters, text messages, emails and other communication methods.

In *Klass v Germany* (1978), the powers of secret surveillance of citizens were tolerable under the ECHR only in so far as strictly necessary for safeguarding the democratic institutions.

This means that, in some circumstances, a public authority may be able to interfere with your right to a private and family life in order to protect public safety or the freedoms of others. This has interesting but untested possibilities, including the operation of the Investigatory Powers Act 2016. This Act legalises a whole range of tools for snooping and hacking by the security services unmatched by any other country in Western Europe and the USA.

We have seen that the right of privacy extends to an office. With respect to private communications made while at work, the case of *Bărbulescu v Romania* (2016) indicates the current position. This decision reflects UK employment law good practice.

Case study

Bărbulescu v Romania (2016)

At his employer's request, Mr Bărbulescu set up a Yahoo Messenger account to deal with client enquiries. However, he also used the account to send personal messages which was not allowed under the company rules. The company investigated his communications including his personal messages and dismissed him for unauthorised use of the internet. The Grand Chamber held that Mr Bărbulescu's employers had breached Article 8 by not striking the right balance between its interests and his right to respect for his private life and correspondence.

The Grand Chamber said that although a right to private life could be reduced in the workplace, an employee could never lose all rights. This right always continued to exist although reduced by the employer's rules in the workplace. The interests of a company wanting to ensure smooth running and the rights of the employee to private life and correspondence had to be balanced.

Restrictions permitted by the ECHR – interception of communications

Most UK employers allow or at least tolerate some personal internet and telephone use at work, so the situation is unlikely to be replicated in the UK. To what extent is it the same for members of the same family or for someone using facilities in a hotel or holiday cottage, or for teachers and pupils at a school?

Look online

Read the article entitled 'Three quarters of secondary schools spying on pupils' devices' at this web address: www.kenilworthweeklynews.co.uk/news/three-quarters-of-secondary-schools-spying-on-pupils-devices-1-7682795.

Make a list of the arguments for and against this form of surveillance being in breach of Article 8 ECHR. Prepare for and hold a debate on whether a school or college is justified legally or morally in 'spying on pupils' devices' and restricting access through school internet servers.

The much-criticised Data Retention and Investigatory Powers Act 2014 gave the Home Office powers to issue a data retention notice to telecommunications operators to retain personal data of subscribers and registered users without overview by a judge. While this piece of legislation has now come to an end as the result of a sunset clause, its replacement has many similar characteristics. The Act required communications companies (telephone companies) to retain data for 12 months following the giving of a notice by the Secretary of State, irrespective of whether the data subject was suspected of committing any crime. This is done in order to combat crime.

Its replacement, the Investigatory Powers Act 2016, has similar provisions. The aims of the Act are to:
- combine the powers already available to law enforcement and the security and intelligence agencies to obtain communications and data about communications
- introduce a 'double-lock' for interception warrants, so that, following Secretary of State authorisation, they cannot come into force until they have been approved by a judge
- create an Investigatory Powers Commissioner to oversee how these powers are used
- ensure the powers are fit for the digital age.

However this may not be seen as being compatible with EU law and the ECHR, as shown in the ruling from the CJEU in the joined cases of *Tele2 Sverige and Watson* (2016).

Case study

Tele2 Sverige and Watson (2016)

The court stated:

> That data taken as a whole is liable to allow very precise conclusions to be drawn concerning the private lives of the persons whose data has been retained, such as everyday habits, permanent or temporary places of residence, daily or other movements, the activities carried out, the social relationships of those persons and the social environments frequented by them ... In particular that data provides the means ... of establishing a profile of the individuals concerned, information that is no less sensitive, having regard to the right to privacy, than the actual content of communications.

Where national legislation provides for data retention, any retention must be strictly necessary for the purposes of investigating serious crime and linked to the investigation of serious crime.

This strongly suggests that the Investigatory Powers Act 2016 is likely not to be compatible under Article 8 as its powers are too wide-reaching and indiscriminate. The challenge now rests in the English courts' hands to decide on this or for the new Act to be amended.

Activity

Research the progress of challenges and changes to the Investigatory Powers Act 2016. You can do this by building up a timeline of events.

Case	Facts	Law
McDonald v McDonald (2016)	The claimant's parents purchased a mortgaged property for her to live in, but ran into financial difficulties. The mortgage company wished to evict her.	Article 8 did not apply in this case so the court did not have to consider proportionality.
Bărbulescu v Romania (2016)	Mr Bărbulescu used a business Yahoo Messenger account to send personal messages. He was dismissed.	Article 8 rights had been engaged, but the employer's interference had been proportionate within the state's margin of appreciation.
Tele2 Sverige and Watson (2016)	A Swedish electronic communications provider refused to retain electronic communications data following the finding in DRI that the Data Retention Directive was invalid was in question.	Where national legislation provides for data retention, any retention must be strictly necessary for the purposes of investigating serious crime and linked to the investigation of serious crime.

Figure 21.4 Key cases for Article 8 –respect for home and correspondence

21.5 Evaluation of Article 8

21.5.1 A qualified right

This wide-ranging right is a qualified right. This means that the state can justify interference with the right. Once a court has found interference with the right, the question is then whether there has been an unlawful interference with the right. As Article 8 is wide ranging, there are many instances of an interference with the right. The court then has to decide whether the interference is justified by the state using the principles of proportionality and margin of appreciation.

With respect to proportionality, the court will consider the effectiveness of the interference related to its legitimate aim; how intrusive the interference is to the individual; whether the interference removes all the protection of the right or sets limits; whether the interference strikes a fair balance between interests of the individual and the community as a whole. Every case is decided on this principle, yet different states have different views about proportionality and even within English law there are some bizarre distinctions drawn such as in *Connors v UK* (2004) and *McDonald v McDonald* (2016).

The margin of appreciation is a controversial principle in itself. A wide margin of appreciation means that a court is more likely to find no violation of the right. There are several factors that influence the width of the margin of appreciation including the lack of a European standard and the way in which the law is expected to change as society evolves. This can be seen in narrowing of the margin of appreciation over time with respect to transsexuals.

There are many areas of possible contention as the law struggles to keep pace with changes in society and its view of morality. The debate about euthanasia and assisted suicide is one that shows different responses across the states that have signed the Convention.

21.5.2 The scope of private life

The scope of private life is very wide – it covers aspects such as self-determination and human dignity and is expanding in meaning as the law develops over time. It was stated in *Peck v UK* (2003) that there is no 'exhaustive definition' of private life. That case involved the later use of unpixelated CCTV images of a young man attempting to commit suicide by slashing his wrists with a kitchen knife to draw attention to the benefits of CCTV. It is clearly beneficial to have this broad definition to cover cases such as this but it does beg the question of the extent to which the state has an obligation to legislate for the protection of individuals.

21.5.3 The scope of family life

The range of relationships that falls within the definition of family life is continuing to develop. Precisely which relationships constitute family rather than private life only is unclear. It can be seen from cases involving immigration rules that the courts are not always consistent and can make decisions that would appear to militate against family life such as the *Agyarco and Ikuga* (2015) case. However, the English courts do try and maintain the general principle that the rights of a child are paramount which also emerges from ECTHR cases such as *Johannsen v Norway* (1996) and *Yousef v Netherlands* (2003).

21.5.4 The meaning of home

The obvious point that the meaning of 'home' does not include the right to a house tends to obscure the rights that are given under the Convention with respect to enjoying your home peacefully. Any investigation as to whether the right has been breached (and there are many circumstances when others are permitted to enter your home without your permission) must be put in the context of public protection. Images of police breaking into a house in the early hours of the morning would be considered horrific by most of us yet be applauded by nearly everyone if the forced entry was to disrupt terrorist bomb makers. While the decision in *Khatun v UK* (1998) is eminently sensible, the later decision in *McDonald v McDonald* (2016) appears less sensible.

21.5.5 The meaning of 'correspondence' and the protection from interference

The right to uninterrupted and uncensored communications is an area of great contention. The right of the state to collect, process and retain personal data should be limited as it should be for all private enterprises. Whether it is the government through GCHQ or Google collecting and mining data, there should be adequate protection for the individual. The state may well claim legitimate aims in this qualified right, but the individual is only protected by the Data Protection Acts in in the UK. In *Bărbulescu v Romania* (2016), the Grand Chamber acknowledged the need to assess whether the applicant was left with a reasonable expectation of privacy after having prior knowledge of a company's internal regulations. This does not in itself secure adequate protection of any employee as an employer will sometimes try to enforce greater rights over the employee than the law apparently allows.

The whole debate about the scope of the Investigatory Powers Act 2016 may prove that UK legislation does not comply with Article 8 given the decision in *Tele2Sverige and Watson* (2016).

Summary

- Article 8 has four protected interests: private life, family life, home, and correspondence.
- Article 8 is a qualified right.
- Under Article 8(2) any limitation must be in accordance with law, necessary and proportionate and for one or more of the five legitimate aims.
- Private life and privacy are not the same.
- Article 8 is not available in private disputes. It can only be raised in cases involving a public authority.
- Family life means that you have the right to enjoy family relationships without interference from the state.
- Respect for home is a right to enjoy your existing home peacefully, rather than a right to a house.
- Respect for correspondence is a right to uninterrupted and uncensored communications with others.

Chapter 22

Article 10: freedom of expression

After reading this chapter you should be able to:
- Understand the scope of Article 10(1) ECHR
- Understand the restrictions permitted by Article 10(2)
- Understand the explanations of Article 10 in the ECtHR
- Understand the ways in which English law has applied Article 10
- Critically evaluate the operation of Article 10 in English law
- Apply the law to given situations

22.1 Article 10 ECHR

" 1 Everyone has the right to freedom of expression. This right shall include freedom to hold opinions and to receive and impart information and ideas without interference by public authority and regardless of frontiers. This Article shall not prevent States from requiring the licensing of broadcasting, television or cinema enterprises.

2 The exercise of these freedoms, since it carries with it duties and responsibilities, may be subject to such formalities, conditions, restrictions or penalties as are prescribed by law and are necessary in a democratic society, in the interests of national security, territorial integrity or public safety, for the prevention of disorder or crime, for the protection of health or morals, for the protection of the reputation or rights of others, for preventing the disclosure of information received in confidence, or for maintaining the authority and impartiality of the judiciary. "

Article 10(1) contains the meaning of expression and Article 10(2) sets out how the state can justify an interference with Article 10(1).

The eighteenth century Scottish philosopher David Hume wrote, in *Essays, Moral and Political* (1741):

" Nothing is more apt to surprize a foreigner, than the extreme liberty, which we enjoy in this country, of communicating whatever we please to the public, and of openly censuring every measure, entered into by the king or his ministers. "

The concept of free speech has been with us for many years, and attempts to restrict it have been met with an outcry throughout history. Speakers' Corner is an area of Hyde Park, London, which is set aside for public speaking. The Parks Regulation Act 1872 passed that anyone can turn up here unannounced to speak on any subject, as long as the police consider their speeches lawful. The spot is near to where the Tyburn gallows were situated, and the creation of Speakers' Corner stems from 1866, when the government suppressed a meeting of the Reform League demanding the extension of the right to vote.

Before HRA 1998, freedom of expression was permitted as long as the law did not prevent it.

Crowds listen to a speaker in Hyde Park

253

22.2 The key provisions of Article 10

Article 10(1) gives everyone the right to freedom of expression, which includes the freedom to hold opinions and to receive and impart information and ideas without state interference. This is much more than free speech. Freedom of expression includes the right to communicate and to express oneself in any medium, including through words, pictures, images and actions. Actions include public protest and demonstrations; this therefore overlaps with Article 11, the right to freedom of assembly and association.

Key term

Freedom of expression – in human rights under Article 11 ECHR, the freedom for a person to hold opinions and to receive and give information and ideas without state interference.

The right to receive information does not, however, have a duty on the state to provide information. In *Guerra v Italy* (1998), a case about toxic emissions, it was stated that freedom to receive information prohibits a government from restricting a person from receiving information that others wish or may be willing to give. There is no positive obligation to collect and disseminate information.

There are three components of the right to freedom of expression:
- freedom to hold opinions
- freedom to impart information and ideas
- freedom to receive information and ideas.

22.2.1 Freedom to hold opinions

Freedom to hold opinions is a prior condition to the other freedoms guaranteed by Article 10. The possible restrictions set out in Article 10(2) do not apply. Any restrictions to this right will be inconsistent with the nature of a democratic society.

This means that states must not try to indoctrinate their citizens and should not be allowed to distinguish between individuals holding one opinion and another. The idea is to prevent prejudice against an individual because of his views by public authorities such as the police or a school. This can be seen in the operation of the equality duty under the Equality Act 2010 where there is a potential conflict with Article 10. For example, a university must prevent unlawful discrimination and promote equality of opportunity, fostering good relationships between different groups, including those with 'protected characteristics' as designated in the Act.

Activity

Read the article at www.theguardian.com/education/2015/feb/02/free-speech-universities-spiked-ban-sombreros.
1 Consider the arguments for and against the bans being outside the apparent scope of freedom of expression under Article 10.
2 Debate this within a small group, and consider the justifications for some bans.
3 Revisit this when you have finished this chapter and review your findings.

This indoctrination could include the promotion of information by the state unless it promotes a balanced view.

An individual's freedom to hold opinions includes the negative freedom of not being forced to communicate his opinions.

22.2.2 Freedom to impart information and ideas

The right to freedom of expression includes the right to 'offend, shock and disturb'. In *Handyside v United Kingdom* (1976) the ECtHR stated:

> The Court's supervisory functions oblige it to pay the utmost attention to the principles characterising a 'democratic society'. Freedom of expression constitutes one of the essential foundations of such a society, one of the basic conditions for its progress and for the development of every man.

Freedom of speech was not applicable only to inoffensive material, but also extends to protect activity which others may find shocking, disturbing, or offensive.

The type of expression protected includes:
- political expression (including comment on matters of general public interest)
- artistic expression
- commercial expression, particularly when it also raises matters of legitimate public debate and concern.

Political expression is given particular precedence and protection. This was the case with respect to Speakers' Corner too. This is described as high-value expression, which means that there is less margin of appreciation.

Freedom of the press

The freedom to impart ideas requires freedom of the press. To ensure that free expression and debate is possible, there must be protection for elements of a free press, including protection of journalistic sources. The public and the media should be able to comment on political matters without hindrance. This includes a journalist being able to protect his sources.

There have been many cases with respect to this aspect of Article 10, such as *Goodwin v United Kingdom* (1996).

This decision was repeated in *Financial Times Ltd v United Kingdom* (2009) when the ECtHR held unanimously that an order requiring various media organisations to disclose original leaked documents which might have led to the revelation of a journalistic source was an unjustified interference with Article 10.

One of the main problems with freedom of the press is the balance between Articles 10 and 8. As we have seen with the limitations under Article 8(2) the balance is difficult.

Tip

Review the material on Article 8, as exam questions may well require a discussion of both Articles.

The case of *Axel Springer AG v Germany* (2012) set out criteria to be used in balancing the two articles. These criteria are:
- whether the information contributes to a debate of general interest
- the notoriety of the person concerned and the subject matter of the report
- the prior conduct of the person concerned
- the method of obtaining the information and its veracity
- the content, form and consequences of the publication
- the severity of the sanction imposed.

Case study

Axel Springer AG v Germany (2012)

A German newspaper published stories and photographs about the arrest and conviction for possession of drugs of an actor, who was well known for his portrayal of a police officer in a television series in Germany. On the facts the court found that his right to privacy under Article 8 outweighed the newspaper's freedom of expression under Article 10. In coming to this conclusion, the court had applied the six criteria set out above.

Activity

Find some recent sensational newspaper headlines about an individual. Consider the criteria for the balance between Articles 8 and 10 for that individual and the newspaper.

Political expression

Meaningful free elections are not possible in the absence of this freedom. A wide range of views were expressed during the 2016 referendum campaign on Britain's withdrawal from the EU, and a Remain-supporting MP, Jo Cox, was murdered by a man who disagreed with her views. In December 2016, after the conviction of Mrs Cox's murderer, a man was arrested over a Twitter post calling for people to 'Jo Cox' an MP.

The difficulty is when political expression contravenes the criminal law relating to protests, or, indeed, as to what is considered political. The limits of acceptable criticism are wider with respect to a politician as such than as regards a private individual. A politician inevitably lays himself open to close scrutiny of his every word and deed by both journalists and the public at large, and therefore must display a greater degree of tolerance. However, the reporting needs to be at the standard of responsible journalism and reportage.

Civil or public interest expression

This is where the expression raises matters of legitimate public debate and concern. This might be with respect to the building of a motorway or rail line, hunting, fracking or activities by commercial enterprises. An example of this is the case of

Steel and Morris v United Kingdom (2005), where the court found that there had been a violation of Article 10.

See Chapter 20, section 20.2.5 for full case details.

Helen Steel and David Morris, who brought a libel case against McDonalds

With respect to the overlap of Articles 8 and 10, where a court was considering whether to interfere with the freedom of the press, any interference has to be justified, even where there is no public interest in the material in question being published. This can be seen in the case of *A v B plc (Flitcroft v MGN Ltd)* (2002).

Case study

A v B plc (Flitcroft v MGN Ltd) (2002)

The newspaper appealed against an injunction preventing it naming a footballer who, it claimed, had been unfaithful to his wife. There remains a distinction between the right of privacy which attaches to sexual activities within and outside a marriage. An order restricting the freedom of the press requires positive and clear justification. The fact that there might be no proper public interest in the material to be published was not itself a sufficient reason.

Artistic expression

This is vital for fostering individual fulfilment and the development of ideas. There is much variety between states as to what is acceptable – in other words, a wide margin of appreciation to reflect different cultures and values in different states.

For example, in *Otto-Preminger-Institut v Austria* (1994) there was a conflict between freedom of expression and religion.

Case study

Otto-Preminger-Institut v Austria (1994)

The institute tried to show a film that offended the Catholic religion and the religious feelings of the people of Tyrol, a region of Austria that consists of a large majority of Catholics in whose lives religion plays a very important role. The authorities had banned the showing of the film in an art cinema and confiscated the film. The institute claimed a violation of its freedom of speech under Article 10 but ECtHR found no violation.

Hate speech or incitement to hatred

Hate speech is dealt with by Article 17, but, confusingly, incitement to racial hatred can be dealt with under Article 10. This can be seen in the case of Garuady v France (2003).

Case study

Garuady v France (2003)

Garuady's book, *The Founding Myths of Modern Israel*, challenged certain historical orthodoxies about the Holocaust and the existence of Hitler's 'final solution'. Criminal proceedings were brought against him and he was found guilty of disputing the existence of crimes against humanity, public defamation of a group of people (the Jewish community) and incitement to discrimination and racial hatred.

He argued that under Article 10, his right to freedom of expression had been unjustifiably infringed. He also argued that his book was a political work written with a view to combating Zionism and criticising Israeli policy, and had no racist or anti-Semitic content. He argued he should have unlimited freedom of expression.

The court found that there could be an interference with his right to freedom of expression. However unpalatable his views, his publication contained ideas, and as such should be protected under Article 10. Therefore there was no breach of Article 10.

Case	Facts	Law
Handyside v United Kingdom (1976)	Handyside was convicted under the Obscene Publications Acts 1959 and 1964.	There was no breach of Article 10 and the UK law fell within the margin of appreciation of the member state.
Goodwin v United Kingdom (1996)	Goodwin failed to disclose the source of company financial information and was fined.	The order for disclosure of the source was not necessary, and so was a breach of Article 10.
Axel Springer AG v Germany (2012)	A newspaper published stories about the arrest and conviction for possession of drugs of a well-known TV actor, together with photographs of him.	The actor's right to privacy under Article 8 outweighed the newspaper's freedom of expression under Article 10. The court had applied six criteria.
Steel and Morris v United Kingdom (2005)	Steel and Morris (and others) libelled and were ordered to pay damages to McDonald's in 1997 after handing out leaflets attacking the company's working practices and policies.	Given the lack of procedural fairness and the disproportionate award of damages, the court found that there was been a violation of Article 10.
A v B plc (Flitcroft v MGN Ltd) (2002)	The newspaper appealed against an injunction preventing it naming a footballer who, it claimed, had been unfaithful to his wife.	The fact that there might be no proper public interest in the material to be published was not itself a sufficient reason for an injunction.
Otto-Preminger-Institut v Austria (1994)	The institute tried to show a film that offended the Catholic religion but the authorities banned it and confiscated the film.	The institute claimed a violation of its freedom of speech under Article 10 of the Convention but failed in its attempt.
Garuady v France (2003)	Garuady was found guilty of disputing the existence of a number of crimes in relation to a book he had written.	However unpalatable his views, his publication contained ideas, and as such should be protected under Article 10. But restriction was justifiable under Article 10(2) (so there had been no breach of Article 10).

Figure 22.1 Key case chart for Article 10 – freedom to impart information and ideas

22.2.3 Freedom to receive information and ideas

The freedom to receive information includes the right to gather information and to seek information through all possible lawful sources, including international television broadcasts and the internet. This freedom enables the media to impart such information and ideas to the public, who have a right to be adequately informed, in particular on matters of public interest. This relates to freedom of information.

This right does not put a general positive obligation to provide the information. This can be seen in *Guerra v Italy* (1998).

Case study

Guerra v Italy (1998)

The applicants complained that the Italian state had failed to provide information about potentially hazardous industry near where they lived.

ECtHR stated that Article 10 of the Convention, 'basically prohibits a government from restricting a person from receiving information that others wish or may be willing to impart to him'. ECtHR stated that the freedom cannot be construed as imposing on a state, positive obligations to collect and disseminate information on its own accord.

In the UK, the Freedom of Information Act 2000 gives everyone the right to access recorded information held by public sector organisations. Any request for information under the Act will be handled under different regulations depending on the kind of information requested, and an organisation could refuse a request if the information is sensitive or the costs are too high.

The other side of freedom of information is the Investigatory Powers Act 2016.

See Chapter 21, section 21.4.5 for more details of the Investigatory Powers Act 2016.

Whether this Act will have an effect on the interpretation of Articles 8 and 10 (as well as other Articles of the ECHR) remains to be seen.

Without interference by public authority

The whole question of freedom of information and when a response can be refused under ECHR has been reviewed in *Magyar Helsinki Bizottság v Hungary* (2016). ECtHR tied access to information to freedom of expression.

The scope of access to information is narrowly defined: it applies to state-held information, and ensures access in the public interest and for recipients who seek access to information in order to contribute to the public debate in a watchdog capacity. The audience's potential 'wish for sensationalism or even voyeurism' is not sufficient reason to provide access to information under Article 10. Where access to the information is 'instrumental' for the individual's exercise of his right to freedom of expression, the information must be disclosed.

Whether it is instrumental requires consideration of four indicative criteria:

- The purpose of the information request – which must be to receive and impart information and ideas to others, and necessary for the exercise of freedom of expression.
- The nature of the information sought – it needs to meet a public interest test in order to prompt a need for disclosure under Article 10.
- The role of the applicant – journalists, social watchdogs, non-governmental organisations (NGOs), researchers and academics are in a privileged position, so long as they seek the information with a view to informing the public in the capacity of a public watchdog.
- Ready and available information.

If the right is engaged (as the court held it was for the NGO in *Magyar*), it is necessary to consider whether the interference is justified under Article 10(2).

'Not prevent States from requiring the licensing of broadcasting, television or cinema enterprises'

This allows the state to license such media companies as, when ECHR was drafted, there were only a limited number of broadcasting frequencies available and most European states had control of these frequencies.

Later ECtHR decisions such as *Groppera Radio AG v Switzerland* (1990) recognised that the technical progress that had been made meant that the justification of these restrictions could no longer be supported on this basis. Public monopolies within the audio visual media were seen by the court as contrary to Article 10.

22.3 Limitations in Article 10

The limitations are set out in Article 10(2). These limitations are only permissible if they fulfil three criteria:

- The interference (formality, restriction, condition, or penalty) is prescribed by law. This means that it is part of the relevant state's law. In the UK this includes statutory and common law rules. For instance, in *Sunday Times v United Kingdom* (1979), the court found that the British common law rules on contempt of court were sufficiently precise as to fall under the requirement 'provided by law'.
- The interference is aimed at protecting one or more of the following legitimate aims:
  - in the interests of national security
  - with respect to territorial integrity or public safety
  - for the prevention of disorder or crime
  - for the protection of health or morals
  - for the protection of the reputation or rights of others
  - for preventing the disclosure of information received in confidence
  - for maintaining the authority and impartiality of the judiciary.

  This list is exhaustive; no other ground may be relied on.
- The interference is necessary in a democratic society. Here the national courts must apply the principle of proportionality, answering the question: 'Was the aim proportional with the means used to reach that legitimate aim?' In *Observer and Guardian v United Kingdom* (1995) the ECtHR stated that 'necessary', within the meaning of Article 10(2), means the existence of a pressing social need.

Where the ECtHR finds that all three requirements are fulfilled, the interference will be considered legitimate. The burden of proof is on the state. The ECtHR examines the three conditions in the order set out. As soon as the state fails to prove one of the three requirements the interference is unjustified, and freedom of expression violated.

Case study

Observer and Guardian v United Kingdom (1995)

The newspapers challenged injunctions from the government preventing their publication of extracts from the *Spycatcher* memoir, authored by Peter Wright, a former member of the British Security Service, without obtaining the authorisation of the Security Service. He asserted that until the late 1970s, the Security Service had been engaged in various unlawful activities, such as bugging and burgling of friendly embassies.

In July 1986 the courts granted an interim injunction to prohibit publication, but by the time of the hearing for a permanent injunction, the book was published abroad including in the USA, and many copies had been imported into the UK.

The ECtHR stated that the temporary injunctions were justified prior to the publication in the United States. At that point, the information lost its confidential character and so the interference was no longer permissible.

Tip

When considering the application of Article 10(2), follow the order set out here to examine the three conditions.

We therefore need to consider how these limitations operate and the reasons of permitted interference by the state, listed under the second bullet point above.

22.3.1 In the interests of national security

We have already seen how this has had a limited protection in the *Spycatcher* case. The court rarely challenges the legitimate national security aim argued by the state. *Hadjianastassiou v Greece* (1992) is an example of this, where a report the applicant had written for a private company gave some hints of the military capabilities of the Greek Air Force where he was an aeronautical engineer.

22.3.2 With respect to territorial integrity or public safety

Territorial integrity means the borders of the state. Public safety would include legislation to prevent bomb hoaxes. There is no public interest defence available to offences under the Official Secrets Act 1989. This was decided in the case of *R v Shayler* (2002).

Case study

R v Shayler (2002)

The defendant had been a member of the security services. He had signed the Official Secrets Act as required by the security services. However he disclosed a number of documents to journalists from the *Mail on Sunday*. A large number of documents were later returned by the newspaper. Most of them appeared to relate to security and intelligence matters and were classified at levels ranging from 'Classified' up to and including 'Top Secret'.

His defence that the disclosures had been made by him in the public or national interest failed.

22.3.3 For the prevention of disorder or crime

The state could try to justify the interference by arguing that it would cause crime or disorder so the criminal offence is needed to protect against it. However, the question is whether the state's actions are proportionate. An example of this (and other limitations) can be seen in the case of *Surek v Turkey* (1999).

Case study

Surek v Turkey (1999)

The applicant was the major shareholder in a company which owned a weekly review. Two readers' articles were published in the weekly review in which the state authorities were severely criticised for their part in the massacres in Kurdistan in south-eastern Turkey. The letters used labels such as 'fascist Turkish army' and 'murder gang' alongside references to 'massacres', 'brutalities' and 'slaughter'. In the Court's view they amounted to an appeal to revenge.

The applicant was convicted of the offence of disseminating propaganda against the indivisibility of the state and provoking enmity and hatred among the people. Surek argued that this was an interference by a public authority under Article 10. However the ECtHR stated that the applicant's conviction was both relevant and sufficient and therefore the interference was proportionate to its legitimate aim so there was no violation of Article 10.

In the UK this can be seen through the mechanisms used by the government to ensure compliance of

legislation with the various Articles in ECHR. For example, the memorandum by the Home Office and Ministry of Justice with respect to the Serious Crime Bill (now the Serious Crime Act 2015) and the impact of ECHR states that:

● Serious Crime Prevention Orders may interfere with a person's rights under Articles 8, 10 and 11
● any order would be in pursuit of a legitimate aim, and necessary in a democratic society, in that the action that interfered with the right would meet a pressing social need and be proportionate to the legitimate aim relied on.

Tip

Legislation may have to reflect more than one Article of the ECHR. Look carefully at the question to make sure you respond to the appropriate Article.

22.3.4 For the protection of health or morals

There are areas of expression that no society or state is likely to allow. This might be incitement to murder or the sale of pornography to or involving children.

However, one difficulty is that different states have a different view of morals and obscenity. In *Müller v Switzerland* (1988) this was one of the main arguments.

Case study

Müller v Switzerland (1988)

This involved a claim that Article 10 had been infringed by the applicant's conviction of an offence of publishing obscene items, consisting of paintings which were said 'mostly to offend the sense of sexual propriety of persons of ordinary sensitivity'. The Court stressed the need to consider the principle of necessity for limitation in this context, and stated: 'The adjective "necessary" implies the existence of a "pressing social need".'

ECtHR recognised that standards of sexual morality do change, but it did not find the view of the Swiss courts to be unreasonable. Therefore, fining the exhibition organisers was not a violation of the right to freedom of expression.

The debate about abortion combines the issues of both health and morality. Article 10's application will reflect the prevailing views at the time of any complaint brought before the court as each case is based on the standards of the day rather than strict precedent. In *Open Door and Dublin Well Woman v Ireland* (1992) the views prevailing then were in issue.

Case study

Open Door and Dublin Well Woman v Ireland (1992)

The applicants were two non-profit organisations which provided information about pregnancy-related options. The Irish Supreme Court prohibited them from providing any information to pregnant women about abortion clinics in Great Britain. The ECtHR stated that this prohibition was a breach of Article 10.

This can also be seen with respect to the law relating to obscenity and outraging public morals, which appears to be largely within the scope of the framework of the ECHR.

Restrictions on human rights law – obscenity

Obscene publications are governed by the Obscene Publications Act 1959 and the Obscene Publications Act 1964. The 1959 Act sets out the legal test for obscenity. Section 1(1) of the Obscene Publications Act 1959 describes an 'obscene' item as one that has the effect of tending to deprave and corrupt persons likely to read, see or hear it. This statutory definition is largely based on the common law test of obscenity, as laid down in the case of *R v Hicklin* (1868), namely:

" whether the tendency of the matter charged as obscenity is to deprave and corrupt those whose minds are open to such immoral influences, and into whose hands a publication of this sort may fall. "

Famous cases in the UK include those of the books *Lady Chatterley's Lover* by D.H. Lawrence and *Last Exit to Brooklyn* by Hubert Selby Jr. The courts have defined 'deprave' as meaning to make morally bad, to debase, to pervert or to corrupt morally, and 'corrupt' as meaning to render morally unsound or rotten, to destroy moral purity or chastity, to pervert or ruin a good quality, and to debase or defile.

The Theatres Act 1968 applies a similar definition of obscenity to plays and performances. This is also extended to live broadcasts under the Broadcasting Act 1990.

There is also a possible lesser offence of outraging public decency. Public decency requires a level of behaviour which is generally accepted in public and is not obscene, disgusting or shocking for the observers. A recent example is the case of a man arrested after being spotted urinating on Manchester's city centre war memorial.

Galleries (and their staff, officers or directors) may be committing a criminal offence if, for example, they sell, show or distribute work that is considered to be obscene or which causes public outrage.

Extension question

In 2015 the Law Commission reported on 'Simplification of Criminal Law: Public Nuisance and Outraging Public Decency' (Law Com. No. 358). Find their main recommendations with respect to outraging public decency, and consider arguments for and against the proposals.

Case	Facts	Law
Guerra v Italy (1998)	The applicants lived about 1 km from a chemical factory and demanded a right to receive information.	The court held there is no positive obligation to collect and disseminate information.
Observer and Guardian v United Kingdom (1995)	The newspapers challenged injunctions preventing their publication of extracts of the *Spycatcher* book.	The ECtHR stated that the temporary injunctions were justified prior to the publication of the book but not thereafter.
R v Shayler (2002)	S had been a member of the security services and disclosed documents to journalists that related to security and intelligence matters.	S argued that the disclosures were in the public or national interest. This defence failed.
Surek v Turkey (1999)	The applicant was convicted of the offence of disseminating propaganda against the indivisibility of the state and provoking enmity and hatred among the people.	S argued that this was an interference by a public authority with his right to freedom of expression. No breach of Article 10 was found.
Müller v Switzerland (1988)	M was conviction of an offence of publishing obscene items, consisting of paintings.	Fining the exhibition organisers was not a violation of the right to freedom of expression.
Open Door and Dublin Well Woman v Ireland (1992)	The applicants were prohibited from providing any information to pregnant women about abortion clinics in Great Britain.	This prohibition was a breach of Article 10.

Figure 22.2 Key case chart for Article 10 – freedom to receive information and ideas (1)

22.3.5 For the protection of the reputation or rights of others

The case of *Bédat v Switzerland* (2016) is interesting as the Grand Chamber of the ECtHR had to balance the conflicting rights of the right to fair trial and presumption of innocence under Article 6 and the right to privacy in Article 8 on the one hand, and freedom of expression under Article 10 on the other hand.

Case study

Bédat v Switzerland (2016)

In 2003 the applicant published an article in *L'Illustré* dealing with criminal proceedings against a motorist who had crashed his car into passers-by on the Lausanne Bridge, resulting in three deaths and injuries to eight people. The article questioned the motorist's state of mind and included a personal description as well as photographs of letters sent by him to the investigating judge. Criminal proceedings were brought against the journalist by the public prosecutor for having published secret documents, in breach of the Swiss Criminal Code.

The Grand Chamber found no violation of Article 10 and found that the fine imposed on Mr Bédat was necessary in a democratic society. In doing so, the Grand Chamber took into account six criteria relating to the case. The Grand Chamber expanded its approach of balancing the competing interests of privacy protection of Articles 8 and 10 to the situation of conflict between the right to fair trial under Article 6 and freedom of expression.

Restrictions on human rights law – defamation

In the UK, the law of defamation sets out a position that is largely compatible with ECHR. Defamation comes in two forms, libel and slander. Libel is defamation in permanent form including broadcasting, slander in transient form – spoken, conduct or gestures. In defamation the words are taken to have their normal or natural meaning.

A claimant needs to show that the statement complained of:
● is defamatory, meaning that an ordinary person would think worse of the claimant as a result of the statement
● identifies or refers to him, and
● is published to a third party.

The Defamation Act 2013 requires claimants to show that the publication of the statement caused them, or is likely to cause them, serious harm. In the case of businesses, serious harm means caused them, or is likely to cause them, serious financial loss.

A claim for slander also requires proof of special damage. This means financial loss. There are two exceptions to this requirement:
● a statement that the claimant has committed a criminal offence punishable by imprisonment, such as 'X is a thief', or
● where the words are calculated to disparage the claimant in any office, profession, calling, trade or business carried on by them at the time of publication such as 'He [or she] is a doctor who is always amputating the wrong limb'.

Defences to a claim for defamation

There are a number of defences in English law with respect to defamation.
● Truth
  This is a statutory defence under s 2 of the Defamation Act 2013. It is a complete defence if the defendant can show that the imputation conveyed is substantially true.
● Honest opinion
  This is a statutory defence under s 3 of the Defamation Act 2013. It provides a defence if the statement complained of was one of opinion which could have been held by an honest person on the basis of any fact which existed at the time the statement was published. If a claimant can show that the defendant did not hold the opinion, the defence will fail.
● Publication on a matter of public interest
  This is set out in s 4 of the Defamation Act 2013. Here the defendant has to show that the statement complained of was, or formed part of, a statement on a matter of public interest, and a reasonable belief that publishing the statement complained of was in the public interest.

  What is in the public interest is potentially very wide. It is not just that it is considered newsworthy. Whether the defendant has a reasonable belief includes attempts made to verify the truth of what is being published, the nature of the sources of information and the extent to which the claimant was given an opportunity to respond or comment. You will often see an article in a newspaper that 'X declined to comment.'

- Internet defences
  There are also a number of defences available to internet intermediaries including innocent dissemination and a website operator's defence as well as defences under the E-Commerce Regulations 2002.
- Privilege – this comes in two forms, absolute and qualified
  Absolute privilege applies if there are clear public policy reasons for ensuring that there is a limit on the freedom of speech. Such situations include statements made in the course of judicial proceedings, parliamentary proceedings or papers, and contemporaneous reports of judicial proceedings.

  Qualified privilege covers the publication of any fair and accurate report or statement on a matter of public interest. This defence can be defeated if there is evidence that the publication was made with malice. Examples of statutory qualified privilege include fair and accurate reports of proceedings in public of Parliament or the courts, or courts or international organisations anywhere in the world, or at a UK public company general meeting, or reporting. This has been extended to cover peer-reviewed statements published in scientific or academic journals.

The Leveson Inquiry and the Crime and Courts Act 2013

The Leveson Inquiry was a judicial public inquiry into the culture, practices and ethics of the British press following the News International phone hacking scandal, chaired by Lord Justice Leveson. The inquiry published the Leveson Report in November 2012, which reviewed the general culture and ethics of the British media, and made recommendations for a new, independent, body to replace the existing Press Complaints Commission, which would have to be recognised by the state through new laws. These laws were set out in the Crime and Courts Act 2013, although much of the relevant sections of the Act have not yet been brought into force.

22.3.6 For preventing the disclosure of information received in confidence

In *Bédat v Switzerland* (2016) the court suggested that the journalist had not obtained the information by unlawful means. However, as a professional journalist he must have been aware of the confidential nature of the information.

In *Guja v Moldova* (2008) it was decided that the public interest in having the information about undue pressure and wrongdoing within public office was so important in a democratic society that it outweighed the interest in maintaining public confidence in that office.

ECtHR used this case to stress that open discussion of topics of public concern, such as the separation of state powers and the independence of investigating authorities, was essential to democracy and it was of great importance for civil servants and members of the public not to be discouraged from voicing their opinions on such matters.

In *Heinisch v Germany* (2011) the ECtHR considered the need to strike a fair balance between the need to protect the employer's reputation and rights on the one hand and the need to protect the right to freedom of expression of the whistleblower on the other. Here the failure of the domestic courts to order the whistleblower's reinstatement (she had been dismissed following her whistleblowing) had violated her rights under Article 10.

In the UK, the Public Interest Disclosure Act 1998 protects workers who disclose information about malpractice at their workplace provided certain conditions are met. The conditions concern the nature of the information disclosed and the person to whom it is disclosed. If these conditions are met, the Act protects the worker who made the disclosure.

However, the English courts tried to limit this right to employees and the public as opposed to members of the firm. It was not until the case reached the Supreme Court in *Clyde & Co. LLP v van Winklehof* (2014) that a member of a limited liability partnership firm of solicitors was able to be within the definition of a worker and so protected.

22.3.7 For maintaining the authority and impartiality of the judiciary

There are usually restrictions on the press disclosing details in advance of a trial so that the case can proceed fairly, without those involved being swayed by the views in the media. There are usually restrictions on recordings and photography in court, punishable as a criminal offence. This is usually less of a problem in the UK than in some other states, but the idea can be seen in the case of *Sunday Times v United Kingdom* (1979). The government justified injunctions against publication of a newspaper article on the basis of this limitation.

Sunday Times v United Kingdom (1979)

The use of the prescribed drug thalidomide resulted in side effects where many children were born with severe malformations. In the UK the drug was produced and sold by Distillers Company Ltd, which withdrew it from the market in 1961. Parents sued the company and negotiations continued for many years. Settlements had to be approved by the courts. This was covered by the press in great detail.

In 1971 the parties started negotiations to set up a charity fund for the children with malformations. In September 1972 the *Sunday Times* published an article entitled 'Our Thalidomide Children: A Cause for National Shame', criticising the company for the financial payments the company was to pay. The *Sunday Times* also announced that it would run a detailed analysis of the circumstances of the tragedy in future editions of the paper.

The Attorney-General asked the Court to grant an injunction against the newspaper as the publication of the announced article would obstruct justice. The *Sunday Times* claimed a violation of Article 10. Since thalidomide cases were still pending before the courts, the Attorney-General claimed that there was no violation of Article 10.

The ECtHR stated that the thalidomide disaster was a matter of public concern. The families involved in the tragedy as well as the public at large had the right to be informed on all the facts of this matter. The Court concluded that the injunction ordered against the newspaper 'did not correspond to a social need sufficiently pressing to outweigh the public interest in freedom of expression within the meaning of the Convention'.

While the *Sunday Times* case was not critical of the judiciary, recent criticisms of the judiciary with respect to the challenge to the UK's handling of the referendum on leaving the EU and Article 50 have led to lively debate.

Look online

Read newspaper articles such as www.theguardian.com/politics/2016/nov/04/enemies-of-the-people-british-newspapers-react-judges-brexit-ruling. List arguments stating whether or not these pieces violate Article 10.

The ECtHR has considered 'maintaining the authority and impartiality of the judiciary' in the case of *Pinto Coelho v Portugal (No. 2)* (2016).

Case study

Pinto Coelho v Portugal (No. 2) (2016)

Ms Pinto Coelho is a journalist and crime reporter for a Portuguese television channel. On 12 November 2005 the news programme on the channel broadcast a report prepared by her about the criminal conviction of an 18-year-old man for aggravated theft of a mobile phone. The programme claimed that the young man was innocent and that the judges had made a mistake. She included in her report shots of the courtroom, extracts of sub-titled sound recordings and the questioning of prosecution and defence witnesses, in which their voices and those of the three judges were digitally altered.

She was fined for broadcasting unauthorised audio recordings of a criminal trial. The ECtHR said that her rights under Article 10 had been breached. The sound recordings were from the official tape recording of the proceedings which was available to the parties, but their use in a broadcast had not been authorised. The Court balanced the rights of the media to report on a matter of public interest with the interests of the participants, witnesses and judiciary and the necessity in a democratic society to impose restrictions on the use of recordings.

There may be a further appeal in this case.

Case	Facts	Law
Bédat v Switzerland (2016)	In 2003 the applicant was fined for publishing an article questioning an accused motorist's state of mind and included a personal description as well as photographs of letters sent by him to the investigating judge.	No violation of Article 10 and the Court found that the fine imposed on Mr Bédat was necessary in a democratic society.
Sunday Times v United Kingdom (1979)	The Attorney-General asked the Court to grant an injunction against the *Sunday Times* as the publication of the article on thalidomide victims would obstruct justice. The *Sunday Times* claimed a violation of Article 10.	This was a matter of public concern. The injunction was not granted.
Pinto Coelho v Portugal (No. 2) (2016)	The applicant was fined for broadcasting unauthorised audio recordings of a criminal trial.	The Court balanced the rights of the media to report on a matter of public interest with the interests of the participants. It found a breach of Article 10.

Figure 22.3 Key case chart for Article 10 – freedom to receive information and ideas (2)

22.3.8 Article 10 and the internet

Technology has progressed significantly since the ECHR was conceived. *Editorial Board of Parvoye Delo and Shtekel v Ukraine* (2011) deals with the internet aspects of Article 10.

Case study

Editorial Board of Parvoye Delo and Shtekel v Ukraine (2011)

Ukrainian legislation exempts journalists from civil responsibility for referencing materials that have already been published by another press outlet. However, the local courts held that the exemption does not apply to material obtained from publications that are not registered with the Ukrainian authorities. However, Ukrainian law does not regulate registration of internet media. *Pravoye Delo*, a Ukrainian newspaper, published an anonymous letter posted on an internet site that accused senior local officials of involvement in various criminal activities.

The ECHR stated that since Ukrainian domestic law was not clear on the use of information received from the internet, the applicants could not have foreseen that the exemption did not apply. Therefore, the Ukrainian ruling failed to meet the Article 10 requirement that any limitation of freedom of expression should be based on a clear, accessible and reasonably foreseeable law.

In *Yildirim v Turkey* (2013) the ECtHR unanimously held that the blanket blocking of access to sites.google.com breached the right to freedom of expression. In *Delfi AS v Estonia* (2015) the Grand Chamber commented:

> While the Court acknowledges that important benefits can be derived from the Internet in the exercise of freedom of expression, it is also mindful that liability for defamatory or other types of unlawful speech must, in principle, be retained and constitute an effective remedy for violations of personality rights.

Activity

Research the following cases (and similar ones you can find). Consider the arguments for and against the merits of the decisions with respect to Article 10 and any other Articles you have studied.

- *Delfi AS v Estonia* (2015)
- *Ashby Donald v France* (2013)

Case	Facts	Law
Editorial Board of Parvoye Delo and Shtekel v Ukraine (2011)	*Pravoye Delo*, a Ukrainian newspaper, published an anonymous letter posted on an internet site that accused senior local officials of involvement in various criminal activities.	The Ukrainian ruling failed to meet the Article 10 requirement that any limitation of freedom of expression should be based on a clear, accessible and reasonably foreseeable law.
Yildirim v Turkey (2013)	The state had ordered blanket blocking of access to sites.google.com.	This breached the right to freedom of expression.

Figure 22.4 Key case chart for Article 10 and the internet

22.4 Evaluation of Article 10

22.4.1 A qualified right

As Article 10 is a wide-ranging qualified right, there are many instances of an interference with the right. As with Article 8, the court then has to decide whether the interference is justified by the state using the principles of proportionality and margin of appreciation.

It should be noted that there is an explicit limitation on expression with the ability of the state to impose licensing conditions on broadcasting. Apart from this, there is a distinction between different forms of expression. For some forms of expression, sometimes referred to as low value forms of expression such as artistic expression, it is easy for the state to restrict it. This allows restrictions on the grounds of morality or public decency that reflect society. High value expression, such as political or religious expression and matters of public interest, is much more difficult for the state to restrict. We can therefore expect to see some form of consistency that reflects the evolving nature of society. However, the conclusion to be drawn from the cases may not be quite what one expect to be the logical conclusion. If we take the case of *Steel and Morris v UK* (2005) (the McLibel case), the logical conclusion would be that legal aid would be available in all libel cases to protect freedom of expression. However, this is not the case as other libel cases may not be considered to be so much in the public interest.

22.4.2 The scope and values of free speech

Freedom of expression is essential in a democracy. This is not just in relation to political arguments but also to artistic matters that are designed to offend or shock, which may or may not have a political purpose. There is however an apparent inconsistency of approach as can be seen in the cases of *Otto Preminger Institut v Austria* (1994) where there was no violation as the ban was justified as the state had a wide margin of appreciation and *Vereinigung Bildender Künstler v Austria* (2008) where an injunction prohibiting exhibition of a painting showing public persons in sexual positions was a violation of Article 10 even though the individual person depicted in part of the painting had complained the painting debased him.

It can be seen from *Garaudy v France* (2003) that 'hate speech' falls outside Article 10 because of Article 17 ECHR which provides that no one may use the rights guaranteed by ECHR to seek the abolition or limitation of other rights guaranteed in the Convention, but if the expression is 'incitement to racial hatred' it can be argued under Article 10 and the state may be able to justify a restriction. This does not seem to be an obvious distinction to try to make and could well lead to injustice. It remains unclear what amounts to hate speech and what amounts to incitement to racial hatred.

22.4.3 Press freedom and free speech

The right of the press to report on matters of public interest and the protections from the law of defamation in the UK gives rise to much debate about the behaviour and role of the press. Recent headlines about the judiciary, about rebel Conservative MPs and historically about the Liverpool football supporters present at the Hillsborough disaster have been in the news recently. Such instances show that there needs to be a balance between public interest, opinions of one or other sector of the press, and the privacy and protection of the individual. Subsequent threats and trolling of those mentioned in reports need to be contained by action by the state to balance the interests of those involved with freedom of expression. The plethora of legislation and protection available is no help when someone is killed or injured.

The behaviour of the press as revealed in the phone hacking scandal in the Leveson Inquiry on the ethics and practices of the press demonstrate that there still needs to be a great deal of regulation of public bodies – not just the press but also the police. Six years after Leveson, there is still not a truly independent way of dealing with complaints about the press.

22.4.4 Article 10 and technology

Quite rightly, human rights law deals with cases on an evolutionary basis. As ever, the difficulty is that technology moves on and the law lags behind. Cyber-crime, discussed in chapter 16, shows the difficulty with controlling, for example, child pornography which would not be considered acceptable within Article 10. However, the ability to access images and writings that are considered a valid freedom of expression in some states, is not considered acceptable in other states. This inconsistency of approach leads to the conclusion that states cannot control the internet and its content even if, perhaps, they should. Most people condemn the restrictions on access to the internet imposed in some states such as China; yet we still see ECtHR cases such as *Yildrim v Turkey* (2013). Should access to the internet be a universal human right, or should it be restricted as, allegedly, President Trump wishes to do, so that there is a two-tier system?

Summary

- Article 10 covers freedom of expression in all its forms.
- Whether a restriction on the right contained within Article 10 can be justified depends on whether it comes within the terms of Article 10(2). The *Sunday Times* case explained that the test is as follows:
  - Is the restriction prescribed by law?
  - Does it have a legitimate aim?
  - Is it necessary in a democratic society?
  - Is it within the margin of appreciation?
- The list of the possible grounds for restricting the freedom of expression is exhaustive; this means no other ground may be relied on.
- There are three components of the right to freedom of expression:
  - freedom to hold opinions
  - freedom to impart information and ideas
  - freedom to receive information and ideas.
- The case of *Axel Springer AG v Germany* (2012) set out criteria to be used in balancing Articles 10 and 8.
- There is a wide margin of appreciation to reflect different cultures and values in different states, as to what is acceptable with respect to artistic expression.
- Incitement to racial hatred can be dealt with under Article 10.
- The freedom to receive information includes the right to gather information and to seek information through all possible lawful sources.
- The interference by a state is aimed at protecting one or more of the following legitimate aims:
  - in the interests of national security
  - with respect to territorial integrity or public safety
  - for the prevention of disorder or crime
  - for the protection of health or morals
  - for the protection of the reputation or rights of others
  - for preventing the disclosure of information received in confidence
  - for maintaining the authority and impartiality of the judiciary.

Chapter 23

Article 11: the right to freedom of assembly and association

After reading this chapter you should be able to:
- Understand the scope of Article 11(1) ECHR
- Understand the restrictions permitted by Article 11(2)
- Understand the explanations of Article 11 in the ECtHR
- Understand the ways in which English law has applied Article 11
- Critically evaluate the operation of Article 11 in English law
- Apply the law to given situations

23.1 Article 11 ECHR

" 1 Everyone has the right to freedom of peaceful assembly and to freedom of association with others, including the right to form and to join trade unions for the protection of his interests.

2 No restrictions shall be placed on the exercise of these rights other than such as are prescribed by law and are necessary in a democratic society in the interests of national security or public safety, for the prevention of disorder or crime, for the protection of health or morals or for the protection of the rights and freedoms of others. This Article shall not prevent the imposition of lawful restrictions on the exercise of these rights by members of the armed forces, or the police, or of the administration of the State. "

There are three rights under Article 11(1):
- freedom of peaceful assembly
- freedom of association with others
- the right to form and to join trade unions for the protection of his interests.

These are qualified rights. The limitations are set out in Article 11(2):
- prescribed by law
- necessary in a democratic society

- for a legitimate aim:
  - in the interests of national security or public safety
  - for the prevention of disorder or crime
  - for the protection of health or morals
  - for the protection of the rights and freedoms of others.

The right must fulfil the criterion of proportionality. This involves looking at the following questions:
- Is the limitation effective?
- Is it the least intrusive measure possible?
- Does it deprive the very essence of the right?
- Is it balanced between the competing interests as a whole?

As with other Articles, the margin of appreciation will vary from case to case. However the Council of Europe has expressed concerns about developments in some states during 2015 such as:
- in Turkey, with the adoption in March 2015 of the Security Bill which extends the powers of the police to use firearms
- in Spain, with the adoption in March 2015 of the law on citizen's security, which allows heavy fines against organisers of spontaneous protests
- in the Russian Federation, with an amendment to the law on public gatherings which permits the detention of any person participating in an unauthorised public assembly.

23.2 The rights under Article 11(1)

Article 11, as interpreted by the courts, has two closely related rights:

- the right not to be prevented or restricted by the state from meeting and associating with others to pursue particular aims, except to the extent allowed by Article 11(2) – a negative obligation
- the duty on the state to take positive measures, even in the sphere of relations between individuals, to ensure that the rights provided are secured – a positive obligation.

Freedom of assembly is not a mere duty on the part of the state not to interfere. Where individuals or businesses act in a way that undermines Article 11 rights, the state may be required to intervene to secure the protection of those rights.

Tip

Keep in mind that Article 11 has both a positive and a negative obligation.

23.2.1 Freedom of peaceful assembly

This applies to static meetings, marches, public processions and demonstrations. The right must be exercised peacefully, without violence or the threat of violence, and in accordance with the law. Freedom of peaceful assembly under Article 11 is broadly interpreted to include the organisation of, and participation in, marches or processions, static assemblies or sit-ins and both public and private events, whether formal or informal. Article 11 will cover any gathering for a common economic or political purpose, but it is unlikely to be applicable to gatherings that are purely social or are sporting in character. This seems to indicate that a football match or an unauthorised music festival will not be covered.

Key term

Peaceful assembly – in human rights under Article 11 a person is allowed to meet in public, march, process and demonstrate without state interference.

A totally peaceful assembly can still be disbanded without a violation of Article 11, as can be seen from the case of *Cisse v France* (2002).

Case study

Cisse v France (2002)

The applicant was a member of a group of people without residence permits who in 1996 decided to take collective action to draw attention to the difficulties they were having in obtaining a review of their immigration status in France. A group of some 200 illegal immigrants occupied a church as a protest about their plight. The Paris Commissioner of Police signed an order for the total evacuation of the church on the grounds that the occupation of the premises was unrelated to religious worship, and there were serious sanitary, health, peace, security and public order risks.

The assembly was peaceful and did not cause any disturbance of public order or prevent churchgoers from attending services. However, after two months of continued occupation of the church, the hunger-strikers' health had deteriorated and sanitary conditions had become wholly inadequate. There was no breach of Article 11.

Assemblies may be peaceful even though they may lead to counter demonstrations. The case of *Plattform 'Ärzte für das Leben' v Austria* (1988) shows that a peaceful demonstration may annoy or give offence to persons opposed to the ideas or claims that the demonstration is seeking to promote.

Case study

Plattform 'Ärzte für das Leben' v Austria (1988)

Plattform 'Ärzte für das Leben' was an association of doctors campaigning against abortion, which organised a religious service and a march to the surgery of a doctor who carried out abortions. The ECtHR stated that a demonstration may annoy or give offence to persons opposed to the ideas or claims that it is seeking to promote. The participants must, however, be able to hold the demonstration without fear of physical violence by their opponents. Fear might deter associations or other groups supporting common ideas or interests from openly expressing their opinions on highly controversial issues affecting the community. While there is a right to counter-demonstrate, sometimes the state must interfere to protect its citizens and maintain order.

Tip

When looking at problem questions, remember that as with Article 10, Article 11 sometimes requires positive measures to be taken.

However, where the assembly is designed to cause disorder, this would not be within Article 11. *G v Federal Republic of Germany* (1989) concerned an illegal demonstration in front of US military barracks in support of nuclear disarmament. Here, demonstrators blocked the road for 12 minutes every hour, but the sit-in still fell within the accepted definition of a 'peaceful assembly'.

In the UK, the position can be seen in the case of *DPP v Jones (Margaret)* (1999).

Case study

DPP v Jones (Margaret) (1999)

There was a peaceful protest on the main road next to the perimeter fence at Stonehenge. Some protesters carried banners saying things such as 'Stonehenge Campaign 10 years of Criminal Injustice'. The officer in charge concluded that they constituted a 'trespassory assembly' and told them so. When asked to move off, some people were determined to remain and were convicted. On appeal, the appeal was allowed. A peaceful assembly on the highway, which did not unreasonably interfere with or obstruct the highway, was not a trespassory assembly. The existence of a public right of way entitled the public to have the right of public assembly so long as such assembly does not unreasonably obstruct the highway.

There is an increasing recognition that some tolerance of demonstrations that may shock, annoy or distress others is an integral part of ensuring that these rights are properly protected. This was the view taken in *Faber v Hungary* (2012) where restriction on the display of flags during a demonstration was a breach of Article 10.

Tip

Note the clear link between Articles 10 and 11 in *Faber v Hungary* (2012).

Where the assembly takes place on private land, the owner of that land is able to prohibit the assembly, providing this does not prevent lawful protest taking place in a suitable alternative place or method. This can be seen in *Appleby v United Kingdom* (2003).

Case study

Appleby v United Kingdom (2003)

The claimants wanted to demonstrate against a development in their town. The shopping mall, which dominated the town centre, had been built by public funds but sold to a private company. The company refused to allow the claimants to demonstrate in the mall or to distribute protesting leaflets. The claimants complained of interference with their rights to free speech and expression.

Shopping centres, though primarily for private commercial interests, increasingly serve as gathering places and events centres. Despite the importance of freedom of expression, Article 11 does not grant any freedom as to where an individual may exercise that right. Therefore, no violation had occurred.

All demonstrations affect others who are not part of it. The authorities must bear that in mind and make a decision that results in any restriction being proportionate. No permissions would ever be granted if any effect of the demonstration on others would always be enough to deny permission.

23.2.2 Freedom of association with others

Freedom of association is the right to come together with others to form an association. This includes the right to form and join trade unions, and to join with others to pursue or advance common causes and interests. Equally, it is the right not to belong to an association. This was stated in *Young, James and Webster v United Kingdom* (1981) where the ECtHR stated:

> Article 11 guarantees not only freedom of association, including the right to form and to join trade unions, in the positive sense, but also, by implication, a 'negative right' not to be compelled to join an association or a union.

Key term

Freedom of association – in human rights under Article 11 ECHR it is the right for a person not to be prevented or restricted by the state from meeting and joining with others to follow a particular aim.

Case	Facts	Law
Cisse v France (2002)	The applicant was a member of a group of people without residence permits who in 1996 decided to take collective action to draw attention to the difficulties they were having in obtaining a review of their immigration status in France.	In the circumstances there was no violation of Article 11. The restrictions on the exercise of the applicant's right to assembly may have become necessary.
Plattform 'Ärzte für das Leben' v Austria (1988)	Plattform 'Ärzte für das Leben' held two demonstrations which were disrupted by counter-demonstrators despite the presence of a large contingent of police.	A demonstration may annoy or give offence to persons opposed to the ideas or claims that it is seeking to promote, but sometimes the state must interfere.
DPP v Jones (Margaret) (1999)	21 people protested peacefully on the verge of the A344, next to the perimeter fence at Stonehenge. The officer in charge concluded that they constituted a 'trespassory assembly'.	A peaceful assembly on the highway, which did not unreasonably interfere with or obstruct the highway, was not a trespassory assembly.
Appleby v United Kingdom (2003)	The claimants wanted to demonstrate against a development in their home town of Washington.	Where the assembly takes place on private land, the owner of that land is able to prohibit the assembly, providing this does not prevent lawful protest taking place in a suitable alternative place or method.

Figure 23.1 Key cases for Article 11 – peaceable assembly

G20 protest march in London, 2009

The meaning of association is not defined as is the case in many states. It is not just spending time in other people's company. This can be seen in *McFeeley v United Kingdom* (1981).

Case study

McFeeley v United Kingdom (1981)

The claimants had been convicted of offences relating to anti-terrorist legislation in Northern Ireland and were serving prisoners in the Maze prison. There was a change of regime imposed in 1976, resulting in them not being permitted association with the rest of the prison community. This and other matters was decided on the basis of Article 3; Article 11 did not apply to association in this sense.

Similarly, association does not include professional regulatory bodies set up by the state to regulate professions as in *Le Compte, Van Leuven and De Meyere v Belgium* (1981), a case involving doctors and their regulatory body.

Political parties have been found to be an association as in *Redfearn v United Kingdom* (2012).

Case study

Redfearn v United Kingdom (2012)

The appellant was a bus driver driving children and adults with physical and mental disabilities. He worked in and around Bradford and most of his passengers were of Asian origin. He was summarily dismissed, after nearly seven months' employment, following his election to the local council representing the British National Party. Concerns were voiced by unions that their members could be at risk of harm or abuse. However, there were no allegations against him and he had been nominated as a 'first class employee' by his line manager, who was of Asian origin.

In the ECtHR, he successfully argued that for an employee to lose his job for exercising his right to freedom of association 'struck at the "very substance" of that right', and that the government had a positive obligation under Article 11 to enact legislation that would protect that right even though he could not claim for unfair dismissal.

Case	Facts	Law
McFeeley v United Kingdom (1981)	The claimants had been convicted of offences relating to anti-terrorist legislation, and after a change of regime imposed in 1976, they were not permitted association with the rest of the prison community.	The meaning of association is not defined, as is the case in many states. It is not just spending time in other people's company.
Redfearn v United Kingdom (2012)	The appellant was a bus driver and elected local councillor representing the British National Party. He was summarily dismissed after this election.	While association does not include professional regulatory bodies set up by the state to regulate professions, it does include political parties so there was a violation of Article 11.

Figure 23.2 Key cases for Article 11 – freedom of association with others

23.2.3 The right to form and to join trade unions for the protection of his interests

Trade unions are specifically recognised as associations, as is the right to form and join one. The state can restrict the right if the restriction can be justified. This might be the restriction on secondary picketing and the right of a trade union to expel members.

23.3 Restrictions set out in Article 11(2)

As this Article contains a qualified right, any interference depends on the conditions set out below.

23.3.1 'Prescribed by law'

This means there must be a clear, precise and predictable legal basis for the interference with Article 11. In the UK there are a number of restrictions. These restrictions come from both the common law and statute.

Common law restrictions

These include:
- a breach of the peace, and
- the law on trespass to land.

Breach of the peace

Breach of the peace is used to prevent unlawful violence against people or property. 'Peace' in this context refers to the Queen's peace. 'Peace' also occurs in the definition of the crime of murder. Peace is the opposite of war. The definition of breach of the peace can be found in *R v Howell* (1981):

'there is a breach of the peace whenever harm is actually done or is likely to be done to a person or in his presence to his property or a person is in fear of being so harmed through an assault, an affray, a riot, unlawful assembly or other disturbance.'

Key term 🔑

Breach of the peace – a criminal offence committed when it is alleged that harm has been done, or is likely to be done, to a person or to property or when a person fears harm by an assault, affray, riot, unlawful assembly or some other disturbance.

The wide powers available to stop or prevent a breach mean that any use of the powers is closely examined by the courts to ensure that there has been no undue interference with respect for human rights. Examples of this can be seen with respect to kettling tactics by the police in *McClure and Moos v Commissioner of Police of the Metropolis* (2012) and *Austin v Commissioner of Police of the Metropolis* (2012).

See Chapter 19, section 19.2.4 on crowd control.

Look online

Read the material at http://criminology.leeds. ac.uk/2013/09/05/kettling-protests-and-the-limits-of-the-european-convention-on-human-rights/.

How does this help to explain the relationship between Articles 5, 10 and 11? Summarise the arguments made in the material you have read.

Trespass to land

Trespass to land is a tort and so the remedies would be damages or an injunction to stop the trespass. It is not a criminal offence unless some special statutory provision makes it so. Any damage done by a trespasser while trespassing may amount to the offence of criminal damage.

Trespass to land consists of any unjustifiable intrusion by a person upon the land in possession of another. It is actionable in the courts, whether or not the claimant has suffered any damage. This rule may seem harsh but in modern practice, an action will not normally be brought for trespass without damage unless the claimant wishes to deter persistent trespassing or there are disputes over boundaries or rights of way.

However, technically the slightest crossing of the claimant's boundary is sufficient to result in a trespass. In the case of *Ellis v Loftus Iron Co.* (1874) the court stated:

> if the defendant place[s] a part of his foot on the claimant's land unlawfully, it is in law as much a trespass as if he had walked half a mile on it.

This principle was used to evict travellers parked on land belong to others, typically the owners of woodland as in the case of *Drury v Secretary of State for Environment, Food and Rural Affairs* (2004) and those involved in sit-ins such as that at Essex University in *University of Essex v Djemal* (1980). These cases had mixed results for the landowners and so the criminal law was strengthened, as will be seen later in this chapter.

Examples of civil trespass include removing any part of the land in the possession of another, or any part of a building or other erection attached to the soil. It can also be a trespass to place something on, or in, land in the possession of another – such as dumping rubbish.

There are a number of legal justifications to trespass, including:
- licence to enter by law
- justification by right of way or easement (the use of someone else's property or land for a stated reason such as permitting the underground services of one property (such as drains) to pass beneath the land of a neighbouring property)
- justification by licence or necessity
- various powers of entry granted to officers of the law, such as the police.

Statutory restrictions

Removing trespassers from land

Section 61 of the Criminal Justice and Public Order Act (CJPOA) 1994 applies to trespassers who are on the land of another with the common purpose of remaining there. This section enables a police officer to direct trespassers on the land to leave the land where the occupier has already taken steps to ask them to do so, and either:
- they have damaged the land
- they have used threatening, abusive or insulting behaviour to the occupier, the occupier's family, employees or agents, or
- between them they have six or more vehicles on the land.

Failure to obey a direction to leave or returning to the land as a trespasser within three months is an offence. This deals with the problems occurring in *Drury v Secretary of State for Environment, Food and Rural Affairs* (2004) and *University of Essex v Djemal* (1980).

Section 62 provides a power for the police to seize vehicles of persons failing to comply with a direction under s 61.

Raves

A rave is defined as a gathering on land in the open air of 20 or more persons at which amplified music is played during the night and, by reason of its loudness and duration and the time at which it is played, is likely to cause serious distress to the inhabitants of the locality.

Section 63 CJPOA 1994 provides the police with powers to direct persons (other than exempt persons such as the occupier of the land and their family or assistants) gathering on land for a rave to leave. Failure to comply with a direction, or returning to the site within seven days are offences.

Aggravated trespass

Section 68(1) CJPOA 1994 as amended states that a person commits the offence of aggravated trespass if he or she trespasses on land and, in relation to any lawful activity which persons are engaging in or are about to engage in on that or adjoining land, does anything there which is intended by him or her to have the effect of:
- intimidating those persons or any of them so as to deter them or any of them from engaging in that activity
- obstructing that activity
- disrupting that activity.

Following the case of *DPP v Chivers* (2010), the word 'land' includes a building.

Case study

DPP v Chivers (2010)

Daniel Chivers locked himself to a stair railing using a D-lock round his neck, Ian Fitzpatrick occupied a stairwell and Carl Von Tonda glued himself to the front door of the building.

The court decided that land includes a building so all three had been correctly charged with aggravated trespass.

The s 68 offence is capable of being committed by hunt saboteurs or motorway protesters or any protesters who are trespassing on land, but it is not formally limited to protest groups. It was used with respect to the UK Uncut protest in Fortnum & Mason.

In the news

Why the Fortnum & Mason protesters' case matters

If 300 football fans chant together and then one assaults a rival supporter, are they all responsible? If you're on a protest and someone commits a crime and you don't leave immediately, can you be held to account for the person's actions? That was the question put before Westminster Magistrates' Court as we, the first ten defendants in the trials of those arrested for staging a sit-in at Fortnum & Mason on 26 March 2011, faced our verdict. We were found guilty of aggravated trespass; nine of us were given a conditional discharge and ordered to pay costs of £1,000 each, while the tenth was also fined.

The prosecution was required to prove an act beyond ordinary trespass — which on its own is not a crime. In this case, it argued that the protesters demonstrated intent to intimidate. Michael Snow, the district judge, accepted in his sentencing that none of us had been personally intimidating towards staff and shoppers, but said that under the terms of 'joint enterprise' we were responsible for the actions of other protesters.

...

There is some evidence that a small number of acts inside the store may have been intimidating. There is no evidence that any of us on trial was responsible for these. .... But the prosecution maintained that we were guilty because we didn't leave when the intimidating acts allegedly took place. We will find out if the high court agrees when we take the case to appeal.

Source: Blog by Adam Ramsay in the *New Statesman* online, 17 November 2011

In *Edward Bauer v DPP* (2013) the appellants appealed a decision of a District Judge convicting them of aggravated trespass following occupation of the Fortnum and Mason's store by demonstrators in protest against tax avoidance. The court upheld the conviction as the demonstration was an additional act distinct from the trespass and it could be inferred that by demonstrating they intended to intimidate.

This additional conduct can be anything. There is no requirement that the additional conduct should itself be a crime, so activities such as playing a musical instrument or taking a photograph would suffice. What limits the scope of anything is the intention that must accompany it: the intention to obstruct, disrupt or deter by intimidating.

Ramblers, for instance, may trespass and may disrupt a lawful activity such as rounding up sheep by doing so, but unless they have the intention to obstruct, disrupt or deter they do not commit the offence of aggravated trespass.

Trespassory assemblies

Section 70 CJPOA 1994 amends the Public Order Act 1986 by inserting two new sections, 14A and 14B, in respect of trespassory assemblies.

A chief officer of police who reasonably believes:
- that an assembly will be held on land (being land to which the public has no or only a limited right of access),
- that the assembly is likely to take place without the permission of the occupier,
- that it may result in serious disruption to the life of the community or damage a site of historical archaeological or scientific importance,

may apply for an order prohibiting the holding of all trespassory assemblies for a period of not more than four days. To organise a prohibited assembly, to take part in one and to incite others to take part in one are all offences.

It is also an offence to fail to comply with a direction not to proceed to a trespassory assembly.

Squatting

Section 144 of the Legal Aid, Sentencing and Punishment of Offenders Act 2012 creates a specific offence of squatting in a residential building.

In order to prove the offence, it must be shown that the defendant:
- is in a residential building as a trespasser having entered as a trespasser
- knows or ought to know that s/he is a trespasser, and
- is living in the building or intends to live there for any period.

To be a 'residential' building, it must be designed or adapted before the time of entry for use as a place in which to live. A person can only commit the offence if he or she has entered and remains in the residential building as a trespasser. So the offence will not apply to a person who entered the building with permission of the property owner, such as a tenant or a workman. This is so even if a tenant subsequently falls behind with rent payments or decides to withhold rent as in a rent strike.

The person must know or ought to know that he or she is a trespasser. The offence will not apply to someone who reasonably believes he or she has permission to enter the property in good faith.

The offence also requires that the trespasser 'is living' or 'intends to live' in the building for any period. A person who enters the front porch of someone's home to deliver junk mail is not liable to be convicted of this offence, even where there is a notice on the gate stating 'no junk mail'.

Using violence to enter premises (squatting)

Sections 6 and 7 of the Criminal Law Act 1977 set out offences relating to entering property without lawful authority and remaining there:

- Section 6 makes it an offence to use or threaten violence to secure entry into premises knowing that there is someone present who is opposed to the entry which the violence is intended to secure. This section does not apply to a person trying to get rid of a trespasser from his property.
- Section 7 makes it an offence for any person on premises as a trespasser to fail to leave those premises on being asked to do so by, or on behalf of, a displaced residential occupier or an individual who is a protected intending occupier.

Damage by trespassers

Any damage done by a trespasser while trespassing may amount to the offence of criminal damage. The elements of that offence are set out in the Criminal Damage Act 1971.

Another possibility to curb persistent trespass by particular children may be the use of anti-social behaviour orders (ASBOs).

The Public Order Act 1986

The Public Order Act 1986 sets out various offences which can occur where there are demonstrations or protests. The Act replaces and largely replicates existing common law offences. Other offences include obstructing the highway under the Highways Act 1980 and aggravated trespass under CJPOA 1994.

This means that when Article 11 is considered, the state may have to show that the offence was committed and that the offence is a proportionate response to a legitimate aim.

Riot

Riot comes under s 1 of the Public Order Act 1986. Riot is defined as:

> Where 12 or more persons who are present together use or threaten unlawful violence for a common purpose and the conduct of them (taken together) is such as would cause a person of reasonable firmness present at the scene to fear for his personal safety, each of the persons using unlawful violence for the common purpose is guilty of riot.

Violent disorder

Under s 2 of the Public Order Act 1986, the offence of violent disorder is defined as:

> Where 3 or more persons who are present together use or threaten unlawful violence and the conduct of them (taken together) is such as would cause a person of reasonable firmness present at the scene to fear for his personal safety, each of the persons using or threatening unlawful violence is guilty of violent disorder.

This is therefore the same as riot but with fewer people involved.

Affray

Under s 3 of the Public Order Act 1986, affray is defined as follows:

> A person is guilty of affray if he uses or threatens unlawful violence towards another and his conduct is such as would cause a person of reasonable firmness present at the scene to fear for his personal safety.

Tip

When looking at a problem, look for information as to how many people are involved so as to decide between riot, violent disorder and affray.

Causing fear or provocation of violence

Under s 4 of the Public Order Act 1986, the offence of causing fear or provocation of violence is defined as:

> if, with intent to cause a person harassment, alarm or distress, he (a) uses threatening, abusive or insulting words or behaviour, or (b) displays any writing, sign or other visible representation which is threatening, abusive or insulting, with intent to cause that person to believe that immediate unlawful violence will be used against him or another by any person, or to provoke the immediate use of unlawful violence by that person or another, or whereby that person is likely to believe that such violence will be used or it is likely that such violence will be provoked.

Causing intentional harassment, alarm or distress

Under s 4A of the Public Order Act 1986 the offence of causing intentional harassment, alarm or distress is defined as:

> A person is guilty of an offence if, with intent to cause a person harassment, alarm or distress, he—
>
> a uses threatening or abusive words or behaviour, or disorderly behaviour, or
>
> b displays any writing, sign or other visible representation which is threatening, abusive or insulting, thereby causing that or another person harassment, alarm or distress.

There is a defence if the accused can prove:
- that s/he was inside a dwelling and had no reason to believe that the words or behaviour used, or the writing, sign or other visible representation displayed, would be heard or seen by a person outside that or any other dwelling, or
- that his/her conduct was reasonable.

Harassment, alarm or distress

Under s 5 of the Public Order Act 1986 the offence of causing harassment, alarm or distress is defined as:

> A person is guilty of an offence if he—
>
> a uses threatening or abusive words or behaviour, or disorderly behaviour, or
>
> b displays any writing, sign or other visible representation which is threatening or abusive, within the hearing or sight of a person likely to be caused harassment, alarm or distress thereby.

There is a defence if the accused can prove:
- that s/he had no reason to believe that there was any person within hearing or sight who was likely to be caused harassment, alarm or distress,
- that s/he was inside a dwelling and had no reason to believe that the words or behaviour used, or the writing, sign or other visible representation displayed, would be heard or seen by a person outside that or any other dwelling, or
- that his/her conduct was reasonable.

This makes it clear that there are many options under UK law to control public order and also restrict the right to freedom of assembly. The situation is difficult for the police who have provided a flow chart for guidance.

Look online

Read through this document to see how the police are trained to respond to protests: http://library.college.police.uk/docs/APPref/police-response-to-protest.pdf.

Outline the key aspects of the training and write down arguments for and against the view that the training needs to be modified to comply with the ECHR.

23.3.2 'Necessary in a democratic society'

'Necessary in a democratic society' implies two conditions:
- there has to be a pressing social need for the interference, and in particular
- the interference should be proportionate to the legitimate aims pursued.

National authorities need to decide whether or not there is a pressing social need in a particular case. There is a margin of appreciation, although the assessment of the national authorities is subject to supervision by the ECtHR. Furthermore, the Court's task is not to substitute its own view for that of the national authorities, but to review under Article 11 the decisions it delivered in the exercise of its discretion. This means that the Court must look at the interference complained of in the light of the case as a whole and determine whether it was 'proportionate to the legitimate aim pursued' and whether the reasons adduced by the national authorities to justify the interference are 'relevant and sufficient.'

In *Ezelin v France* (1991) the ECtHR said:

> the freedom to take part in a peaceful assembly – in this instance a demonstration that had not been prohibited – is of such importance that it cannot be restricted in any way, even for an *avocet* (a French lawyer roughly equivalent to a barrister), so long as the person concerned does not himself commit any reprehensible act on such an occasion.

In *Ziliberberg v Moldova* (2004) the court observed at the outset of its findings that:

> the right to freedom of assembly is a fundamental right in a democratic society and, like the right to freedom of expression, is one of the foundations of such a society.

The question of proportionality arose in the case of *R (Laporte) v Chief Constable of Gloucestershire* (2006).

Case study

R (Laporte) v Chief Constable of Gloucestershire (2006)

Officers from seven police forces, acting under the direction of the Gloucestershire constabulary, stopped three coaches from London carrying 120 anti-Iraq war protesters in March 2003. The protesters had been planning to join thousands of people in a demonstration against the war at RAF Fairford in Gloucestershire, from which part of the US-led attack on Iraq had been launched two days before. At least some of the protesters, including Laporte, had purely peaceful intentions, but some items which suggested a more violent intent were apparently discovered by the police on the coaches.

The coaches were returned to London under police escort, without any opportunity for any of the passengers to get off the coaches. It was decided that the Chief Constable's actions were unlawful because they were not prescribed by law and were disproportionate.

23.3.3 'For a legitimate aim'

The legitimate aim must fall under one of the following categories:

- in the interests of national security or public safety
- for the prevention of disorder or crime
- for the protection of health or morals
- for the protection of the rights and freedoms of others.

In the interests of national security or public safety

The *Laporte* case considered above may well be argued on the basis of public safety as well as the prevention of disorder or crime. This will include counter-terrorism measures and counter-extremism measures, and will inevitably overlap with freedom of expression. The Court seems quite willing to accept that the state has a wide margin of appreciation on this.

For the prevention of disorder or crime

The majority of references to ECtHR are dismissed as the Court takes the view that each state recognises the need to protect public safety. We have seen the one example of the state being heavy-handed in the *Laporte* case. However, states have a relatively wide margin of appreciation in this area as we have seen in *Cisse v France* (2002).

For the protection of health or morals

One case with respect to Article 11 and health and morals is *Larmela v Finland* (1997). Here the Cannabis Association of Finland aimed 'to influence intoxicant policy and legislation with a view to making the personal use of cannabis legal for Finnish citizens'. The Finnish Minister of Justice refused to register the association. The state was permitted to deny this association registration with the aim of protecting the health and morals of the country.

This would also apply to banning a march in favour of drug-taking if the authorities thought this would have a detrimental effect on the health or morals of the country.

For the protection of the rights and freedoms of others

When deciding in the case of *Countryside Alliance v Attorney General* (2007), Baroness Hale said:

> Article 10 protects freedom of expression, the freedom to hold opinions and to receive and impart information and ideas. But it does not expressly protect the right to meet or associate with other people in order to do this. This, it might be said, is separately provided for in Article 11. It protects the freedom to meet and band together with others in order to share information and ideas and to give voice to them collectively. While democracy values each individual, it also knows that individuals cannot get much done unless they band together. These articles, then, are designed to protect the

freedom to share and express opinions, and to try to persuade others to one's point of view, which are essential political freedoms in any democracy. On this view, the right of the hunt and its followers to gather together publicly to demonstrate in favour of their sport and against the ban, perhaps even by riding over the countryside to demonstrate what they do, is protected by Article 11. But the right to chase and kill the fox or the stag or the mink or the hare is not. "

Activity

Construct a chart that lists all the statutory offences available to the authorities with respect to assemblies. Alongside each offence, give a brief note that helps you identify the key aspects of that offence.

23.4 Evaluation of Article 11

23.4.1 A qualified right

Unlike Articles 8 and 10, this qualified right to assembly and association is a collective right as it protects the rights of individuals to join together to take part in collective action. As with other qualified rights, the court then has to decide whether the interference is justified by the state using the principles of proportionality and margin of appreciation. The limitations must be prescribed by law and necessary in a democratic society.

The assembly must be a peaceful one to have the positive obligation of protection of those assembling peacefully. This would include protection from violence or fear of violence from a counter-demonstration. Any counter-demonstration would also have to be protected providing it is peaceful.

In the UK, two clashing demonstrations are usually kept apart by the police. This potentially affects an individual's freedom generally as they may be prevented from going where they wish to go or, indeed, be prevented from going anywhere. This can then lead to kettling, excessive force by the authorities or other interferences with human rights as we have seen.

The case of *Plattform 'Ärzte für das Leben' v Austria* (1988) shows that the protection is not an absolute guarantee, but does raise the question whether the protection given is sufficient and is given even-handedly to opposing views. In *Fáber v. Hungary* (2012), a case based on Article 10, the court ruled that Hungary was wrong to arrest and fine Fáber who waved a flag with Fascist connotations, less than 100 metres away from an anti-racism demonstration. It could be argued that this was sufficient protection for the anti-racist demonstration but could be said to be excessive force being used against Fáber with respect to his demonstration.

23.4.2 Police powers and the right to demonstrate

Restrictions on the right to demonstrate are always controversial and the courts have to rule on the balance between protecting the workers at the site, the right to protest, the need to protect public order and the rights of others. The anti-fracking protests in North Yorkshire in 2017 are an obvious example of the different interests involved – the protestors who believe fracking is bad for the environment; people who wish to travel past the protest site; those living in the locality whose lives are disrupted; those who have to pay for the police presence; the disruption and cost to the fracking business; those supplying materials to the fracking site and so on. Depending on your point of view, there is always an argument that the state through the police did or did not do enough.

Case	Facts	Law
DPP v Chivers (2010)	The activity complained of took place inside a house.	s 68 could be used as the court decided that land includes a building.
R (Laporte) v Chief Constable of Gloucestershire (2006)	Police officers stopped three coaches from London carrying 120 anti-Iraq war protesters in March 2003, and returned the coaches to London. Some protesters had purely peaceful intentions, but police discovered some items which suggested a more violent intent.	The Chief Constable's actions were unlawful because they were not prescribed by law and were disproportionate.

Figure 23.3 Key cases for Article 11 – limitations under Article 11(2)

The state is obliged to deal with these conflicting interests using the principle of proportionality. Proportionality is the balance between the individual right and the community. The criteria used for this include the effectiveness of the measures taken, the balance achieved, whether the actions of the state operate in the least intrusive manner possible and whether the effect is to deprive the individual of the right under Article 11.

23.4.3 Variation in the margin of appreciation between different states

We have seen that the Council of Europe has commented unfavourably on the variation in the margin of appreciation in different states, with particular reference to Spain, Turkey and Russia. It is interesting to note that in all these countries there has been, arguably, a further erosion of human rights particularly under Article 11. People turn to Article 11 when the state attempts to stop a demonstration going ahead, takes steps in advance to disrupt a demonstration or store personal information on those taking part.

Extension question

Review the last year and list events in the UK and also within other signatories to ECHR that may be a violation of Article 11. Compare your list with others and explain to each other why you think there might be a violation of Article 11.

Where there has been a violation of Article 11, the state may then have to change its law to ensure no further breach of the convention. This is often a lengthy process in the UK and it can be argued that remedying the law is not seen as a serious and urgent matter by the UK government. It would be interesting to speculate as the changes to police powers that have occurred since Laporte decision in 2006.

Summary

- Article 11 has three protected interests:
  - freedom of peaceful assembly
  - freedom of association with others
  - the right to form and to join trade unions for the protection of his interests.
- Article 11 is a qualified right.
- Under Article 11(2) any limitation must be in accordance with law, necessary and proportionate and for one or more of the four legitimate aims.
- As with other Articles, the margin of appreciation will vary from case to case.
- There are restrictions under common law and statute.
- The common law restrictions are breach of the peace and trespass to land.
- Restrictions under statute are many and varied, so that the authorities have a variety of possible offences available to help control assemblies of people.

Chapter 24

Enforcement of human rights laws

After reading this unit you should be able to:
- Understand the role of domestic courts in enforcing human rights laws
- Understand the process of judicial review
- Understand the role of the ECtHR

24.1 The role of domestic courts in enforcing human rights laws

24.1.1 The role before 2000

The UK has been subject to the ECHR since it came into force in 1953. But it was not until 1966 that the UK recognised the power of the ECHR to hear complaints from UK citizens and allowed an individual claiming breach of a Convention right to bring a case in the ECtHR.

There had been a debate over many years whether the ECHR should be incorporated into English law. The consequences of non-incorporation were that an individual had to take an action in the ECtHR rather than in English courts but only when all domestic remedies had been exhausted. This was unsatisfactory for individuals and the judiciary. For the judiciary, it was unsatisfactory as it had to make decisions in line with UK law, knowing there was a strong possibility of the decision being overturned on appeal to the ECtHR. It was also a concern that the jurisprudence of the ECtHR was being developed without any input from UK law. However there were means of indirectly incorporating the effect of the ECHR by interpreting legislation using the purposive approach and in the spirit of decisions of the ECtHR.

In 1997 a White Paper, 'Rights Brought Home: The Human Rights Bill' said:

> It takes on average 5 years to get an action into the ECtHR once all domestic remedies have been exhausted; and costs an average of £30,000. Bringing these rights home will mean that the British people will be able to argue for their rights in the British courts – without this inordinate delay and cost. It will also mean that the rights will be brought much more fully into the jurisprudence of the courts throughout the UK and their interpretation will thus be far more subtly and powerfully woven into our law. **"**

This resulted in the Human Rights Act 1998 which came into force in October 2000, incorporating the ECHR into UK law and allowing an individual to assert his convention rights in English courts

24.1.2 The role after 2000

For courts, s 2(1) of HRA 1998 says:

> A court or tribunal determining a question which has arisen in connection with a Convention right must take into account any—
>
> a   judgment, decision, declaration or advisory opinion of the European Court of Human Rights **"**

The effect of this section is to require courts to take into account any previous decisions of the ECtHR. This affects judicial precedent as it allows the overruling of any previous English precedent that was in conflict with the ECHR.

This provision was commented on by Lord Slynn in *R (Holding & Barnes plc) v Secretary of State for the Environment, Transport and the Regions* (2001):

> Your Lordships have been referred to many decisions of the ECtHR on Article 6 of the Convention. Although the Human Rights Act 1998 does not provide that a national court is bound by these decisions, it is obliged to take account of them so far as they are relevant. In the absence of some special circumstances it

seems clear to me that the court should follow any clear and constant jurisprudence of the ECtHR. If it does not do so there is at least a possibility that the case will go to that court which is likely in the ordinary case, to follow its own jurisprudence. "

In relation to legislation, s 3 HRA 1998 says:

" 1 So far as it is possible to do so, primary legislation and subordinate legislation must be read and given effect in a way which is compatible with the Convention rights. "

This section has the potential to invalidate previously accepted (pre-2000) interpretations of Acts which were made without reference to the ECHR.

By s 4, if the court is satisfied that a provision of primary legislation is incompatible with a Convention right, it may make a declaration of that incompatibility. Note that the court cannot strike down the legislation, as can happen in some other countries; it can only make a declaration, which will have to be considered by Parliament. This power of a declaration is limited to the High Court, the Court of Appeal and the Supreme Court.

24.2 Judicial review

Judicial review is a form of court proceeding, usually in the Administrative Court, in which the judge reviews the lawfulness of a decision or action, or a failure to act, by a public body exercising a public function. It is only available where there is no other effective means of challenge. The Administrative Court is part of the Queen's Bench Division of the High Court.

Judicial review is concerned with whether the law has been correctly applied, and the right procedures have been followed. The court's decision must be followed, but its role is supervisory only and any remedies are discretionary.

In order to succeed, the claimant will need to show that:

- a public body is under a legal duty to act or make a decision in a certain way and is unlawfully refusing or failing to do so, or
- a decision or action has been taken by a public body that is beyond the powers it is given by law.

24.2.1 Whose decisions can be challenged by judicial review?

Decisions made by public bodies in a public law capacity may be challenged by judicial review.

Examples of the bodies whose decisions can be challenged are:

- government ministries and departments
- local authorities
- health authorities
- chief constables
- prison governors
- some tribunals (but not if an appeal is available to a higher tribunal or court).

If a public body is not exercising a public function, for example where it is an employer, or there is a claim of negligence against it, its actions are governed by private laws of employment and tort, not public law. These actions will not be subject to judicial review.

If public functions are contracted out to a private company, for example a private company that is running a prison, it is carrying out a public function. Its actions in the running of the prison are governed by public law and are therefore subject to judicial review.

24.2.2 Who can bring a judicial review action?

The person bringing the action has to have an interest in the decision being challenged. This is called 'standing'. That means that the claimant has to have sufficient connection to the subject matter of the claim.

24.2.3 Alternatives to a judicial review

If there are other ways of challenging a decision or a delay, such as an appeal, those avenues have to be followed. If there are issues of maladministration, then a case should be made to the relevant ombudsman.

24.2.4 Time limits

A judicial review case must be brought before the court quickly, and in any event within three months of the decision or action being challenged.

24.2.5 The grounds for judicial review

Illegality

Public bodies can only generally do what the law allows them to do. The law setting out their powers is usually contained in legislation. Public bodies may also have guidance and policy on the exercise of their legal powers. Guidance and policy do not have to be followed, but they should be followed unless there is good reason not to. Public bodies must correctly understand and apply the law that regulates their decision-making powers. If they do not follow the law correctly, then action or failure to act will be unlawful. This is known as being *ultra vires* and the decision will be void and of no effect. An action or decision may be unlawful if:

● the decision-maker had no power to make it
● the decision-maker exceeded the powers given to him
● it misapplies the law
● the correct procedure was not followed.

Case studies

Attorney-General v Fulham Corporation (1921)

An Act gave the Corporation the power to set up a clothes washing facility for the local population to use. The Corporation set up a commercial laundry where its employees washed the residents' clothes. This was decided by the court to be *ultra vires* and illegal as the Act did not give any power to the Corporation to wash clothes for others.

Agricultural, Horticultural and Forestry Training Board v Aylesbury Mushrooms (1973)

The government minister failed to follow the correct procedures when introducing a new regulation. The procedure allowed for consultations with appropriate organisations but this procedure was not followed. In particular, the minister failed to consult the Mushroom Growers' Association, which represented the industry. Government proposals requiring the establishment of a training board were, as a result, *ultra vires* and void.

Fairness

A public body should never act so unfairly that it amounts to an abuse of power. If there are set procedures laid down by law that it must follow in order to reach a decision, then it must follow them. Claimants must be given a fair hearing which includes knowing the case against them, and having the opportunity to present their case.

A public body must be impartial and not biased.

The public body must consult people it has a duty to consult before a decision is made, or who have a legitimate expectation that they will be consulted, perhaps because they have been consulted in the past or they have an obvious interest in a matter.

A public body must keep its promises unless there is a good reason not to.

Irrationality and proportionality

The court may quash a decision when it is considered to be so demonstrably unreasonable as to be 'irrational' or 'perverse'. In practice this is very difficult to show, and it is usually argued alongside other grounds. The test was given by Lord Greene in *Associated Provincial Picture Houses Ltd v Wednesbury Corporation* (1948):

> If a decision on a competent matter is so unreasonable that no reasonable authority could ever had come to it, then the courts can interfere ... but to prove a case of that kind would require something overwhelming.

The test is a lower one, of proportionality, where human rights issues are involved. The concept of proportionality involves a balancing exercise between the legitimate aims of the state on one hand, and the protection of the individual's rights and interests on the other. The test is whether the means employed to achieve the aim correspond to the importance of the aim, and whether they are necessary to achieve the aim.

Case study

R (Rogers) v Swindon NHS Trust (2006)

A woman with early stage breast cancer was prescribed the drug Herceptin by her GP. The NHS Trust refused to supply the drug as it said it was non-approved and because – it said – her case was not exceptional. The Trust was not able to put forward in court any clear reasons for allowing some patients to have the drug treatment and not others, and it was ruled as irrational and unreasonable.

24.2.6 The approach of the Administrative Court

There are special procedures for handling judicial review claims:

● It proceeds as far as possible on the basis of agreed facts. The rules do not easily accommodate cases where the facts are in dispute.
● Both parties are expected to co-operate with the court and to take an open approach to the issue.
● The court will sometimes act proactively – bringing issues into play which have not been raised by either party.

- Depending on the nature of the decision being challenged, the court may show a degree of deference to the decision-maker, given their democratic mandate, or special expertise; the court may be reluctant to intervene in matters of public policy or in areas where a specialist expertise is needed.

The orders that the court can make

When a case is being brought for judicial review, a remedy will also be asked for. The Administrative Court can give these remedies:

- Quashing order – an order which overturns or undoes a decision already made.
- Prohibiting order – this stops a public body from taking an unlawful decision or action it has not yet taken.
- Injunction – a temporary order requiring a public body to do something or not to do something until a final decision has been made.
- Mandatory order – this makes a public body do something the law says it has to do.
- Declaration – the court can state what the law is or what the parties have a right to do.
- Damages – these may be awarded where a public body has breached the claimant's human rights.

Note that the remedies outlined above are discretionary. Even if the court finds that a public body has acted wrongly, it does not have to grant a remedy. It might decide not to do so if it thinks the claimant's own conduct has been wrong or unreasonable; for example, where the claimant has delayed unreasonably, has not acted in good faith, or where a remedy would impede a public body's ability to deliver fair administration.

There is a right of appeal from the Administrative Court to the Court of Appeal. The party that wants to appeal must first ask permission from the Administrative Court, and if that is refused, it can ask permission from the Court of Appeal directly. A further appeal may lie to the Supreme Court if the case is one of public importance.

24.3 The role of the ECtHR

The court can deal with complaints from one state against another state and from an individual against a state. The ECtHR has been successful in dealing with a large number of cases dealing with Convention rights. However a problem of being accessible to every individual within the states in the Council of Europe is the sheer number of cases referred to it. Delay undermines the work of the Court and access to justice for people who may be suffering a violation of their rights. Another criticism is that only about 6 per cent of cases referred to it are admitted for hearings.

Protocol 14 was brought into force in 2010. The current structure of dealing with a case is shown in Figure 24.1.

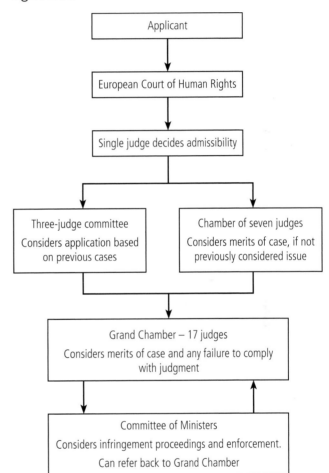

Figure 24.1 Claims procedure in ECtHR

Some specific points about the court which were introduced by Protocol 14 were:

- A judge will serve a single term of nine years.
- A single judge initially rules on the admissibility of the case – his decision is final.
- The three-judge committee can make a decision on the merits of the case if there is well-established case law on the issue.
- If the point has not previously been considered by the court it must go before a chamber of seven judges.

- Infringement – if the Committee of Ministers (by 3–2 majority) finds a state refusing to abide by a judgment of the court, it can be referred back to the Grand Chamber for an infringement finding, which will then be referred back to the committee to take action.
- An application is only admissible if the applicant has suffered a significant disadvantage.

Protocols 15 and 16 have been agreed in principle but are not yet in force. They were agreed after the Brighton Declaration on the future of the European Court of Human Rights 2012 in an attempt to reduce the number of cases referred. In 2014 there were 78,000 applications pending (down from 122,450 the year before). The focus of the protocols is subsidiarity – attempting to get referrals dealt with locally.

24.3.1 Criteria for admission

Under the ECHR, the admissibility criteria is as follows:
- The person referring the issue has to be a victim and directly affected by the act complained of (Article 34).
- Domestic remedies have to be exhausted (Article 35).
- An application has to be made within six months of the final decision of the domestic court – to be reduced to four months by Protocol 15.
- The complaint cannot be anonymous (Article 35).
- It cannot be substantially the same issue as a previously examined case (Article 35).
- It cannot be incompatible with the Convention, or ill-founded, or an abuse of process (Article 35).
- The individual must have suffered a significant disadvantage (Article 35).

24.3.2 The functions of the ECtHR

A living instrument

It is the role of the ECtHR to interpret the rights contained in the ECHR, and this interpretation should be followed in all member states.

The court is not bound by previous precedent which allows it to develop human rights protections following changes in society; it can depart from previous approaches, which it has done in matters relating to the death penalty and prisoners' rights.

Example

In *Rees v United Kingdom* (1981) the applicant was a transsexual who wanted to change his name on his birth certificate. The ECtHR found there was a lack of common approach among member states on this issue and found there was no violation of ECHR.

In *Cossey v United Kingdom* (1991) the claimant was a transsexual who could not change her birth certificate sex to allow her to marry a man. The ECtHR found that there had been some developments in the approach of member states since the decision in *Rees*, but not enough to rule that there had been a violation of Article 8.

In *Goodwin v United Kingdom* (2002) the applicant was transsexual. In addition to the complaint of *Cossey*, she could not change her National Insurance details and was still regarded as male for pension purposes. She alleged this caused her to be discriminated against. The ECtHR recognised in this case that there had been scientific and social developments in the field since the previous decisions and that there had been a violation of Article 8.

Effectiveness

The court has emphasised that it is important for individuals to be able to access Convention rights and that the court will enforce them.

Case study

Golder v United Kingdom (1975)

The applicant, a prisoner, was denied the right to see a lawyer. The court interpreted Article 6 as reading the right to access to a court, allowing the protection of Articles 5 and 6.

Autonomy

The court can give a meaning to legal words that may be different from their meaning in member states. This provides a common meaning across all member states and can prevent states interpreting meanings narrowly. This has been the case with the phrase 'criminal charge'.

Positive obligations

Convention rights are negative in the sense that they require the state not to act in a certain way that violates the right. However the ECtHR interprets the

Convention to require a state to take positive steps to prevent violations. This approach may place a burden on the state in terms of economic or social policy in order to meet its obligations, not so they are excessive.

The ECtHR has a vertical relationship between itself and the applicant who brings the case. Note that the applicant can only bring an action against a state and not another person. However, if a state is under a positive obligation, it may be required to control the behaviour of individuals within the state (such as in criminal law) or to take steps to protect a person from other individuals.

Tip

Make sure you understand in which court a claimant can bring an action alleging breach of a right and the orders that the court can make.

Activity

In which courts can the claimants in the following cases bring a claim?

1   Janice has been told by her doctor that he cannot prescribe a course of treatment to her because the local health authority refuses to approve that treatment. She has found out that authorities in other parts of the country allow this treatment.

2   Toby intends to make a claim against the police as he was detained for several hours without reason during a demonstration.

    Would your answer be different if the demonstration had taken place in 1998?

3   A tribunal has ordered Santi to be deported from the UK. Santi did not know that a hearing was taking place and was not given an opportunity to put forward any reasons why he should be allowed to stay.

24.4 How well does the UK enforce ECHR rights?

As stated at 24.1.2 above, a domestic court should take account of any previous decision of the ECtHR and this is supported by Lord Steyn's comments. Domestic courts can go further than the ECtHR but can also depart from ECtHR decisions. If a court is faced with a domestic decision which conflicts with a ECtHR decision, then it should follow the domestic decision and refer the case to appeal.

The procedures to enforce ECHR rights are in place but there are obstacles for an individual to enforce their rights before the ECtHR. Firstly, there is the necessity to exhaust all domestic remedies before bringing a claim to the ECtHR. Potentially, this can mean appealing all the way to the Supreme Court. Then, there will be the cost of taking such action as well as the ECtHR when no state funding will be available. Further, there will be the need to find a suitably specialised lawyer who is able and willing to pursue the claim.

It will have to be considered who a claim can be made against. Under s 6 HRA the Act only applies to public bodies carrying out public functions. Increasingly, former public services such as residential care and social housing have been contracted out to private bodies which are not covered by the Act. Despite calls for legislation to define what a public authority is, it is often left to the courts to decide. The provision can also operate to the detriment of an individual depending on who the claim is made against, even if the claim is based on similar grounds. This can be shown in *McDonald v McDonald* (2016) at 21.1.4 above where the vulnerable claimant was left without any remedy, whereas another claimant such as in *Connors v UK* (2004) was protected under the HRA.

Finally, even if a claim is accepted and reaches the ECtHR, the court may apply the margin of appreciation doctrine which considers the amount of discretion allowed to the state when considering alleged violations of qualified rights. For example, in *Laskey, Jaggard and Brown v UK* (1997) (an appeal to the ECtHR from the case of *R v Brown* (1994) referred to at 1.2.2) where the court considered that outlawing homosexual sado-masochistic activity between consenting adults was acceptable for public health reasons. This doctrine can also be illustrated in the cases involving transsexuals above. In this area the court initially decided there was a lack of European consensus or standards and it took over 20 years before a claim was accepted.

Case name	Facts	Legal principle
Attorney-General v Fulham Corporation (1921)	A council had power to set up a washing facility but instead set up a commercial laundry	The council's decision was *ultra vires* and unlawful as it did not have the power to set up the laundry
Agricultural, Horticultural and Forestry Training Board v Aylesbury Mushrooms (1973)	A minister did not consult the mushroom industry representatives before introducing new rules, as he was required to do.	The government proposals were ultra vires and void as required procedures had not been followed
R (Rogers) v Swindon NHS Trust (2006)	An NHS trust refused to supply a cancer drug	The decision was irrational and unreasonable as no reasons were put forward for the refusal. The decision was set aside

Figure 24.2 Key cases for the ECHR

Summary

- The UK has been subject to the ECHR since 1953.
- Cases brought by a UK citizen alleging breach of a Convention right have only been heard by the ECtHR since 1966
- Before 2000 a UK citizen had to exhaust all domestic court actions before bringing a claim before the ECtHR
- Since 2000 a claim can be brought before a UK court alleging breach of a Convention right
- The decision of a UK public body can be challenged by a judicial review action. The claimant has to have an interest in the action which must be brought within 3 months of the decision being challenged.
- Actions can be brought on the grounds of illegality, unfairness or unreasonableness.
- If judicial review is granted the Administrative Court can make various orders at its discretion
- The ECtHR interprets the ECHR and is not bound by precedent.

Chapter 25

The rules and theory of contract law

> After reading this chapter you should have:
> - An outline of the rules of the law of contract
> - An overview of the theory of the law of contract

25.1 Introduction to the law of contract

A contract can be defined as an agreement that the law will enforce. The following areas need to be studied for the OCR specification Paper 3, Section B, Option 1 – The Law of Contract:

- Agreement – this is all about making an agreement to do something, for example buy a car. This area of the specification must be evaluated as well as known, understood and applied.
- The validity of that agreement – the area of law is known as 'vitiating factors', in other words factors that may make a contract invalid. Here we are considering the law of misrepresentation and economic duress. Misrepresentation might be where the seller of the car stated its mileage was 20,000 when in fact it was 80,000.
- The terms of the contract – the terms are the obligations and rights of each party to the contract. At its simplest, these would be to pay the agreed price for the car and to hand over legal ownership of the car to the buyer. However, some terms are specifically agreed by the parties while others are implied, that is, they are part of the contract whether or not the parties have thought about it. This area of the specification must be evaluated as well as known, understood and applied.
- Discharge of contract – this involves examining exactly what amounts to performance of a contract, when there is breach of contract through non- or part-performance, and what happens when performance of the contract is prevented by events outside the control of the parties to the contract.
- Remedies – this is all about what legal remedies a party to the contract can seek when the contract has been breached (broken) or the contract has been affected by a vitiating factor.

25.2 An outline of the rules of the law of contract

Contract law is largely derived from the common law – case law. The principles have been developed over many years – we will consider *Pinnel's case* (1602) in Chapter 27. Originally, itinerant justices travelled the land making judgments to settle disputes. Cases involving the buying and selling of goods were often decided according to local rules or customs. These rules were gradually extended over wider areas, eventually becoming the common law of the land. These were developed and refined into the modern law of contract.

Equity provides some ways of overcoming aspects of inherent unfairness in the common law. We can see this, for example, with equitable remedies available for breach of contract.

There are some Acts of Parliament that have been passed to deal with problems that have arisen in the common law. The Sale of Goods Act 1979 is a modern incarnation of the Sale of Goods Act 1893. This first Act was created by Parliament to reflect the then current law on sale of goods as part of the Victorian idea to codify commercial law so that it could easily be used throughout the world. It therefore reflected the case law on sale of goods that existed at that time.

European law has influenced today's contract law by making regulations that are often designed to help consumers. The Unfair Terms in Consumer Contracts Regulations 1999 are one example. These regulations are now subsumed in the Consumer Rights Act 2015.

25.3 An overview of the theory of the law of contract

25.3.1 Freedom of contract

The usual principle of the common law is freedom of contract and the sanctity of contracts. The nineteenth-century definition of a contract is 'a promise or set of promises which the law will enforce'. That is, there are mutual promises between the promisor and the promisee. The rights and obligations or duties are created by the agreement between the parties to the contract.

Under this theory, contract law is based on promising. To promise is to assume an obligation to the promisee by means of a communication to the promisee to that effect. An agreement is taken to entail the making of a promise in return for a promise (or for performance), and if an agreement is recognised as a contract in law, the law recognises a contracting party as having incurred a legal obligation to perform his promise.

There is also a reliance theory: an agreement states the performance required of a contracting party, but that party does not promise the performance and does not incur an obligation to provide it. Contract is not based on promising it, but on what is described as the 'assumption of responsibility'. A contracting party assumes responsibility for reliance incurred by the other party on the assumption that the specified performance will be provided.

Whichever theory is considered, the agreed terms must be certain, which is a principle in contract law. An offer must be certain before it can be accepted, so in the case of *Guthing v Lynn* (1831) the offer to pay £5 more for a horse if it was 'lucky' was too vague and not an offer. This leads to problems where two businesses try to deal with each other, but both businesses have their own conditions of trading. If there is no certainty, then there would appear to be no contract, but the parties have gone on with the deal without formally agreeing whose terms are the contract terms.

This can be seen in *Butler Machine Tool Co. Ltd v Ex-Cell-O Corporation* (1977) where Lord Denning said:

> I have much sympathy with the judge's approach to this case. In many of these cases our traditional analysis of offer, counter-offer, rejection, acceptance and so forth is out of date. This was observed by Lord Wilberforce in *New*

Zealand Shipping Co. Ltd v A M Satterthwaite [(1975)]. The better way is to look at all the documents passing between the parties and glean from them, or from the conduct of the parties, whether they have reached agreement on all material points, even though there may be differences between the forms and conditions printed on the back of them. [Applying *Brogden v Metropolitan Railway Co.* (1877)] it will be found that in most cases when there is a 'battle of forms' there is a contract as soon as the last of the forms is sent and received without objection being taken to it. Therefore, judgment was entered for the buyers.

Lord Denning is suggesting that the subjective view of the contract terms that the parties to the contract have, is replaced by an objective view the parties must have agreed, as is the case with implied terms in a contract. *Reveille Independent LLC v Anotech International (UK) Ltd* (2016) is another example of the courts concluding what the terms of a contract actually were from the dealings between the parties.

Implied terms are also placed in a contract that neither party may have agreed. In *Marks and Spencer plc v BNP Paribas Securities Services Trust Company (Jersey) Ltd* (2015) Lord Neuberger emphasised that construing the express words of a contract is a different exercise from implying words which are not there to be construed. So, for example, reasonableness is to be judged objectively – in considering what the parties would have agreed. Here,

> one is not strictly concerned with the hypothetical answer of the actual parties, but with that of notional reasonable people in the position of the parties at the time at which they were contracting.

This is moving away from the idea that a contract is a freely negotiated deal under the freedom of contract theory.

Freedom of contract is eroded when Parliament creates an Act that implies terms in a contract. At one extreme is the Consumer Rights Act 2015 that inserts terms, rights and remedies that cannot be excluded by a business. Even the Sale of Goods Act did this, although most of the terms implied could be excluded by the parties to a contract. That right to exclude the implied terms became less likely under the Unfair Contract Terms Act 1977.

The argument is that there is still freedom of contract. If you do not like the terms of a contract, then do not enter the contract. You may have no choice but to agree to the terms (as in a music streaming contract), but you still have freedom of choice.

Look online

Research legal professionals' advice about freedom of contract. Note their views and general advice to clients. Think about how this affects the traditional view of freedom of contract.

Websites should be from the UK, such as www.shoosmiths.co.uk/client-resources/legal-updates/guidance-freedom-contract-not-open-interpretation-11014.aspx and www.greenwoods.co.uk//knowledge-base//essentials//freedom-of-contract-cakes-and-other-goods-services.

25.3.2 Good faith

The ideas of reliance and responsibility are also present in English contract law. For contracts and commerce to work, there must be an expectation that both parties will do what they said they will do. If they do not do so, then the law will settle the dispute. Criminal sanctions are reserved for the worst cases (fraud) but even these are extended by Parliament with respect to many aspects of trading.

Corrective justice can be seen to be applied in contract law. The basis of assessment of damages is loss of bargain: the claimant is placed in the position they would have been in had the contract been performed. In other words, responsibility for the losses is taken by the person at fault, and both parties entered the contract relying on each other to perform their obligations.

However, only losses that are reasonably within the contemplation of the parties may be recovered, as can be seen in *Victoria Laundry v Newman* (1949).

Case study

Victoria Laundry v Newman (1949)

The defendant had been late in fitting a boiler. As a result the claimant had suffered not only normal business losses, but also exceptional losses through losing a special contract with the Ministry of Supply. As the latter were not within the contemplation of the parties at the time of the contract, they were not recoverable.

In *Wellesley Partners LLP v Withers LLP* (2015) the basic rule in contract was summarised:

> A contract breaker is liable for damage resulting from his breach, if at the time of making the contract, a reasonable person in his shoes would have had damage of that kind in mind as not unlikely to result from a breach.

This is another objective test that may not, therefore, reflect the freedom of contract principle. This would seem to indicate that contracts are expected to be made between the parties in good faith.

Good faith is incorporated as an underlying principle in contracts of insurance where all material facts must be disclosed if there is not to be a misrepresentation. However, imposing a duty of good faith in all contracts would run contrary to the general principle of contract law. Businesses enter into contracts and their aim is to make as much profit as possible within a competitive market, subject to the law as it stands at the time. However, contract parties are involved in a competitive situation and cannot be expected to disclose every aspect of their business deal. What the law does is to attempt to balance the interests of the parties to a contract by legislation, interpretation of the contract and the common law with a smattering of equity. The results of this however lack certainty.

Article 7 of the United Nations Convention on Contracts for the International Sale of Goods (1980) states:

> In the interpretation of this Convention, regard is to be had to its international character and to the need to promote uniformity in its application and the observance of good faith in international trade.

Interestingly, most international commercial contracts state as a term of the contract that English Law will apply and disputes will be settled in accordance with English law in London. So much for good faith.

25.3.3 Balancing interests and justice

We have seen that judges often have to balance competing interests in their judgments. This can lead to unusual results. Parliament also sets out to balance rights between contracting parties, which seems to go against the theory of freedom of contract. As we have seen, parties to a contract may try to limit their liability by relying upon exclusion clauses. The traditional rule of *caveat emptor* (let the buyer beware) could operate harshly against the interests of the weaker bargaining party.

There are apparently conflicting decisions such as:

- *Olley v Marlborough Court Hotel* (1949) – the exclusion clause was invalid as it had not been brought to Mrs Olley's attention when she made the contract.
- *Thompson v LMS Railway* (1930) – an exclusion clause was implied even though the claimant could not read the printed terms which referred to another document she would have had to locate.

However, if we are aware of a risk and take it, why should death and personal injury not be excluded from a voluntary contract?

Only a party to a contract can take legal action on it. This could lead to injustice, despite the legal position of an agent.

Key term 🔑

Agent – a person who is authorised to act for another (the principal) in the making of a contract with third parties. The resulting contract is made between the principal and the third party, and not with the agent.

In *Jackson v Horizon Holidays* (1975) the claimant succeeded in seeking damages for himself and for members of his family after a package holiday failed to match the advertised description, even though only he, and not his family members, had signed the contract.

The Contract (Rights of Third Parties) Act 1999 modified the law by allowing third parties to make a claim where the contract expressly provided for it, or where the contract purported to confer a benefit on them. Obvious injustices such as *Tweddle v Atkinson* (1861) are remedied, but the provisions of the Act are frequently excluded in standard form contracts and so the benefit of the Act is largely negated for consumers.

The law with respect to frustration of contract has also been modified by Parliament. The Law Reform (Frustrated Contracts) Act 1943 enabled the courts to apportion the losses more fairly between the parties: the court may order 'a just sum' to be paid where either expenses have been incurred or a valuable benefit obtained.

25.3.4 The principle of fault

The principle of fault has two distinct elements:

- the degree of responsibility for actions
- the liability under the law.

Responsibility is seen as one theory in contract law.

A misrepresentation is an untrue statement of fact made by one party to the contract which induces the other party to enter into the contract. It is a vitiating factor in a contract and the remedies vary in accordance with the type of misrepresentation. These are categorised as innocent, negligent or fraudulent; in other words, by the perceived amount of blameworthiness or fault. Sometimes statements are recognised as no more than advertising slogans, and so do not create liability.

Case study

Smith v Land and House Property (1884)

A tenant was described by the defendant as 'most desirable'. In fact, the tenant was completely unreliable. As this misrepresentation was relied upon by the other party, the maker of the statement could be sued – at fault for the statement and therefore for the loss it caused.

Generally, silence will not amount to misrepresentation. After all, there is freedom of

contract, and if you do not ask about something, there is no obligation to be told about it unless it is a contract where good faith is required, such as one of insurance. This was shown in *Fletcher v Krell* (1873). However, where there is a deliberate attempt to conceal an important fact, there will be liability. This occurred in *With v O'Flanagan* (1936).

See Chapter 30, section 30.2.1 for full details of these cases.

Breach of contract depends on the level of blameworthiness to determine the injured party's rights. This will determine whether a person can end the contract or must continue it, but claim some compensation. The cases of *Poussard v Spiers* (1876) and *Bettini v Gye* (1876) illustrate this point.

In 1995 the Law Commission reported on damages which considered the situation where there could be punitive damages. The recommendation was that punitive damages must not be awarded for breach of contract. However, the law on penalty clauses in contract seems to allow what might appear to be punitive damages, subject to the judicial view as to what is commercially justifiable.

In *ParkingEye v Beavis* (2015) Mr Beavis parked in the car park, but overstayed the two-hour limit by almost an hour and the charge of £85 was upheld by the court. Lords Sumption and Neuberger placed some emphasis on the context in which the contract was made in reaching their decision:

'The penalty rule is an interference with freedom of contract. In a negotiated contract between properly advised parties of comparable bargaining power, the strong initial presumption must be that the parties themselves are the best judges of what is legitimate in a provision dealing with the consequences of breach.'

25.3.5 Morality

A rule is something that influences the way in which we behave, either because we submit ourselves to it voluntarily, as with moral rules, or because it is enforceable by some authority as with laws.

Many rules are neither morally binding, nor do they ultimately have the force of law attached to them. They are kept because of the context in which they operate. For example rules, sometimes called laws, define a sport and how it is played. These have evolved to cope with new situations, improve the sport and protect participants. There are sanctions here too, and some of the sanctions may be the result of a legal

contract when taking out membership of a sporting body or club.

Rules might also come about through custom or practice, and involve the disapproval of the community rather than any legal sanction if such a rule is broken.

Morality is generally to do with beliefs, so may be affected by religion. We all have a moral code of some kind which defines what we think is and is not acceptable behaviour. Morality can differ from culture to culture and from individual to individual, although some behaviour is universally unacceptable. Morality is most obviously intertwined with criminal law, but aspects of contract law are also affected by morality.

Contracts can be declared void because of their association with immorality. In *Pearce v Brooks* (1866) a cab owner's contract with a prostitute to use his cabs for her trade was void because it was a contract for immoral purposes.

Other examples of contracts being void because of illegality include:
- *Parkinson v The College of Ambulance* (1925) where the whole purpose of the contract was to buy an honour (knighthood, OBE, etc.) – i.e. corruption in public life.
- *Dann v Curzon* (1910) – the courts were not prepared to enforce a contract to commit a tort or a crime.
- *Napier v National Business Agency* (1951) – the courts will not allow parties to take advantage of contracts that set out to defraud.

Today, there are frequent press reports about contracts obtained as a result of bribery and contracts made to hide the true situation with respect to tax. These contracts may be viewed as immoral, but are only illegal if involving tax evasion rather than tax avoidance. The same may be said for methods to avoid contractual obligations with respect to wages and minimum wage regulation.

Economic duress may be considered immoral (as would physical duress). Equity reflects morality when the principle of equitable estoppel is applied.

 Key term

Estoppel – a principle of contract law that prevents one party to a contract from denying or alleging a fact owing to their previous conduct, allegation, or denial.

This can be seen in:

- *Central London Property Trust Ltd v High Trees House Ltd* (1947) – a morally correct response to the situation that became the legal principle.
- *D and C Builders v Rees* (1965) – Mrs Rees' behaviour may be seen as immoral and certainly had no legal effect.

Equitable remedies are a reflection of morality and justice in contract law.

The area of fraudulent misrepresentation developed in *Derry v Peek* (1889), while based on the tort of deceit, still reflects the view in contract law that it would be wrong to allow a contract to be obtained by fraud.

Freedom of contract allows, subject to illegality, any contract to be made. It may, however, be viewed that some contracts are so outrageous that they are immoral, but they are rarely illegal. Under the Victorian Moneylenders Acts, any contract to lend money with a rate of interest above 50 per cent was unenforceable in a court of law. Today we allow much higher rates of interest to be used and enforced, despite most religions taking a strong view about charging interest to lend money. Is this a changing view of morality in business?

Summary

- Contracts have a number of elements that can be considered as a whole or individually.
- Contract law is largely based on common law so most of the law comes from decided cases.
- The elements that come from Acts of Parliament are mostly to do with consumer protection.
- The main theory of contract law is freedom of contract. This means that a person can make any contract he or she likes even if it is disadvantageous to him/her. There is, however, some statutory protection.
- The principle of good faith is an underlying principle; a person assumes that the other party will fulfil his promise and that the law will help when he or she does not.
- The law tries to balance interests between parties, particularly where exclusion clauses are concerned.
- The concept of fault applies particularly to the law on misrepresentation in contracts.
- Morality is present in contract law, particularly with illegal contracts, economic duress, terms imposed in contracts and equitable remedies.

Chapter 26

Formation of contract (1): offer and acceptance

After studying this chapter you should be able to:
- Understand offer and acceptance, including the rules of communication and revocation
- Evaluate formation of contract (in relation to offer and acceptance)
- Apply the law to given situations

26.1 The offer

This chapter deals with the idea of agreement in formation of a contract. This requires an offer and acceptance. These, and the relevant rules, are explored in this section of the chapter and evaluated in the next section.

26.1.1 What is an offer?

An offer is the starting point for a contract. Contract law sets out what amounts to an offer, when the offer comes into existence and when it comes to an end. Once an offer is communicated to the offeree by the offeror, the offeree can choose whether to accept that offer or not until such time as the offer ends.

Key terms

Offer – a statement of the terms upon which a person is prepared to be bound by a contract.
Offeree – in contract law the person to whom an offer is made.
Offeror – in contract law the person who makes an offer to another.

The offer must be definite in its terms. Words such as 'might be prepared to' or may be able to' indicate uncertainty. Therefore, it is likely that the statement will be an invitation rather than an offer. This can be seen in the case of *Gibson v Manchester City Council* (1979).

Case study

Gibson v Manchester City Council (1979)

Mr Gibson was a council tenant. The council wrote to him stating:

> The Corporation may be prepared to sell the house to you ... If you would like to make formal application to buy your Council house, please complete the enclosed application form.

He completed the application but the council refused to accept his application.

It was decided that the council's letter was not an offer. His formal application was the offer that the council could accept or reject.

An acceptance of the offer forms the basis of a valid contract. The difficulty is in deciding whether a statement amounts to an offer or whether it is just a statement preparatory to an offer which is known as an invitation to treat.

Key term

Invitation to treat – an indication that one person is willing to negotiate a contract with another, but that he or she is not yet willing to make a legal offer.

26.1.2 An offer or an invitation to treat?

The law distinguishes between an offer and an invitation to treat. An invitation to treat is not an offer and therefore it cannot be accepted to make a contract. There are a number of examples of invitations to treat.

Advertisements

Generally, an advertisement cannot be an offer, and is thus only an invitation to treat. This can be seen in the case of *Partridge v Crittenden* (1968).

Case study

Partridge v Crittenden (1968)

Crittenden placed an advertisement stating 'Bramblefinch cocks, bramblefinch hens, 25s (£1.25) each'. He was prosecuted for 'offering for sale' a wild bird under the Protection of Birds Act 1954. He was not guilty as the advertisement was not an offer but an invitation to treat. This meant he could not make a contract to sell the birds as there was no offer by him. Any offer leading to a contract would be made by the person responding to the advertisement.

Exceptionally, if an advertisement contains a clear indication that there is an 'offer' because it is expected to be taken seriously, then the court may well decide it is an offer. This usually occurs in a unilateral rather than a bilateral contract.

A unilateral contract occurs where there is a promise to perform an obligation with no corresponding obligation on the other party to the contract to do anything. Typically, this is a reward for doing something; so if a reward is offered for an act and the act is performed the offeror is bound to pay the reward, but the offeree is not obliged to perform the act. This might arise in the situation of a reward poster for return of a missing cat. There is no obligation to look for the cat, but if you find it, the reward must be paid.

Each party in a bilateral contract must do something under the contract; for example, pay the price for goods bought.

Key terms 🔑

Unilateral contract – there is an obligation on one party to the contract only, the offeror.

Bilateral contract – this requires both offeror and offeree to do something.

A unilateral contract can be seen in the case of *Carlill v Carbolic Smoke Ball Co.* (1893).

Case study

Carlill v Carbolic Smoke Ball Co. (1893)

The company advertised a patent medicine, the smoke ball. The advertisement stated that if a purchaser used it correctly and still got flu, then the company would pay him £100. Mrs Carlill did get flu after using the smoke ball as instructed. The court awarded her the £100. The promise was an offer that could be accepted by anyone who used the smoke ball correctly and still contracted the flu as the advertisement was a unilateral offer.

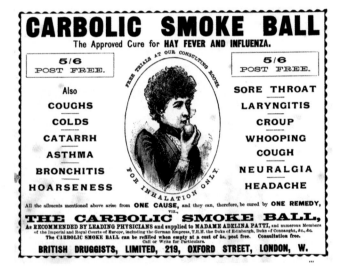

Advertisement from 1897

Goods in a shop window or on a shop shelf

This principle makes good sense. A seller of goods is not obliged to sell the goods to you. The goods might be a display item, even with a price ticket on the item. There may be none left to sell or there may be legal restrictions on the sale of the goods. Examples include the cases of *Fisher v Bell* (1961) and *Pharmaceutical Society of Great Britain v Boots Cash Chemists* (1953).

Case studies

Fisher v Bell (1961)

A shopkeeper displayed a flick-knife with a price tag in his window for sale. He was charged with 'offering it for sale', an offence under the Offensive Weapons Act 1959. The display of the knife in the window was an invitation to treat so the knife had not been offered for sale. He was therefore not guilty of the offence.

Lord Justice Parker said:

> It is perfectly clear that according to the ordinary law of contract the display of an article with a price on it in a shop window is merely an invitation to treat. It is in no sense an offer for sale the acceptance of which constitutes a contract.

Pharmaceutical Society of Great Britain v Boots Cash Chemists (1953)

Boots were charged with selling controlled pharmaceutical products other than under the supervision of a pharmacist. The shop was a self-service shop where the items that had to be sold by a pharmacist were on a shelf for customers to select. They were found not guilty as the offer was made by the customer at the till and acceptance of the offer was approved by a pharmacist in accordance with the Act controlling such sales.

The goods on the shelf are an invitation to treat and remain so when put in the customer's basket. The contents of the basket become an offer when the customer presents them to the checkout operator (or self-service scanner). The shop then accepts or declines the customer's offer through its checkout operator or assistant at the self-service scanner.

Lots at an auction

At an auction the bidder makes the offer that the auctioneer then accepts by banging his hammer. This means that the lots available at an auction are an invitation to treat. This can be seen in the case of British Car Auctions v Wright (1972).

Case study

British Car Auctions v Wright (1972)

The auctioneers were prosecuted for offering to sell an unfit vehicle at an auction. However, the prosecution failed because there was no offer, only an invitation to treat.

A request for information

A request for information and a reply to such a request is not an offer. This might be just a general enquiry such as when an item displayed for sale does not have a price in it. This can be seen in the case of Harvey v Facey (1893).

Case study

Harvey v Facey (1893)

Harvey wanted to buy Facey's farm and sent a message: 'Will you sell me Bumper Hall Pen [the farm]? State lowest price.'

Facey replied: 'Lowest price acceptable £900.'

Harvey tried to buy the farm for £900 but could not as the reply was merely a reply to the request for information, not an offer.

Offer or invitation to treat?	Brief legal rule	Case example
An advertisement	An advertisement is usually an invitation to treat, not an offer.	Partridge v Crittenden (1968)
An advertisement containing an offer	Where there is a unilateral contract, the advertisement may be an offer rather than an invitation to treat.	Carlill v Carbolic Smoke Ball Co. (1893)
Goods in a shop window	An invitation to treat.	Fisher v Bell (1961)
Goods on a supermarket shelf	An invitation to treat.	Pharmaceutical Society of Great Britain v Boots Cash Chemists (1953)
Goods at an auction	Each lot is an invitation to treat; offer made by bidder.	British Car Auctions v Wright (1972)
Request for information and reply to the request	An invitation to treat.	Harvey v Facey (1893)

Figure 26.1 Key facts chart for invitation to treat

26.1.3 Who can make an offer?

An offer can be made by anyone. This can be by an individual, a partnership, limited company or other organisation. An offer made other than by an individual is made by an employee of the business or an agent. It can also be made through a notice or a machine as in Thornton v Shoe Lane Parking (1971).

Case study

Thornton v Shoe Lane Parking (1971)

Mr Thornton put money into a machine and was given a ticket at the entrance to a car park. The offer was made by the machine on behalf of the company owning the car park. The acceptance was made by putting the money into the machine. This was where the contract was made which dictated what terms were in the contract – the terms displayed by the machine.

26.1.4 How long does an offer last?

An offer can only be accepted while it is open. Once an offer has ended, it cannot be accepted and cannot form the basis of a contract. It is therefore essential to establish when an offer starts and when it ends.

An offer comes into existence when it is communicated to the offeree. Communication requires the offeree to know of the existence of the offer. This can be seen in the case of *Taylor v Laird* (1856).

Case study

Taylor v Laird (1856)

Taylor gave up the captaincy of a ship overseas. He needed to get back to England. He worked as an ordinary crew member on the ship in order to get back to England, but received no wages. The ship owner had not received any communication of his offer to work as an ordinary crew member. Therefore no contract could exist for the payment of wages on this voyage.

Exact timing can be critical – this can be seen in the case of *Stevenson v McLean* (1880).

Case study

Stevenson v McLean (1880)

On Saturday, the offeror offered to sell iron to the offeree. The offer was stated to be open until Monday. On Monday at 10 a.m., the offeree sent a telegram asking if he could have credit terms, but got no reply. At 1.34 p.m. the offeree sent a telegram accepting the offer, but at 1.25 p.m. the offeror had sent a telegram: 'Sold iron to third party' arriving at 1.46 p.m. The offeree sued the breach of contract but the offeror argued that the query about credit was a counter offer so there could be no acceptance. It was decided that the query about credit was only an enquiry, so a binding contract was made at 1.34 p.m.

26.1.5 How an offer can end

An offer can come to an end in the following ways:
- revocation
- rejection
- lapse of time
- death
- acceptance.

Revocation

An offer can be revoked (withdrawn) at any time before acceptance. The offeror must communicate the revocation to the offeree before it is effective, as in *Routledge v Grant* (1828).

Case studies

Routledge v Grant (1828)

Grant had offered his house for sale, stating that the offer would remain open for six weeks. When he told Routledge that he no longer wished to sell the house, this was effective revocation of the offer even though it was within the six-week period. Routledge could no longer accept the offer as it had ended.

Dickinson v Dodds (1876)

Dodds had offered to sell houses to Dickinson. When a reliable person known to both of them told Dickinson that Dodds had withdrawn the offer, this was effective revocation.

Tip

Note that an offer is revoked as soon as the revocation is communicated to the offeree. You can exemplify this from *Stevenson v McLean* (1880) as well as *Routledge v Grant* (1828).

However, an offeree can make a separate contract with the offeror to keep the offer open, or only to sell to him. This is known as a collateral contract which can be enforced if the offeror refuses to sell within the agreed period or sells the item to someone else.

Communication of revocation does not have to be from the offeror directly, if the person communicating the revocation is reliable. There are no particular categories of 'reliable person' but evidence could be given that the communication took place and could be expected to be taken seriously:
- In *Routledge v Grant* it was the offeror who communicated the revocation of the offer to the offeree.

- In *Dickinson v Dodds* the offeree heard about the revocation of the offer from a reliable source. This was effective communication of revocation.

Rejection

Once an offer is rejected, it cannot be accepted by the person rejecting the offer as the rejection ends the offer. If the offer is made to more than one person, rejection by one person does not mean the other offerees can no longer accept the offer. The rejection must be communicated to the offeror before it is effective. A counter offer is a rejection of an offer. This often occurs when negotiating the price of an item such as a car where there are often multiple offers and counter offers.

An example of rejection occurs in *Hyde v Wrench* (1840).

Case study

Hyde v Wrench (1840)

Wrench offered to sell his farm for £1000 to Hyde. Hyde replied with a counter offer of £950. Wrench rejected this counter offer. Hyde then replied that he accepted Wrench's earlier offer to sell for £1000. However, the counter offer ended Wrench's original offer, so Hyde could not accept it. Wrench could have accepted Hyde's offer of £1000 but did not do so.

Sometimes there are enquiries during negotiations. As has been seen in *Stevenson v McLean* (1880), these are generally treated as requests for information and not counter offers.

Tip

It is not always easy to decide whether there has been a request for information or a counter offer. One argument you can make is that a request for information does not seem to imply a rejection of the offer made.

Lapse of time

An offer can come to an end by lapse of time. If a fixed period for the duration of the offer is stated, then as soon as that expires there is no offer to accept. The problem arises when no time is set. In this situation the time is a reasonable time. This is clearly going to vary depending on the nature of the offer. You would expect a longer time for the duration of an offer to sell a metal tank than an offer to sell a cake. An example is *Ramsgate Victoria Hotel v Montefiore* (1866).

Case study

Ramsgate Victoria Hotel v Montefiore (1866)

On 8 June, Montefiore offered to buy shares at a fixed price in the hotel. On 23 November, his offer was accepted but he no longer wanted them as the share price had fallen so he refused to pay. It was held that the long delay between the offer and the acceptance meant the offer had lapsed and could no longer be accepted.

Death

The effect of the death of either the offeror or the offeree depends on which party died and the type of contract involved. If the offeree dies then the offer ends and those dealing with his estate cannot accept on his behalf. The executors or administrators of his estate can make a new offer as can the offeror.

When an offeror dies, acceptance can still take place until the offeree learns of the offeror's death. However, this is obviously not the case where the offer is to perform some personal service such as to provide personal tuition.

Situation	Brief legal rule	Case example
Offer not communicated to offeree	No offer exists.	*Taylor v Laird* (1856)
Offer must exist to be open for existence.	Exact timing of duration of offer is critical.	*Stevenson v McLean* (1880)
Revocation of offer	Can be made at any time.	*Routledge v Grant* (1828)
Communication of revocation of offer	Must be effectively communicated, not necessarily by offeror.	*Dickinson v Dodds* (1876)
Offer rejected	Once rejected, offer ends and cannot be accepted.	*Hyde v Wrench* (1840)
Offer lapsed	Lapses after end of fixed time, or if no time, after a reasonable time.	*Ramsgate Victoria Hotel v Montefiore* (1866)
Death of one party	Ends the offer when known or if offer is for personal services by deceased.	

Figure 26.2 Key facts chart for duration of an offer

Acceptance

Once an offer has been accepted there is agreement, and assuming that the other essential features of a contract have been fulfilled, there is a legally binding contract.

26.2 Acceptance of the offer

Acceptance must be positive and unqualified. It must be acceptance of the whole offer and all the terms in it. There is no acceptance if the response to the offer is 'Yes, if ...' or 'Yes, but ...'. Where there is a 'Yes, if ...' or 'Yes, but ...', then this is a counter offer unless it can be seen as just a request for information.

Acceptance of all the terms in a contract can be seen when you tap on 'I agree' to accept your iTunes contract on your phone or computer. This then incorporates all the terms and conditions that you have indicated you have read, whatever they might be.

26.2.1 How do you accept an offer?

Usually acceptance can be in any form provided it is unequivocal and communicated to the offeror. It does not have to be in the same format so an email can be responded to by a text, letter, telephone call, etc. However, acceptance cannot be by silence; there must be some positive act for acceptance. This can be seen in the case of *Felthouse v Bindley* (1863).

Case study

Felthouse v Bindley (1863)

There were discussions about the purchase of a horse. The final letter stated, 'If I hear no more, I consider the horse mine'. There was no further response, but the court decided there was no contract as an offer could not be accepted by silence or inactivity.

There can be acceptance by positive conduct. This was obviously the case in *Carlill v Carbolic Smoke Ball Co.* (1893).

If the offer requires a particular manner of acceptance, then that must usually be complied with if there is to be a valid acceptance. There can sometimes be a waiver of the requirement stated. This can be seen in the case of *Yates v Pulleyn* (1975).

Case study

Yates v Pulleyn (1975)

An option to purchase land was required to be agreed by notice in writing 'sent by registered or recorded delivery post'. When a letter was sent by ordinary post it was argued that there was no acceptance. This argument was rejected as it was a convenience for the offeree to ensure certainty that the acceptance had arrived. Lord Denning made the distinction between the requirement being mandatory and being directory. A mandatory instruction would have to be followed exactly (acceptance must be registered post). A directory instruction only requires completion within the time frame set – so any form of post would do.

26.2.2 When does acceptance take place?

As we have seen in *Stevenson v McLean* (1880), the actual time of revocation of an offer is critical. This is equally important with acceptance. The general rule is that acceptance takes place when the acceptance is communicated to the offeror. There are three ways of accepting an offer that need special attention. These are:

- acceptance by conduct
- acceptance by use of the post – the postal rules
- electronic methods of communication.

Acceptance by conduct

This has been seen in *Carlill v Carbolic Smoke Ball Co.* (1893). The case of *Reveille Independent LLC v Anotech International (UK) Ltd* (2016) reflects what occurs quite often in business contracts – the job proceeds before the formal contract is agreed in all its detail, with numerous offers and counter offers.

Case study

Reveille Independent LLC v Anotech International (UK) Ltd (2016)

In common with many contracts, there was a written offer document which stated that it was not binding until signed by both parties. The offeree made some alterations and signed the document but as the alterations amounted to a counter offer the document remained unsigned. There was performance of the 'contract' in accordance with its terms. The dispute concerned whether a binding contract came into existence by which Reveille agreed to integrate and promote products in three episodes of Season 2 of MasterChef US, as well as other matters. The promotions took place but the document remained unsigned. ➡

The counter offer had been accepted by conduct, because the prescribed mode of acceptance was said to have been waived by the original offeror. Acceptance was by the conduct of the offeree, as, objectively, it was intended to be acceptance.

Acceptance by use of the post – the postal rules

The postal rules were developed in the nineteenth century to deal with the problem of when a contract came into existence and, should a letter not be delivered correctly, where the loss should fall. The rule also adapted the idea that once you have posted a letter you cannot get it back.

The rules only apply to letters of acceptance, not to offers or counter offers.

The rules are:

1 The rules only apply if post is the usual or expected means of communication.
2 The letter must be properly addressed and stamped.
3 The offeree must be able to prove the letter was posted.

If the rules apply, acceptance takes place at the moment the letter is posted.

The rules were set out in the case of *Adams v Lindsell* (1818).

Case study

Adams v Lindsell (1818)

Lindsell wrote to Adams offering to sell them some wool and asking for a reply 'in the course of post'. The letter was delayed in the post. On receiving the letter Adams posted a letter of acceptance the same day. However, because of the delay Lindsell assumed Adams did not want the wool and sold it to someone else. However there was a valid contract because acceptance took place as soon as the letter was placed in the post box and there had been no communication about revoking the offer.

Electronic methods of communication

The law has struggled to deal with the issues arising from modern methods of communication. The principle is that acceptance, apart from the postal rules, occurs when the offeror is aware of the acceptance. This can be seen in the statement of Lord Denning in *Entores v Miles Far East* (1955):

> If a man shouts an offer to a man across a river but the reply is not heard because of a plane flying overhead, there is no contract. The offeree must wait and then shout back his acceptance so that the offeror can hear it.

The case of *Brinkibon Ltd v Stahag Stahl* (1983) dealt with the problem of out-of-hours messages. These are only effective once the office is reopened. Fax, text and email are more modern forms of communication and the same problems and the same principles very often apply.

The Consumer Protection (Distance Selling) Regulations 2000 give consumers a number of rights in addition to those within the Consumer Rights Act 2015. If the obligations with respect to providing key information to the consumer are omitted, then no contract is formed. The Regulations apply to telephone, fax, internet shopping, mail order, email and television shopping.

Article 11 of the Electronic Commerce (EC Directive) Regulations 2002 states that where a buyer is required to give his consent through technological means (such as clicking on an icon), the contract is made when the buyer has received from the service provider, electronically an acknowledgement of receipt of the acceptance. This means that the seller makes the acceptance, but the acceptance only takes place when the buyer can access the communication accepting his offer. For this reason, many online businesses state, 'Your order has been received and is now being processed' or words to that effect, rather than 'Your order has been accepted'. This ensures that online sellers are not required to accept the order at this point.

	Brief legal rule	Case example
Acceptance by conduct	Valid. Particularly in unilateral contracts.	*Carlill v Carbolic Smoke Ball Co.* (1893)
Prescribed method of acceptance may be waived	Acceptance by different method to that in offer may be permitted.	*Reveille Independent LLC v Anotech International (UK) Ltd* (2016)
Postal rules	If they apply, acceptance takes place at moment of posting of letter.	*Adams v Lindsell* (1818)
Electronic methods of communication	Acceptance occurs when the offeror is aware of the acceptance.	Art 11 of Electronic Commerce (EC Directive) Regulations 2002

Figure 26.3 Key facts chart for acceptance of an offer

Tip

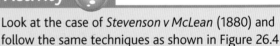

Examinations often include offer and acceptance problems that need to be decided upon. A logical approach is needed to give a precise answer.

Your answer needs to be justified by reference to authority – usually decided cases. See Figure 26.4 for the steps to take.

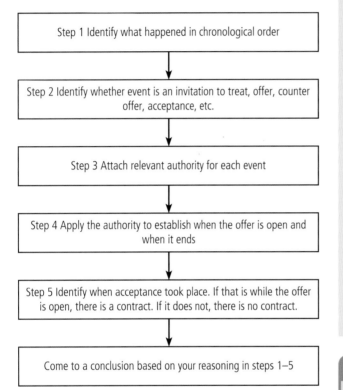

Step 1 Identify what happened in chronological order

↓

Step 2 Identify whether event is an invitation to treat, offer, counter offer, acceptance, etc.

↓

Step 3 Attach relevant authority for each event

↓

Step 4 Apply the authority to establish when the offer is open and when it ends

↓

Step 5 Identify when acceptance took place. If that is while the offer is open, there is a contract. If it does not, there is no contract.

↓

Come to a conclusion based on your reasoning in steps 1–5

Figure 26.4 Steps to take to decide whether an offer has been accepted

Examples

Consider the facts of *Adams v Lindsell* (1818). Assume that A found out (from L or a reliable source) that L had sold the wool on 9 Sept:

2 Sept   L wrote to A offering to sell wool
5 Sept   A received the letter
5 Sept   A sent a letter of acceptance
8 Sept   L sold the goods to X
9 Sept   L received the letter of acceptance

The offer opened when A received the letter. The offer ended when A learned the wool had been sold (9 September). The acceptance took place when the letter of acceptance was posted. The contract was therefore made on 5 September between A and L.

A slightly more complicated case is *Byrne v Van Tienhoven* (1880):

1 Oct   V T posted a letter offering goods for sale
7 Oct   Letter of 1 Oct arrived with B
8 Oct   V T revoked the offer in a letter
11 Oct   B accepted the offer by telegram
15 Oct   B posted a letter confirming acceptance
20 Oct   Letter of revocation arrived with B

Here the revocation was not effective until it was received on 20 October. This was too late as the contract was made on 15 October when the letter of acceptance was posted or when the telegram arrived, whichever is earlier.

Activity

Look at the case of *Stevenson v McLean* (1880) and follow the same techniques as shown in Figure 26.4 to decide when the contract was made.

Case	Judgment
Gibson v Manchester City Council (1979)	An offer must have definite terms, not vague such as 'may be prepared to'.
Partridge v Crittenden (1968)	An advertisement is usually an invitation to treat and not an offer.
Carlill v Carbolic Smoke Ball Co. (1893)	Here the advertisement contained promises that were intended to be taken seriously so it was an offer leading to a unilateral contract.
Fisher v Bell (1961)	Goods in a shop window are an invitation to treat.
Pharmaceutical Society of Great Britain v Boots Cash Chemists (1953)	Goods in a self-service shop are an invitation to treat.
British Car Auctions v Wright (1972)	The bidder makes the offer at an auction; the auctioneer accepts it.
Harvey v Facey (1893)	A request for information and the response to the request are not an offer.
Thornton v Shoe Lane Parking (1971)	In a vending machine, or ticket machine, the offer is made by the person inserting the coin.
Taylor v Laird (1856)	An offer only comes into existence when it is communicated to the offeree.

Case	Judgment
Stevenson v McLean (1880)	Exact timing of offer and acceptance is critical in deciding when a contract comes into existence.
Routledge v Grant (1828)	An offer can be revoked at any time, providing revocation is communicated to the offeree.
Dickinson v Dodds (1876)	Revocation can be via a reliable source rather than directly communicated.
Hyde v Wrench (1840)	Once an offer is rejected it cannot be accepted.
Ramsgate Victoria Hotel v Montefiore (1866)	An offer ends through lapse of time when a reasonable time has elapsed.
Felthouse v Bindley (1863)	Acceptance cannot be made through silence.
Yates v Pulleyn (1975)	A mandatory method of acceptance by a particular method must be complied with.
Reveille Independent LLC v Anotech International (UK) Ltd (2016)	Where acceptance is directed to be by a particular method, but that method is not mandatory, the directed method may be found to have been waived.
Adams v Lindsell (1818)	If the posting rules apply, acceptance takes place at the moment of posting.
Entores v Miles Far East (1955)	With non-postal acceptance, acceptance takes place when the offeror is aware of the acceptance.
Brinkibon Ltd v Stahag Stahl (1983)	Acceptance takes place when a message is opened.
Byrne v Van Tienhoven (1880)	An example of the working of offer and acceptance issues in negotiations.

Figure 26.5 Key cases chart for offer and acceptance in contract law

26.3 Critical evaluation of formation of contract (in relation to offer and acceptance)

In this section we will look at how well the law operates and the balance between the two parties to a contract.

26.3.1 Offer and invitation to treat

The distinction between an offer and an invitation to treat is confusing to both parties to a contract. The differences between an invitation to treat and an offer are often very slight.

Goods in a shop window

In *Fisher v Bell* (1961), the justification for the decision is based on the traditional view of freedom of contract. If the shop window display was an offer, this would remove the shop owner's right to decide whether to contract with that particular customer or not. The customer could enter the shop and accept the offer and create a legally binding contract. The shop owner may then be liable for selling prohibited goods to a person who is under a particular age, for example a knife.

Goods on a shop shelf

In a self-service shop, people generally believe the goods can be bought there and then, or at least when brought from a store room. If the goods are not in stock, the customer believes the seller will be able to provide them at a later date but recognises that both sides have the option to decline the contract. It has been suggested that all invitations to treat should be treated as offers so the law would mirror the public's belief in the situation. However, this would again cause problems with respect to age-restricted goods.

If the item on the shelf had the status of an offer, then once the item is placed in the customer's basket a contract, arguably, would be made and the customer would then be bound to pay for the item or possibly charged with theft. This would also prevent a customer changing his mind without being in breach of contract. If there was a pricing error, neither party could rectify the situation.

It appears that the word 'offer' is generally used to encompass invitations to treat. This is not just in the general public's mind, but can be seen in most guidance given to retailers by local authorities. It would seem that the term 'invitation to treat' is redundant except to lawyers.

Advertisements and unilateral contracts

There is much legislation about misleading advertisements which suggests that these advertisements only have legal significance if they lead to a contract; while the legislation leads to criminal sanctions, the individual affected by the advertisement is usually only left with a claim for misrepresentation unless some part of the advertisement has become a term of the contract or there is protection under the Consumer Rights Act 2015. The only remaining value of *Carlill* appears to be in genuine reward cases – the missing cat advertisement!

26.3.2 Duration of offer, information or counter offer?

The law can be confusing as to what exactly forms the offer and how long it remains open. There are many ways an offer can come to an end. A counter offer ends the original offer, but it is not clear when there is a counter offer and when there is just a request for information. This confusion can be seen from the status of an enquiry about credit in *Stevenson v McLean* (1880).

If you state the length of time the offer will be open, you can still change your mind, as in *Routledge v Grant* (1828). If you do not state the length of time it will be open, then it is for a reasonable time as in *Ramsgate Victoria Hotel v Montefiore* (1866). How long is a reasonable time? The answer is that it all depends on the circumstances. This leads to confusion. The balance is between doing what is morally right and losing money or arguing the point and losing goodwill. This seems to be a poor choice for a business.

A counter offer ends the original offer and this may take place on several occasions during negotiations. This seems a perfectly fair rule as an attempt to go back to the original offer is rarely refused during negotiations – the price rarely goes up during negotiations.

26.3.3 Acceptance

Whatever method of acceptance is used, the way in which the rules work is open to criticism.

Silence

The courts claim the law on formation of contracts will consider what the parties intended to do. This is a subjective approach. In practice, an objective test is often applied disguised as a subjective judgment. In *Felthouse v Bindley* (1863) both parties wanted there to be a contract. The court said that from an objective viewpoint there was no evidence of an acceptance from the nephew. In fact the nephew had contacted the auctioneer holding the horse to remove it from the auction, which might contradict that view.

However, for the court to decide there is a valid contract there should be clear and identifiable evidence. The offer has to be communicated and so, logically, must the acceptance.

Silence as a form of acceptance creates many problems, so the Unsolicited Goods and Services Act 1971 states that, for example, where goods are received without request, there can be no contract unless the acceptance is communicated to the sender. So the individual may benefit and the business may lose out and be prosecuted, but is it morally right to keep the goods?

Of course the need to communicate an acceptance may be said to have been waived as in *Carlill* and in *Reveille*.

The postal rules

The postal rule appears to be unfair on an offeror who may never receive the letter of acceptance or it is late. The offeror is a party to a legally binding contract without realising so. The offeror may have contracted with another party in the meantime so the courts have to make a decision that is only satisfactory to one of the offerees.

A further problem with the postal rule is whether it applies to any other method of communication. The *Entores* and *Brinkibon* cases above indicate the courts' unwillingness to expand the rule to more modern methods of communication. This unwillingness may be due to the courts' belief that an offeree should take reasonable steps to ensure the acceptance is received and that the postal rule is outdated in any event and should therefore be restricted.

Modern communication methods

If the obligations with respect to providing key information to the consumer are omitted, then no contract is formed. However, the seller may still have received payment and it may be difficult to regain the payment made under the non-existent contract.

As we have seen, Article 11 of the Electronic Commerce (EC Directive) Regulations 2002 sets out when acceptance takes place. Thus many online businesses state, 'Your order has been received and is now being processed' or words to that effect, rather than 'Your order has been accepted'. This ensures that online sellers are not required to accept the order at that point, but merely acknowledge receipt of the order, that is the offer to buy the goods or service. The question remains as to when they have accepted the customer's offer and when, more importantly, they can take the money from the buyer's bank, details of which will have inevitably been given.

Summary

- Agreement in the formation of contract requires an offer to be accepted while it is open.
- An offer is a statement of the terms upon which a person is prepared to be bound by a contract.
- An offer differs from an invitation to treat as only an offer can form the basis of a contract.
- An advertisement is an invitation to treat. It can only be an offer when there is a unilateral contract.
- Other invitations to treat include goods in a shop window or on a shop shelf, lots at an auction and requests for information.
- It is essential to know when an offer has been communicated so that it is open, and when it ends.
- An offer can end through revocation, rejection, lapse of time, death and when accepted.
- Acceptance must be communicated to be effective; there are special rules in some circumstances where there is acceptance using the post.
- Evaluation of offer and acceptance includes the distinctions between an offer and an invitation to treat and how the rules with respect to acceptance are dealt with in the modern world.

Chapter 27

Formation of contract (2): intention to create legal relations, consideration and privity

After studying this chapter you should be able to:
- Understand intention to create legal relations: domestic and commercial, presumptions and rebuttals
- Understand consideration: adequacy, sufficiency, past consideration, pre-existing duties
- Understand privity: the rights of third parties under the Contract (Rights of Third Parties) Act 1999 and common law exceptions
- Evaluate the law relating to the consideration and intention to create legal relations
- Apply the law to given situations

27.1 Intention to create legal relations – domestic and commercial, presumptions and rebuttals

Once offer and acceptance have taken place and an agreement is formed, then it would appear that there is a contract. However as a contract is an agreement that the law will recognise, there must be an intention to create legal relations and make the contract legally binding. This is presumed in a business agreement and is presumed not to exist where the agreement is purely of a social and domestic nature.

Key term

Intention to create legal relations – the parties to a contract expressly or impliedly agree that the contract is legally binding and therefore enforceable in court.

27.1.1 Business agreements

Business agreements are presumed to be legally binding. This is quite logical but does not take into account the fact that the presumption can be rebutted by showing the opposite is the case. This can be seen in a so-called gentlemen's agreement which is usually discovered by a term that states the contract is binding in honour only, as in the case of *Jones v Vernons Pools* (1938).

Case study

Jones v Vernons Pools (1938)

Mr Jones claimed that he had a winning football pool coupon. The coupon, which he signed, stated that the transaction was 'binding in honour only'. He was not entitled to have his claim decided in court as the agreement was based on the honour of the parties and thus not legally binding.

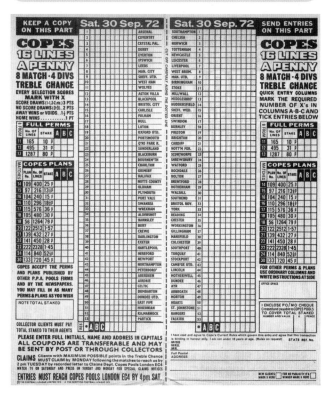

A pools coupon from the 1970s

There are other situations which would appear to be ones where there may be no legal intention. The burden of proof is on the person seeking to establish there is no legal intention, i.e. that the presumption has been rebutted.

An example of this is seen in *Edwards v Skyways Ltd* (1969).

Case study

Edwards v Skyways Ltd (1969)

Skyways tried to avoid making an agreed ex gratia payment in a redundancy. This failed because, while ex gratia suggests a voluntary payment with no liability to make it, the agreement to actually pay it is binding.

The offer of a free gift also creates problems. Where this is to promote a business it can still be held to be legally binding, as in *Esso Petroleum Co. Ltd v Commissioners of Customs and Excise* (1976).

Case study

Esso Petroleum Co. Ltd v Commissioners of Customs and Excise (1976)

Esso gave a World Cup coin with every four gallons of petrol purchased. Should this free gift attract tax? As Esso was clearly trying to gain more business from the promotion, there was held to be intention to be bound by the arrangement, so tax was payable.

Another situation is where prizes are offered in competitions. Just as the free gift is designed to promote the company offering it, the same occurs where a company offers a competition prize, as in *McGowan v Radio Buxton* (2001).

Case study

McGowan v Radio Buxton (2001)

The claimant entered a radio competition. The prize was stated to be a Renault Clio car. The winner was given a four-inch scale model of a Renault Clio. Radio Buxton argued that there was no intention to create legal relations. The court decided that there was legal intention in line with previous cases.

The same problem arises with a letter of comfort which is not usually intended to be legally binding.

Key term

Letter of comfort – a written assurance usually provided by a parent company in respect of its subsidiary's financial obligations to a bank. It is usually where the parent company wishes to give some assurance to the lender in respect of the subsidiary's ability to repay the loan but has no obligation to pay on its behalf.

This can be seen in *Kleinwort Benson Ltd v Malaysian Mining Corporation* (1989) where the courts found that there is no legal contractual obligation but only a moral obligation.

Case study

Kleinwort Benson Ltd v Malaysian Mining Corporation (1989)

Kleinwort lent £10 million to Metals Ltd, a subsidiary of the Malaysian Mining Corporation (MMC). MMC would not guarantee this loan but issued a comfort letter stating its intention to ensure Metals had sufficient funds for repayment. When Metals went out of business without repaying Kleinwort, a claim based on the comfort letter failed as there was no legal intention. If Kleinwort had required a guarantee it should have insisted on one.

27.1.2 Business or domestic agreement?

It has been suggested in *Sadler v Reynolds* (2005) that there may be situations which fall into a sort of 'halfway house' between domestic and commercial, and that in this case the burden of overturning the presumption may be affected.

Case study

Sadler v Reynolds (2005)

The alleged contract was between a journalist and a businessman who were friends. The journalist wanted to ghost-write the autobiography of the businessman. The judge suggested that the agreement fell 'somewhere between an obviously commercial transaction and a social exchange'.

The burden was on the journalist to prove that there was an intention to create legal relations, that it was a business agreement and not a social one.

27.1.3 Social and domestic arrangements

These are presumed not to be legally binding, but the presumption can be rebutted. The most usual distinction can be seen in *Balfour v Balfour* (1919) and *Merritt v Merritt* (1971).

Case study

Balfour v Balfour (1919)

A husband worked abroad. His wife stayed in England. He promised her an income of £30 per month. Later the marriage failed and she petitioned for divorce and claimed her £30 per month. As it had been made at an amicable point in their relationship, not in contemplation of divorce, it was a purely domestic arrangement and not legally enforceable.

However, where husband and wife are already separated, an agreement between them may be taken as intended to be legally binding.

Case study

Merritt v Merritt (1970)

Mr Merritt had left his wife. An agreement to pay the wife an income if she paid the outstanding mortgage was held to be intended to create legally binding obligations and was enforced by the court.

Sometimes families make arrangements that appear to be business arrangements because of the nature of what they are doing. In such cases, the court must examine the real purpose of the arrangement – was it purely a social matter or something with much more legal intent?

Case study

Jones v Padavatton (1969)

A mother had persuaded her daughter to come to England to study for the Bar, promising to allow her to stay in her house. Several years later, the daughter had still not passed any Bar examinations. They fell out, and the mother wanted to evict her. The daughter said that there had been a contract for her to stay there.

At the time when the first arrangement was made, the mother and daughter were very close, so the court was satisfied that neither party at that time intended to enter into a legally binding contract.

If money has changed hands, then even if the arrangement is made socially, it is more likely to be a business arrangement and therefore legally binding, as in *Simpkins v Pays* (1955).

This is usually the case with arrangements such as lottery ticket syndicates. It is, of course, wise to make some record of the agreement as it is difficult to decide whether an agreement has been made or it is merely social chatter with insufficient evidence of a binding agreement, as in *Wilson v Burnett* (2007).

Case study

Simpkins v Pays (1955)

A lodger and two members of the household entered competitions in the lodger's name but paid equal shares of the entry money on the understanding that they would share any winnings. Their action succeeded as this was more than just a social arrangement.

If parties put their financial security at risk for an agreement, then it must have been intended that the agreement should be legally binding.

Case study

Parker v Clarke (1960)

A young couple were persuaded by an older couple to sell their house to move in with them, with the promise also that they would inherit the property on their death. Later, the couples fell out and the young couple was asked to leave. The young couple successfully argued that they had a legally binding agreement. Giving up their security indicated that the arrangement was intended to be legally binding.

	Brief legal rule	Case example
The presumption with business contracts	Business agreements are presumed to be legally binding.	*Edwards v Skyways Ltd* (1969)
Rebutting the presumption in business contracts	The presumption can be rebutted by showing the opposite is the case.	*Jones v Vernons Pools* (1938)
The position of letters of comfort	A letter of comfort is not usually intended to be a legally binding document but, confusingly, it may give rise to a legally binding obligation depending on the wording.	*Kleinwort Benson Ltd v Malaysian Mining Corporation* (1989)
The presumption with social and domestic arrangements	Social and domestic arrangements are presumed not to be legally binding.	*Balfour v Balfour* (1919)
Rebutting the presumption in social and domestic arrangements	The presumption can be rebutted by showing the opposite is the case.	*Merritt v Merritt* (1971)
Social arrangements can be like business arrangements	If money has changed hands, then even if the arrangement is made socially, it is more likely to be a commercial arrangement and therefore legally binding.	*Simpkins v Pays* (1955)

Figure 27.1 Key facts chart for intention to create legal relations

Case	Judgment
Edwards v Skyways Ltd (1969)	The agreement to actually pay redundancy package is binding even though it is described as ex gratia.
Jones v Vernons Pools (1938)	The football pool coupon, which he signed, stated that the transaction was 'binding in honour only'. This rebutted the presumption in the business contract.
Esso Petroleum Co. Ltd v Commissioners of Customs and Excise (1976)	As Esso was clearly trying to gain more business from the promotion, there was held to be legal intention in the arrangement.
McGowan v Radio Buxton (2001)	A prize in a competition is part of a legally binding contract.
Kleinwort Benson Ltd v Malaysian Mining Corporation (1989)	The claim based on the comfort letter failed as there was no legal intention. If Kleinwort had required a legally binding guarantee it should have insisted on one.
Sadler v Reynolds (2005)	There may be situations which fall into a sort of 'halfway house' between domestic and commercial. The person alleging it is legally binding must show that is the case.
Balfour v Balfour (1919)	The agreement was not binding as it was a domestic arrangement between an amicable married couple.
Merritt v Merritt (1971)	The agreement was binding as it was an arrangement between a separated married couple about future maintenance payments.
Jones v Padavatton (1969)	There is a presumption that cohabitants would not intend to create enforceable contractual obligations between themselves.
Simpkins v Pays (1955)	If money has changed hands, then even if the arrangement is made socially, it is more likely to be a commercial arrangement and therefore legally binding.
Parker v Clarke (1960)	If parties put their financial security at risk for an agreement, then it must have been intended that the agreement should be legally binding.

Figure 27.2 Key cases chart for intention to create legal relations

 Activity

Here are two short scenarios. For each scenario, write down the arguments for and against there being a valid contract on the basis of intention to create legal relations. Discuss your arguments in a group and come to a justified conclusion.

1   Three students share a flat. They take it in turns to buy milk for the fridge. As people often forget to do this, they have instituted a fine system of 50p each time someone forgets his turn. All money collected will go towards a meal at the end of term. One member of the flat refuses to pay the 50p fine.

2   Anna's Uncle Paul said he would let her have his car if she got into a degree course at a top university. She has now achieved this, but he refuses to give her his car as he has just spent most of his savings on a brand new Ferrari.

27.2 Consideration – adequacy, sufficiency, past consideration, pre-existing duties

Consideration is essential for every valid contract because contract law requires a bargain and not a gift. This means that both parties to a contract will give something to the other by way of exchange. In our everyday contracts this might be paying money for a newspaper. When the consideration has been performed it is said to be executed; if it is yet to be performed, it is said to be executory.

> **Key terms**
>
> **Executed consideration** – where the consideration has been carried out.
>
> **Executory consideration** – a promise to perform acts in the future.

Consideration is defined in *Currie v Misa* (1875) as 'some right, interest, profit or benefit accruing to one party or some forbearance, detriment, loss or responsibility given, suffered or undertaken by the other'.

27.2.1 The rules of consideration

Over time a number of rules have been developed that are applied to the principle of consideration and to which there are some exceptions. These rules are:

- Consideration need not be adequate but must be sufficient.
- Past consideration is not good consideration.
- Consideration must move from the promisee.
- Performing an existing duty cannot be the consideration for a new contract.
- Consideration may be found where contractual duties are owed to a third party.

- A promise to accept part payment of a pre-existing debt in place of the whole debt is not consideration.

Consideration need not be adequate but must be sufficient

The idea of adequacy is that the parties to the contract themselves agree that the value of things being exchanged is acceptable. The law does not concern itself with the equality of consideration between the parties. This can be seen in the cases of *Thomas v Thomas* (1842) and *Chappell v Nestlé Co. Ltd* (1960).

> **Case studies**
>
> ### *Thomas v Thomas* (1842)
>
> Before he died, a man expressed the wish that his wife should be allowed to remain in the house after he died. This wish was not stated in his will. The executors carried out this wish and charged the widow a nominal rent of £1 per year. When they later tried to evict her they failed. Consideration was not the moral obligation to carry out the dead man's wishes but the payment of the very small rent was.
>
> ### *Chappell v Nestlé Co. Ltd* (1960)
>
> Nestlé's customers were able to claim a recording of a song at a fraction of the normal cost if the customer sent in some of their chocolate bar wrappers. The chocolate bar wrappers amounted to consideration for the record.

Sufficiency means the consideration must be real, and have some value. Real means the consideration must exist. Consideration must be definite and having some value means it has at least a nominal amount of value (as in *Chappell v Nestlé Co. Ltd*).

However, there is little consistency in approach – *White v Bluett* (1853) and *Ward v Byham* (1956) show conflicting decisions.

Case studies

White v Bluett (1853)

A son owed his father money and had given him a promissory note to cover the debt. The father died with the promissory note unpaid. The father's executors sued for the money. The son claimed that his father had promised to write off the debt if he stopped complaining about the way his father was handing out his assets, which he had done. There was no consideration as he had no legal right to complain, and natural love and affection were not consideration so he still had to pay the debt.

Ward v Byham (1956)

The parties were the parents of an illegitimate daughter. The child lived with the father at first, but the mother asked for the child to live with her. The father agreed subject to a letter saying: 'Mildred, I am prepared to let you have Carol and pay you up to £1 per week allowance for her providing you can prove that she will be well looked after and happy and also that she is allowed to decide for herself whether or not she wishes to come and live with you.'

The father eventually stopped making the payments. The court said he ought to honour his promise, and he ought not to avoid it by saying that the mother was herself under a duty to maintain the child. Effectively natural love and affection were considered to be consideration.

Past consideration is no consideration

'Past consideration is no consideration' means that consideration has no value where it has already been done at the time the agreement is made. This can be seen in *Re McArdle* (1951).

Case study

Re McArdle (1951)

Mrs McArdle carried out work on the bungalow which she lived in with her husband and his mother. The bungalow formed part of the estate of her husband's father who had died leaving the property, after his wife's death, to Mr McArdle and his brothers and sisters. After the work had been carried out the brothers and sisters signed a document stating 'in consideration of you carrying out the repairs we agree that the executors pay you £488 from the estate'. The promise to make payment came after the work had been done, so it was past consideration and of no value; she could not recover the £488.

There is an exception to this rule when there is an implied promise to pay for a particular task. This is often the case in commercial agreements such as *Re Casey's Patent* (1892), and occasionally can be seen in other 'important' matters such as in the case of *Lampleigh v Braithwait* (1615).

Case studies

Re Casey's Patent (1892)

The claimant worked on patents for a company. The company later promised him a one-third share in the patents. The company then refused to hand over the share of the patents on the basis that there was no contract as the consideration was past consideration. The court decided he was entitled to the share as it was implied that when he worked on the patents he would receive some payment.

Lampleigh v Braithwait (1615)

Braithwait had been convicted of murder and was to be hanged. Lampleigh agreed to do what he could to obtain a royal pardon (the only way to avoid being executed). Lampleigh negotiated the pardon, and Braithwait then promised to pay him £100, but did not do so. Braithwait's argument was that the gaining of the pardon was past consideration so there was no obligation to pay the £100. The court decided that although the consideration had preceded the promise, the actions taken were at the defendant's request and were so important that a fee must have been implied.

Consideration must move from the promisee

Key terms

Promisee – in contract law a person to whom a promise is made.

Consideration moving from the promisee means that a person cannot sue or be sued under a contract unless he or she has provided consideration for it. Central to this idea is privity of contract, dealt with later in section 27.3.

An example can be seen in *Tweddle v Atkinson* (1861).

Case study

Tweddle v Atkinson (1861)

Both fathers of a young couple who intended to marry agreed in writing to each give a sum of money to the couple. The woman's father died before giving over the money and the husband then sued the executors of the estate when they refused to pay the money. Even though the husband was named in the agreement, his claim failed because he had given no consideration and was not a party to the agreement himself.

Performing a pre-existing duty cannot be the consideration for a new contract

A pre-existing duty is something that you are already legally required to do. Examples include a public duty as in the case of *Collins v Godefroy* (1831) or an obligation under an existing contract as in *Stilk v Myrick* (1809).

Case studies

Collins v Godefroy (1831)

A policeman was under a court order to attend and give evidence at a trial. It was important to the defendant that the policeman attended, so he promised to pay him some money to make sure he did. There was no consideration as the policeman was already under a duty to be in court.

Stilk v Myrick (1809)

Stilk agreed to sail as crew with Myrick for £5 per month. Part way through the voyage, two of the crew deserted and the captain asked the remaining crew to do the extra work, sharing the wages saved. The claim for the additional wages failed as there was no consideration as crew agree to do everything possible in the event of emergencies.

However, if there is an extra element required for the new payment, there is consideration. This was demonstrated in *Glasbrook Bros v Glamorgan County Council* (1925) and in *Hartley v Ponsonby* (1857).

Case studies

Glasbrook Bros v Glamorgan County Council (1925)

During a strike a pit-owner asked for extra protection from the police. He wanted them to live on site. For this there would be a payment. When the strike was over the pit-owner refused to pay, arguing that the police were in any case bound to protect his pit. As the police had provided more men and in a different way than they would normally have done, there was consideration for the promise.

Hartley v Ponsonby (1857)

This case involved similar facts to *Stilk v Myrick* (1809). However, after desertion only 19 members of a crew of 36 remained. A similar promise to pay more money to the remaining crew was enforceable because the reduction in numbers made the voyage much more dangerous, so there was an extra element amounting to good consideration.

More modern examples can be seen in which the courts give commercial effect to arrangements that might appear to have no consideration. The current situation can be seen in *Williams v Roffey Bros and Nicholls (Contractors) Ltd* (1990).

Case study

Williams v Roffey Bros and Nicholls (Contractors) Ltd (1990)

Roffey sub-contracted the carpentry on a number of flats it was refurbishing to Williams for £20,000. Williams had underquoted for the work and ran into financial difficulties. There was a clause in Roffey's building contract that it would have to pay its client if the flats were not finished on time. Therefore, Roffey agreed to pay Williams another £10,300 if he would complete the carpentry on time.

Williams completed the work on time but Roffey failed to pay the extra £10,300. Even though Williams was only doing what he was already contractually bound to do, Roffey was gaining the extra benefit of not having to pay the money for delay to its client. Williams was thus providing consideration for Roffey's promise to pay him more for the work merely by completing his existing obligations on time.

Consideration may be found where contractual duties are owed to third party

Where someone is under a contractual duty to a third party, sometimes the performance of that duty provides good consideration for a contract. This stems from the cases of *Scotson v Pegg* (1861) and *Shadwell v Shadwell* (1840).

Case studies

Shadwell v Shadwell (1840)

The defendant promised the claimant £150 a year until his income as a chancery barrister reached 600 guineas. In 'consideration' (return) the claimant was to marry Ellen Nicholl whom he had already promised to marry anyway.

This promise to marry was seen as consideration so the contract could be enforced.

Scotson v Pegg (1861)

A purchaser of coal paid the defendant to carry and unload it. The claimant was the supplier of the coal who had also paid the defendant to carry and unload the coal. The claimant argued that the defendant was already under an existing duty to carry and unload the coal and thus provided no consideration.

The court stated that an existing contractual duty owed to a third party to the contract can amount to valid consideration for a new promise.

Scotson v Pegg was approved by the Privy Council in the case of *Pao on v Lau Yiu Long* (1979).

Pao on v Lau Yiu Long (1979) is discussed later in Chapter 30, section 30.4.2.

A promise to accept part payment of an existing debt in place of the whole debt is not consideration

This rule arises from *Pinnel's case* (1602). In that case the judge said that the payment of a lesser sum on the day a debt is due cannot be in satisfaction of the greater debt.

This means that a creditor is able to claim the reminder of a debt even if he or she has agreed with the debtor that a part payment will clear the debt, unless there is early repayment or something additional given. This rule was confirmed in the case of *Foakes v Beer* (1884) where an agreement to pay a debt by instalments was no consideration for not claiming the whole debt at once.

Case study

Foakes v Beer (1884)

Dr Foakes owed Mrs Beer £2,090 after a court gave judgment in favour of Mrs Beer. The two reached an agreement for Foakes to pay in instalments, with Mrs Beer agreeing that no further action would be taken if the debt was paid off by an agreed date. Later Mrs Beer demanded the interest to which she was entitled under a judgment debt and sued when Foakes refused to pay. She was successful following the rule in *Pinnel's case*.

The law in *Pinnel's case* is harsh, so two exceptions to the rule have developed:

1 The principle of accord and satisfaction – where there is agreement (accord) to end a contract and satisfaction (consideration) that has been acted upon voluntarily. Thus accepting something other than money for the whole debt is good consideration, even if it is not of equal value to the debt.

2 The doctrine of promissory estoppel – if one party to an existing contract agrees to vary the contract and the other party relies on that promise, then the promisor cannot go back on the agreement as he or she is estopped from breaking the promise.

Key term

Promissory estoppel – an equitable doctrine which can prevent a person going back on a promise which is not supported by consideration.

Promisor – in contract law a person who makes a promise to another.

This was seen in *Central London Property Trust Ltd v High Trees House Ltd* (1947).

Case study

Central London Property Trust Ltd v High Trees House Ltd (1947)

The owner of a block of flats agreed with the company to which he leased the block that only half rent was to be paid during the Second World War. The agreement was made as finding individual tenants for the flats in London was very difficult. After the war finding tenants was easy so the landlord claimed the full rent for the period after the war had ended. The owner was entitled to the full rent after the war.

Even though there was no consideration from the tenant for the reduction in rent, he had relied on and acted on the owner's promise. The owner had accepted the reduced rent without question, so both parties had acted voluntarily on the agreement and so the agreement was valid. However, the owner would not have been entitled to the foregone half rent accrued during the war.

This appears to be in direct conflict with the decision in *Foakes v Beer*. If Mrs Beer could break her promise not to sue for more, how and why is the landlord in the *High Trees* case not allowed to break his promise? The decision seems to indicate that consideration was not a crucial element of a contract and the courts have been reluctant to develop this idea. An example is *Re Selectmove Ltd* (1995).

Case study

Re Selectmove Ltd (1995)

Selectmove Ltd owed tax to the Inland Revenue (now HM Revenue & Customs). An agreement was reached that the tax owed would be paid by instalments and the company started payment of the instalments. The Revenue then claimed the whole debt and wanted to put the company into liquidation. The company argued that it had relied on the Revenue's promise not to claim the whole debt while payments were being made and that equitable estoppel applied.

As the Inland Revenue is not bound to accept payment by instalments, no additional consideration had been given. As the company had failed to pay future tax instalments on time, which was part of the agreement, the revenue could then claim the whole debt.

Equitable (promissory) estoppel did not apply in this case as the company had failed to make payments as they had agreed. This meant that the Revenue were entitled to claim the full debt as the company had not acted as agreed unlike in High Trees.

However, in *D and C Builders v Rees* (1965) the full debt was recoverable because the agreement to accept less was made under pressure which would not be equitable.

Case study

D and C Builders v Rees (1965)

The builders had been chasing payment of about £480. Knowing that the builders were in financial difficulties, Mrs Rees offered £300, saying that if it was not accepted, the builders would get nothing and therefore be likely to go bankrupt. She made the payment in full and final satisfaction of the debt which the builders reluctantly accepted.

The builders' claim for the balance succeeded. The pressure applied had been improper so equitable estoppel did not apply.

Tip

When faced with a question involving payment of a lesser sum than what is due, look for something which can amount to good consideration for the creditor abandoning the rest. If there is nothing, consider equitable estoppel, but remember that it only applies when it is inequitable for the creditor to insist on his full rights.

	Brief legal rule	Case example
Consideration must be sufficient	Sufficiency means the consideration must be real, and have some value.	*Chappell v Nestlé Co. Ltd* (1960) *White v Bluett* (1853)
Past consideration is no consideration	Consideration has no value where it has already been done at the time the agreement is made.	*Re McArdle* (1951)
Consideration must move from the promisee	A person cannot sue or be sued under a contract unless he or she has provided consideration for it.	*Tweddle v Atkinson* (1861)
Performing an existing duty is not consideration	Performing an existing duty cannot be the consideration for a new contract.	*Stilk v Myrick* (1809)
Consideration may be found where contractual duties are owed to a third party	Consideration may be found where contractual duties are owed to a third party.	*Scotson v Pegg* (1861) *Shadwell v Shadwell* (1840)
Where there is acceptance of part payment of a debt	Payment of a lesser sum on the day a debt is due cannot be in satisfaction of the greater debt.	*Foakes v Beer* (1884)
Promissory (equitable) estoppel	An equitable doctrine which can prevent a person going back on a promise which is not supported by consideration.	*Central London Property Trust Ltd v High Trees House Ltd* (1947)

Figure 27.3 Key facts chart for consideration

Case	Judgment
Thomas v Thomas (1842)	Payment of the very small rent was consideration, not the moral obligation to carry out the dead man's wishes.
Chappell v Nestlé Co. Ltd (1960)	The chocolate bar wrappers amounted to consideration for the record.
White v Bluett (1853)	An intangible benefit is not consideration.
Ward v Byham (1956)	Going beyond one's existing legal duty can amount to consideration.
Re McArdle (1951)	The promise to make payment came after the work had been done, so it was past consideration and of no value.
Re Casey's Patent (1892)	The court can find an implied term as to make some payment to circumvent the past consideration rule.
Lampleigh v Braithwait (1615)	The matter was so important that some payment could be implied as intended by the parties.
Tweddle v Atkinson (1861)	The claim failed because he had given no consideration and was not a party to the agreement himself.
Collins v Godefroy (1831)	There was no consideration for it as he was already under a duty to be in court.
Stilk v Myrick (1809)	A pre-existing contractual obligation was not sufficient consideration to create a contract.
Shadwell v Shadwell (1840)	A promise to marry a third party amounted to consideration.
Scotson v Pegg (1861)	A second contract to perform the same task by a third party is valid consideration (there can only be payment once).
Glasbrook Bros v Glamorgan County Council (1925)	As the police had provided more men and in a different way than they would normally have done, there was consideration for the promise.
Hartley v Ponsonby (1857)	A great change in circumstances and workload amounted to consideration.
Williams v Roffey Bros and Nicholls (Contractors) Ltd (1990)	The extra benefit of not having to pay a sum for delay to a client is consideration.
Pinnel's case (1602)	Payment of a lesser sum on the day a debt is due cannot be in satisfaction of the greater debt.
Foakes v Beer (1884)	*Pinnel's case* was applied.
Central London Property Trust Ltd v High Trees House Ltd (1947)	Both parties had acted voluntarily on the agreement. The agreement was valid as equitable estoppel applied.
Re Selectmove Ltd (1995)	No additional consideration had been given so the agreement to pay by instalments was invalid.
D and C Builders v Rees (1965)	Mrs Rees had not acted equitably, so the principle of equitable estoppel could not apply.

Figure 27.4 Key cases chart for consideration

27.3 Privity

27.3.1 The general principle of privity of contract

The rule of privity can be seen in *Dunlop Pneumatic Tyre Co. Ltd v Selfridge & Co. Ltd* (1915). However, the rule has been modified by the Contracts (Rights of Third Parties) Act 1999. The Act allows that someone who is not a party to a contract (a 'third party') may enforce the contract against either or both of the actual parties to the contract if:
- the third party is expressly identified by name, or as a member of a class or as answering a particular description, and
- the contract expressly provides the third party may enforce the contract, or
- the contract term is an attempt to confer the benefit of the term on the third party.

This seems to get round the difficulty that occurred in *Beswick v Beswick* (1967).

Case study

Beswick v Beswick (1967)

Mr Beswick made a contract with his nephew to sell his coal merchant's business in exchange for weekly payments to the uncle for life and, after his death, to his wife, the nephew's aunt. After the death of the uncle the nephew refused to pay the weekly payments to his aunt. The court decided that the aunt was not a party to the contract and so there was no privity of contract.

The Contracts (Rights of Third Parties) Act 1999 would now allow her claim.

The parties to the contract have the right to exclude the Act from benefiting a third party. Most commercial contracts now include such a term so the Act is not as useful as might be hoped.

However, in consumer contracts there are often rights where goods are bought for someone else, such as when a gift receipt is obtained.

Case study

Dunlop Pneumatic Tyre Co. Ltd v Selfridge & Co. Ltd (1915)

Dunlop manufactured tyres and sold some to Dew who agreed not to resell them below a certain price. Dew resold to Selfridge on the basis of the same term not to resell below a certain price. Selfridge then resold below this price. As Dew refused to sue Selfridge, Dunlop sued Selfridge. Because Dunlop was not a party to the contract between Dew and Selfridge, it could not sue Selfridge for selling below the agreed price.

27.3.2 The relationship between privity and consideration

The rule of privity can be seen as based on the rule that consideration must move from the promise, as in *Tweddle v Atkinson* (1861).

This rule is seen as causing injustice and the courts have tried to find ways of avoiding the rule. In *Jackson v Horizon Holidays Ltd* (1975), the rule would prevent all members of a family party as he had made the booking for everyone.

Case study

Jackson v Horizon Holidays Ltd (1975)

Mr Jackson booked a holiday for himself and his family. The holiday was very disappointing. He sued for damages for himself and his family. The court decided that it would be unfair to limit the award of damages to Mr Jackson. Damages awarded reflected all the members of the holiday party.

Extension question

Research and look for legal justifications in other cases such as those discussed in this article about *Jackson v Horizon Holidays*: **www.lawgazette. co.uk/law/claiming-damages-for-a-ruined-holiday/55929.article**.

27.3.3 General exceptions

There are some exceptions when the rule of privity does not apply.

Agency

An agency arises when one person, the agent, is authorised to make a contract on behalf of another person, the principal. The effect is that the principal will be bound by the terms of the contract even though he or she did not make the contract him/herself. The principal and the agent are treated as being the same person so the principal is a party to the contract. This occurs, for example, when an employee makes a contract on behalf of a company.

Collateral contracts

The court may be able to avoid the strict rule of privity by finding a second contract alongside the main agreement as in the case of *Shanklin Pier Ltd v Detel Products Ltd* (1951).

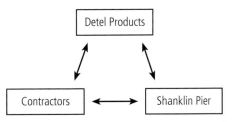

Figure 27.5 *Shanklin Pier Ltd v Detel Products Ltd* (1951)

Case study

Shanklin Pier Ltd v Detel Products Ltd (1951)

Contractors employed to paint the pier were told by the pier company to use paint manufactured by Detel. The paint was bought by the contractors from Detel. Detel made a representation to the pier company that the paint would last for seven years. The paint only lasted three months.

As there was no privity of contract between the pier company and the defendant paint manufacturer, the court found that there was a collateral contract between them to the effect that the paint would last for seven years, the consideration for which was the instruction given by the pier company to its contractors to order the paint from the defendants.

Restrictive covenants

Key term

Restrictive covenant – an agreement between land owners where one party will restrict the use of its land in some way for the benefit of another's land.

In English land law, if a purchaser of land promises the seller in his/her contract for the purchase of land that s/he will not do something on the land, then this is a restrictive covenant. This becomes part of the title to land that an owner has. That promise will 'run with the land', which means that all subsequent purchasers of that land are legally bound by that promise even though they are not parties to that initial contract. This can be seen in the case of *Tulk v Moxhay* (1848).

Case study

Tulk v Moxhay (1848)

Tulk sold the garden in Leicester Square, London to Elms. The contract for the sale of this land contained a restrictive covenant that Elms would not build on this land. Elms sold the land to Moxhay who intended to build on the land. However, Tulk could enforce the covenant against Moxhay even though there was no direct contract between them. This was because the covenant had run with the land and Moxhay was therefore bound by it.

	Brief legal rule	Case example
The rule of privity of contract	Only those who are parties to a contract are bound by it and can benefit from it.	*Dunlop Pneumatic Tyre Co. Ltd v Selfridge & Co. Ltd* (1915)
Relationship with consideration	In certain circumstances the courts try to avoid the strict rule of privity by allowing for damages for distress.	*Jackson v Horizon Holidays Ltd* (1975)
Agency provides an exception to privity	An agent is authorised to make a contract on behalf of another person, the principal.	
Collateral contacts can provide an exception to privity	The court may be able to avoid the strict rule of privity by finding a second contract alongside the main agreement.	*Shanklin Pier Ltd v Detel Products Ltd* (1951)
Restrictive covenants can provide an exception to privity	A restrictive covenant is an agreement between land owners where one party will restrict the use of its land in some way for the benefit of another's land.	*Tulk v Moxhay* (1848)
Contracts (Rights of Third Parties) Act 1999	The Act allows someone who is not a party to a contract (a 'third party'), in some circumstances, to enforce the contract against either or both of the actual parties to the contract.	*Beswick v Beswick* (1967)

Figure 27.6 Key facts chart for privity of contract

Case	Judgment
Dunlop Pneumatic Tyre Co. Ltd v Selfridge & Co. Ltd (1915)	As Dunlop was not a party to the contract between Dew and Selfridge it could not sue Selfridge for selling below the agreed price.
Jackson v Horizon Holidays Ltd (1975)	It would be unfair to limit the award of damages to Mr Jackson. The claims of his family were allowed even though, strictly, they were not parties to the holiday contract.
Shanklin Pier Ltd v Detel Products Ltd (1951)	There was found to be a collateral contract between them to the effect that the paint would last for seven years.
Tulk v Moxhay (1848)	The covenant had run with the land and Moxhay was bound by it.
Beswick v Beswick (1967)	As the aunt was not a party to the contract there was no privity of contract.

Figure 27.7 Key cases chart for privity of contract

27.4 Critical evaluation of formation – legal intention and consideration

27.4.1 Intention to create legal relations

The first issue is whether the parties intend to form a contract at all. In *Kleinwort Benson Ltd v Malaysian Mining Corporation* (1989) the courts had to decide whether or not the document was in fact intended to be legally binding. Courts can view individual letters of comfort as a contract or not, depending on all the evidence in the case.

Whether the contract is commercial or social is a question that also has to be resolved. It has been suggested in *Sadler v Reynolds* (2005) that there may be situations which fall into a sort of 'halfway house' between domestic and commercial. If that is the case, then the presumption will vary depending on which side the decision is made.

The two presumptions created by the courts have proved helpful when deciding if an agreement has legal validity or not. However, the court will always consider all the circumstances surrounding the case and, particularly in respect of social and domestic arrangements, the final decision will not always be obvious:

- The case of *Jones v Padvatton* (1968) divided the Court of Appeal as to the existence of legal intent.
- In *Hardwick v Johnson* (1978) the agreement had legal intent.
- In *Ellis v Chief Adjudication Officer* (1997) there was not a legally binding contract as the court found that the parties did not intend that to be the case.

The presumption against legal intent for social and domestic arrangements is understandable but by considering the surrounding circumstances the courts reach inconsistent decisions.

This is also the case in a business situation. In *Esso Petroleum Ltd v Commissioners of Customs and Excise* (1976) the court, by a majority, considered that the offer of the free coin was enough to allow the presumption for legal intent to remain as it was inextricably linked to the purchase of fuel.

It can also be argued that there should be no need to prove legal intent. Offer, acceptance and consideration are the foundations on which a contract is made. If these elements are all present and there is no clear statement that the agreement is not to be legally binding, then it should be a valid contract. Indeed, it has been argued that this should be the case even where there is no consideration. A straightforward objective test might be a satisfactory solution to the issue.

Extension question

In *Hardwick v Johnson* (1978) the agreement had legal intent and in *Ellis v Chief Adjudication Officer* (1997) there was no legally binding contract. Research these cases and note the arguments made for and against legal intention in each case.

27.4.2 Consideration

Consideration confirms that the law is concerned with bargains and not gifts. So a 'free gift' attached to a contract appears not to form part of the consideration as the recipient gives no additional value for it. Despite this, we would expect the 'free gift' to be safe and to be provided as the contract can be seen as the main item plus the 'free gift' in exchange for the other party's consideration, usually money. This can be seen in cases such as *Chappell v Nestlé Co. Ltd* (1960) and *Esso Petroleum Co. Ltd v Commissioners of Customs and Excise* (1976).

The law on consideration has not been the subject of proposals for reform since a 1937 Law Commission report which effectively led to no change. What reform there has been, has been in the area of third party rights and legislation referred to below.

The most radical proposal for reform is to abandon the concept of consideration and thus allow gifts to be legally actionable. This is unlikely to be adopted as there is a fear of spurious claims as there is with legal intention reform.

If the law were reformed to redefine consideration by looking at factual benefits rather than legal benefits, then the recent legislation would be easier to apply and would have less focus on consumers only. This could also be a mechanism for preventing general use of an exclusion clause with respect to the 1999 Act.

The development of the law on economic duress is effectively avoiding the reliance on the apparent use of consideration that is not freely given, as is seen in Chapter 30.

Sufficiency

The rule of consideration that it must be sufficient, as in the *Nestlé* case, may be viewed by a member of the public as ridiculous as the chocolate wrapper has no value in the real world. The justification for this rule is often said to be the courts' willingness to validate an agreement.

If a party wishes to give something to another party and this is to form the basis of the agreement, then the court will always attempt to allow the agreement to exist and be enforceable. This means that anyone who understands the courts' attitude need not use a deed of gift, but can merely agree to sell something at a gross undervalue to achieve the objective. This was the case in *Thomas v Thomas* (1842). This may then conflict with the criminal law of fraud, or be evidence of coercion on the part of the beneficiary that may be more difficult to prove where there is a deed.

Past consideration

Re McArdle (1951) explains past consideration. However, it seems that the court can sometimes find an implied promise to pay, as in *Lampleigh v Braithwait* (1615).

The argument against allowing past consideration as a valid form of consideration is made to prevent opening the floodgates to dubious cases. This would seem a poor argument as few minor cases would ever go to court given the cost of litigation. Bigger cases

tend to be resolved on the basis of commercial reality and the expectation of payment of a reasonable sum on the basis of quantum merit, which might well be agreed after the event.

Performing an existing duty cannot be the consideration for a new contract

This rule concerns variation of contract, interpretation of terms in a contract or replacement by a new contract to be decided.

In *Stilk v Myrick* (1809) the crew members did not receive the extra payment as they were only carrying out an existing duty – an interpretation of the terms. The same could be said in *Hartley v Ponsonby* (1857) except for the greater number of crew members who had deserted, so there was a variation of the terms of the contract or possibly a new contract.

- In *Stilk* there was a hint of pressure from the crew on the captain for the extra payment or they would all desert.
- In *Hartley* the remaining crew had to get the ship to its destination under the possible threat of desertion if they did not.
- In *Williams v Roffey Bros and Nicholls (Contractors) Ltd* (1990) there was no pressure as it was the defendant builder who offered the extra payment to the claimant roofer.

Today's courts take the view that there is a commercial reality in applying the strict rules of consideration.

A promise to accept part payment of the existing debt in place of the whole debt is not consideration

It has always been a commercial reality that some customers will be unable to pay their debts as they fall due. The idea of bankruptcy and company insolvency rules recognise this and provide a means of distributing assets in the event of insolvency. The development of rules to combat agreements made near to the date of insolvency such as those on fraudulent preference reflect this. Many businesses accept a part payment in settlement of a debt as they will have to wait longer and possibly receive less if there is an insolvency.

The strict legal position would appear to be modified only by the very special circumstances in the *High Trees* case. The doctrine of promissory estoppel only applies when it is inequitable for the creditor to insist on his full rights. Practical considerations mean that, subject to the principle of fraud and duress, the reality reflects the principle of freedom of contract. There is a conflict between the morality of breaking a promise and the strict rule of law that consideration is required for a valid contract.

27.4.3 Privity

The decision in *Tweddle v Atkinson* (1861) does not give effect to the arrangement made by the families. It would appear to be more than just a social arrangement yet fails to be enforced on the basis that the young couple were not a party to the agreement. A similar result was the outcome in *Beswick v Beswick* (1967). In that case the aunt did in fact succeed as she could carry out her late husband's contracts in her capacity as the executor of his estate.

The 1999 Act would apply in the situations in *Tweddle v Atkinson* and *Beswick v Beswick*. However, the parties to the contract may specifically exclude the Act's application so that a carefully drafted contract will not allow a third party to obtain the benefit of the contract. Many commercial contracts contain such an exclusion. The question remains as to whether these exclusions are unfair contract terms under the Unfair Contract Terms Act 1977 for business-to-business contracts or under the Consumer Rights Act 2015 for consumers.

Summary

- There must an intention to create legal relations for there to be a valid contract.
- There is a distinction between business or commercial contracts and those that are of a social and domestic nature.
- Consideration involves each party to a contract giving something of value to the other.
- There are five rules with respect to what amounts to consideration.
- Privity of contract means that only a party to the contract can take legal action on it.
- There are exceptions to the doctrine of privity, both from case law and statute.

Chapter 28

Terms (1): express and implied terms

> After reading this chapter you should be able to:
> - Understand express and implied terms, including the Consumer Rights Act 2015
> - Understand types of term: conditions, warranties, innominate terms
> - Apply the law to given situations

28.1 Express and implied terms

The terms of a contract are what the parties to the contract have agreed. These terms can either be:
- specifically agreed between the parties, known as express terms, or
- implied in the contract.

Terms define the obligations of each party to the contract. For example, if I buy a cup of coffee for £1, the stated terms are coffee and £1 which represents the consideration in the contract. Other terms may be implied in the contract, for example that the coffee will be hot.

Express and implied terms may be of different types which, if not complied with, have different consequences.

28.2 Types of term

Terms in a contract can be categorised as:
- a condition
- a warranty
- an innominate term.

The type of each individual term depends on the evidence, particularly on any description of the term in a contract. Any term that is not clearly a condition or a warranty is an innominate term.

28.2.1 Condition

A condition is a term in a contract so important that a failure to perform the obligation would destroy the main purpose of the contract. For example, if I make a contract to buy a phone, it is central to the contract that it can make and receive calls when attached to a phone network. The reason this is important is that if a condition is broken, the person suffering the failure is entitled to end the contract. This ending of the contract is known as repudiation.

> **Tip**
>
> It is easy to confuse repudiation with rescission. Repudiation is done by the party to the contract bringing it to a premature end. This can be done for a breach of condition but not a breach of warranty.

> **Key terms**
>
> **Condition** – a term in a contract that is central to the contract, breach of which may allow the contract to be repudiated.
> **Repudiation** – the ending of the contract due to a refusal by one of the parties to perform the duty or obligation owed to the other party.
> **Rescission** – this is an equitable remedy that is made at the discretion of the court. If granted it places the parties back in their pre-contractual position.

A condition is said to go to the root of a contract. This can be seen in the case of *Poussard v Spiers and Pond* (1876).

Case study

Poussard v Spiers and Pond (1876)

An actress agreed to perform the lead role in a production. She failed to attend the first few performances. Her role was given to an understudy. When she did attend, she was not allowed to take up the role. She had in fact broken her contract by not turning up for the performances. As the lead, her presence was central. It was therefore a condition in the contract so the contract could be repudiated.

28.2.2 Warranty

A warranty is a minor term of the contract. Only damages can be claimed for a breach of warranty – the contract is not ended and the main purpose of the contract can continue to be performed despite the breach. For example, for a phone, it is not central to the contract if the phone will only store 99 contacts rather than the 100 stated in the contract.

There is no right of the injured party to repudiate the contract. An example is *Bettini v Gye* (1876).

Key term

Warranty – a minor term in a contract, breach of which does not end the contract but allows a claim for damages only.

Case study

Bettini v Gye (1876)

A singer was contracted to perform at a series of concerts and six days of rehearsal. He failed to attend the first three days of rehearsals. He was replaced as the singer for his failure to turn up to these rehearsals. When he did turn up, he was not permitted to continue the contract.

This was a breach of warranty, so the concert organiser could not repudiate his contract which continued. The singer was, therefore, awarded damages for loss of earnings for the breach of his contract.

28.2.3 Innominate term

An innominate term is a term in a contract that is not clearly a condition or a warranty. The effect of its breach may be viewed as a condition or a warranty depending on the consequences.

Key term

Innominate term – a term in a contract that is not defined as a condition or a warranty. Whether it is a condition or a warranty depends on the consequences of any breach of the term.

Many terms in contracts are not clearly either a condition or a warranty until the breach of that term has occurred, as in *Hong Kong Fir Shipping Co. Ltd v Kawasaki Kisen Kaisha Ltd* (1962).

Case study

Hong Kong Fir Shipping Co. Ltd v Kawasaki Kisen Kaisha Ltd (1962)

The defendants chartered a cargo ship from the claimants for two years. A term in the contract required that the ship should be 'in every way fitted for ordinary cargo service'. In fact there were problems with the ship's engine and the ship was not fully seaworthy. Eighteen weeks' use of the ship was lost while the ship was being repaired. The defendants repudiated the contract. Was the term a condition or a warranty?

The court said that not all contract terms could be simply divided into conditions and warranties; many contracts are more complex and

> some breaches will, and others will not, give rise to an event which will deprive the party not in default of substantially the whole benefit which it was intended that he should obtain from the contract.

Unless expressly provided for in the contract, the classification depends on the consequences of the breach. Such terms are known as innominate terms. In fact the court decided this was only a breach of warranty so only damages could be awarded.

This is a straightforward solution to the problem where general terms can have a variety of breaches. The proper remedy is only discovered after the consequences of the breach have been identified. However, there is an element of uncertainty to the innominate term. The outcome of a particular breach is uncertain until the term has been construed.

	Brief legal rule	Case example
Condition in a contract	A term in a contract that is central to the contract, breach of which may allow the contract to be repudiated.	*Poussard v Spiers and Pond* (1876)
Warranty in a contract	A minor term in a contract, breach of which does not end the contract but allows a claim for damages only.	*Bettini v Gye* (1876)
Innominate term in a contract	A term in a contract that is not defined as a condition or a warranty. Whether it is a condition or a warranty depends on the consequences of any breach of the term.	*Hong Kong Fir Shipping Co. Ltd v Kawasaki Kisen Kaisha Ltd* (1962)

Figure 28.1 Key facts chart for terms in a contract

Case	Judgment
Poussard v Spiers and Pond (1876)	Her presence was central to the production; it was a condition entitling the producers to repudiate her contract for her non-attendance.
Bettini v Gye (1876)	The rehearsals were not central to the contract to sing, so the concert organiser could not repudiate his contract. He had not broken a condition in the contract.
Hong Kong Fir Shipping Co. Ltd v Kawasaki Kisen Kaisha Ltd (1962)	Not all contracts could be simply divided into terms that are conditions and terms that are warranties. Many contracts are more complex.

Figure 28.2 Key cases chart for terms in a contract

28.3 Is a statement a representation or a term of the contract?

When negotiations are taking place, many things are discussed so that the terms of the contract are agreed. If what is said is a representation, then if it is untrue it will be a misrepresentation as we will see in Chapter 30. The difficulty is deciding whether what is said is a term or a representation.

The courts will take into account the following factors:
● the importance attached to the representation
● special knowledge or skill of the person making the statement
● any time lag between making the statement and making the contract
● whether there is a written contract.

28.3.1 The importance attached to the representation

Where the statement is obviously important to the contract, it will be seen as a term of the contract. This was demonstrated in *Couchman v Hill* (1947).

Case study

Couchman v Hill (1947)

An auction catalogue stated that a heifer was unserved (not pregnant). The auctioneer and the farmer selling the animal confirmed this. In fact the heifer was pregnant and died while calving. The statement was clearly important to the purchaser of the animal and so was taken as a contract term rather than a representation.

28.3.2 Special knowledge or skill of the person making the statement

There are two contrasting cases which show the importance of the skill expected of a person making a statement, *Oscar Chess v Williams* (1957) and *Dick Bentley v Harold Smith Motors* (1965).

Case studies

Oscar Chess v Williams (1957)

The private seller of a car believed it to be a 1948 model but it was actually much older. This statement was not a term of the contract.

Dick Bentley v Harold Smith Motors (1965)

The car dealer stated the car had done 20,000 miles when in fact it had done 100,000 miles. Even though that statement was not written in the contract, it was taken to be a term of the contract rather than a mere statement.

This distinction is important as the purchaser of the car could take action for breach of contract rather than for misrepresentation. In the *Dick Bentley* case it is crucial because the purchaser of the car would have lost his rights under misrepresentation – the law at the time would only have allowed a claim for rescission, which was not available in his case.

28.3.3 The time lag between the statement and the contract

Where a contract is made later and does not refer to the statement, it is likely that the statement does not become a term of the contract. This can be seen in *Routledge v Mackay* (1954).

> **Case study**
>
> **Routledge v Mackay (1954)**
>
> The contract was made later and did not refer to the date of the vehicle. The time lag was seven days. The actual date of manufacture of the vehicle was not seen as important, so the statement was a representation and not a term of the contract.

28.3.4 Whether there is a written contract

As we have seen in *Routledge v Mackay*, the court tends to presume that everything the parties wanted to include as a term of the contract is put in the written contract.

	Brief legal rule	Case example
The importance attached to the representation	Where the statement is obviously important to the contract it will be seen as a term of the contract.	*Couchman v Hill* (1947)
Special knowledge or skill of the person making the statement	Where there is special knowledge or skill, the statement is more likely to be a term of the contract.	*Oscar Chess v Williams* (1957) *Dick Bentley v Harold Smith Motors* (1965)
The time lag between making the statement and making the contract	Where a contract is made later and does not refer to the statement, it is likely that the statement does not become a term of the contract.	*Routledge v Mackay* (1954)
Whether there is a written contract	The court tends to presume that everything the parties wanted to include as a term of the contract is put in the written contract.	*Routledge v Mackay* (1954)

Figure 28.3 Key facts chart for term or representation in a contract

Case	Judgment
Couchman v Hill (1947)	The statement was clearly important to the purchaser of the animal and so was taken as a contract term rather than a representation.
Oscar Chess v Williams (1957)	A private seller of a car believed it to be a 1948 model but it was actually much older. This statement was not a term of the contract, just a representation.
Dick Bentley v Harold Smith Motors (1965)	The misleading mileage of a car was a term of the contract rather than a mere statement.
Routledge v Mackay (1954)	It was presumed that the actual date of manufacture of the vehicle was not seen as important as it was not in the written contract.

Figure 28.4 Key cases chart for term or representation in a contract

28.4 Terms implied by common law or statute

Terms can be implied into the contract by the common law or by statute. Statutory implied terms are seen in different Acts depending, for example, on whether the contract is business-to-business or business-to-consumer:

- In business-to-business contracts the law is contained in acts such as the Sale of Goods Act 1979 and the Sale of Goods and Services Act 1982.
- A contract between a business and a consumer is in the Consumer Rights Act 2015.

However, as the Consumer Rights Act 2015 has similar provisions to the Sale of Goods Act 1979 and the Sale of Goods and Services Act 1982, interpretation of the earlier Acts will inform the meaning of the provisions of the Consumer Rights Act 2015.

28.4.1 Terms implied by common law

Terms can be implied by common law in two ways:
- through business efficacy and the officious bystander test
- by custom or prior dealings between the parties.

Terms implied through business efficacy and the officious bystander test

The courts will imply a term into a contract if the term is necessary to make sure that the contract works on a business-like basis. There is a two-part test for this:

- Is the term necessary to make the contract effective?
- If the parties to the contract had thought about it, would they have agreed that the suggested term was obviously going to be in the contract?

Business efficacy

An example of this can be seen in the cases of *The Moorcock* (1889) and *Schawel v Reade* (1913).

Case studies

The Moorcock (1889)

The defendants owned a wharf with a jetty on the River Thames. They agreed to dock a ship and unload cargoes at the wharf. Both parties were aware at the time of contracting that this could involve the vessel being there at low tide, and that then the ship would rest on the bottom. When the ship grounded it broke up on a ridge of rock. The defendants stated there was no term covering this. The court implied a term that the ship would be at a safe mooring that would not be damaged.

Schawel v Reade (1913)

The claimant wanted to buy a stallion for stud purposes. At a stud farm the defendant stated, 'You need not look for anything: the horse is perfectly sound. If there was anything the matter with the horse I would tell you.'

The claimant did not inspect the horse further and bought it. In fact the horse was unfit for stud purposes. The court decided that the defendant's statement was not an express term as to fitness for stud, but there was an implied term in the contract that it would be fit for stud.

The officious bystander test

The test can be seen in *Shirlaw v Southern Foundries Ltd* (1939) where it was stated:

> *Prima facie* that which in any contract is left to be implied and need not be expressed is something so obvious that it goes without saying; so that if, while the parties were making their bargain, an officious bystander were to suggest some express provision for it in their agreement, they would testily suppress him with a common 'Oh, of course!'

In *Hollier v Rambler Motors* (1972) the court accepted that a failure to sign a document on one occasion did not prevent the terms in that document being present in the contract, if it was merely an oversight in not signing the document on that particular occasion.

Terms will not be implied if the parties would never have agreed to them had they thought about them. This was shown in *Shell UK Ltd v Lostock Garage Ltd* (1977).

Case study

Shell UK Ltd v Lostock Garage Ltd (1977)

In the contract, Shell supplied petrol and oil to Lostock who in return agreed to buy these products only from Shell. Shell later supplied petrol to other garages at lower prices as part of a price war. This forced Lostock to sell at a loss. Lostock argued there was a term in the contract that Shell would not abnormally discriminate against Lostock. This argument failed as Shell would never have agreed to such a term.

Genuinely implied terms are what a reasonable person would have understood to be the intention of both parties in the context of the contract. *Egan v Static Control Components (Europe) Ltd* (2004) is a good example.

Case study

Egan v Static Control Components (Europe) Ltd (2004)

SCC supplied Egan's company with components. Before 1999 Egan had signed three guarantees making him personally liable for the company's debts up to £75,000. In 1999 with the debt rising Egan was asked to repay in six instalments at weekly intervals and to sign a new guarantee for up to £150,000 in the same form as the previous guarantees. When the company went into liquidation Egan tried to argue that the 1999 guarantee only applied to goods supplied after it was signed. The court decided that a reasonable person would assume that the guarantee applied to both existing and future debts.

In a recent case, *Marks and Spencer plc v BNP Paribas Securities Services Trust Company (Jersey) Ltd* (2015), the Supreme Court has clarified the law relating to implied terms in contracts.

Reasonableness is to be judged objectively – in considering what the parties would have agreed,

> one is not strictly concerned with the hypothetical answer of the actual parties, but with that of notional reasonable people in the

position of the parties at the time at which they were contracting. **"**

Fairness and acceptability to the parties are not enough – the fact that a term appears fair or that one considers that the parties would have agreed to it if it had been suggested are necessary but not sufficient grounds for implying it.

The requirement for reasonableness and equitableness will usually add nothing to the other tests – 'if a term satisfies the other requirements, it is hard to think that it would not be reasonable and equitable'.

The business efficacy and officious bystander tests are not cumulative – they can be alternatives in that only one needs to be satisfied, 'though it would be a rare case where only one of those two requirements would be met'.

The officious bystander test may not be straightforward – it is important to formulate the question to be posed by the officious bystander 'with the utmost care'.

The test of necessity for business efficacy involves a value judgment – it is not a test of absolute necessity, because the necessity is judged by reference to business efficacy. Lord Sumption suggested that it may be more helpful to say that 'a term can only be implied if, without the term, the contract would lack commercial or practical coherence'.

Terms implied by custom

Much of English law is founded on the law of custom. Some local customs survive, such as the one in the case of *Hutton v Warren* (1836).

Terms implied by prior dealings between the parties

The prior conduct of the parties may indicate terms to be implied, as shown in *Hillas v Arcos* (1932).

	Brief legal rule	Case example
Business efficacy and the officious bystander test (1)	Is the term necessary to make the contract effective?	*The Moorcock* (1889)
Business efficacy and the officious bystander test (2)	If the parties to the contract had thought about it, would they have agreed that the suggested term was obviously going to be in the contract?	*Schawel v Reade* (1913)
Terms can be implied by custom	The terms of the lease must be viewed in the light of the custom.	*Hutton v Warren* (1836)
Terms can be implied by a course of dealing between the parties	The court may imply a term that reflects the previous dealings between the parties.	*Hillas v Arcos* (1932)
Terms will not be implied if the parties would never have agreed to them had they thought about them	Terms will not be implied if the parties would never have agreed to them had they thought about them.	*Shell UK Ltd v Lostock Garage Ltd* (1977)
The implied terms reflect the clear intention of the parties	Genuinely implied terms are what a reasonable person would have understood to be the intention of both parties in the context of the contract.	*Egan v Static Control Components (Europe) Ltd* (2004)
Reasonableness is to be judged objectively	It is not strictly concerned with the hypothetical answer of the actual parties, but with that of notional reasonable people in the position of the parties at the time at which they were contracting.	*Marks and Spencer plc v BNP Paribas Securities Services Trust Company (Jersey) Ltd* (2015)

Figure 28.5 Key facts chart for implied terms in a contract

Case	Judgment
The Moorcock (1889)	There was an implied undertaking that the ship would be at a safe mooring that would not damage the ship.
Schawel v Reade (1913)	The court decided that the defendant's assurances were not an express term as to fitness for stud but there was an implied term in the contract that it would be fit for stud.
Hutton v Warren (1836)	Local custom meant that at the end of an agricultural lease, a tenant farmer was entitled to an allowance for seed and labour on the land.
Hillas v Arcos (1932)	While the option clause lacked specific detail, nevertheless it was in the same terms as the contract of sale that had been completed if the option were to be taken up.
Hollier v Rambler Motors (1972)	A failure to sign a document on one occasion did not prevent the terms in that document being present in the contract, if it was merely an oversight in not signing the document on that particular occasion.
Shell UK Ltd v Lostock Garage Ltd (1977)	Lostock argued there was a term in the contract that Shell would not abnormally discriminate against them. This argument failed as Shell would never have agreed to such a term.
Egan v Static Control Components (Europe) Ltd (2004)	The court decided that a reasonable person would assume that the guarantee applied to both existing and future debts.
Marks and Spencer plc v BNP Paribas Securities Services Trust Company (Jersey) Ltd (2015)	The court set out the current position with respect to when terms may be implied in a contract.

Figure 28.6 Key cases chart for implied terms in a contract

28.4.2 Terms implied by statute

For business-to-business contracts, we will consider the Sale of Goods Act 1979 and the Sale of Goods and Services Act 1982. Where the contract is between a business and a consumer we will consider the Consumer Rights Act 2015.

Implied terms under the Sale of Goods Act 1979

The Act contains a number of these terms which provide protection to a purchaser of goods. These implied terms only apply to business-to-business contracts and consumer-to-consumer contracts. We will consider three sections that are similar to the rights of a consumer in the Consumer Rights Act 2015, ss 9–11. It seems that the consumer rights in these sections will use the case law under the Sale of Goods Act 1979 where interpretation may be needed.

Section 13 – the implied condition as to description

In a sale of goods contract, the goods must correspond to any description applied to them. This has been seen to include the way in which goods are packaged.

The result can be harsh, as in *Re Moore & Co. and Landauer & Co.'s Arbitration* (1921), and also very sensible, as in *Beale v Taylor* (1967).

Case studies

Re Moore & Co. and Landauer & Co.'s Arbitration (1921)

The contract was for tinned peaches packed in cartons of 30 tins. When the goods were delivered, many of the cartons contained 24 tins although the total number of the tins was correct. This was a breach of s 13.

Beale v Taylor (1967)

The car had in fact been welded together from two different models, one of which was an earlier model. The buyer successfully argued breach of s 13.

Tip

Remember *Re Moore & Co.* when you look at the idea that performance must be complete and exact in Chapter 31 on discharge of contract.

Section 14(2) (as amended) – the implied condition that the goods are of satisfactory quality

What is 'satisfactory' includes:

- fitness for all purposes for which goods of the kind in question are commonly supplied

- appearance and finish
- freedom from minor defects
- safety and durability.

However, the section does not apply if the defects were brought to the buyer's attention, or the goods were examined and the defect should have been noticed. Many sale goods are reduced due to a small defect, such as a missing button. If the buyer is told of this, or it is obvious, then s 14 cannot be relied on with respect to the defect noticed or which should have been noticed.

Section 14(3) – the implied condition that the goods are fit for their purpose

This applies if the buyer:

> either expressly or impliedly makes known to the seller any particular purpose for which goods are being bought regardless of whether or not that is a purpose for which goods of that kind are commonly supplied.

Therefore, if the buyer is relying on the skill and judgement of the seller in buying the goods and has expressed a particular purpose for which the goods are required, the implied condition will be in the contract. This can be seen in *Baldry v Marshall* (1925).

Case study

Baldry v Marshall (1925)

The buyer had asked the seller to supply him with a fast, flexible and easily-managed car that would be comfortable and suitable for ordinary touring purposes. He then claimed that a Bugatti car sold to him was not fit for the purpose. The court agreed.

There is no need to state a purpose where the goods are being bought for their normal use, as in *Grant v Australian Knitting Mills Ltd* (1936) which involved underwear. There was no need to state that they were for wearing for the section to apply.

The Supply of Goods and Services Act 1982

This Act implies terms into contracts where the contract is for a service and where goods are supplied when services are being provided. There are terms equivalent to ss 13, 14(2) and 14(3) of the Sale of Goods Act 1979 with respect to description, satisfactory quality and fitness for purpose under ss 3 and 4 of the 1982 Act.

Sections 13 and 14 of the Supply of Goods and Services Act 1982 set out terms with respect to carrying out the service with reasonable care and skill and within a reasonable time. These implied terms are not stated to be conditions, so will be treated as innominate terms.

Section 13 – the implied term that the service will be carried out with reasonable care and skill

In a contract for the supply of a service, there is an implied term that the supplier will carry out the service with reasonable care and skill. The standard of care is equivalent to the standard of care expected in a claim in the tort of negligence. This is decided on a case-by-case basis. This can be seen in the cases of *Thake v Maurice* (1986) and *Wilson v Best Travel* (1993).

Case studies

Thake v Maurice (1986)

Mr and Mrs Thake already had five children so decided that the husband should have a vasectomy. However, after the operation Mrs Thake became pregnant again and sued for breach of contract. There was an implied term that the surgeon would perform the operation to the standard of care and skill of a competent surgeon. The evidence was that he had reached that level of care and skill so the claim was unsuccessful.

Wilson v Best Travel (1993)

While on holiday in Greece the claimant fell through a glass door and suffered injuries. The glass conformed to Greek but not British safety requirements. The court stated that as the tour company had checked the premises to ensure the local safety regulations had been complied with and the danger posed by the glass would not cause 'reasonable holidaymakers' to decline to stay there, they had not breached the implied term.

Section 14 – the implied term that the service will be carried out within a reasonable time

In a contract for the supply of a service, there is an implied term that the supplier will carry out the service within a reasonable time. Again this term is only implied when the supplier is acting in the course of a business. This term applies where the contract does not have a term with respect to time and the service has not been completed or has taken longer than expected. What is a reasonable time is a question of fact which will depend on the circumstances.

	Brief legal rule	Case example
s 13 of the Sale of Goods Act 1979	The goods must correspond to any description applied to them.	*Re Moore & Co. and Landauer & Co.'s Arbitration* (1921)
s 14(2) of the Sale of Goods Act 1979	There is an implied condition that the goods are of satisfactory quality.	
s 14(3) of the Sale of Goods Act 1979	There is an implied condition that the goods are fit for their purpose.	*Baldry v Marshall* (1925)
s 3 of the Supply of Goods and Services Act 1982	There is an implied condition as to description as in the Sale of Goods Act 1979.	
s 4 of the Supply of Goods and Services Act 1982	There are implied conditions as to satisfactory quality and fitness for purpose as in the Sale of Goods Act 1979.	
s 13 of the Supply of Goods and Services Act 1982	There is an implied term that the service will be carried out with reasonable care and skill.	*Thake v Maurice* (1986)
s 14 of the Supply of Goods and Services Act 1982	There is an implied term that the service will be carried out within a reasonable time.	

Figure 28.7 Key facts chart for implied terms in a contract as a result of statutes

Case	Judgment
Re Moore & Co. and Landauer & Co.'s Arbitration (1921)	Although the total number of tins was the total number in the contract, this was a breach of s 13 as the way they were packed was incorrect.
Beale v Taylor (1967)	The description applies to all the contracted items.
Baldry v Marshall (1925)	The buyer made clear the purpose for which he wanted the car. The court agreed the car supplied was not fit for that purpose.
Grant v Australian Knitting Mills Ltd (1936)	s 14(3) of the Sale of Goods Act 1979 also applies implicitly when goods are bought for their ordinary normal use
Thake v Maurice (1986)	There was an implied term that the surgeon would perform the vasectomy to the standard of care and skill of a competent surgeon. The evidence was that he had reached that level of care and skill so the claim was unsuccessful.
Wilson v Best Travel (1993)	s 13 meant the tour operator should take reasonable care not to offer holiday accommodation which was of such a nature that clients could not stay in safety. Checks made in this case had complied with this requirement.

Figure 28.8 Key cases chart for implied terms in a contract as a result of statutes

28.4.3 Implied rights under the Consumer Rights Act 2015

The Consumer Rights Act 2015 brings together rights and remedies available to consumers when making a contract with a business. These contracts are defined as being between consumer and trader in the Act, with both 'consumer' and 'trader' being defined. With these contracts, terms are not implied in the contract but 'rights' are given to the consumer and there is, therefore, a corresponding duty on the trader.

See Chapter 15, section 15.4.3 for Wesley Hohfeld's viewpoint on rights and duties.

The Act also reforms and consolidates the law relating to unfair terms in consumer contracts, and sets out specific remedies available to consumers in contracts to which the Act applies. The law also makes it clear what is to happen for contracts involving digital content. This area of law was not necessarily clear under the existing law.

Much of the law set out in the Act with respect to consumer contracts for the sale of goods and services is very similar to the law we have considered under the Sale of Goods Act 1979 and the Supply of Goods and Services Act 1982. You will recognise the terms.

To whom does the Consumer Rights Act 2015 apply?

The Act applies to contracts and notices between a 'consumer' and a 'trader'.

Key term 🔑

Consumer – described in the Consumer Rights Act 2015 as 'an individual acting for purposes that are wholly or mainly outside that individual's trade, business, craft or profession'.

This definition is wider than existing definitions as it includes individuals who enter into contracts for a mixture of business and personal reasons. This means that if an author of a textbook, who is otherwise retired from work, buys computer software for his/her home computer and then uses the software to write part of the book, s/he will still be classified as a consumer. It is the trader who has to prove that an individual is not a consumer in the circumstances.

Key term

Trader – described in the Consumer Rights Act 2015 as 'a person acting for purposes relating to that person's trade, business, craft or profession, whether acting personally or through another person acting in the trader's name or on the trader's behalf'.

This expressly provides that traders remain liable when dealing through a third party, as, for example, when dealing through an agent.

The first implied term relates to pre-contract information. This includes things such as:
- the total price of the goods or services, including all taxes
- information on any additional delivery charges
- arrangements for payment, delivery or performance and the time that you will take to deliver the goods or perform services, where applicable
- your telephone number, fax number and email address, where applicable
- the identity and geographical address of any third party trader
- the address which complaints should be sent to.

The specific required information varies with the type of contract – on-premises contracts, off-premises contracts and distance contracts including those concluded by electronic means.

Application of the implied rights with respect to the supply of goods

The Consumer Rights Act 2015 applies to contracts of:
- sale
- hire
- hire-purchase
- other contracts for the transfer of goods.

The right of satisfactory quality

Section 9 of the Consumer Rights Act 2015 states, 'Every contract to supply goods is to be treated as including a term that the quality of the goods is satisfactory.'

Satisfactory quality is defined as being where the goods meet the standard that a reasonable person would consider satisfactory, taking account of:
- any description of the goods
- the price or other consideration for the goods (if relevant)
- all the other relevant circumstances.

The Act goes on to explain that the quality of goods includes their state and condition and takes into account:
- the fitness for all the purposes for which goods of that kind are usually supplied and their durability
- the goods' appearance and finish
- the goods' freedom from minor defects
- the safety of the goods.

However, this will not apply:
- with respect to defects specifically drawn to the consumer's attention before the contract is made
- where the consumer examines the goods before the contract is made, or
- where the goods have been sold after inspection of a sample and the defect would have been apparent on a reasonable examination of the sample.

This is very similar to the law under the Sale of Goods Act 1979 studied above, and we can assume that the case law under that Act will continue to apply.

The right of fitness for particular purpose

Section 10 of the Consumer Rights Act 2015 applies to a contract to supply goods if, before the contract is made, the consumer makes known to the trader (expressly or by implication) any particular purpose for which the consumer is contracting for the goods. In these circumstances there is an implied term that the goods are reasonably fit for that purpose, whether or not that is a purpose for which goods of that kind are usually supplied.

This term is again much the same as the provision in the Sale of Goods Act 1979.

The right relating to description

Section 11 of the Consumer Rights Act 2015 states, 'Every contract to supply goods by description is to be treated as including a term that the goods will match the description.'

This is again much the same as the equivalent term in the Sale of Goods Act 1979. The description can be an implied description, for example when the goods are on a display. The description also includes relevant information that must be included in any statutory information relating to goods as set out in the Consumer Contracts (Information, Cancellation and Additional Charges) Regulations 2013.

There is also a provision that where the supply of goods is by reference to a model seen or examined by the consumer, then the goods supplied must match the model.

Remedies for failure to provide the rights with respect to supply of goods

If the goods do not conform to the contract because of a breach of any of the rights we have studied, then there are new rights available to the consumer. These rights are cumulative, and are in addition to the usual contract remedies such as damages. The rights are:

- the short-term right to reject under s 20
- the right to repair or replacement under s 23
- the right to a price reduction or the final right to reject under s 24.

The short-term right to reject under s 20 must be exercised within 30 days. Obviously the period will be shorter where the goods are perishable. Exercise of this right must be made clear to the trader. The consumer is then entitled to a full refund.

The trader must bear any reasonable costs of returning the goods, other than any costs incurred by the consumer in returning the goods in person to the place where the consumer took physical possession of them. This is particularly important with respect to distance selling.

A refund must be given without undue delay, and in any event within 14 days, beginning with the day on which the trader agrees that the consumer is entitled to a refund. The refund must be given using the same means of payment as the consumer used, unless the consumer expressly agrees otherwise and the trader must not impose any fee on the consumer for making the refund.

If this right is not exercised by the consumer, they will have the Right to Repair or Replacement under s 23. If the consumer requires the trader to repair or replace the goods, the trader must do so within a reasonable time and without significant inconvenience to the consumer, and bear any necessary costs incurred in doing so. This includes the cost of any labour, materials or postage relating to the exercise of this right.

The consumer cannot require the trader to repair or replace the goods if it would be impossible, or disproportionate compared to other remedies. The trader must carry out any repairs within a reasonable time. This takes into account the nature of the goods, and the purpose for which the goods were acquired. The fault complained of must have been present at the time of the original delivery.

If this is not satisfactory, then the consumer has the right to a price reduction or a final right to reject the goods and claim a refund under s 24. The trader can have only one attempt at repair or replacement for the consumer to have this right. Any refund is subject to a deduction for use. During the first six months any deduction for use is, at present, limited to motor vehicles.

The implied rights with respect to the supply of services

Section 49 states that a contract to supply a service is to be treated as including a term that the trader must perform the service with reasonable care and skill.

Section 52 states that the service has to be performed within a reasonable time where the contract does not expressly fix the time for the service to be performed, and does not say how it is to be fixed.

These two rights and the right of the trader to be paid a reasonable sum where no price is agreed are subject to the possibility of pre-contract statements being incorporated into the contract. These are more likely to be quite detailed, particularly where the contract is for building work.

Remedies for failure to provide the rights with respect to supply of services

If the service does not conform to the contract, the consumer's rights are:

- the right to require repeat performance
- the right to a price reduction.

The right to repeat performance is a right to require the trader to perform the service again, to the extent necessary to complete its performance in accordance with the contract. If the right is demanded, and assuming that performance is not impossible, the trader must then provide it within a reasonable time and without significant inconvenience to the consumer. The trader must also bear any necessary costs incurred in doing so such as the cost of any labour or materials.

The right to a price reduction under s 56 is to reduce the price to the consumer by an appropriate amount for the trader's failure to perform the contract. This may result in the trader giving a refund, up to the full contract price.

Contract parties	Business and business	Business and consumer	Consumer and consumer
Implied terms – sale of goods	Sale of Goods Act 1979	Consumer Rights Act 2015*	Sale of Goods Act 1979
Implied terms – sale of goods and services	Supply of Goods and Services Act 1982	Consumer Rights Act 2015*	Supply of Goods and Services Act 1982

Figure 28.9 Summary of implied terms statutory provisions. *The implied terms are called rights of the consumer. The Consumer Rights Act 2015 also includes specific remedies for consumers.

See Chapter 29, section 29.3 for critical evaluation of terms in a contract.

See Chapter 29, section 29.3 for critical evaluation of terms in a contract.

Activity

Read this scenario:

You have just bought a cup of coffee at a café. You have a loyalty card with the café and as you have enough points on the card you are given a free toy.

The coffee makes you ill.

You give the toy to your niece but when she opens the box, the toy is broken.

1 List the express and implied terms or rights in each part of the scenario.

2 What rights do you have, and what rights does your niece have?

Summary

- Terms are of three types:
  - conditions
  - warranties
  - innominate terms.

- The courts have to decide whether a statement is a representation or a term.
- Terms can be implied in a contract by the common law and/or by statute.
- Breach of a term gives rise to different possible remedies.
- The Consumer Rights Act 2015 uses the nomenclature of 'rights' rather than terms.

Chapter 29

Terms (2): exclusion and limitation clauses

After reading this chapter you should be able to:
- Understand exclusion and limitation clauses
- Understand the Unfair Contract Terms Act 1977 and the Consumer Rights Act 2015
- Evaluate formation and contract terms, including ideas for reform a terrorist suspect may be made subject to this order which places conditions on their residence, movement and activities.
- Apply the law to given situations

29.1 Exclusion and limitation clauses

Exclusion clauses are terms in a contract that exclude or limit liability for a breach of the contract. They may also attempt to exclude liability in other areas of law, for example under the tort of negligence. Exclusion clauses also include terms in a contract that limit liability for a breach of contract or other loss. They are often found in standard form contracts and on notices.

Courts generally accept that the parties to a contract can agree any terms they like under the principle of freedom of contract. However, this view is balanced by the idea that often, during negotiations, one party is in a much stronger position than another. For example, as an individual or even as a business, you have little opportunity to negotiate the terms of a contract for a rail ticket or a mobile phone contract.

The courts and Parliament have tried to find ways of limiting the effectiveness of an exclusion clause.

Tip

When writing about exclusion clauses, first look at the common law approach through case law and see the result. If the clause is effective to exclude or limit liability, then look at the statutory provisions and see whether they reduce its effectiveness.

Key terms

Exclusion clause – a term in a contract that prevents one party being liable for a breach of contract.
Limitation clause – a term in a contract that sets an upper limit on liability for breach of contract.

29.1.1 The courts' approach – common law controls

A clause in a contract that seeks either to limit or exclude liability for breaches of the contract, is subject to all of the normal rules regarding terms, particularly those concerning incorporation of the term. Such terms are likely to seriously limit a party's rights under the contract. The first question to be considered by the court is whether the term is part of the contract. There are three matters to consider:
- whether the agreement is signed
- whether any notice with the term in it is incorporated in the contract
- whether the term is incorporated as a result of the previous dealings of the parties.

Whether the agreement is signed

Where a party has signed a written agreement, they are bound by that agreement as in *L'Estrange v Graucob* (1934).

However, where the meaning of the clause or its consequences have been queried before signing the document, the exclusion clause may be construed as the oral statement suggests rather than as it is actually written. This was shown in *Curtis v Chemical Cleaning and Dyeing Co. Ltd* (1951).

Whether any notice with the term in it is incorporated in the contract

This involves incorporating notices and forms into a contract, typically an unwritten contract.

Incorporation can only happen if, at the time the contract was made, the unsigned document was brought to the attention of the person suffering the exclusion clause.

Any attempt to introduce new terms to the contract after acceptance will fail unless there is a new contract varying the original one or the original contract allows for variation of the terms. An example of price variation can be seen in most mobile phone contracts.

The problem of incorporation arises when the terms are not made clear when the contract is made. This can be seen in *Olley v Marlborough Court Hotel* (1949).

The key point is whether it was brought to the attention of the other party before the contract was made. In *Olley v Marlborough Court* it had not. The combination of notices, tickets and other documents may make it difficult for someone trying to rely on an exclusion clause to prove it was brought to the attention of the other party.

Activity

1   Compare the three ticket cases above and decide whether the exclusion clause in each case has been incorporated. You will need to justify your decision.

2   Find full reports of these cases online and discover the decisions made by the courts.

Case studies

Chapelton v Barry Urban District Council (1940)

Mr Chapelton hired two deckchairs on the beach at Barry Island, and received two tickets from the council's beach attendant on paying the hire charge for the chairs. Next to the deckchairs was a sign which gave the price and time limit, but did not refer to any exclusion clauses. However, on the back of the tickets it stated, 'The council will not be liable for any accident or damage arising from the hire of the chair'.

Mr Chapelton did not read the ticket as he thought it was merely a receipt so he would not be asked to pay again during the day. The canvas on one chair was defective and the chair collapsed, injuring him. The council tried to rely on their exclusion clause as a defence to a claim for his injuries.

Thompson v London, Midland and Scottish Railway Co. (1930)

Mrs Thompson was illiterate and could not read. She went on a railway excursion, and was given a ticket with the words 'Excursion: for conditions see back'.

On the back of the ticket was a notice referring customers to the conditions printed in the company's timetables. These conditions excluded liability for any injury. She was injured on the journey and claimed for damages.

Thornton v Shoe Lane Parking Ltd (1971)

The claimant was injured in a car park owned by the defendants. At the entrance to the car park by the barrier where a ticket was issued by a machine, there was a notice that, as well as giving the charges, stated that parking was at the owner's risk. On the ticket was printed the words 'This ticket is issued subject to the conditions of issue as displayed on the premises'.

Notices inside the car park then listed the conditions of the contract including an exclusion clause covering both damage and personal injury.

On this basis, an exclusion clause will only be incorporated into a contract when on an objective analysis it is contained in a document that has contractual significance.

Whether the term is incorporated as a result of the previous dealings of the parties

As we saw in Chapter 28 in *Hollier v Rambler Motors* (1972), if the parties have dealt on the same terms in the past, it is possible to imply knowledge of the clause from the past dealings, provided there has been a consistent course of dealing. However, the courts are reluctant to find that to be the case, for example in *McCutcheon v David MacBrayne Ltd* (1964).

Case study

McCutcheon v David MacBrayne Ltd (1964)

The claimant had often used the defendants' ferries. Sometimes, but not always, he was asked to sign a document including an exclusion clause. On this occasion, one of his relatives took the car to the ferry. The relative received a receipt on which the exclusion clause was printed. He did not read it, and was not asked to sign it. The ferry sank and the car was destroyed. The court decided there was no consistent course of action that allowed them to assume that the claimant knew that the exclusion clause was always present, so it was not incorporated in the contract.

29.1.2 The effect of exclusion clauses on third parties to the contract

As we have seen, the doctrine of privity usually prevents a third party from relying on the terms of a contract. This means an exclusion clause in a contract may not offer protection to parties other than the parties to the contract. In *Scruttons Ltd v Midland Silicones Ltd* (1962) the defendant was sued for damages resulting from its negligent handling of goods. The defendant could not take advantage of an exclusion clause in the contract between the owner of the goods and the owner of the ship.

The Contracts (Rights of Third Parties) Act 1999 means that third parties can now rely on an exclusion clause, providing the other requirements of the Act are met, and the Act itself is not excluded.

29.1.3 The *contra proferentem* rule

The *contra proferentem* doctrine is there to remove doubt, not create it, so if the exclusion clause is clear, *contra proferentem* does not apply.

Key term

Contra proferentem – where there is doubt about the meaning of a term in a contract, the words will be construed against the person who put them in the contract.

The actual operation of the rule has been examined in the case of *Transocean Drilling UK Ltd v Providence Resources plc* (2016).

Transocean Drilling UK Ltd v Providence Resources plc (2016)

This case involved a claim for loss of use by Providence of oil exploration rigs off the coast of Ireland. Normally, it is assumed that exclusion clauses should be construed *contra proferentem*. However, the agreement in this case was a sophisticated arrangement which was drawn up for parties of equal bargaining power. The exclusion clause benefited both parties, and was part of a scheme for allocating losses between the parties.

The court stated that the *contra proferentem* principle is an approach to be used where the term is both one-sided and ambiguous. If the meaning of the words is clear, then the rule is not to be used.

	Brief legal rule	Case example
Exclusion clause definition	Exclusion clauses are terms in a contract that exclude or limit liability for a breach of the contract.	
Is the term incorporated in the contract (1)	Where a party has signed a written agreement, then they are bound by that agreement.	*L'Estrange v Graucob* (1934)
Is the term incorporated in the contract (2)	Whether exclusion clauses are only incorporated into a contract requires the party subject to the clause to know of the clause at the time the contract was made.	*Olley v Marlborough Court Hotel* (1949)
Is the term incorporated in the contract – the ticket cases	The combination of notices, tickets and other documents may make it difficult for someone trying to rely on an exclusion clause to prove it was brought to the attention of the other party.	*Chapelton v Barry Urban District Council* (1940) *Thompson v London, Midland and Scottish Railway Co.* (1930) *Thornton v Shoe Lane Parking Ltd* (1971)
Is the term incorporated in the contract (3)	Is the term incorporated as a result of the previous dealings of the parties?	*McCutcheon v David MacBrayne Ltd* (1964)
The *contra proferentem* rule	The *contra proferentem* principle is an approach to be used only where the term is both one-sided and ambiguous.	*Transocean Drilling UK Ltd v Providence Resources plc* (2016)

Figure 29.1 Key facts chart for exclusion clauses

Case	Judgment
L'Estrange v Graucob (1934)	Mrs L'Estrange was bound by the exclusion clause in the contract for the cigarette vending machine, regardless of the fact that she had not read it.
Curtis v Chemical Cleaning and Dyeing Co. Ltd (1951)	The cleaners could not rely on the exclusion clause because of the oral explanation made to Mrs Curtis that they were only excluding liability for damage to beads and sequins.
Olley v Marlborough Court Hotel (1949)	The clause was not incorporated in the contract since it was on a notice on a wall inside the Olleys' bedroom in the hotel and could not have been known about when they made the contract.
Chapelton v Barry Urban District Council (1940)	It was unreasonable to assume that Mr Chapelton would automatically understand that the ticket was a contractual document, and the council was liable for his injuries.
Thompson v London, Midland and Scottish Railway Co. (1930)	It was common knowledge that railway journeys were contracts and that there were terms of carriage involved. The fact that Mrs Thompson was illiterate and could not read did not alter the legal position.
Thornton v Shoe Lane Parking Ltd (1971)	The customer is bound by the terms of the contract as he can assume that all the terms are set out in the first notice as in *Chapelton v Barry Urban District Council*.
McCutcheon v David MacBrayne Ltd (1964)	Previous dealings are only relevant if they prove knowledge of the terms is actual and not constructive assent to them.
Transocean Drilling UK Ltd v Providence Resources plc (2016)	If the exclusion clause is clear, *contra proferentem* has no application.

Figure 29.2 Key cases chart for exclusion clauses

29.2 Statutory controls

If an exclusion clause has not been successfully incorporated into a contract according to the normal rules, it will be inoperable anyway.

There are two principal provisions provided by Parliament:

- the Unfair Contract Terms Act 1977 – applies to exclusions for liability in tort as well as contractual breaches
- the Consumer Rights Act 2015 – applies to contracts between traders and consumers.

The current state of play can be seen in Figure 29.3.

Contract parties	Business and business	Business and consumer	Consumer and consumer
Implied terms – sale of goods	Sale of Goods Act 1979	Consumer Rights Act 2015*	Sale of Goods Act 1979, s 12 (right to sell) and s 13 (description)
Exclusion clauses	Unfair Contract Terms Act 1977	Consumer Rights Act 2015*	Limited protection under Sale of Goods Act 1979

Figure 29.3 Summary of implied terms statutory provisions. *The implied terms are called rights of the consumer. The Consumer Rights Act 2015 also includes specific remedies for consumers.

29.2.1 The Unfair Contract Terms Act 1977

The Unfair Contract Terms Act 1977 provides the main protection against exclusion clauses in non-consumer contracts.

It contains a test of reasonableness to be applied to exclusion clauses.

Exclusions and limitations made void by the Act

Certain types of exclusion clauses are invalidated by the Act and will therefore be unenforceable:

- Under s 2(1) a person cannot exclude liability for death or personal injury caused by negligence.
- Under s 2(2) in the case of other loss or damage, a person cannot exclude or restrict his liability for negligence except in so far as it is reasonable to do so.
- Under s 6(1) the implied condition as to title (the Sale of Goods Act 1979 and s 7 of the Supply of Goods and Services Act 1982) cannot be excluded.

Exclusions depending for their validity on a test of reasonableness

Section 3 imposes a reasonableness test to contracts where one party is subject to the other's standard written terms of business.

The test of reasonableness

Guidelines on what is reasonable are contained in both s 11 and Sch 2 of the Act. As these are only guidelines, the test is one that depends on all the circumstances of the case, and ultimately is for judges to interpret.

Section 11(5) requires the party who inserts the clause in the contract, and who seeks to rely on it, to show that it is reasonable in all the circumstances. An example is *Warren v Trueprint Ltd* (1986).

Case study

Warren v Trueprint Ltd (1986)

This case involved the development and printing of photographs. The contract contained a limitation clause where the defendants were responsible only for a replacement film in the event of failure to develop and print the photographs. Trueprint was unable to show that this clause was reasonable when it lost a couple's silver wedding photos.

There are three tests of reasonableness:

1 Section 11(1) concerns exclusion clauses in general. The test is whether the insertion of the term in the contract is reasonable in the light of what was known to the parties at the time when the contract was made. This is sometimes called the knowledge test. This can be seen in the case of *Smith v Eric S. Bush* (1990).

Case study

Smith v Eric S. Bush (1990)

Surveyors negligently carried out a paid-for valuation on a building and a defect was missed which later resulted in loss to the purchaser. The surveyors and the mortgage application contained clauses excluding liability for the accuracy of the valuation report. The inclusion of the exclusion clause was not reasonable.

2 Section 11(2) covers exclusion clauses involving breaches of the implied conditions in the Sale of Goods Act 1979 and Supply of Goods and Services Act 1982 in business-to-business dealings. The criteria are set out in Sch 2 of the Unfair Contract Terms Act 1977:

- the strength of the bargaining position of the parties relative to each other, taking into account (among other things) alternative means of meeting the customer's requirements
- whether the customer received an inducement to agree to the term, or in accepting it had an opportunity of entering into a similar contract with other persons, but without having to accept a similar term
- whether the customer knew of the existence and extent of the term (knowing, among other things, any custom of the trade and any previous dealing between the parties)
- where the term excludes or restricts any relevant liability if some condition is not complied with, whether it was reasonable at the time of the contract to expect that compliance with that condition would be practicable
- whether the goods were manufactured, processed or adapted to the special order of the customer.

An example of an exclusion clause being found to be reasonable can be seen in *Watford Electronics Ltd v Sanderson CFL Ltd* (2001).

Case study

Watford Electronics Ltd v Sanderson CFL Ltd (2001)

The claimant bought software from the defendant. The system failed to perform. In the defendant's standard terms there was a clause limiting any liability to the price of the goods supplied. The court said that it was a reasonable term since the parties were of equal bargaining power and the limitation clause was subject to negotiation when the contract was made.

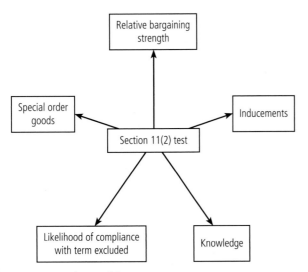

Figure 29.4 The s 11(2) test

3 Section 11(4) specifically relates to limitation clauses. There are two criteria:
- the resources which the defendant could expect to be available for meeting his liability, should it arise
- how far it was open to the defendant to cover himself by insurance against any successful claim.

An example is *George Mitchell Ltd v Finney Lock Seeds Ltd* (1983).

Case study

George Mitchell Ltd v Finney Lock Seeds Ltd (1983)

The claimant ordered winter cabbage seed from the defendant at a cost of £201.60. The seed did not match the description and produced plants that were unfit for resale. The entire crop was lost, at a cost of £61,000.

The contract limited liability to replacement of the goods or a refund in price. The court stated the clause was not reasonable because:
- the breach arose from the seller's negligence
- the seller could have insured against crop failure at a modest cost
- in the past the seller had settled claims which exceeded the limitation sum – this showed that the seller himself did not always consider the clause fair and reasonable.

Case	Judgment
Warren v Trueprint Ltd (1986)	s 11(5) of the Unfair Contract Terms Act 1977 requires the party who inserts the clause in the contract, and who seeks to rely on it, to show that it is reasonable in all the circumstances.
Smith v Eric S. Bush (1990)	The test is whether the insertion of the term in the contract is reasonable in the light of what was known to the parties at the time the contract was made. This is sometimes called the knowledge test.
Watford Electronics Ltd v Sanderson CFL Ltd (2001)	The exclusion clause was a reasonable term since the parties were of equal bargaining power and the limitation clause was subject to negotiation when the contract was made.
George Mitchell Ltd v Finney Lock Seeds Ltd (1983)	s 11(4) of the Unfair Contract Terms Act 1977 specifically relates to limitation clauses and not exclusion clauses as in this case.

Figure 29.5 Key cases chart for statutory controls of exclusion clauses

29.2.2 The Consumer Rights Act 2015

The Consumer Rights Act 2015 covers contracts between traders and consumers. It includes:
● a 'fairness test' for enforceability of terms and consumer notices
● a provision that the main subject matter of the contract or terms that set the price are only exempt from the test of fairness if they are 'transparent and prominent'
● a 'grey list' of potentially unfair clauses in consumer contracts.

Bars on exclusion clauses

There are three main sections of the Act which set out the bars – ss 31, 57 and 65.

Section 31 prohibits a term excluding or limiting liability for the following sections of the Act with respect to sale of goods:
● s 9 (goods to be of satisfactory quality)
● s 10 (goods to be fit for particular purpose)
● s 11 (goods to be as described)
● s 14 (goods to match a model seen or examined)
● s 15 (installation as part of conformity of the goods with the contract)
● s 16 (goods not conforming to contract if digital content does not conform)
● s 17 (trader to have right to supply the goods, etc.).

Section 57 prohibits a term excluding or limiting liability for the supply of services under the following sections of the Act:
● s 49 (service to be performed with reasonable care and skill)
● s 50 (information about trader or service to be binding)
● s 51 (reasonable price)
● s 52 (reasonable time).

Section 65 prohibits exclusion or restriction of liability for death or personal injury resulting from negligence.

General fairness of terms

Under s 62 there is a requirement for all consumer contract terms and notices to be fair. The Act defines 'unfair' terms as those which put the consumer at a disadvantage, by limiting the consumer's rights or disproportionately increasing his obligations as compared to the trader's rights and obligations. However, a court should take into account the specific circumstances existing when the term was agreed, other terms in the contract and the nature of the subject matter of the contract.

This fairness test is supplemented by a so-called 'grey list' of terms. This is a non-exhaustive list of terms that may be unfair.

Look online

The 'grey list' of terms are defined on page 64 of the government's 'Unfair Contract Terms Guidance' document. Find this online at www.gov.uk/government/publications/unfair-contract-terms-cma37.

In particular, terms relating to the main subject matter of the contract or terms that set the price are not subject to the test of fairness, if they are both:
● transparent – in plain and intelligible language and, if in writing, legible, and
● prominent – brought to the consumer's attention in such a way that the average consumer would be aware of the term.

Written terms in consumer notices must also be transparent. So this could be in any communication or announcement, as long as it is reasonable to assume it can be seen or heard by a consumer.

29.3 Critical evaluation of contract terms

29.3.1 The distinction between different types of term

Until the development of the idea of innominate terms, the distinction between types of term was straightforward. Today the important question is how the court will interpret the terms of a contract. Judges use the following principles:
● Where terms are implied by law, judges apply the classification given to them in the statute.
● Where terms are implied by fact, the judges will construe them according to the presumed intention of the parties.
● Where terms have been expressed by the parties who have identified how the terms are to be classified or what remedies attach to them, the judges will usually try to give effect to the express wishes of the parties.
● Where the terms are express but the parties have not identified what type they are or what is the appropriate remedy in a breach, judges will construe those terms according to what they believe is the true intention of the parties.

In doing this, the court might ignore the literal interpretation of the words used and look at context and background if it feels that there is some error in expression of the intention of the parties in the formal agreement.

An example of how these rules can be bypassed by a stronger party to the contract is seen where all terms in a contract are stated to be conditions. Judges may feel that it is impossible to follow the express classification of the terms. In this way, a term stated as being a condition may be construed in fact as a warranty. This can lead to different approaches depending on whether the court thinks the term is clear or is open to different interpretations as evidenced by cases such as *Arnold v Britton* (2015) and *Rainy Sky v Kookmin Bank* (2011).

Case studies

Arnold v Britton (2015)

A standard lease of plots on a caravan park stated that the rent would increase by 10 per cent in each year. The tenants argued that such a substantial increase could not have been intended. However, the tenants' appeal failed as the words were clear, and even though they might lead eventually to an absurdly high service charge, they remained the primary source for any interpretation of the lease.

When interpreting a written contract, the court is concerned to identify the intention of the parties by reference to 'what a reasonable person having all the background knowledge which would have been available to the parties would have understood them to be using the language in the contract to mean'. The court was to discover what had actually been agreed, and not what should have been agreed. It was not the court's job to save a party from a bad decision or from imprudent advice.

Rainy Sky v Kookmin Bank (2011)

The court was asked as to the role of commercial good sense in the construction of a term in a shipbuilding contract which was open to alternative interpretations. Here the court stated that in such a case the court should have the ultimate aim of determining what the parties meant by the language used. This involves ascertaining what a reasonable person who has all the background knowledge would believe it meant.

Lord Clarke said:

> the ultimate aim of interpreting a provision in a contract, especially a commercial contract, is to determine what the parties meant by the language used, which involves ascertaining what a reasonable person would have understood the parties to have meant

and particularly approved the dissenting opinion of Sir Simon Tucker in the CA.

If there are two possible constructions, the court is entitled to prefer the construction which is consistent with business common sense and to reject the other.

29.3.2 The use of the officious bystander test

See Chapter 28, section 28.4.1 for a description of the officious bystander test.

The officious bystander test is still used, and on the face of it is an adequate way of showing that the court is giving effect to the presumed intention of the parties. However, it imposes a very strict standard and possibly an unrealistic one. While one party will usually be all too willing to accept that the implied term at issue was what they actually intended to be part of the contract, the other party almost inevitably will be arguing the exact reverse, or there would be no dispute.

As a result, there are circumstances when the 'officious bystander rule' cannot apply.

One example is where one party is totally unaware of the term which the other suggests should be implied into the agreement. In this case it could never have been his intention to include it, so the test fails.

29.3.3 Non-incorporation of previous terms

In *Hollier v Rambler Motors* (1972), it could be argued that the court was trying to avoid an exclusion clause in a standard form contract. Hollier had been to this garage on three or four occasions in the past five years before, and he had usually signed an invoice which said, 'the company is not responsible for damage caused by fire to customers' cars on the premises'.

Had he taken the car to the garage on the occasion in question, he would no doubt have signed the document with the exclusion clause in it.

29.3.4 Departure from the principle of freedom of contract

The courts will be very careful when departing from the common law principle of freedom of contract. They will therefore be reluctant to imply terms into a contract, especially in cases where this would set a general implication of a term into all contracts of a similar nature.

It could be argued that the courts try to avoid this because of the long-debated criticism of judge-made law, and the argument that Parliament should make changes to the law. However, when Parliament changes the law, we tend to get a confusing situation where the clarity and extension of rights in one situation, for example the Consumer Rights Act 2015, is balanced by areas which lack clarity. For example, what protection is afforded by the law, if any, for the purchaser of goods in a private sale? Is a sale on eBay a private sale?

29.3.5 Lack of certainty in implied terms

The traditional use of conditions and warranties promotes certainty. If a condition is breached and the contract has not been fully performed, then it may be terminated. But if it is a warranty, there is no right to terminate. This approach is inflexible and can lead to unfair results, as it does not consider the consequences of a breach.

A minor breach of a condition gives the right to terminate the contract. This is always the case except when there is a contract for the sale of goods when s 15A of the Sale of Goods Act 1979 applies. This is where the buyer has the right to reject the goods because the seller breached one of the implied terms in ss 13–15 of the Act, but the breach is so slight that it would be unreasonable for him to reject them. In this case the breach is not to be treated as a breach of condition, but may be treated as a breach of warranty.

There is, however, an exception to this exception. This section applies unless a contrary intention appears in, or is to be implied from, the contract. Presumably this means that a term of a contract stating that all terms, express or implied, are to be treated as conditions would then nullify this section of the Sale of Goods Act 1979. Of course that term may be an unfair contract term and be found to be ineffective on that basis.

A similar effect is produced as a result of s 5A of the Supply of Goods and Services Act 1982. However, if an innocent party suffers a major breach of a warranty, no termination is possible.

The innominate terms approach is less certain. It can be difficult to decide if the effect of the breach is sufficiency serious to justify termination. This is important in relation to remedies available and may mean that if a party purports to terminate when they are not entitled to do so, they will be in breach of the contract.

Despite the problems that could be caused, it is possible to see that the innominate terms approach of considering the effect of the breach is more flexible. This is particularly true as many terms are put in contracts to protect the party with the stronger bargaining power. There would be one fewer hurdle for the weaker party if all terms were innominate terms.

29.3.6 Implied terms are default terms

In contracts for the sale of goods and the supply of services, both for businesses and consumers, there are a number of implied terms and terms that are implied not to exist. Examples include goods corresponding with description, care and skill in carrying out a service and the inability to exclude liability for death or personal injury.

We can make sense of the emphasis that the House of Lords placed in *Liverpool City Council v Irwin* (1977) on the courts only implying a term by law into a contract when it is necessary to do so. However, 'necessary' here is not the same as 'necessary to give business efficacy' to the contract.

29.3.7 The Supreme Court is still trying to decide how to imply terms in a contract

The Supreme Court has apparently clarified the law on when the court can imply a term in a contract. They have endorsed the traditional approach that the term either must be so obvious as to go without saying, or must be necessary to give business efficacy to the contract. But which test is favoured?

In *Marks and Spencer plc v BNP Paribas Securities Services Trust Company (Jersey) Ltd* (2015) the court considered the Privy Council's decision in *Attorney General of Belize v Belize Telecom* (2009), which had generally been accepted as the leading modern case on the implication of terms.

In *Belize*, Lord Hoffmann suggested that in the process of implying terms, the only question was whether a reasonable reader of the contract, with the relevant background knowledge, would understand the term to be implied. That decision led to a great deal of academic debate as to whether it had changed the law, so that reasonableness could now be seen as a sufficient ground for implying a term.

In the *Marks and Spencer* case, the Supreme Court is unanimous in emphasising that *Belize* should not be taken as having watered down the traditional, highly restrictive approach to the implication of terms. The upshot of the decision is that reasonableness in itself is not sufficient; the tests of obviousness or business efficacy must be met. There still remains an alternative.

29.3.8 Two different approaches to the purpose of exclusion clauses

- One approach would use the whole of the contract, including any exclusion clauses, to define the obligations set out in it.
- The other approach would be to define the obligations set out in the contract without reference to the exclusion clauses. The exclusion clauses would then be used as defences when necessary.

Cheshire, Fifoot and Furmston's Law of Contract suggests that the approach usually depends upon the wording of the exclusion clause being considered. However, exclusion clauses are more commonly viewed as a defence.

Activity

Look back at the scenario in Chapter 28, page 330.

You discover that the café limits liability for its food and drink to the price paid for the food and drink. Additionally, the loyalty card specifically excludes the Contracts (Rights of Third Parties) Act 1999.

How would this change your answers to that scenario?

Summary

- Exclusion clauses are sometimes excluded from a contract by the operation of the common law.
- Judges have done their best to make the exclusion clauses ineffective.
- Statutory protection is more geared to consumers than to businesses.
- Different statutes cover different types of contract, which can lead to confusion.
- The Consumer Rights Act 2015 may need to be interpreted by reference to cases on legislation such as the Sale of Goods Act 1979.
- The combined effect of terms and restrictions on their use is beneficial to consumers, but goes against the principle of freedom of contract.

Chapter 29 Terms (2): exclusion and limitation clauses

Chapter 30

Vitiating factors

After reading this chapter you should be able to:
- Understand the concept of a vitiating factor in a contract
- Understand misrepresentation, including omission in consumer contexts, and remedies
- Understand economic duress and its remedies
- Apply the law to factual situations

30.1 What is a vitiating factor?

A vitiating factor makes a contract void or voidable. A contract is void if it has no legal standing.

In this chapter, we will consider two vitiating factors that make a contract voidable:
- misrepresentation
- economic duress.

> ### Key term
>
> **Vitiating factor** – something that makes a contract void or voidable.

30.2 What is misrepresentation?

A misrepresentation only occurs during the formation of a contract. Representations are statements that influence a decision on whether or not to make a contract, and are misrepresentations when false. The effect of misrepresentation is to make the contract voidable. This means that the contract is valid unless the person who has suffered the misrepresentation takes action to end the contract. This is known as rescission of the contract.

> ### Key term
>
> **Misrepresentation** – a false statement of material fact made by a party to the contract that induces the other party to enter the contract.

We need to explore the following elements of this definition:
- a false statement
- material fact
- made by a party to the contract
- induces the other party to enter the contract

30.2.1 False statement

The statement made must be false, meaning it is not true or accurate. The extent of the person's knowledge of the accuracy of the statement when it is made defines the type of misrepresentation it might be.

Because there must be a statement to be a misrepresentation, silence cannot be a misrepresentation. There is no obligation on a person wishing to enter a contract to make any statement about what is being offered – but anything said in that respect must be true, as in *Fletcher v Krell* (1873).

> ### Case study
>
> #### *Fletcher v Krell* (1873)
>
> A woman applied for a job of governess. She was not asked and she did not state that she was divorced. In Victorian times this would mean she would not be offered the job. The court decided that there was no misrepresentation as she was under no duty to disclose her marital status and she had not been asked about it.

However, once a statement has been made, even if it is true when made, it can become a misrepresentation if it becomes false before the contract is made. This was shown in *With v O'Flanagan* (1936).

Case study

With v O'Flanagan (1936)

A doctor accurately stated the profits of his medical practice made with a view to inducing purchasers to buy the practice. However, between the statement and the contract being made, the doctor fell ill and many of the patients left the practice. This made the original statement inaccurate. The court decided he had to tell the purchaser of the changed situation.

Therefore, a person must correct information where the situation has changed between making the representation and the acceptance of the offer.

Similarly, silence can be a misrepresentation where a statement made is a half-truth. What is not said is a non-disclosure, and may be a misrepresentation as the maker of the statement has a duty to reveal the whole truth of the situation. This can be seen in the case of *Dimmock v Hallett* (1866).

Case study

Dimmock v Hallett (1866)

A seller of land told the purchaser truthfully that there were tenants on the land. This was exactly what the purchaser wanted. However, he did not complete the statement by telling the purchaser that all the tenants were leaving. The court decided that this part-truth was a misrepresentation.

Where the relationship between the parties is based on trust, then silence may be a misrepresentation. This was shown in *Tate v Williamson* (1866).

Case study

Tate v Williamson (1866)

A financial adviser advised his client to sell some land for less than half its value so that his client could clear his debts. The adviser then purchased the land himself but did not tell his client that he had done so. The court decided that the adviser's failure to disclose that he was intending to buy the land personally was a breach of trust and was therefore a misrepresentation.

Where a contract is a contract of 'utmost good faith' (*uberrimae fidei*) then all material facts must be disclosed whether asked about or not. This is most commonly seen in contracts of insurance, for

example in *Lambert v Co-operative Insurance Society* (1975). There is now clearer guidance as to what must be disclosed and how insurance companies remind their customers of this in the Consumer Insurance (Disclosure and Representations) Act 2012.

Look online

The Association of British Insurers has set out guidance on the Act for consumers and their agents at **www.abi.org.uk/data-and-resources/tools-and-resources/how-to-buy-insurance/what-the-consumer-insurance-act-means-for-customers/**. There are two pdfs at the bottom of this web page.

Case study

Lambert v Co-operative Insurance Society (1975)

A woman renewed her jewellery insurance policy. She did not tell the insurance company that her husband had recently been convicted of conspiracy to steal. This was an important fact which would have affected the insurance company's decision whether to renew the insurance and, if so, at what premium. Her silence about the conviction was a misrepresentation. The company was entitled to avoid the policy and refuse to pay her claim.

The statement does not have to be written or verbal. It could also be anything that would influence the other's decision, as in *Spice Girls Ltd v Aprilia World Service BV* (2000).

Case study

Spice Girls Ltd v Aprilia World Service BV (2000)

The Spice Girls had signed a sponsorship agreement with Aprilia. While the agreement was being negotiated, unknown to Aprilia a member of the group, Geri Halliwell, had given notice to leave the group. Filming of promotional material took place with all the girls together, but when one left it made the films worthless for promotional purposes. The court decided that by all of them attending, the group represented that none of them intended to leave the group and none of them was aware that one member intended to. This was a misrepresentation.

30.2.2 Material fact

The misrepresentation must be of a material fact. This means that it would have led a reasonable person to make the contract and did in fact influence the mind of the person making the contract.

It must be a statement of fact rather than a statement of opinion. A statement of future intention is not a fact. However, if it can be shown that the person making the statement could not have held such an opinion or had no such intention, then there will be a misrepresentation. This can be seen in the cases of *Bisset v Wilkinson* (1927) and *Edgington v Fitzmaurice* (1885).

Case studies

Bisset v Wilkinson (1927)

The seller of farmland that had never had sheep on it was asked by the buyer how many sheep it could take. Although not a sheep farmer, he stated that he thought it would support about 2,000. This turned out to be false. However, as he genuinely believed his opinion to be accurate, it was not a misrepresentation.

Edgington v Fitzmaurice (1885)

The claimant invested in a company. The directors of the company falsely stated that the investment was to be used to complete alterations to the buildings of the company and other developments. In fact it was used to pay off existing debts. The representation was seen as a statement of fact rather than just future intention, as they did not have the intention to make alterations, etc. This was a misrepresentation.

30.2.3 Made by a party to the contract

This means that a person is not liable for statements made by others unless they are their agent. This means, for example, that a newspaper review of an item cannot be a misrepresentation.

30.2.4 Induces the other party to enter the contract

This means that the statement must lead the other party into making the contract, and must be a critical part of making the decision. The statement must be important to the person making the contract, and they must have relied on the statement made rather than their own judgment or information they obtained elsewhere for there to be a misrepresentation. This was shown in *Attwood v Small* (1838).

Case study

Attwood v Small (1838)

The seller of a mine made a false statement to the purchaser about the earnings from a mine. The buyer instructed a surveyor to confirm this statement, which he did (incorrectly). The purchaser bought the mine and then discovered the statement to be untrue. There was no misrepresentation as the purchaser relied on the survey report and not the seller's statement.

It does not matter if the victim could have discovered the truth by taking reasonable steps or it was unreasonable to rely on the untrue statement. The fact that the untrue statement was relied upon is enough to make it amount to a misrepresentation, as in *Redgrave v Hurd* (1881).

Case study

Redgrave v Hurd (1881)

The purchaser of a solicitor's practice was given a set of accounts to look at. The seller verbally misled the purchaser as to the true earnings. He relied on the statement and did not look at the accounts. Had he done so, he would have seen that the seller's statement was false. He was entitled to rely on the seller's statement, which, as it was untrue, was a misrepresentation.

In *Museprime Properties Ltd v Adhill Properties Ltd* (1990) it was decided that what the reasonable person would, or would not, have done is irrelevant.

Case study

Museprime Properties Ltd v Adhill Properties Ltd (1990)

The purchaser of property relied on inaccurate statements about rents made in auction particulars. The defendant argued that no 'reasonable' purchaser would have relied on these statements and would have made other enquiries. However, as the purchaser had relied on the statements, there was reliance and so there could be a misrepresentation.

30.2.5 Misrepresentation – omissions in consumer context

Section 12 of the Consumer Rights Act 2015 covers pre-contract information included in a contract to supply goods. The trader has to provide certain information to the consumer before the contract becomes binding. A change to any of that information, made before entering into the contract or later, is not effective unless expressly agreed between the consumer and the trader.

Under the Consumer Protection (Amendment) Regulations 2014, a misleading omission is where a trader deliberately misses out key information that the consumer might need to make an informed decision about the purchase of goods or services. All consumer information must be displayed clearly. For the purposes of the

Regulations, it is considered misleading if a trader does any of the following:

- omits material information that the average consumer needs, according to the context, to make an informed transactional decision
- hides or provides material information in an unclear, unintelligible, ambiguous or untimely manner
- fails to identify the commercial intent of the commercial practice if not already apparent from the context.

In effect, the obscure presentation of consumer information will be treated as a misleading omission.

	Brief legal rule	Case example
Misrepresentation definition	Misrepresentation is a false statement of material fact made by a party to the contract that induces the other party to enter the contract.	
There must be a false statement.	If nothing is said or asked it cannot be a statement and, if false, misrepresentation.	*Fletcher v Krell* (1873)
Silence is not usually a misrepresentation unless there are changed facts.	A statement which is true when made but becomes false before the contract is made must be corrected.	*With v O'Flanagan* (1936)
The statement does not have to be written or verbal.	The statement can be made pictorially or by appearance.	*Spice Girls Ltd v Aprilia World Service BV* (2000)
The misrepresentation must be of a material fact.	It must be a statement of fact rather than a statement of opinion.	*Bisset v Wilkinson* (1927)
It must induce the other party to enter the contract.	The statement must be important to the person making the contract and they must have relied on the statement made rather than their own judgment.	*Redgrave v Hurd* (1881)

Figure 30.1 Key facts chart for misrepresentation

Case	Judgment
Fletcher v Krell (1873)	There was no misrepresentation as she was under no duty to disclose her marital status and she had not been asked about it.
With v O'Flanagan (1936)	There was a continuing representation; he had to tell any prospective purchaser of changes to the situation.
Dimmock v Hallett (1866)	A part-truth was a misrepresentation.
Tate v Williamson (1866)	The adviser's failure to disclose that he was intending to buy the land personally was a breach of trust and was therefore a misrepresentation.
Lambert v Co-operative Insurance Society (1975)	Where a contract is a contract of 'utmost good faith' (*uberrimae fidei*) then all material facts must be disclosed whether asked about or not. An example is a contract of insurance.
Spice Girls Ltd v Aprilia World Service BV (2000)	By all the Spice Girls attending photos for an advertising campaign, the group represented that none of them intended to leave the group and none of them was aware that one member intended to.
Bisset v Wilkinson (1927)	An expression of the seller's honestly held opinions was not a misrepresentation.
Edgington v Fitzmaurice (1885)	A statement of future intention can be seen as a statement of fact if it was proved that the maker had no such intention and therefore can be a misrepresentation.
Attwood v Small (1838)	A person must have relied on the statement made rather than his own judgement or information he obtained elsewhere for there to be a misrepresentation.
Redgrave v Hurd (1881)	The fact that the untrue statement was relied upon is enough to make it amount to a misrepresentation even if he could easily have found out the truth.
Museprime Properties Ltd v Adhill Properties Ltd (1990)	What the reasonable person would, or would not, have done is irrelevant; if there is reliance on the false statement, it can be a misrepresentation.

Figure 30.2 Key cases chart for misrepresentation

30.3 Different types of misrepresentation

There are three possible types of misrepresentation:
- innocent
- negligent
- fraudulent.

Each has different possible remedies.

30.3.1 Innocent misrepresentation

The Misrepresentation Act 1967 clarifies the definition of innocent misrepresentation as one which is genuinely held on reasonable grounds. This is a false statement made honestly – the person making the statement always believed it to be true. The remedy is either rescission or damages instead of rescission. This is under the courts' discretion as stated in the Misrepresentation Act 1967.

Rescission and damages are not both available for innocent misrepresentation (as for fraudulent and negligent misrepresentation) but only as alternative remedies.

30.3.2 Negligent misrepresentation

Historically, any misrepresentation that was not fraudulent was an innocent misrepresentation, and the only possible outcome was if the court was minded to award rescission. The law on negligent misrepresentation started with the case of *Hedley Byrne v Heller* (1964) with the possibility of a claim in the law of tort.

Negligent misrepresentation is a false statement made by a person who had no reasonable grounds for believing it to be true. It is not a deliberate lie, but there is nothing to suggest that the maker of the statement believed it to be true.

There are two types of negligent misrepresentation:
- under the common law tort of negligence
- under the Misrepresentation Act 1967.

Under the common law tort of negligence

In the case of *Hedley Byrne & Co. Ltd v Heller & Partners Ltd* (1964), the court suggested that a claim for a misrepresentation based on negligence would be allowed.

Under the Misrepresentation Act 1967

Section 2(1) of the Misrepresentation Act created a statutory liability for negligent misrepresentation which does not require there to be a special relationship between the parties. All that is needed is for there to be a misrepresentation which results in a contract and the victim suffers loss. This is much broader than any of the previous possible claims. It is particularly appropriate where the claimant is unable to prove fraud.

Under the Act, once the victim has proved there was a misrepresentation the burden of proof is then on the person making the statement that there were reasonable grounds to believe the statement was true. This reverses the usual burden of proof in civil cases when it is for the victim to prove the case. This means the Act is preferable for the victim to use than the *Hedley Byrne* principle. An example can be seen in the case of *Howard Marine v Ogden & Sons* (1978).

Case study

Howard Marine v Ogden & Sons (1978)

Ogden hired two dredgers from Howard Marine for £1800 per week to carry out works for Northumbrian Water Authority. So as to complete a tender for the work, Ogden asked Howard for the capacity of the barge. Howard checked Lloyds Register which stated the capacity was 850 cubic metres. In fact the entry was incorrect and the capacity was much lower. Therefore the work carried out by Ogden took much longer and cost a great deal more to perform.

Howard argued that they had reasonable grounds for believing the statement to be true as they had checked Lloyds Register. However, as they had the registration document of the barge which stated the correct capacity, this argument failed.

30.3.3 Fraudulent misrepresentation

Fraudulent misrepresentation has its origins in the tort of deceit. *Derry v Peek* (1889) set this out and stated that fraudulent misrepresentation is when there is a statement which the person making the representation knows to be untrue, or is reckless as to whether or not it is true.

Case study

Derry v Peek (1889)

A tram company used horses to pull its trams. The directors of the company believed that under a recent Act of Parliament, the Board of Trade would consent to the company using motor-driven trams and that this consent was a formality, but did not check. The use of powered trams would make the company more profitable and the directors advertised for investors for the company on this basis. The company did not obtain the consent and the company shares dropped in value. The purchasers of the shares sued for their losses.

There was no fraudulent misrepresentation because the issuers of the prospectus had applied for permission and reasonably expected it to be granted. The directors were only careless as to whether what they said was true (possibly either innocent or negligent misrepresentation).

In the news

Developer loses £5 million lawsuit

Richard Butler-Creagh hoped to make millions by acting as an intermediary in the sale of Fawley Court near Henley-on-Thames in Buckinghamshire. He went to court to sue the company involved for the disputed £5 million fee. But Mr Justice Eady threw out the legal action against Aida Hersham and her company Cherrilow Ltd after he found that Mr Butler-Creagh had constructed an elaborate scheme to convince the defendants to pay him millions for doing 'effectively nothing'.

Mr Butler-Creagh had acquired the contract for the grand house from the Marian Fathers, a Roman Catholic order, for £22.5 million in 2008. He claimed Ms Hersham owed him a £5 million 'facilitating fee' after he agreed to let her 'step into his shoes' and buy the impressive property. Ms Hersham denied that there had been any such agreement. Cherrilow eventually bought the property for £13 million.

Mr Justice Eady threw out the action after finding Mr Butler-Creagh had failed to establish his case, adding that it was clear the developer had a scheme in mind. He said, 'In truth, and in law, he had no other role than as an officious bystander.' Mr Butler-Creagh, added the judge, 'told lie after lie' in his dealings with the Marian Fathers and Ms Hersham.

The judge concluded that Cherrilow did rely, as always intended by Mr Butler-Creagh, on false misrepresentations of fact and had it not done so, the purchase would not have been made. The company claims it has lost £9,864,940 from the transaction.

Source: Adapted from an article by Damien Gayle in the Daily Mail online, 7 October 2011

A fraudulent misrepresentation is not only an out-and-out incorrect answer to an inquiry but can also be an overly rose-tinted view of the position. This was shown in *Greenridge Luton One Ltd v Kempton Investments Ltd* (2016).

Case study

Greenridge Luton One Ltd v Kempton Investments Ltd (2016)

A buyer of a commercial property was entitled to the return of its deposit and an award of damages. It had relied on an untrue representation made in replies to enquiries, which played down the reason that a major tenant had not paid the service charge. It was told that this was because of 'historical issues', but in fact there was a pending dispute. This amounted to a fraudulent misrepresentation.

30.3.4 Remedies for innocent misrepresentation

The remedy of rescission

Rescission is an equitable remedy. All equitable remedies are discretionary, which means that the court will only award it if it is fair to do so in all the circumstances. The idea of rescission means the parties are returned to the positions they were in before the contract was made. The justification for this rule is that the misrepresentation induced the contract, and had the misrepresented party known the truth there would have been no contract.

However, the remedy of rescission will not be available in the following situations:
- restitution to the original pre-contract position is impossible
- the contract is affirmed
- delay
- a third party has gained rights over the property.

Restitution to the original pre-contract position is impossible

This was shown in *Clarke v Dickson* (1858).

Case study

Clarke v Dickson (1858)

The claimant was misled into becoming a partner. Rescission was not available – he could not return the partnership as the firm had become a limited company.

The contract is affirmed

Affirmation is where the innocent party decides to carry on with the contract despite being aware of the misrepresentation. The right to seek to rescind the contract is then lost, as demonstrated in *Long v Lloyd* (1958).

Case study

Long v Lloyd (1958)

The claimant was told by the seller that a lorry was in excellent condition, but shortly after the sale it broke down. The claimant noticed faults with the lorry and contacted the defendant who offered to pay half the repairs, which he agreed to.

The lorry broke down again shortly afterwards and the claimant wanted to rescind the contract. The court refused to grant rescission because by persevering with the lorry after the first breakdown and agreeing the share of the cost of repairs, he had indicated his willingness to continue with the contract and so affirmed the contract.

Delay

One maxim of equity is that delay defeats equity. The idea behind this is that once a contract has been completed, any complaints are likely to arise within a short time and after that you can assume there are no major problems. This can be seen in *Leaf v International Galleries* (1950).

Case study

Leaf v International Galleries (1950)

In 1944, the claimant had purchased a picture of Salisbury Cathedral from the defendant. He was told that it was by Constable but found out it was not by the famous artist when he tried to sell it five years later. Even though he had no means of finding out the truth until he came to sell the painting, rescission was not allowed because of the delay in bringing his claim.

A third party has gained rights over the property

Where someone else has gained an interest in the goods, then rescission will not be granted as this would be unfair on the innocent third party. This was shown in *Lewis v Averay* (1972).

Case study

Lewis v Averay (1972)

Lewis sold his car and let the buyer take the car away in exchange for a cheque. The cheque was worthless. He had accepted it as he was persuaded by the fraudster that he was the well-known actor Richard Green who had played Robin Hood in the television series. The fraudster then sold the car on to the defendant, an innocent third party.

The original seller's only effective remedy was to claim rescission and to ask for the car to be returned to him by the innocent third party. The claim for rescission failed as, between the two innocent parties, it would be more unfair to deprive the third party of the car purchased in good faith.

The remedy of damages

There is no right to damages for an innocent misrepresentation. The court has discretion to award damages instead of rescission under s 2(2) of the Misrepresentation Act 1967. In *Government of Zanzibar v British Aerospace (Lancaster House) Ltd* (2000) it was stated that damages under s 2(2) were awarded in place of rescission – this meant that a party who had lost the right to rescind the contract, for example because of delay, could also not claim damages under this section.

30.3.5 Remedies for negligent misrepresentation

The remedies for negligent misrepresentation are rescission and/or damages. The remedy of rescission has been discussed above. The remedy of damages, if the *Hedley Byrne* principle is applied, are calculated according to the law of tort. It also means that the principle of contributory negligence under the Law Reform (Contributory Negligence) Act 1943 will apply, so damages may be reduced accordingly.

See *OCR AS/A Level Law Book 1* Chapter 25 for more information on the award of damages in tort.

If the claim is under the Misrepresentation Act 1967, damages are again calculated according to a tort measure, because a claim under the Act is made where fraud cannot be proved. In *Royscot Trust Ltd v Rogerson* (1991) the Court of Appeal decided that the measure of damages under s 2(1) is the same as in fraud.

Royscot Trust Ltd v Rogerson (1991)

A car dealer negligently misrepresented to a finance company the amount of a deposit paid for a car by a purchaser. The finance company lost money when the purchaser defaulted on the hire-purchase agreement. The court decided that the damages for negligent misrepresentation under the Act are the same as for fraud.

30.3.6 Remedies for fraudulent misrepresentation

The remedies are rescission and damages in the tort of deceit. Both of these have been discussed above. An example of damages in the tort of deceit can be seen in the case of *Smith New Court v Scrimgeour Vickers* (1996) where the court awarded the victim damages based on the difference between the amount paid for shares and the final sale price – more than the usual award of damages in a contract.

Damages based on fraudulent misrepresentation aim to put the victim in the position they were in

before the tort (the misrepresentation) occurred. However, the court seems willing to take the view that contractual damages may be appropriate in certain circumstances. In *East v Maurer* (1991) the Court of Appeal stated that it was possible in principle to recover damages for loss of profit following a fraudulent misrepresentation.

East v Maurer (1991)

The claimant had bought a hairdressing salon from the defendant, who continued to trade from another salon he owned, despite telling the purchaser that he did not intend to continue to work at his other salon. As a result, the purchaser lost business to the defendant. The victim suffered a loss of profit as a result which was only recoverable under breach of contract, not fraudulent misrepresentation.

The court decided the victim would have purchased a different business if the truth had been known. The tort calculation of damages awarded him the profit he would have earned from that business.

Type	Level of truth	Remedy	Example
Innocent misrepresentation	The maker of the statement always believes it to be true.	Rescission or damages under Misrepresentation Act 1967.	*Leaf v International Galleries* (1950)
Negligent misrepresentation	The maker of the statement had no reasonable grounds for believing it to be true.	Rescission and damages in the tort of negligence.	
Fraudulent misrepresentation	The maker of the statement knew the statement to be false.	Rescission and damages in the tort of deceit.	*Cherrilow Ltd v Butler-Creagh* (2011)

Figure 30.3 Summary chart of types of misrepresentation

	Brief legal rule	Case example
Rescission definition	The equitable remedy of rescission means the parties are returned to the positions they were in before the contract was made.	
Rescission is not allowed (1) – cannot restore the pre-contract situation	Rescission is not allowed if the parties cannot be restored to their pre-contractual position.	*Clarke v Dickson* (1858)
Rescission is not allowed (2) – affirmation	Affirmation is where the innocent party decides to carry on with the contract despite being aware of the misrepresentation.	*Long v Lloyd* (1958)
Rescission is not allowed (3) – delay	A delay in bringing the claim for misrepresentation to court will mean rescission is not available as a remedy. Delay defeats equity.	*Leaf v International Galleries* (1950)
Rescission is not allowed (4) – a third party has gained rights over the property	Where someone else has gained an interest in the goods then rescission will not be granted as this would be unfair on the innocent third party.	*Lewis-v-Averay* (1972)

Figure 30.4 Key facts chart for remedies for misrepresentation

Case	Judgment
Clarke v Dickson (1858)	Rescission was not available as the victim could not return to the original position.
Long v Lloyd (1958)	By persevering with the lorry after the first breakdown, he had indicated his willingness to continue with the contract and so affirmed the contract.
Leaf v International Galleries (1950)	Even though he had no means of finding out the truth until he came to sell the painting, rescission was not allowed because of the delay in bringing his claim.
Lewis v Averay (1972)	The claim for rescission failed as in the circumstances it would be unfair to deprive the third party of the car purchased in good faith.
Hedley Byrne & Co. Ltd v Heller & Partners Ltd (1964)	There could be a duty of care in negligence even though there was no contractual relationship.
Howard Marine v Ogden & Sons (1978)	They had not discharged the burden of proof by demonstrating they had reasonable grounds for believing it to be true; they had the registration document of the barge which stated the correct capacity, so it could not be innocent misrepresentation.
Royscot Trust Ltd v Rogerson (1991)	The measure of damages for negligent misrepresentation under the Misrepresentation Act 1967 is the same as for fraud.
Derry v Peek (1889)	The directors of the company were only careless as to whether what they said was true, so it was not fraudulent misrepresentation.
Smith New Court v Scrimgeour Vickers (1996)	In fraudulent misrepresentation the remedies are rescission and damages in the tort of deceit.
East v Maurer (1991)	It is possible to recover damages for loss of profit following a fraudulent misrepresentation.

Figure 30.5 Key cases chart for remedies for misrepresentation

Activity

Read this scenario and answer the questions that follow:

Dodd G. Motors has sold several cars this week, but not all the customers are happy.

Alphonso knew nothing about cars so just asked for an Italian car. He was sold a car made for an Italian company in Poland.

Beryl wanted a car with low mileage. She was sold a car with the odometer showing 17,000 miles. Dodd G. Motors knew that it had done 70,000 miles.

Cal asked for a particular make and model of car with the more powerful engine option. The car he was sold had the less powerful engine. Dodd G. Motors could have checked this from the car's identity but did not bother to do so.

Desi bought a car that was described as 'one owner'. The car's document showed one registered keeper, but did not show that it had been specially imported to the UK from Japan where it had had two previous owners. Dodd G. Motors had no reason to believe the car was an import.

1 Decide what type of misrepresentation is present (if any) in each scenario.
2 Explain what remedies might be available in each possible claim against Dodd G. Motors.

30.4 Economic duress

30.4.1 What is economic duress?

Any contract made where one party is forced into it should not be valid. This could be as a result of undue influence, duress or economic duress.

- Undue influence occurs where one party entered the contract as a result of pressure. This is presumed where the relationship is one of trust and one party will benefit at the expense of another. This includes relationships such as doctor and patient, solicitor and client and religious adviser and disciple, where there is a presumption of undue influence. An example is *Allcard v Skinner* (1882) where a novice nun gave nearly all her money to the mother superior. In that case it was said,

> The court interferes, not on the ground that any wrongful act has in fact been committed by the donee, but on the ground of public policy, and to prevent the relations which existed between the parties and the influence arising therefrom being abused.

- A contract signed under duress might involve threats, such as blackmail, or even violence to persuade one party to sign the contract. For example, in *Barton v Armstrong* (1976) death threats were made. Threats to property were not always treated as duress but the situation today is that the combination of the ideas of undue influence and duress have led to the development of economic duress.

- Economic duress – the threat to damage a business or personal financially – is a common form of duress, and the court will consider each case involving economic duress according to its individual circumstances.

Key terms 🔑

Undue influence – a principle of contract law where one party exploits their dominant position to gain an unfair advantage over the other party.

Duress (2) – in contract law where one of the parties alleges they have been forced to enter into a contract as a result of threats made by another person.

Economic duress – when someone enters into a contract as a result of financial threats.

30.4.2 Economic duress in context

In the case of *Skeate v Beale* (1840), the court had decided that a threat towards property did not constitute duress. However, in the case of *The Siboen and The Sibotre* (1976), the court said that serious threats should be considered as duress. This was developed in *Atlas Express v Kafco* (1989).

Case study

Atlas Express v Kafco (1989)

Atlas agreed to transport Kafco's goods for many months. A rate was agreed, but Atlas later insisted on minimum quantities to be delivered. Kafco argued that its agreement to the new term had been obtained by economic duress.

Kafco would have been forced out of business if Atlas refused to carry its goods as the goods were to be transported to its major customer. Economic duress was established as the agreement was induced by illegitimate pressure. There was also no consideration for its promise to pay more money on the basis that Atlas was merely performing an existing contractual duty.

Every case where economic duress is argued is considered on its particular circumstances. The key requirements for economic duress are that there must be pressure. This involves:

- a practical effect that there is compulsion on, or a lack of practical choice for, the victim
- the pressure must be illegitimate
- the illegitimate pressure is a significant cause of making the contract.

This can be seen in *Universe Tankships v International Transport Workers Federation* (1983).

Case study

Universe Tankships v International Transport Workers Federation (1983)

International Transport Workers Federation blocked a ship, *The Universe Sentinel*, to prevent it from leaving port. They made several demands in relation to pay and conditions and also demanded the ship owners pay a large sum of money to the Seafarers International Welfare Fund. The ship owners agreed so the ship could leave port. The court decided that the money had been extracted as a result of economic duress and must be repaid.

The question is what makes the pressure illegitimate. Factors to consider were set out in *Pao on v Lau yiu Long* (1979).

Case study

Pao on v Lau yiu Long (1979)

The claimant had threatened not to complete a large contract for the purchase of shares unless subsidiary agreements including a guarantee were signed. The court said that there must be some factor 'which could in law be regarded as a coercion of his will so as to vitiate his consent'.

The court then identified factors to help decide whether economic duress was present:
- Did the person claiming to be coerced protest about the pressure?
- Did that person have any other available course of action that was reasonable?
- Was he independently advised before taking the action?
- After entering into the contract, did he take steps to make the contract void?

In *CTN Cash & Carry v Gallagher* (1994) it was decided that duress was not available when the action threatened was lawful.

CTN Cash & Carry v Gallagher (1994)

Gallagher sent a consignment of cigarettes to the wrong address and the cigarettes were stolen. Gallagher believed that the cigarettes were at CTN's risk and sent them an invoice for the cigarettes. Gallagher then threatened to withdraw the claimant's credit facility unless the invoice was paid. CTN needed the credit facilities and so paid the invoice. Was this economic duress?

The court decided that the threat to withdraw the credit facility was a lawful threat as, under the credit agreement, credit could be withdrawn at any time. This was not economic duress.

However, in *Progress Bulk Carriers Ltd v Tube City* (2012) it was decided that pressure could be illegitimate even when lawful.

Case study

Progress Bulk Carriers Ltd v Tube City (2012)

There were delays in making an agreed ship available. The owners then promised to provide another ship and to pay full compensation for any loss. They identified a substitute ship and suggested dates for its availability. This was reluctantly agreed. The value of the cargo was falling and the costs of using the new ship were more. There was no other way to ship the goods and there would be 'catastrophic' losses if they delayed any longer.

The ship owners refused to supply the substitute ship unless they agreed to waive all claims against them arising from the breach. Since they had no practical alternative, the charterers, under protest, did as the owners asked. They then claimed the waived losses from the owners, claiming their agreement to waive their claim was obtained by economic duress.

Cooke J said:

> It is, in my judgement, clear from the authorities that 'illegitimate pressure' can be constituted by conduct which is not in itself unlawful, although it will be an unusual case where that is so, particularly in the commercial context. It is also clear that a past unlawful act, as well as a threat of a future unlawful act can, in appropriate circumstances, amount to 'illegitimate pressure'.

Tip

When looking at a scenario in which a person is in financial difficulties, consider whether economic duress might be present.

30.4.3 Effect of a finding of duress

The effect of a finding of duress is always to make the contract voidable. This is exactly the same as for misrepresentation. In other words, it is a valid contract until avoided by the innocent party – the one who has suffered the economic duress.

30.4.4 Remedies for economic duress

A claim based on economic duress does not result in an award of damages. The courts can make an order for the restitution of property or money extracted under such duress, and also the avoidance of any contract that has been induced by it. Restitution is an equitable remedy that restores a person to the position they would have been in if not for the improper action of another. Being an equitable remedy, it is discretionary, as we have seen for rescission.

	Brief legal rule	Case example
Economic duress definition	The threat to damage a business or person financially.	
Economic duress does not normally cover a threat towards property	Economic duress does not normally cover a threat towards property except in severe circumstances.	*Atlas Express v Kafco* (1989)
Economic duress involves (1) – compulsion or a lack of practical choice for the victim	A practical effect must be that there is compulsion on, or a lack of practical choice for, the victim.	*Universe Tankships v International Transport Workers Federation, The Universe Sentinel* (1983)
Economic duress involves (2) – illegitimate pressure	Commercial pressure is not enough to amount to economic duress. There are a number of factors to consider.	*Pao on v Lau yiu Long* (1979)
Economic duress involves (3) – actions that are not lawful	Duress was not available when the action threatened was lawful.	*CTN Cash & Carry v Gallagher* (1994)
Economic duress involves (4) – pressure could be illegitimate even when lawful	'Illegitimate pressure' can be constituted by conduct which is not in itself unlawful, although it will be an unusual case where that is so.	*Progress Bulk Carriers Ltd v Tube City* (2012)

Figure 30.6 Key facts chart for economic duress

Case	Judgment
Atlas Express v Kafco (1989)	Economic duress was established as the agreement was induced by illegitimate pressure of great magnitude.
Universe Tankships v International Transport Workers Federation, The Universe Sentinel (1983)	Several demands made in relation to pay and conditions as well as that the ship owners pay a large sum of money to the Seafarers International Welfare Fund amounted to compulsion.
Pao on v Lau yiu Long (1979)	The court identified four factors to be considered if there was to be economic duress.
CTN Cash & Carry v Gallagher (1994)	The threat to withdraw the credit facility was a lawful threat so there was no economic duress.
Progress Bulk Carriers Ltd v Tube City (2012)	The charterers had no other way to ship the goods, and faced 'catastrophic' losses if they delayed any longer. The agreement to waive all claims against them arising from the breach was obtained by economic duress.

Figure 30.7 Key cases chart for economic duress

Summary

- Vitiating factors include misrepresentation and economic duress.
- Misrepresentation occurs where a person is induced to enter a contract as a result of statements made that are false.
- There are three types of misrepresentation, each with its own remedies: innocent, negligent and fraudulent.
- Economic duress arises where there is the threat to damage a business or a person financially. The court will consider each case involving economic duress according to its individual circumstances.

Chapter 31

Discharge

After reading this chapter you should be able to:
- Understand the concept of discharge of contract
- Explain discharge by performance
- Explain discharge by frustration and relevant remedies
- Explain breach of contract: actual and anticipatory breach, and relevant remedies
- Apply the law to given situations

31.1 What is discharge of contract?

The usual method of discharge of a contract is through performance. Both parties have done what they agreed in the contract. But, if the contract has not been performed as agreed, it may be discharged by breach. However, not every breach of contract discharges the contract. The question here is to decide the effect of an individual breach of contract.

A contract may be discharged by frustration where unforeseen events outside the control of the parties makes performance impossible.

This chapter looks at discharge, and Chapter 32 considers the possible remedies for a breach of contract.

31.2 Discharge by performance

The strict rule of discharge by performance is that performance must be complete and exact.

An early case showing the rule is *Cutter v Powell* (1795).

Case study

Cutter v Powell (1795)

Cutter agreed to work as second mate on a voyage for a fixed fee. Unfortunately Cutter died near the end of the voyage. His widow sued for a proportion of his fee. However, she was entitled to nothing as he had agreed to work the entire voyage and had not done so.

Another example is *Re Moore & Co. and Landauer & Co.'s Arbitration* (1921).

See Chapter 28, section 28.4.2 for full case details of *Re Moore & Co. and Landauer & Co.'s Arbitration* (1921).

The harshness of the rule has been tempered in several ways:
- divisible contracts
- substantial performance
- prevention of full performance
- acceptance of part performance.

Activity

Jen arranged a minicab home from a club late one night for £20. She had given the driver her precise address. The driver was in a hurry to pick up his next, very lucrative, fare so told Jen to get out at the end of her street, about 100 metres from her house, as it was a one-way street and would require him to take a long and time-consuming detour.

- Do you think she should pay the driver £20, a little less than £20 or nothing?
- If you think she should pay nothing, how close do you think the driver should get to her house to be paid?
- Write down the arguments for Jen and the minicab driver.

31.2.1 Divisible contracts

Where a contract can be seen as being separate parts, then non-completion of one part is not a breach of the whole contract. So, if Mr Cutter's contract in *Cutter v Powell* had been described as, for example, £1 per day, then the contract for the voyage would have been divisible. This can be seen in *Ritchie v Atkinson* (1808).

Case study

Ritchie v Atkinson (1808)

A ship owner agreed to carry a cargo at an agreed rate per ton. He carried only a part of the cargo. The ship owner was entitled to be paid for the part of the cargo he had carried at the agreed price per ton, but was liable in damages for breach of contract for not carrying the whole cargo.

31.2.2 Substantial performance

If a party has done substantially what was required under the contract, then the doctrine of substantial performance may apply. Where it does apply, there must be payment of the amount appropriate to what has been done.

This does not apply where the contract is considered to be an entire contract where all of the obligations in the contract are seen as a single transaction that cannot be broken down, as in *Cutter v Powell*.

Substantial performance often occurs in large contracts where little things are not performed exactly, as in *Dakin & Co. v Lee* (1916).

Case study

Dakin & Co. v Lee (1916)

Builders agreed to repair the defendant's premises for £1500. They performed the contract completely but there were three relatively poorly performed aspects. These cost £80 to rectify. The court decided that the contract had been substantially, if not precisely performed. The fact that the work was done badly did not mean it had not been performed at all. The builder was entitled to be paid the price subject to a deduction for the defective work.

The difficulty is in establishing what amounts to substantial performance. No specific percentages for completion are specified as to when work has been substantially completed. It is decided on the circumstances of each case. Two contrasting examples are *Hoenig v Isaacs* (1952) and *Bolton v Mahadeva* (1972).

Case studies

Hoenig v Isaacs (1952)

A decorator contracted to decorate and furnish a room for £750. Some of the furniture was defective but could be repaired for £55. The court decided that the contract was substantially completed on a financial basis. The decorator was entitled to be paid for what he had done on a *quantum meruit* basis.

Bolton v Mahadeva (1972)

A builder agreed to install a central heating system for £560. However, the installation was defective, as the system gave off fumes and did not work properly. Repairs cost £170. The court decided that the builder was entitled to nothing, as there had not been substantial performance of the contract.

Key term

Quantum meruit – as much as it is worth.

See Chapter 32, section 32.2.5 for more information on *quantum meruit*.

There is uncertainty as to when and whether the exception applies. This is a disadvantage but is inevitable so as to allow the courts some use of discretion in cases. An example of the court's use of discretion to reach a just and fair decision can be seen in *Young v Thames Properties Ltd* (1999).

Case study

Young v Thames Properties Ltd (1999)

A contract was made for resurfacing a car park, but the contractor did not resurface to the exact specifications with respect to depth of some of the materials. The court decided that the defects made little difference to the quality of the car park, so the contractor was entitled to the contract price less the savings to the contractor of not completing the contract with the correct depth of materials.

31.2.3 Prevention of full performance

If one party prevents the other from carrying out his contract, then the innocent party can claim to be paid on a *quantum meruit* basis. This can be seen in *Planche v Colburn* (1831).

Planche v Colburn (1831)

A publisher hired an author to write one of a series of books. When the publisher decided to abandon the whole series, the author was prevented from completing the work through no fault of his own. He was entitled to recover a fee for his wasted work.

31.2.4 Acceptance of part-performance

If one party has agreed the other party need not complete the entire contract, then the contract must be paid for on a *quantum meruit* basis. However, the consent must be in the form of a specific acknowledgement that the defaulting party is entitled to be paid for what they have completed so far and the agreement made without undue pressure. If the innocent party has no option but to take the benefit of the work done, this is not considered consent to part-performance. This was shown in *Sumpter v Hedges* (1898).

Sumpter v Hedges (1898)

A builder agreed to build two houses. He completed just over half of the work and then ran out of money. The customer completed the outstanding work. The builder argued that in completing the work himself, the defendant accepted part-performance.

The court said the defendant had no choice but to accept part-performance as he was left with half a completed house on his land. Therefore, the builder was not entitled to be paid for the work he had done so far. The customer had no alternative but to complete the work himself and had not, therefore, consented to the builder's part-performance. There was insufficient work done for substantial performance.

31.2.5 The effect of a term as to time for performance of a contract

In many contracts it is useful to have a term as to time inserted. This is particularly important when an item is needed at a particular time (for example, a wedding dress). There are often terms in contracts about the time for performance of the contract. The question here is, how exactly must terms as to time be performed? If it is exact, can the injured party repudiate the contract for breach of this term?

The court regards time as a condition if:

- the parties have expressly stated in the contract that time is of the essence of the contract
- in the circumstances time for completion of the contract is critical, or
- one party has failed to perform on time and the other has insisted on a new date for completion of the contract.

If none of the above apply, then the time for performance is treated as a warranty rather than a condition.

Exceptions to the rules can be seen in cases such as *Charles Rickards Ltd v Oppenheim* (1950) and *Union Eagle Ltd v Golden Achievement Ltd* (1997).

Charles Rickards Ltd v Oppenheim (1950)

A buyer of a Rolls-Royce car chassis agreed for a body to be built upon it by a fixed date. The body was not completed by that date. The buyer kept pushing for delivery and eventually gave notice that unless delivery of the car with a completed body was ready within four weeks he would cancel the contract. The car was not delivered within the period of four weeks. When the car was completed, he rejected it. He was entitled to cancel the contract as time had been made of the essence and that term had not been complied with.

A mechanic working on a car

Most contracts for the sale of land including houses have terms in them with respect to time for performance of the contract. It is essential that once time being of the essence has been waived, it is then reinstated as a term by giving notice if such a term is to be relied on. This is apparent from the case of *Hakimzay Ltd v Swailes* (2015), a case involving the sale of a residential property.

	Brief legal rule	Case example
Discharge by performance – general rule	Performance must be complete and exact.	*Cutter v Powell* (1795)
Some contracts can be seen as divisible contracts	If a contract can be seen as being separate parts, then non-completion of one part is not a breach of the whole contract.	*Ritchie v Atkinson* (1808)
The doctrine of substantial performance	If a party has done substantially what was required under the contract, then the doctrine of substantial performance can apply.	*Dakin & Co. v Lee* (1916)
Full performance prevented by actions of the other party	If one party prevents the other from carrying out his contract, then the innocent party can claim to be paid on a *quantum meruit* basis.	*Planche v Colburn* (1831)
One party accepts part performance	If one party has agreed that the other party need not complete the entire contract, then the strict rule will not apply.	*Sumpter v Hedges* (1898)
The effect of a term as to time for performance of a contract	A term as to time is treated as a condition if it falls within one of three categories. If not, it is treated as a warranty.	*Union Eagle Ltd v Golden Achievement Ltd* (1997)
Time can be made of the essence of a contract	This also means the right to treat it as a condition can be waived.	*Charles Rickards Ltd v Oppenheim* (1950)

Figure 31.1 Key facts chart for discharge by performance

Case	Judgment
Cutter v Powell (1795)	As the contract was for the whole voyage, he had not performed his contract.
Ritchie v Atkinson (1808)	The ship owner was entitled to be paid for the part of the cargo he had carried as the contract was divisible.
Dakin & Co. v Lee (1916)	Substantial performance applied as there were relatively minor defects in the work.
Hoenig v Isaacs (1952)	*Quantum meruit* was used to establish payment to be made.
Bolton v Mahadeva (1972)	The defects were too great to amount to substantial performance.
Young v Thames Properties Ltd (1999)	The court used its discretion to reach a just and fair decision.
Planche v Colburn (1831)	An author was prevented from carrying out his contract so was paid on a *quantum meruit* basis.
Sumpter v Hedges (1898)	The builder was not entitled to be paid for the work he had done so far as the customer had no alternative but to complete the work himself. He had not consented to the builder's part performance.
Union Eagle Ltd v Golden Achievement Ltd (1997)	The time for completion of the contract had been specified as 5 p.m. and time was expressly stated to be 'of the essence'. The purchaser delivered the purchase price at 5.10 p.m. and the seller was entitled to repudiate the contract.
Charles Rickards Ltd v Oppenheim (1950)	He was entitled to cancel the contract as time had been made of the essence and that term had not been complied with.

Figure 31.2 Key cases chart for discharge by performance

31.3 Discharge by frustration

Historically the law held that a party was bound to perform his obligations under the contract, whatever happened. In *Paradine v Jane* (1647) the defendant was still liable to pay rent on land even though he had been forced off the land by an invading army during the English Civil War!

The injustice of this strict rule led, in the nineteenth century, to the development of a new doctrine. If a party to a contract was prevented from keeping the promise because of an unforeseeable, intervening event, they would not be liable for a breach of contract. This was shown in *Taylor v Caldwell* (1863).

Case study

Taylor v Caldwell (1863)

The owner contracted to rent out his music hall. Through no one's fault, and before the rental could take place, the music hall burned down. The hirer had spent money advertising the events for which he would not be paid until after the events. As it was now impossible to complete the contract, it was frustrated. This ended the contract and there was no recompense for the wasted expenses.

Many contracts contain a force majeure clause.

Key term

> **Force majeure clause** – a clause often found in commercial contracts. It excludes liability for the parties for delay in performance or the non-performance if there are extraordinary events.

If the contract does not contain a force majeure clause, then it may still be possible to rely on frustration to avoid being in breach of contract. However, what may constitute a frustrating event depends on the circumstances of each case.

Frustration requires performance as envisaged in the contract to become impossible as a result of outside events beyond the control and contemplation of the parties. These events are sometimes categorised as:

- impossibility of performance
- the contract becoming illegal to perform
- a radical change of circumstances.

31.3.1 Impossibility of performance

We have already seen this in the destruction of the music hall in *Taylor v Caldwell*. Frustration also applies where the subject matter becomes unavailable through no fault of the contacting parties. An example is *Jackson v Union Marine Insurance Co. Ltd* (1874).

Case study

Jackson v Union Marine Insurance Co. Ltd (1874)

A ship was chartered to sail from Liverpool to Newport and from there load a cargo for San Francisco. It ran aground and could not be loaded for a long time. This was seen as 'the perils of the sea'. The court agreed there was an implied term that the ship should be available for loading in a reasonable time, so the long delay frustrated the contract.

In a contract for services, the frustrating event may be the unavailability of the party who is to perform the service because of illness, as in *Robinson v Davidson* (1871), or failure to perform on medical advice as in *Condor v The Baron Knights* (1966).

Case studies

Robinson v Davidson (1871)

A pianist made a contract to perform. Some hours before the performance was due she became ill and her husband informed the claimant that she would be unable to attend. The court decided that the contract was conditional on the woman being well enough to perform and her illness was a frustrating event.

Condor v The Baron Knights (1966)

A contract entered into by a band required all members of the band to be available to perform for seven evenings a week if necessary. The drummer became ill and was advised to work no more than four nights per week. On occasion, he ignored this advice, but the court still held that the contract was frustrated since it was necessary to have a stand-in musician in case he fell ill.

31.3.2 The contract becoming illegal to perform

A contract may be frustrated as the result of a change in the law that makes the contract illegal to perform, for example, as a result of war. Examples include *Denny, Mott & Dickson Ltd v James B Fraser & Co. Ltd* (1944) and *Re Shipton Anderson & Co. and Harrison Bros & Co.* (1915).

Case studies

Denny, Mott & Dickson Ltd v James B. Fraser & Co. Ltd (1944)

The court said that a contract to import certain goods would be frustrated if importing goods of that kind became illegal after the contract was made.

Re Shipton Anderson & Co. and Harrison Bros & Co. (1915)

A cargo of grain was sold, but before it could be delivered, war broke out. The government requisitioned the cargo so the contract was frustrated.

There is a radical change of circumstances

If the main purpose of the contract is based on a particular event and the event will not take place, then the contract may be frustrated. The contrasting cases of *Krell v Henry* (1903) and *Herne Bay Steamboat Co. v Hutton* (1903) illustrate this.

Case studies

Krell v Henry (1903)

A man hired a hotel room in order to view Edward VII's coronation procession. The prince became ill and the coronation and procession were postponed. The court said that the event was the main purpose of the contract; as it would not occur, the contract was frustrated even though the room could still have been used.

Herne Bay Steamboat Co. v Hutton (1903)

Hutton hired a boat in order to see the fleet when the king reviewed it as part of his coronation celebrations. Hutton claimed he did not have to pay as the king was ill and did not attend. However, the court said the contract was not frustrated as one main reason for the contract still remained, to view the fleet. All that was missing was the king's presence. This was not enough to frustrate the contract.

31.3.3 When frustration cannot apply

These events are sometimes categorised as:
- self-induced frustration
- the contract becoming less profitable
- the event being a foreseeable risk or one that was mentioned in the contract.

Self-induced frustration

Frustration will not apply when the frustrating event is within the control of one party. This can be seen in *Maritime National Fish Ltd v Ocean Trawlers Ltd* (1935).

Case study

Maritime National Fish Ltd v Ocean Trawlers Ltd (1935)

A fishing company owned two trawlers and had a contract to hire a third. The company needed a licence for each vessel but was only allocated two licences, which it allocated to its own boats. The company then claimed frustration of the hire contract as it could not use the hire boat. The court held frustration did not apply and the contract was still valid. The 'frustrating' event was within the company's control as it could have allocated a licence to the hired boat rather than one of its own.

This can be contrasted with *Gamerco SA v ICM Fair Warning (Agency) Ltd and Missouri Storm Inc.* (1995).

Case study

Gamerco SA v ICM Fair Warning (Agency) Ltd and Missouri Storm Inc. (1995)

A Spanish concert promoter and the defendant rock group, Guns N' Roses (their corporate persona is Missouri Storm Inc.) agreed to put on a concert at Atletico Madrid's stadium. Shortly before it was due to take place, the stadium was deemed unfit and its licence withdrawn by the Spanish authorities. No other stadium was available.

The contract had been frustrated, the promoter could not erect the stage and the band could not perform.

Find the full law report for this case online. It is interesting to read, in terms of the way in which a large rock tour is organised and the amount of money involved.

Guns N' Roses concert, Los Angeles, 2016

The contract has becoming less profitable

A contract becoming less profitable or more difficult to complete is not a reason for frustration of that contract. This can be seen in *Davis Contractors Ltd v Fareham Urban District Council* (1956).

The event being a foreseeable risk or was mentioned in the contract

In *Amalgamated Investment & Property Co. Ltd v John Walker & Sons Ltd* (1977) there was a foreseeable risk.

Case study

Amalgamated Investment & Property Co. Ltd v John Walker & Sons Ltd (1977)

This involved a contract to sell a building to the investment company who wanted it for redevelopment. Unbeknown to either party and after the contract was made, the Department of the Environment made the building a listed building, meaning that it could not be used for development. This resulted in a huge drop in the value of the building.

The court rejected a claim of frustration, as listing was a risk associated with all old buildings, of which the developers should have been aware. The pre-contract enquiries showed they were aware of the possibility of the building becoming listed so the contract was not radically different from that contemplated by the parties.

In general, the courts are reluctant to find that there has been frustration of contract. This can be seen in the recent case of *Armchair Answercall v People in Mind* (2016).

Case study

Armchair Answercall v People in Mind (2016)

The contract for services was commercially undermined when third party franchisees refused to agree to vary the way the business was carried out. The court said this was not frustration of contract. People in Mind's role was to support Armchair Answercall in moving the business to a new management model for existing franchisees and potential new customers. It had not anticipated that the franchisees would withdraw, but that was in fact foreseeable. The inference was therefore that 'one or other party [had] assumed the risk of the occurrence of the event'.

31.3.4 Remedies for frustration – Law Reform (Frustrated Contracts) Act 1943

At common law the frustrating event automatically terminates the contract at the time of the event. Obligations already existing must be completed but future obligations are terminated. This explains why the customer in *Krell v Henry* (1903) did not have to pay for the room as the payment was an obligation that only became effective when the room was actually used. This can be contrasted with *Chandler v Webster* (1904) where the room had to be paid for in advance. The court decided the contract was frustrated so he still had to pay for the room. His obligation to pay (in advance – on making the booking) arose before the frustrating event (the postponement of the coronation).

The outbreak of the Second World War led to more cases of frustration. This fact and in particular the *Fibrosa* case (*Fibrosa Spolka Ackyjna v Fairbairn Lawson Combe Barbour Ltd* (1943)) led to the passing of the Law Reform (Frustrated Contracts) Act 1943.

The Act does not affect the law on the situations when frustration may occur; it only applies to situations where frustration is found to exist. What it does is to set out the way in which frustrated contracts are settled.

The rules are set out in the Law Reform (Frustrated Contracts) Act 1943, s 1(2) and (3) as follows:

- Money already paid (such as a deposit) is recoverable and money already due under the contract (as in *Chandler*) is not payable.

- The court can use its discretion to order compensation to be paid for work done and expenses incurred under the contract before the frustrating event (provided there was an obligation to pay money before the frustrating event).

	Brief legal rule	Case example
Discharge by frustration – general rule	Where a party to a contract was prevented from keeping the promise because of an unforeseeable, intervening event, it would not be liable for a breach of contract.	*Taylor v Caldwell* (1863)
For there to be frustration the contract must be impossible to perform	The court must decide whether performance is impossible in fact.	*Jackson v Union Marine Insurance Co Ltd* (1874)
Subsequent illegality can amount to frustration of contract	A contract becoming illegal to perform after it is made frustrates the contract.	*Denny, Mott & Dickson Ltd v James B. Fraser & Co. Ltd* (1944)
A radical change of the main purpose of the contract can amount to frustration of contract	The main purpose of the contract must be affected by the change, not just some aspect of it.	*Krell v Henry* (1903) *Herne Bay Steamboat Co. v Hutton* (1903)
Self-induced frustration is breach not frustration	Frustration will not apply when the frustrating event is within the control of one party.	*Maritime National Fish Ltd v Ocean Trawlers Ltd* (1935)
A contract becoming less profitable is not frustration	Merely because a contract becomes less profitable or more difficult to complete is not a reason for frustration of that contract.	*Davis Contractors Ltd v Fareham Urban District Council* (1956)
Remedies for frustration of contract	These are dealt with in the Law Reform (Frustrated Contracts) Act 1943.	

Figure 31.3 Key facts chart for discharge by frustration

Case	Judgment
Taylor v Caldwell (1863)	As the destruction of the music hall was not the fault of either party, so the contract was frustrated.
Jackson v Union Marine Insurance Co. Ltd (1874)	The long delay in loading caused by it running aground amounted to frustration of the contract.
Robinson v Davidson (1871)	Illness of a person who is to perform personally can amount to frustration.
Condor v The Baron Knights (1966)	Acting on medical advice can be sufficient for frustration of contract.
Denny, Mott & Dickson Ltd v James B. Fraser & Co. Ltd (1944)	The law was changed so that importing goods of that kind became illegal after the contract was made. This frustrated the contract.
Re Shipton Anderson & Co and Harrison Bros & Co (1915)	The government requisitioned the cargo so the contract was frustrated.
Krell v Henry (1903)	The event, which was the main purpose of the contract, would not occur therefore the contract was frustrated.
Herne Bay Steamboat Co. v Hutton (1903)	The contract was not frustrated as one main reason for the contract still remained.
Maritime National Fish Ltd v Ocean Trawlers Ltd (1935)	The choice of which boat to allocate a licence to amounted to self-induced frustration.
Gamerco SA v ICM Fair Warning (Agency) Ltd and Missouri Storm Inc (1995)	The license was withdrawn by a third party so the contract was frustrated.
Armchair Answercall v People in Mind (2016)	In general, the courts are reluctant to find there has been frustration of contract.

Figure 31.4 Key cases chart for discharge by frustration

- The quantification of the amount due is based on the principle of *quantum meruit*.
- The court may order compensation to be paid for any valuable benefit one party may acquire under the frustrated contract.

31.4 Discharge by breach

When a party fails to perform his obligations under a contract, that party may be sued for breach of contract. The victim will always be entitled to claim for damages, but terminating the contract depends on the type of term that has been breached.

See Chapter 28 for more information about breach of contract.

Breach can be a total failure to perform, for example non-delivery or non-payment, or it can be failure to perform in accordance with the terms of the contract that could be seen as part-performance.

The three sets of circumstances giving rise to a breach of contract are:

- renunciation by a party of his liabilities under it
- impossibility created by his own act
- total or partial failure of performance.

In the case of the first two circumstances, the renunciation may occur or impossibility be created either before or at the time for performance. These are anticipatory breach. In the case of the third circumstance, it can occur only at the time or during the course of performance and is, therefore, actual breach.

Key terms

Anticipatory breach – when a party to a contract gives notice in advance to the other party that they will not be performing or completing the contract.

Actual breach – in contract law where the breach occurs at the time of, or during the course of, performance.

31.4.1 Anticipatory breach and actual breach

An anticipatory breach occurs when a party to a contract gives notice in advance to the other party that they will not be performing or completing the contract. The innocent party in this situation has a choice – to sue immediately for breach of a condition, or to wait for the time agreed for performance of the contract and to sue if performance does not take place then. This means they can treat the contract as repudiated and/or claim damages. An example is *Hochster v de la Tour* (1853).

Case study

Hochster v de la Tour (1853)

Hochester agreed to work as a courier on a tour due to start in June. However the company told him in May that it no longer required his services. In that situation he was entitled to sue immediately and did not have to wait until the actual breach of contract, which would have occurred in June.

This is a good right to have, as by waiting to see if performance will take place, the company could fall into financial difficulties or there might be other events that result in discharge by frustration.

If one of the parties to a contract, either expressly or by conduct, leads the other party to the reasonable conclusion that they do not mean to carry out the contract, this amounts to a repudiation. The other can treat the contract as at an end.

In *Geden Operations Ltd v Dry Bulk Handy Holdings Inc (The Bulk Uruguay)* (2014) the principle was summarised as:

> the conduct ... [that would be] sufficient to entitle the other contracting party to treat himself as discharged from further performance [would either be] renunciation, [i.e.] words or conduct which evince an intention by the contracting party no longer to be bound by his contractual obligations[; or] self-induced impossibility, [i.e.] conduct by the contacting party which puts it out of his power to perform his contractual obligations.

In both cases, the inevitability of non-performance entitled the innocent party to treat the contract as at an end prior to the time for performance. However, unlikelihood or uncertainty in future performance do not suffice.

31.4.2 Remedies for breach

If the victim claims an anticipatory breach, then the victim may claim damages immediately. These damages are to put the victim in the same position they would have been in had the contract been completed. However, the victim must take reasonable steps to mitigate their losses.

The victim may choose not to accept the anticipatory breach but to see if the defendant commits an actual breach at the time performance is due. Here, the damages are assessed at the time when performance should occur, and the loss might increase due to a change in market factors. Alternatively, an event may occur which discharges the contract, such as frustration of contract for which there are different remedies.

The victim may also repudiate the contract under anticipatory breach. The result is that the victim is no longer bound to perform any obligations under the contract.

For a breach of condition, the right of the victim is to claim for damages and/or repudiation. Damages are again based on putting the victim in the position they would have been in had the contract been completed.

For a breach of warranty, the claim is limited to damages.

	Brief legal rule	Case example
Discharge by breach – general rule	When a party fails to perform his obligations under a contract, then that party may be sued for breach of contract.	*Poussard v Spiers and Pond* (1876) (see Chapter 28, section 28.2.1)
Types of breach	Breach can be actual breach or anticipatory breach.	*Hochster v de la Tour* (1853)
When can it be taken as anticipatory breach?	This can be by renunciation or self-induced impossibility. Unlikelihood or uncertainty in future performance do not suffice.	*Geden Operations Ltd v Dry Bulk Handy Holdings Inc (Bulk Uruguay)* (2014)
Effect of breach	This depends on the type of term broken.	

Figure 31.5 Key facts chart for discharge by breach

Case	Judgment
Hochster v de la Tour (1853)	An anticipatory breach occurs when a party to a contract gives notice in advance to the other party that he will not be performing the contract.
Geden Operations Ltd v Dry Bulk Handy Holdings Inc (Bulk Uruguay) (2014)	Sets out when a breach can be treated as an anticipatory breach.

Figure 31.6 Key cases chart for discharge by breach

Summary

- A contract can be discharged by performance (the usual method), frustration or breach (failure to perform in whole or in part).
- Performance must be complete and exact, but there are exceptions such as where part-performance is accepted.
- If the contract is not discharged by frustration, there will be a breach of contract.
- Breach and frustration have different remedies.
- Breach can be of a condition, a warranty or an innominate term.
- Breach can be actual or anticipatory.

Chapter 32

Remedies

After reading this chapter you should be able to:
- Understand the way in which damages are assessed in contract law: compensatory damages; causation and remoteness of damage; mitigation of loss
- Understand equitable remedies
- Understand consumer remedies under the Consumer Rights Act 2015
- Apply the law to given situations

32.1 What is a remedy?

Remedies in contract law are divided into:
- legal remedies
- equitable remedies
- remedies under a specific statute.

Legal remedies are available against a person in breach of contract as of right. These can be damages, which is financial compensation, or remedies against the goods.

Equitable remedies are discretionary. This means you do not have a right to an equitable remedy, but the court may award one if it thinks the legal remedies are not the most appropriate remedy in the circumstances.

Some Acts of Parliament provide for specific remedies in certain situations. The Acts we have considered in previous chapters are the Law Reform (Frustrated Contracts) Act 1943 and the Consumer Rights Act 2015.

32.1.1 Legal remedies

Legal remedies are damages or rights with respect to the goods. So if the goods do not match those required by the contract, the goods can be rejected. There is also the right to repudiate the contract, in other words to treat the contract as at an end.

At common law (therefore not including statutory rights), breach can result in the ending of the contract if the affected party so chooses where:
- there is a breach of a condition or breach of an innominate term construed as a condition

- one party refuses to perform his obligations under a contract at all or the substantial part of its obligations, including anticipatory breach
- one party makes it impossible to perform the contract.

Rights against the goods

Rights against the goods include the right to reject the goods for breach of contract. We have already seen this, along with consumer remedies under the Consumer Rights Act 2015. Many contracts between businesses include a reservation of title clause in them whereby the title (ownership) of goods remains with the seller until the buyer has paid for them. The Sale of Goods Act 1979 ss 38–48 also provides three specific rights for an unpaid seller of goods:
- A lien, which is a right to retain possession of the goods of the debtor until paid. This is an unpaid seller's lien. There are also other liens such as a repairer's lien.
- In case of the insolvency of the buyer, a right of stopping the goods in transit and regaining possession of the goods from a carrier.
- A right of resale as limited by the Act.

Key term

Lien – the right to retain possession of the goods of the debtor until paid.

We have seen that consumers have rights and remedies with respect to the goods. These are:

- the short-term right to reject under s 20
- the right to repair or replacement under s 23
- the right to a price reduction or the final right to reject under s 24.

32.2 Damages

A claim for damages is always available, as of right, to the claimant when a contractual term has been broken. This means that if the claimant has not suffered any loss, the court must still make an award of damages.

The purpose of damages is to put the victim in the position they would have been in if the contract had been properly completed and performed by the defendant. The court is therefore looking at what should have happened and the consequences of non- or part-performance.

32.2.1 Types of damages

The problem for the courts is to establish how much the loss will be. As damages are compensatory, they will only include losses that are too remote to be awarded. Compensatory damages are the main type of damages, but other types need to be briefly explained first.

Nominal damages

If no loss is actually suffered but there is breach, the court may award 'nominal damages'. In *Staniforth v Lyall* (1830) the award of nominal damages was made as the claimant had made no loss. In fact, the main purpose of bringing the case was to have proof that the contract was at an end.

Therefore, there was no danger of being unable to rehire the boat to someone else, which he did at a greater profit.

In some cases, substantial damages have been awarded where traditionally nominal damages might have been considered more appropriate. One example is *Experience Hendrix LLC v PPX Enterprises Inc.* (2003) where an equitable remedy was refused and no monetary loss was provable.

This is sometimes called a 'Wrotham Park' award following the case of *Wrotham Park Estate Co. Ltd v*

Parkside Homes Ltd (1974). Instead of working out how much the innocent party has lost, or how much the wrongdoer has gained, Wrotham Park damages try to quantify the sum which might reasonably have been negotiated between the parties for giving permission to the wrongdoer to act as they did, rather than according to the contract.

The difficulty with Wrotham Park damages is that it is not clear when they should be awarded. In *Morris-Garner v One Step (Support) Ltd* (2016) it was stated that Wrotham Park damages will be awarded where the claimant would have very real problems in establishing financial loss, it is a 'just' response to a breach of contract and such damages should not be restricted to exceptional circumstances.

Extension question

Research the *Morris-Garner* case. Write down the decision and consider how this case might be used to illustrate the concept of law and justice studied in Chapter 14.

Speculative damages

The courts have been careful to avoid granting damages of a speculative nature when considering the idea of loss of a chance. In *Addis v The Gramophone Company* (1909) the court refused a claim for damages in contract for injury to reputation and the mental distress caused by the humiliating manner of Mr Addis's dismissal from his job, as this was a matter for the law of tort. He was awarded damages only for the loss of salary and commission owed.

However, contract law has developed cases allowing damages of a highly speculative nature for mental distress, while also recognising the problems with respect to privity of contract – such as *Jackson v Horizon Holidays* considered earlier in this book (see Chapter 27, section 27.3.2) and *Jarvis v Swan Tours Ltd* (1973).

More recently, damages for loss of amenity have been allowed where the sole purpose of the contract was for the provision of a pleasurable amenity. In *Ruxley Electronics and Construction Ltd v Forsyth* (1996) damages were awarded for loss of amenity.

Ruxley Electronics and Construction Ltd v Forsyth (1996)

The contract for a swimming pool stated the depth but the builder completed the pool with a depth about 10 per cent less. There was nothing wrong with the pool apart from the depth – it was still worth its cost, it did not affect the value of the property as a whole and it could still be used as originally intended. The cost to correct the pool was £21,650, which was equivalent to the original cost of building the pool.

The court stated that in building contracts there are two bases for quantification of damages – the cost of reinstatement or the difference in value. The cost of reinstatement was totally unreasonable in this case. As there was no real difference in value of the pool technically, Mr Forsyth was entitled to nothing. However, as he had not received that which he had contracted for, the court awarded him £2500 for loss of amenity.

32.2.2 Causation and remoteness of damage

Compensatory damages are relevant once it has been established which losses are to be compensated. This is remoteness of damage.

Remoteness of damage does not establish how much compensation will be payable (damages), but merely which losses can be the subject of compensation (damage).

Tip

To remember the difference between damage and damages, think of damages as being money – damage$.

The test of remoteness was set out in *Hadley v Baxendale* (1854).

The test is in two parts:

- The first part is measured objectively according to what loss is a natural consequence of the breach – in this case, late delivery.
- The second is subjective, based on specific knowledge of potential losses in the minds of both parties when the contract is formed – did the carrier know that the mill could not operate without the crankshaft?

Case study

Hadley v Baxendale (1854)

A mill owner made a contract with a carrier to deliver a crankshaft for his mill. The mill was unable to operate as the existing crankshaft was broken. The carrier did not know this. The carrier was late with delivery. The mill owner sued unsuccessfully because the carrier was unaware of the importance of prompt delivery.

Baron Alderson stated:

> Where the parties have made a contract which one of them has broken, the damages which the other party ought to receive in respect of such breach of contract should be such as may fairly and reasonably be considered arising either naturally, i.e. according to the usual course of things, from such breach of contract itself, or such as may be supposed reasonably to have been in the contemplation of both parties at the time they made the contract as the probable result of the breach.

The test is the starting point for remoteness of damage, although it has been modified on occasions as in *Victoria Laundry Ltd v Newman Industries Ltd* (1949).

Case study

Victoria Laundry Ltd v Newman Industries Ltd (1949)

There was a contract to deliver a boiler to the laundry company but it was not delivered until five months after the contract date. The laundry successfully sued for loss of its usual profits from the date of the breach. This was a natural consequence loss.

It also sued in respect of additional lost profits from a special contract that it had been unable to take up without the boiler. This claim failed as the special contract was unknown to the defendants at the time the contract was made.

The test is:

- recoverable loss should be measured against a test of reasonable foreseeability
- foreseeability of loss is itself dependent on knowledge at the time the contract was made
- knowledge is of two types: common knowledge and actual knowledge of the defendant, as in *Hadley v Baxendale* (1854).

Knowledge can be implied on the basis of what a reasonable man may have contemplated in the circumstances. This is shown in *Czarnikow Ltd v Koufos (The Heron II)* (1969).

This principle was considered in *H Parsons (Livestock) Ltd v Uttley Ingham* (1978).

Thus it is crucial to determine what was in the contemplation of the parties at the time that the contract was made. The case of *Transfield Shipping Inc. v Mercador Shipping Inc. (The Achilleas)* (2008) suggested that the test also concerns whether the damage is of a type that the defendant ought reasonably to have accepted responsibility for.

This has been reviewed again in *Wellesley Partners LLP v Withers LLP* (2015) where the law as it stands was summarised:

> A contract breaker is liable for damage resulting from his breach, if at the time of making the contract, a reasonable person in his shoes would have had damage of that kind in mind as not unlikely to result from a breach.

This case also clarified the position where a claim is made in both contract and negligence, by stating that the contract interpretation of the law as set out here should prevail.

Once the tests of causation and remoteness have established that there is liability for the loss claimed, the court then has to determine how much the claimant can recover.

	Brief legal rule	Case example
Remoteness of damage	This establishes which losses can be the subject of compensation	*Hadley v Baxendale* (1854)

Figure 32.1 Key facts chart for remoteness of damage

Case	Judgment
Hadley v Baxendale (1854)	Sets out the two-part test for remoteness of damage.
Victoria Laundry Ltd v Newman Industries Ltd (1949)	Modifies the test set out in *Hadley v Baxendale* (1854).
Czarnikow Ltd v Koufos (The Heron II) (1969)	The court decided that under the subjective part of the test in *Hadley v Baxendale* it was only necessary to show that the losses were in the reasonable contemplation of the parties as a possible result of the breach.
H Parsons (Livestock) Ltd v Uttley Ingham (1978)	The court must determine what was in the contemplation of the parties at the time that the contract was made.
Wellesley Partners LLP v Withers LLP (2015)	Summarises the current position on damage.

Figure 32.2 Key cases chart for damage

32.2.3 Assessing compensatory damages

There are many ways to assess awards of damages in contract claims.

Loss of a bargain

The idea here is to place the claimant in the same financial position as if the contract had been properly performed. This can be seen in a number of ways:

1 The difference in value between the goods or services required in the contract and those actually provided. An example of this is *Bence Graphics International Ltd v Fasson UK Ltd* (1996).

Case study

Bence Graphics International Ltd v Fasson UK Ltd (1996)

The defendant supplied vinyl film on which the claimant printed decals to put on bulk containers. There was an implied term that the decals would survive in a readable form for five years, but they lasted only two years. The court awarded damages amounting to the actual loss incurred by having to replace the decals.

2 Where there is a market, damages will be the difference between the contract price and the price in the market. If the claimant's profit remains, there is no loss. This can be seen in the case of *Charter v Sullivan* (1957). However, if there is no available market then the claimant can recover the full loss, as in *W L Thompson Ltd v Robinson Gunmakers Ltd* (1955).

Case studies

Charter v Sullivan (1957)

The defendant contracted to buy a Hillman Minx then refused to take delivery. Because demand for this particular car easily outstripped supply, the seller could easily sell the car and make his profit. Therefore, only nominal damages were awarded.

W L Thompson Ltd v Robinson Gunmakers Ltd (1955)

The defendant agreed to buy a Standard Vanguard but later refused to accept and pay for it. Supply of Standard Vanguard cars exceeded the demand. Had the garage found another customer and sold to him as well as the defendant, then there would have been two sales and two profits. Therefore damages were awarded for the loss of profit on one sale.

3 Loss of profit not just for goods, but also in other contracts – as in *Victoria Laundry Ltd v Newman Industries Ltd* (1949) where the claimant recovered the profit that he would have been able to make but for the breach of contract.

4 Loss of a chance – generally a speculative loss is not recoverable in contract, and most cases are based in negligence rather than contract. There was an exception in *Chaplin v Hicks* (1911) where an actress had a contractual right to attend an audition and she was wrongly prevented from attending. The court stated that the mere fact that damages were difficult to calculate should not prevent them being awarded.

Reliance loss

This is the expense incurred by a claimant who relied on a contract being performed. A claimant may also recover expenses s/he has had to spend in advance of a contract that has been breached. An example of this can be seen in *Anglia Television Ltd v Reed* (1972).

Case study

Anglia Television Ltd v Reed (1972)

Anglia TV spent a lot of money preparing for a film including fees paid to the director, designer and stage manager. Robert Reed agreed to be the main actor but then pulled out. A suitable replacement could not be found so the film was not made. As Anglia TV could not predict what its profit on the film would have been, the court awarded damages based on reliance loss. Robert Reed must have known that such expenditure was likely and was liable for the expenses incurred by Anglia TV, both before and after the contract was made, up to breach.

It is also possible sometimes to recover damages for the loss of an amenity, as in *Farley v Skinner* (2001).

Case study

Farley v Skinner (2001)

The claimant asked the defendant surveyor whether the house he was to buy was subject to aircraft noise. The surveyor incorrectly reassured him that it was not. The court said that an innocent party was entitled to be placed in the position that he would have been in had the party in breach exercised due care.

Damages were recoverable for distress and inconvenience where the matter was important to the claimant, that had been made clear to the defendant, and the required action had been incorporated into the contract. The court viewed an award of £10,000 pounds for the discomfort of suffering aircraft noise.

Restitution

This is simply a repayment of any money or other benefits passed to the defendant in advance of the contract that is breached.

	Brief legal rule	Case example
Damages – purpose	The purpose of damages is to put the victim in the position they would have been in if the contract had been properly completed and performed by the defendant.	
Nominal damages	If no loss is actually suffered but the breach has been established, then the court may award 'nominal damages'.	*Staniforth v Lyall* (1830)
Wrotham Park damages	Awarded where the claimant would have very real problems in establishing financial loss and it is a 'just' response to a breach of contract.	*Wrotham Park Estate Co. Ltd v Parkside Homes Ltd* (1974)
Damages for loss of a bargain	The idea here is to place the claimant in the same financial position as if the contract had been properly performed.	*Bence Graphics International Ltd v Fasson UK Ltd* (1996)
Damages where there is a market	Where there is a market, damages will be the difference between the contract price and the price obtained or required to be paid in the market.	*Charter v Sullivan* (1957)
Damages for future contracts	There can be a claim for the profit that they would have been able to complete but for the breach of contract.	*Victoria Laundry Ltd v Newman Industries Ltd* (1949)
Damages for loss of a chance	In rare circumstances the courts have allowed claimants to recover a loss that is entirely speculative; such claims are normally based on negligence.	*Chaplin v Hicks* (1911)
Reliance loss	This refers to the expenses incurred by a claimant who relied on a contract being performed, but it was not performed.	*Anglia Television Ltd v Reed* (1972)
Restitution	A repayment of any money or other benefits passed to the defendant in advance of the contract that is breached.	
Speculative damages	Contract law has developed cases allowing damages of a highly speculative nature for mental distress while also recognising the problems with respect to privity of contract.	*Ruxley Electronics and Construction Ltd v Forsyth* (1996)

Figure 32.3 Key facts chart for damages

Case	Judgment
Staniforth v Lyall (1830)	Upon breach, the claimant hired the boat to someone else for a greater profit than he would have made. As he had suffered no loss, he was awarded a nominal sum as damages.
Wrotham Park Estate Co. Ltd v Parkside Homes Ltd (1974)	The claimant had suffered no loss but damages were awarded on the basis of the hypothetical sum the claimant could have charged to release the covenants.
Experience Hendrix LLC v PPX Enterprises Inc. (2003)	The court decided that the publisher should pay a reasonable sum to Hendrix's estate, even though Hendrix's estate had suffered no actual loss.
Bence Graphics International Ltd v Fasson UK Ltd (1996)	Damages are assessed according to the difference in value.
Charter v Sullivan (1957)	Where demand exceeds supply, the claimant can still make his profit so there is no loss to be compensated.
W L Thompson Ltd v Robinson Gunmakers Ltd (1955)	Supply exceeded demand; had the claimant found another customer and sold to him as well as the defendant, then there would have been two sales and two profits. So loss of profit is the measure of damages.
Victoria Laundry Ltd v Newman Industries Ltd (1949)	The claimant may recover for the profit that he would have been able to complete but for the breach of contract.
Chaplin v Hicks (1911)	The mere fact that damages were difficult to calculate should not prevent them being awarded.
Anglia Television Ltd v Reed (1972)	The main actor pulled out and a suitable replacement could not be made so a film was not made. The question of damages was decided that as Anglia TV could not predict what its profit on the film would have been, the court awarded damages based on reliance loss.
Farley v Skinner (2001)	It is possible to recover damages for the loss of an amenity under reliance loss.
Ruxley Electronics and Construction Ltd v Forsyth (1996)	As he had not received the exact swimming pool that he had contracted for, the court awarded him £2500 for loss of amenity.

Figure 32.4 Key cases chart for damages

32.2.4 The duty to mitigate the loss

The injured party must take reasonable steps to minimise the effects of the breach. This is mitigation of loss. How this works can be seen in *British Westinghouse Electric v Underground Electric Railways* (1912).

> **Mitigation of loss** – in contract law the party who has suffered loss must take reasonable steps to minimise the effects of a breach of contract.

Case study

British Westinghouse Electric v Underground Electric Railways (1912)

The goods delivered were defective. The railway company purchased replacements, which turned out to more efficient than the original ones. They obtained benefits over and above what they would have got from the original contract. The court said that additional benefits obtained as a result of taking reasonable steps to mitigate loss were to be accounted for when calculating damages. The court will balance loss against gain when calculating the amount of damages.

However, a claimant is not bound to go to extraordinary lengths to mitigate the loss, only to do what is reasonable in the circumstances. In an anticipatory breach, they are not bound to sue immediately they know of the possibility of the breach, but may continue until the breach is an actual breach. This can be seen in *White and Carter v McGregor* (1962).

Case study

White and Carter v McGregor (1962)

The agreement was to buy advertising space on litter bins to be fitted by the claimants to lamp posts. When the defendant wrongfully ended the contract, the claimants continued to fit the bins. The argument that the claimants might have mitigated the loss by not continuing to fit the bins failed.

The case of *Thai Airways v K I Holdings* (2015) confirms the principle of mitigation in computation of damages.

Case study

Thai Airways v K I Holdings (2015)

The defendant company had contracted to supply the claimant with seats for its aircraft, but seats were delivered either late or not at all. The airline leased substitute planes to mitigate its loss. The lease of substitute aircraft which were more fuel-efficient had to be taken into account.

32.2.5 Liquidated damages

Liquidated damages are where the amount of damages has been fixed by a term in the contract. However, the courts will only accept this sum as the award of damages if the sum identified in the contract represents an accurate and proper assessment of loss. If it is not, it is seen as a penalty and will be unenforceable. The courts developed rules for determining the difference between genuine liquidated damages and a penalty. The case of *Dunlop Pneumatic Tyre Co. v New Garage and Motor Co.* (1914) set out the position:

- An extravagant sum will always be a penalty.
- Payment of a large sum for failure to settle a small debt is probably a penalty.
- A single sum operating in respect of a variety of different breaches is likely to be a penalty.
- The wording used by the parties is not necessarily conclusive.
- It is no bar to recovering a liquidated sum that actual assessment of the loss was impossible before the contract.

Key term

> **Liquidated damages** – where the amount of damages has been fixed by a term in the contract.

However the Supreme Court has in effect rewritten the rule on penalties. The new rule is found in the conjoined appeals of *Cavendish Square Holding BV v Talal El Makdessi* (2015) and *ParkingEye Ltd v Beavis* (2015).

Cavendish Square Holding BV v Talal El Makdessi (2015)

This involved the sale of a Middle Eastern media business. The contract stated that if the seller did not comply with the terms of the contract preventing him from competing with the buyer, then he would lose his right to future payments that would otherwise have been due to him, and he would have to sell his remaining shares to the buyer at a greatly reduced price.

The court held that the provisions contained in the agreements were there to protect the legitimate interests of the buyer.

ParkingEye Ltd v Beavis (2015)

An £85 parking fine was given for overstaying the two-hour parking limit at a privately owned car park. Mr Beavis tried to argue that the fine was a penalty and therefore unenforceable.

Lord Hodge stated:

> the correct test for a penalty is whether the sum or remedy stipulated as a consequence of a breach of contract is exorbitant or unconscionable when regard is had to the innocent party's interest in the performance of the contract.

Under the new test, the party seeking to rely on a penalty clause must be able to show that the clause is to protect a legitimate interest, and that the penalty is not exorbitant or unconscionable. The following principles will also apply:

- The penalty no longer has to be a genuine pre-estimate of loss.
- The penalty rule applies to commercial and consumer cases.
- The party seeking to rely on the clause does not have to have suffered loss.
- The purpose of the clause can be to act as a deterrent against a specific breach of contract.
- The penalty does not have to be financial.
- The penalty can only apply to a breach of a primary obligation, not a secondary one, such as not paying a contractual penalty.
- The traditional tests in the *Dunlop* case are useful for cases concerning standard damages clauses but are of little use in more complex cases. The tests are not fixed rules of general application to all situations and were never intended to be this.

- In more complex cases, a broader approach, which focuses on the nature and extent of the innocent party's interest in the performance of the relevant obligation, is more suitable.
- A term with respect to damages may be justified by some consideration apart from the desire to recover compensation for a breach. This is the commercial justification approach.
- The penalty rule is an interference with freedom of contract. In a negotiated contract between properly advised parties of comparable bargaining power, the strong initial presumption must be that the parties themselves are the best judges of what is legitimate in a provision dealing with the consequences of breach.

This significantly widens the position in relation to the enforceability of penalty clauses. In determining whether such a clause is enforceable, the court will be obliged to consider the wider commercial context of the agreement. If it can be shown that there is a legitimate reason why breach of contract damages would not be sufficient in the case in question, then even if the amount stated in the penalty clause seems to have no correlation to the actual loss suffered, it may be enforceable.

Quantum meruit

We have seen the operation of *quantum meruit* in relation to part-performance in Chapter 31.

There are three common circumstances in which such an award is made:

- In a contract for services where no part is stated, as in *Upton Rural District Council v Powell* (1942): a retained fireman provided services with no fixed agreement as to wages – the court awarded a reasonable amount.
- Where the circumstances of the case show that a fresh agreement can be implied in place of the original one, as in *Steven v Bromley* (1919): Steven had agreed to carry steel at a specified rate. When the steel was delivered it contained extra goods. Steven was able to claim extra for the additional items.
- Where a party has elected to consider the contract discharged by the other's breach, or where a party has been prevented from performing by the other party. In either case they might claim for work they have already done as in *De Barnady v Harding* (1853): a principal wrongly revoked his agent's authority to act on his behalf. The agent was then entitled to claim for the work he had already done and for expenses incurred.

	Brief legal rule	Case example
The duty to mitigate the loss	The party injured by a breach of contract must take reasonable steps to minimise the effects of the breach.	*Westinghouse Electric v Underground Electric Railways* (1912)
Liquidated damages	Liquidated damages are where the amount of damages has been fixed by a term in the contract.	*Dunlop Pneumatic Tyre Co. v New Garage and Motor Co.* (1914)
Quantum meruit	Recovery of an unqualified sum for services already rendered.	*Upton Rural District Council v Powell* (1942)

Figure 32.5 Key facts chart for mitigation of loss and terms attempting to quantify damages

Case	Judgment
Westinghouse Electric v Underground Electric Railways (1912)	It was necessary to balance loss against gain when the amount of the damages was being calculated.
Thai Airways v K I Holdings (2015)	The lease of substitute aircraft which were more fuel efficient had to be taken into account.
Dunlop Pneumatic Tyre Co. v New Garage and Motor Co. (1914)	The case sets out the traditional rules as to when the term is a liquidated damages clause or a penalty.
Cavendish Square Holding BV v Talal El Makdessi and *ParkingEye Ltd v Beavis* (2015)	Sets out new tests for being able to rely on a penalty clause.
Upton Rural District Council v Powell (1942)	Where a contract for services that is silent on the issue of remuneration, *quantum meruit* applies.
Steven v Bromley (1919)	Where the circumstances of the case show that a fresh agreement can be implied in place of the original one, *quantum meruit* applies.
De Barnady v Harding (1853)	Where a party has elected to consider the contract discharged by the other's breach or where a party has been prevented from performing by the other party *quantum meruit* applies.

Figure 32.6 Key cases chart for mitigation of loss and terms attempting to quantify damages

32.3 Equitable remedies

Equitable remedies are awarded where damages is an inadequate remedy and justice would not be served merely by damages. Equitable remedies are at the discretion of the court.

32.3.1 Injunction

An injunction in contract law is a court order instructing someone not to breach a term of his contract. The idea is that the prohibition will prevent someone interfering with the rights of another. This is the most usual type of injunction and is known as a prohibitory injunction.

Key term

Prohibitory injunction – a court order instructing someone to not to do something. Breach of the order can lead to further sanctions.

An injunction can be permanent or temporary, for example until a full trial of the issues in a dispute. A temporary injunction is called an interim injunction. Injunctions are often applied for with respect to intellectual property rights which companies protect fully, and also in employment contracts to prevent an employee competing when leaving employment or when a business owner is selling the business. This can be seen in the case of *A B v C D* (2014).

Case study

A B v C D (2014)

The dispute involved intellectual property rights. An interim injunction was granted to prevent the defendant's alleged breach of contract, on the basis that damages would not be an appropriate remedy because of a limitation clause on damages in the contract.

Occasionally an injunction will order a party to do something. This is known as a mandatory injunction.

Key term

Mandatory injunction – a court order requiring a party to do something.

However, an injunction will not be awarded for a party to complete a personal service as the court is unable to supervise such an order. This was shown in *Page One Records Ltd v Britton* (1967).

Case study

Page One Records Ltd v Britton (1967)

The Troggs agreed that Page One Records would be their manager and sole agent for five years. The Troggs agreed not to appoint anyone else as a manager during the contract. The relationship broke down.

Page wanted an injunction to prevent The Troggs from appointing a new manager. The injunction was refused and Page could only claim damages. This was because the contract involved obligations of trust and confidence. An injunction would amount to forcing the band to remain idle, or to continue to employ a manager and agent in whom the band had lost confidence. Forcing them to work together could not be supervised by the court.

Tip

When suggesting that an injunction is the most appropriate remedy in a scenario, suggest the wording of the injunction to be sought. For example, 'The defendant shall not sell the (named) Picasso painting without permission of the court.'

32.3.2 Specific performance

This equitable remedy is the opposite of an injunction. It is a court order compelling someone to do something, rather like a mandatory injunction. An example is *Airport Industrial G P Ltd v Heathrow Airport Ltd* (2015). This complex case concerned car parking on a site at Heathrow Airport. Here the judge was concerned that exercising his discretion to make an order for specific performance would inevitably force a company into liquidation, so did not make such an order.

Activity

Review the scenarios in previous chapters.

1 Where there has been a breach of contract, state the appropriate remedies.
2 Consider, in each case, whether the Consumer Rights Act 2015 would apply, and how remedies under that Act would differ from the remedies where the Act does not apply.

	Brief legal rule	Case example
Injunction	An injunction in contract law is a court order instructing someone to not breach a term of his contract	*A B v C D* (2014)
Specific performance	This is a court order compelling someone to do something, typically hand over property that has been agreed under a contract.	*Airport Industrial G P Ltd v Heathrow Airport Ltd* (2015)

Figure 32.7 Key facts chart for equitable remedies

Case	Judgment
A B v C D (2014)	An interim injunction was granted to prevent the defendant's alleged breach of contract on the basis that damages would not be an appropriate remedy.
Page One Records Ltd v Britton (1967)	An injunction will not be awarded for a party to complete a personal service as the court is unable to supervise such an order.
Airport Industrial G P Ltd v Heathrow Airport Ltd (2015)	Specific performance was not ordered as it would inevitably force a company into liquidation which would be unjust in the circumstances.

Figure 32.8 Key cases chart for equitable remedies

See Chapter 28, section 28.4.3 for information about remedies under the Consumer Rights Act 2015.

Summary

- Remedies for breach of contract can be either legal or equitable remedies.
- Compensatory damages are the most common form of damages and are compensation for losses suffered.
- In specific circumstances, more than the actual loss suffered will be awarded.
- Contracts sometimes try to establish what damages will be payable if there is a breach. These are valid terms if considered liquidated damages, but not if they are considered a penalty.
- Equitable remedies are discretionary.
- Injunctions usually aim to prevent a breach of contract.
- Specific performance requires delivery of goods but is not available for contracts of service.

Glossary

Actual breach – in contract law where the breach occurs at the time of, or during the course of, performance.

Agent – a person who is authorised to act for another (the principal) in the making of a contract with third parties. The resulting contract is made between the principal and the third party, and not with the agent.

Anticipatory breach – when a party to a contract gives notice in advance to the other party that they will not be performing or completing the contract.

Attempt – in criminal law an attempt occurs where a person with the relevant *mens rea* does an act which is more than merely preparatory to the commission of an offence.

Automatism – a complete defence where the defendant proves that the body acted without any control by the mind due to an external factor.

Basic intent offences – offences where recklessness is sufficient for the *mens rea*. These include offences such as assault, battery, ss 47 and 20 OAPA 1861 and manslaughter.

Bilateral contract – this requires both offeror and offeree to do something.

Breach of the peace – a criminal offence committed when it is alleged that harm has been done, or is likely to be done, to a person or to property or when a person fears harm by an assault, affray, riot, unlawful assembly or some other disturbance.

Burglary (1) – a crime when a person enters any building or part of a building as a trespasser with intent to steal, inflict GBH, or damage the building or anything in it.

Burglary (2) – a crime when a person, having entered a building or part of a building as a trespasser, steals or attempts to steal anything in the building or inflicts or attempts to inflict GBH on any person in the building.

Civil liberties – freedoms that are guaranteed to people to protect them from an over-powerful government. They are found in democratic states such as the UK but are not found in undemocratic states such as North Korea.

Condition – a term in a contract that is central to the contract, breach of which may allow the contract to be repudiated.

Conflict theory – society is in a state of perpetual conflict due to competition for limited resources.

Consensus theory – consensus theory is a social theory that holds that a particular political or economic system is a fair system, and that social change should take place within the social institutions provided by it.

Consent – where the victim agrees to suffer an injury. It is a defence to some, less serious, non-fatal offences.

Consumer – described in the Consumer Rights Act 2015 as 'an individual acting for purposes that are wholly or mainly outside that individual's trade, business, craft or profession'.

Contra proferentem – where there is doubt about the meaning of a term in a contract, the words will be construed against the person who put them in the contract.

Corrective justice – this is sometimes known as restorative justice, and is when the law restores the imbalance that has occurred between two individuals or an individual and the state.

'Correspondence' – with regard to Article 8 ECHR, this means the right to uninterrupted and uncensored communications with others.

Derogation – in human rights where there is an exemption from, or relaxation of, rules which would otherwise apply.

Diminished responsibility – a partial defence to a charge of murder which reduces the offence to one of voluntary manslaughter under s 2 Homicide Act 1957 as amended by s 52 Coroners and Justice Act 2009.

Duress (1) – a full defence to certain crimes where the defendant alleges he has been forced to commit the crime.

Duress (2) – in contract law where one of the parties alleges they have been forced to enter into a contract as a result of threats made by another person.

Economic duress – when someone enters into a contract as a result of financial threats.

Estoppel – a principle of contract law that prevents one party to a contract from denying or alleging a fact owing to their previous conduct, allegation, or denial.

'Everyone' – so far as Article 8 ECHR is concerned, this includes businesses.

Exclusion clause – a term in a contract that prevents one party being liable for a breach of contract.

Executed consideration – where the consideration has been carried out.

Executory consideration – a promise to perform acts in the future.

'Family life' – with regard to Article 8 ECHR, the right to enjoy family relationships without interference from the state.

Force majeure clause – a clause often found in commercial contracts. It excludes liability for the parties for delay in performance or the non-performance if there are extraordinary events.

Freedom of association – in Human Rights under Article 11 ECHR, it is the right for a person not to be prevented or restricted by the state from meeting and joining with others to follow a particular aim.

Freedom of expression – in Human Rights under Article 11 ECHR, the freedom for a person to hold opinions and to receive and give information and ideas without state interference.

Gillick competence – a term used to help assess whether a child has the maturity to make their own decisions and to understand the implications of those decisions. The term is taken from the case of *Gillick v West Norfolk and Wisbech Area Health Authority* (1984).

Gross negligence manslaughter – a form of involuntary manslaughter committed where D is grossly negligent in breach of a duty of care towards V and this results in V's death.

Habeas corpus – a writ issued by the court which required the immediate production of a detained person so the court could hear arguments for and against the continuation of the detention.

'Home' – with regard to Article 8 ECHR, this is a right to enjoy your existing home peacefully, rather than a right to a house.

Human rights – rights and freedoms that everyone in a country and the world are entitled to because they are human.

Innominate term – a term in a contract that is not defined as a condition or a warranty. Whether it is a condition or a warranty depends on the consequences of any breach of the term.

Insanity – a full defence to a criminal offence requiring *mens rea*. The defendant must be labouring under such a defect of reason, from disease of the mind, as not to know the nature and quality of the act they were doing, or if they did know it, that they did not know they were doing what was wrong.

Intention to create legal relations – the parties to a contract expressly or impliedly agree that the contract is legally binding and therefore enforceable in court.

Invitation to treat – an indication that one person is willing to negotiate a contract with another, but that he or she is not yet willing to make a legal offer.

Labelling theory – most people commit deviant and criminal acts but only some are caught and berated, ostracised or punished for them.

Legal positivism – the theory of law that is based on the idea that laws are valid where they are made by the recognised legislative power in the state and do not have to satisfy any higher authority.

Legal realism – an understanding of the law as it is practised in reality, not presented in statutes or academic theories.

Letter of comfort – a written assurance usually provided by a parent company in respect of its subsidiary's financial obligations to a bank. It is usually where the parent company wishes to give some assurance to the lender in respect of the subsidiary's ability to repay the loan but has no obligation to pay on its behalf.

Lien – the right to retain possession of the goods of the debtor until paid.

Limitation clause – a term in a contract that sets an upper limit on liability for breach of contract.

Liquidated damages – where the amount of damages has been fixed by a term in the contract.

Loss of control – a partial defence to a charge of murder which reduces the offence to one of voluntary manslaughter under s 54(1) of the Coroners and Justice Act 2009.

Mala in se – this term means 'intrinsically wrong'.

Mala prohibita – this term means 'forbidden conduct'.

Mandatory injunction – a court order requiring a party to do something.

'McKenzie friend' – the court may allow a legally unqualified and unpaid adviser to represent the defendant and speak for them in a civil case.

Misrepresentation – a false statement of material fact made by a party to the contract that induces the other party to enter the contract.

Mitigation of loss – in contract law the party who has suffered loss must take reasonable steps to minimise the effects of a breach of contract.

Murder – 'the unlawful killing of a reasonable person in being and under the King's (or Queen's) Peace with malice aforethought, express or implied'.

Natural law – a moral theory of jurisprudence, which maintains that law should be based on morality and ethics.

Offer – a statement of the terms upon which a person is prepared to be bound by a contract.

Offeree – in contract law the person to whom an offer is made.

Offeror – in contract law the person who makes an offer to another.

Peaceful assembly – in Human Rights under Article 11 a person is allowed to meet in public, march, process and demonstrate without state interference.

Phishing – a form of online fraud when an attacker represents him or herself as being reputable and tries to learn information in order to defraud an innocent victim.

Pluralist society – a diverse society, where minority groups maintain their independent cultural traditions and all members tolerate each other's beliefs even when they don't match their own.

'Private life' – with regard to Article 8 ECHR, this includes matters such as the physical and psychological integrity; sex life and gender; personal data; reputation, names and photos.

Private nuisance – where an action will be taken because someone's use or enjoyment of their property is affected by the unreasonable behaviour of a neighbour.

Privity of contract – only those who are parties to a contract are bound by it and can benefit from it.

Procedural justice – this is concerned with making and implementing decisions according to fair processes.

Prohibitory injunction – a court order instructing someone to not to do something. Breach of the order can lead to further sanctions.

Promisee – in contract law a person to whom a promise is made.

Promisor – in contract law a person who makes a promise to another.

Promissory estoppel – an equitable doctrine which can prevent a person going back on a promise which is not supported by consideration.

Public nuisance – where a group of people is affected by the use of land in the locality.

Quantum meruit – as much as it is worth.

Repudiation – the ending of a contract due to a refusal by one of the parties to perform the duty or obligation owed to the other party.

Rescission – this is an equitable remedy that is made at the discretion of the court. If granted it places the parties back in their pre-contractual position.

'Respect' – with regard to Article 8 ECHR, this requires the state not to interfere and has positive aspects.

Restrictive covenant – an agreement between land owners where one party will restrict the use of its land in some way for the benefit of another's land.

Robbery – a crime when a person steals and immediately before, or at the time of doing so, and in order to do so, he uses force on any person or puts or seeks to put any person in fear of using force.

Rule – this has been defined by Twining and Miers in *How to Do Things with Rules* (2014) as 'a general norm mandating or guiding conduct'.

Rylands v Fletcher – where a person's property is damaged or destroyed by the escape of non-naturally stored material onto adjoining property.

Social control – the ways in which our behaviour, thoughts and appearance are regulated by the norms, rules, laws and social structures of society.

Specific intent offences – criminal offences for which the required *mens rea* is intention only.

Substantive justice – the content of the law itself must be just.

Terrorism Prevention and Investigation Measures (TPIM) – a terrorist suspect may be made subject to this order which places conditions on their residence, movement and activities.

Theft – A person is guilty of theft if they dishonestly appropriate property belonging to another with the intention of permanently depriving the other of it.

Trader – described in the Consumer Rights Act 2015 as 'a person acting for purposes relating to that person's trade, business, craft or profession, whether acting personally or through another person acting in the trader's name or on the trader's behalf'.

Trespass to land – an unlawful and unjustifiable intrusion by a person onto the land of another – there is no need to show that any damage has been caused.

Undue influence – a principle of contract law where one party exploits their dominant position to gain an unfair advantage over the other party.

Unilateral contract – there is an obligation on one party to the contract only, the offeror.

Unlawful act manslaughter – where the defendant causes a death through doing an unlawful act that is objectively dangerous with the necessary *mens rea* for the unlawful act.

Vexatious litigant – a person who regularly issues civil court proceedings. Once an order is made that a person is a vexatious litigant, s/he can only bring a further action with the permission of the court.

Vicarious liability – where a third person has legal responsibility for the unlawful actions of another. It is commonly seen in employment where the employer is responsible for the actions of an employee who acted in the course of their employment.

Vitiating factor – something that makes a contract void or voidable.

Voluntary manslaughter – the verdict where the defendant has a partial defence to murder where the killing was carried out when the defendant was suffering from diminished responsibility or loss of control.

Warranty – a minor term in a contract, breach of which does not end the contract but allows a claim for damages only.

Practice questions

Component 3

Section A (Chapters 1–16)
Nature of law: crime

Barry suffered from a personality defect which tended to cause him to exaggerate in his own mind the behaviour of others around him. This could make him angry when he thought that he was being made fun of. One evening, while he was in a club, and on a number of occasions during the evening, he saw Helen look at him and make some comments to her friends, at which they all laughed. As he was leaving, Barry noticed Helen at the top of some stairs. He followed her and pushed her. She fell down the stairs, broke her neck and died.

Barry then went to sleep in a bus shelter and started behaving very oddly, claiming that he was directed by 'voices'. The next day Issy, a charity worker, tried to offer him food and accommodation in a hostel. As he thought that she was trying to take him away and have him locked up, he kicked her in the leg. She fell and became unconscious as she hit her head on the ground. Barry watched her for a time but then walked away without helping her or calling for help. Issy was later found to have died from swallowing her tongue.

1 Advise whether Barry could avoid liability for a charge of murder by using the defences of diminished responsibility or loss of control.
2 Advise whether Barry is liable for the unlawful act (constructive) manslaughter of Issy and whether he is liable for the gross negligence manslaughter of Issy.

Nature of law: tort

Gerard owned a large detached house which had formerly been surrounded by farmland, but which now, to his great annoyance, was bordered by a large housing estate. He enjoyed holding weekly outdoor parties for his friends and family which regularly continued until the early hours. One neighbour, Peter, complained to Gerard but his complaint resulted in abuse from Gerard and music being played even louder and later. The music also annoyed Gerard's daughter, Anna who was revising for her exams.

Bob encouraged local residents to empty their used cooking oil into a storage tank in his front garden so that he could recycle the oil as fuel for his minibus. On his smallholding next to Bob's house Roger grew fruit and vegetables which he sold in the local farmer's market. One day he discovered that all his plants had died and, subsequently, nothing would grow on a large area of his land near to the storage tank which was found to be leaking. A neighbour suggested that, one night, he had seen a stranger fiddling with the valve on the storage tank.

1 Advise whether Peter and Anna can make successful claims in private nuisance
2 Advise whether Roger would be successful in a claim in Rylands v Fletcher against Bob.

Section B Option 1 (Chapters 17–24)
Human rights

Anton is a homeless man in a big English city. He has been told that the local Council have recently sold the small park in which he has slept for many years to a developer, Bighouse plc. Anton considers the park his home and the Council have never attempted to remove his small tent that is in a hidden corner of the park. Anton has been told by Council officials that he must leave the park immediately and take all his belongings with him. Anton does not do so and remains in his tent in the park. The Council start eviction proceedings against Anton.

Bighouse plans to build 20 luxury houses on the park with no social or affordable housing. They have started to put a high fence round the park with many notices stating the park is closed and will be patrolled by a guard dog. Anton continues to sleep in his tent, and one day he gives the guard dog some meat laced with a strong tranquiliser. The next morning, the dog is found asleep, but fully recovers over the next few days. Anton is arrested and charged with respect to the incident. He is not allowed to contact anyone until he has made a statement to the police and he is not offered legal advice. Finally he is bailed on the conditions that he cannot return to the park, he has to live at least 15 miles from the park and he must report to a police station another 5 miles away. Six months later, at the first hearing of his case at the Magistrates Court he is accompanied by Cara, a law student of extremely unconventional appearance and dress, who befriended him as part of a student outreach group. The Magistrates refuse to allow Cara to sit next to Anton in court to give him advice as she is deemed not to be 'suitably dressed for court'. Anton cannot understand the court procedure or what he has been charged with. No evidence is called and he is told that he has been convicted based on the statement he gave at the police station.

1 Advise whether and how Anton could use Article 8 ECHR to prevent the action by the council.
2 Discuss whether there have been any breaches of Articles 5 and 6 ECHR.

Section B Option 2 (Chapters 25–32)

Contract

Dan, a butcher, decided to buy 400 chickens from Edie. They agreed a price of £800. She promised to deliver them on Thursday so his shop had a good stock for his busiest day – Saturday. Edie failed to deliver on Thursday.

On Friday morning, Dan ordered 400 chickens from Farouk at a price of £900, which were delivered immediately. On Saturday lunchtime Edie tried to deliver the chickens which Dan refused to take or pay for.

Dan's customers liked the Farouk chickens. Therefore, Dan decided to set up a standing order with Farouk for 400 chickens per week at a price of £850, payable in advance, to be delivered each Thursday for the next 13 weeks. After four weeks, Farouk, despite having received the next week's payment, told Dan he could no longer supply the chickens because his farm was in a 25 mile exclusion zone set up by the government to try to stop the spread of a fatal chicken disease. Chickens from elsewhere in the country were still available but at a much higher price.

1 Advise what rights and remedies Dan might have against Edie.
2 Advise whether Farouk will be liable to pay any money to Dan and whether Farouk might be entitled to treat the contract as frustrated.

Index

377